MILITARY MEMOIRS
OF A
CONFEDERATE

General E. P. Alexander

MILITARY MEMOIRS OF A CONFEDERATE

A Critical Narrative

by

GENERAL
EDWARD PORTER ALEXANDER

with a new introduction by
GARY W. GALLAGHER

DA CAPO PRESS

Library of Congress Cataloging in Publication Data

Alexander, Edward Porter, 1835-1910.
  Military memoirs of a Confederate: a critical narrative / by Edward
Porter Alexander; with a new introduction by Gary W. Gallagher. – 1st Da
Capo Press ed.
      p.   cm.
  Originally published: New York: Charles Scribner's Sons, 1907.
  ISBN 0-306-80509-X
  1. United States – History – Civil War, 1861-1865 – Campaigns. 2. Alex-
ander, Edward Porter, 1835-1910. 3. Confederate States of America –
History, Military. 4. United States – History – Civil War,
1861-1865 – Personal narratives, Confederate. I. Title.
E470.A373 1993   92-40371
973.7′3 – dc20   CIP

First Da Capo Press edition 1993

This Da Capo Press paperback edition of *Military Memoirs of a Confederate*
is an unabridged republication of the edition published in New York in 1907,
with the addition of a new introduction by Gary W. Gallagher.

5   6   7   8   9   10   02   01

Published by Da Capo Press, Inc.
A member of the Perseus Books Group

TO

𝕿𝖍𝖊 𝕸𝖊𝖒𝖔𝖗𝖞 𝖔𝖋 𝖙𝖍𝖊 𝕯𝖊𝖆𝖉

WHOSE BRAVERY WON THE GLORY

WHICH THE LIVING ENJOY

THE BAND IN THE PINES

Oh, band in the pine-wood, cease!
  Cease with your splendid call;
The living are brave and noble,
  But the dead were bravest of all!

They throng to the martial summons,
  To the loud triumphant strain;
And the dear, bright eyes of long dead friends
  Come to the heart again.

They come with the ringing bugle,
  And the deep drum's mellow roar,
Till the soul is faint with longing
  For the hands we clasp no more.

Oh, band in the pine-wood, cease,
  Or the heart will melt in tears
For the gallant eyes and the smiling lips
  And the voices of old years.

JOHN ESTEN COOKE,
Ordnance Officer, Stuart's Cavalry.

THE POINT OF VIEW

THE *raison d'être* of the following pages is not at all to set forth the valor of Confederate arms nor the skill of Confederate generals. These are as they may be, and must here take their chances in an unpartisan narrative, written with an entirely different object. That object is the criticism of each campaign as one would criticise a game of chess, only to point out the good and bad plays on each side, and the moves which have influenced the result. It is far from being a grateful task, and the writer is, moreover, painfully conscious of his limitations in his effort to perform it adequately.

But it is of great importance that it should be attempted even approximately not only for the benefit of general history, but more particularly for that of military students and staff-officers. These will find much of value and interest in the details, pointing out how and why the scale of battle was turned upon each occasion. It is only of recent years — since the publication by the War Department of the full Official Reports of both armies, in 135 large volumes—that it has become possible to write this story, even approximately. History, meanwhile, has been following the incomplete reports of the earlier days which, sometimes, as at Seven Pines (or Fair Oaks), have deliberately concealed the facts, and has always felt the need of the personal accounts covering the incidents of every march, skirmish, and battle.

Only among these can be traced the beginnings, often obscure and accidental, of the most important events; and these must ever form an inexhaustible mine for the study by the staff-officer of the practical working and details in every department of an army.

As to the causes of the war, it will, of course, be understood that every former Confederate repudiates all accusations of treason or rebellion in the war, and even of fighting to preserve the institution of slavery.   The effort of the enemy to destroy it without compensation was practical robbery, which, of course, we resisted.   The unanimity and the desperation of our resistance — even to the refusal of Lincoln's suggested compensation at Fortress Monroe, after the destruction had already occurred — clearly show our struggle to have been for that right of self-government which the Englishman has claimed, and fought for, as for nothing else, since the days of King John.

It has taken many years for these truths to gain acceptance against the prejudices left by the war, even though it has been notorious from the first that no legal accusation could be brought against any one, even Mr. Davis.   With the adoption of this view by leading English authorities, not to mention distinguished Northern and Republican authors, the South may be content to leave all such questions to the final verdict of history, admitting itself too close to the event to claim impartiality.

One thing remains to be said.   The world has not stood still in the years since we took up arms for what we deemed our most invaluable right — that of self-government.   We now enjoy the rare privilege of seeing what we fought for in the retrospect.   It no longer seems so desirable.   It would now prove only a curse.   We have good cause to thank God for our escape from it, not alone for our sake, but for that of the whole country and even of the world.

Had our cause succeeded, divergent interests must soon have further separated the States into groups, and this continent would have been given over to divided nationalities, each weak and unable to command foreign credit.   Since the days of Greece, Confederacies have only held together against foreign enemies, and in times of peace have soon disintegrated.   It is surely not necessary to contrast what would have been our prospects as citizens of such States with our condition now as citizens of the strongest, richest, and — strange for us to say who once called ourselves " conquered " and our cause " lost " — the freest nation on earth.

The statistics of our commerce, our manufactures, and our

internal improvements are an object-lesson of the truth of old Æsop's fable, pointing out the increased strength of the separate sticks when bound together into a fagot. That the whole civilized world shares with us in the far-reaching blessings and benefits of our civilization, wealth, and political power is manifest in our building the Panama Canal, and again, in the Treaty of Peace between Russia and Japan, negotiated through the influence of our President. These are but the first-fruits of what the future will develop, for our Union is not built to perish. Its bonds were not formed by peaceable agreements in conventions, but were forged in the white heat of battles, in a war fought out to the bitter end, and are for eternity.

E. P. A.

CONTENTS

CHAPTER VII

SEVEN DAYS' CAMPAIGN. THE ATTACK

CHAPTER VIII

SEVEN DAYS' CAMPAIGN. THE PURSUIT

CHAPTER IX

THE ESCAPE. BATTLE OF MALVERN HILL

CHAPTER X

CEDAR MOUNTAIN

CHAPTER XI

SECOND MANASSAS

CHAPTER XII

BOONSBORO OR SOUTH MOUNTAIN, AND HARPER'S FERRY

CHAPTER XIII

SHARPSBURG OR ANTIETAM

CHAPTER XVI

GETTYSBURG: THE FIRST DAY

CHAPTER XVII

GETTYSBURG: SECOND DAY

CHAPTER XVIII

GETTYSBURG: THIRD DAY

CHAPTER XIX

Battle of Chickamauga

CHAPTER XX

Battle of the Wilderness

CHAPTER XXI

The Movement against Petersburg

CHAPTER XXII

The Mine

CHAPTER XXIII

The Fall of 1864

INTRODUCTION

Edward Porter Alexander lived a life resonant with accomplishment. As a Confederate staff officer and artillerist, he distinguished himself in virtually all the great campaigns of the Army of Northern Virginia. A succession of senior commanders, including P. G. T. Beauregard, Joseph E. Johnston, R. E. Lee, and James Longstreet, relied heavily on Alexander's engineering skills, imagination, and aptitude for handling men. He combined in remarkable fashion a scholar's intellect and the capacity for decisive action in combat – attributes that set him apart from nearly all of his peers. In the years after Appomattox, Alexander turned his formidable talents to a range of activities, gaining success first as an educator and later as a businessman. He published prolifically on subjects ranging from technical railroad questions to patterns of weather. His most enduring writings related to the Civil War, and that body of work constitutes Alexander's greatest legacy. Among those publications, *Military Memoirs of a Confederate: A Critical Narrative* stands as a landmark in the literature on the war, rivaled in value and influence by only a handful of other accounts by participants.[1]

A few words about Alexander will set the stage for a closer consideration of *Military Memoirs.* Born into a prominent slaveholding family in Washington, Georgia on May 26, 1835, he received his early education from private tutors. He entered the United States Military Academy in 1853, graduated third in the class of 1857, and took a commission as brevet second lieutenant of engineers. Superiors predicted success for him from the beginning. Over the next three years, he taught at the Academy, participated in the final stage of the Mormon War, and assisted Albert J. Meyer in developing the "wig-wag" system of motion telegraphy. He found himself a second lieutenant of engineers at Fort Steilacoom, Washington Territory, when sectional tensions exploded into the secession crisis of 1860-61. Although a political moderate, Alexander left the army upon hearing in February 1861 that Georgia had seceded. He arrived in Richmond, Virginia on June 1, 1861, and learned that he had been commissioned a captain of engineers in the Confederacy's fledgling army.[2]

No other Confederate officer played more varied roles or worked closely with a larger number of famous figures. Alexander joined P. G. T. Beauregard's staff as chief signal officer in late June 1861 and subsequently assumed the responsibilities of chief of ordnance as well. In the wake of First Manassas, Beauregard lauded Alexander's "skillful management" of the signal corps, which rendered "most important service preceding and during the engagement."[3] From the summer of 1861 until the close of the 1862 Maryland Campaign, Alexander held the posts of chief signal officer and chief of ordnance under Beauregard, Joseph E. Johnston, and R. E. Lee. He kept arms and ammunition flowing to the army under difficult circumstances during the Peninsula Campaign, the Seven Days, Second Manassas, and Sharpsburg. Somehow, he also found time to offer a plan for reorganizing the army's artillery, coordinated intelligence operations, supervised the use of a balloon during the Seven Days (he was aloft for part of the battle of Gaines's Mill), performed reconnaissance, and carried out various engineering tasks. Promoted twice in 1862, Alexander became a major of artillery on April 18 and a lieutenant colonel in the "Long Arm" on July 17.

R. E. Lee appreciated Alexander's manifold talents but discerned a special aptitude for artillery. When Stephen D. Lee transferred to the West after Sharpsburg, the army commander selected Alexander to head Lee's battalion of artillery in James Longstreet's wing of the Army of Northern Virginia. Reorganization during the winter of 1862-63 placed six battalions in each of the army's two corps. "We have no more accomplished officer," wrote chief of artillery William Nelson Pendleton in recommending that Alexander be promoted and given a batallion in Longstreet's First Corps (the two wings under Longstreet and "Stonewall" Jackson had become corps after Sharpsburg). Lee agreed, and Alexander, made a full colonel on March 3, 1863, found a secure place in the branch where he would earn a dazzling reputation. "He was far and away the superior of all others in his arm . . . ," observed the leading student of Lee's artillery in assessing the young Georgian some fifty years after the war. "Like Gen. [Henry J.] Hunt of the Federal Army, he was preeminent in the Artillery of his army."[4]

Alexander immediately excelled in his new position. He arranged the guns at Fredericksburg that helped decimate Union attackers on the plain below Marye's Heights on December 13, 1862. At Chancellorsville, he directed the movement of Confederate artillery to Hazel Grove, key ground from which southern guns overwhelmed Union artillery at Fairview Cemetery and enabled Lee to reunite the two wings of his army. Alexander handled Longstreet's artillery on July 2 and 3 at Gettysburg, rendering his most famous service as coordinator of the artillery barrage that preceded the Pickett-Pettigrew assault. Accompanying Longstreet's corps to north Georgia in September 1863, he just missed the battle of Chickamauga but fought at Chattanooga and Knoxville later that year.

On all of these fields, Alexander functioned as Longstreet's tactical chief of artillery. It made sense for the best gunner in the army to control as many batteries as possible in combat; however, Colonel John B. Walton, formerly of the Washington Artillery and a friend of Longstreet's, remained titular head of the First Corps guns. A situation frustrating to all concerned ended on March 19, 1864, when Alexander, promoted to brigadier general on March 1, replaced Walton.[5] Joseph Johnston had forced a resolution of the situation that spring by requesting Alexander's promotion to brigadier and transfer to the Army of Tennessee. Jefferson Davis discussed Johnston's proposal with Lee, who refused to let Alexander go. The President subsequently told one of Alexander's sisters that her brother was "one of a very few whom Gen. Lee would not give to anybody."[6]

Alexander maintained his high reputation through the Overland Campaign of 1864, the siege of Petersburg, and the retreat to Appomattox. Drawing on his engineering expertise, he helped lay out part of the defensive line outside Richmond. Lee eventually expanded his authority to cover all artillery between the James and Appomattox rivers. On April 9, 1865, as Grant's army crowded in from several directions, Alexander drew the last battle line of the Army of Northern Virginia.[7] Thus ended the memorable military career of the Confederacy's finest artillerist.

Despite the demands of a successful postwar career, Alexander found opportunity to study and write about the war. His initial project was a history of the First Corps, begun at Longstreet's request, which he abandoned in the late 1860s because of the press of business and the difficulty of procuring sufficient information from former comrades. "What I want is not the general facts that everybody knows but the *details*," he wrote Thomas Jewett Goree of Longstreet's old staff, "& they only exist in the memories of survivors & I have to elicit them by correspondence & you *cannot imagine* how utterly hopeless a task this seems."[8]

Returning to his historical work in the 1870s, he published several pieces in the *Southern Historical Society Papers* and two in *The Century*'s hugely successful *Battles and Leaders of the Civil War*.[9] All of these articles exhibited scrupulous attention to detail and an absence of special pleading nearly unique among writings by participants. Robert Underwood Johnson, one of the co-editors of *Battles and Leaders*, aptly described Alexander as a man of such "integrity and candor" that anything he wrote could be relied upon.[10]

Alexander undertook a full-scale memoir of the war in the late 1890s. Sent by President Grover Cleveland to Greytown, Nicaragua in May 1897 as an arbitrator in a boundary dispute, Alexander acceded to his daughter Bessie Alexander Ficklen's request that he write his recollections of the war. He began slowly but soon warmed to the task. Relying on a small library that included the popular edition of *Battles and Leaders*, his own brief diaries and journals that covered part of the war, and a limited correspondence with former officers, Alexander retraced the campaigns of the Army of Northern Virginia. He intended to let no one but family and close friends see the finished work; however, he sought to achieve the greatest possible accuracy. He explained to one of his sisters that the recollections were not "to publish, but only for my children, so of course they are very personal." "But partly to tell them the real *story* of the war, & partly because I was often concerned in important affairs which they will be interested to understand," he added in a passage describing the purpose and scope of the recollections, "I have written, along with my own little doings, a sort of critical narrative of the military game wh[ich] was being played, & I have not hesitated to criticise our moves as I would moves in chess – no matter what general made them." He considered his manuscript in Greytown only a first draft. Upon returning home, he would "go over it all at leisure, with all my military library at hand to put on finishing touches, & fill some few gaps." Alexander projected that two years of revision would be necessary to get the recollections in a form suitable for distribution to the family.[11]

He completed a draft of the recollections just before leaving

Greytown in October 1899. The narrative totaled more than 1,200 pages and offered innumerable insights into Lee's campaigns as well as a bountiful supply of anecdotes about Alexander's activities. Bluntly honest in a text he believed never would circulate outside his family and selected friends, Alexander dissected campaigns with an impartial eye, criticized R. E. Lee, Stonewall Jackson, and others in the southern pantheon, and shunned the romanticism and partisan agenda that tainted so many Confederate reminiscences. The distortions characteristic of southern accounts influenced by the Myth of the Lost Cause found no place in the Greytown manuscript. Ninety years after Alexander wrote them, these reminiscences appeared as *Fighting for the Confederacy: The Personal Recollections of General Edward Porter Alexander*.[12]

Military Memoirs grew out of the manuscript completed in Greytown. The deaths of his wife in November 1899 and a daughter five months later staggered Alexander, who grieved for several months on his plantation on South Island off the coast of Georgetown, South Carolina. A determination to revise his reminiscences helped pull him out of mourning: "I've actually *begun* in rewriting my Recollections," he reported in September 1900, "& that puts an end to every idle moment – for I try to write a *little bit* every day." At first he sought only to correct errors and fill in gaps in the existing narrative; however, by the summer of 1901 he had decided to make significant changes. "I want to tell the story *professionally*," he explained in August 1901, "& to comment freely on every professional feature as one w[oul]d comment on moves of chess."[13] Discussions with William A. Dunning, Frederick Bancroft, and other historians sustained his belief that much of the personal material should give way to a more formal critique of operations.[14]

Six years passed before Alexander completed his task. The revised text for *Military Memoirs* differed from the Greytown manuscript in several important ways. Most of the personal anecdotes disappeared, though a few wonderful vignettes, such as his exchange with Longstreet on the afternoon of July 3 at Gettysburg, remained to enliven the narrative. Alexander also softened or cut some harsh estimates of friends and foes – yet still assessed Lee far more rigorously than almost any other ex-Confederate. Finally, he added chapters on the 1862 Valley Campaign, Hood's Tennessee Campaign, and other events in which he had played no part. In all, Alexander deleted about one-third of the original material (in-

cluding an introductory section on his youth), altered much of the
rest, and added several new sections. In terms of emphasis, the
original allocated about 33 percent of its text to events before Gettysburg compared to about 57 percent in *Military Memoirs;* each
devoted roughly 13 percent to Gettysburg; and the Greytown
manuscript allotted 47 percent to campaigns after Gettysburg con-
trasted to about 28 percent in *Military Memoirs.*

Published by Charles Scribner's Sons in 1907, *Military Memoirs
of a Confederate: A Critical Narrative* quickly gained the status of a
classic.[15] "I have so thoro[ugh]ly enjoyed your 'Military Memoirs,'"
President Theodore Roosevelt informed Alexander shortly after
the book appeared, "that I must write to tell you so." The *Army and
Navy Journal* pronounced it "one of the most valuable of all books
on the war."[16] Although many southerners complained of Alexander's sometimes hard evaluation of Lee or took exception to his
lack of regret over the demise of the Confederacy, they generally
admitted considerable admiration for the book. Typical of these in-
dividuals was W. Gordon McCabe, a former officer in William R. J.
Pegram's battalion of artillery. McCabe expressed disappointment
at Alexander's statement that Confederate independence would
have proved a curse in the long run; however, he believed it "no exaggeration to call this a great book . . . by one of the most high-
minded, resolute, and resourceful officers" in Lee's army.[17]

Later historians echoed the initial enthusiasm. Douglas Southall
Freeman leaned heavily on Alexander's book, which he considered
"the most valuable single commentary on the operations of the Army of Northern Virginia." In an introduction to an earlier reprint of
Military Memoirs, T. Harry Williams observed: "Probably no book
by a participant in the war has done so much to shape the historical
image of that conflict. As Alexander drew lessons from the battles,
so a lesson can be drawn from his book – that the finest military
history may be written by a soldier who is also a scholar." Another
careful student of Confederate literature called the book a "hard-
hitting, authoritative narrative by one of Lee's finest young
officers" that contains "assessments of the military operations of
the Army of Northern Virginia [that] are honest, fair, and sound."[18]
The principal criticism registered by modern historians concerns
Alexander's decision to restrict the amount of personal material in
Military Memoirs – a failing remedied by the publication of

Fighting for the Confederacy. Taken together, Alexander's two books complement each other beautifully and constitute a matchless contribution to the literature on the military side of the war.[19]

Military Memoirs will remain one of the most-quoted books by any participant in the Civil War. In terms of objectivity and analytical power, Alexander quite simply has no peer among the Union and Confederate veterans who wrote about their experiences. Much of *Military Memoirs* reads like a work of modern scholarship, reflecting its author's judicious use of the *Official Records* and other printed and unpublished primary sources. Yet Alexander occasionally stops to paint a splendid word picture, as when he describes the scene on December 11, 1862, as Ambrose E. Burnside's mighty Army of the Potomac crossed the Rappahannock River at Fredericksburg:

> The city, except its steeples, was still veiled in the mist which had settled in the valleys. Above it and in it incessantly showed the round white clouds of bursting shells, and out of its midst there soon rose three or four columns of dense black smoke from houses set on fire by the explosions. The atmosphere was so perfectly calm and still that the smoke rose vertically in great pillars for several hundred feet before spreading outward in black sheets. The opposite bank of the river, for two miles to the right and left, was crowned at frequent intervals with blazing batteries, canopied in clouds of white smoke.
>
> Beyond these, the dark blue masses of over 100,000 infantry in compact columns, and numberless parks of white-topped wagons and ambulances massed in orderly ranks, all awaited the completion of the bridges. The earth shook with the thunder of the guns, and, high above all, a thousand feet in the air, hung two immense balloons. The scene gave impressive ideas of the disciplined power of a great army, and of the vast resources of the nation which sent it forth.[20]

The combination of scholarship and descriptive strength in *Military Memoirs* ensures that readers will be both enlightened and entertained. The Da Capo edition marks the first appearance in softcover of this cornerstone of any library of the Confederacy. It should reach a new group of readers who will discover for themselves why previous generations have lavished such praise on *Military Memoirs*.

—GARY W. GALLAGHER
Pennsylvania State University
September, 1992

ENDNOTES

1. By far the best treatment of Alexander's life is Maury Klein, *Edward Porter Alexander* (Athens, Georgia: University of Georgia Press, 1971). Klein accords Alexander's wartime and postwar careers approximately equal attention. For a shorter sketch, see Charles L. Dufour, *Nine Men in Gray* (Garden City, N.Y.: Doubleday & Company, 1963), 299-339.
2. Alexander's promotion to second lieutenant in the United States Army had come on October 18, 1858. For his pre-war ranks, see Francis B. Heitman, *Historical Register and Dictionary of the United States Army, From Its Organization, September 29, 1789, to March 2, 1903,* 2 vols. (1903; reprint ed., Urbana, Ill.: University of Illinois Press, 1965), 1:156. Alexander's commission as a captain in the Confederate army carried the date March 16, 1861. Information on all of Alexander's promotions during his Confederate service are in Compiled Service Records of Confederate General and Staff Officers and Nonregimental Enlisted Men, M331, Roll 2, National Archives, Washington, D.C.
3. U.S. War Department, *The War of the Rebellion: A Compilation of the Official Records of the Union and Confederate Armies,* 128 vols. (Washington: GPO, 1880-1901), ser. I, vol. 2:446.
4. Ibid., ser. I, vol. 25, pt. 2:616; Jennings C. Wise, *The Long Arm of Lee, or, The History of the Artillery of the Army of Northern Virginia, With a Brief Account of the Confederate Bureau of Ordnance,* 2 vols. (1915; reprint ed., Richmond, Va.: Owens Publishing Company, 1988), 2:758.
5. For a postwar exchange of correspondence beetween Longstreet and Walton that underscores the latter's sensitivity on this subject, see J. William Jones and others, eds., *Southern Historical Society Papers,* 52 vols. and 3-vol. index (1876-1959; reprint ed., Wilmington, N.C.: Broadfoot Publishing Company, 1990-92), 5:47-53.
6. The quotation is from Edward Porter Alexander, *Fighting for the Confederacy: The Personal Recollections of General Edward Porter Alexander,* ed. Gary W. Gallagher (Chapel Hill, N.C.: University of North Carolina Press, 1989), 336-37.
7. The noted illustrator Allen C. Redwood, who had served in Lee's army, portrayed Alexander and his last battle line at Appomattox in a postwar engraving reproduced in James Longstreet, *From Manassas to Appomattox: Memoirs of the Civil War in America* (Philadelphia: J. B. Lippincott Company, 1896), opposite p. 624, and in Helen D. Longstreet, *Lee And Longstreet at High Tide: Gettysburg in Light of*

the Official Records (Gainesville, Ga.: privately printed by the author, 1904), opposite p. 212.

8. Edward Porter Alexander to Thomas Jewett Goree, April 24, 1868, in Langston James Goree V, ed., *The Thomas Jewett Goree Letters: Volume I, The Civil War Correspondence* (Bryan, Tex.: Family History Foundation, 1981), 281-82.

9. Alexander's contributions to the *Southern Historical Society Papers* include "The 'Seven Days Battles'" (1:61-76); "Letter from General E. P. Alexander, late Chief of Artillery First Corps, A. N. V." (4:97-111); "Sketch of Longstreet's Division. Winter of 1861-62" (9:512-18); "Sketch of Longstreet's Division – Yorktown and Williamsburg" (10: 32-45); "The Battle of Fredericksburg. Paper No. 1" (10:382-92); "The Battle of Fredericksburg. Paper No. 2 – (Conclusion.)" (10:445-64); and "Confederate Artillery Service" (11:98-113). His two pieces in *Battles and Leaders of the Civil War* are "The Great Charge and Artillery Fighting at Gettysburg" and "Longstreet at Knoxville" (3:357-68, 745-51).

10. Robert Underwood Johnson, *Remembered Yesterdays* (Boston: Little, Brown, 1923), 197.

11. Edward Porter Alexander to Louise Alexander Gilmer, July 2, October 2, 1899, folder 4, Minis Family Papers, Southern Historical Collection, Wilson Library, University of North Carolina, Chapel Hill, North Carolina (repository cited hereafter as SHC).

12. For a discussion of the Greytown manuscript, as well as the tendency of modern scholars to confuse it with draft chapters of *Military Memoirs,* see Gary W. Gallagher's introduction to *Fighting for the Confederacy,* xiii-xxiii.

13. Edward Porter Alexander to William Mason Alexander, September 26, 1900, folder 49, Edward Porter Alexander Papers, SHC; Edward ·Porter Alexander to My Dear Hal, August 20, 1901, folder 51, Alexander Papers, SHC.

14. In *Edward Porter Alexander,* 220-21, Maury Klein explores Alexander's relationship with several historians.

15. Scribners reprinted the book in 1908, 1910, 1912, 1914, and 1918. In 1962, Indiana University Press (Bloomington, Ind.) offered an edition with an introduction by T. Harry Williams as part of its "Civil War Centennial Series"; in 1977, the Press of Morningside Bookshop (Dayton, Ohio) published another hardcover edition with a fine introduction by Maury Klein and new illustrations.

16. Theodore Roosevelt to Edward Porter Alexander, July 16, 1907, folder 67, Alexander papers, SHC; excerpt from a review in *Army and Navy Journal* quoted in an ad for *Military Memoirs* in *Confederate Veteran* 15 (June 1907): third page of advertisements inside the front cover.

17. McCabe's quotation is in *Confederate Veteran* 23 (June 1915):252. In *The South to Posterity: An Introduction to the Writing of Confederate History* (1939; reprint ed., Wendell, N.C.: Broadfoot's Bookmark, 1983), 178, Douglas Southall Freeman commented on the reaction of ex-Confederates to Alexander's book: "At the time [of its publication], the book caused mutterings because General Alexander was thought by some veterans to have been unduly critical of General Lee."

18. Douglas Southall Freeman, *R. E. Lee: A Biography*, 4 vols. (New York: Charles Scribner's Sons, 1934-36), 4:566; introduction by T. Harry Williams in Indiana University reprint of *Military Memoirs*, xxxv; Richard Barksdale Harwell, *In Tall Cotton: The 200 Most Important Confederate Books for the Reader, Researcher, and Collector* (Austin, Tex.: Jenkins Publishing Company & Frontier America Corporation, 1978), 1.

19. For representative comments on the absence of personal anecdotes, see T. Harry Williams's introduction to the Indiana University Press reprint of *Military Memoirs*, xxxiv-xxxv, and James I. Robertson, Jr., "The War in Words," *Civil War Times Illustrated* 14 (Oct. 1975):44.

20. The quotation is on p. 291.

MILITARY MEMOIRS OF A CONFEDERATE

CHAPTER I

FROM THE U.S.A. INTO THE C.S.A.

Mormon War. Return to West Point. The Plains in 1858. The Signal System. Fort Steilacoom, 1860. Leaving Steilacoom. At San Francisco. Interview with McPherson. Resign from U. S. Army. New York to Georgia. Captain of Engineers, C.S.A. Impressions of Travel. The First Blow. Instructions to Maj. Anderson. Anderson's Second Excuse. Third Excuse. Buchanan's Excuse.

THE year 1861 found me a second lieutenant of Engineers, U.S.A., on duty with Co. A, Engineer troops, at Fort Steilacoom, Washington Territory. I had entered West Point from Georgia in 1853, and graduated in 1857. For three years after my graduation I served, generally at the Military Academy, as an assistant instructor, but on two occasions was absent for six month at a time upon special details.

On the first, with Capt. James C. Duane and 64 men of the Engineer Company, we were sent out to Utah for duty with Gen. Albert Sidney Johnston in what was then called the Mormon War. In 1857 the Mormons had refused to receive a governor of the territory, appointed by President Buchanan, and assumed a hostile attitude. Johnston was sent with about 2000 men to install the new governor, Alfred Cumming of Georgia. The Mormons took arms, fortified the passes of the Wasatch Mountains, and captured and burned trains of supplies for the troops.

The near approach of winter decided the War Department to halt Johnston and put him in winter quarters at Fort Bridger, east of the Wasatch, until he could be heavily reënforced in the spring. Six columns of reënforcements were ordered from

Fort Leavenworth, and, of these, our detachment and the 6th Infantry composed column No. 1, and marched on May 6, 1858.

The only travelled route at that time passed by Fort Kearney, Fort Laramie, and the Great South Pass. Our column was ordered to open a new route, following the South Platte to Lodge Pole Creek, and up that stream to its headwaters in the Southern Black Hills, and thence, via Bridger's Pass, to join the old road a short distance east of Fort Bridger. Only Frémont, some years before, had ever gone through by that route, and it was thought to be materially shorter. When we got into the mountains we found it necessary to leave the 6th Infantry in camp, and to go ahead with our company to make a practicable road. We also had to ferry, using iron wagon bodies as boats, the Laramie, the North Platte, and Green rivers. Fort Bridger was reached on Aug. 1 — 86 days, 970 miles. The new route proved to be 49 miles shorter than the South Pass road.

Without mails for six weeks, it was only on arrival at Fort Bridger we learned that the "Mormon War" was over. Brigham Young, on seeing the large force prepared to install his rival, Gov. Cumming, had wisely concluded to submit and forego his dream of independence. Perhaps he was the wisest leader of a people seeking freedom, of all his generation. At first, the Mormons deserted their homes, and proposed to burn them and migrate to Mexico. Neither Confederate nor Boer was more devoted to his cause than the Mormons to their own. But Brigham Young knew when the time to surrender had come, and he deserves a monument for knowing it and acting upon the knowledge; even though by doing so he greatly disappointed many young officers, myself among them, anxious to see active service.

Meanwhile an important Indian war had broken out in Oregon, and the detachment of our company which had been left at West Point was now on its way there via the Isthmus under Lts. Casey and Robert. Orders had, therefore, been issued recalling our detachment to West Point, and directing the 6th Infantry to march on by land to Oregon.

On Aug. 9 we set out via the South Pass and Fort Laramie route and reached Leavenworth, 1019 miles, on Oct. 3, 56 days. We lay over eight Sundays, and one day at Laramie, and made

47 marches averaging 22 miles each. The longest march was 27 miles. These figures are of interest for comparison with marches made on special occasions in the war. The conditions of the march were the most favorable possible, being over good roads, in good weather, by a small body, with all ammunition and knapsacks carried in a train of nearly empty wagons, and officers and men all anxious to make a quick trip. Distances were carefully measured by an odometer. Rests during the march were about 10 minutes in each hour, and the average rate of movement on good ground was a mile in 20 minutes. From Leavenworth we took a boat to St. Louis, and thence rail to New York and West Point, arriving Oct. 13.

The Plains at this period were in their pristine wildness, and I had enjoyed the march greatly. Buffalo and antelope were abundant, and I was fond of hunting. The Indians were armed but with bows and arrows, and dressed only in breech clouts, blankets, feathers, and paint. Gold was first discovered on Cherry Creek, near what is now Denver, during this summer, and on our return we met the earliest emigrants going out to that section. Within two years there was a considerable city there, with theatres and daily papers.

I remained at West Point a year as Assistant Instructor in Engineering, and during the summer of 1859 was put in charge of the Department of Fencing and Target Practice. In Oct., 1859, I was assigned to special duty with Assistant-Surgeon A. J. Myer to experiment with a system of military signals which he had devised and offered to the War Department. It was based upon the use of Baine's telegraphic alphabet, which formed the letters by the use of only two elements — dot and dash. The Morse alphabet uses four — dot, short dash, long dash, and interval between dashes. Myer had originally suggested its use as a language for the deaf and dumb, when he was a medical student. By the waving of anything to the left for dot, and to the right for dash, any letter could be indicated by a few waves.

For three months we experimented with flags, torches, and glasses between Fort Hamilton and Sandy Hook, and, in Jan., 1860, we reported to the War Department in Washington with what has been since known as the "Wig-wag" Signal

System. A bill was introduced into Congress to adopt the system and Myer and I were directed to exhibit it to the Military Committees. I was also assigned to temporary duty on a board of officers experimenting with breech-loading rifles, of which there were several models being offered to the War Department.

By April, 1860, the Signal Bill having been favorably reported, I was relieved from special duty and ordered back to West Point, but was given a leave of absence for 60 days. During this leave I married Miss Bettie Mason of King George Co., Va. Soon after returning to West Point I was ordered to relieve Lt. Robert at Fort Steilacoom in Washington Territory with the detachment of our company. With my wife I sailed on the steamer *Northern Light* for Aspinwall on Aug. 10; by the *John L. Stephens* from Panama on the 19th; and by the *Cortes* from San Francisco on Sept. 8; landing at Steilacoom City on Sept. 20. All steamers of those days were side wheelers.

The post was commanded by Col. Silas Casey of the 9th Infantry, and garrisoned by two companies of the 9th Infantry and our detachment of 36 Engineer troops under Lt. Thomas L. Casey. There were no duties but those of company routine. The post was a very pleasant one, the woods and waters abounded in game and fish, the climate was mild and open, and the fall and winter passed rapidly. But it was a period of great anxiety to Southern officers whose native states, after debating the question of secession, began one after another to take the step.

There was generally little active interest taken by army officers in political questions, but, with few exceptions, the creed was held that, as a matter of course, in case war should result from secession, each officer would go with his state. In Feb. we received news of the secession of Georgia. There seemed then, however, strong probability of a peaceful separation. In March came orders for the return of our detachment to West Point.

No vessel was then running to any port in Puget Sound, and we had to wait until special arrangements for our transportation could be made. Our Quartermaster Department, however, maintained an armed vessel, the *Massachusetts*, upon the Sound to keep off invasions of the Stikane Indians, who made raids from Alaska in their immense war canoes. This vessel was directed to take us to Port Townsend, and there the *Cortes*, which ran between San Francisco and Vancouver's Island, would call and get us.

We sailed from Steilacoom City in the afternoon of April 9, 1861. Four years later, to an hour, I saw Gen. Lee ride back to his lines from Appomattox Court House, where he had just surrendered his army. On April 12 we took the *Cortes*, and, after touching at Squimault and Portland, we reached San Francisco on the 20th. We were too late to catch the Panama steamer of that date, as we had hoped, and the next boat was May 1.

As our steamer made fast to the wharf all my personal plans were upset. A special messenger, waiting on the wharf, came aboard and handed me an order by telegraph and Pony Express relieving me from duty with my company, and ordering me to report to Lt. McPherson in charge of Alcatraz Island, San Francisco harbor.

I was very sorry to receive this order, as it deprived me of transportation, leaving me, with my wife, over 6000 miles from home by the only available route, and it precipitated my own resignation, which I might have reasonably delayed until I was back in the East.

But there was now no longer any doubt that war was inevitable, and, indeed, within a day or two the Pony Express and telegraph line brought news of the fall of Fort Sumter.

So when I reported to McPherson, in obedience to my orders, I told him that I must resign and go with my state, and I begged that he would forward my resignation, and at the same time give me a leave of absence, which would allow me to go home and await the acceptance of my resignation there. He had authority to give such leave, and, unless he gave it, I would be compelled to remain in San Francisco, which would detain me at least two months.

While McPherson proved himself afterward to be a great soldier, he was also one of the most attractive and universally beloved and admired men whom I have ever met. His reply to my request was like a prophecy in its foresight, and its affectionate kindness appealed to me very deeply. I have always remembered the conversation vividly. He said: —

"If you must go, I will give the leave of absence, and do all in my power to facilitate your going. But don't go. These urgent orders to stop you here are meant to say that, if you are willing to keep out of the war on either side, you can do so. They mean that you will not be asked to go into the field against your own people, but that you will be kept on this coast, upon fortification duty, as long as the war lasts. Gen. Totten likes you and wants to keep you in the Corps. That is what these orders mean. This war is not going to be the ninety days affair that papers and politicians are predicting. Both sides are in deadly earnest, and it is going to be fought out to the bitter end. If you go, as an educated soldier, you will be put in the front rank. God only knows what may happen to you individually, but for your cause there can be but one result. *It must be lost.* Your whole population is only about eight millions, while the North has twenty millions. Of your eight millions, three millions are slaves who may become an element of danger. You have no army, no navy, no treasury, and practically none of the manufactures and machine shops necessary for the support of armies, and for war on a large scale. You are but scattered agricultural communities, and you will be cut off from the rest of the world by blockade. Your cause must end in defeat, and the individual risks to you must be great. On the other hand, if you stay out here, you will soon be left the ranking engineer officer on this whole coast. Every one of the older officers will soon be called East for active service, and there will be casualties and promotion, and probably increase of the Corps. Meanwhile you will have every chance to make a reputation for yourself as an engineer, and you will have charge of this big Lime Point reservation, about 10,000 acres, all covered with wild oats. Buy a flock of sheep and put on it, hire a Mexican to herd them, and in four years you will be a rich man. The city of San Francisco, too, is filling in water lots, and the Engineer officers are consulted in fixing the harbor lines. This will give you information and opportunities in making good investments. Briefly, remaining here you have every opportunity for professional reputation, for promotion, and for wealth. Going home you have every personal risk to run, and in a cause foredoomed to failure."

I could not but be greatly impressed by this appeal. It made me realize, as I had never done before, the gravity of the decision which I had to make. But one consideration was inexorable: *I must go with my people.* So I answered: —

"What you say is probably all true. But my situation is just this. My people are going to war. They are in deadly earnest, believing it to be for their liberty. If I don't come and bear my part, they will believe me to be a coward. And I shall not know whether I am or not. I have just *got* to go and stand my chances."

His reply was, "In your situation I would probably feel the same way about it." So I wrote my resignation, dating it May 1, and McPherson gave me leave of absence, and did everything possible to make my going easy and comfortable. I never saw him again after our sad parting on the dock, for, as he had foreseen, he was ordered East, and, having been made a major-general and won high distinction, was killed at Atlanta in July, 1864.

My resignation was duly accepted, and notice reached me in August, before the mails to the South through Kentucky were entirely discontinued. We sailed on May 1 in the *Golden Age*, crossed the Isthmus on the 14th, and arrived in New York on steamer *Champion* on the 24th, having lost two days in a severe gale. We landed early, and had intended remaining in New York for a day or two, but while we had been upon our journey, events had been in progress.

President Lincoln had called for 75,000 troops. All of the border states had refused to furnish troops, and had taken part with those which had seceded, and a small Federal army had been collected at Washington. On the night before our arrival a part of this force was marched across into Virginia, and occupied Alexandria.

Col. Ellsworth, commanding the leading regiment, had entered a hotel and torn down a secession flag from its roof. The proprietor, Jackson, had shot Ellsworth dead as he came downstairs, and had been killed himself.

My wife and I were shopping in Canal Street about noon, when a man rushed into the store and shouted out this news. The excitement which this caused, and the hostility to all Confederates evident in general conversation, warned me that if I were known to be a resigned officer on my way to enter the Confederate army I might encounter trouble.

We cut short our shopping and decided to leave for Louisville by the first train. Kentucky was endeavoring to take a position of neutrality in the conflict, and through that state we could

make our way to Georgia.   We left at 5 P.M. on 26th by the
Erie road, and going through Cleveland, Cincinnati, Seymour,
and Jefferson, we reached Louisville on the 27th and Chattanooga on May 28.   Here I met the Confederate Secretary of
War, Hon. L. P. Walker, on his way to Richmond, Va., now
the capital of the Confederacy.

I called on him and was told that a commission as captain of
Engineers was awaiting my acceptance.   Of course I accepted,
and promised to report in Richmond as soon as I could leave
my wife in Washington, Ga., at my father's home.   We spent
that night in Atlanta, and reached Washington, Thursday, May
30.   The next day I left for Richmond and arrived there Saturday night, June 1.

One feature of this eight days' journey, which I recall very
distinctly, was the comparative impressions made upon me by
the camps, and the preparations for war, which I saw everywhere, both at the North and in the South.   They recalled
McPherson's comparison of the military strength of the two
sections, and did not discredit his predictions.

The camps near the principal Northern towns were all of regiments.   Those in the South were mostly of a company each.
The arms of the Northern troops were generally the long-range
rifled muskets.   Those of the Southern troops were almost universally the old-fashioned smooth-bore muskets.   The Northern
troops were always neatly uniformed in blue, their camps seemed
well equipped, and there was generally some visible show of military discipline about them.   The Confederate uniforms were
blue, gray, or brown, and sometimes uniforms were lacking.
There was, too, a noticeable contrast in the physical appearance
of the men, the Northern and Western men having more flesh
and better color.   As physical machines, to withstand hardships,
a casual observer would have pronounced them superior to their
antagonists.   But I lived to see that appearances may deceive.
Indeed, it became a never-ceasing wonder, to the very end at
Appomattox, to see how our lean, ill-equipped ranks would fight,
all the harder, it seemed, as the men grew thinner and more
ragged and hungry looking.

Here it is in order to speak briefly of one of the incidents leading up to the attack upon Fort Sumter, the history of which is instructive.

This attack is often spoken of as the first hostile act of the war. Really the first hostile act was the transfer of the garrison of Fort Moultrie into Fort Sumter, stealthily accomplished during the night of Dec. 26, 1860, the guns of Moultrie being spiked, and their ammunition destroyed. It was a military measure which utterly changed the *status quo*.

Both the S.C. authorities and President Buchanan were earnestly anxious to maintain this status, and the War Department, in its anxiety, had sent a specially detailed officer, Maj. Don Carlos Buell (afterward Maj.-Gen.) to impress the importance of it upon Maj. Anderson in command. His instructions were to be delivered *verbally*, which is, surely, always a mistake in a matter of grave importance. Conversations are too often and too easily misunderstood, and exact words forgotten. In this case, it is hard to believe that Maj. Anderson *could* have so forgotten, not to say deliberately disobeyed, his instructions as he did, *had they been given in writing*. In that view of the matter, it may be said that the war was precipitated by giving *important orders verbally*. Another example will be found in the story of the battle of Seven Pines which Gen. Joseph E. Johnston lost by trusting to instructions given verbally.

Maj. Buell's memorandum of the verbal instructions given is a paper of over 300 words, and is a fair sample of explicit language. Here is the sentence especially referring to any change of position of the garrison of Fort Moultrie: —

" You are to carefully avoid every act which would needlessly tend to provoke aggression, and for that reason you are not, without evident and imminent necessity, to take up any position which could be construed into the assumption of a hostile attitude."

These instructions were given Dec. 11. The Carolina authorities were entirely satisfied with the assurances given that the status would be preserved.

Both sides were, therefore, taken completely by surprise when the morning of Dec. 27 dawned, and disclosed what Anderson had done. The Secretary of War telegraphed him as follows:

"Intelligence has reached here this morning that you have abandoned Fort Moultrie, spiked your guns, burned the carriages, and gone to Fort Sumter. It is not believed, because there is no order for any such movement. Explain the meaning of this report."

Anderson made in all three explanations. One had been written before being called for, at 8 P.M. the night before, when his movement was barely completed. It was as follows: "The step which I have taken was in my opinion necessary to prevent the effusion of blood." Next, on receipt of the telegraphic demand for explanation, he replied: —

"I abandoned Fort Moultrie because I was certain that if attacked my men must have been sacrificed and the command of the harbor lost."

As the entire garrison numbered but 75, including officers, this was probably true. But he had instructions from the Secretary of War reading: —

"It is neither expected nor desired that you should expose your own life, or that of the men under your command, in a hopeless conflict in defence of these forts. If they are invested or attacked by a force so superior that resistance would in your judgment be a useless waste of life, it will be your duty to yield to necessity and make the best terms in your power."

Anderson had been selected for the command, as a native of a neutral state, Kentucky, and as one who, it was hoped, would not be stampeded by imaginary danger. But his correspondence had indicated nervousness, and this had probably inspired the instructions here quoted. They evidently, however, failed of their intended effect.

After sending the telegram, Maj. Anderson, for the first time apparently, recalled that he had been strictly cautioned against a needless stampede, and that he would be expected to show some more pressing necessity for his action. He accordingly wrote a third explanation as follows: —

"In addition to my reasons given in my telegram, and in my letter of last night, I will add, as my opinion, that many things convinced me that the authorities of the state designed to proceed to a hostile act."

A weaker defence of such gross disobedience of orders cannot be conceived. In all the acrimony of the times, no one ever alleged the existence of any design to violate the status.

President Buchanan felt himself pledged, and decided to order Anderson back to Fort Moultrie, and acquainted the Attorney-General, Stanton, with his decision. Mr. Stanton immediately set to work to defeat this intention. He summoned Dan Sickles, and planned with him to have at once salutes of 100 guns fired in New York and Philadelphia in honor of Anderson's act, and to have telegrams in hundreds showered on the President, congratulating him as a second Jackson, and a saviour of the country by his firmness.[1]

These demonstrations were effectively made under the joint action of Sickles and John Russell Young in Washington, of Dougherty in Philadelphia, and of Rynders in New York. They worked upon the weak side of Buchanan's character, and Anderson was allowed to remain in Fort Sumter.

Buchanan excused himself to the Carolinians by saying that he would have ordered Anderson back, had they given him time before themselves taking possession of Moultrie, and raising their flag over it. It was a poor excuse, but it was an occasion when any excuse would do. Passion was inflamed on both sides and recriminations began. The position occupied by Anderson was one of unstable equilibrium, impossible to be long maintained. He had indeed saved the "effusion of blood" *of his own command*, but the act made inevitable a deluge of other blood.

The crisis came in April, when Fort Sumter ran short of provisions, and here the Confederate leaders lost the opportunity of their lives in not allowing provisions to be supplied, and otherwise maintaining the *then* status. They might thus have avoided at least the odium of firing the first gun, and gained valuable time for preparation, or for possible compromises through the influence of the border states. But no compromise is ever possible after the firing of the first gun. There is in it some quality which stirs the human heart as nothing else can do. Had the British not fired upon the Colonials at Lexington in 1775, we might all have been Colonials yet. For blood is thicker than water, and were it not so, the development of nations would often prove painfully slow.

[1] *Men and Memories*, Mrs. J. R. Young, p. 25.

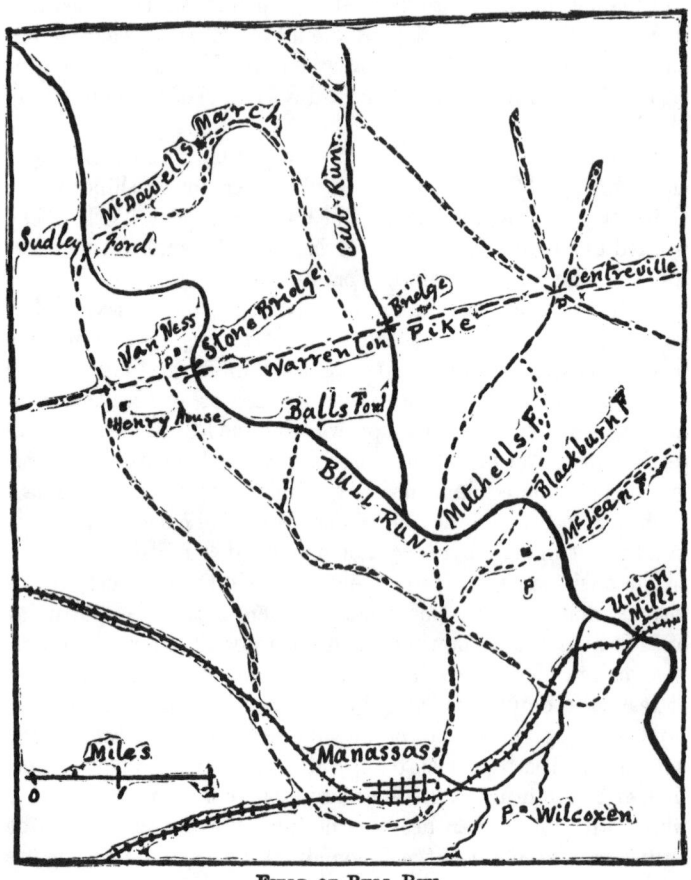

FIELD OF BULL RUN

CHAPTER II

THE BATTLE OF BULL RUN (JULY, 1861)

At Richmond. Gen. Robert S. Garnett. Orders Received. At Manassas. Installing Signal Stations. Strategic Opportunities. Beauregard's Suggestions. McDowell's Moves. Orders sent Johnston. Johnston Marches. Patterson remains Ignorant. The Odds against Us. Marked Batteries, etc. Blackburn's Ford. An Infantry Skirmish. An Artillery Duel. New Plan Needed. Plan Adopted. McDowell Over-persuaded. In the Confederate Lines. McDowell's New Plan. Beauregard's Plan. How it Failed. Tyler at Stone Bridge. At the Signal Station. Beauregard Informed. A Pause. The Dust Cloud. The Action Begun. Bee and Bartow come in. The Generals go to the Left. Watching the Battle. Johnston and Beauregard Arrive. Reënforcement sent for. McDowell's Four Idle Brigades. Two Hours' Fighting. The Henry House Hill. Cummings's Brilliant Coup. The Federal Collapse. Leaving Signal Station. Stragglers in the Rear. Davis and Jackson. Lost Opportunities. Order checking Kershaw. Order stopping Pursuit. Affairs on the Right. Jones and Longstreet. Bonham takes the Lead. Bonham Halts. Overcaution in New Commanders. The Final Scene. Return from the Field. Hill's Report. Inaction of Council.

I ARRIVED in Richmond, Saturday night, June 1, reported for duty Monday morning, and received my commission as captain of Engineers. Engineer officers were in demand, but President Davis remembered my appearing with Maj. Myer before the Military Committee of the Senate, in connection with the system of signals, and I was first ordered to start in Richmond a little factory of signal apparatus, such as torches, poles, and flags. I was told that I would soon be sent to install the system in some one of the small armies being collected at several points.

I was quickly ready, and anxious for orders, which for some cause were delayed. Gen. Robert S. Garnett was in Richmond at the time, organizing a force for service in West Virginia, and made application for me upon his staff, but it was refused. He had been Commandant of the Corps of Cadets during my first year at West Point, and the impression I formed of him as a soldier is not lower than that formed of any other officer I have ever known. In every one else I have seen some mere human traits, but in Garnett every trait was purely military. Had he lived, I am sure he would have been one of our great generals.

He lost his life, however, in his first affair, July 13, 1861, near Carrick's Ford, Va., and in a characteristic manner. With ten of his men, who were raw troops, he had halted to delay the enemy at a creek crossing. His men were nervous under a sharp fire, and Garnett remarked that "they needed a little example." He stepped out in full view of the enemy and walked slowly back and forth, a target for the sharpshooters. He was presently shot dead, just when he was prepared to withdraw.

Nearly the whole of June passed while I was kept, from day to day, awaiting orders. Near the end of June, I was ordered to organize five batteries of artillery into a battalion, and prepare them for the field. I was forming classes for the instruction of officers, and making requisitions for supplies when new orders came, sending me to signal duty with Beauregard at Manassas.

I had just decided to have my wife come on to Richmond, and she was *en route* when I had to leave. I regretted giving up the Artillery Battalion. It would have been a decided step in advance had we inaugurated, so soon, a battalion organization of several batteries. We came to it about a year later, but meanwhile our batteries had been isolated and attached to infantry brigades. So they fought singly, and in such small units artillery can do little.

On July 2, I arrived at Manassas, reported to Beauregard, was assigned to duty upon his staff, and ordered to install the system of signals for use in the coming battle. It was certain that a battle must be fought soon.

Federal armies were being collected in West Virginia under McClellan; on the upper Potomac threatening Winchester, under Patterson; at Alexandria under McDowell; and, at Fortress Monroe, under Butler. These armies were mostly raw troops, but among them were the 75,000 three-months men, first called out in April, and they were now fairly well disciplined.

Their terms of service would begin to expire soon after the middle of July, and it was sure that some use would sooner be made of them. For we were then less a military nation than ever before or since, and neither side recognized its own unpreparedness.

By June 24 McDowell had submitted a plan of aggressive operation, and July 8 had been named as the date of the proposed movement. Gen. Scott had urged longer delay, and that the three-months men should be allowed to go, and their places supplied with the three-years men now being enlisted. Political necessities, however, overruled his objections. Fortunately for the Confederates, with all their resources the Federal forces were not able to move before the 16th, and when they did move, they consumed four days more, from the 17th to the 20th inclusive, in about 20 miles of marching and in preliminaries. Battle was only delivered on July 21, and the crisis of this battle occurred about 3.30 P.M.

We shall see that not only every day of that delay, but even every hour of it, was essential to the Confederate victory which resulted.

So on my arrival at Manassas, July 2, there was really more time to install the signals than I expected, for "rumors of the foe's advance" now swelled upon almost every breeze. I had brought with me from Richmond all necessary equipment and I had only to select men and train them. I soon made acquaintances and got the names of some intelligent privates, who might later be promoted. I had these detailed and put upon a course of instruction and practice. Meanwhile I procured a horse, and between times began an exploration of the country to find what facilities it offered for lines of signals.

The topography was far from favorable. Our line of battle had been chosen behind the stream of Bull Run, about three miles north of Manassas, and the course of the stream was generally wooded and bordered with small fields and pastures, giving few open stretches. I was not sanguine of rendering any valuable service, but fortunately had time to examine the country, and, as will be seen, the line was found which disclosed the enemy's attack in time to defeat it.

About a mile east of Manassas, on the farm of a Mr. Wilcoxen, was a high rocky point having a good outlook over a valley to the north and west.   I made this point a central station, and by a little clearing here and there got two straight six-mile ranges.   One was northwest to a bluff over Bull Run valley on our extreme left, near the house of Van Ness, just above the Stone Bridge by which the Warrenton Turnpike crossed Bull Run. The other was north, to Centreville, about three miles beyond the Run, opposite our centre.   A third station was found near the house of McLean, opposite our right centre, and a fourth near our headquarters at Centreville.   This was the utmost the topography permitted, and the men were encamped at the stations and set to practising by day and night.

Where the opponents have each two armies in the field, each has the opportunity to combine his whole force upon his adversary.

This was the situation in Northern Virginia.   McDowell, at Alexandria with 35,000 men, and Patterson near Harper's Ferry, about 50 miles away, with 15,000, were opposed by Beauregard at Manassas with 22,000, and Johnston at Winchester with 11,000.

No effort was made by the Federal commander-in-chief to unite Patterson's force with McDowell's, but McDowell was assured that Patterson should threaten Johnston, and keep him in the Valley, so that McDowell would have Beauregard only to deal with.   The Confederate armies, unfortunately, had no commander-in-chief.

In theory the power resides with the President, but his action is apt to be slow and comparatively inefficient.   In the approaching battle this was well illustrated.   Although the enemy was so slow as to allow amazing time, and the battle was saved, it was, as it were, "by the skin of our teeth" and without any of the fruits of victory.

Beauregard had proposed to the President on June 12 to take the aggressive and unite the two armies in an attack upon Alexandria.   It was disapproved, but Beauregard did not let the matter drop.

On July 13 he sent Col. Chestnut, a staff-officer, to Richmond to urge the concentration of the two armies and a prompt offensive movement. A formal hearing was had by the President, with Cooper and Lee, but the proposition was rejected, on the good ground that the enemy was as yet practically within his fortified lines, where he could not be attacked, and could bring up, at his leisure, Patterson and other reënforcements. The only effective way to combine the two armies was to make it a surprise to the enemy when away from his fortifications.

About noon, July 16, McDowell put his army in motion. There were ten brigades in four divisions, comprising about 30,000 men, with 49 guns. He did not bring his whole force, but left in reserve, in the works behind him, Runyon's division of over 5000 men. This large division would have been of greater value on the field, and he should have had at least 100 guns, for artillery is the best arm against raw troops. The four divisions moved by different roads, converging toward our advanced positions about Fairfax. They made on the first day only short marches of six or eight miles, going into camp far outside of our picket lines, so as not to divulge the movement. This was so well managed that, although rumors reached the Confederates, yet nothing was known until next morning. Then our advanced posts were driven in and a few of our pickets were captured. At this moment Johnston's army should have been ready to march to Beauregard over roads previously selected and reconnoitred. The men should even have been kept for days encamped where they could quickly stretch out on the proper roads. For many contingencies beset all marches, and preparation saves hours big with fate.

The whole day of the 17th was lost to the Confederates by the news having to go to the President. Beauregard, sometime during the day, telegraphed him as follows: —

"MANASSAS, July 17, 1861.

"The enemy has assailed my outposts in heavy force, I have fallen back on the line of Bull Run, and will make a stand at Mitchell's Ford. If his force is overwhelming, I shall retire to the Rappahannock railroad bridge, saving my command for defence there, and for future operations. Please inform Johnston of this, via Staunton, and also Holmes. Send forward any reënforcements at the earliest possible moment, and by every possible means. — G. T. BEAUREGARD."

Apparently after some deliberation, the Executive acted, for about 1 A.M. on July 18, Johnston in Winchester received a telegram. It is worthy of study as a model *not* to be followed in such cases. It was as follows : —

"RICHMOND, July 17, 1861.

"Gen. Beauregard is attacked. To strike the enemy a decisive blow all of your effective force will be needed. If practicable, make the movement, sending your sick and baggage to Culpeper C. H. either by railroad or by Warrenton. In all the arrangements exercise your discretion. — S. COOPER, Adj't. and Ins. General."

When Johnston came to make his report of the battle of Bull Run he wrote as follows of this message : —

"About one o'clock in the morning of July 18 I received from the Government a telegraphic despatch informing me that the northern army was advancing upon Manassas, then held by Gen. Beauregard, and directing me, if practicable, to go to that officer's assistance, after sending my sick to Culpeper C. H. In the exercise of discretion conferred by the terms of the order, I at once determined to march to join Gen. Beauregard."

President Davis took great offence at this language and ordered the word "after" before the words "sending your sick" to be erased from the report in the records. He resented also Beauregard's speaking of this order in his report as only permissive, and not mandatory. And even in his book, written after the war, he claims that the order was a "positive" one, and considers it "strange that any one has construed it otherwise."

The words "if practicable" are always of such doubtful interpretation that they should be excluded from all important orders. They leave matters in doubt. Every order should be distinctly either the one thing or the other. Lee used the phrase at Gettysburg, in ordering Ewell to press a routed enemy, and lost his victory by it.

It is notable, too, that this order not only failed to urge haste, but, by injunctions concerning sick and baggage by rail, implied that time would permit, which it did not. Exclusive use of the railroad by the troops was absolutely necessary.

Had Johnston felt any reluctance to the movement, or had Patterson's attitude been in the least threatening, excuses would have been easy to make for non-compliance. But Johnston was a good soldier, and he lost no time in taking the road. He quickly arranged for the best route of march, and for the indispensable help of the railroad in moving his infantry. His leading brigade was under command of Jackson, soon to show the world the stuff of which he was formed, and to earn an immortal name. Jackson's brigade left camp at noon, and at ten o'clock that night bivouacked at Paris, 17 miles, fording the Shenandoah and crossing the Blue Ridge *en route*. This is an average of about one and three-quarters miles an hour and is an excellent march under the circumstances.

The other three brigades, Bee's, Bartow's, and Elzey's, made about 13 miles, and encamped at the Shenandoah, itself a good march. Next morning, Friday, the 19th, Jackson's brigade covered the remaining six miles from Paris to the railroad station at Piedmont, 34 miles from Manassas by 8 A.M. Trains were awaiting it, and by 10 A.M. it was off, arriving at Manassas about 1 P.M. say, 2500 strong and coming 57 miles in 25 hours. The other brigades arrived at Piedmont during the afternoon; but although the railroad had promised to deliver all four brigades in Manassas by sunrise Saturday, the 20th, only two more regiments, the 7th and 8th Ga., of Bartow's brigade — about 1400 men — were sent. The cavalry and artillery continued their march by the wagon road, but the infantry waited at Piedmont, some of it for two days, and without rations. The trouble was that the railroad had no relays of employees, and was unable to hold its men at constant work.

On the 20th Johnston himself went with the 4th Ala., the 2d Miss., and two companies of the 11th Miss., about a thousand men. These were the last troops to arrive in time for the opening of the battle.

During the night, the 6th N.C., 10th Va., 3d Tenn., and 1st Md. were taken — about 2000 men — under Kirby Smith and Elzey. These, arriving at Manassas before noon on Sunday, were hurried to the battlefield, six miles, arrived at the critical moment at the critical point, and changed defeat into victory. The remaining 2500 of Johnston's 11,000 (the 9th Ga., 2d Tenn., 13th Va., the Ky. Battalion, and eight companies of the 11th

Miss.) only arrived the day after the battle, having been nearly four days making the 57 miles.

On the 19th, while Johnston was waiting at Piedmont, one of Beauregard's staff arrived to suggest that Johnston should march by Aldie, and fall upon McDowell's flank at Centreville, while Beauregard attacked from Bull Run. It was an unwise scheme, and Johnston's decision to unite the two armies out of the presence of the enemy was safest.

Meanwhile, by monumental mismanagement, Patterson's army might as well have been upon another planet. He had been notified that McDowell would advance on the 16th, and that he must hold and occupy Johnston. Accordingly, on the 15th he advanced from Martinsburg to Bunker Hill. He remained all day on the 16th at Bunker Hill, and on the 17th moved as far as Charlestown, in the direction of Harper's Ferry. Here he remained until after the battle on the 21st. On the 18th he telegraphed : —

"The enemy has stolen no march on me. I have kept him actively employed and, by threats and reconnoissances in force, caused him to¸be reënforced. I have accomplished, in this respect, more than the General-in-Chief asked, or could well be expected in face of an enemy far superior in numbers." Only on the 20th did he find out that something had happened, and he reports: "With a portion of his force Johnston left Winchester by the road to Millwood on the afternoon of the 18th. His whole force was about 35,200."

These telegrams are fair specimens of the colossal misinformation often conveyed in official reports. Johnston, in his narrative, humorously suggests that the overrating of each other's strength, by opposing commanders, resulted probably from the same feeling which made his antagonist's sword seem to Gil Blas "d'une longueur excessive." If Johnston's sword had been as long as Patterson believed, it would have been creditable in the latter to approach even within 14 miles.

And now, at sunrise on the 17th, McDowell is in front of our pickets at Fairfax, and within 10 miles of our line of battle, and he is to have us at the mercy of his superior force until the afternoon of the 21st — say four days and a half. If the shades of departed warriors watched the contest, the odds among them against us at this stage must have been high. Against their force, our position and our organization were both inferior. Our line of battle was nearly seven miles long, and communications in rear of it were poor and crooked. Our six brigades were all independent of each other, no divisions having been formed, and there were, besides, several unbrigaded regiments and batteries, making a command too complex to be efficiently handled, especially with an inexperienced staff. Apart from their superior numbers, the effective division organization of the Federals, and especially their batteries of regular artillery with each division, would seem enough to insure Federal victory even for a front attack by brute force. This might have been made, even on the afternoon of the 17th, by a bold pursuit of our advanced guard, which comprised but one brigade.

For the slowness of the Federal advance that day (it holds the record for slowness) McDowell was personally responsible. He had issued to his troops a good order of march, in which he called attention to the strength of each column, and its ability to cope with all it was likely to meet, even without the help of the other columns. But he had spoiled the moral effect of his own language and practically demoralized his brigade commanders by one unwise caution.

It "would not be pardonable in any commander to come upon a battery or breastwork without a knowledge of its position." That caution meant more to McDowell's officers than appears on its face. For the newspaper reporters of those days, with the appetite for sensations which still distinguishes the craft, had made a great bugbear of "masked batteries." The term originated at the attack upon Fort Sumter, where a certain battery was constructed, masked by a house which was destroyed just before opening fire. After that masked batteries figured on every field and in every event. When Butler was repulsed at Big Bethel it was a masked battery which did it. When Schenck's railroad reconnoissance from Alexandria on June 17, accidentally ran into Gregg's reconnoissance from Manassas at Vienna, and was fired into by Kemper's six-pounders, the mysterious masked battery got the credit. Soon, to read the newspapers, one might believe the woods were infested with such batteries, not to mention "Louisiana Tigers" and "Black Horse Cavalry," two other scarecrow names which had caught the reporters' fancies, and been made to do enormous duty.

Now, the threat conveyed in McDowell's order implied the real existence of formidable dangers, and is doubtless responsible for the excessive caution which consumed the day in making an advance scarcely over five miles. Beauregard's advanced guard had not sought to delay the Federals, but had fallen back beyond Centreville, where it bivouacked; and, early next morning, it crossed Bull Run and took position in the Confederate line of battle.

Beauregard had concentrated the bulk of his force between Union Mill's Ford, on the right, and Mitchell's Ford on the left, in which space — about three miles — he had, in order from the right, Ewell's, D. R. Jones's, Longstreet's, and Bonham's brigades, with only Early in reserve some 250 yards behind Longstreet. Cocke's brigade held Ball's Ford, and Evans with the 4th S.C. and Wheat's La. Battalion held the Stone Bridge, two and three miles to the left.

On the morning of the 18th the slow advance of the Federals was resumed, and about noon Tyler's division occupied the hills overlooking the valley of Bull Run, opposite Blackburn's and Mitchell's fords. McDowell was not with his advanced forces. He had ridden far to the left to reconnoitre, with a view to turning our right flank — a duty he might have more wisely confided to his staff. During his absence a small affair occurred at Blackburn's Ford, terminating favorably for the Confederates.

Tyler's instructions were to reconnoitre our position and to threaten our left so as to draw attention to that quarter, but not to bring on a general engagement. These instructions were our salvation, for our army was weak and badly posted and could not have withstood a vigorous attack by the force in front of us. Both of our flanks were in the air, and Bull Run could be crossed by infantry in many places. Our centre was a large salient whose lines the enemy could enfilade. The ground on their side was commanding and afforded close approach under excellent cover. On our side it was low and gently rising to the rear, giving no cover whatever, except of the woods. Our whole force present on the field was about 21,000, of whom about 5000 (Evans's and Cocke's commands) were too far to the left to be available. McDowell's force available was about 37,000.[1]

Tyler, about noon, brought up some guns and began firing at the few points in our territory where he could discern signs of our presence.[2]

After cannonading for some time without drawing reply, Tyler ordered Richardson's brigade to scour the woods in front, and a squadron of cavalry with two guns to advance on the road to Mitchell's Ford. Two of our guns under Kemper fired upon the cavalry when it came into view. It was quickly withdrawn, and Tyler soon decided to withdraw Richardson also. Meanwhile, this brigade had suddenly become engaged. It had found itself on a low bluff overlooking Bull Run, scarcely 50 yards away, a thin fringe of woods intervening. Just across the creek was Longstreet's brigade, about 1400 strong, occupying the low opposite bank of the stream. Immediately both sides opened fire, and a portion of Longstreet's men, finding themselves in the lower position and on open ground, broke to the rear badly. Longstreet rode among and rallied them, and soon led them back, the enemy's line having also withdrawn under cover. Longstreet called upon Early for reënforcement, and the 7th La. was sent forward to him. Meanwhile the Federals made a second advance and poured in another volley and fell back. These tactics were repeated several times, Longstreet meanwhile attempting to cross some of his men over the ford to meet the enemy. The 7th La., however, on one of the Federal advances, had opened fire while still behind Longstreet's line. This fire in the rear threw Longstreet into such confusion that the order to cross was recalled. Our line was in bad shape

[1] O. R. 2, 309.

[2] One of these was the Wilmer McLean residence, on a shady knoll in the cultivated fields a half mile in the rear of Bull Run, which Beauregard had announced as his headquarters for the battle. One of the earliest shots struck the kitchen and ruined the dinner being prepared. Within a year the family were compelled to abandon the plantation and remove to another, which they owned, at Appomattox C. H., Va. Here, by remarkable coincidence on April 9, 1865, the last fighting between the same two armies took place, upon their land as the first had done. Grant made his headquarters in their residence, and in it Lee made the surrender of his army.

when the Federal attack ceased and their force was rapidly withdrawn. Two companies, however, under Captain Marye had crossed the stream, and these pursued the enemy's retreat for some distance and brought back some 20 prisoners and 100 muskets. This gave an air of victory to the termination of the infantry combat.

There then followed a sharp artillery duel, for about 45 minutes. The Federals engaged eight guns (two 20-Pr. and two 10-Pr. Parrott rifles; two 6-Pr. guns and two 12-Pr. howitzers), and fired 415 rounds. The Confederates engaged seven guns, four 6-Pr. guns and three 3-inch iron rifles, made in Richmond, firing a 6-Pr. Burton and Archer projectile. They fired 310 rounds. Our guns stood in the open plateau about 150 yards behind our infantry line, and were hidden from the enemy's view by the thin fringe of tall timber along the creek. This saved us from a speedy defeat, for our limbers and caissons were without cover until Longstreet ordered them brought forward on the flanks, and kept them behind the trees. Thus neither of the combatants could see more of the other than the smoke of his guns, and the fire was but little better than random.

Our guns belonged to the Washington Arty. of New Orleans, the oldest and best drilled organization of artillery in the Confederacy, and it illustrates the lack of professional skill among our volunteers to know that a favorable report was made upon the Burton and Archer projectile, from its performance in this affair, where it was used for the first time. Yet, the first competent test, made of it a few weeks later, showed it to be entirely worthless and caused its manufacture to be at once discontinued. It would not fly point foremost, but "tumbled" and had no range.

Besides these three rifles with ineffective ammunition, a fourth Confederate gun, a brass 6-Pr., soon became useless from an enlarged vent. During the first half of the affair, however, the enemy's fire was not accurate and all went well. There was then a pause during which they managed to improve their aim, and, when they resumed, our men soon realized how they were overmatched. Capt. Eshleman was wounded and Capt. Squires called for reënforcement. Longstreet had no more artillery

available, and ordered Squires to withdraw gradually, one gun
at a time, but meanwhile to keep up a slow reply.

Just then, as so often happens when a battle is becoming
desperate, the enemy ceased to fire, and allowed Squires, who
deserved it, the honor of the last shot, and Beauregard the invaluable morale of the first victory. In this duel the Confederates had one killed, five wounded, and six horses disabled. The
Federals two killed, two wounded. In the whole affair the losses
were : —

Confederate:	15 killed,	53 wounded,	0 missing	68 total
Federal:	19 "	38 "	26 "	83 "

On the night of the 18th McDowell found himself compelled
to make a change in the plan of attack which had been decided
on in Washington before starting. That had contemplated
turning of our right flank. But his reconnoissance in that direction had found the country so wooded and broken, and with
so few good roads, as to be unfavorable for operations. His
next thought was of direct attack upon our front. That was,
beyond question, his best opportunity.

We had, practically, no intrenchment, and there were gaps,
sometimes wide ones, between our brigades. Holmes's brigade
of two regiments (the 2d Tenn. and 9th Ark.), coming from
Acquia Creek, did not arrive until late on the 19th. The confusion caused in our ranks by Tyler's demonstration — for it
can scarcely be called an attack — indicates that a serious
effort with the whole force at hand would have succeeded.

McDowell had disapproved of Tyler's affair, upon his return
from his reconnoissance, and seems to have misunderstood the
facts. In his official report he writes that this affair had shown
us to be too strong to be attacked at Blackburn's Ford. He also
states that the Stone Bridge was mined and defended by a
battery and a heavy abattis, and that his only alternative was
to seek a route to turn our left flank. No one of these statements was correct. At Stone Bridge there was neither abattis,
earthwork, nor mine. There were only two 6-Pr. guns with
the 4th S.C. regiment and Wheat's La. battalion — say 1400
men. There were no other supports within a mile.

The movement decided upon, however, promised excellent results if it could be carried out before Beauregard was reënforced. It was decided to turn the Confederate left by crossing Bull Run above the Stone Bridge. This involved further loss of time in reconnoissance, but confidence was felt that Patterson would keep Johnston in the valley, so the engineers were ordered to find the desired roads. It was not dreamed that Johnston's forces were crossing the Blue Ridge as the sun was setting that afternoon.

McDowell proposed to make his reconnoissance by main force, driving in our pickets and developing our exact position and strength, but he weakly allowed himself to be persuaded, instead, into a reconnoissance by stealth, which is less to be depended upon.

It is worthy of note that upon three occasions in this advance McDowell was persuaded by his leading subordinates to modify orders which he had issued and these modifications lost him the battle. The first occasion was on the 17th, when his army only marched some five or six miles, as already noted. McDowell wished to have the march prolonged to 12 miles, but yielded to persuasion to go into bivouac when half the distance was covered. That practically lost the entire day.

The second occasion was the reconnoissance by stealth to which he now consented. It occupied a day and a half and went miles astray, as may now be seen, in finding the shortest route. It was noon on the 20th when the engineers made their report of having found a concealed road crossing Bull Run at Sudley Ford, and the march was decided upon. From their present camps the average distances to be covered by the turning brigades were between nine and ten miles. McDowell proposed that they should make four miles that afternoon, leaving only six for the next morning. For the third time his officers proposed, and McDowell consented to, a change. It would be more convenient, they urged, to remain in their camps that afternoon and night, and to march a couple of hours earlier in the morning, say at 2.30 A.M. Orders were issued, accordingly, for the 21st. When they came to be executed, the routes of various commands were found to interfere, and although there was a bright moon, and the country was open and roads good, the head of column was about four hours in covering the first four miles. This involved a further loss of at least two hours.

It is now time to revert to the Confederate lines and note what had happened on the 19th and 20th. An attack in force by the Federals had been expected each morning, and its non-occurrence gratefully appreciated. It might be supposed that our time would have been busily used to intrench, erect batteries, and provide abattis and obstructions, but almost nothing of the sort was done. It required a year's experience to educate our army to the value of such work, although the enemy meanwhile not only set us many examples, but had given us some severe object lessons. On the 19th Holmes's brigade had arrived from Acquia Creek. It took position behind Ewell, on our right flank. Jackson's brigade also arrived and was placed in reserve behind Mitchell's Ford. On the 20th Johnston arrived in person, also the 7th and 8th Ga. of Bartow's brigade, the 4th Ala., and the 2d Miss. of Bee's. These troops were placed in reserve behind Blackburn's Ford. As already told, these were the only troops of Johnston's army to arrive in time for the beginning of the battle, though another brigade under Kirby Smith arrived in time to turn the wavering scale about 3 P.M. on the 21st.

It is strange that all this could go on in such close proximity to the Federal army without discovery through some negro or deserter. It is still stranger that McDowell seems to have had no scouts out, upon either flank, who might easily have learned it. Only one intimation reached him of what was going on, and that he refused to credit. Gen. Tyler was an experienced railroad manager, and from the hills north of Bull Run, on the 19th, he had listened to the exhaust of many engines bringing heavy loads into Manassas from the direction of the Valley. He correctly guessed that they were bringing Johnston's army, and reported the facts and his conclusions to McDowell, not only on the 19th, but again on the 20th. The suggestions were received very coolly, and no steps were taken to find out.

From Centreville the Warrenton pike runs straight southwest

for many miles. At two miles it crosses Cub Run, a tributary of Bull Run, on a high wooden bridge. In the retreat this bridge became blocked and many guns were lost there. At four miles it crosses Bull Run on Stone Bridge. A little beyond Cub Run a farm road to the right, by a circuitous route of six miles, leads to Sudley Springs ford of Bull Run, which is two miles above Stone Bridge in an air-line. From Sudley, on the south side of Bull Run, a road to the southeast crosses the Warrenton pike a mile beyond Stone Bridge and leads to Manassas. McDowell's plan was as follows: Tyler with three brigades was to take position opposite the Stone Bridge, make demonstrations, and be prepared to cross. McDowell in person would conduct the five brigades of Hunter's and Heintzelman's divisions by the circuitous road, cross Bull Run at Sudley Ford, and attack Stone Bridge in the rear. As soon as it was carried Tyler's three brigades would cross, and the eight brigades, united behind our left flank, could easily sweep our entire line.

There was, however, one bad feature. The circuitous route by which the five brigades would march would take them dangerously far from his other forces, should Beauregard take the offensive and attack his left at the moment when this turning column was entangled in the circuitous road. The fear of such an attack induced McDowell, while actually on the march, to halt his rear brigade — Howard's — and leave it behind, until the four other brigades had crossed Bull Run and were in action on the south side. That brigade was thus out of use for four critical hours, and when it rejoined, the battle had been lost. Its only service was in covering the retreat.

Meanwhile, by a coincidence, Beauregard had planned to make the very attack which McDowell had feared, and at the very time when he was stretched out on the circuitous road. As Johnston was Beauregard's senior, he was now in command of the joint forces, but as Beauregard was more familiar with the situation, it was left to him to decide upon the order of battle. By uniting the two armies, the Confederates had prepared a surprise for the Federals, but, to reap the full benefit, it should be sprung upon them before they became aware of their danger. Beauregard's order of battle proposed to cross Bull Run with our three right brigades, envelop the enemy's exposed left flank, and drive it toward Centreville. As soon as this battle was joined it would be taken up to the left, by adjoining brigades, in succession. We now had eight brigades concentrated on a front of about three miles, and, opposed to them, McDowell had left but three brigades. We could never hope for a more favorable opportunity to quickly crush these three brigades and be prepared to meet in detail those which McDowell would have to bring back from his right. Unfortunately, however, we failed to improve the opportunity, and it vanished. The history of our failure is as follows: —

Had Beauregard been in command, the so-called "orders" issued would have been immediate, and have been put into process of execution at dawn. But, presumably by Johnston's wish, they were merely instructions to each brigade to "place itself in position of attack upon the enemy," and await orders. The "orders to attack would be given by the Commander-in-Chief." These instructions were sent out at 5 A.M. and were differently understood by the officers addressed. Ewell, with Holmes, did not advance across Bull Run, but simply held himself in readiness on the south side. Jones and Longstreet crossed their brigades and took position on the north bank. Bonham's brigade did not move.

Johnston had expected the arrival during the night of his troops still in the rear. When he found that they had not arrived, he determined not to attack, but to await developments. He consented, however, to a demonstration by Beauregard's right, and orders were sent Ewell and Jones to advance. The order to Ewell was lost. It never reached him and was never found or accounted for afterward. Jones crossed and waited for two hours before the situation was developed. It was then thought too late, and he was withdrawn.

About 6 A.M. Tyler's division appeared before our force under Evans at Stone Bridge, and presently opened a slow fire with a 30-Pr. Parrott rifle. The movement of Tyler toward Stone Bridge early in the morning had been discovered by Longstreet's scouts. He writes of it in his book (page 45): "Their report was sent promptly to headquarters, and, after a short delay, the brigade [Longstreet's] was ordered back to its position behind the Run."

About 8 A.M. Johnston and Beauregard, accompanied by staffs and couriers, rode to the vicinity of Mitchell's Ford, where they left their party under cover, and took position on an open hill some 200 yards to the left of the road. On the Federal side of the Run, the three brigades, left to amuse our line while the flanking column made its march around us, had taken position on the hills about a half-mile north of the creek, started to protect itself with abattis, and opened fire with a few guns upon all movements which they could discover on our side. To this fire we made no reply and kept our positions concealed, but we did nothing to strengthen them.

As he rode out in the morning, Beauregard directed me to go with a courier to the Wilcoxen signal station and remain in general observation of the field, sending messages of all I could discover. I went reluctantly, as the opportunity seemed very slight of rendering any service. There were but two signal stations on our line of battle, — one in rear of McLean's Ford, and one near Van Ness' house, on a bluff a few hundred yards to the left and rear of the Stone Bridge. Beyond the latter station the broad, level valley of Bull Run for some miles, with its fields and pastures, as seen through the glass, was foreshortened into a narrow band of green.

While watching the flag of this station with a good glass, when I had been there about a half-hour, the sun being low in the east behind me, my eye was caught by a glitter in this narrow band of green. I recognized it at once as the reflection of the morning sun from a brass field-piece. Closer scrutiny soon revealed the glittering of bayonets and musket barrels.

It was about 8.45 A.M., and I had discovered McDowell's turning column, the head of which, at this hour, was just arriving at Sudley, eight miles away.

I appreciated how much it might mean, and thought it best to give Evans immediate notice, even before sending word to Beauregard. So I signalled Evans quickly, "Look out for your left; you are turned." Evans afterwards told me that a picket, which he had had at Sudley, being driven in by the enemy's advance guard, had sent a courier, and the two couriers, one with my signal message and one with the report of the picket, reached him together. The simultaneous reports from different sources impressed him, and he acted at once and with sound judgment. He left four companies of his command to watch the bridge and the enemy in his front, — Tyler and his three brigades. With the remainder of his force (six companies of the 4th S.C. and Wheat's La. battalion) he marched to oppose and delay the turning column, at the same time notifying Cocke, next on his right, of his movement. But he sent no word to Beauregard, whom he supposed that I would notify.

Having sent Evans notice of his danger, I next wrote to Beauregard, as follows: —

"I see a body of troops crossing Bull Run about two miles above the Stone Bridge. The head of the column is in the woods on this side. The rear of the column is in the woods on the other side. About a half-mile of its length is visible in the open ground between. I can see both infantry and artillery."

In his report of the battle, Beauregard does not mention this note, but says, generally, that Capt. Alexander gave him "seasonable and material assistance early in the day with his system of signals."

Johnston, in his report, says: —

"About eight o'clock Gen. Beauregard and I placed ourselves on a commanding hill in rear of Gen. Bonham's left. Near nine o'clock, the signal officer, Capt. Alexander, reported that a large body of troops was crossing the valley of Bull Run some two miles above the bridge. Gen. Bee, who had been placed near Col. Cocke's position, Col. Hampton' with his legion, and Col. Jackson from a point near Gen. Bonham's left, were ordered to hasten to the left flank."

Bee's force comprised the 4th Ala. and 2d Miss., with the 7th and 8th Ga. under Bartow. The Hampton Legion was one regiment, and Jackson had five regiments, the 2d, 4th, 5th, 27th, and 33d Va. So 10 regiments, with an average distance of about three miles to go, were now *en route* to reënforce Evans with his two half-regiments.

Now, for an hour and a half, nothing took place but the enemy's desultory artillery firing across Bull Run. McDowell's turning column was arriving at Sudley, crossing the creek and having a half-hour to rest, drink, and fill their canteens. Evans was getting into a position on the road from Sudley to Manassas, about a mile in front of McDowell, and three-quarters of a mile north of the Warrenton turnpike. Bee and Bartow were marching to join Evans. Hampton's Legion was following, and behind it Jackson's brigade was also coming. In order toward the right were Cocke, Bonham, Longstreet, and Early, south of the Run; Jones north of it; and Ewell, with Holmes, south of it at Union Mill's Ford, on the extreme right.

Meanwhile, from my signal station, I had watched McDowell's column arrive at Sudley, and about 10 A.M. reported the rear of it — except Howard, left halted, as already told, some four miles behind. Soon after that picket firing was heard and presently an occasional gun. About 10.30, as the sun grew hotter, an immense column of dust began to develop, apparently about 10 miles to the northwest. I afterward acquired more experience with army dusts than I then possessed, but never during the war did I see a dust cloud tower higher or rise more densely than this. It proved, finally, to be the wagon trains of Johnston's forces on their march down from the Valley. But, as Patterson's army might be expected to follow Johnston, this portentous dust seemed at first an important phenomenon. So I determined to be my own messenger to tell of it, and perhaps to point it out to the generals as it had now risen to a high altitude.

This I was able to do, and Johnston refers to it as follows: —

"The signal officer soon called our attention to a heavy cloud [of dust to the northwest and about ten miles off, such as the march of an army would raise. This excited apprehensions of Gen. Patterson's approach."

Meanwhile, quite a fire of both musketry and artillery was beginning to develop on the left, where McDowell's advance had now come in collision with Evans's little force.

As a bystander I soon appreciated that Johnston believed the battle was to be fought upon the left and wished to go there, but Beauregard was reluctant to give up the proposed attack on Centreville by his right.

Evans, with his 11 companies and two guns, maintained a good fight. He was fighting for time, and he managed to delay the Federal advance for about an hour. The fighting was not bad for beginners. Wheat's Tigers (the 1st La. battalion) lost 38 in killed and wounded, and Evans's six companies of the 4th S.C. regiment doubtless lost at least 50; though the exact figures in the reports are consolidated with other companies. It was doubtless influenced by the morale gained on the 18th. The Federal tactics were poor and timid. The engagement was begun by a single regiment, and this was reënforced by others successively, but there was lack of concert and combined power. New troops going into action are very prone to "fire and fall back," — to touch and let go,— as one handles a piece of hot iron when uncertain how hot it may be. There were cases of this among the volunteer regiments upon both sides.

When Jackson, at Chancellorsville, turned Hooker's flank, he formed his force into a double line of battle, with an interval of about 200 yards between the lines, before he made his attack.[1] When made it was irresistible and produced an immediate panic. Had he begun it by piecemeal, it would have proved a failure. Had McDowell first advanced even two brigades, formed in a double line, Evans's force could scarcely have detained them ten minutes.

As it was, he was able to hold on until he was reënforced by Bee and Bartow with their four regiments. But soon after these had prolonged Evans's line of battle, facing the troops advancing from Sudley, their right was taken in flank and rear by Sherman's and Keyes's brigade of Tyler's division, which had found fords and crossed Bull Run about halfway between the Stone Bridge and Sudley, which McDowell's reconnoissance on the 19th had missed. The roar of the young battle now swelled in volume. There came crashes of musketry which told that whole brigades were coming in, and the fire of the guns increased.

Of course the Confederate line could not be held long against the odds now opposed to it, but the fight which it made has seldom been excelled by such raw troops. Jackson's brigade,

[1] Jackson gave order to form three lines, but gave signal for advance before the third line had gotten up and it followed in column.

later that day, by steadfast fighting, conferred the immortal name of Stonewall upon its commander. The killed and wounded in its five regiments were 561, an average of 112 each. The killed and wounded in Bee's and Bartow's four regiments were 658, an average of 164 each. The 8th Ga., Bartow's own regiment, lost 200, and the 4th Ala. 197. Equally to their credit is the fact that though forced back a half-mile they were not demoralized, but on meeting the reënforcements many were rallied and re-formed, and fought throughout the day. It was in this later fighting that both Bee and Bartow were killed. The victory could never have been won without them.[1]

We must now return to the hill near Mitchell's Ford occupied by the two generals. When the sudden increase of fire broke out, which marked the arrival on the field of Bee and Bartow, Johnston seemed so restless that Beauregard was moved to despatch a staff-officer, Maj. Stevens, with a half-dozen couriers, under orders to ride rapidly, learn the situation, and send back a messenger every ten minutes. Not a word of information had yet come from the left, except what I had seen from the signal station. About 11.30 A.M., Stevens having gone less than a half-hour, there came a further access of fire both of musketry and artillery. It was doubtless due to the attack of Sherman and Keyes upon the flank of Bee and Bartow. No one who heard it could doubt its import. No messages from the left were needed now. All paused for a moment and listened. Then Johnston said, "The battle is there! I am going." Walking rapidly to his horse, he mounted and set off at a gallop, followed by his own staff, as fast as they could get their horses.

---

[1] In this connection mention should be made of Maj. Robert Wheat of the La. battalion, known as "The Tigers." As a boy, Wheat had run away from home in Baltimore and served gallantly in the Mexican War, and, after that, in desperate fighting with Walker in Nicaragua. In his report Evans writes that he was much indebted to Major Wheat "for his great experience and his excellent advice." He doubtless advised Evans in his movement to the left. Early in the action he fell, shot through the lungs. He survived and in June, 1862, again led his battalion in the bloody charge at Gaines Mill. Just before starting, to a friend who gave a greeting, he said, "Something tells Bob that this is his last." He had advanced but a short distance when he fell, only living to exclaim, "Bury me on the field, boys!"

Beauregard only paused to give a few brief orders. Holmes's and Early's brigades, and two regiments of Bonham's with Walker's and Kemper's batteries, were to march to the firing. Jones's brigade was to be recalled to our side of Bull Run. I was ordered to return to my signal station, which I did reluctantly. From it I watched the progress of the battle for hours, but could only distinguish a single event to be reported. This was the arrival at Sudley Ford between one and two o'clock of another Federal brigade. This, I afterward learned, was Howard's brigade, now tardily brought forward.

I was able to follow the progress of the conflict by the rising clouds of smoke and the gradual approach of the musketry for an hour or two, after which, for a long time, there was little change, and the battle seemed to stand still. When Evans and Bee were broken by Sherman's attack upon the flank, their retreat was specially pressed by the Federal artillery. On reaching the Warrenton pike they were met by the Hampton Legion, and Hampton made an earnest effort to rally the retreating force upon his command. The ground, however, was unfavorable, and though Hampton made a stubborn fight (losing 121 out of 600) and delaying the advance near two hours before leaving the pike, our whole line then fell back under the enemy's fire. Here, however, its tenacity was rewarded. A fresh brigade was drawn up in line on the elevated ground, since known as the Henry house hill, and its commander, till then unknown, was henceforth to be called Stonewall. Bee rode up and said to him, "General, they are driving us." "Then, sir," said Jackson, "we will give them the bayonet."

The hill was really a ridge, with a plateau-like top, some 200 yards more across. The inner edge of such a ridge is a fairly good position for a defensive line of battle. It affords some cover both from view and from fire. If the enemy bring their artillery to the front edge of it, they are within musket range, and are also near enough to be charged. There was a good fringe of young pines, masking the inner edge of the hill. Jackson, while marching to the firing, had recognized this comparatively good position and occupied it. Bee galloped among his retreating

men and called out to them, "See Jackson standing like a stone
wall. Rally behind the Virginians." [1]

It was at this moment, when Jackson's 3000 men and Hampton's 600 were the only organized troops opposing the Federal
advance, and Bee, Bartow, and Evans were attempting to rally
their broken forces, that Johnston and Beauregard reached the
field. A heavy Federal fire was being poured after the fugitives.
The two generals had picked up and brought with them two
batteries, Pendleton's and Alburtis's, of four guns each. Their
first efforts were to rally the stragglers and, by example, to
encourage the whole line. Both were veterans at such work.
Johnston took the colors of the 4th Ala. and established it
in the line of battle. His ordnance officer, Col. Thomas, was
placed in command of a battalion formed of fragments of all
commands. Thomas was killed while leading them through the
day. Beauregard had his horse killed under him. When the
line of battle seemed well established, it was agreed that its
immediate conduct should be left to Beauregard, and that
Johnston should take his position at the Lewis house, a short
distance in the rear, whence he could control the movements of all
forces, and direct the reënforcements as they approached the field.

Two incomplete regiments of Cocke's brigade, the 8th Va.,
of seven companies, and the 49th, of three companies, were
brought from Ball's Ford. Ewell's brigade was sent for from
Union Mills. Orders to hasten were sent the two regiments under
Kershaw, and Early's and Holmes's brigades already on the
march. Longstreet, at his own request by courier, was authorized to cross Bull Run and make demonstrations against the
enemy in his front, and Jones was authorized to join him.

Besides these there was also on the way Kirby Smith's brigade,
which, as before told, had arrived at Manassas during the morning, and was at once started to the field.

Beauregard's task, therefore, was to hold his line of battle

---

[1] It is a coincidence that the same comparison was made the same afternoon by Gen. Johnston. I was acting as his guide late in the evening,
and, in speaking of the fighting, he instanced the 4th Va. regiment of
Jackson's brigade, under Col. James F. Preston, and said, so impressively
that I always remembered it, " Preston's regiment stood there like a stone
wall."

until some of these six bodies of reënforcements could reach him. It was his last chance. And to do it he had about 3000 fresh infantry, and about as much more which had been engaged and driven back, and he had about 16 guns, mostly 6-pounders. His great advantage was that he had a fairly good position and was on the defensive.

It was McDowell's task—and it was his last remaining of all the chances on his side at the beginning — to crush Beauregard's line before reënforcements could reach it. He had eight brigades, about 20,000 men, and 24 guns, mostly 12-pounders, and rifles. But he set about the work with only four brigades. Howard's brigade, as has already been told, had been left miles behind, when he felt uneasy about the long flank march. He sent for it about this time, but it arrived too late.

Burnside's brigade he had weakly permitted Burnside to beg off for a rest, and to replenish ammunition. It was lying in the woods, in rear of where it was first engaged in the morning, and from Burnside's report it lay there nearly five hours and was not again engaged.

The third brigade missing from the fighting line was Keyes's. It had followed Sherman closely in its arrival on the field, and had borne some part in driving back the Confederate line. Then it had borne to its left, and gotten into the valley of Bull Run. There was no Confederate infantry there, but it took shelter in the valley from a few guns which looked after our flank and rear in that direction. Here it was out of touch with everything. McDowell did not even know where it was. Had it advanced upon the Confederate guns, or had it communicated with Schenck's brigade on the north side of Bull Run, and the two moved on Cocke's brigade at Ball's Ford, — had it, in short, tried *anything*, it might have accomplished important results. The fourth brigade missing was Schenck's, which never crossed Bull Run. Schenck still believed that the bridge was mined, but he had ventured to cross axemen, one at a time, and had them cutting out the forest trees which had been felled across the Warrenton pike in the low ground beyond the bridge. The axemen got their task completed just in time for Keyes's brigade to retreat by that route.

The absence of these four brigades, and the losses suffered by the other four, probably reduced McDowell's fighting line to about 9000 men, and Beauregard's advantage in the defensive equalized the remaining differences. For McDowell made the further mistake of continuing to fight in front instead of hunting for a Confederate flank.

So now, for over two hours, these lines of battle fired away at each other, across the front ridge of the plateau, neither one's fire being very murderous, as each fired mostly at random at the other's smoke. That, indeed, is the case in nearly all battles since long-range guns have come into use. It is rare that hostile lines get so near together, and are so exposed to each other's view, that men can select their targets. When this does occur, some decisive result is apt to be reached quickly. Fighting rarely consists now in marching directly upon one's enemy and shooting him down at close range. The idea is now a different one. It rather consists in making it rain projectiles all over the enemy's position. As far as possible, while so engaged, one seeks cover from the enemy's fire in return. But the party taking the offensive must necessarily make some advances. The best advance is around the enemy's flanks, where one meets less fire and becomes opposed by smaller numbers. But here, McDowell, encouraged by his early success, endeavored to push straight forward. All along Young's Branch, at the foot of the rolling slopes, was more or less cover in which his troops could form. They could then advance, sheltered from view until their heads would begin to show over the front edge of the plateau, to the Confederate line along its rear edge. Then they would receive an accelerated and more accurate fire. They would return a volley or two and then run back down the hill until they found cover again. Some commands would try it over and over again, a number of times, but none ever made a lodgment.

If McDowell had had some of his absent brigades at hand, he would doubtless have sent a single column to do the work in a single charge. But his successive attacks in partial force were only consuming time, while the Confederate reënforcements were already beginning to arrive on the field. And as they came,

Johnston, with good judgment, hurried them to the left and extended the Confederate flank.

At length, as his infantry could not make a lodgment, McDowell determined to try it with a dozen guns, manned by Griffin's and Ricketts's splendid companies of regulars. A gentle swale in the face of the ascending slope left the Henry house on a sort of knoll between the swale and the Sudley-Manassas road. Griffin's and Ricketts's batteries were ordered to advance to the Henry house, and two or three regiments were directed forward to their support. This was about 3 P.M.

The Henry house was a two-story frame, of about two rooms on each floor, in open grass land, with a small flower garden and a few locust trees by it. Heretofore it had not been in the line of fire, but there had been enough near to drive off all occupants except Mrs. Henry herself, who, old and bedridden, had to be left. The house now became suddenly the focus of a heavy fire. Mrs. Henry was killed in her bed, struck by a cannon shot and several musket balls. The enemy was within canister range of our lines, and the battle waxed hot. A regiment of Zouaves, following in support of the Federal batteries, were charged by a company of cavalry under Col. Stuart. The Zouaves took cover in a body of woods, and the cavalry lost 9 men and 18 horses in a very few minutes. Other Federal regiments sent in support entered the woods, to the right and rear of the batteries, and found them being occupied from the other direction by the Confederate reënforcements which Johnston was now directing to our left flank.

Meanwhile, Griffin and Ricketts had fired but a short while when the 33d Va., under Col. A. C. Cummings from Jackson's left, leaving the shelter of the ridge and thickets, and, partly obscured from view by a fence, marched boldly out toward them. Col. Cummings moved of his own accord and without orders, tempted by the enemy's near approach. The day had been very dusty, and all uniforms, blue and gray, were now of the same dusty color. All over the field, and on both sides, cases of confusion had occurred, but the most important of all took place now. Griffin saw the regiment coming, and prepared to give them a blizzard of canister. But the Federal chief of artillery, Maj. Barry, stopped him, saying that it was a Federal regiment coming to his support. One can scarcely imagine an intelligent officer becoming so confused as to points of the compass, but it is often seen upon battle-fields. A few zigzag changes of direction upon unfamiliar ground will upset the "orientation" of many men. Maj. Barry had been fighting that regiment in Jackson's line for some hours, yet he let it march up to a fence within 70 yards and deliver a volley. That volley was the end of the two batteries. About 40 men and perhaps 75 horses were killed or disabled by it. Ricketts was badly wounded and captured, and his first lieutenant, Ramsay, was killed. Griffin managed to drag off three of his guns, but the other nine were left isolated between the two armies, surrounded by the dead and wounded men and horses.

McDowell, however, did not tamely abandon his guns. The 33d Va. soon found itself too far from home to maintain its position, and it had to leave its captures and fall back. Then there were two or three efforts on each side to hold them before the final one, about 4 P.M. Then Beauregard advanced his whole line of battle. The Hampton Legion and the 18th Va. finally swept over the captured guns, and Ferguson and Chisolm, of Beauregard's staff, turned some of them upon the Federal forces now dissolving into rout.

Within the last half-hour, Kirby Smith's brigade had reached the field, closely followed by Early's brigade, and with them came Beckham's battery. As Kirby Smith led in his troops, extending our line on the left, he was severely wounded and had to turn over the command to Elzey. Early took Stuart's cavalry and Beckham's battery and advanced across the Warrenton turnpike, where the ground is rolling and open. Beckham came into action in a position taking the Federal forces in flank. Having lost Griffin and Ricketts from their right flank, there was little artillery available to fight Beckham, and meanwhile, Beauregard, in the front, was now taking the aggressive. The Federal soldiers appreciated that the long and crooked road by which they had advanced would be peculiarly exposed in retreat, and great numbers dissolved ranks and started back to Centreville by the route they had come. Only Keyes's brigade, and some of those nearest the left, took the Warrenton pike and crossed on the Stone Bridge. Early's brigade and the cavalry followed the fugitives who went by Sudley. The infantry could do but little in this pursuit, and the cavalry by nightfall had loaded themselves with as many prisoners as they could care for, so most of these commands halted at Sudley and bivouacked for that night.

We may now return briefly to my signal station, whence at 1.15 P.M. I sent my last message, reporting what I now know to have been Howard's brigade arriving at Sudley Ford, and two dust columns, both made by Johnston's wagons coming from the valley. My message was dated at 1.15 P.M. and was as follows: —

"Large reënforcements are pushing toward the enemy, crossing Bull Run far above Stone Bridge. The column of dust, which has come down from toward the mountains, is going straight toward Manassas Station. It now appears about three miles from the Junction. Another column is visible in the far distance toward Paris. Six pieces in battery at Butler house, Centreville road."

After two o'clock the roar of the battle began to increase again, and about three, a new battery opened fire from a point farther to my left than any previous firing. It was plainly engaged in enfilading one of the opposing lines, and I watched anxiously to see which. Presently one of its shells burst high in the air over the Federal position. I was satisfied that I could be of no further service at the signal station, and I rode for the field. Had I not seen the direction in which that new battery was firing I would soon have believed our army to have been already defeated from the swarms of stragglers met upon my road. A few had flesh wounds, and all had stories of disaster which had left few survivors of their commands. President Davis had arrived at Manassas from Richmond, early in the afternoon, and, even then, stragglers from the field had met the train at the Junction, a half-mile from the station, with such alarming stories that the conductor feared to carry the train farther. After persuasion, however, he sent the President and an aide up to the station on a locomotive.

At the station horses and a guide were procured, and Mr. Davis rode to the field.   He soon encountered the procession of stragglers and heard their stories.   He was so impressed by their numbers that he said to an officer riding with him, "Fields are not won where men desert their colors as ours are doing."

Quite near the field, the road crossed a small stream.   Here the surgeons had established field hospitals, and about these and under shade of the trees the crowd of wounded, attendants, and stragglers was extensive.   As he had ridden along the road, the President had frequently called upon men to turn back to the field, and some had done so.   Here he seemed to fear that the whole army was in retreat.   As he rode his horse into the stream he drew his rein, and with a pale, stern face, and in a loud, ringing voice he shouted, "*I am President Davis. Follow me back to the field!*"   Not far off, Stonewall Jackson, who had been shot through the hand, but had disregarded it until victory was assured, was now having his hand dressed by Surgeon Hunter McGuire.   Jackson did not catch the President's words, and McGuire repeated them to him.   Jackson quickly shouted: "We have whipped them!   They ran like sheep!   Give me 5000 fresh men, and I will be in Washington City to-morrow morning."   In that sentence, as we shall see, appears almost the only evidence of appreciation among our leaders, on that field, of the great opportunity now before them.

The enemy were routed.   Jackson saw their demoralization, and felt that, if rapidly followed up, it would spread and might involve the capital itself.   And every soldier should have seen in it at least a good chance to cut off and capture many thousands of fugitives retreating by long and roundabout roads.

There was little effort, worthy of the name, even to do this. Our small bodies of cavalry did their best and captured about as many prisoners as they could handle.   In all 871 unwounded were taken.   But to fully improve such an opportunity much more was necessary.   All the troops best situated to cut the line of retreat should have been put in motion.   Not only staff-officers, but generals themselves, should have followed up to inspire and urge pursuit.   The motto of our army here would seem to have been, "Build a bridge of gold for a flying enemy."

Jackson's offer to take Washington City the next morning

with 5000 men had been made to the President as he arrived
upon the field, probably about five o'clock. It was not sunset
until 7.15, and there was a nearly full moon. But the President
himself and both generals spent these precious hours in riding
over the field where the conflict had taken place. Doubtless it
was an interesting study, the dead and badly wounded of both
sides being mostly where they had fallen, but it was not war
to pause at that moment to consider it. One of the generals —
Beauregard, for instance — should have crossed Bull Run at Ball's
Ford or Stone Bridge with all the troops in that vicinity, and
should have pushed the pursuit all night. Johnston should
have galloped rapidly back to Mitchell's Ford and have marched
thence on Centreville with Bonham, Longstreet, and Jones, who
had not been engaged. No hard fighting would have been
needed. A threat upon either flank would doubtless have been
sufficient; and, when once a retreat from Centreville was started,
even blank volleys fired behind it would have soon converted it
into a panic.

It would be vain to speculate how far the pursuit might have
been pushed or what it might have accomplished had all the
available force been energetically used. We were deficient in
organization, discipline, and transportation, but these deficiencies
are no sufficient excuse for not attempting the game of war. In
that game, to use the slang of more modern days, it was now
"up to the Confederates" to pursue their routed enemy to the
very utmost. His line of retreat was circuitous and offered us
rare opportunity to cut it at Cub Run by a short advance from
Stone Bridge; or at Centreville, by an advance of three miles
from Mitchell's Ford. Johnston and Beauregard both sent orders
to different commands to make such advances, *but neither went
in person to supervise and urge forward the execution of the orders,
though time was of the very essence.* Both generals and the President spent the valuable hours of daylight still left in riding over
the battle-field, as Napoleon lost his opportunity to crush
Wellington at Quatre Bras by wasting hours in riding over the
field of Ligny. Owing to their absence from the field, the
advance from Mitchell's Ford was countermanded by Major
Whiting of Johnston's staff, and that from the Stone Bridge,

after being first checked, was later countermanded by Beauregard on receipt of a false rumor, which would not have been credited had the orders been in process of execution.

It was my fortune to carry the first order checking the pursuit, and my recollection of the circumstances is vivid. When I reached Beauregard, coming from the signal hill, the enemy was in full flight, some retreating across the Stone Bridge and others toward Sudley; and orders were being despatched to different commands concerning the pursuit. Kershaw, with the 7th and 8th S.C. regiments, was ordered to pursue across the Stone Bridge and along Warrenton pike. I accompanied the general in riding over the field and in looking after minor matters for some time. About 6 P.M. I happened to be the only one of his personal staff with him. Rather abruptly, and apropos of nothing that I saw or heard, he said to me: "Ride across the Stone Bridge and find Col. Kershaw, who is conducting the pursuit along the pike. Order him to advance very carefully and not to attack."

I had recently read accounts of the affair at Big Bethel, Va., June 10, in which Magruder had repulsed Butler, whose troops fell back to Fortress Monroe in a panic, though entirely unpursued. I noted two facts: (1) That Magruder's cavalry, which had been ordered to pursue, had allowed itself to be "bluffed" by Greble's U. S. Battery. This was entirely out of ammunition, but it had turned back pursuit of our cavalry by unlimbering their empty guns. (2) That though victorious, Magruder retreated to Yorktown the same afternoon, though perhaps with less haste than was used in Butler's return to Fortress Monroe. It seemed to me now that peremptory orders "not to attack" might result in another such scandal. I hesitated to make any suggestion, remembering army stories of replies by old generals to young aides who had volunteered advice. But I ventured to say: "Shall I tell him not to attack under *any circumstances*, no matter *what* the condition of the enemy in his front?" He replied: "Kemper's battery has been ordered to join him. Let him wait for it to come up. Then he can pursue, but cautiously, and he must not attack unless he has a decided advantage."

Better satisfied, I rode on my errand. A mile beyond the Stone Bridge a member of Congress, Mr. Ely of N.Y., was brought out of the woods a prisoner, as I passed, and turned over to the guard. A half-mile farther I overtook Kershaw forming in line of battle, a Federal gun, near the bridge over Cub Run, having opened fire upon his column. After a few minutes, during which skirmishers were advanced, Kemper's battery arrived and opened fire with two guns on the position at Cub Run.

I then turned back to rejoin Beauregard, and, at the Stone Bridge, met Elzey's brigade coming over. It was now nearly seven o'clock and the sun about a half-hour high when on the Stone Bridge I met Ferguson of Beauregard's staff, bearing orders not only to stop the pursuit, but to recall all troops to the south side of Bull Run. I asked the reason and was answered that a message had been brought to the generals, who were still on the battle-field, that a force of the enemy had been seen south of Bull Run in rear of our right flank. Ferguson pronounced the message as absurd, and was carrying the orders reluctantly. I soon rejoined the two generals upon the field, and among the staff-officers found that no regard was being paid to the story. But the orders already despatched were not recalled, and, until late at night, all the troops on the north side were being brought back.

Meanwhile, Kemper's fire on the bridge at Cub Run had wrecked a team on the bridge, and caused a panic and an inextricable jam of over fifty vehicles, including guns, caissons, wagons, and ambulances, from which the drivers had cut many of the teams. Hundreds of the infantry also had thrown their guns into the stream as they crossed the bridge. Here Kershaw was joined by some of our cavalry which had crossed Bull Run at Ball's Ford, and later, by some which had followed the enemy via Sudley. When the orders to return to the south side were received, he left one of his regiments of infantry and this cavalry in charge of the situation. These during the night cleared up the blockade and in the morning brought to Manassas 17 guns, including the 30-pounder Parrott, with over 20 caissons and many other vehicles.

It now only remains of the battle, to give the brief story of the five brigades of our right and centre which held the line of Bull Run, opposite Centreville, and were confronted by Miles with three brigades. Under the confusion of orders in the morning which has been mentioned, Ewell, about 10 A.M., started to cross Bull Run, was recalled; was again sent across and a mile and a half in advance; was again recalled, and, about 2 P.M., was ordered to march to the battle-field. Here he was followed by Holmes. They reached the vicinity of the field after the rout of the enemy. Then, on the false alarm about 6.30 P.M., they were ordered to march back to Union Mills, where they arrived late at night, worn out with dust, heat, and fatigue, without having fired a shot all day.

Next to Ewell and Holmes came Jones, who had crossed early and waited for Ewell, as has been told. He was also recalled about 11 A.M. About noon he was ordered to cross again and to make some demonstrations. He did so and attempted to charge a battery with Jenkins's S.C. regiment, but became entangled in difficult ground under sharp artillery fire. After losing 14 killed and 62 wounded, and finding his effort isolated and hopeless, he fell back. Next to the left of Jones was Longstreet. He also crossed and recrossed Bull Run in the morning, and crossed again about noon as Jones did. In the afternoon about four he was called back to the south side by orders from Johnston. But he had scarcely completed the movement, when, about half-past five, there came from Johnston orders for Bonham and Longstreet to advance upon Centreville and intercept the routed forces from Stone Bridge. Neither of the generals came to see this order executed, and the manner in which it was ignored and disobeyed is instructive. It shows that the giving of orders *to go into action* is but one-half of the duty of a commanding general.

Here, time was of the essence, as the sun was less than two hours high. Longstreet's brigade, having the advantage in position, got the lead. It was the strongest brigade, having five regiments present. Bonham also had five, but two, under Kershaw, were now across Stone Bridge, as has been told. Longstreet, with superfluous caution, left one regiment to hold Blackburn's Ford. With the other four he was well under way when Bonham, holding the older commission, claimed command of the joint operation, and put his own brigade in front. Longstreet had to yield and halt, and half the precious daylight was sacrificed to this vain whim. In the Federal official reports are noted several incidents showing that, even after all this delay, the enemy were caught retreating and might have been attacked at much disadvantage. For instance, Lt. Edwards, commanding a battery, says that he marched close along the front of a Confederate regiment, drawn up in the woods, on the side of the road he was following. He says: —

"It was the most dangerous position occupied during the day. One shot was fired over the battery, and there was a simultaneous movement of muskets along the line as if to continue the fire. Fortunately it was not followed up."

After Bonham took the lead, the advance was continued but a short distance, when it was halted and a small squad of cavalry was sent ahead to reconnoitre, — a timid waste of time. They came back and reported the enemy drawn up on the hills about Centreville. The rest of the daylight was consumed in deploying the column on both sides of the road, and then, *after resting a half-hour*, they fell back to Bull Run without firing a single shot.

From all accounts of the condition of the enemy at this time, had Bonham even stood still and fired blank cartridges to make a great roar and pretend that he was coming, the panic at Centreville would have been doubled, and soon he could have advanced and found it deserted.

His report of this episode is an instructive picture of how opportunities may be lost from overcaution, bred by the sense of responsibility in commanding officers not inured to its weight. Few who have never felt it can realize what this may be. Bonham had served in Florida and Mexico and had been wounded at Contreras. He was personally brave, but had here no major-general to give him orders, and the responsibility overwhelmed him. To nothing else can we attribute the excessive caution which here characterized the conduct of both our generals and of the President. Similar instances may be found in the stories of many battles. Magruder had already illustrated it at Big Bethel. Meade afterward did likewise at Gettysburg, and, even in our most recent war, the siege of Santiago narrowly escaped being terminated by a retreat. The capture of the Spanish fleet at Manila was delayed by a suspension for breakfast, and for an unnecessary inventory of ammunition. All these events took place under the pressure of new responsibilities.

Longstreet, in his book, *Manassas to Appomattox*, p. 52, gives the following account of the final scene: —

"When within artillery range of the retreating column passing through Centreville, the infantry was deployed on the sides of the road under cover of the forest, so as to give room for the batteries ordered into action in the open. Bonham's brigade on the left, the other on the right.

"As the guns were about to open there came a message that the enemy, instead of being in precipitate retreat, was marching around to attack the Confederate right. With this report came orders, or reports of orders, for the brigades to return to their positions behind the Run. I denounced the report as absurd, claimed to know a retreat, such as was before me, and ordered that the batteries open fire, when Maj. Whiting, of Gen. Johnston's staff, rising in his stirrups, said, —

"'In the name of Gen. Johnston, I order that the batteries shall not open.'

"I inquired, 'Did Gen. Johnston send you to communicate that order?'

"Whiting replied, 'No, but I take the responsibility to give it.'

"I claimed the privilege of responsibility under the circumstances, and when in the act of renewing the order to fire, Gen. Bonham rode to my side and asked that the batteries should not open. As the ranking officer present, this settled the question. By that time, too, it was near night. Col. G. W. Lay, of Johnston's staff, supported my views, notwithstanding the protest of Maj. Whiting.

"Soon there came an order for the brigades to withdraw and return to their positions behind the Run. Gen. Bonham marched his brigade back, but, thinking there was a mistake somewhere, I remained in position until the order was renewed, about ten o'clock. My brigade crossed and recrossed the Run six times during the day and night.

"It was afterwards found that some excitable person seeing Jones's brigade recrossing the Run, from its advance under previous orders, took them for Federal troops crossing at McLean's Ford, and, rushing to headquarters at the Junction, reported that the Federals were crossing below and preparing for attack against our right. And upon this report one of our staff-officers sent orders, in the names of the Confederate chiefs, revoking the orders for pursuit."

On my return from the message to Kershaw I rejoined Beauregard on the field, and was with him until after dark, when I was sent to escort Gen. Johnston back to Manassas Junction by the Sudley-Manassas road. On the road we were overtaken by President Davis with Beauregard and most of his staff. Between 10 and 11 P.M. we all arrived at the headquarters in the village. After supper a conference was held between the President and the two generals in an upper room. While it was in progress, probably about midnight, there arrived Maj. R. C. Hill, a staff-officer in Johnston's command, who had taken part in the pursuit in the afternoon, and who now came to report that he had "made his way into Centreville, and had found it entirely deserted, and the streets blockaded with abandoned artillery and caissons."

This was the first intimation which reached headquarters that the enemy's retreat, even without any pursuit, had degenerated into a panic, and Maj. Hill was taken at once upstairs to make his report in person to the generals and the President. He was well known under the sobriquet of "Crazy Hill," to distinguish him from another Hill, classmate at West Point. Nothing that he had ever done had justified his nickname, but it arose from something peculiar in his eye, tones, and manner, all suggestive of suppressed excitement. As a matter of fact, he had not been to Centreville, but only to Cub Run bridge. He had come upon the field with a company of cavalry, and had seen the blockaded guns and caissons. There was no other such blockade, at Centreville or elsewhere.

The details of what took place in the council, after Hill had told his story and been dismissed, indicate that the case was one where too many cooks spoiled the broth. Immediate advance should have been made. While Hill had not really been at Centreville, an advance there after midnight would have found it nearly if not entirely deserted, and might have overtaken the rear of the retreating Federals. Mr. Davis suggested immediate pursuit, and there was some discussion as to which troops were in best condition and most conveniently situated. Johnston, who was the commander-in-chief, offered no definite motion, and there ensued a pause. Beauregard's adjutant, Col. Jordan, then asked the President if he would dictate an order. He complied and dictated one for immediate pursuit. Conversation began on whether pursuit at dawn would answer, and also as to Hill and his story. It was brought out that Hill was known as "Crazy Hill," and, though no one knew him personally, some doubt was felt, and the order was modified into one directing a reconnoissance at dawn by Bonham's and Cocke's brigades and infantry.

At dawn next morning it was pouring rain and it continued most of the day. This heavy precipitation has often been appealed to by the rain-makers as confirmation of their theories that rain may be induced by heavy cannonading.

The reconnoissances ordered were made and, of course, found the country deserted. Our cavalry followed the retreat beyond Fairfax Court House, and picked up a few stragglers and about 20 wagons. These small matters and the artillery captured at Cub Run and brought in during the day amused and interested us while the last hours of our opportunity passed away. Never did an enemy make a cleaner escape out of such an exposed position after such an utter rout.

CASUALTIES. BULL RUN, JULY 21, 1861

CONFEDERATE

BRIGADES		KILLED	WOUNDED	MISSING	TOTAL
Army of Potomac					
Bonham	(5 Reg'ts)	10	66		76
Ewell	(3 ")	3	23		26
Jones	(3 ")	13	57		70
Longstreet	(4 ")	2	12		14
Cocke	(3½ ")	23	79	2	104
Early	(4 ")	20	117	6	143
Evans	(6 Co's.)	8	38	2	48
Hampton	(6 Co's.)	19	100	2	121
Total		98	492	12	602
Army of Shenandoah					
Jackson	(5 Reg'ts)	119	442		561
Bartow	(2 ")	60	303		363
Bee	(2⅕ ")	72	260	1	333
Elzey	(3 ")	8	18		26
6th N.C.	(1 ")	23	50		73
Total		282	1073	1	1356
Total		380	1565	13	1958

FEDERAL.   1ST DIVISION.   TYLER

	KILLED	WOUNDED	MISSING	TOTAL
Keyes	19	50	154	223
Schenck	19	15	16	50
Sherman	20	208	253	481
Richardson		not	engaged.	
Total	58	273	423	754

2D DIVISION.   HUNTER

	KILLED	WOUNDED	MISSING	TOTAL
Porter	84	148	245	477
Burnside	40	88	61	189
Total	124	236	306	666

3D DIVISION.   HEINTZELMAN

	KILLED	WOUNDED	MISSING	TOTAL
Franklin	71	197	26	294
Wilcox	71	172	186	429
Howard	50	115	180	345
Total	192	484	392	1068

5TH DIVISION.   MILES

	KILLED	WOUNDED	MISSING	TOTAL
Blenker	6	16	94	116
Davies	1	2	1	4
Total	7	18	95	120
Aggregate	481	1011	1216	2708

CHAPTER III

ON the day after Bull Run I was appointed Chief of Ordnance
of Beauregard's corps, and within a few days Johnston extended
my office over the whole army, which, about this period, took
the name ever afterwards used, — "The Army of Northern Virginia." The enemy, about the same time, adopted their equally
well-known title, "The Army of the Potomac."

My new duties largely absorbed my time, but I remained in
charge of the signal service, the work being now confined to
sending instructed parties to all parts of the Confederacy where
they might be of use. During the fall a "Department of Signals" was organized in Richmond, and the charge of it, with the
rank of colonel, was offered me, but declined, as I was unwilling
to leave the field. As head of a department I was soon made
Major, and, later, Lieutenant-Colonel of Artillery. Col. William
Norris of Baltimore became the Chief Signal Officer.

Briefly, my duties embraced the supply of arms and ammunition to all troops in the field, — infantry, artillery, and cavalry.
I organized the department, with an ordnance officer or sergeant in
every regiment, from whom I received weekly statements showing the arms and ammunition on hand in cartridge boxes and
regimental wagons. Reserve storehouses were provided at the
nearest railroad points, and reserve trains for brigades and divisions, to run between the storehouses and the troops. For emergency, under my own control was held a train of ammunition
and battery wagons equipped with tools and expert mechanics
for all sorts of repairs from a broken mainspring to a spiked

fieldpiece. I was fortunate in securing for superintendent of this train, Maj. George Duffy, an expert from Alexandria, who became an institution in the army, and remained with it throughout the war.

In its early stages we had great trouble with the endless variety of arms and calibres in use, scarcely ten per cent of them being the muzzle-loading rifled musket, calibre 58, which was then the regulation arm for United States infantry. There were several breech-loading small-arms manufactured at the North, but none had secured the approval of the United States Ordnance Department, although many of them would have made more formidable weapons than any muzzle-loaders.

The old idea was still widely entertained that, because the percentage of hits is always small, the fire of infantry should not be rapid, lest the men waste too much ammunition. After a year or two some of the best breech-loaders got admission among cavalry regiments, and common sense and experience gradually forced a recognition of the value of a heavy fire. By 1864, the Spencer breech-loading carbine had been adopted as the regulation arm for the Federal cavalry, and by the fall of that year brigades of infantry began to appear with it.

On October 7, 1864, on the Darbytown road, Field's division was easily repulsed by two brigades armed with Spencers, with severe loss, including Genls. Gregg killed and Bratton wounded; and on Nov. 30, 1864, at Franklin, Tennessee, Casement's brigade with these arms decided that battle with terrific slaughter, It was written of this fight that "never before in the history of war did a command, of the approximate strength of Casement's. in so short a period of time kill and wound as many men."

There is reason to believe that had the Federal infantry been armed from the first with even the breech-loaders available in 1861 the war would have been terminated within a year.

The old smooth-bore musket, calibre 69, made up the bulk of the Confederate armament at the beginning, some of the guns, even all through 1862, being old flint-locks. But every effort was made to replace them by rifled muskets captured in battle, brought through the blockade from Europe, or manufactured at a few small arsenals which we gradually fitted up. Not until after the battle of Gettysburg was the whole army in Virginia equipped with the rifled musket. In 1864 we captured some Spencer breech-loaders, but we could never use them for lack of proper cartridges.

Our artillery equipment at the beginning was even more inadequate than our small-arms. Our guns were principally smoothbore 6-Prs. and 12-Pr. howitzers, and their ammunition was afflicted with very unreliable fuses. Our arsenals soon began to manufacture rifled guns, but they always lacked the copper and brass, and the mechanical skill necessary to turn out first-class ammunition. Gradually we captured Federal guns to supply most of our needs, but we were handicapped by our own ammunition until the close of the war.

No department of our government deserves more credit than our Ordnance Bureau in Richmond under Gen. Josiah Gorgas, for its success in supplying the enormous amount of ordinance material consumed during the war. Although always economical of ammunition, yet we never lost any action from the lack of it. We were, however, finally very near the end of our resources, in the supply of one indispensable article. To make percussion caps nitric acid, mercury, and copper were required. Our Nitre and Mining Bureau had learned to make saltpetre from caves, and the earth under old barns and smoke houses, and from all kinds of nitrogenous waste material. From the saltpetre our chemists could make nitric acid. Our quicksilver came from Mexico, but after the fall of Vicksburg we were cut off from it, and about the same time the supply of sheet copper was exhausted. The chemists found out a mixture of chlorate of potash and sulphuret of antimony which they could use in place of fulminate of mercury; and we collected all the turpentine and apple-brandy stills in the country and sent them to Richmond to be cut up and rerolled into copper strips.

From this copper and the above chemical mixture all the caps were made which we used during the last year of the war, but at its close the copper stills were exhausted. It is hard to imagine what we would then have done had not the surrender at Appomattox relieved the quandary.

In August our line of pickets was advanced within five miles of the Potomac, opposite Washington, and it included two hills, Munson's and Mason's, from which many houses in Washington were plainly visible. This suggested opening a line of secret signals from a window in one of these houses to an observation room on the top of a residence on Mason's Hill. A powerful telescope was borrowed from Charleston, and an intelligent signal employee, E. P. Bryan, of Maryland, was sent in disguise to Washington to find a room with an available window, and to install himself therein. The scheme was entirely feasible, but before it could be put into operation Johnston decided that it was unwise to hold our lines so close to the enemy, and they were withdrawn, giving up the positions on the two hills.

Bryan then established a signal line across the Potomac, some 15 miles below Alexandria, with messengers from its termini to Manassas and to our secret agents in Washington. The principal business of these agents was to supply us with the Northern papers, although for some time careful account was kept of arrivals of new troops at Washington. But this was found less reliable than the accounts in the daily papers. From them we learned not only of all arrivals, but also of assignments to brigades and divisions, and, by tabulating these, we always knew quite accurately the strength of the enemy's army.

Why the enemy, by similar obvious methods, did not, also, always know our strength, remains a mystery. But McClellan had a bureau under Pinkerton to estimate for him, from the reports of spies, prisoners, and deserters, and implicitly believed, by preference, the most absurd and impossible of all their reports. As an illustration may be taken his report in October, 1861, in which he estimates the Confederate army on the Potomac as "not less than 150,000 strong, well-drilled and equipped, ably commanded and strongly intrenched."

In fact, the Confederate army at the time was only about 40,000 strong. It was very poorly drilled and wretchedly equipped, and it had, practically, no intrenchments whatever. And although it numbered able officers among its generals, it was badly commanded, in that it was not organized into divisions, and could not have been well handled either on a march or in action.

McClellan, though unfit to command in battle, had no superior in organizing an army to take the field as a thoroughly fit machine, able to concentrate its energies wherever needed. By the end of October he might easily have advanced upon the Confederates with a force three to one in numbers and twice better armed and organized.

Public opinion would have forced McClellan into making an attack, but for the moral effect of the imaginary battalions which Pinkerton's Bureau had conjured into existence and drilled and equipped so easily. And as so good a fighting machine of American soldiers would do hard fighting, even without a general at their head, as was abundantly shown by McClellan's subsequent career, it is entirely possible that the Confederates may owe their escape from a defeat in November, 1861, as much to yarns spun by their deserters as to their own impudent attitude in the field.

After the battle of Bull Run it was apparent that if the South sat quietly in a defensive attitude until the enemy was ready to advance again, he would come in overwhelming force. Consequently the burden was upon us to bring on the collision while our comparative resources were greatest. Johnston and Beauregard recognized this, but deferred action from day to day, hoping to receive reënforcements worth waiting for, and to accumulate transportation and supplies. President Davis recognized it also, and sent some new regiments from time to time, but the demands upon him were very great. He had urgent appeals for more troops from every quarter, from the Potomac to the Rio Grande. And, as scarce as men were, arms were even scarcer. He divided out all he had according to his best judgment, but it must be admitted that this was often mistaken. Troops were certainly held at Pensacola, Savannah, Charleston, Norfolk, and in West Virginia, which might have given the needed strength to the army at Manassas to enable it to take the offensive. As it was, the new troops sent were little more than enough to make good the losses from sickness which befell the army in the summer of 1861.

The entire country about Bull Run was malarial, and the troops were badly equipped and ignorant about sanitary measures. All our new regiments from country districts were great sufferers from measles, which often reduced their effective force one-half.

In the latter part of Sept., feeling that the opportunity was about to pass, President Davis was induced to visit Johnston, Beauregard, and Smith at Manassas, and this matter was discussed. The three generals asked for 10,000 or 20,000 more men than the 40,000 they had. With this addition to their numbers they proposed to cross the Potomac and make an offensive campaign in Maryland. Mr. Davis seemed greatly disappointed to find so few troops available. He acknowledged the force of the argument for the offensive, but he could not see his way to taking troops from other points, and he could not provide more men until he could procure more arms.

On Oct. 21 an accidental affair took place at Ball's Bluff, near Leesburg, Virginia, which greatly elated the Confederates. Evans's brigade, of four regiments and a battery, was held at Leesburg in observation of the Potomac, and of a force under Gen. Stone on the Maryland shore. On Oct. 19, McClellan had sent out a strong reconnoissance toward Leesburg from his main body covering Washington. The reconnoissance was scarcely extended half-way to Leesburg, but McClellan thought that it might alarm Evans and cause him to fall back nearer to Manassas; so on Oct. 20 he wired Stone, suggesting a demonstration on his part. Stone made it by crossing the river at two points, Edward's Ferry and Ball's Bluff, about three miles apart. Both parties crossed without opposition, but the Ball's Bluff party, having occupied the high bluff on the Virginia shore, pushed out a reconnoissance through the woods toward Leesburg, some two miles off.

Evans, with three of his regiments and his battery, was observing the Edward's Ferry body, which had taken a strong position and intrenched itself. His fourth regiment, the 18th Miss., came in contact with the Ball's Bluff advance, and drove it back to the main body at the top of the bluff. There the fight grew hotter. Gen. Baker, commanding the Federals, brought up his whole brigade of five regiments and three pieces of artillery, — about 3000 men, — and Evans sent two of his three regiments, the

8th Va. and 17th Miss., from in front of Edward's Ferry, making the Confederate force engaged about 1600. After a sharp and well-conducted fight under the inspiration of Col. Jenifer, Baker was killed, his artillery captured, and his entire force driven into the river, many being drowned. The casualties were: —

Federal:	Killed 49,	wounded 158,	missing 714,	total 921
Confederate:	" 36,	" 117,	" 2,	" 155

This affair, so soon following Bull Run, had a powerful influence upon the Confederate morale. About this period we unmasked on the Potomac, near the mouth of the Occoquan, some heavy batteries, which, for some weeks, we had been secretly constructing to blockade the river. The enemy submitted to this blockade during the whole winter, although a well-planned attack at any time might have captured the batteries and established a very threatening lodgment upon our right flank.

McClellan's apparent apathy in this matter, taken in conjunction with the disaster at Ball's Bluff, gradually gave rise in Mr. Lincoln's mind to a loss of confidence in him as a leader which was never fully restored, and which materially influenced the course of events. Lincoln was now accumulating a force which seemed enormous. The expense incurred was certainly very great, and he became impatient to see reprisals. McClellan calmly advised waiting until he had collected and thoroughly organized an army of about 273,000 men, which he said would take the blockading batteries without firing a gun. Lincoln submitted, but his discontent was increased.

Meanwhile winter put in its appearance. The vicinity of each army became a vast quagmire, and all military operations became impossible. The Confederate army was withdrawn to Centreville and the vicinity of Bull Run, where it went into winter quarters. Soon after this Beauregard was transferred to the Western Army under Gen. A. S. Johnston. His position in Virginia had been that of a supernumerary, and in his new position it was little better until after the battle of Shiloh, where Johnston was killed as he was about to grasp a victory. Beauregard was not yet immune to attacks of overcaution, the bane of new commanders, and his excellent chance to win a great success was lost. He recalled his attack just at the critical moment when it gave every promise of developing a panic among the enemy.

Gen. Joseph E. Johnston at this time had organized his army into four divisions, two of four brigades each, commanded by Van Dorn and G. W. Smith; and two of five each, under Longstreet and E. Kirby Smith. These 18 brigades averaged about four regiments, and the regiments averaged about 500 men each. Besides these there were other troops under Jackson in the valley and under Holmes near Acquia. The total effective strength on February 28, 1862, was 47,617, with about 175 guns.

Early in March the Federal army was organized into five army corps under McDowell, Sumner, Heintzelman, Keyes, and Banks. Each corps was generally composed of three divisions, each division of three brigades, and each brigade of four regiments. The regiments were generally fuller than ours, and would average about 700 men. The total effective strength of all arms on February 28, 1862, was 185,420, with 465 field guns, of which 100 were massed in a reserve under the Chief of Artillery.

During the winter the Federal engineers had completely surrounded Washington with a cordon of fortifications consisting of detached forts impregnable to assault, with heavy guns and permanent garrisons connected by infantry parapets, and batteries for field guns. Within these lines a small movable force could defy any adversary not able to sit down and resort to siege operations. This was amply shown when Lee, in August, 1862, drove Pope into Washington, and also in July, 1864, when Early made his demonstration, but withdrew without venturing to attack.

The Federal government, however, had received such a scare in the Bull Run campaign that it had small confidence in fortifications without a big army to hold them. So when McClellan proposed to make his next advance upon Richmond, from Fortress Monroe as a base, Mr. Lincoln gave but reluctant consent, as it involved the removal of a large body of troops from their position between the enemy and the capital. At length he agreed that about 73,000 would be enough to keep for the

defence of Washington. This would allow McClellan to have
about 150,000 at Fortress Monroe. Early in April, however,
under some strong political pressure, Mr. Lincoln detached
Blenker's division, about 10,000 men, from McClellan's force
and sent them to Frémont in West Virginia.

Before taking up the history of this campaign, it will be
interesting to take a general view of all routes to Richmond
which were tried during the war.

There were seven campaigns under as many different commanders.

First. McDowell set out to follow the Orange and Alexandria Railway, but was defeated at Manassas in his first battle.

Second. McClellan set out from Fortress Monroe via the
York River. As we shall see, he had some success. His advance was within six miles of Richmond when he was beaten
at Gaines Mill. He found a refuge on the James River, but his
army was soon recalled to Washington.

Third. Pope, in August, 1862, followed in McDowell's foot-
steps along the railroad from Alexandria, and was defeated upon
nearly the same ground which had witnessed McDowell's defeat.

Fourth. Burnside took the railroad via Fredericksburg, and
in December, 1862, met a bloody repulse at that point and gave
up his campaign.

Fifth. Hooker also took the Fredericksburg route, but was
attacked at Chancellorsville so severely that he also gave up
his campaign early in May, 1863.

Sixth. Meade, after repulsing Lee at Gettysburg in July,
1863, in November essayed an advance from Alexandria upon
Lee's right flank at Mine Run, about halfway between the two
railroad lines. He found Lee so strongly intrenched that he
withdrew without attacking.

Seventh. On May 4, 1864, Grant, with the largest force yet
assembled, set out from Alexandria on a line between Meade's
Mine Run and Hooker's Spottsylvania routes. Lee attacked
his columns in the Wilderness. The battle thus joined raged for
over 11 months, and only ended at Appomattox on April 9, 1865.
Our only concern here is to note the advantages and the disadvantages of the different lines. The overland route again

proved a failure.   At Spottsylvania, North Anna, Totopotomoy, Cold Harbor, and Petersburg, Grant found Lee across his path, and was unable to drive him off.   His only recourse, on each occasion, was to move to his left and try the next road to the eastward.   And now every intermediate road had been tried, and, after losing 65,000 men, he was only on the James River with Fortress Monroe as his base, where his fleet might have landed him at the beginning and without losing a man.

Here at last, literally *driven* into the location in front of Petersburg, Grant found himself in a position of rare strategic advantage; certain to give him possession of Richmond when properly utilized.   Indeed, it seems strange that it had not been realized in 1862, that the position astraddle both rivers at the junction of the James and Appomattox was the key to Richmond. For it would force Lee to hold an exterior line of such enormous length — from the Chickahominy River to the south of Petersburg, nearly 30 miles — that it could not be long maintained.

As McClellan selected the York River line before the James River was opened (by the loss of Norfolk and of the ironclad *Merrimac*), he is entitled to the credit of having selected the best route available at the time.   After his retreat from Richmond, he very nearly had stumbled into the key position itself. His army was recalled to Washington by the Executive, against his strong protests and appeals.

Johnston fully realized that his inferiority of force left him no recourse but to stand upon the defensive, and watch to take advantage of any blunders his enemy might make.   And it was ordered from Richmond, very prudently, that the army should be withdrawn from Manassas before the roads became good.

Johnston's movement was accordingly begun on March 8, which was some weeks before it would have been possible for McClellan to move his army.   He followed Johnston's withdrawal slowly, for a short distance, but there was no collision. A considerable loss of provisions resulted to the Confederates from the condition of the roads, and the fact that their Commissary Department had established a meat-packing depot on the Manassas Gap Railroad at Thoroughfare Gap, and accumulated there an amount of stores much greater than the railroad could remove upon short notice.

The army paused for a while behind the Rappahannock, but then took a better position behind the Rapidan, where it awaited developments.

Meanwhile on March 23, something took place in the Valley. Stonewall Jackson had been in command there of two small brigades through the winter, but had fallen back, about 40 miles south of Winchester, when Johnston's army abandoned Manassas. Banks's Federal Corps had been opposed to him, and it was now ordered to Manassas. Jackson learned of the movement in progress, and, believing that he might surprise its rear, and at least disconcert plans, he made a march of 36 miles in a day and a half, and fell upon his enemy at Kernstown.

His attack was so vigorous that, for a while, it bore promise of success, but the Federal force at hand was largely greater than had been anticipated. It consisted of Shields's division of three brigades, about 10,000 men. Jackson had upon the field only about 3500. Consequently, when the battle became fully developed, Jackson was driven off with a loss of 455 killed and wounded and 263 captured. Shields lost 568 killed and wounded, and 22 captured. It was a small affair, and apparently a Federal victory, but it was bread cast upon strategic waters.

There soon followed a serious development. Jackson's name and aggressiveness, and the fierceness of his attack, all tended to increase Mr. Lincoln's reluctance to see Washington stripped of any force available for its defence. He had already taken Blenker's division of 10,000 men from McClellan, and now, on April 4, he took also McDowell's corps of 37,000, ordering it to report to the Secretary of War. As the result of that order was to keep McDowell out of the "Seven Days" battles in June, Jackson's battle at Kernstown, though generally reckoned a defeat, was really the first step to Lee's victory in June.

CHAPTER IV

YORKTOWN AND WILLIAMSBURG

McClellan at Fortress Monroe. Johnston goes to Yorktown. Reorganization. Dam No. 1. Yorktown Evacuated. Retreat from Yorktown. Battle of Williamsburg. Early's Attack. Hancock's Report. Casualties. Eltham's Landing.

IN the latter part of March, the Confederate signal lines began to report the movement of a great army down the Potomac, and it was soon discovered that it was being concentrated at Fortress Monroe. On April 5, some five divisions of Federal infantry, with cavalry and artillery, from that point, approached the Confederate lines across the Peninsula at Yorktown. These were held by Gen. Magruder, whose force at the time was only about 13,000 men. They occupied a line about 12 miles in length — partly behind the Warwick River, and partly protected by slight earthworks. Another opportunity as good as that offered McDowell at Bull Run was here offered to McClellan, who could have rushed the position anywhere. He contented himself, however, with some cannonading and sharp-shooting. Of course, he was still under the Pinkerton delusion as to the enemy's strength. Magruder, who was expecting reënforcements, made the bravest possible display, exhibiting the same troops repeatedly at different points. It was just at this juncture, when a great success was in McClellan's grasp, had he had the audacity to risk something, that the news reached him that Lincoln had taken from him McDowell's 37,000 men. This, doubtless, had its effect in discouraging him and leading him to resort to siege operations against Yorktown instead of attempting to pass the position by main force.

Meanwhile, Johnston had been summoned to Richmond, and had advised Davis that a defence of Yorktown involved great risk, and at best could gain no important result. He advocated its abandonment, and the concentration at Richmond of all forces from Virginia to Georgia. With these McClellan's force should be attacked when it came near Richmond.

A conference was called, which included Lee, Longstreet, G. W. Smith, and the Sec. of War, Randolph. It was advocated by Lee, and finally determined, that Johnston should risk making all the delay possible at Yorktown. This was a safe conclusion to reach, only in view of the cautiousness of McClellan.

Johnston had already begun sending some reënforcements to Magruder, and had brought a large part of his army near Richmond. About Apr. 15 he went to Yorktown, taking Smith's and Longstreet's divisions, which gave him a total force of 55,633.

In the whole course of the war there was little service as trying as that in the Yorktown lines. There was much rain and the country was low and flat, so that the trenches were badly drained and would frequently be flooded with water. The general flatness left no cover in rear of the lines. The enemy's rifle-pits were within range and view at many points, and the fire of sharp-shooters with telescopic rifles was incessant, and that of artillery was often severe. At many important points, the crowded ranks in the trenches had to either sit or crouch behind the parapet, in water up to their knees, from daylight until darkness permitted one to rise upright or to step outside of the trench. The only rest at night was to sleep in the universal mud and water. Although the men in the worst locations were relieved as often as possible, an unusual amount of sickness resulted. Gen. D. H. Hill wrote in his official report: —

"Our Revolutionary sires did not suffer more at Valley Forge than did our army at Yorktown, and in the retreat from it. Notwithstanding the rain, mud, cold, hunger, watching, and fatigue I never heard a murmur or witnessed an act of insubordination. The want of discipline manifested itself only in straggling which was and still is the curse of our army. This monstrous evil can only be corrected by a more rigid government and a sterner system of punishment than have yet been introduced into our service."

During our stay here a reorganization of the army took place. The majority of our troops had enlisted for a year in the spring of 1861. It was now necessary to reënlist them for the war. Congress had enacted that reënlistment furloughs should be given to a few men at a time, and that a reëlection of officers should take place in each regiment. This feature was very detrimental to the standard of good discipline.

During the whole of the siege there was but one affair of any consequence, and it is of interest principally as indicating the great improvement wrought in the Federal troops by the discipline which had been given them during the fall and winter.

On Apr. 16, a Federal reconnoissance was made by W. F. Smith's division, of a position on our lines called Dam No. 1. Here our intrenchment, at the upper part of Warwick Creek, was protected by inundations. Just below Dam No. 1 the inundation from No. 2 was only about waist deep and perhaps 100 yards wide, thickly grown up with trees and undergrowth. These facts were discovered by a bold reconnoissance under cover of a heavy fire. Four companies of the 3d Vt. were ordered to cross the inundation and develop what we had on the other side.

They made their advance very handsomely, fording the overflow, and actually got possession of our line of infantry parapet some 20 yards on the farther side. This was occupied at the time by only a picket line of the 15th N.C., Col. McKinney, the rest of the regiment being at work upon a second line 200 yards in the rear. McKinney promptly formed his regiment and moved forward to drive the enemy out, but was killed, and his men repulsed in confusion, the enemy fighting from the far side of our parapet. Presently, however, the brigade commander, Howell Cobb, arrived, and as the enemy were not reenforced, after holding their ground for perhaps a half hour, they retreated, losing 83 men out of 192 who crossed the stream. The entire casualties of the Federals were 165. The casualties of the 15th N.C. were 12 killed and 31 wounded.

It was plain from this affair that the fighting we would soon have to face was to be something better than that of 1861.

Meanwhile McClellan was preparing for Yorktown a terrific bombardment by which he hoped to wreck our water batteries so that his fleet could pass us. Siege batteries mounting 71 guns, including two 200-Pr. rifles and five 100-Prs. and several 13-inch mortars were being rapidly mounted. On May 1 his

100-Pr. rifles opened fire, and by May 6 he expected all the other batteries to be able to join in. But Johnston had never intended to risk siege operations at this point, and at sundown on May 3 put his army in motion toward Richmond. His heavy guns were fired actively all the day before, and until midnight, when the artillerists spiked them and withdrew.

I recall that night's march as particularly disagreeable. The whole soil of that section seemed to have no bottom and no supporting power. The roads were but long strings of guns, wagons, and ambulances, mixed in with infantry, artillery, and cavalry, splashing and bogging through the darkness in a river of mud, with frequent long halts when some stalled vehicle blocked the road. Then men from the nearest ranks would swarm in to help the jaded horses pull the vehicle out. Meanwhile, everything in the rear must halt and wait, and so it went on all night — a march of one or two minutes, and halt for no one could guess how long. The average time made by the column was under a mile an hour.

Our movement was not discovered by the enemy until after daylight on the 4th. His cavalry was at once started in pursuit, and these were followed during the day by five divisions of infantry under Smith, Hooker, Kearney, Couch, and Casey, the whole under command of Sumner. Besides these, Franklin's division was loaded upon transports during the day, and early on the 6th sailed up the York to intercept us near West Point. Two other divisions, Sedgwick's and Richardson's, were also to have been sent by water, and McClellan remained in Yorktown to see them loaded and despatched. But the fighting next day at Williamsburg proved so severe that he rode to the front and had both divisions to follow him.

Near Williamsburg, Magruder had, some months before, selected a line of battle across the Peninsula four or five miles long, on which he had at a few places some slight intrenchments with slashings of timber in front, and, about the centre, an enclosed fort of some size, called Fort Magruder.

As the rear of our column came into Williamsburg during the afternoon of the 4th, the enemy's cavalry suddenly appeared so near to this fort, that Semmes's tired infantry brigade had to be taken back at the double quick to occupy it, and a sharp skirmish was fought before sundown. McLaws reënforced Semmes with Kershaw and two batteries, and we captured one of the enemy's guns, stuck in the mud, ten horses being unable to get it off. After dark Kershaw and Semmes were relieved by Anderson's and Pryor's brigades of Longstreet's division.

That night we stayed at Williamsburg, and it poured rain all night. About 2 A.M. the leading divisions were pushed forward. Johnston was anxious to get his troops ahead to meet the forces he expected McClellan to send by water to West Point.

To hold the enemy in check at Williamsburg, Longstreet retained his whole division of six brigades as a rear-guard. Soon after daylight on the 5th, the enemy developed their presence before Pryor and Anderson. Hooker's and Smith's Federal divisions had reached the field about dark on the 4th.

The fighting began with fire upon our lines from artillery and skirmishers, and gradually increased in volume. The whole of Longstreet's division was brought up, and advanced upon the enemy in the edge of the wood, where it captured one of his batteries. Toward noon, when it became evident from the slow progress of the marching columns that the enemy would have to be held off until night, Johnston returned to the field, and the division of D. H. Hill, which had only advanced a short distance from Williamsburg, was brought back as a reserve. One of its brigades, Early's, was divided, two regiments sent into the fight on our right, and the other four sent out in observation beyond our left flank.

D. H. Hill and Early both went with this left column, and got into trouble from a little superfluous aggressiveness.

On the extreme right of the Federals, Gen. Hancock had discovered some vacant intrenchments — part of Magruder's old line, before mentioned. With five regiments, parts of two brigades, and 10 guns, he occupied a commanding ridge, and opened artillery toward the Confederate lines. Early, on lower ground and in the woods, could not see Hancock's position, but suggested an attack to Hill. Hill approved, but referred the question to Johnston. Johnston, who had left the battle entirely to Longstreet's direction, referred it to the latter. Longstreet very

properly refused to give permission, as we fought only to cover
our retreat up the Peninsula, and it was assured. But this
message taken to Hill did not satisfy him. He was a brother-
in-law of Stonewall Jackson and was a soldier of the same type.
He visited Longstreet in person, and Longstreet now weakly
yielded to his appeal. Rains's brigade had meanwhile been
brought up behind Early's, and it would have been possible to
organize an attack which might have routed Hancock. But
Hill, to lose no time, began the formation of the four regiments
for the charge. The distance to be traversed was over half a
mile, much of it wood and swamp. Hill placed the four regiments in a line of battle extending through a wood, with Early
leading the two left regiments, while he led the two right. But
Early mistook one of Hill's commands to his own wing, for
the order to charge, and he led off at once with his left regiment, the 24th Va., which had open ground before it.
Hill's extreme right regiment, the 5th N.C., also had open
ground in front, and, soon becoming aware that a charge had
been begun, it also advanced without orders. Hill, tangled
in wood and swamp with the two centre regiments, could do
nothing. After passing the wood between them, the two outside regiments could see each other and the Federal guns, now
scarcely 500 yards distant in front. These guns immediately
opened a severe fire of shell and canister. The 5th N.C.
obliqued to its left to close the wide gap between them and
both advanced to the charge, reserving their fire generally until
within 150 yards of the enemy. A large portion of Hancock's
infantry lay concealed behind the crest of the ridge until the
two regiments, now with ranks disorganized by their advance,
were within 30 yards, when the Federals raised and fired, advancing over the crest and continuing the fire for 15 or 20 rounds.
    Hancock says in his official report : —

"The plunging fire from the redoubt, the direct fire from the right and
the oblique fire from the left, were so destructive that, after it had been
ordered to cease and the smoke arose, it seemed that no man had left
the ground unhurt who had advanced within 500 yards of our line.
    "The enemy's assault was of the most determined character. No troops
could have made a more resolute charge. The 5th North Carolina

was annihilated. Nearly all of its superior officers were left dead or wounded on the field. The 24th Virginia suffered greatly in superior officers and men."

Gen. Early, Col. Terry, and Lt.-Col. Hairston of the 24th Va. all fell severely wounded, and the regiment lost: killed 30, wounded 93, missing 66, total 190. In the 5th N.C. Lt.-Col. Badham was killed, and the regiment lost "about fifty per cent" of its members, but no official report was made.

Hancock reported his losses in the affair as: killed 10, wounded 88, missing 31, total 129. This affair about terminated the fighting. It had rained nearly all day, and on our right Longstreet simply kept back the enemy's advance by fire, and by threatening their flanks.

The total Federal casualties as reported were: killed 456, wounded 1410, missing 373, total 2239. The Confederate casualties [reported by Longstreet only] were: officers 102, men 1458, total 1560. We captured 12 guns of which five were brought off, five were chopped down with axes, and two had to be left, as neither horses or axes were available. We also brought off about 400 prisoners.

As far as possible the wounded were brought into Williamsburg, and soon after dark our march was resumed over roads now even worse than any we had had before. I rode with Johnston's staff, and late in the forenoon of May 6 we were at Barhamsville, and the greater part of the army was halted and resting in the vicinity.

It had been a special feature of McClellan's strategy that on our retreat from Yorktown we should be intercepted at Eltham's landing by a large force. But our battle at Williamsburg had proved a double victory, for it had prevented Franklin's division from being reënforced so as to be either formidable or aggressive. It arrived at the mouth of the Pamunkey at 5 P.M. on the 6th. During the night it disembarked and next morning reconnoitred its vicinity and took a defensive position, sending Newton's and Slocum's brigades through a large wood to examine the country beyond.

On the far edge of that wood about 9 A.M. their skirmishers ran into those of Hood's and Hampton's brigades of Whiting's division, which were there to see that our trains passed without interruption.

The Federals fell back and were followed until they were under the protection of Franklin's intrenched camp, and all our trains passed unmolested.

The Federals reported: killed 48, wounded 110, missing 28, total 186.

The Confederate loss was but 8 killed, and 40 wounded, and they captured 46 prisoners. There was no further effort to interfere with our retreat. This was continued at leisure until the 9th, when we halted on the north bank of the Chickahominy.

CHAPTER V

SEVEN PINES OR FAIR OAKS

Drury's Bluff. The Situation. Attack Planned. Johnston's Plan
Changed. Johnston's Problem. Battle of Seven Pines or Fair Oaks.
A Misunderstanding. Longstreet's Mistake. Huger Delayed. Huger
unjustly Blamed. Signal Given. Hill's Battle in Brief. Losses.
Reënforcements. Reports. Wilcox's Report. Couch's Position.
Johnston's Battle. Whiting's Advance. A Second Attack. Johnston
Wounded. G. W. Smith in Command. Smith's Battle, June. The
Confederates Withdraw. Lee placed in Command. Résumé. Staff
and Organization. Artillery Service. Davis and Johnston.

MEANWHILE, Norfolk had now been evacuated by our forces,
which were withdrawn at first to Petersburg and then to Richmond. Our ironclad, the *Virginia* (the old *Merrimac*), drawing
too much water to ascend the James, had been blown up. This
river was now open to the Federal fleet, except for some hurriedly
built batteries at Drury's Bluff, about six miles below Richmond,
covering obstructions made of a row of piles and some sunken
schooners.

On May 15 the fleet, which included three ironclads, the
Monitor, *Galena*, and *Naugatuck*, attacked the batteries, but was
repulsed with 25 killed and wounded, and considerable injury
to some of the vessels. Until that time Johnston had contemplated fighting on the north of the Chickahominy, but he
now decided to concentrate his army nearer Richmond, and on
May 17 it was all encamped within three or four miles to the
east of the city.

The situation had grown very threatening; for McDowell's
army, still at Fredericksburg with 31,000 men, had again been
assigned to McClellan. He only awaited the arrival of Shields,
marching to join him with 11,000 more, before advancing.

If it was now in Johnston's power to do anything to save
Richmond, it must be done before McDowell arrived. It was

not likely that McClellan would himself seek battle when such
a large reënforcement was near.   Johnston's only chance, therefore, lay in taking the offensive.   He had no such works to rely
upon as the Federals had around Washington.   There were, indeed, a few small enclosed forts, erected during the first year of
the war, each armed with a few of the smooth-bore guns of that
day, but they were located too near the city limits to have any
value.

The lines in which we afterward fought were but light infantry

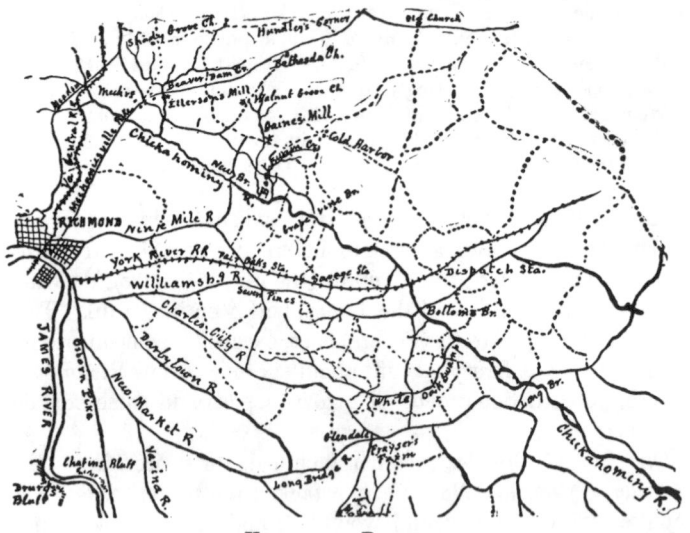

VICINITY OF RICHMOND
(The dotted lines show roads of minor importance.)

trenches with occasional barbette batteries, usually thrown up
by the troops under emergency.

The enemy soon followed us up and established a line of battle, upon which at different points earthworks began to appear.

His right flank, on the north bank of the Chickahominy,
rested upon Beaver Dam Creek, a strong position which Johnston's engineers had selected for our own left flank, before we
left Yorktown, when Johnston contemplated fighting on that
bank.   Thence, the Federal line extended southeast along the

Chickahominy some three miles to New Bridge. Then, crossing this stream, it bent south and ran to White Oak Swamp, where the left rested, giving about four miles on the south side in a line convex toward Richmond, and scarcely six miles away at its nearest point.

In observation of McDowell at Fredericksburg was Gen. J. R. Anderson at Hanover Junction with about 9000 men; and near Hanover C. H. was Branch's brigade, about 4500. Johnston directed that these forces should be drawn behind the Chickahominy, on our left, and united into a new division under A. P. Hill. Before this could be accomplished, however, Branch was attacked by Morell's division and Warren's brigade of Porter's corps, and was forced back with a loss of about 300 killed and wounded, and 700 prisoners, the enemy reporting 62 killed, 223 wounded, and 70 missing, total 355.

At Fredericksburg, McDowell's column was at last joined by Shields, who had been detached from Banks in the Valley, and on May 26 McDowell was put in motion. In the forenoon of the 27th notice of his advance reached Johnston, who at once recognized that he must now attack before McDowell could unite with McClellan.

The latter had moved so cautiously as to offer no favorable opportunity until his last move which had put his army astride of the Chickahominy. That presented as fair a chance as Johnston could now expect. So he immediately determined to attack on the 29th. As McDowell was approaching behind the enemy's right, his strongest effort would be made to crush that flank. On the 28th Johnston got his troops into position to attack at dawn on the 29th. Three of his seven divisions (Whiting's, A. P. Hill's, and D. R. Jones's) were to attack Porter's corps at Beaver Dam. The other four divisions on the south side of the Chickahominy (McLaws's, Longstreet's, D. H. Hill's, and Huger's) would be held in observation, ready to cross when Porter's corps was driven back. Everything was in readiness by sundown on the 28th, when further news was received. McDowell had suddenly stopped his advance, and his troops seemed to be falling back toward Manassas. What had happened was that Jackson had again broken loose in the Valley and defeated Banks at Strasburg on May 23, and at Winchester on May 25, and was moving on the Potomac, as will be told more fully in a later chapter.

This had created a panic at Washington, for rumor had magnified Jackson's forces greatly, and McDowell, just in the nick of time for us, had been turned back for the defence of the capital.

Johnston was glad of a respite, and an opportunity to consider as an alternative an attack upon McClellan's left. The strength of the position at Beaver Dam Creek made any direct attack very dangerous, and to turn it would consume time. To attack the enemy's left was certainly a safer proposition. On the south side his force was smaller and was much more easily gotten at. And while it was already partially fortified by abattis and trenches, quickly constructed in flat and wooded country, yet they had had time to do but little. Longstreet urged going on with the attack for which the troops were already in position, but Johnston decided to withdraw the troops north of the Chickahominy during the night of the 28th, and to have reconnoissances made to discover the location and strength of the enemy's position on the south side. Accordingly, on the 29th, and again on the 30th, one or two regiments were advanced and drove in the enemy's pickets on our extreme right flank, developing his presence and that he was fortifying. This being reported to Johnston by D. H. Hill soon after noon on the 30th, Hill was informed in reply that "he would lead an attack upon the enemy next morning."

There was nothing to gain by further delay; for, by the arrival at Richmond of Huger's division from Norfolk on the 29th, Johnston now had all the force possible to get. His problem was to defeat four divisions of the enemy, 12 brigades fortified, and crush them before assistance could cross the Chickahominy to their relief. If he could do this quickly his chance was good to involve in the defeat also some of the reënforcements the enemy would be sending across the bridges. He had seven divisions, 27 brigades, numbering about 60,000 infantry and artillery. The four divisions to be attacked numbered about 37,000. Considering the morale of our men, which will appear more fully after a description of the battle, the proposition was an easy one, if only we could succeed in bringing our fighting strength to bear in the right places and at the right times. But just there lay our greatest difficulty and weakness. Our army was not yet organized into corps, our divisions were often too large, and our staff service, by which information and orders were disseminated, was insufficient in amount and deficient in technical training and experience. Johnston was endeavoring to remedy some of these evils by assigning his ranking officers, G. W. Smith, Longstreet, and Magruder, to command two or more divisions each, which he called wings and centre, but such temporary arrangements are always more apt to mar than to promote unity of action. And our general himself was impatient and unmindful of small detail. Let us now have the story of what happened.

To use the slang expression, it was "up to" Johnston to play, and in a conference with Longstreet during the afternoon of May 30, the battle for the next day was planned in accordance with the intimation given D. H. Hill about noon.

The conference was prolonged by the coming up of a violent rain-storm, scarcely second to any in violence, according to my recollection, that I saw during the war. Over three inches of rain must have fallen in the first two hours, and it kept up, more or less, until late at night. It was hoped that this rain would make our task easier by rendering the Chickahominy impassable for reënforcements to the enemy. Indeed, it did have this effect, but not until the night of the day after the rain. The immediate effect was only to make all of our marchings and manœuvres slower and more difficult, and the flat, swampy country of much of the battle-field was entirely inundated.

During this afternoon — prolonged by the rain-storm — Johnston gave verbal instructions to Longstreet as to the battle of the next day, and it is hard to imagine how any serious misunderstanding of such a simple movement could have taken place in a conversation prolonged for hours. One would need to have heard the whole of it to tell how it arose. But Johnston afterward recognized the fact that it had occurred, and wrote to G. W. Smith that the misunderstanding "may be my fault, as I told you at the time." Smith, however, denies recollection of any such telling.

The following sketch will illustrate the misunderstanding:

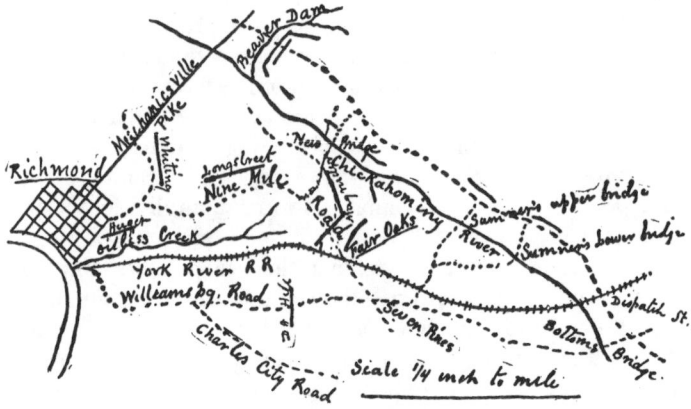

Johnston intended to have the battle begun at an early hour by D. H. Hill's division of four brigades, three of which were already in position, in the front line, on our extreme right on the Williamsburg road. Rodes was on picket on the Charles City road, not far off, and, unfortunately, Johnston's plan included his being relieved and joining his division before the attack was begun. Any preliminary movement, however simple it may appear, will usually turn up fated to cause unexpected delay. Rodes is ordered to be relieved by a brigade of Huger's division, of three brigades, now in camp on the north bank of Gilliss Creek, near Richmond. This is ordered at an early hour to go down the Charles City road and relieve Rodes, after which it will guard and protect Hill's right flank and render it aid if opportunity offers.

Longstreet's division of five brigades is in camp on the Nine Mile road nearest the Chickahominy on our left. Johnston's plan is that it shall march straight down that road, perhaps three miles, pass our line of battle, here held by Magruder's division, form line of battle, and listen for the sounds of battle begun by D. H. Hill's attack upon Casey's division, which will be within a mile or two of his front and right. He will be in a position to take Casey on the right flank and with Hill's four brigades, having abundant force, can hope to make short work of it.

Meanwhile, Whiting's division of five brigades (considered a part of Smith's "Wing") had been a part of the attack proposed two days before, and were still encamped farther up the Nine Mile road. After Longstreet left Johnston's headquarters, the rain having slacked, the latter sent word to Smith to order Whiting to march down the Nine Mile road early in the morning and take position at our line of battle behind Longstreet, to further reenforce him in the battle.

Smith came in person, some five miles, arrived at 4.30 A.M., and now first learned of the proposed attack, and had it all explained. Johnston proposed to make his own headquarters on the Nine Mile road where he could observe any efforts of the enemy to cross the Chickahominy. It would have been much wiser to have first visited the right and seen his battle started. The whole Confederate plan at Bull Run had gone astray for the lack of this precaution, and now it turned out that Longstreet had understood him either to order or to consent that his division was to be marched across from the Nine Mile road to the Williamsburg road and to go into action behind D. H. Hill's division. It will soon appear how utterly this wrecked and ruined Johnston's excellent and simple plan. How the misunderstanding occurred has never been explained, for neither Johnston or Longstreet in their official reports or other writings ever gave any explanation or even admitted openly that a mistake was made. But Johnston induced G. W. Smith to change his official report, to avoid its being made public therein. The official reports also disclose that on that day Longstreet was anxious to have Huger's division recognized as under his command, although Huger was the senior officer. Possibly Longstreet made some request of Johnston for authority over Huger, and Johnston in complying may have thoughtlessly used some expression which Longstreet interpreted as permission to go to the right. But the whole history of this battle remains a monument of caution against verbal understandings.

Longstreet's division was early upon the road, and it soon developed that its route to the Williamsburg road cut off and blocked the prescribed marches of both Whiting's and Huger's divisions as they respectively came up.

After some delay, Whiting sent a note to Johnston's headquarters, complaining that his march was obstructed by Longstreet. Johnston, supposing only that Longstreet was preceding
Whiting down the Nine Mile road, as ordered to do, answered
to that effect, and G. W. Smith, who was still with Johnston,
sent an aid, Capt. Beckham, down the Nine Mile to overtake
Longstreet and learn the cause of any delay. Beckham followed
this road to Magruder's line, and, not finding Longstreet, guessed
that he had gone across to the Williamsburg road. So he sent
back a note saying that he would continue his search in that
direction.

When this note was shown Johnston about 9 A.M., he was still
so convinced that Longstreet was upon the Nine Mile road that
he despatched his aide-de-camp, Lieut. Washington, down the
same road to find him.

Washington pushed his investigation so far as to follow the
Nine Mile into the enemy's pickets where he was captured about
10 A.M.   His capture, and his disturbed manner when some firing
was soon after heard, convinced Gen. Keyes that an attack was
on foot, and Keyes was accordingly alert and prepared.

Meanwhile, Longstreet's column, having delayed Whiting on
the Nine Mile road for two or three hours (for the column took
its wagons along), found itself next blocking the column of
Huger at Gilliss Greek.   The creek was bank full from the rain.
Longstreet says: —

"The delay of an hour to construct a bridge was preferred to the
encounter of more serious obstacles along the narrow lateral road flooded
by the storm.   As we were earlier at the creek, it gave us precedence of
Huger's division, which had to cross after us."

As Longstreet knew that one of Huger's brigades must relieve Rodes's brigade, on the Charles City road, and let it rejoin
Hill's division before the battle could commence, it would have
saved much to waive this precedence at least for one brigade.

Colston, commanding one of these brigades, wrote as follows
of this occasion: —

"A little brook near Richmond was greatly swollen, and a long time was
wasted crossing it, on an improvised bridge, made of planks, a wagon
midstream serving as a trestle.   Over this the division passed in single

file, you may imagine with what delay.   If the division commander had given orders for the men to sling their cartridge boxes, haversacks, etc., on their muskets and wade, without breaking formation, they could have crossed by fours with water up to their waists, and hours would have been saved.   *When we got across we received orders to halt on the roadside until Huger's division passed us.   There we waited five or six hours.*"

He had just passed Huger, and now he waits for Huger to pass him!

When one contemplates the fact that there was a commanding officer, hoping to win a great victory, then at his headquarters within two miles of this spot where nine brigades were thus wasting the precious hours passing and repassing each other, the whole performance seems incredible.   And when it is further said that six of these brigades were lost, with their commander, and that the staff of the general was seeking them at that moment, high and low, miles away along the picket-line, it is almost ludicrous.   And any friends of Huger may be excused for finding even a tragic side to the situation.   For when the whole affair was over, and had ended in defeat, Johnston and Longstreet laid the entire blame upon Huger.   I give as il'ustrations two quotations from Johnston, and there were equally disparaging statements by Longstreet.

"General Longstreet, unwilling to make a partial attack instead of the combined movement which had been planned, waited from hour to hour for Huger's division." — "Had Huger's division been in position and ready for action when those of Smith, Longstreet, and Hill moved, I am satisfied that Keyes's Corps would have been destroyed instead of being merely defeated.   Had it gone into action even at four o'clock the victory would have been much more complete."

After the battles were over and Johnston was recovering from his wound, Huger made vain effort to have the injurious statements corrected and applied for a Court of Inquiry.   This was promised by the War Department, but it was to be held "as soon as the state of the service will permit."   The state of the service never permitted, and the court was never held.

About 1 P.M., however, Rodes's brigade was relieved on the Charles City road, and hurried to join the other three brigades under Hill, who had fretted greatly under the delay. He started his two brigades on the left of the road as soon as he saw Rodes approaching.

The formation was Garland's brigade on the left of the road, followed by G. B. Anderson; Rodes's brigade on the right, followed by Rains. Each brigade marched in column until the enemy were met, when it formed line. The rear brigades formed about 300 yards behind the leading ones.

In *Johnston's Narrative*, he states that "Longstreet as ranking officer of the three divisions to be united near Hill's camp, was instructed verbally to form his own and Hill's division in two lines crossing the Williamsburg road at right angles and to advance to the attack in that order." But the circumstantial evidence is overwhelming that on the morning of the battle, Johnston was expecting Longstreet to be in position on the Nine Mile road, and to support Hill's attack upon the Williamsburg road by his attack down the Nine Mile. That was the only quick way of bringing his large force into proper action, and it is hard to see how the two divisions could have failed to crush the enemy in their front.

It is no wonder that Johnston said when he found out where Longstreet was, that he wished the troops were all back in their camps, for the victory was surely his if only he could play his game correctly.

It was being started badly. It was on a front of only two brigades, supported by two in a second line, while nine other brigades encumbered the one good road leading to the battle. From a glance at the field one might now confidently predict the outcome.

It is D. H. Hill's division, about 8500 strong, excellent troops, and there is not living a more honest fighter than D. H. Hill. They will first meet Casey's division, of about equal strength, partly fortified with trenches and abattis. Behind Casey are three other divisions holding two other lines partly intrenched. Hill may carry the first line and even have some success against the second. But, by that time, he will be worn out, and the daylight will be gone before enough of the nine brigades (those behind him) can be gotten to him in force to cut any figure. The fight on this road cannot amount to more than a bloody draw, prolonged until night.

That is what any one, knowing the conditions, might have predicted, and that is just what happened. To follow all the details is useless, but the list of casualties, and some brief descriptions of incidents will give a good idea of the fighting.

The Confederate reports of casualties, particularly in battles fought during active campaigns, are far from being full, and are not at all uniform in their shape and detail. Complete figures, therefore, for the whole division cannot be given.

Of Rains's brigade, the official report only states that its losses were one-seventh of the force. The reports show that this brigade was employed in a flank movement around the enemy's left which it executed successfully, but did not repeat it. Hill expressed disappointment and says that Rains might have saved Rodes's brigade from suffering 500 casualties.[1] Rains fought on the left. Had Longstreet's division that morning not gone astray, all of its brigades would have been on the enemy's flank, and have had similar chances. The other three brigades reported their strength and losses as follows: —

SEVEN PINES, MAY 31, 1862

Position	Brigade	Present	Killed	Wounded	Missing	Total	Per Cent
Front right	Rodes	2200	241	853	5	1099	50
Front left	Garland	2065	98	600	42	740	37
Rear left	Anderson, G. B.	1865	149	680	37	866	47
		6130	488	2133	84	2705	44

This record shows great fighting power, and will compare favorably for a half-day's fighting of an equal body of men, with any records of the war.

[1] Rains was a graduate of West Point of class of 1827, and was now fifty-nine years of age. He had had some Indian fighting in Florida, and had been wounded, but he was not in the Mexican War. He was an expert and enthusiast upon explosives, and, soon after the action at Seven Pines, he was relieved of his brigade and assigned to the Torpedo Bureau, which was organized for submarine defence of our rivers and harbors.

At Waterloo, the losses were: Allies 20 per cent, French 34 per cent, British regulars 29 per cent. At Balaklava, the Light Brigade (600) lost 49 per cent.

On the Federal side the battle was opened by Casey's division, moderately well fortified with trenches, batteries, and abattis, and soon supported by Peck's brigade of Couch's division. These four brigades were finally routed from their first line by the Rains's flank movement. They then fell back upon the second intrenched line, where they united with Couch's two remaining brigades. Rains's brigade now dropped out of the fight.

The three other brigades pushed their attack upon the enemy's second line, which was now being reënforced by Kearny's division, but Hill received also a reënforcement of R. H. Anderson's brigade, which he divided. Two regiments under Jenkins he sent to the left and the remainder under Anderson to his right. A little later also he received two regiments, the 11th Ala. and the 19th Miss., of Wilcox's brigade. With this help the second line was carried. Four Federal regiments and a battery retreated north toward the Chickahominy unpursued. The remainder fell back slowly and night put an end to the fighting. Kemper's brigade also arrived, brought by Longstreet to Hill's aid. It came upon the field, but too late to take effective part. On the Federal side Hooker's division also came up as the fighting ceased.

Hill's division was now worn out, and Longstreet relieved it from the seven idle brigades still left on the Charles City and Williamsburg roads.

Hill's forces during the battle had averaged about four brigades, for R. H. Anderson had come up, after Rains dropped out with a loss of only 14 per cent. Anderson's losses are not given, but they were severe and probably equalled the average of Hill's. Jenkins's official report says: —

"We never fought twice in the same place, nor five minutes in one place, and steadily on the advance; were under fire from 3 P.M. to 7.40 P.M. The service we did will be evidenced by our list of killed and wounded. In my two color companies out of 80 men who entered, 40 were killed or wounded, and out of 11 in the color guard 10 were shot down, and my colors, pierced by 9 balls, passed through four hands without touching the ground."

The following shows a comparison of the total casualties of Hill's part of the battle, as nearly as they can be ascertained, including the three brigades already given: —

CASUALTIES. HILL'S BATTLE. WILLIAMSBURG ROAD, MAY 31, 1862

	Division	Strength	Killed	Wounded	Missing	Total
Keyes's Corps	Casey	8,500	177	927	325	1429
Keyes's Corps	Couch [1]	8,500	195	773	127	1095
Heintzelman's	Kearny	8,500	193	816	82	1091
Federal	Total	25,500	565	2516	534	3615
Confederate	Total [2]	12,000	608	2751	156	3515

The Confederates captured 10 guns, 5000 muskets, and about 400 prisoners. The following extracts from official reports give an idea of the fighting. Rodes writes: —

"The total number of men carried into action was about 2200. The aggregate number present at camp was, however, 2587. The 6th Ala. lost nearly 60 per cent of its aggregate force. Some of its men were drowned after having been wounded, as they fought at times in a swamp in which the water was from six inches to two feet in depth. The right company of the 6th Alabama was thrown back at right angles to the line of battle by Col. Gordon, to protect his rear, and engaged the enemy at such close quarters that its brave commander, Capt. Bell, after having fallen wounded mortally, was able to use his revolver with effect upon the enemy. The company fought with great heroism. Its loss was 21 killed and 23 wounded out of a total of 55 " (80 per cent).

It remains to say a few words of the movements of the unengaged troops on the Williamsburg and Charles City roads. Longstreet at 3.30 P.M. placed Wilcox in charge of his own, Pryor's, and Colston's brigades, and ordered him to follow and support Huger. Soon after this order was modified and Wilcox was ordered to precede Huger. But, having moved to the front, he was soon countermarched and ordered to return to the Williamsburg road, and then to follow that road to the front. He had retraced his steps about a mile when his fourth order

[1] This includes 12 killed, 45 wounded, 12 missing, total 69, which occurred in Johnston's battle on the left.

[2] This omits Kemper, who was not seriously engaged.

again reversed his direction. He was now to follow down the Charles City road, keeping abreast of the firing which was heavy. And soon a fifth order came, of which Wilcox writes in his report: —

"Again orders were received in writing to move across to the Williamsburg road, following country roads and paths through woods and fields, a guide being furnished to conduct the command. The intervening distance between the two roads was low and flat, and in many places covered with water, at one point waist deep. The march was of necessity very slow. It was about 5 P.M. when the head of the column reached the Williamsburg road."

It was at this time that the 11th Ala. and 19th Miss. of Wilcox's brigade were sent into the action, as has already been told. Later, these brigades with the others of Longstreet and Huger, which were brought up, relieved the troops which had been so heavily engaged.

So terminated what should properly be called "D. H. Hill's Battle," for the whole, as we shall see, embraced three minor battles, at different times and places, and under different commanders. Hill's battle was fought principally against Keyes's corps; and we have seen that Couch with four regiments and a battery retreated northward toward the Chickahominy.

Here he soon found friends. Sumner's corps on the north side of the river had been formed about 1 P.M., and moved toward two recently constructed roadways and bridges across the Chickahominy. At 2.30 P.M. orders to cross were received, and Sumner, having two roads, was able to cross quite rapidly. The river was high and rising, and by nightfall and until next morning the stream was impassable.

Now we enter upon the second, which may be called "Johnston's Battle."

It has been told how his original plans were destroyed by Longstreet's taking his division to the Williamsburg road. It must have been near eleven o'clock when Johnston learned where Longstreet was, and realized that it was too late to get the troops back for that day. He hesitated whether to wait and prepare for the morrow or to go on, and unfortunately decided to let it go on. He took no measures to supply the

place on the Nine Mile road of the six brigades of Longstreet.
Whiting's five brigades, however, were at hand.   Three of them,
Whiting's, Hood's, and Pettigrew's, were at the fork of the Nine
Mile and New Bridge roads; Hatton's and Hampton's in re-
serve near by.

Toward noon Johnston left his headquarters, which were on
the Nine Mile road about three miles from Richmond, and took
his position at a house near the fork of the Nine Mile and New
Bridge roads.   His intention now was to send Whiting's division
down the Nine Mile road to coöperate with D. H. Hill's attack
down the Williamsburg road.

By coincidence of bad luck, his right wing having lost several
hours in the morning, his left wing lost about three hours in
the afternoon.   The signal for Whiting's advance was to be
the sound of Hill's musketry on the Williamsburg road, two
miles southeast, through a wooded country.   This musketry
began about one o'clock, and was heard in the Federal lines,
five miles northeast; also, near Richmond five miles west; but
was not audible two miles to the northwest at the position occupied by Whiting's division and by Gen. Johnston.[1]

Longstreet reports having sent a message, upon the capture
of Casey's first line, but it was not received, and Johnston's first
knowledge of the battle came about four o'clock, from an officer
whom he had sent at three to investigate and report.

Soon after 4 P.M., Whiting's five brigades were put in motion,
with Hood in front.   Hood was directed to leave the Nine Mile
road to his left and to push over toward the York River Railroad, and find Hill's troops, while the remaining brigades moved
down the railroad.   Already there had been upon the railroad
all day Pickett's brigade of Longstreet's division, sent there by
Longstreet before the beginning of the action, "to report any
advance of the enemy up that road."   It is remarkable that
Longstreet contented himself with this, and did not utilize this
road as a route of advance for some of his many brigades.   Be-

---

[1] Such phenomena, called acoustic shadows, are of common occurrence
and are to be expected upon every battle-field, in *some* direction; especially
in wooded localities.   Here the intervening ground was moderately wooded.
The artillery could be distinguished, but the amount of it was not great.

sides his own six he could have called on some of Huger's three, and have led a strong attack down the railroad, turning Casey's right flank. An opportunity for one of the most brilliant strokes in the war was here overlooked and lost. Soon after five o'clock, Whiting's four rear brigades had straightened out upon the Nine Mile road, with Whiting's own brigade in front near Fair Oaks Station, when a battery opened fire upon the column from its left.

It was the battery with four regiments of Couch's division, which had been cut off from Casey's second line and had retreated northward, unpursued, toward the Sumner bridges. Here it had met Sedgwick's division of Sumner's corps and Richardson's division was not far away. Johnston was riding with Whiting when the Federal battery opened fire, but supposing the Chickahominy to be impassable, he thought that there could be no great force there, and Whiting was ordered to charge the position with his brigade. Near the Chickahominy the ground was rolling, and the enemy's guns secured fine positions. For fully 800 yards the Confederate advance was exposed to fire.

The reception which it met, however, made it speedily apparent that the errand upon which it had been sent was much beyond the dimensions of a brigade.

Johnston was impatient, and directed the attack to be renewed at once by all the brigades present. Hood's brigade might have been recalled, and several batteries of artillery, not far off, could have found positions against the two batteries the enemy presently had in action. But a very hurried formation of the three remaining brigades—Hatton's, Hampton's, and Pettigrew's—was made, and the attack was renewed without bringing up artillery, although there was much of it near. It was met by Sedgwick's division and Abercrombie's four regiments, and received a bloody repulse, to which the enemy's artillery contributed largely, having a fair sweep and no artillery opposing them. Hatton was killed, Pettigrew wounded and captured, and Hampton wounded.

The casualties of the division for the day were reported as follows:—

Johnston's Battle	Strength	Killed	Wounded	Missing	Total
Hood's Brigade	1,922		13		13
Hampton's	2,225	45	284		329
Whiting's (Law)	2,398	28	286	42	356
Pettigrew's	2,017	47	240	54	341
Hatton's	2,030	44	187	13	244
Total Confederate	10,592	164	1010	109	1283
Sedgwick's Division	8,000	62	282	3	347
Abercrombie's Brigade	2,000	12	45	12	69
Total Federal	10,000	74	327	15	416

Before sundown Johnston recognized that his attack was a failure, and he was about to arrange that his troops should sleep on their arms and renew the fight at dawn, when he received two wounds. The first was a flesh wound in the shoulder from a musket ball, and the second, a few moments later, was a blow in the chest from a heavy fragment of shell, knocking him from his horse. He was placed in an ambulance and started toward his headquarters, but suffered such pain from the motion caused by the fearful roads that a litter had to be substituted. He was incapacitated for service until the middle of November, when he was assigned to the principal command of the Army in the West.

G. W. Smith succeeded Johnston in the command, and the action of the next day is therefore to be called "Smith's Battle." It is sometimes stated in Confederate accounts, that this day offered the Confederates their best opportunity to crush the enemy, because it is supposed that the Chickahominy was now entirely impassable. This is a mistake. The railroad bridge had been repaired and covered with plank, and was always available for infantry and for horses, though not for vehicles. By 8 A.M., June 1, the Federal engineers had built a pontoon bridge at the site of the New Bridge, but it was under Confederate fire, and the approaches to it were impassable during the flood. By noon Sumner's upper bridge was again practicable for infantry, and by dark the lower one. By morning, June 1, therefore, the Federal army was practically safe from any Confederate attack. It had six divisions on the ground and a good line of battle, extending across the railroad nearly parallel to the Nine Mile road, with its left flank retired and protected by White Oak Swamp. The only chance of a successful assault by the Confederates would have been with a heavy artillery fire upon the obtuse angle where Sedgwick's line bent back to connect with the other divisions. The condition of the ground, as well as the unorganized state of the Confederate artillery service, made such an attack impossible, and no effort at it seems to have been made. Late at night, May 31, Longstreet reported to Smith, and received orders to attack in the morning from the Williamsburg road northward, Smith proposing to take up the battle, with Whiting and other troops, when it was well developed.

It is easy to see that the Federals had nothing to fear from anything the Confederates were likely to do.

Early in the morning there was some sharp firing at many points along the line, where daylight brought into view troops and skirmishers which had been posted after dark; and, in accordance with Smith's instructions, four of Longstreet's brigades — Pickett's, Wilcox's, Pryor's, and Colston's — and two of Huger's, Mahone's and Armistead's, advanced upon the enemy's position, which ran largely through the woods. There resulted a number of more or less severe affairs at different points, which were waged with varying fortunes for some hours. The brigades which had been engaged the day before were held in reserve near the captured redoubt. Meanwhile, with daylight, the enemy's position of the afternoon before, opposite Whiting, showed itself strengthened by intrenchments, and Smith thought there was evidence of additional reënforcements being sent from the north side. So the battle in Whiting's front was not renewed. Longstreet, too, soon began to call for reënforcements. The following notes were received from him in quick succession: —

"June 1st. Yours of to-day received. The entire army seems to be opposed to me. I trust that some diversion may be made in my favor during these attacks, else my troops cannot stand it. The ammunition gives out too easily."

"10 A.M., June 1. Can you reënforce me? The entire army seems to be opposed to me. We cannot hold out unless we get help. If we can fight together, we can finish the work to-day and Mac's time will be up. If I can't get help, I fear that I must fall back."

On receipt of these notes, Smith ordered 5000 men to

be withdrawn from Magruder's force along the Chickahominy, above New Bridge, and sent to Longstreet, but meanwhile D. H. Hill, seeing that the fighting was accomplishing nothing, sent orders withdrawing the troops to the line of the night before. This was done rapidly at some points, and more slowly at others, but the enemy made no marked advance, and the action soon died out, it being now about 11 A.M.

About 1.30 P.M. President Davis arrived at Smith's headquarters, and informed him that Lee had been assigned to the command of the army, and Lee himself soon arrived. The party then rode over to Hill's position, whence Magruder's troops, which had arrived, were ordered back to the Chickahominy. After dark orders were received by Hill from Longstreet for all troops to return to their camps within the Confederate lines. In his official report, Hill says : "The thirteen brigades were not got together until near midnight. . . . We regained our own intrenchments near sunrise." The moon that night was about five days old.

The official reports do not show separately the casualties either of this last action or of Hill's battle on the 31st, though those of Johnston's battle are given by both sides. But Kearny's division and some of Longstreet's brigades were engaged both on the 31st and the 1st, and, on the latter day, two of Huger's. The totals of the whole affair, as nearly as can be estimated, are shown in the following table, averaging where exact figures are wanting:—

TOTAL CASUALTIES. SEVEN PINES OR FAIR OAKS

BATTLE		ENGAGED	KILLED	WOUNDED	MISSING	TOTAL
Hill's	Confederate	11,642	608	2751	156	3515
May 31	Federal	18,000	565	2516	534	3615
Johnston's	Confederate	10,592	164	1010	109	1283
May 31	Federal	10,500	74	327	15	416
Smith's	Confederate	14,136	208	988	140	1336
June 1	Federal	17,000	151	751	98	1000
Aggregate	Confederate	36,370	980	4749	405	6134
	Federal	45,500	790	3594	647	5031

A glance at this table suggests at once the weakness of our army. Three separate times we advanced to give offensive battle, expecting to meet and to crush two Federal corps which we knew would average over 15,000 men each. We had about 50,000 men to do it with, and it was necessary to do it quickly when once begun, for three other Federal corps were close at hand. On neither of the three occasions did we succeed in getting over about 14,000 men into action at all.

The fighting qualities of the troops engaged proved excellent, but the trouble was in our organization, which could not handle the available force effectively. That was due partly to our lack of staff-officers trained to military routine, partly to the unwieldy structure of our army into large divisions, instead of into corps, and partly to the personal peculiarities of our commander, whose impatience of detail appears in the misunderstanding between himself and Longstreet, and in the lack of written orders to officers charged with carrying into effect important plans.

Perhaps our greatest deficiency at this period was in the artillery service. None of our batteries were combined into battalions, but each infantry brigade had a battery attached to it. There were no field-officers of artillery, charged with combining batteries and massing them to concentrate heavy fire upon important points. There was never greater need or better opportunity for this than in Johnston's battle of the 31st. The enemy had but two batteries, Kirby's and Brady's, and no more were available. They did not receive a single hostile cannon shot, and were able to devote their whole fire to our infantry lines, which in every case seemed to be finally repulsed only by heavy canister at close quarters.

We had no lack of batteries. The roads were full of them, but there was no organization to make them effective. Both roads and open fields were in very miry condition, and all movements would have been slow, but a competent officer by doubling teams could have brought up guns with little delay.

The opportunity to place Lee in command of the army was a very gratifying one to President Davis, and it increased our chances of success to have cordial relations established between the War Department, under the Chief Executive, and the army under its commander.

Relations had not been cordial before, and at this particular time the strain upon them was being increased daily by Davis's feeling that he was not being taken into Johnston's confidence as to his plans.

In Volume II of his *Rise and Fall of the Confederacy*, Davis writes of this period as follows: —

"Seeing no preparation to keep the enemy at a distance, and kept in ignorance of any plan for such purpose, I sent for Gen. Lee, then at Richmond in general charge of army operations, and told him why and how I was dissatisfied with the condition of affairs.

"He asked me what I thought it was proper to do. I answered that McClellan should be attacked on the other side of the Chickahominy before he matured his preparations for a siege of Richmond. To this he promptly assented, as I anticipated he would, for I knew it had been his own opinion. He then said: 'Gen. Johnston should, of course, advise you of what he expects or proposes to do. Let me go and see him and defer this discussion until I return.'"

No date is given, but in the War Records the following letter from Lee to Johnston appears, and it was probably the result of this conversation:—

"May 21, 1862.
" (Wednesday.)

" GEN. JOSEPH E. JOHNSTON : —

"General: The President desires to know the number of troops around Richmond, how they are posted, and the organization of the divisions and brigades; also the programme of operations which you propose.

"The information relative to the composition and position of your army can readily be furnished, but your plan of operations, dependent upon circumstances, perhaps yet to be developed, may not be so easily explained, nor may it be prudent to commit it to paper. I would, therefore, respectfully suggest that you communicate your views on this subject personally to the President, which perhaps would be more convenient to you and satisfactory to him. I am, etc.,

" R. E. LEE, General."

The War Records follow this letter with a statement of the army's complete organization, and its strength (53,688), but there is nowhere record of any other reply. From Mr. Davis's narrative it is clear that no further communication took place. The narrative goes on: —

"When Gen. Lee came back, he told me that Gen. Johnston proposed, on the next Thursday, to move against the enemy as follows: Gen. A. P. Hill was to move down the right flank and rear of the enemy; Gen. G. W. Smith, as soon as Hill's guns opened, was to cross the Chickahominy at the Meadow bridge, attack the enemy in flank, and by the conjunction of the two it was expected to double him up. Then Longstreet was to cross on the Mechanicsville bridge, and attack him in front. From this plan the best results were hoped for by both of us."

The "next Thursday" was May 29. In the Records appear no signs of battle until May 27. On that day came news that McDowell was starting south from Fredericksburg. Johnston immediately ordered troops into position for the attack at dawn on the 29th. But, as has been told, on the 28th he received news of McDowell's recall north. That night he countermanded the battle orders, and had the troops withdrawn under cover of darkness from all advanced positions.

The President's narrative goes on: —

"On the morning of the day proposed, I hastily despatched my office business and rode out toward the Meadow bridge to see the action commence. On the road I found Smith's division halted, and the men dispersed in the woods. Looking for some one from whom I could get information, I finally saw Gen. Hood, and asked him the meaning of what I saw. He told me that he did not know anything more than that they had been halted. Riding on to the main road, which led to the Mechanicsville bridge, I found Gen. Longstreet, walking to and fro in an impatient, it might be said, fretful manner. Before speaking to him, he said his division had been under arms all day waiting for orders to advance, and that the day was now so far spent that he did not know what was the matter. Thus ended the offensive-defensive programme from which Lee expected much, and of which I was hopeful."

But two days afterward, May 31, the President rode out again late in the afternoon, and when on the Nine Mile road, heard firing in the direction of Seven Pines. Mr. Davis writes: —

"As I drew nearer I saw Gen. Whiting with part of Gen. Smith's division file into the road in front of me; at the same time I saw Gen. Johnston ride across the field from a house before which Gen. Lee's horse was standing.[1] I turned down to the house and

---

[1] Among the staff-officers who saw this incident, it was believed that Gen. Johnston saw Mr. Davis approaching, and that he sought to avoid a meeting by mounting quickly and riding rapidly to the extreme front, where he remained until he received his wounds. I was a witness of the scene.

asked Gen. Lee what the musketry firing meant. He replied by asking whether I had heard it, and being answered in the affirmative, he said he had been under that impression himself; but Gen. Johnston had assured him that it could be nothing more than an artillery duel. It is scarcely necessary to add that neither of us had been advised of a design to attack the enemy that day."

It seems clear from this narrative that Gen. Johnston entirely disregarded the letter of May 21, so far as it required him to acquaint the President with his proposed programme of operations. The verbal message conveyed by Lee, that he proposed to attack north of the Chickahominy on the 29th, may serve to acquit him of literal disobedience; but the change of programme was neither notified beforehand, or explained afterward, nor was any notice given of the attack at Seven Pines on the 31st, although there was ample opportunity to do so.

It is not probable, however, that Johnston intended his course to be one either of disrespect or disobedience. It had its source, doubtless, in his aversion to detail, or to committing himself as to what he proposed to do, when he was fighting a superior force and was really waiting for opportunities to turn up.

It must be admitted that at Seven Pines our prospects, had Johnston not been wounded, would have been dismal. Besides the lack of cordial relations between the President and Johnston, the latter's effort to handle the army in battle had been an utter failure. His orders were given, he says, " for the concentration of 23 of our 27 brigades against McClellan's left wing." Yet nowhere were ever over four brigades in action at one time. No complaint is made of any disobedience, slowness, or nonperformance, by any officer, except Huger, and the facts in his case distinctly relieve *him* from any blame whatever. Indeed, it is almost tragic the way in which he became the scapegoat of this occasion, the true history of which is even yet not generally understood. Gen. Smith, however, in 1891, published all the facts for the first time with documentary proof.

CHAPTER VI

Jackson's Valley Campaign

The Valley. Jackson's Plan. Battle of McDowell. Shields joins Mc-
Dowell. Jackson attacks Front Royal. Banks Retreats. Winchester
Captured. Cavalry not at Hand. Steuart's *Faux Pas*. Jackson's
Report. McDowell's Delay. Lincoln keeps Sunday. Panic in Wash-
ington. Jackson keeps Sunday. Jackson's Retreat. Race down the
Valley. Death of Ashby. Port Republic, June 8. Cross Keys,
June 8. Port Republic, June 9. Winder Repulsed. Taylor's Charge.
After Effects.

BEFORE taking up the history of affairs before Richmond in
June, 1862, with Lee at the head of the army, it is necessary to
review events in the Valley of Virginia.

This Valley constituted the only route by which a Confederate army could invade Maryland and threaten Washington
City in rear.

Cool judgment at the head of affairs, after Washington had
once been fortified against an attack by open assault, might
have laughed at any idea of real danger from such an invasion.
It should have been clear to all that no invasion could maintain
itself long enough to carry on a siege, or to do more than to fight
one great battle. The trouble was the lack of railroad transportation. Wagons alone would have to be relied upon to
bring all supplies from Staunton, Va., a distance via the Valley
roads of nearly 200 miles to Washington. But fear, approaching panic, took possession of Washington whenever a Confederate
force appeared in the Valley, and every other operation would
be suspended to concentrate all efforts upon driving it out.

This oversensitiveness of the Federals cut its greatest figure
in 1862, and was, more than once, the only salvation of Richmond. For the Confederate generals understood it, and as the
situation in front of Richmond became more threatening, they
sought more earnestly to reënforce the Valley.

It happened that Stonewall Jackson had been assigned as the commander of the Valley District in Nov., '61, and the reader has already been told of the battle of Kernstown, which he fought there on Mar. 23, '62.

After that battle he had fallen back with his division, about 8000 strong, to Swift Run Gap. Ewell, with about as many more, was at Gordonsville, and Edward Johnson, with about 3000, was near Staunton.

The Federals had made in West Virginia two separate departments. That of the Shenandoah, under Banks, included the Valley in which Banks had, in April, about 19,000 men near Harrisonburg.

About 40 miles west in the mountains was Frémont, commanding what was called the Mountain Department, in which he had about 15,000 men. About 3700 of these, under Milroy, were at McDowell, a point 25 miles west of Staunton.

On April 29, Jackson proposed to Lee in Richmond that he, Jackson, should unite his own force and Johnson's and attack Milroy and Frémont, and drive them back into the mountains. Then returning quickly, and being joined by Ewell, his whole force should fall upon Banks. Lee approved the project and committed its entire execution to Jackson.

Ewell's division was brought up to Swift Run Gap to observe Banks, while Jackson concealed his object by marching his own division back across the Blue Ridge toward Charlottesville, and moving from a railroad station near Charlottesville by rail to Staunton. Here he united with Johnson and marched rapidly upon Milroy. He had started on April 30, and, taking a country road, had been three days in moving his guns and trains through 12 miles of mud to reach a metalled road. He had intended to rest over Sunday, May 4, but news of Frémont's cavalry having advanced, induced him reluctantly to put his infantry upon the cars and move to Staunton on that day. On May 7, he left Staunton, and on May 8 he confronted Milroy at McDowell. Milroy had been reënforced by Schenck's brigade. Jackson kept most of his force concealed, and about 2500 Federals were advanced against him in the afternoon. A sharp affair ensued with about 2800 of Jackson's force, holding the crest of a steep

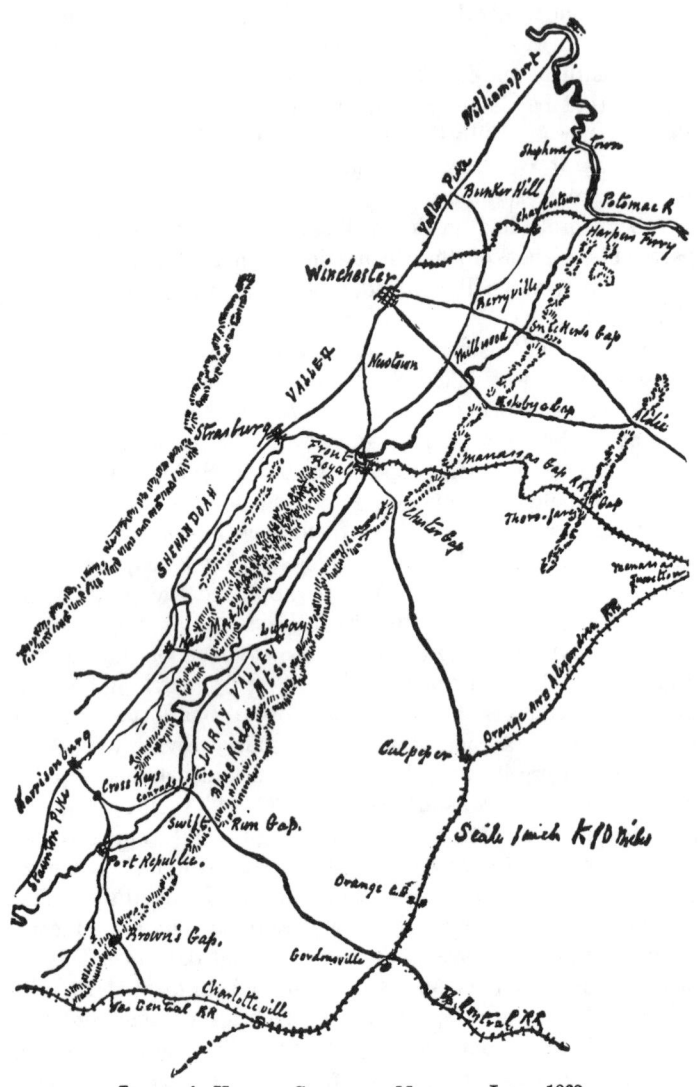

JACKSON'S VALLEY CAMPAIGN, MAY AND JUNE, 1862

ridge more exposed to fire than was the enemy. The latter only lost about 250 killed and wounded, while the Confederates lost 498; but next morning the Federals had retreated. Jackson pursued for two or three days, going nearly to Franklin, and then on May 12 turned back, damaging and obstructing all roads behind him, and thus practically neutralizing for a while Frémont's whole force. He now marched to unite with Ewell and to strike at Banks. Friday, May 16, had been appointed by the Confederate President a day of fasting and prayer, and it was spent in camp at Lebanon Springs near Staunton.

Meanwhile, during Jackson's absence, the situation in the Valley had changed. Shields's division, about 9000 men, had been taken from Banks and ordered to join McDowell at Fredericksburg, where the latter would await it before advancing to join McClellan before Richmond. This reduced Banks's force to about 10,000, and he had been withdrawn down the Valley to Strasburg, which he was ordered to fortify and hold.

Jackson had now with Ewell's division about 16,000 men. On May 20 he arrived at New Market, whence there were two roads to Winchester. The western, the most direct and shortest, going by Strasburg, and the eastern, crossing the Massanutten Mountains to Luray, followed the valley of the South Fork of the Shenandoah to Front Royal, about 12 miles east of Strasburg. Then, crossing the river, it united with the direct road at Newtown, within 12 miles of Winchester.

His march was by the eastern route and was conducted with such secrecy that the enemy had no idea that he was within 60 miles, when, at 1 P.M., May 23, his skirmishers attacked a Federal outpost at Front Royal held by Col. Kenly with about a thousand men and two guns. Kenly, seeing a much superior force, set fire to his camp, and, crossing the Shenandoah, also set fire to the bridge behind him, but Jackson's men rushed in and saved it, though so damaged as to make the use of it slow and difficult.

Jackson, crossing at a ford with the 6th Va. Cav., under Col. Flournoy, charged the enemy, capturing the two guns and 600 prisoners, the enemy losing 154 killed and wounded, and the Confederates only 26.

Even a more brilliant success might have resulted here but for an unfortunate failure of our staff service, as follows: —

As he approached Front Royal from the south, about three and a half miles from the town, a rough country road diverged to the east and gave a second approach to the town by an obscure route of about eight miles over some steep hills.

The more surely to avoid the enemy's pickets and to execute a surprise, Jackson had taken the head of his column by this road. But after striking the enemy's pickets near Front Royal, he sent back orders for the rear brigades to follow the short and nearly level highway to the town. As usual at that time in the Confederate armies, the courier service was performed by a small detachment of cavalry, temporarily detailed; not by specially selected men, as was later practised.

In this case the courier selected to carry the order not only failed to deliver it, but took himself off, and was never heard of again. It resulted that Jackson waited in vain the whole afternoon for the coming up of most of his artillery and infantry. Part of it only arrived after dark, completely exhausted by its laborious march; and one of his brigades, tired out, encamped four miles short of Front Royal. The cream of the whole occasion was thus lost.

Banks did not appreciate the situation until next morning, and only toward 10 o'clock did he get off from Strasburg in retreat for Winchester. Jackson, too, was able to make only a late start, and, being delayed by forces sent out by Banks to protect his right flank, he missed, by two hours, intercepting Banks's infantry, though he captured and destroyed about 100 wagons, and took some prisoners. There was much delay, also, from poor discipline in both the Confederate infantry and cavalry, especially in the latter. It was not easy for either to resist the temptations offered by so many wagons loaded with articles of food and clothing, calculated to appeal strongly to Confederate wants.

But if time was thus wasted, Jackson made it up by pushing his march for the greater part of the night. It was 3 A.M. when he finally allowed his exhausted men to lie down and sleep, and they were now near enough to Winchester to make it sure that Banks could not get away without a battle.

Early in the morning Jackson attacked Winchester. The enemy made a stubborn resistance, having good position but an inferior force. He was finally, however, broken and driven from the town in great confusion. Jackson, in his official report, says of the occasion : —

"Never have I seen an opportunity when it was in the power of cavalry to reap a richer harvest of the fruits of victory. Hoping that the cavalry would soon come up, the artillery, followed by infantry, was pressed forward for about two hours for the purpose of preventing by artillery fire a re-forming of the enemy; but as nothing was heard of the cavalry, and as but little or nothing could be accomplished without it in the exhausted condition of our infantry, between which and the enemy the distance was constantly increasing, I ordered a halt and issued orders for going into camp and refreshing the men."

This had been the critical moment of Jackson's whole strategic movement. He had successfully concentrated a superior force upon his enemy, and routed him, and needed but his cavalry to reap the full fruits of a great success. He had three regiments of cavalry, — the 7th under Col. Turner Ashby, and the 2d and 6th, which, the day before, had been placed under the command of Gen. Geo. H. Steuart. Ashby's regiment was recruited in the Valley and was noted for every good quality except discipline. Being near their homes, the opportunity to loot the captured trains had been peculiarly seductive, and the regiment for some days was but little more than a company. With his small force remaining, Ashby, unfortunately, the night before, had ridden to Berryville, fearing the enemy might attempt to escape by Snicker's Gap. The 2d and 6th regiments under Steuart were with Ewell's troops on the right of the attack, Jackson being with the left. There was no reason, therefore, except our fatal facility of blundering, why these two regiments should not have been promptly at hand, and, for once, the spectacle be seen of a Confederate army reaping the fruits of victory.

The story is a curious one, and is told in Jackson's official report as follows : —

"I had seen but some 50 of Ashby's cavalry since prior to the pillaging scenes of the previous evening, and none since an early hour of the past night. The 2d and 6th Va. regiments of cavalry were under the command of Brig.-Gen. Geo. H. Steuart of Ewell's command. After the pursuit had been continued for some distance beyond the town, and seeing nothing of the cavalry, I despatched my aide-de-camp, Lt. Pendleton, to Gen. Steuart with an order 'to move as rapidly as possible and join me on the Martinsburg turnpike and carry on the pursuit of the enemy with vigor.' His reply was that he was under the command of Gen. Ewell and the order must come through him. Such conduct and consequent delay has induced me to require of Lt. (now Maj.) Pendleton a full statement of the case, which is forwarded herewith."

Pendleton tells how Steuart, who was a graduate of West Point and an officer of the old army, had refused and failed to obey Jackson's order for immediate action, because not given through a division commander.

Gen. Jackson then goes on to say:—

"About an hour after the halt of the main body had been ordered, Brig.-Gen. Geo. H. Steuart, with his cavalry, came up, and renewing the pursuit pushed forward in a highly creditable manner and succeeded in capturing a number of prisoners; but the main body of Banks's army was now beyond the reach of successful pursuit, and effected its escape across the Potomac.

"Before reaching Bunker Hill Gen. Steuart was joined by Gen. Ashby with a small portion of his cavalry. Upon my inquiring of Gen. Ashby why he was not where I desired him at the close of the engagement, he stated that he had moved to the enemy's left for the purpose of cutting off a portion of his force. Gen. Steuart pushed on to Martinsburg, where he captured a large amount of army stores.

"There is good reason for believing that had the cavalry played its part in this pursuit as well as the four companies had done under Col. Flournoy two days before in the pursuit from Front Royal, but a small portion of Banks's army would have made its escape to the Potomac."

This narrative shows how our efficiency was impaired by our deficiencies of discipline. Our strategy, marching and fighting, had all been excellent. Yet, owing to the failure of one courier, and a single mistake of narrow-mindedness in a general, Banks had escaped with but trifling loss of men or material. The campaign, however, had not been undertaken to capture men or material. Its great object was to break up McDowell's proposed march from Fredericksburg to reënforce McClellan in front of Richmond.   This, it will be seen, was fully accomplished by the help of the following chapter of accidents and just at the critical moment.

McDowell had been ordered to march as soon as he was joined by Shields's division.   It arrived on May 22.   Only one day was needed to equip it for the march to Richmond, but the loss of three days followed.   Its artillery ammunition had been condemned by an inspector and a second day was lost, waiting for ammunition which had been delayed by the grounding of a schooner near Alexandria.   Everything, however, was ready by the night of the 24th, and McDowell was anxious to march on Sunday, the 25th.   But a third day's delay now ensued from Mr. Lincoln's superstitious feeling that his chances of success might be improved by showing some special regard for the Sabbath.

McDowell's official report says: [1] —

"I was now ready to march with over 40,000 men and over 100 pieces of artillery.   Though I could have started, and would have started, Sunday, yet it was resolved not to march till Monday; this out of deference to the wishes of the President, who was with me at the time, having come down Friday night, and with the concurrence of the Secretary of War, on account of the day."

When it is remembered that the distance to unite with McClellan could have been easily covered within three marches, one is impressed with the influence of small events upon great matters, especially when the small events involve the loss of time, even of hours.   It has already been told how McDowell did actually start, but, *having made only a part of a day's march, he was recalled*, and sent after Jackson.   Had he made even a full day, it is very doubtful if he would have been recalled.

On the morning of Sunday, the 25th, everything in Washington was serene.   Those best posted, and in highest authority, confidently expected the early fall of Richmond, and had good reason for their expectations   Indeed, the *New York Herald* that morning had had a leader headed, "Fall of Richmond."   By noon the papers were issuing extras headed, "Defeat of Banks, Washington in Danger."   A volcanic eruption could scarcely have startled

[1] O. R. 15, 282.

the administration more. Telegrams were sent the governors of a dozen states calling for instant help to save the capital. Reënforcements were rushed to Williamsport and Harper's Ferry to assist Banks. McDowell's march, already begun before orders could reach it, was countermanded, and half his force, under Shields and Ord, was hurried to the Valley to attack Jackson from the east, while Frémont's 15,000 attacked from the west.

McDowell, who was a good soldier, appreciated that no force possible for Jackson to have collected, could accomplish any serious results, and remonstrated, and begged in vain, to be allowed to carry out his projected march upon Richmond. When this was refused, he suggested that he be directed upon Gordonsville, but this too was overruled, and Shields and Ord were directed to march upon Strasburg, toward which point also Frémont was approaching.

Meanwhile, Jackson, having gone into camp about noon on Sunday, the 25th, when his infantry and artillery could no longer pursue the enemy, felt moved, even as Lincoln had done, to recognize the Sabbath by making up for the services missed in the morning.

His official report says: —

"On the following day (the 26th), divine service was held for the purpose of rendering thanks to God for the success with which He had blessed our arms, and to implore His continued favor."

During the next two or three days he made demonstrations toward the Potomac, advancing his troops to Charlestown, and within two miles of Harper's Ferry; but these demonstrations were only for their moral effect at the North, and to occupy time, while he filled his wagons with captured stores and prepared a convoy of a double line of wagons near seven miles long and about 2300 prisoners. Only on the 30th did he put his columns in motion toward the rear.

Had his opponents acted boldly and swiftly, their positions would now have enabled them to cut off Jackson's retreat and to overwhelm him. But the moral effect of his reputation doubtless caused some hesitation, and Jackson's entire force and his whole convoy, with some skirmishing at Front Royal with

Shields, and at Wardensville with Frémont, passed between his converging foes at Strasburg on the 31st, a portion of one of his brigades making in one day a march of 36 miles.

Besides the prisoners and stores brought off, Jackson left about 700 Federal sick and wounded at Winchester, and burned many stores for which he had no transportation. Two guns and over 9000 muskets were saved.

After passing Strasburg on the 31st, the race was continued up the main Shenandoah Valley, with Jackson leading and Frémont following in his tracks, while Shields advanced up the Luray Valley on the east.

At New Market the road from Luray enters the Valley through Massanutten Gap, but Jackson had sent cavalry ahead who burned the bridges by which Shields might have had access.

At Conrad's store another bridge across the South Fork gave a road to Harrisonburg, and Shields rushed his cavalry ahead to gain possession of it, but again he was too late. Meanwhile, there had been a severe rain-storm on June 2, and though Shields could hear the guns of Jackson's rear-guard and Frémont's advance on the other side of the Massanutten Mountains, he was powerless to cross.

On Thursday, June 5, Jackson reached Harrisonburg, and here diverged east to cross the South Fork upon the bridge at Port Republic. On the 6th, in a severe cavalry affair of the rear-guard, Gen. Turner Ashby was killed. Of the civilian soldiers whom the war produced, such as Forrest, Morgan, and others, scarcely one gave such early and marked indication of rare military genius as Ashby.[1]

---

[1] Col. Henderson writes of Ashby as follows:—

" The death of Ashby was a terrible blow to the Army of the Valley. From the outbreak of the war he had been employed on the Shenandoah, and from Staunton to the Potomac his was the most familiar figure in the Confederate ranks. His daring rides on his famous white charger were already the theme of song and story, and if the tale of his exploits, as told in camp and farm, sometimes bordered on the marvellous, the bare truth stripped of all exaggeration was sufficient in itself to make him a hero. His reckless courage, his fine horsemanship, his skill in handling his command, and his power of stimulating devotion, were not the only attributes which incited admiration. With such qualities, it is said, were united the utmost generosity and unselfishness, and a delicacy of feeling equal to a woman's."

On the 7th Jackson's advance at night reached the vicinity of Port Republic. This village is situated in the angle between the North and South rivers, which here unite and form the South Fork of the Shenandoah. The North River is the larger of the two, and the road from Harrisonburg crosses it by a wooden bridge. The South River was fordable.

On the morning of Sunday, the 8th, Jackson had sent two companies of cavalry across the river to scout on the Luray road toward Shields's advance. About 8 A.M. these companies were driven back in a rout and followed into the village by a body of Federal cavalry, who, with four guns and a brigade of infantry following, formed Shields's advance.

Jackson himself was in the village and narrowly escaped capture, riding across the bridge over the North River. Three of his staff were captured, but afterward escaped. Three brigades of infantry, however, and three batteries were near at hand, and the Federals were soon brought under a fire that sent them back in confusion with a loss of about 40 men and two guns, which had been brought across the South River. As their leading brigade, Carroll's, fell back, it met a second brigade of Shields's division, Tyler's, with artillery, and the two brigades, selecting a position about two miles north, decided to await the arrival of Shields with the rest of the division.

Jackson left two brigades to protect the bridge, and with the remainder of his force marched back about four miles to Cross Keys, where he had left Ewell's division holding a selected position against Frémont. Frémont was now in reach of Jackson, and, by all the maxims of war, should have exerted his utmost strength to crush him. He could afford to risk fighting his last reserves, and even to wreck his army, if he might thereby detain or cripple Jackson, for other armies were coming to his help and were near at hand. His attack, however, was weak. He had about 10,000 infantry, 2000 cavalry, and 12 batteries. Ewell had at first but 6000 infantry and 500 cavalry. Frémont brought into play about all of his artillery, but he advanced only one brigade of infantry from his left flank. This was repulsed and followed, and the whole of Frémont's left wing driven back to the shelter of his line of guns. Elsewhere there was no more than skirmishing and artillery duelling, of which the Federals usually had the best with their superior metal and ammunition. It was Jackson's rôle to fight only defensive battle, until he had shaken off the superior force which beset him; so the battle lingered along all day, the casualties being: —

Federal: killed 114,   wounded 443,   missing 127,   total 684
Confederate: "   41,   "   232,   "   15,   "   288

During the night of the 8th, Jackson returned to Port Republic and improvised a foot-bridge to carry his infantry dry shod across the South River. Early next morning, leaving a rear-guard of two brigades under Trimble and Patton to delay Frémont, the rest of his force was put in motion to find and attack Shields's two brigades, which had unwisely halted about two miles from Port Republic the day before.

I say unwisely, because they were only about 4000 men and 16 guns, but they had a position so beautiful that they were excusable just for the chance of fighting from it.

From the river on the right it extended straight across a mile of open plain, along a hollow road running between good banks, strongly fenced, to a considerable ravine in the wooded foot-hills of the Blue Ridge. The key of the position was a high retired shoulder on the Federal left, on which were posted seven guns, strongly supported by infantry sheltered in the near-by wood, and commanding every foot of the plain.

Jackson, this morning, proposed to himself a double victory, and he built the foot-bridge across the South River to enable him to win it. He intended, by making a very early start, to fall upon Shields's two brigades and crush them, and then doubling back upon his track to recross the rivers and meet Frémont, whom he would expect to find advancing toward Port Republic, against the opposition which Trimble and Patton would make. It was a good plan and entirely feasible, but two things went wrong in its execution.

The first was with the foot-bridge over the South River. This was rudely constructed of a plank footway, supported upon the running-gear of wagons standing in the stream, which was about breast deep. Such a bridge may be made quite serviceable, but this one was not strongly built, and before it had been in use long, it became impassable, except in single file. This made the passage of each brigade over twice as long as it should have been.

The second trouble was Jackson's impatience, which defeated his own purpose. Winder's brigade, leading his column, began to cross the bridge about 4.45 A.M., and Jackson was near the head of the column. When the enemy's position was discovered, it was plain that the key position above noted was its most assailable point. Time and blood would both have been saved by bringing up at once a force amply sufficient to overwhelm it. As he had five brigades at hand, and an abundance of artillery, there need have been no failure, and no more delay than the time needed to bring up his troops. Going into battle before enough troops were brought up, was sure to result in more or less disaster.

Winder's brigade, about 1500 strong, with two batteries, first attacked the Federal centre. It was not only badly repulsed, but the enemy gave a counterstroke, pursuing the fugitives and capturing a gun which they succeeded in carrying off. Other troops were arriving to reënforce Winder, but they were arriving too slowly. The Federal commander saw a chance to defeat his adversary by taking him in detail, and was swift to take advantage of it. He brought forward two fresh regiments from his left to reënforce an advance from his centre.

In vain Jackson himself rode among his own old brigade, exposing his life freely and endeavoring to rally them. Their thin lines had been for the time practically wrecked against superior numbers in a position almost impregnable. Fortunately, at the critical moment, relief came suddenly.

Jackson had recognized the key position held by the enemy's seven-gun battery, early in the morning, and had directed Taylor's fine La. brigade to attack it, and later, sent a second brigade to follow Taylor.

Their approach was made through forest, and the enemy were unaware of it. Taylor urged his march to the utmost, and was admonished by the sounds of the battle in the open country on his left that his friends were in need of assistance. So, without waiting for the brigade which followed him, he broke cover and charged boldly on the Federal battery at just the critical moment for Jackson on the left.

The sudden bursting out of so severe a battle at this vital point at once relieved the pressure upon Winder's centre. Taylor had a desperate fight, the battery being taken and retaken and taken again, before six of its guns and all of its caissons were finally held, and its fire opened upon the now retreating Federals. Taylor's brigade lost 288 men in this action, but accomplished its victory before the arrival of its support.

It was now about 10.30 A.M. About nine Jackson had realized that he would not be able to accomplish the double victory he had hoped for, and had sent word to Patton and Trimble to come across the bridges at Port Republic and to burn them. They had not been followed closely by Frémont. He only showed up on the opposite bank at noon, having had but seven miles to come.

He had a pontoon train, but made no effort to cross, and confined his activity to cannonading the Confederates from the north bank, wherever he could find an opportunity, during the whole afternoon. It accomplished little harm except to the Federal wounded, driving off the ambulances which were gathering them.

Jackson pressed the retreat of Tyler's two brigades for about nine miles down the river, capturing about 500. He then withdrew by roads which avoided Frémont's guns on the west bank, and went into camp between midnight and dawn on the 10th in Brown's Gap on the Blue Ridge, some of his regiments having marched over 20 miles.

The casualties in this action were as follows, the Federals having but two brigades engaged and the Confederates four: —

Confederate: killed 94, wounded 703, missing 36, total 833
Federal: "   67,   "   393,   "   558,   " 1018

The entire casualties for the whole campaign sum up as follows for the two armies: —

Confederate: killed 266, wounded 1580, missing 36, total 1903
Federal: "   269,   "   1306,   "   2402, "   3977

When, in his retreat, Jackson had gotten safely past Strasburg, the Federal War Department gave up all hope of capturing him, and began to take measures to renew McDowell's advance upon Richmond. One of McDowell's divisions, McCall's, had been held at Fredericksburg, and, about June 6, it had been sent by water to join McClellan upon the Peninsula. On the 8th orders were sent for McDowell himself with Shields's and Ord's divisions to march for Fredericksburg; but before these orders could have any effect there came the news of Jackson's sharp counterstrokes at Cross Keys and Port Republic, which had the purely moral effect of causing the order to be countermanded. It remained countermanded, and McDowell and his two divisions were kept in the valley about Front Royal until June 20.   This delay took away his last possible chance to reënforce McClellan before Lee took the offensive.   Indeed, the movement to Fredericksburg, resumed about June 20, was stopped on June 26 by the formation of a new army to be commanded by Gen. John Pope.   It comprised the entire forces of Frémont, Banks, and McDowell, and was charged with the duty of overcoming the forces under Jackson.

So we may now leave him and his gallant but wearied foot cavalry to enjoy about five days of rest on the banks of the Shenandoah, and take up the story of Lee before Richmond.

SEVEN DAYS' CAMPAIGN. THE ATTACK

Lee in Command. Ives predicts Lee's Audacity. Lee's Plan. McClellan's Delay. Lee's Opportunity. Lee's Order. Stuart's Raid. Intimations to the Enemy. Conference of Officers. Jackson's First Failure. Jackson's March. Stuart and Trimble. Branch Moves. A. P. Hill Moves. Battle of Mechanicsville. Porter's Retreat. A. P. Hill's Advance. Gaines Mill Position. The Chances. Jackson at Cold Harbor. Porter's Account. Hill's Account. Lee's Account. Jackson ordered in. General Advance. Enemy's Escape. Casualties. Remarks.

WHEN Gen. Lee, on June 1, 1862, took command of the Army of Northern Virginia, he brought with him his personal staff, — Col. R. H. Chilton, Adjutant, Col. A. L. Long, Military Secretary, and Majs. Taylor, Venable, Marshall, and Talcotts, as Aides. He retained the chiefs of all departments, — Corley as Quartermaster, Cole as Commissary, Guild as Medical Director, and myself as Ordnance Officer, — and all matters of routine went on as before.

The chances of a successful campaign against McClellan had increased greatly when Johnston fell, wounded, as has been already told. Johnston had proposed the concentration at Richmond of a large force, to be drawn from points farther south. Lee would be able to bring this about more effectively, occupying, as he had done, the position of Military Adviser to the President. He had, as yet, never commanded an army, and his accession to his present command did not at once inspire popular enthusiasm. His only active service had been in West Virginia, where he was Department Commander in the fall of 1861. This campaign had generally been considered a failure, but should have been recognized as a success, for there had been at least no loss of men, nor any serious reverse. It was absurd for the Confederacy to seek to occupy so extensive and mountainous a country as West Virginia, so close to the great state of Ohio, and with a population strongly favoring the Federal cause. It was impossible to supply our armies over their long and difficult roads. Mountain barriers in that section not only gave the country to the Federals, but proclaimed peace. This came to be recognized after one compaign. With this for a result, and no battles having been fought, an idea arose that Lee would not be an aggressive commander. This was strengthened when Lee's first care was to select a line of battle and begin to fortify it. To some of the amateur critics, who wrote for the public press, this seemed little better than a confession of cowardice.

The *Richmond Examiner*, edited by Pollard, was conspicuous in the bitterness of its attacks. Through some of these I chanced upon an interview which impressed me very forcibly at the time, and which proved to be quite a prophetic estimate of Lee as a commander. It came about as follows : On the staff of the President was Col. Joseph C. Ives, a graduate of West Point in the class of '52. He was born in New York and appointed from Connecticut, but had married in the well-known Semmes family of Georgia and Alabama, and had joined his fortunes with the South. He served on the staff of President Davis during the whole of the war. While in no way conspicuous, he impressed all who met him as particularly intellectual, and as an unusually accomplished officer.

When Lee had been in command about two weeks, I had a long ride with Ives about our lines, one afternoon, during which he referred to these newspaper attacks and asked if I thought they in any way impaired the confidence of the army in Lee. I had seen no such effect and told him so, and then went on to say: "Ives, tell me this. We are here fortifying our lines, but apparently leaving the enemy all the time he needs to accumulate his superior forces, and then to move on us in the way he thinks best. Has Gen. Lee the *audacity* that is going to be required for our inferior force to meet the enemy's superior force,—to take the aggressive, and to run risks and stand chances?"

Ives's reply was so impressive, both in manner and matter, that it has always been remembered as vividly as if to-day. He reined up his horse, stopped in the road, and, turning to me, said: "Alexander, if there is one man in either army, Confederate or Federal, head and shoulders above every other in *audacity*, it is Gen. Lee! His name might be Audacity. He will take more desperate chances and take them quicker than any other general in this country, North or South; and you will live to see it, too."

It is needless to say that I did live to see it many times over. But it seems, even yet, a mystery how, at that time, Ives or President Davis or any other living man had divined it. No one could meet Lee and fail to be impressed with his dignity of character, his intellectual power, and his calm self-reliance; but all those qualities might be recognized without deducing from them, also, the existence of such phenomenal audacity, except by an inspiration of genius.

The principal feature of Lee's proposed plan had long been the bringing down of Jackson from the Valley to attack the enemy's right wing. Even before Jackson had extricated himself from the pursuit of his enemies, on June 8, Lee had written him to set on foot the arrangements to mislead the enemy as to his intentions.

The arrangements adopted were both elaborate and effective. Not only were all sorts of exciting false rumors set on foot throughout the Valley, but Whiting's division, from before Richmond, and Lawton's large brigade — arriving from Georgia nearly 4000 strong — were sent by rail from Richmond to Staunton about June 11, to create the impression that Jackson's raid was about to be repeated with a much larger force. Meanwhile, Jackson's force was marched again to the Shenandoah near Port Republic, about the 11th, after Shields and Frémont had fallen back to the neighborhood of Strasburg. Here Jackson took five days of rest preparatory to the movement upon Richmond.

During most of this period, by all the rules of the game, McClellan was in default for not attacking. He had come within arm's length, but allowed the initiative to Lee. McDowell had been taken from him, so that he had nothing to gain by waiting, while his enemy had the opportunity both of reënforcement and of fortification. Lee was, indeed, doing his utmost in each direction. McClellan seemed to have been subconsciously aware that he ought to attack, and that his advantage was being lost by every day's delay; for his reports to Washington represented his army, from day to day, as being only held back from a general advance by waiting for some slight additional advantage, which a day or two would bring.

On June 2, which was his best opportunity, he was only waiting for the water to fall in the Chickahominy. On June 7 he was waiting for McCall's division (about 10,000 strong) which arrived on the 12th and 13th. On June 16 he was waiting for two days to let the ground harden. On June 18 the general engagement might begin at any hour. On June 25 "the action will probably occur to-morrow, or within a short time." And at last he was right, for Lee began it on the 26th, and during the interval, since June 2, the advantage had shifted from McClellan's side to Lee's.

As the game and the players now stood, the game was Lee's for a great success, — the greatest ever so fairly offered to any Confederate general. His strategy had been good and had been carried through without a flaw. Jackson's entire army, reënforced by Whiting's division and Lawton's brigade, had been brought down secretly from the Valley and, on the night of June 25, was encamped at Ashland within 13 miles of Mechanicsville. It was about 18,500 strong. Meanwhile, Lee had drawn together, available for battle, around Richmond, about 65,000 other troops, and had fortified his lines on the southeast between the Chickahominy and the James, enough to make them quite secure with half his force. McClellan's right flank was but a single corps, Porter's not over 30,000 strong, and separated from the Federal centre by the Chickahominy River and about four miles of distance. Under these circumstances, with even fairly good tactics, Porter's corps should have been practically destroyed, and with it the Federal line of supply from the York River. That once accomplished, the capture or destruction of the remainder of McClellan's army, during their retreat to the James River, would have been an easier task than the first.

All this was in the game which Lee set out to play on June 26, and the stakes were already his if his execution were even half as good as his plan.   At the beginning there was every promise that it would be.   Two days before, a confidential order had been issued to general officers and heads of departments, which is given in part, in contrast with Johnston's method, as developed at Seven Pines.

"GENERAL ORDERS No. 75.

"Headquarters in the field, June 24, 1862.

"Gen. Jackson's command will proceed to-morrow from Ashland toward the Stark (or Merry Oaks) Church, and encamp at some convenient point west of the Central Railroad.   Branch's brigade of A. P. Hill's division will also, to-morrow evening, take position on the Chickahominy near Half-Sink.

"At three o'clock Thursday morning, 26th inst., Gen. Jackson will advance on the road leading to Pole Green Church, communicating his march to Gen. Branch, who will immediately cross the Chickahominy and take the road leading to Mechanicsville.

"As soon as the movements of these columns are discovered, Gen. A. P. Hill, with the rest of his division, will cross the Chickahominy near Meadow Bridge and move direct upon Mechanicsville.

"To aid his advance the heavy batteries on the Chickahominy will, at the proper time, open upon the batteries at Mechanicsville.   The enemy being driven from Mechanicsville and the passage across the bridge opened, Gen. Longstreet, with his division and that of Gen. D. H. Hill, will cross the Chickahominy at or near that point, Gen. D. H. Hill moving to the support of Gen. Jackson, and Gen. Longstreet supporting Gen. A. P. Hill.   The four divisions keeping in communication with each other and moving *en echelon* on separate roads, if practicable, the left division in advance, with skirmishers and sharp-shooters extending their front, will sweep down the Chickahominy and endeavor to drive the enemy from his position above New Bridge, Gen. Jackson bearing well to his left, turning Beaver Dam Creek, taking the direction toward Cold Harbor.

"They will then press forward toward the York River Railroad, closing upon the enemy's rear and forcing him down the Chickahominy. Any advance of the enemy toward Richmond will be prevented by vigorously following his rear and crippling and arresting his progress. . . ."

But one grave error had been committed.   Among the preparations which Lee had made for the occasion had been a forced reconnoissance of the enemy's rear, which was made by his cavalry commander, Stuart, between June 11 and 15.   Stuart, with about 1200 men and two guns, passing well behind the enemy's right, had gotten into his rear and discovered that his right flank did not extend for any distance northward from the Chickahominy and rested on no natural obstacle. But the expedition could not safely return, Stuart thought, by the route taken in going. He determined, therefore, to make the circuit of the Federal army, crossing the Chickahominy below by a bridge which he expected to find.

In this he was disappointed, but with great resource he got safely across, partly by swimming, and partly by rebuilding a bridge, and brought off his guns and a few prisoners.

But this raid, though ordered by Lee and handsomely conducted, had one unfortunate effect. It would have been much better to have obtained the necessary information by scouts. It seriously alarmed McClellan for his rear. But for it the probabilities are that he would never have given the subject any thought, and he would certainly not have been prepared with a fleet of loaded transports on hand when he was, soon after, forced to change his base to Harrison's Landing on the James River. It is hard to estimate the difference in the result, had McClellan been taken by surprise on this occasion and been forced, perhaps, to retreat down the Peninsula. On the whole, therefore, the _éclat_ of our brilliant raid cost us much more than its results were worth. Where important strategy is on foot, too great care can scarcely be used to avoid making any such powerful suggestions to the enemy as resulted in this case.

It is interesting to note that the enemy got no intimations of what was going on until June 24. On that day a deserter from Jackson's force was brought in. After trying in vain to pass himself off as a Union prisoner, escaped from Jackson, he had told of Jackson's march and its supposed intent to attack McClellan's flank.

McClellan wired the story to Stanton, and also sent out two negroes to go along the railroad and investigate, but Stuart's pickets were too vigilant for the negroes to pass them. Stanton gave some credence to the deserter's story, but it cut small figure among the rumors which McClellan was receiving from his detective bureau. He believed that Beauregard had arrived and that Lee now had 200,000 men.

On June 25 he made his first forward movement by advancing

the skirmish-lines of several brigades and taking up a portion of the neutral ground in front of our picket-lines, near the Williamsburg road. Sharp skirmishing ensued and lasted all day, the Federal losses being reported as about 700, and our own about 400. The affair was called Orchard or Oak Grove Skirmish.

Before issuing order of battle No. 75, Lee had had on June 23 Longstreet, A. P. Hill, D. H. Hill, and Jackson, to meet in conference at his headquarters to arrange all details. Longstreet had asked Jackson to fix the date on which the attack should be made. The latter named June 25. Longstreet suggested that he allow more time, and the 26th was agreed to.

When summoned to this meeting by Lee on Saturday, June 21, Jackson was near Gordonsville. He started on a freight train bound to Richmond, but left the train before midnight that night at a station where he spent Sunday, attending church twice.[1] At midnight he set out on horseback for the conference at Richmond about 50 miles away, arriving about 3 P.M.

Had he kept on the freight train to Richmond, he would have arrived early Sunday morning. His brigades on the march also kept Sunday in camp. It was usually the general's custom to keep account of Sundays spent in fighting or marching, and to make up for each by a week-day rest, and sermons, at the earliest opportunity.

On the march from Gordonsville the railroad was utilized for the infantry, as far as could be done, by picking up the rear brigades and carrying them forward. Artillery and cavalry marched all the way.

On Tuesday morning, June 24, Jackson's infantry was at Beaver Dam Station, on the Virginia Central road, about 18 miles from Ashland, where they were expected to encamp that night, and about 25 miles from the Virginia Central R.R. near the Stark Church, whence order No. 75 required Jackson to march at 3 A.M., Thursday, June 26.

We now enter upon the story of performances. The orders governing the beginning of the action were simple and explicit. Every officer must have realized the supreme importance of

[1] Henderson says it was Frederick Hall, other reports say Louisa C. H.

time, even without the hint given by Lee in his order fixing the hour of Jackson's march at 3 A.M.

It is, therefore, a great surprise to see that instead of crossing the Virginia Central R.R. at 3 A.M. on the 26th, they do not begin to cross it until 10 A.M. on that date. That is practically a whole day late, because, with the distance still to be traversed, it will be too late to commence the great battle intended, in time to win it and gather the fruits of victory.

Had Jackson pushed his march to Ashland on the night of the 24th, about 18 miles from Beaver Dam, as Lee's order contemplated, he would have had only six miles to march on the 25th, and his men would have been in excellent condition to set out at 3 A.M. on the 26th, with less than 10 miles to go to reach the enemy. The result of crossing the Central R.R. at 10 A.M. was to fight the battle a day late and at Gaines Mill, three miles nearer McClellan's main army, thus losing the opportunity to cut off Porter's corps at Beaver Dam. This opportunity, the cream of the whole campaign, was lost by Jackson's not demanding of his troops better marching on the 24th and 25th.

His biographers have found many excuses for him, but, however good or bad these excuses may be, they will not be dwelt upon here for two reasons: —

First. The object of the narrative is neither praise nor blame, but only that military students may realize, more fully than they could without such an example, the infinite value of hours when a battle is on foot, and how easily hours may be lost.

Second. The excuses of the biographers will best be given after finishing the whole story; for, unfortunately, this loss of the first day is not the only, nor is it the worst, failure of Jackson during these Seven Days, to come to time as was expected of him. He nowhere, even distantly, approached his record as a soldier won in his every other battle, either before or afterward. As one reads of his weak and dilatory performance day after day, and recalls what he had always been before, and always was afterward, one feels that during these Seven Days he was really not Jackson. He was a different individual. He was under a spell! Nothing that he had to do was done with the vigor which marked all the rest of his career.

Crossing the Central R.R. at 10 A.M. on the 26th, he marched but eight miles farther that day, going into bivouac about five o'clock, at Hundley's Corner. He was here in easy reach of Porter's rear and in full hearing of the heavy cannonading and musketry going on at Mechanicsville, which will be told of presently.

He describes the march, as follows, in his official report:—

"Pursuing the Ashcake road we crossed the Central R.R. about 10 A.M. Approaching the Totopotomoy Creek, the Federal picket crossed to the south side of the stream, and partially destroyed the bridge, and, by felling trees across the road farther on, attempted to delay our advance. After the Texas skirmishers had gallantly crossed over, Reilly shelled the woods for the purpose of driving the enemy from it, in order that we might safely effect a lodgment beyond the creek. Whiting rapidly repaired the bridge and the march was resumed. That night the three divisions bivouacked near Hundley's Corner. . . . We distinctly heard the rapid and continued discharges of cannon which announced the engagement of Gen. A. P. Hill with the extreme right of the enemy."

Gen. Stuart, in his official report, says:—

"At Dr. Shelton's we awaited the arrival of Gen. Jackson, sending a squadron in advance to seize and hold the bridge at the Totopotomoy. The enemy, anticipating us, had torn up the bridge, and held the opposite bank, and obstructed the road, without, however, making any determined stand. Capt. W. W. Blackford, Corps of Engineers, assigned to duty with my command, set about repairing the bridge, and in a half-hour, with the details furnished him, the bridge was ready. Passing Pole Green Church, Gen. Jackson's march led directly toward the crossing of Beaver Dam Creek opposite Richardson's. Reaching that point he bivouacked for the night."

Gen. Trimble, in his official report, writes:—

"On the 26th we moved, with the army, from Ashland in a southerly direction, passing to the east of Mechanicsville in the afternoon, and at 4 P.M. distinctly heard the volleys of artillery and musketry in the engagement of Gen. Hill with the enemy. Before sundown the firing was not more than two miles distant, and, in my opinion, we should have marched to the support of Gen. Hill that evening."

Now we will go back to the Chickahominy, where Branch's brigade, some eight miles above the rest of A. P. Hill's division at Meadow Bridge, is under arms and expecting to receive the signal to advance not later than 4 A.M. It does not come until after 10 o'clock. As soon as it was received, Branch crossed the Chickahominy and moved toward Mechanicsville, the enemy's pickets falling back before him.

At one point the road pursued by Branch approached, within a short distance, a road upon its left, which was being followed by Ewell's column, and the two generals had a brief meeting, but there was no other communication between the columns until the next day. Meanwhile, since an early hour in the morning, the divisions of A. P. Hill at Meadow Bridge, and of D. H. Hill and Longstreet at the Mechanicsville bridge, two miles below, had been under arms and anxiously awaiting the sound of Jackson's guns.

President Davis was on the ground, having ridden out from Richmond, not only to see, but anxious to participate in, the coming battle. A few siege-guns had been mounted on the low bluffs along the Chickahominy Valley, and they were now manned for use, in case our crossing at the Mechanicsville bridge was resisted. But hour after hour passed, and there came no sound of conflict from the direction of Jackson's advance.

At 3 P.M. A. P. Hill, of his own motion, decided to wait for Jackson no longer. It is strange that he should have taken this responsibility without orders from Lee, who was within two miles, and who, it seems, would not have approved it. Henderson states that, "A message from Lee, ordering Hill to postpone all further movement, arrived too late." [1] Doubtless Lee wished, now, to make a fresh start on the morrow, as Johnston had wished at Seven Pines.

The enemy made slight resistance to Hill's advance, and fell back through Mechanicsville to his works behind Beaver Dam Creek, opening the road to Longstreet's and D. H. Hill's divisions. A. P. Hill's division moved so rapidly that it arrived at Mechanicsville a mile and a half ahead of Branch's brigade. No advantage was gained, however, by thus anticipating the coming up of Jackson. The enemy held, behind Beaver Dam Creek, an intrenched position quite impregnable to assault.

[1] Hend. II., 16.

It had not been intended to attack it with infantry, but to threaten it with artillery, while Jackson passed to the rear and cut off the enemy's retreat.

Already Jackson, in spite of his slow march and the time wasted at Totopotomoy Creek, was within three miles of the enemy's line of retreat and with no force opposing him but a few cavalry. But here he stopped his march, which had only been about 13 miles that day, and went into bivouac, regardless of the roar, not only of artillery, but, presently, of musketry also, appealing to him from Mechanicsville. For with haste and poor judgment Davis, Lee, Longstreet, and the two Hills, not content to merely cannonade the enemy in his position, were beginning to wreck whole brigades of infantry, as must now be told.

The position was one in which good troops could repulse treble their numbers if assailed in front, but it was easily turned. Jackson, three miles off to the northeast, was already in easy reach of Porter's line of retreat, and had but to push his advance a mile or two, and Porter would have been compelled to retreat precipitately or be caught in a trap.

On the 26th of June, in the latitude of Richmond, the sun rises at 4.38 A.M. and sets at 7.27 P.M. and twilight lasts until about 8.30 P.M. There was no moon. As already told, Gen. Jackson arrived at Hundley's Corner at 4.30 P.M. and went into bivouac there for the night, after having marched from Ashland about 11 miles off in an air line, and perhaps 12 to 14 by the roads traversed.

At Mechanicsville the firing commenced at three o'clock, and rapidly grew heavy. It was at first a long-range duel with the Confederate siege-guns on the Chickahominy, and then with the field-batteries accompanying Confederate brigades as they came up. A. P. Hill's five brigades of infantry were also put into action as soon as they could be formed, and advanced within range of the enemy's intrenched lines, when they opened fire both of artillery and infantry. Thus the battle was maintained until dark. Meanwhile, as the hours of daylight were closing, under urgent messages from Lee and President Davis, two regiments of Ripley's brigade of D. H. Hill's division were launched in a direct charge on perhaps the very strongest point

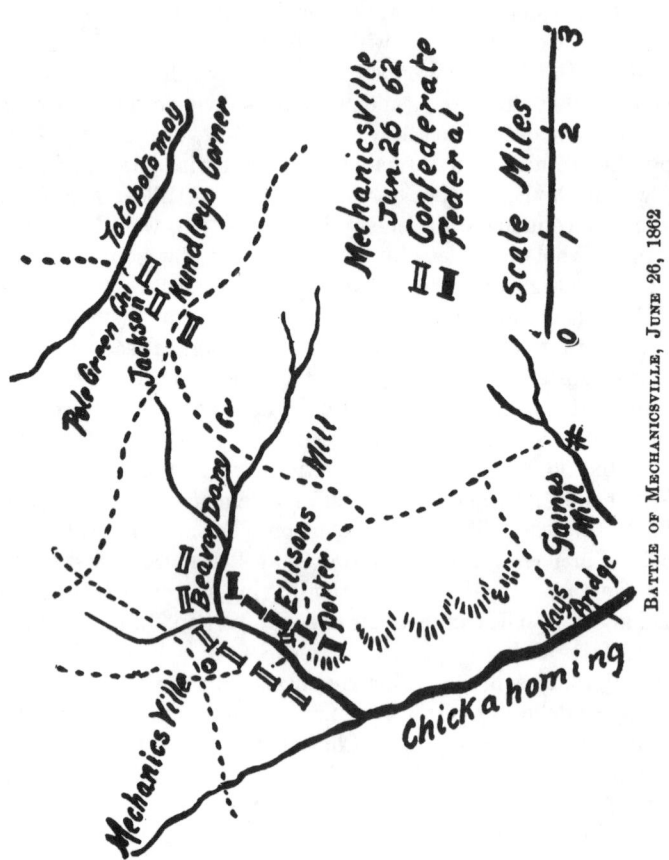

BATTLE OF MECHANICSVILLE, JUNE 26, 1862

of the whole Federal position. A more hopeless charge was never entered upon. They were the 1st N.C. and the 44th Ga., raw regiments, which had never before been under fire. Their behavior illustrated the morale inspiring the army. Had they been given anything to do which it was possible to do, they would have done it, and become seasoned veterans in their first battle.

They dashed across a wide plain through a storm of musketry, shells, and canister, and some even went across Beaver Dam and into the entangled slashing close under the Federal lines. There they were killed until their bodies lay, as a Federal account described it, "as thick as flies in a bowl of sugar," before the survivors realized the trap into which they had been sent, and got back as best they could.

The 1st N.C. suffered 142 casualties, including all three field-officers and the adjutant. The 44th Ga. lost 335, including its Col. and Lt.-Col., — a regimental loss seldom equalled in so short a time. The total casualties of this battle were about 1350 and included 14 field-officers. The Federals reported their loss as 361.

Porter, in his report, says that only during the night, by reports from scouts and outposts, did the Federals become aware of the close proximity of Jackson's force, and it was recognized at once that McClellan's army was in a very critical condition. He writes: —

"But for the conception of the idea of a flank movement, changing our base by the left flank to the James River, our position would have left but one alternative — a hasty abandonment of our attack on Richmond, and a retirement by the way we had advanced."

This conception, as before told, had been developed two weeks before by Stuart's raid, and it had not only been developed, but, what was much more important, already transports had been loaded and many important preparations for carrying it into execution had been made in advance. The matter was decided in McClellan's mind during that night, though no orders were issued. Porter's corps was ordered to withdraw to a strong position upon the north bank of the Chickahominy in close connection with the rest of his army.

This position, about three miles in rear of Beaver Dam, had already been noted and selected by the Chief Engineer, Gen. Barnard.

Porter, however, remained in his intrenched position until daylight, and then began to withdraw down the Chickahominy in good order, carrying with him guns of position which had been posted along the Chickahominy. The Confederate batteries reopened their fire at dawn, and the Federal rear-guard replied heavily for over two hours. Had Jackson's corps made an early start, and been pushed as Jackson was wont to push, both before and after this Seven Days' spell, he would have struck Porter's corps on the flank as it marched toward Cold Harbor. But the advance was so late and slow that when at last, about eight o'clock, it appeared in rear of Porter's position, having marched about three miles, the last Federal soldier had withdrawn, and Jackson's artillery fired by mistake into the head of Hill's advancing column. The trap was sprung, but the bird had flown.

Gen. Gregg gives the following account: —

"Early in the morning of the 27th I received orders from Gen. A. P. Hill to take the advance with the 2d brigade and to drive the enemy from their position on Beaver Dam Creek at Ellison's Mill. The brigade advanced to the attack. Slight resistance was made here by the enemy, and the passage of the stream, which presented a strong natural obstacle, was gained. Many Confederate soldiers, wounded or killed in a preceding unsuccessful assault, lay in the road toward the crossing of the creek, and had to be moved aside to allow the passage of our artillery. A small bridge, broken up by the enemy, had also to be repaired. This was toward eight o'clock in the morning. Crossing Beaver Dam Creek, the brigade advanced along the road among piles of knapsacks and other property, and burning stores abandoned by the enemy, with skirmishers — out to the front and left. Coming into the edge of an open field, Capt. Cordero's company, 1st S.C., deployed as skirmishers, were fired on by artillery in front, and Lt. Heise and a soldier were wounded. Capt. W. T. Haskell's company of the same regiment, advancing in open order, discovered that the forces meeting us in front from the left were those of Maj.-Gen. Jackson, and entered into communication with them so as to to avoid the risk of future mischiefs."

At last then, the morning half gone, the four Confederate divisions were united and within three miles of the enemy. Porter had gone into the position selected behind Boatswains'

Creek, with three divisions of infantry, six regiments of cavalry, and 20 batteries, — in all about 27,000 men and 80 guns. The position was naturally strong, and it was being strengthened hourly with abattis and rifle-pits.

Its development covered only about two miles of convex front. Its left flank rested on the open Chickahominy bottom, where heavy batteries from the south side secured it from being turned. Its right flank was its weak point, its protection there being only tangled thickets which also covered much of the front. Where this was lacking were generally three lines of infantry, partially under cover, and abundant artillery so placed that its fire was over the heads of the infantry. His force was enough to cover his front six deep. Two bridges gave connection to the south side, and over them, during the action, McClellan sent Slocum's division (9000) of Franklin's corps with two batteries, and French's and Meagher's brigades of Sumner's corps, as re-enforcements, — say about 14,000 men. Porter himself was, perhaps, the hardest opponent to fight in the Federal army. No one in it knew better how to occupy and prepare his ground for defence, or was more diligent to do it; and in his corps were concentrated all of the regular regiments of the old Federal army.

To attack such a position was no easy proposition, and Lee's force, checked and 1300 weakened by the ill-advised affair at Mechanicsville, had no margin to spare over the size of its task. Indeed, had McClellan reënforced Porter as he should have done, with a whole corps, he might have won a great victory. But he allowed himself to be imposed upon by the demonstrations made by Magruder and Huger, under orders from Lee, and neither attacked with his left, nor strengthened his right sufficiently. He weakly left the question of sending reënforcements to his four corps commanders. Franklin sent Slocum's division, and Sumner sent French's and Meagher's brigades, but Keyes and Heintzelman reported that they could spare nothing.

As it was, therefore, the fight should result in Lee's favor by a reasonable margin, provided it was well managed and its force not squandered in partial attacks. But this took place to an extent perilously near losing the battle. It did lose the precious hours of daylight necessary to gather any fruits of victory, and made the victory much more bloody than it need have been. The importance of time should have been appreciated and the march pushed to locate the enemy's new position and develop it with strong skirmish-lines. Then, at the most favorable points, our utmost strength should have been marshalled and concentrated for simultaneous assaults of infantry, supported upon each flank by concentrations of batteries. It was but waste of time and blood to launch any small assault against that position, as had been done at Beaver Dam.

The fact that we finally carried the position by a general charge, after the repulse of many partial ones, shows that our men were good enough and that we had enough of them to have made a success early in the afternoon, had our energies been first concentrated for the effort.

During the morning of the 27th, the Confederates moved with a slowness only to be understood by remembering the inexperience, in handling such large bodies, of many of our generals and staff-officers. By noon, however, we had developed the enemy's position. On our left Jackson was at Cold Harbor with four divisions,—his own, Ewell's, Whiting's, D. H. Hill's, — and Lawton's large brigade in addition. He confronted the Federal right. A. P. Hill, with Longstreet in reserve, confronted their left.

Porter, in the *Century*, writes: —

"The advance column of these troops [Jackson's] came a little earlier than those under Longstreet and A. P. Hill, but were more cautious, and, for some hours, not so aggressive."

What happened was this: D. H. Hill's division, crossing the Chickahominy behind A. P. Hill, had been pushed out to the left by Lee's battle order and brought up behind and in support of Jackson's forces early on the 27th. But in the slow marching of the morning, D. H. Hill, with characteristic aggressiveness, had managed to pass Jackson's force and to take the lead. On approaching Cold Harbor and discovering the enemy's position, Hill at once moved his division up to the edge of the swamp held by the enemy upon the other side, and opened upon them with a battery. His battery was quickly answered by 10 guns, and after a brief action was withdrawn, crippled. Just at that juncture came orders from Jackson withdrawing Hill into some woods in rear, where the head of Jackson's long column was already standing halted. In his official report, Jackson thus explains his object in this manœuvre: —

"Soon after, Gen. A. P. Hill became engaged, and, being unacquainted with the ground, and apprehensive, from what appeared to me to be the respective positions of the Confederate and Federal forces engaged, that, if I then pressed forward, our troops would be mistaken for the enemy and be fired into, and hoping that Gen. A. P. Hill and Longstreet would drive the Federals toward me, I directed Gen. D. H. Hill to move his division to the left of the road, so as to leave between him and the wood on the right of the road [from which he is withdrawing D. H. Hill], an open space across which I hoped the enemy would be driven. Thus arranged, it was in our power to distinguish friend from foe in case the enemy should be driven as expected."

It is not necessary to comment upon this too elaborate explanation of how more than a half of Lee's army was paralyzed for three hours, just on the verge of battle, further than to say that the inaction, and the excuse for it, are both unlike anything ever seen in Jackson before or after these Seven Days. D. H. Hill was withdrawn about 2 P.M. It was about 2.30 P.M. when A. P. Hill's advance, pressed as rapidly as he was able to bring up his six brigades, developed into a battle.

Porter, in *Battles and Leaders*, further describes the fight made by this single division (about 12,000 men) which had had, only the evening before, sharp losses at Ellison's Mill.

"Soon after 2 P.M., A. P. Hill's force, between us and New Cold Harbor, again began to show an aggressive disposition, independent of its own troops on its flanks, by advancing from under cover of the woods, in lines well formed and extending, as the contest progressed from in front of Martin's battery to Morell's left.

"Dashing across the intervening plains, floundering in the swamps, and struggling against the tangled brushwood, brigade after brigade seemed to almost melt away before the concentrated fire of our artillery and infantry; yet others pressed on, followed by supports as dashing and as brave as their predecessors, despite their heavy losses and the disheartening effect of having to clamber over many of their disabled and dead, and to meet their surviving comrades rushing back in great disorder from the deadly contest. For nearly two hours the battle raged, extending more or less along the whole line to our extreme right.

"The fierce firing of artillery and infantry, the crash of the shot, the bursting of shells, and the whizzing of bullets heard above the roar of artillery and the volleys of musketry, all combined, was something fearful.

"Regiments quickly replenished their exhausted ammunition by bor-

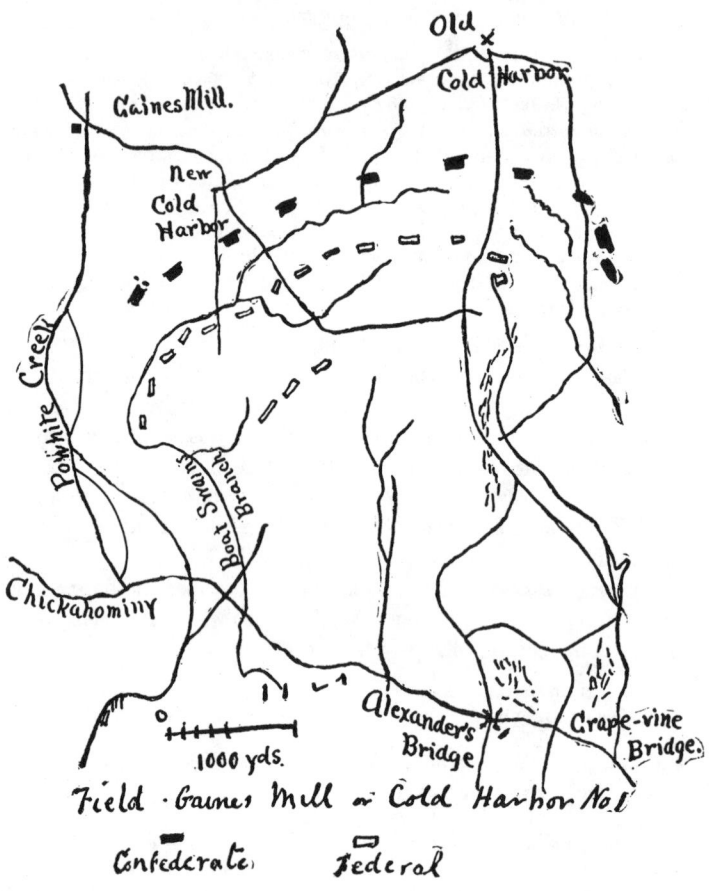

Field · Gaines Mill or Cold Harbor No. 1

rowing from more bountifully supplied and generous companions; some withdrew temporarily for ammunition, and fresh regiments took their places, ready to repulse, sometimes to pursue, their desperate enemy, for the purpose of retaking ground from which we had been pressed, and which it was necessary to occupy in order to hold our position."

It is to make one almost sick of regret to read of such desperate valor so lavishly wasted upon an impossible effort, while three times as many men stood by and looked on. A. P. Hill's account of it in his official report is as follows: —

"The incessant roar of musketry and deep thunder of artillery told that the whole force of the enemy was in my front. Branch becoming hard pressed, Pender was sent in to his relief. Field and Archer were also directed to do their part in this murderous contest. Braxton's battery, accompanying Archer, had already opened. They were ordered to turn the enemy's left. These two brigades under their heroic leaders, moving across the open field, met the enemy behind an abattis and strong intrenchments at the base of a long wooded hill, the enemy being in three lines on the side of this declivity, its crest falling off into a plateau, and this plateau studded with guns.

"My front now presented a curved line, its convexity toward the enemy. Desperate but unavailing attempts were made to force the enemy's positions. The 14th S.C., Col. McGowan (having hurried up from picket duty on the other side of the Chickahominy, and arriving in the thickest of the fight), on the extreme left, made several daring charges. The 16th N.C., Col. McElroy, and 22d, Lt.-Col. Gray, at one time carried the crest of the hill, and were in the enemy's camp, but were driven back by overwhelming numbers. The 35th Ga., Col. Thomas, also drove through the enemy's line like a wedge, but it was all of no avail. Gregg and Branch fought with varying success, Gregg having before him the vaunted Zouaves and Sykes's regulars. Pender's brigade was suffering heavily, but stubbornly held its own. Field and Archer met a withering storm of bullets, but pressed on to within a short distance of the enemy's works, but the storm was too fierce for such a handful of men. They recoiled and were again pressed to the charge, but with no better success. These brave men had done all that any soldiers could do. Directing their men to lie down, the fight was continued and help awaited. From having been the attacking, I now became the attacked, but stubbornly, gallantly, was the ground held. My division was thus engaged fully two hours before assistance was received. We failed to carry the enemy's lines, but we paved the way for the successful attacks afterward, in which attacks it was necessary to employ the whole of our army on that side of the Chickahominy.

"About four o'clock reënforcements came up on my right from Gen. Longstreet, and later, Jackson's men on my right and centre, and my division was relieved of the weight of the contest. It was then continued on more equal terms, and finally the extreme left of the enemy's line was most gallantly carried by Hood's brigade.

"At seven o'clock the General-in-chief, in person, gave me an order to

advance my whole line and to communicate this order as far as I could
to all commanders of troops. This was done, and a general advance
being made, the enemy were swept from the field and the pursuit only
stopped by nightfall, and the exhaustion of our troops. The batteries
of Crenshaw, Johnson, Braxton, and Pegram were actively engaged,
Crenshaw and Johnson pretty well knocked to pieces. Pegram, with
indomitable energy and earnestness of purpose, though having lost 47
men and many horses at Mechanicsville, had put his battery in condition
for this fight also."

Lee's official report of this battle was not written until eight
months afterward, during which period Jackson's great military
genius had manifested itself undimmed by any spell; and with
increasing brilliancy on the fields of Cedar Mountain, Second
Manassas, Harper's Ferry, Sharpsburg, and Fredericksburg.
There was, most wisely and properly, every disposition to ignore
and forget the disappointments felt during the Seven Days, and
the facts are glossed over with but brief and, as it were, casual
mention, but they are plainly apparent.

Lee by no means designed that A. P. Hill should alone engage
the whole of Porter's force. He had had a personal interview
with Jackson during the morning, and he knew that the head
of his column was at Cold Harbor before 2 P.M. He expected it
to immediately envelop and to turn Porter's right. He says
that Hill —

"Immediately formed his line nearly parallel to the road toward
McGehee's house, and soon became hotly engaged. The arrival of Jackson on our left was *momentarily expected*, and it was supposed that his
approach would cause the extension of the enemy's line in that direction.
Under this impression *Longstreet was held back* until this movement
should commence."

Hill went into action anticipating that Jackson's whole force
would almost immediately be demonstrating or attacking upon
the enemy's right flank. Why were they not? The head of
the column was up, but it was hidden from the enemy's view
in the woods, and its whole length, stretching for miles back,
was simply standing idle in the road. Had the divisions even
been closed up and disentangled from ordnance wagons, artillery,
and ambulances, and massed near Cold Harbor, the time would
not have been entirely wasted, but this was not done. Stern

necessity, at length, forced Lee to call upon Longstreet's division to aid A. P. Hill.   Three brigades were advanced within musket range as supports, but held back from the charge while the remaining three were held near at hand and ready for action.   At length, — probably about 4.30, — aroused to action both by the receding sounds of A. P. Hill's battle, and by urgent messages from Lee, Jackson sent D. H. Hill's division back into the wood from which he had withdrawn it before two o'clock.   He also sent a staff-officer to his other divisions with instructions, quoted by Henderson, as follows : —

"The troops are standing at ease along our line of march.   Ride back rapidly along the line, and tell the commanders to advance instantly *in echelon* from the left.   Each brigade is to follow as a guide, the right regiment of the brigade on the left, and to keep within supporting distance. Tell the commanders if this formation fails at any point, to form line of battle and move to the front, pressing to the sound of the heaviest firing, and attack the enemy vigorously wherever found.   As to artillery, each commander must use his discretion.   If the ground will at all permit, tell them to take in their field-batteries and use them.   If not, post them in the rear."

That the troops were still standing halted along the line of march appears in the official reports, as well as in the time consumed before they were able to make their power felt in the battle.   This required from one to two hours.

Winder, commanding Jackson's division, reports : —

"Left bivouac near Totopotomoy Creek at about 5 A.M., being in the rear of the column, except one brigade.   The march was slow and tedious [about seven miles during the whole day].   Firing was heard on the right.   Between 4 and 5 P.M. I received orders from Gen. Ewell to move up rapidly.   I ordered the ordnance wagons and artillery to halt, and moved the brigade from the column filing to the right through a wood and swamp, to the point where I heard the heaviest fire."

Lawton's official report says : —

"In the order of march toward the battle-field on that day my brigade brought up the rear of Gen. Jackson's army, and was, therefore, the last to engage the enemy.   I had remained at a halt for several hours, more than two miles from the point where the brigade afterward entered the field, and was not ordered forward until nearly 5 P.M.   I then marched rapidly on, retarded much by the artillery and ambulances which blocked up the narrow road."

While Jackson's troops were being brought up, the noise of battle waned, until an ominous silence seemed to possess the field as the sun drew near the horizon. Then the storm arose again and soon swelled to a magnitude never before heard on this continent.

It was about seven o'clock when at last D. H. Hill, Ewell, Lawton, and a part of Winder were all hotly engaged in the swampy tangle in front of the Federal right, and, though in great confusion, were making headway through it, and several Confederate batteries were returning the Federal fire. Opposite their left, Whiting's two brigades had just arrived, being directed by Lee as they approached from Cold Harbor, and two of Winder's brigades were also close at hand. A. P. Hill's brigades, though much diminished, were still holding their lines, and Longstreet was all in position. It was, practically, anybody's fight. A fresh division to Porter would have easily held his lines until night. It might even have enabled him to make an effective counterstroke, though the natural obstacles behind which his lines were located, offered but one or two possible opportunities. Two fresh brigades, French's and Meagher's, were *en route* to him, but were yet too far off to lend any aid.

But Lee, at last, was putting forth his whole strength. He issued orders for an advance of every command, regardless of the troops upon its right or left. A general advance was made, not simultaneous in its beginnings, but pressed to success by Whiting's two brigades supported by Longstreet on our extreme right, by Lawton's and Winder's brigades in the centre, and by D. H. Hill with Garland's and parts of Ripley's and Rodes's brigades upon our left.

Had it been made two hours earlier, the fruits of the victory would have been important. As it was, they were so trifling as scarcely to be worth mention. Porter fell back in fairly good order under cover of his superior artillery, and our artillery could not be gotten forward across the swamps. Blessed night, for which the defeated pray, had let down her mantle while the firing was still severe, and before we could even feel fully assured of our victory. Under its friendly cover, and the protection of the French and Meagher brigades, by 4 A.M. the whole Federal army had crossed the Chickahominy, damaging the bridges behind them, and leaving us, as the fruits of victory, but 22 guns, 2836 prisoners, and about 10,000 small-arms.

The Federal casualties were reported as: killed 894, wounded 3107, missing 2836, total 6837.

The Confederate casualties cannot be exactly divided, but I estimate the total losses of the different divisions for this battle, as follows: —

A. P. Hill's	division,	6	brigades,	2688	
Longstreet's	"	6	"	1883	(Only 5 engaged.)
D. H. Hill's	"	5	"	1423	
Whiting's	"	2	"	1017	
Ewell's	"	3	"	764	
Jackson's	"	3	"	91	(Only 1 engaged.)
Lawton's	brigade	1	"	492	
Totals		26		8358	

The heavy character of much of the fighting is shown by some of the regimental losses, although in many instances the reports give only the total casualties for the Seven Days, and do not distinguish between the battles. The charge by Whiting's two brigades, under Hood and Law, was notable for being driven home on the first effort, without halting to open fire. The 4th Tex., the first regiment to enter the enemy's works, lost 44 killed and 206 wounded. There was no thicket or obstruction to seriously check the advance at this portion of the field, and part of the ground traversed was exposed to but little artillery fire.

Trimble, of Ewell's division, made the following observations in his official report: —

" The subjoined list of killed and wounded best shows the severity of the conflict, and a comparison of those of different regiments fairly illustrates the superiority of a rapid charge over a standing fight, not only as the best mode of securing victories, but doing it with smaller loss. The 15th Ala. and 21st Ga., numbering 1315 men, stood under a destructive fire for an hour or more, returning the enemy's volleys all the time, and advanced half a mile, with only fragments of companies, at the close of the day. Their loss in killed and wounded was 251 men. The 16th Miss. and 21st N.C., numbering 1244 men, passed under as hot a fire an equal distance in 15 minutes, losing in killed and wounded only 85 men."

Briefly, it may be said of this battle that it seems to have been left in the hands of the division commanders until it was nearly lost.   Only at the last moment was the hand of the general in command revealed.   But had Jackson's march that morning been pushed with the fierce swiftness natural to him on such occasions, and had he, during A. P. Hill's attack, thrown his whole force upon McClellan's right, a comparatively easy victory would have resulted.   As has been stated, the enemy's right flank was his weakest point.   It was not found.   D. H. Hill would have attacked it even before A. P. Hill's battle, had not Jackson stopped and withdrawn him, instead of reënforcing and pushing him, as it was naturally expected that Jackson would do — although no man ever needed pushing less than D. H. Hill. In the *Century War Book*, he wrote of this occasion : —

"Had Jackson's command gone in on the left of the road running by the McGehee House, Porter's position would have been turned and the line of retreat cut off."

CHAPTER VIII

Seven Days' Campaign. The Pursuit

June 28. June 29. Magruder's Report. Jackson's Report. Lee's Report. Lee to Magruder. Savage Station. June 30. Waiting in vain for the Signal. Holmes's Division. Huger's Division. Wright meets Jackson. Huger's Report. Jackson, June 29. Lee to Magruder. Jackson, June 30. White Oak Swamp. Franklin's Report. Jackson's Account. The Cannonade. Munford's letter. Hampton's Crossing. Franklin's Comments. D. H. Hill's Explanation. Battle of Frazier Farm. Bayonet Fighting. A Successful Ruse. Lee's Report.

THE day after the battle, Saturday, the 28th, was given to the care of the wounded, the burial of the dead, and the collection of the scattered troops. During the night McClellan had begun his retreat to the James, ordering Keyes, with the 4th corps, to cross White Oak Swamp and take position to cover the passage of his trains, which were put in motion early on the 28th. On the 28th, also, the troops which had fought under Porter on the 27th were sent forward across White Oak Swamp.

On the Confederate side it was not yet clear what the enemy would do. Ewell's and Jackson's divisions had not been seriously engaged, and Ewell's was sent down the Chickahominy about seven miles to Despatch Station, to see if they showed any disposition to cross the stream and retreat down the Peninsula. Stuart's cavalry followed the railroad toward White House. Bottom's bridge was found burned, and the next morning White House was also burned and evacuated. On Sunday morning, the 29th, the enemy's intrenchments opposite Magruder and Huger were found abandoned, and his camps and depots were being burned. It was then apparent that his destination was the James River, and Lee, no longer hesitating, issued orders to his whole army for a vigorous pursuit. His best chance, that of destroying Porter's corps, had been lost; but his adversary was on foot in the woods, encumbered with enormous trains which he would try to defend, and there should be opportunities to overwhelm him in detail, and unprotected by breastworks.

Magruder, immediately behind the enemy on the Williamsburg road, was ordered to pursue down that road. Huger, on the Charles City road, was ordered down that road. From the battle-field of the 27th, A. P. Hill and Longstreet were ordered to cross the Chickahominy at New Bridge, and passing in rear of Magruder and Huger to move by the Darbytown, the next road to the right. Ewell from Despatch Station was to rejoin Jackson. Jackson, with the largest force, was directed to pursue by the shortest and most direct route. He was to cross the Chickahominy over the Grapevine bridge, across which Porter had retreated, and which he had partially torn up, and to press directly upon McClellan's rear with his whole force. This comprised his own three brigades under Winder, Ewell's three, D. H. Hill's five, Whiting's two, and Lawton's one, — in all 14 brigades, nearly 25,000 strong.

Looking back upon the course of events, it is interesting to inquire wherein lay the weakness of this order, apparently so simple and obvious in its execution. Yet the pursuit, from this moment, was bootless and a failure. It did capture a few guns and prisoners, but it paid for them in blood a price far beyond their value. There were two ways in which Lee might have pursued. One is that just set forth. The recommendation of that method is that it seemed to reach the enemy with his largest forces by the shortest roads. But, *per contra*, is the consideration that on the shortest roads will be found the enemy's most formidable rear-guards and obstructions. With energetic lieutenants these may be overcome; but the chance exists whether the proper leaders will be at the right places. The alternate course would have been to leave the direct pursuit over the obstructed roads, and against the enemy's rear-guards, to but two divisions, — those of Magruder and Huger, — while Lee himself with Jackson, Longstreet, and A. P. Hill, moving swiftly around the rear by good roads, and reënforced by Holmes, put the bulk of his army, flushed with its recent victory, directly across McClellan's path near Malvern Hill.

Not only would it count for a great deal that all the divisions should be under the personal eye of the commander, but there was strong probability that Lee might be able to force upon McClellan the disadvantage of having to take the offensive. On this occasion, as it turned out, Jackson was still under his "spell," and did nothing. Lee, having gone with Longstreet and A. P. Hill, lost touch of all three, — Jackson, Magruder, and Huger, — and entirely failed to get any service from them for the two critical days, the 29th and 30th.

The orders for the pursuit were given soon after sunrise on Sunday, the 29th. Magruder had not entirely absorbed Lee's confidence that McClellan did not have in him the risking of a counterstroke. He knew that there were on the south side fully 60,000 Federals, and that between them and Richmond there were now but 25,000 Confederates. His official report thus describes the situation : —

"I received repeated instructions during Saturday night from Gen. Lee's headquarters enjoining upon my command the utmost vigilance, directing the men to sleep on their arms, and to be prepared for whatever might occur. These orders were promptly communicated by me to the different commanders of my forces, and were also transmitted to Gen. Huger on my right. I passed the night without sleep and in superintendence of their execution. Had McClellan massed his whole force in column and advanced against any point in our line . . . though the head of his column would have suffered greatly, its momentum would have insured him success. His failure to do so is the best evidence that our wise commander fully understood the character of his opponent.

"Our relief was therefore great when intelligence reached us almost simultaneously from Col. Chilton and one of my staff, that the enemy, whose presence had been ascertained as late as 3.30 A.M., had evacuated his works and was retreating.

"Col. Chilton, who rode into my camp on Sunday morning, hurried me off to see Gen. Lee on the Nine Mile road, and I gave, while riding with him, the necessary orders to put in motion my whole command, which extended over a distance of some miles, directing Gen. Griffith's brigade, which was nearest to the road, to advance at once from the centre, and ordering Gen. Jones's division, in advancing, to incline toward Fair Oaks Station, as I had been informed that Maj.-Gen. Jackson had crossed, or was crossing, the Grapevine bridge, and would operate down the Chickahominy. Having overtaken Gen. Lee, we rode together down the Nine Mile road, and the general informed me of the plans which he had adopted for the pursuit of the enemy. They were as follows: Longstreet's division was to have crossed the New Bridge and to take position on our extreme right, so as to intercept the enemy in his attempt to reach James River; Huger's division to march down the Williamsburg road on my right flank, and Maj.-Gen. Jackson's division, which he stated had crossed or was crossing the Grapevine bridge, over the Chickahominy River, was to operate down that river on its right bank, while my own command would press him vigorously in front.

"At Fair Oaks Station . . . Gen. Lee, having repeated his instructions, left the ground. . . .

"I also despatched a staff-officer toward Grapevine Bridge, some three miles off, to ascertain the position of Maj.-Gen. Jackson's troops, which I had supposed from the statements above given had already crossed. . . . In the meantime, Maj. Bryan, the staff-officer who had been sent to Maj.-Gen. Jackson, returned with his [Jackson's] engineer, Lt. Boswell, who reported that Maj.-Gen. Jackson was compelled to rebuild the bridge, which would be completed in about two hours. Maj. Bryan reported that Maj.-Gen. Jackson had crossed but a small portion of his infantry, not more than three companies, over the broken bridge."

It is plain from this narrative that Lee's orders to Jackson to pursue by the Grapevine bridge road, above referred to, contemplated immediate performance on Jackson's part, and were given at an early hour on Sunday, the 29th. The name Grapevine, applied to this bridge, was taken from a ford of the Chickahominy well known in the neighborhood, and reached by a country road which crossed the swamp by the ford. In building a bridge the Federals utilized the road, and built the bridge near it, but without disturbing the ford, which was practicable at this time, the river being low, even while waiting to repair the bridge.

Meanwhile, too, New Bridge and another bridge, three-quarters of a mile above it, were opened by Lee's order on Saturday, the 28th. The extra distance, which would have been involved in marching from the battle-field to Savage Station by the New Bridge, instead of by the Grapevine route, was only about three miles. But this was Sunday, and Jackson gave it strict observance. The greater part of his troops remained in camp all day and until after midnight Sunday night. Then they made a start at, or before, 2.30 A.M. His official report entirely ignores the receipt of any orders from Gen. Lee, but says: —

"The 28th and 29th were occupied in disposing of the dead and wounded and repairing Grapevine bridge over the Chickahominy, which McClellan's forces had used in their retreat and destroyed in their rear. During the night of the 29th we commenced crossing the Chickahominy, and on the following morning arrived at Savage Station."

Lee, in his official report, written as before told, eight months later, accepts the excuse of Grapevine bridge, as follows: —

"Jackson's route led to the flank and rear of Savage Station, but he was delayed by the necessity of reconstructing Grapevine bridge. Late in the afternoon, Magruder attacked the enemy with one of his three divisions [two brigades each], and two regiments of another. A severe action ensued, and continued about two hours, when it was terminated by night. The troops displayed great gallantry, and inflicted heavy loss upon the enemy; but, owing to the lateness of the hour and the small force employed, the result was not decisive, and the enemy continued his retreat under cover of darkness, leaving several hundred prisoners, with his dead and wounded, in our hands."

This was the insignificant outcome of the day, and in his reference to Jackson's delay and to the lateness of the hour and the small force engaged, one may easily read that he had hoped to have had a very different story.

After giving Magruder his orders, but unfortunately without waiting to see that Jackson failed to arrive, Lee had gone over to the Charles City road, where Huger was advancing, and thence he passed on to the Darbytown road to join A. P. Hill and Longstreet. Soon after being left alone, finding that Jackson was not near, Magruder became alarmed at a demonstration of the enemy's rear-guard, and sent such urgent calls for aid to Huger that the latter halted two of his four brigades, and marched back with them to Seven Pines. This lost for his division the cream of the day. Here he discovered the needlessness of Magruder's alarm, and, getting urgent messages from Lee, he returned to the Charles City road, marched down it until he found the enemy's pickets, late in the afternoon, and went into bivouac.

Lee was much disappointed that evening at the lack of results, and wrote Magruder the following note:[1] —

[1] O. R. 13, 687.

"General, I regret much that you have made so little progress to-day in the pursuit of the enemy. In order to reap the fruits of our victory the pursuit should be most vigorous. I must urge you then again to press on his rear, rapidly and steadily. We must lose no more time or he will escape us entirely."

This note had also a postscript which will be quoted presently in another connection.

Magruder had only brought into action two brigades, — Kershaw's and Semmes's, — and a half of Barksdale's. The force engaged against him had been Sumner's corps, and Smith's division of Franklin's. Heintzelman's corps had also been present in the morning, but in the afternoon it had crossed White Oak Swamp at Brackett's Ford. The remaining nine Federal brigades were, doubtless, too heavy a task for Magruder with only six, but had Jackson with his 14 brigades been present in the morning, the enemy should have been routed. Doubtless Magruder should have employed twice the force he did engage, and taken chances. His two and a half brigades were overmatched, though they fought until dark, losing over 400 men, and capturing prisoners from each of the three divisions opposed to them. They reported next morning 400 dead left by the enemy on the field, but such reports are always overestimated.

Jackson arrived in person at Magruder's headquarters near Savage Station at 3.30 A.M. on Monday, the 30th, and informed Magruder that his troops would be up soon after daylight.

During the night, the entire Federal force had crossed the White Oak Swamp and McClellan had accomplished one-half his retreat safely. He had had only about 16 miles to traverse, and his trains were now upon the last half of it, with his army well concentrated to protect his flank. With one more day his column would be so shortened that no exposed flank would be left, and his whole army could be united in the rear of the train.

This was, therefore, the critical day. Serious blows had threatened the Federals on the 26th at Beaver Dam, on the 27th at Gaines Mill, and on the 29th at Savage Station; but all had been escaped by bad handling on the part of the Confederates. Now a final opportunity was offered to repair all shortcomings, and every condition seemed favorable. Holmes's division, 6000 strong, with six batteries, had been brought from south of the James River, and was at New Market at 10 A.M. on the 30th. Longstreet, with his own and A. P. Hill's divisions, had bivouacked on the Darbytown road, the night before, and this morning they moved into the Long Bridge road, and soon found the enemy's line covering Charles City cross-roads at Frazer's Farm or Glendale, and extending down the Quaker road toward Malvern Hill. These three divisions, 14 brigades, numbered about 23,000 men.

In addition to these, Lee, early on the 30th, had withdrawn Magruder's six brigades, now about 12,000 strong, from Savage Station, and brought them down the Darbytown road within striking distance by 2 P.M., and had halted them at that hour near Timberlake's store.

Huger's four brigades, about 9000 men, were advancing down the Charles City road, and were expected to open the action on this part of the field at an early hour. Either his guns or Jackson's would be the signal for Longstreet and A. P. Hill to take up the battle.

Meanwhile, Jackson, only four miles off in an air line, but all of 15 miles by the public roads, — the only ones generally known, — was confidently expected to make up for his non-appearance of the day before by an early and very vigorous one this morning, assaulting the enemy's rear-guard with his 14 brigades, 25,000 strong, and emulating the reputation he had made in the Valley. Thus, with 44,000 men, all close at hand upon the enemy's flank, and Stonewall Jackson with 25,000 in his rear, fortune seemed at last about to smile broadly for once upon the Confederate cause. Unknown to us, another circumstance was rarely in our favor. The Federal army was temporarily without a head. On the 29th, 30th, and July 1, McClellan, on each day, left his army without placing any one in command during his absence, while he did engineer's duty, examining the localities toward which he was marching. Had the Confederates accomplished their reasonable expectations, the criticism of McClellan would have been very severe.

On the Confederate side, Lee, with Longstreet and Hill, in a field of broom-grass and small pines, waited impatiently for the signal.

He was so close in rear of his line of battle that men and horses among the couriers and staff, were wounded by random shots. For quite a time, too, President Davis and his staff were present, in conference with the generals, while missiles grew more frequent, and wounded men began to come in from the front.

For hours we stood there waiting — waiting for something which never happened. Every minute that we waited was priceless time thrown away. Twelve o'clock came and the precious day was half gone. One o'clock, two o'clock, three o'clock followed. Even four o'clock drew near, and now, whatever was started, would be cut short by night. Our great opportunity was practically over, and we had not yet pulled a trigger. We had waited for either Huger or Jackson or both to begin, and neither had begun. As Beauregard, at Bull Run, had sent word to Ewell to begin, and then had gone to the centre and waited; as Johnston, at Seven Pines, had given orders to Hill and Longstreet about beginning, and then gone to the left and waited; so now, Lee, having given orders beforehand to both Jackson and Huger, had passed on to the right and was waiting; and in every case the opportunity passed unimproved.

Briefly, this is what had happened, beginning with the extreme right column under Holmes, which, with Magruder's column, was to support Longstreet's right: —

The river road from New Market to Harrison's Landing passed under and around Malvern Heights, between them and the river. From a point on this road, perhaps a mile and a half from the river, across low, flat ground, one could see a considerable expanse of the Malvern Heights, 1000 yards off across the meadows on the left; and over these heights were passing many of the 5000 wagons composing McClellan's trains. No target is more attractive to an artillerist than his enemy's wagon train, and six rifle guns of Holmes's were sent down in the meadows to fire upon these wagons. Lee also saw the position, and approved the attack, and directed Holmes to bring up his whole division to support the guns. But no sooner did the six guns open than they were replied to by 30 of the heaviest rifles of the Federal Artillery Reserve, which, escorted by only about 1500 infantry under Fitz-John Porter, had just arrived on Malvern Heights to occupy the position. The fierce fire of this great battery was quickly aided by the fire of heavy guns from the gunboats in the James — lying in Turkey Bend, and directing their fire by wigwag signals between their mastheads — and the Federals on the Heights. The six guns were quickly wrecked. Two caissons were exploded, and so many horses killed that the guns were with difficulty withdrawn. No fire is so appalling to un-seasoned troops as that of heavy artillery received in a thick wood where every shot cuts limbs and smashes trees around them, even though the actual damage from it may be trifling. Holmes's whole division, concealed in the woods in the vicinity of the six guns engaged, was now exposed to such a fire, converging from opposite quarters. There was but one thing to do, and that was to get away. Some commands, especially among the infantry, behaved well, and withdrew in perfect order; some were thrown into confusion, and among some cavalry commands and light artillery a stampede took place. Two guns which had not been engaged were entangled in the woods and abandoned, and many men were run over and injured. Altogether, the con-fusion was so great that Lee directed Magruder's six brigades to march to Holmes's support, though they could have done no good, as there was nothing for them to attack or defend.

Thus, Holmes and Magruder, 18,000 men, were diverted from the real work of the day. This was just about to begin when this side issue of the cannonade of Malvern Hill was ventured upon. The total casualties in Holmes's division (including 15 wounded among the six guns) were two killed and 49 wounded, besides some injured in the stampede.

Let us next turn to Huger's division. On Sunday, the 29th, the division made but a very short distance down the Charles City road for two reasons. Two of its brigades were called back, and had some miles of extra marching and countermarching in the hot sun by Magruder's false alarm when he found that he was not supported by the proximity of Jackson, as has been already told.

The other two brigades thought it imprudent to pass any road on their left leading across White Oak Swamp, until it had been reconnoitred, as it was known that a large force of the enemy was still on the other side.

At the first of these cross-roads, a force of the enemy was discovered attempting to cross to the south side. It was driven back, and the resulting skirmish consumed the day.

It seems strange that Lee, though at no great distance on the next day (the 30th), should have still failed to see Huger, and either to bring him to the battle, which was waiting for his arrival, or to order it to proceed without him. But there is no intimation in the reports, of any communication; nor, in Huger's proceedings, of any consciousness that important action was waiting upon him.

At another swamp crossing, called Fisher's, Huger's column, Monday morning, discovered that the enemy's forces on the opposite side had been withdrawn. Wright's brigade was then ordered to investigate. He crossed the swamp with his brigade and got into the deserted camps of the enemy on the north side, picking up a few prisoners and finding some abandoned stores.

By 2.30 P.M. he had made his way entirely across to the main road where Jackson, as is yet to be told, with his 14 brigades, was standing at bay at the main crossing, called the White Oak Bridge. Jackson seems to have taken no special interest in Wright's arrival, though it proved that at least one unobstructed crossing of the swamp was within three miles. Jackson ordered Wright to return along the edge of the swamp, to look for crossings as he went, and if he found one, to try and force it; but he sent neither staff-officer to bring back a report, or reenforcements to aid if any favorable point should be found. Apparently, he was satisfied to remain where he was and to do only what he was doing — nothing. Wright started back, and at one and a half miles came to Brackett's Ford, a well-known road, across which a large part of the Federal forces had crossed during the night, and which they had then obstructed by cutting down trees and destroying a small bridge. Pushing two companies of skirmishers through the swamp, Wright captured the enemy's picket force on the south side, but saw, beyond the picket, a force of the enemy with artillery, too strong for his brigade; so he withdrew. Continuing his march along the edge of the swamp another mile and a half, he found a cow trail which led him across it about three-fourths of a mile below his crossing of the morning, and here he encamped. The occupation of Huger's other brigades during the day is given as follows in his official report: —

"The troops bivouacked in their position while it was dark, and resumed the march at daylight (Monday, June 30). Mahone advanced cautiously, captured many prisoners, and killed some cavalry scouts, one bearing an order to Kearny to retire and keep a strong battery of artillery with his rear-guard. After passing Fisher's house, we found the road obstructed by trees felled all across it. Gen. Mahone found it best to cut a road around the obstructions. For such work we were deficient in tools. The column was delayed while the work was going on, and it was evening before we got through and drove off the workmen who were still cutting down other trees. As we advanced through the woods and came to an open field on high ground (P. Williams on map), a powerful battery of rifled guns opened on us. Gen. Mahone disposed his troops and advanced a battery of artillery, Moorman's, and a sharp artillery fire was kept up for some time. The enemy's fire was very severe and we had many men killed and wounded. List of casualties sent herewith (25 killed, 53 wounded, total 78). I went to the front and examined the position. I withdrew most of our guns, and only kept up a moderate fire. On our left the White Oak Swamp approached very near. The right appeared to be good ground, and I determined to turn the battery by moving a column of infantry to my right. It was now dark."

It seems incredible that this division, within four miles of Lee, could have been allowed to spend the whole day in a mere contest of axemen, wherein the Federals, with the most axes, had only to cut *down*, and the Confederates, with the fewest, to cut *up* and remove. The result could scarcely have been doubtful. Our army at this time compared with an organized and disciplined army about as a confederacy would compare with a nation. Each division was an allied but independent command, rather than a part of a single army.

This will be even more evident in the story of Jackson's column, now to be told. His command had always before acted alone and independently. Lee's instructions to him were very brief and general, in supreme confidence that the Jackson of the Valley would win even brighter laurels on the Chickahominy. The shortest route was assigned to him and the largest force was given him. Lee then took himself off to the farthest flank, as if generously to leave to Jackson the opportunity of the most brilliant victory of the war.

His failure is not so much a military as a psychological phenomenon. He did not try and fail. He simply made no effort. The story embraces two days. He spent the 29th in camp in disregard of Lee's instructions, and he spent the 30th in equal idleness at White Oak Swamp. His 25,000 infantry practically did not fire a shot in the two days.

Here is the story: It has already been related that early Sunday morning, Lee, coming from Jackson's direction, told Magruder that Jackson had been ordered to pursue, and was even then supposed to be crossing the Chickahominy. Magruder was also ordered to attack the enemy, and he and his lieutenants soon sent messengers to establish communication with Jackson. Later, Magruder received a severe shock in the following note from Gen. Jones, commanding one of his three divisions, of two brigades each: —

"Maj.-Gen. Magruder:

"My line is formed to the left and somewhat to the front of Gen. Cobb. . . . I do not think it prudent for me to attack with my small force, unless there be a simultaneous attack all along our lines. I will keep a good lookout on my left. *I had hoped that Jackson would have coöperated with me on my left, but he sends me word that he cannot, as he has other important duty to perform.*[1]

"Respectfully, D. R. Jones, Brig.-Gen."

This note, taken in connection with the withdrawal of the two brigades which Huger had sent, depressed Magruder very much. Later in the evening he received some encouragement. Maj. Taylor of Lee's staff, bearing a message, arrived, hunting for Jackson. Upon being told that Jackson had been "ordered elsewhere," as Magruder loosely quoted his message to Jones, Taylor did not hesitate to say that there must be some mistake. As he did not know the country, and Magruder had upon his staff a Chaplain Allen who did know it, the message for Jackson

[1] 13 W. R., 675, incorrectly dated June 28. On the 28th the retreat of the enemy was not known, and there were no orders to attack, or for Jackson to cross the Chickahominy. The situation is that of the 29th. The italics are mine.

was intrusted to Allen, and Taylor returned to Lee.   But Lee's
note that night to Magruder, already quoted (p. 138), contained
a postscript, as follows: —

"P.S.   Since the above was written I learn from Maj. Taylor that
you are under the impression that Gen. Jackson has been ordered not
to support you.   On the contrary, he has been directed to do so, and to
push the pursuit vigorously."

It scarcely needs the corroboration of Lee's word to know that,
upon his discovery of McClellan's retreat, and his putting the
rest of his army in motion with orders to press the enemy, he must
have given similar orders to Jackson; and his statement to
Magruder, that Jackson was even then crossing at Grapevine
bridge, and his sending Taylor later with a message to Jackson,
show that he believed his orders were being executed.

The explanation of Jackson's message to Jones is clear in the
light of his regard for the Sabbath and from the particular expression used.   He mentions no physical obstacle nor any other
demand upon his troops, who, indeed, are all resting quietly in
their camps, but the "*important duty*" to be performed seems to
concern himself rather than his command, and to be entirely
personal in character.   Evidently, Jackson excused not only
himself, but his troops also, because it was Sunday.   He certainly considered attendance upon divine service an "important duty" of the first magnitude.   He confidently believed
that marked regard for the Sabbath would often be followed by
God's favor upon one's secular enterprises.   If so, why not upon
a battle or a campaign?   We have seen even Lincoln share the
same belief when he stopped the advance of McDowell from
Fredericksburg on Sunday, and thus broke up McClellan's
campaign, as has been told. (See p. 101.)

The rebuilding of Grapevine bridge was not a serious matter.
Lee clearly anticipated no delay there whatever.   Jackson's
engineer, early Sunday morning, reported that it would be finished
in two hours.   There was a ford close by, and other bridges within
a few miles, but most of Jackson's troops spent the entire day in
camp.

His early start next morning would seem to promise more vigor in the performance for that day, but its history does not bear out the promise. It was but seven miles from the bivouacs which his men left about 2.30 A.M. to White Oak Bridge where they went into bivouac at night. No obstacle to a swift march existed, but the earliest arrival noted in the reports is at 9.30 A.M. by Col. Crutchfield of the Artillery. Jackson himself puts it later.

White Oak Swamp rises between the Charles City and the Williamsburg road near where the Confederate lines crossed them, five miles from Richmond. The course of the stream is southeast, almost parallel to that of the Charles City road for about six miles. Then it turns and runs directly toward the Chickahominy some three miles away. Just above this bend was Brackett's Ford, and about a mile below it was the main road crossing at which Jackson arrived about 9.30 A.M., Monday. The stream itself was a small creek, averaging 10 to 15 feet wide and six inches deep, with sandy bottom. The swamp was merely a flat area densely grown up in trees and bushes, more or less wet in places, but generally with firm footing. Small farms and settlements were scattered along its edges, and residents and cattle had many paths in and through it. It was widest near its source, where the country was flatter. Near the bridge the country was rolling and the swamp grew narrow. Four crossings above the bridge were well known to the natives,—Chapman's (or Goodman's), Jourdan's, Fisher's, and Brackett's,—and one below called Carter's; but besides these were many less-known paths.

The road crossing was held by Franklin, who thus describes the operations of the day in his official report:—

"About noon I was directed by the commanding general to assume command at the position guarding the crossing of the swamp, and repaired there at once. I found that a terrific cannonade had been opened by the enemy upon the divisions of Gen. Smith and Gen. Richardson and the brigade of Gen. Naglee. The two latter had been placed under my command by the commanding general. The casualties in Richardson's division were quite numerous, but I have received no report of the action from him. In Gen. Smith's division and in Gen. Naglee's brigade the number lost was insignificant.

"The enemy kept up the firing during the whole day and crossed some infantry below our position, but he made no very serious attempt to cross during the day, and contented himself with the cannonading and the firing of his sharp-shooters. Nightfall having arrived, and the wagons having all disappeared, I took the responsibility of moving my command to the James River by a road to the left which had not been much used, and arrived at headquarters safely about daylight."

The infantry referred to by Franklin as having crossed were only D. H. Hill's skirmish-line. No effort was made to cross anything more. Jackson's own account of the day is as follows: —

"About noon we reached White Oak Swamp, and here the enemy made a determined effort to retard our advance, and thereby prevent an immediate junction between Gen. Longstreet and myself. We found the bridge destroyed and the ordinary place of crossing commanded by their batteries on the opposite side and all approach to it barred by detachments of sharp-shooters concealed in a dense wood close by. A battery of 28 guns from Hill's and Whiting's artillery was placed by Col. Crutchfield in a favorable position for driving off or silencing the opposing artillery. About 2 p.m. it opened suddenly upon the enemy. He fired a few shots in reply, and then withdrew from that position, abandoning part of his artillery. Capt. Wooding was immediately ordered near the bridge to shell the sharp-shooters from the woods, which was accomplished, and Munford's cavalry crossed the creek, but was soon compelled to retire. It was soon seen that the enemy occupied such a position beyond a thick intervening wood on the right of the road as enabled him to command the crossing. Capt. Wooding's batteries turned in the new direction. The fire so opened on both sides was kept up until dark. We bivouacked that night near the swamp.

"A heavy cannonading in front announced the engagement of Gen. Longstreet at Frazier's Farm and made me anxious to press forward, but the marshy character of the soil, the destruction of the bridge over the marsh and creek, and the strong position of the enemy for defending the passage prevented my advancing until the following morning. During the night the Federals retired."

Considered as an excuse for Jackson's inaction during the whole day this report is simply farcical.

It appears from subordinate reports that the long delay between the arrival of the head of Jackson's column and the opening of his 28 guns was caused by cutting a road to enable the guns to be kept concealed while getting position. Concealment here was of little value, and the time thus lost by the artillery, and the sending across of Munford's cavalry at the road crossing, illustrate the prominent feature of Jackson's conduct during the whole Seven Days, — to wit: a reluctance to bring his infantry into action. Here infantry alone could accomplish anything, but only cavalry and artillery were called upon. He could have crossed a brigade of infantry as easily as Munford's cavalry, and that brigade could have been the entering wedge which would split apart the Federal defence and let in the 13 brigades which followed. The bridge, whose destruction is mentioned, was not necessary to a crossing. It was only a high-water bridge with a ford by it which was preferably used except in freshets. Now the floor of the bridge, made of poles, had been thrown into the ford, but Munford's cavalry got through without trouble, and infantry could have swarmed across.

The cannonade, which was kept up during all the rest of the day, was not only a delusion, but a useless burning both of daylight and ammunition, for it was all random fire. The Federal and Confederate artillery could not see each other at all. They could scarcely even see the high-floating smoke clouds of each other's guns. They fired by sound, at a distance of three-quarters of a mile, across a tall dense wood, until they exhausted their ammunition. One Federal battery reported the expenditure of 1600 rounds. The noise was terrific, and some firing was kept up until nine o'clock at night, but the casualties on each side were naturally but trifling. Only one Confederate battery, Rhett's, mentions any, and it reported but two killed and five wounded.

No reconnoissance was made for other crossings, even of Brackett's, over which much of the Federal force had passed, until Wright's brigade arrived and was sent back, as has been told. Meanwhile, two other crossings available for infantry were discovered within a very short distance below, and were both at once reported to Jackson by the officers discovering them — Col. Munford, commanding his cavalry, and Gen. Hampton, commanding the 3d brigade of Jackson's division. I have in possession letters from Munford to Hampton, and from Hampton to myself, giving the following details.

I have already quoted from Jackson's report that his cavalry, sent across the creek at first, was forced to retire. Col. Munford in a letter to Gen. Hampton, dated Mar. 23, 1901, writes: —

"At the battle of White Oak Swamp, after Col. Crutchfield's artillery had disabled one gun, and driven the cannoneers from the battery which commanded the crossing at the old bridge at White Oak Swamp, Gen.

Jackson directed me to cross the creek, with my regiment, at the ford, and to secure the guns in front of us. The enemy's sharp-shooters were stationed in rear of the building overlooking the ford ; and as soon as we neared the abandoned battery of the enemy, these sharp-shooters, and another battery stationed in the road at the edge of the woods, and commanding the road and the ford over which we had passed, opened a furious fire upon us, and I was forced to move a quarter of a mile lower down the creek, where I found a cow path which led me over the swamp. But *en route*, I found where Gen. Franklin's troops had been located, having now changed front. They had left a long line of knapsacks and blankets, from which I allowed my men to take what they pleased; and among their things were many late newspapers from Washington, which I despatched by a courier to Gen. Jackson, giving him full information of what I had seen and *how* and *where* I had crossed.

"Thirty-nine years is too long a time to attempt to say what I wrote him, but I know that I thought, all the time, that he could have crossed his infantry where we recrossed. I had seen his infantry cross far worse places, and I expected that he would attempt it.

"We remained near where we recrossed all day, with a vidette on the other side of the swamp. He put his sharp-shooters in on the right of the ford, and made no attempt to cross where we recrossed.

"Why, I never understood.

"Yours sincerely, THOMAS T. MUNFORD."

All the crossings so far described were paths already marked by use of men and cattle, but another opportunity was discovered and brought to Jackson's notice by Hampton, who was an expert woodsman and hunter. While the infantry stood idly by and the useless cannonade went on, nothing was more natural to Hampton than a personal reconnoissance in front. He found a crossing and the flank of the enemy's infantry line. He returned and reported it to Jackson. In the last year of his life he wrote out the story as given below. He has only omitted from it, modestly, the fact that, when he reported to Jackson his discovery, he begged permission to take his brigade across immediately and attack it. This request was at first put off by the order to go and build a bridge. After the bridge was reported finished, the whole matter was silently ignored, as his narrative describes.

Hampton's narrative is as follows: —

"We left the Chickahominy on Monday morning, June 30, though my impression is that the Grapevine bridge could have been used on Sunday, and at any rate there was a good ford of the stream not far below the bridge, near the road followed by the retreating enemy. Early on the morning of Monday we reached the White Oak crossing, my brigade being in advance; and about the same time the 2d Va. Cav. under Col. Munford came up. This regiment had accompanied Gen. Jackson from the Valley covering his advance.

"We found a large hospital tent on the brow of the hill overlooking the crossing of the small stream over which a little bridge of poles had been made. The enemy had pulled off the poles and thrown them in the stream above the bridge, and a battery of four guns on the opposite hill commanded the causeway and the ford of the stream. Gen. Jackson ran up some guns and soon silenced those of the enemy, disabling one of them. The battery was withdrawn, and Gen. Jackson, accompanied by the regiment of cavalry, crossed with a view, I suppose, of capturing the disabled gun, or of ascertaining the position of the enemy—none of whom were in sight except those manning the gun. In a few minutes the General returned alone, while Munford took his regiment a short distance down the stream, where he crossed without difficulty. As there were no further hostile demonstrations where we were, I placed my brigade in a pine forest on the left of the road leading to the ford, directing the men to lie down; and, desiring to ascertain the character of the ground in front of us, I rode to the edge of the swamp, accompanied by Capt. Rawlins Lowndes, and my son Wade, who was serving on my staff at that time. The swamp was comparatively open, the ground not at all boggy, and we soon struck the stream.

"This was very shallow, with a clear sandy bottom, and not more than 10 or 15 feet wide. Crossing this, we soon came in sight of the open land opposite our position.

"We could see a very wide and deep ravine in which was a line of Federals lying down in line of battle, and evidently expecting, if any attack was made upon them, it would be from the open field below the ford of the stream. In this event their position would have been very strong.

"Withdrawing without attracting their notice, I returned across the swamp and gave to Gen. Jackson all the facts stated above.

"He asked if I could make a bridge across the stream, to which I replied that I could make one for the infantry, but not for artillery, as cutting a road would disclose our position. He directed me to make the bridge. Ordering a detail of my men to cut some poles where they were standing and to carry them into the swamp, a bridge was made in a few minutes. I then again reconnoitred the position of the enemy whom I found perfectly quiet — unsuspecting. On my return to our side of the swamp, I found Gen. Jackson seated on a fallen pine alongside of the road that led down to the ford, and seating myself by him, I reported the completion of the bridge and the exposed position of the enemy. He drew his cap down over his eyes which were closed, and after listening to me for some minutes, he rose without speaking, and the next morning we found Franklin with the rest of the Federal troops concentrated on Malvern Hill.

"While we were waiting at the White Oak crossing we heard the noise of Longstreet's battle at Frazier's Farm, and Capt. or Maj. Fairfax of Longstreet's staff came with a message from the general to Gen. Jackson. Though I heard this message, I cannot recall it. . . .   In speaking to Gen. Lee in 1868 on this subject he expressed the greatest surprise at my account of this matter, and he said that he never had understood why the delay had occurred. . . .

" Gen. Jackson was too great a soldier, and I was too much attached to him, for me to venture to criticise his actions or his plans, but it seems to me that everything which throws light on the plans of our great chief, Gen. Lee, should go down in history. I believe that if Franklin, who opposed us at White Oak, could have been defeated, the Federal army would have been destroyed. . . .

"Yours truly,

"WADE HAMPTON."

Much comment suggests itself, but little is needed : Who that fought with Lee can picture to himself without emotion what might have happened had the Jackson of the Valley had the opportunity presented to him which Gen. Hampton has described as offered in vain to the Jackson of the Chickahominy.

Franklin, commanding the Federal force here opposed to Jackson, wrote of this occasion as follows (*Battles and Leaders*, II., 381) : —

"Jackson seems to have been ignorant of what Gen. Lee expected of him, and badly informed about Brackett's Ford. When he found how strenuous was our defence at the bridge, he should have turned his attention to Brackett's Ford, also. A force could have been as quietly gathered there as at the bridge ; a strong infantry movement at the ford would have easily overrun our small force there, placing our right at Glendale, held by Slocum's division, in great jeopardy, and turning our force at the bridge by getting between it and Glendale. In fact, it is likely that we should have been defeated that day, had Gen. Jackson done what his great reputation seems to have made it imperative he should have done."

D. H. Hill (who was Jackson's brother-in-law), writing in the *Century* of this occasion many years after the war, says : —

"Our cavalry (Munford's regiment) returned by the lower ford and pronounced it perfectly practicable for infantry ; but Jackson did not advance. Why was this ? It was the critical day for both commanders, but especially for McClellan. With consummate skill he had crossed his vast train of 5000 wagons, and his immense parks of artillery, safely over White Oak Swamp, but he was more exposed now than at any time in his flank march. Three columns of attack were converging on him and a strong corps was pressing upon his rear. Escape seemed impossible for him, but he did escape. . . . Gen. Lee, through no fault in his plans, was to see his splendid prize slip through his hands. Longstreet and A. P. Hill struck the enemy at Frazier's Farm (or Glendale) at 3 P.M., and both being always ready for a fight, immediately attacked. . . . There were five divisions within sound of the firing and within supporting distance, but not one of them moved. . . . Maj. Dabney, in his life of Jackson, thus comments on the inaction of that affair: 'On this occasion it would appear, if the vast interests dependent upon Gen. Jackson's coöperation with the proposed attack upon the centre were considered, that he came short of the efficiency in action for which he was elsewhere noted.'

"After showing how the crossing of White Oak might have been effected, Dabney adds: 'The list of casualties might have been longer than that presented on the 30th, of one cannoneer wounded, but how much shorter would have been the bloody list filled up the next day at Malvern Hill? This temporary eclipse of Jackson's genius was probably to be explained by physical causes. The labor of the previous days, the sleeplessness, the wear of gigantic cares, with the drenching of the comfortless night, had sunk the elasticity of his will and the quickness of his invention, for the nonce, below their wonted tension.'"

D. H. Hill does not comment upon this explanation, but it will not bear examination. For two days Jackson and his command had been quietly in camp; and his lapse from duty, while culminating only on June 29 and 30, in fact dated from the very first of the Seven Days. Hill submits his own explanation of the matter as follows: —

"I think that an important factor in this inaction was Jackson's pity for his own corps, worn out by long and exhausting marches, and reduced in numbers by its numerous sanguinary battles. *He thought that the garrison of Richmond ought now to bear the brunt of the fighting.*" [1]

This last expression is but another form of a rumor which, to my knowledge, had private circulation at the time among the staff-officers of some of the leading generals. It was reported that Jackson had said that "he did not intend that *his* men should do all the fighting."

[1] The italics are mine.

Jackson's troops (his own and Ewell's divisions) had had a sharp campaign in the Valley, but the rest of the army at York-town, Williamsburg, and Seven Pines had suffered just as many hardships, and done even more severe fighting, as the casualties will attest.   There were no arrears to be made up.   The total killed and wounded of Jackson's six brigades in the Valley campaign from Kernstown (March 23) to Port Republic (June 9) were but 2311.   Three brigades—Rodes's, Garland's, and G. B. Anderson's of D. H. Hill's division—had had killed and wounded the first day at Seven Pines 2621.   During the Seven Days they lost 2277 more, while Jackson's six brigades lost but 1152.

It is only natural and right that every division commander should feel both pity and affection for his own men, but to manifest either by shirking battle is no real kindness to them, apart from the tremendous consequences to the army and the nation.

We may now return to Lee, Longstreet, and A. P. Hill at Frazier's Farm or Glendale, where we left them waiting vainly for the sounds of battle from Huger and Jackson.   Between three and four o'clock the enemy, aware of their proximity, unwisely increased the fire of one of their batteries.   Longstreet ordered Jenkins, second to none in either courage or ambition, to charge it.   Jenkins charged the battery and got possession, but was attacked by the infantry in support.   This brought on the battle at once, though not in the best shape; for, instead of one simultaneous attack by the whole force, more time was wasted, and the brigades came in in piecemeal.   A very desperate fight ensued, and lasted until long after dark, with varying fortunes.   There were present but the two Confederate divisions, 12 brigades, which had borne the brunt of the 27th at Gaines Mill, and had lost 4300 men out of 22,000 engaged. They were taking the aggressive against Kearny's, McCall's, and Hooker's divisions (about 25,000 men), carefully posted, with some protection and obstructions.

A fourth division, Sedgwick's, was in reserve in a second line behind McCall, and a fifth, Slocum's, was near on the right, each over 8000 strong.   Almost the whole of these 40,000 troops took part in the battle.   Within an hour's march were Richardson's and Smith's divisions and Naglee's brigade, 23,000 more, which could have been called in if needed. It goes without saying that while the Confederates might have more or less success, at the beginning, depending upon the coöperation of their brigades, only the approach of night could prevent their being finally repulsed and driven from the field, with losses proportionate to the persistence of their attacks.

No more desperate encounter took place in the war; and nowhere else, to my knowledge, so much actual personal fighting with bayonet and butt of gun. Randol's battery, over which it began, was taken and retaken several times. Once, when in possession of the 11th Ala. regiment of Wilcox's brigade, it was charged by McCall's Pa. Reserves, and after a desperate bayonet fight each side fell back to adjacent woods, leaving the guns deserted, but under fire from both sides. Wilcox's report gives illustrations of the character of the fighting: —

"Capt. W. C. Y. Parker had two successive encounters with Federal officers, both of whom he felled with his sword, and, beset by others of the enemy, he was severely wounded, having received two bayonet wounds in the breast and one in his side, and a musket ball breaking his left thigh.

"Lt. Michie had a hand-to-hand collision with an officer, and having just dealt a severe blow upon his adversary, he fell, cut over the head with a sabre-bayonet from behind, and had afterward three bayonet wounds in the face and two in the breast, — all severe wounds which he survived, however, for three days."

A little later, Field's brigade of Hill's division, in a counter-charge, again had bayonet fighting, and drove McCall's line back for a half-mile, and held the ground until the captured guns were carried safely to the rear. Severe fighting continued to take place until after dark. The enemy became so aggressive that Lee felt it necessary to send for Magruder's six brigades which had been unwisely marched to reënforce Holmes, and which had lost distance and time by confusion of roads and guides. These unfortunate troops, which had been marching all day, were now marched and countermarched until long after midnight, so that they were thoroughly exhausted when they reached the field, and were put in front of those who had been equally worn out in the desperate fighting. Meanwhile a ruse which had been practised seems to have been successful in bringing the pressure of the enemy's fresh battalions to an end. A. P. Hill thus describes it: —

"About dark the enemy were pressing us hard along our whole line, and my last reserve, Gen. J. R. Anderson, with his Ga. brigade, was directed to advance cautiously, and be careful not to fire on our friends. His brigade was formed in line, two regiments on each side of the road, and, obeying my instructions to the letter, received the fire of the enemy at 70 paces before engaging themselves. Heavy reënforcements to the enemy were brought up at this time, and it seemed that a tremendous effort was being made to turn the fortunes of the battle. The volume of fire that, approaching, rolled along the line, was terrific. Seeing some troops of Wilcox's brigade, with the assistance of Lt. Chamberlayne and other members of my staff, they were rapidly formed, and being directed to cheer long and loudly moved again to the fight. This seemed to end the contest, and in less than five minutes all firing ceased and the enemy retired."

In this battle the losses of Longstreet's division were about 2600 and in A. P. Hill's about 1700; total 4300. The Federal losses are not given separately, but were, doubtless, not very unequal. McCall was captured, riding into our lines by mistake, and we also secured 18 guns, besides some prisoners, and the gleanings of the field in small-arms.

Lee, an example for all time of restraint in expressing personal feeling, wrote in his report of this battle: —

"Could the other commands have coöperated in this action, the result would have proved most disastrous to the enemy."

I have often thought that in his retrospect of the war no one day of the whole four years would seem to him more unfortunate than June 30, 1862. It was, undoubtedly, the opportunity of his life, for the Confederacy was then in its prime, with more men available than ever before or after. And at no other period would the moral or the physical effect of a victory have been so great as upon this occasion.

CHAPTER IX

The Escape. Battle of Malvern Hill

Enemy's New Position. Line Formed. Pendleton's Artillery. Artillery
Combats. Whiting's Report. Sumner seeks Cover. Lee's Recon-
noissance. Lee Misled. Attack Begun. Wright's Report. Semmes
and Kershaw. D. H. Hill's Report. Toombs's Report. Casualties.
Lee's Report. Stuart shells a Camp. McClellan Writes. Stuart's
Report. Attack Abandoned. Casualties. An Artillery Raid. The
South Side. Our Balloon.

Next morning (Tuesday, July 1) we began to pay the pen-
alty for our unimproved opportunity of the day before.

Of course, the enemy was gone, and about three miles down the
road we came upon his whole army, now united and massed, upon
Malvern Hill.

This position is a high plateau stretching north from the low-
lands along the valley of James River, over which it dominates
in high steep hills, with Turkey Run on the west, and Western
Run on the east. It is about a mile wide and, for two miles
from the river, is open land, rolling and sloping toward the
north where it ends in a heavy forest, intersected by marshy
streams, with only one good road leading through the forest out
upon the plateau. The Rev. L. W. Allen, already mentioned as
on the staff of Magruder, was a native of this section, and had described to D. H. Hill its striking features, noting, —

"its commanding height, the difficulties of approach, its amphitheatri-
cal form and ample area, which would enable McClellan to arrange his
350 field guns, tier above tier, and sweep the plain in every direction."

Hill writes in the *Century Magazine:* —

"Jackson moved over White Oak Swamp on July 1, Whiting's division leading. Our march was much delayed by the crossing of troops
and trains. At Willis's Church I met Gen. Lee. He bore grandly his
terrible disappointment of the day before, and made no allusion to it.
I gave him Mr. Allen's description of Malvern Hill and presumed to say,

'If Gen. McClellan is there in force, we had better let him alone.' Long-street laughed and said, 'Don't get scared, now that we have got him whipped.'"

Reconnoissance, ordered by Longstreet on the right, found a position favorable if we could employ a heavy force of artillery. A hill across Turkey Creek on the west gave ground whence 40 or more guns could enfilade the enemy's batteries and lines of battle. A wheat-field to the northeast gave positions whence a hundred guns could cross fire with them. Could we mass and open two such batteries, and follow their fire by a simultaneous charge of heavy columns, we would have a chance of winning a victory. Lee ordered the plan carried into effect. Meanwhile, a line of battle had been formed through the woods and fields. Whiting was on the left with three brigades (one of Jackson's under Hampton, and two of his own). D. H. Hill came next with five, then two of Huger's, six of Magruder's, and two more of Huger's, including Ransom's, detached from Holmes's division. The remainder of Holmes's was held on the River road, and was not engaged. Longstreet and Hill were in reserve behind Magruder; and Ewell's and Jackson's own division, behind Jackson. The enemy's batteries kept up a severe fire through the woods and along the roads, and the gunboats in the James participated for some hours with their heavy guns, until at length some shells burst prematurely over their own lines, when their fire was ordered to cease.

The order to charge the enemy's lines was, however, not made absolute. Magruder, Huger, and D. H. Hill, with their 14 brigades, were notified as follows about noon: —

"July 1, 1862.
"Batteries have been established to rake the enemy's line. If it is broken, as is probable, Armistead, who can witness the effect of the fire, has been ordered to charge with a yell. Do the same. By order of Gen. Lee.
"R. H. CHILTON, A. A. G."

The charge, therefore, was made to depend upon our being able to inaugurate and conduct with success an artillery duel of some magnitude.

Pioneers were sent to open a road to the left, and it was expected that artillery would act upon both flanks; but here our organization broke down.   Gen. Pendleton, Lee's Chief of Artillery, had a large artillery reserve, organized in four battalions of several batteries each, including our best rifled guns; but he was not able to bring a single one of his batteries into action. His official report of the day is as follows: —

"Tuesday, July 1, was spent by me in seeking, for some time, the commanding general, that I might get orders, and, by reason of the intricacy of routes, failing in this, in examining positions near the two armies toward ascertaining what could be best done with a large artillery force, and especially whether any position could be reached whence our large guns could be used to good purpose.   These endeavors had, of course, to be made again and again under the enemy's shells ; yet no site was found from which the large guns could play upon the enemy without endangering our own troops, and no occasion was presented for bringing up the reserve artillery.   Indeed, it seemed that not one-half of the division batteries were brought into action on either Monday or Tuesday.   To remain near by, therefore, and await events and orders in readiness for whatever service might be called for, was all that I could do.   Here again it was my privilege to be thrown with the President, he having arrived sometime after nightfall at the house near the battle-field, where I had just before sought a resting-place."

Between the lines one can but read a disappointing story. Pendleton did not find Lee all day long, nor did any orders from Lee find him.   He implies that his reserve artillery was not expected to go in until all the division batteries were first engaged. The division batteries were not organized into battalions, and, acting separately, were easily overpowered when brought out, one by one, in the face of many guns already in position.   Pendleton's battalions of from three to six batteries each, would have stood much better chances; and while there were not many places, there were two extensive ones, in either of which all of these battalions could have been used — Poindexter's field, and the position on Magruder's right, to which Lee made the pioneers open a road.   As matters were, our whole reserve artillery stood idle all day.

Pendleton graduated at West Point in 1830, one year after Lee.   He resigned in 1833, and entered the ministry in 1837. In 1861, he returned to military life, and was appointed Chief of Artillery of the Army about Oct., 1861, under Gen. Johnston. His command did little during the Seven Days, and Col. Brown, commanding his largest battalion, in his report mentions "the great superabundance of artillery and the scanty use that was made of it."

Col. Cutts, commanding another battalion, also reported: —

"My own small command (seven guns) was assigned a place near the battle-field of Tuesday, the 1st inst., and although I am sure that more artillery could have been used with advantage in this engagement, and also that my company could have done good service, yet I received no orders ; therefore, I have not had the honor to participate in any of the many engagements for the protection of our capital."

Several field-batteries were brought in, one or two at a time, upon both flanks, but each was quickly overwhelmed. The artillery under D. H. Hill, which had been engaged at White Oak Swamp the afternoon of the 30th, had entirely exhausted its ammunition and been sent to the rear to replenish. In the demand for guns, A. P. Hill sent two of his batteries, Davidson's and Pegram's. Pegram had been engaged in every battle, beginning with Mechanicsville. Including Malvern Hill, he had 60 casualties out of 80 men, and was only able to man a single gun at the close. This fighting, the artillery part of the action, began about noon and continued until about half-past three o'clock. D. H. Hill thus describes that in his front, —

"Instead of ordering up 100 of 200 pieces of artillery to play on the Yankees, a single battery, Moorman's, was ordered up, and knocked to pieces in a few minutes. One or two others shared the same fate of being beat in detail. Not knowing how to act under the circumstances, I wrote to Gen. Jackson that the firing from our batteries was of the most farcical character."

Whiting, on Hill's left, says: —

"To our left was a very large wheat-field which afforded a good view of the enemy's position, and fair opportunities for artillery. Batteries were ordered up. . . . The first battery ordered into Poindexter's field found itself exposed to a vastly superior cross-fire and was soon compelled to retire with loss. Balthis's battery, better posted and better covered by the ground, fought well and continued the action until their ammunition was exhausted. Other batteries were ordered up. Our gunners replied with spirit, but from want of ammunition the contest was too unequal, and I caused them successively to withdraw. This cross-fire was excessively severe upon the supporting troops."

Of the artillery fighting on the right flank, Gen. Armistead reported : —

"By a reconnoissance first made by Col. E. C. Edmonds of the 38th Va. . . . I found that the enemy were in, near, and around Crew's house, and that the hill in front of the ravine we occupied was a good position for artillery. It was asked for, and Capt. Pegram's and Grimes's batteries were sent. The fire was a terrible one and the men stood it well. The enemy must have had 30 or 40 pieces opposed to ours and of superior calibre. No men could have behaved better than Capts. Pegram and Grimes. They worked their guns after their men were cut down, and only retired when entirely disabled. I sent for more artillery repeatedly."

These extracts sufficiently illustrate the character of the fighting during the hours devoted in theory to bringing a heavy enfilading and cross-fire of artillery to bear upon the enemy in his crowded position. The one advantage which we had was that all our shots were converging toward his centre, and stood fair chances of finding some of his troops, even when they missed their special targets. And, thin, scattered, and meagre as our artillery fire was, — "almost farcical," as D. H. Hill pronounced it, and directed entirely at the enemy's batteries, its effect upon his infantry lines was such that Sumner withdrew his whole corps from their positions, and took refuge under the crest of the hills nearest the river, and he ordered Porter also to withdraw. Porter reports that he —

"protested against such a movement as disastrous to us, adding that as the major-general commanding had seen and approved my disposition, and also Gen. Couch's, I could not change without his order, which could soon be obtained if desirable. He desisted and the enemy was soon upon us, compelling him to recall his own corps."

How eloquent is this episode of what might have been the effect of bold and energetic use, early in the day, not only of our large artillery reserve, but of all our brigade and division batteries, brought in under their protection, as might have been done under efficient management.

As it was, this inefficient artillery service so discouraged the prospects of an assault that before three o'clock Lee abandoned his intention to assault. Longstreet was informed,[1] but no no-

---

[1] His report says, — "A little after 3 P.M., I understood that we would not be able to attack the enemy that day, inasmuch as his position was too strong to admit of it."

tice was sent to other generals, as there seemed no apparent need. The aggressive efforts had grown gradually weaker, and by three o'clock the firing on both sides had almost ceased.

Shortly before this, Lee had taken Longstreet and ridden over to our left in search of some route by which the enemy's position could be turned.

This should have been done early that morning, not by Lee in person, but by staff-officers under cavalry escorts. Jackson, on the left flank, had with him a fair supply of staff, and Munford's regiment of cavalry. In the Valley he would have done it without waiting for orders. By a movement inaugurated that day, a force might easily have reached the high ground known as Evelington Heights, overlooking Westover (of which there will be more to tell later), or any nearer point threatening the enemy's line of retreat, where a Confederate force in position might compel the enemy to take the offensive at a disadvantage.

A short reconnoissance induced Lee to order Longstreet at once to move his own division and Hill's to the left: Longstreet had rejoined his troops and was putting them in motion, when, to his surprise, he heard the sounds of battle break forth. He thought the enemy had taken the offensive, and that Magruder would soon be calling for reënforcements. His two divisions were, therefore, moved up to secure the right flank, though they did not become engaged.

Longstreet, in his narrative, states that the battle was precipitated by accident, but this is a mistake. It was begun by a direct order from Lee given hastily under the influence of a misapprehension of fact, which occurred as follows: —

When Sumner withdrew his corps under the cover of the hills, as has been told in the quotation from Porter, the movement was observed from our left by Whiting. He reported to Lee that the enemy were withdrawing both trains and troops. About the same time, a body of the enemy's skirmishers being advanced in front of Armistead's brigade, was attacked and easily driven back by three of his regiments. These followed the fugitives a short distance and occupied advanced ground, in a swale which afforded some shelter. This affair was considered a success, and it was also reported to Lee as he was returning from his reconnoissance with Longstreet. Had Sumner's movement, and the advance and easy retreat of the Federal skirmishers, been planned as a ruse to decoy us into a charge, its success would have been brilliant. That part of our plan which had called for a tremendous preliminary cannonade was forgotten. Lee believed that his enemy was retreating and about to escape him, and he hastened to send a verbal order to Magruder through Capt. Dickinson of Magruder's staff, who wrote the order as follows: —

"Gen. Lee expects you to advance rapidly. He says it is reported the enemy is getting off. Press forward your whole line and follow up Armistead's success."

Under Magruder's orders the advance was commenced by Wright's Ga. and La. brigade, followed by Mahone's Va. brigade, both of Huger's division. These two brigades formed our extreme right, and went into action only about 2500 strong, many stragglers having been lost from the ranks in the marchings and skirmishes of the three previous days.

To the left of Wright was Armistead of Huger's division, followed by Cobb's and Semmes's brigades. In support of these were all the rest of Magruder's and Huger's 10 brigades, Ransom, of Holmes's division, being also temporarily attached to Huger. Farther to the left came D. H. Hill's five brigades. Magruder's brigades consumed a little time in developing a full roar of musketry, but no sooner was it heard than D. H. Hill's division was also put in.

Fitz-John Porter, in *Battles and Leaders*, thus describes the opening of the battle from the Federal point of view: —

"The spasmodic, though sometimes formidable, attack of our antagonists, at different points along our whole front, up to about four o'clock were, presumably, demonstrations or feelers preparatory to their engaging in more serious work. An ominous silence, similar to that which had preceded the attack in force at Gaines' Mill, now intervened, until, at about 5.30 o'clock, the enemy opened upon both Morell and Couch with artillery from nearly the whole of his front, and soon after pressed forward in columns of infantry, first on one, then on the other, or on both.

"As if moved by a reckless disregard of life equal to that displayed at Gaines Mill, with a determination to capture our army or destroy it by driving us into the river, brigade after brigade rushed at our batteries;

but the artillery of both Morell and Couch mowed them down with shrapnel, grape, and canister, while our infantry, withholding their fire until the enemy were in short range, scattered the remnants of their columns, sometimes following them up and capturing prisoners and colors."

One can scarcely read the full story of this charge without believing that, made early in the day with the aid of all our reserve artillery on the flanks and of the 22 brigades of infantry who were spectators, we might, by main force, have crushed the enemy's army as it stood. Porter himself, who was practically in command of the field, and the most accomplished of the Federal corps commanders, records that, at one period of the action, as he rode to bring up reënforcements, he felt such apprehensions of soon becoming our prisoner, that he took from his pocket and tore up his "diary and despatch book of the campaign."

That the ground was less unfavorable for an assault from our right flank appears from the reports of Wright and Mahone, whose small force was not driven back at all, but made a lodgment and held their ground all night. Gen. Wright reports as follows: —

"At 4.45 o'clock I received an order from Gen. Magruder through Capt. Henry Bryan, one of his staff, to advance immediately and charge the enemy's batteries. No other troops had yet come upon the field. I ordered my men forward, and, springing before them, led my brigade, less than 1000 men, against a force I knew to be superior in the ratio of at least 20 to 1. Onward we pressed, warmly and strongly supported by Gen. Mahone's brigade, under a murderous fire of shot, shell, canister, and musketry. At every step my brave men fell around me, but the survivors pressed on until we had reached a hollow about 300 yards from the enemy's batteries on the right. Here I perceived that a strong force had been sent forward on our left, by the enemy, with a view of flanking and cutting us off from our support, now more than 1000 yards in our rear. I immediately threw the left of the 3d Ga. a little back along the upper margin of the hollow, and, suddenly changing front of the regiment, poured a galling fire upon the enemy, which he returned with spirit, aided by a fearful direct and cross-fire from his batteries. Here the contest raged with varying success for more than three-quarters of an hour; finally the line of the enemy was broken, and he gave way in great disorder.

"In the meantime, my front, supported by Gen. Mahone, had been subjected to a heavy fire of artillery and musketry, and had begun to waver, and I feared I would be compelled to fall back. Just at this moment firing was heard far away to our left, and soon we saw our columns advancing upon the enemy's centre. This diverted a portion of the enemy's fire from us, and I succeeded in keeping my men steady. We had now approached within a few hundred yards of the enemy's advanced batteries, and I again gave the order to charge, which was obeyed with promptness and alacrity.

"We rushed forward, up the side of the hill under the brow of which we had been for some time halted, and dashing over the hill, reached another hollow or ravine immediately in front of, and, as it were, under, the enemy's guns. This ravine was occupied by a line of Yankee infantry posted there to protect their batteries. Upon this we rushed with such impetuosity that the enemy broke in great disorder and fled. . . .

"The firing had now become general along the left and centre of our line, and night setting in, it was difficult to distinguish friend from foe.

"Several of my command were killed by our own friends, who had come up on our immediate left, and who commenced firing long before they came within range of the enemy. This firing upon us from our friends, together with the increasing darkness, made our position peculiarly hazardous, but I determined to maintain it at all hazards, as long as a man should be left to fire a gun. The fire was terrific now, beyond anything I had ever witnessed, — indeed, the hideous shrieking of shells through the dusky gloom of closing night, the loud and incessant roll of artillery and small-arms, were enough to make the stoutest heart quail. Still my shattered little command, now reduced to less than 300, with about an equal number of Gen. Mahone's brigade, held our positions under the very muzzles of the enemy's guns, and poured volley after volley with murderous precision into their serried ranks. . . .

"Just at this time a portion of Col. Ramseur's 49th N.C. regiment, having got lost upon the field, was hailed by me and ordered to fall in with my brigade. A strong picket was advanced all around our isolated position, and the wearied, hungry soldiers threw themselves upon the earth to snatch a few hours' rest. Detachments were ordered to search for water and administer to our poor wounded men, whose cries rent the air in every direction. Soon the enemy were seen with lanterns, busily engaged in moving their killed and wounded, and friend and foe freely mingled on that gloomy night in administering to the wants of wounded and dying comrades. . . .

"Early on the morning of July 2, Gen. Ewell rode upon the field, and coming to the position where my men lay, I reported to him and was relieved from further watching on the field. . . . My loss in this engagement was very severe, amounting to 55 killed, 243 wounded, and 64 missing (total 362). I have no means of determining the loss of the enemy, though I am satisfied it was very heavy."

Gen. Mahone reports that his brigade carried into action 1226, and lost 39 killed, 164 wounded, and 120 missing (total 323).

Wright's report gives a clear idea of the fighting upon our right flank. Next, on the left, Semmes and Kershaw also made, perhaps, the farthest advance of the attack, actually getting among the enemy's guns, where lay the body of a handsome young Louisiana officer, next morning, the farthest jetsam of the red wave which had stained all the green fields of our advance. Both of these brigades had been forced to fall back, not so much from the fire of the enemy in their front, as from that of their friends farther on the left, advancing on converging lines in the dusk. There were more troops concentrated in the forest in a small space than could be well handled, even in daylight; and the plateau over which their charge was to be made, when they got free of the wood, was so bare of shelter, and swept by such fire of musketry and artillery, that not a single brigade faced it long without being driven back. The official reports show that in the storm and smoke around them single brigades often thought themselves to be the only ones engaged.

D. H. Hill, whose advance was across the plateau, thus describes the attack by his division: —

"While conversing with my brigade commanders, shouting was heard on our right, followed by the roar of musketry. We all agreed that this was the signal agreed upon, and I ordered my division to advance. This, as near as I could judge, was about an hour and a half before sundown. . . .

"The division fought heroically and well, but fought in vain. Garland, in my immediate front, showed all his wonted courage and enthusiasm, but he needed and asked for reënforcements. I sent Lt.-Col. Newton, 6th Ga., to his support, and, observing a brigade by a fence in our rear, I galloped back to it and found it to be that of Gen. Toombs. I ordered it forward to support Garland, and accompanied it. The brigade advanced handsomely to the brow of the hill, but soon retreated in disorder. Gordon, commanding Rodes's brigade, pushed gallantly forward and gained considerable ground, but was forced back. The gallant and accomplished Meares, 3d N.C., Ripley's brigade, had fallen at the head of his regiment, and that brigade was streaming to the rear. Colquitt's and Anderson's brigades had also fallen back. Ransom's brigade had come up to my support from Gen. Huger. It moved too far to the left and became mixed up with a mass of troops near the parsonage on the Quaker road, suffering much and effecting little. Gen. Winder was sent up by Gen. Jackson, but he came too late, and also went to the same belt of woods near the parsonage, already overcrowded with troops. Finally Gen. Ewell came up, but it was after dark, and nothing could be accomplished. I advised him to hold the ground he had gained and not to attempt a forward movement."

Gen. Toombs's account of the advance of his brigade will give some idea of the confusion of commands upon the field after the battle was in full tide : —

"Accordingly, I advanced rapidly in line of battle through the dense woods, intersected by ravines, occasionally thick brier patches, and other obstructions, guided only by the enemy's fire in keeping direction, frequently retarded and sometimes broken, by troops in front of me, until the command reached the open field on the elevated plateau immediately in front of, and in short range of, the enemy's guns. Here, coming up with a portion of the troops which I was ordered to support, I halted my line for the purpose of rectifying it and of allowing many of the troops whom I was to support, to pass me and form. These objects were but imperfectly accomplished by me, as well as by the rest of the troops within my view, from the great confusion and disorder in the field — arising much from the difficulties of the ground over which they had to pass, and in part from the heavy fire of grape and canister and shells, which the enemy's batteries were pouring in upon them. But, having accomplished what could be done of this work, I ordered my brigade to advance. It moved forward steadily and firmly until it came up with the troops in advance, who had halted. I then ordered it to halt, and ordered the men to lie down, which they did, and received the enemy's fire for a considerable time, when an order was repeated along my line, coming from the left, directing the line to oblique to the left. This order I immediately and promptly countermanded as soon as it reached the part of the line where I stood, and arrested it in part. I saw that the immediate effect of the movement was to throw the troops into the woods and ravines on the left of the plateau, and necessarily throw them into great confusion. . . .

"In the meantime Gen. Kershaw came into the field with his brigade, near one of my regiments, the 2d Ga., which still remained in very good order; and my adjutant, Capt. Du Bose, proposed to him to unite that, and some other companies of other regiments, with his command in the attack on the enemy's batteries, to which he assented; and this command, under Cols. Butt and Holmes, accompanied by Capt. Du Bose and Maj. Alexander (my quartermaster, who acted as one of my aides on the field) advanced with Gen. Kershaw's brigade beyond the edge of the wood into the open field, but, under the destructive fire of the enemy's cannon and small-arms, wavered and fell back into the road skirting the pine thicket. . . .

"My losses were very severe, the total being 194 killed and wounded, out of about 1200 carried into action. I am happy to add that the disorders which did arise were due rather to the difficulties of the ground, and the nature of the attack, than from any other cause, and that as far as my observation went, they extended to all troops engaged on the plateau in front of the enemy's guns. This is further evidenced by the fact that at roll-call next morning over 800 of my command answered to their names, leaving under 200 unaccounted for, many of whom soon made their appearance.''

There is no doubt that the entire force which had been engaged was wrecked for the time being, and that, had the enemy been in position for a counterstroke, the fragments could have made but little opposition. But A. P. Hill and Longstreet were close in rear, and Whiting's, Jackson's, and Ewell's divisions were on the left, and Holmes a few miles off on the right. The enemy, moreover, having sent ahead all of their trains, were now very low both in ammunition and provisions, and could scarcely have ventured anything serious.

Whiting's division had suffered 175 casualties in its two brigades, and 19 in Hampton's brigade, from the enemy's artillery fire, while lying in support of our artillery in Poindexter's field. Including with these the losses in Jackson's and Ewell's divisions and Lawton's brigade, the casualties were 599. In Magruder's division the casualties were 2014, and in Huger's, including Ransom's brigade, 1609. In Rodes's, Colquitt's, and Ripley's brigades of D. H. Hill's division, the casualties were making 889, a total, so far, of 5111. The other two brigades, Anderson's and Garland's, report only their total casualties for the campaign as 863 and 844, a total of 1707. A half, 854, is a moderate estimate for their losses at Malvern.

This would make our total losses 5965 or more; those of the enemy could scarcely have reached 2000, but the casualties of different battles are not separated.

Of Jackson's part in this action there is very little to be said. He took no initiative, though complying promptly with orders or requests as received. But had he been the Jackson of the Valley, being on the left flank that morning, he would have turned Malvern Hill by his left, and taken position commanding the road somewhere beyond Turkey Creek. Malvern should not have been attacked; only the enemy observed and held by Longstreet, while Jackson got a position which they would be forced to assault.

Lee's report sums up the subsequent operations briefly, as follows : —

"On July 2, it was discovered that the enemy had withdrawn during the night, leaving the ground covered with his dead and wounded, and his route exhibiting abundant evidence of precipitate retreat. The pursuit was commenced, Gen. Stuart with his cavalry in the advance, but a violent storm which prevailed throughout the day greatly retarded our progress. The enemy, harassed and followed closely by the cavalry, succeeded in gaining Westover and the protection of his gunboats. He immediately began to fortify his position, which was one of great natural strength, flanked on each side by a creek, and the approach to his front commanded by the heavy guns of his shipping in addition to those mounted in his intrenchments. It was deemed inexpedient to attack him, and in view of the condition of our troops, who had been marching and fighting almost incessantly for seven days, under the most trying circumstances, it was determined to withdraw in order to afford them the repose of which they stood so much in need."

One episode of the pursuit, however, is worthy of note. On July 2, but little progress was made by the infantry, owing to the heavy rain-storm, but Stuart's cavalry (which had recrossed the Chickahominy by fording at Forge Bridge on the afternoon of July 1) followed the enemy and endeavored to shell his columns wherever opportunity offered. About 5 P.M. the last of these columns had arrived at its destination on the James River, Harrison's Landing, — a peninsula about four miles long by one and a half wide, formed by Herring Creek on the northeast, running for that distance nearly parallel to the James before emptying into it. At its head a small inlet from the river on the southwest left but a narrow front exposed to attack.

But, across Herring Creek, an extensive plateau called Evelington Heights dominates the upper part of this peninsula so that, if held by artillery, the enemy would be forced to attack at a disadvantage — the creek being impassable for some distance above. During Wednesday night, Stuart received a report from Pelham, commanding his artillery, describing this position and recommending its being seized. He forwarded the report to Lee, through Jackson, and early on the 3d, with a few cavalry and a single howitzer, nearly out of ammunition, he ran off a Federal squadron and took possession of the heights. It is a pity that there was *any* ammunition, for Stuart writes that —

"the howitzer was brought in action in the river road to fire upon the enemy's camp below. Judging from the great commotion and excitement below, it must have had considerable effect."

It did have considerable effect of a most unfortunate kind for us. It awaked the enemy to instant appreciation of the fact that it was essential for him to hold that ground, and that it behooved him to take it before we brought up any more force. A military lesson is to be learned from the result, to wit, that dangers lurk in excess of enterprise as well as in its deficiency. In this campaign our cavalry affords two instances. Stuart's zeal, without necessity, led him to make the circuit of McClellan's army, June 11–15. The result was that McClellan was prepared to change his base to the James as soon as he found Lee threatening his communications. Now, the temptation to shell a camp and wagon trains loses to our army its last chance to take a position which would compel the enemy to assume the offensive. One howitzer could, of course, accomplish nothing but to alarm the enemy, and precipitate their attack.

When Stuart opened fire, he thought that both Longstreet and Jackson were near. In fact, neither was within miles. Jackson had been sent in direct pursuit, being nearest the most direct roads, and his troops having been least engaged during the Seven Days. Two of the four brigades of his own division had been so little exposed as to have had together but two killed and 26 wounded, in the whole campaign. His 3d brigade, Winder's, had had but 75 casualties at Gaines Mill, and 104 at Malvern. Lawton's brigade, and Ewell's and Whiting's divisions, had only been severely engaged at Gaines Mill.

Longstreet, with A. P. Hill's and his own divisions, was on the 2d moved around the field of battle to Poindexter's house, and on the 3d was sent by roads to the left of Jackson. By mistake of the guides he was conducted too far to the left, and only reached Evelington Heights about dark on the 3d; Jackson's troops came up at the same time by the direct road.

Jackson's official report says: —

"On the morning of the 3d, my command arrived near the landing and drove in the enemy's skirmishers," but the date is shown by all other reports to be a clerical error for the 4th.

Had Stuart not opened fire, the enemy would not have disturbed him that day. During it McClellan wrote to the Secretary of War, as follows: —

"I am in hopes the enemy is as completely worn out as we are. He was certainly very severely punished in the last battle. The roads are now very bad. For these reasons I hope we shall now have enough breathing space to reorganize and rest the men, and get them into position before the enemy can attack again. . . . It is, of course, impossible to estimate, as yet, our losses, but I doubt whether there are to-day more than 50,000 men with their colors."

By the next morning 21 Confederate brigades had arrived and would have been upon Evelington Heights had Stuart not forced the enemy to come over and occupy them. McClellan's 50,000 men would then have had the task of removing them.

Stuart thus describes his resistance : —

"I held the ground from 9 A.M. till 2 P.M., when the enemy had contrived to get one battery into position on this side the creek. The fire was, however, kept up until a body of infantry was found approaching by our right flank. I had no apprehension, however, as I felt sure Longstreet was near by, and, although Pelham had but two rounds of ammunition left, I held out, knowing how important it was to hold the ground till Longstreet arrived.

"The enemy's infantry advanced, and his battery kept up its fire. I just then learned that Longstreet had taken the wrong road and was then at Nance's shop, six or seven miles off. Pelham fired his last round, and the sharp-shooters, strongly posted in the skirt of woods bordering the plateau, exhausted every cartridge, but had at last to retire. . . . The next day, July 4, Gen. Jackson's command drove in the enemy's advanced pickets. I pointed out the position of the enemy, now occupying, apparently in force, the plateau from which I shelled their camp the day before, and showed him the routes by which the plateau could be reached, to the left, and submitted my plan for dispossessing the enemy and attacking his camp. This was subsequently laid before the commanding general."

From the Federal reports it appears that the enemy occupied the heights on the afternoon of July 3 with Franklin's division. The next morning Longstreet was up with his own and A. P. Hill's division and two brigades of Magruder's. Jackson was also up with his own, Ewell's, Whiting's, and D. H. Hill's divisions. Lee did not reach the field until noon, and, as Longstreet ranked Jackson, he ordered the enemy's pickets driven in and preparation made for an attack.

A favorable opportunity was presented to regain the Evelington Heights by main force. They were occupied by but one division, and, being across Herring Creek from the rest of the Federal army, it could not have been rapidly reënforced.   There would have been very small risk in making the effort so earnestly urged by Stuart, for McClellan would never have dared a counter-stroke, had we failed.   The enemy's gunboats could have rendered little assistance, as their own camps and lines intervened. Briefly, the game seems to have been worth the candle, and it should have been played.

Jackson's troops, however, were in front, and Jackson protested against the attack, saying that the troops were not in proper condition, and asking for delay until Lee should reach the field.   To this Longstreet consented, and when Lee arrived, Jackson's arguments prevailed and the attack was given up. It was entirely unlike Lee, and he must have reluctantly yielded to Jackson's persuasion.   Evidently, Jackson was still not the Jackson of the Valley.

The next day the troops were moved back toward Richmond, and the campaign was ended.

The total casualties of the two armies for the Seven Days were : —

Confederate : killed 3286, wounded 15,909, missing 946, total 20,141
Federal: "   1734,   "   8,062,   "   6053,   "   15,849

Including the Federal wounded, we took about 10,000 prisoners and captured 52 guns and about 35,000 muskets.   We lost two guns in the stampede in Holmes's division.

For a week after McClellan had established himself at Westover, he neglected to occupy the opposite bank of the James. As the fire of his gunboats commanded it, he could do so at pleasure, but as long as he did not, it was much better for us that he should not.   Again, however, the temptation to shell a camp proved irresistible, and Lee was persuaded to authorize an expedition for the purpose under Pendleton's supervision.

On July 12 some 47 rifled guns were collected, positions chosen, and ranges marked for night firing.   After midnight they opened fire upon the Federal transports, wharves, and camps, and used up their small supplies of ammunition in a random cannonade. The enemy replied in like fashion, both from the shore and from gunboats.   Of course, there was much commotion in the Federal camps, but the actual damage done was trifling. Some 40 casualties are reported among the Federals, and two or three among the Confederate artillerists.

The next day the Federals established themselves on the South Side. The strategic advantages of a position astraddle of the James River have already been referred to (page 61, Chap. III.), but they were not yet generally appreciated. Fortunately for us, Lincoln and Halleck recalled McClellan and his army to Washington without ever realizing them; although McClellan had tried hard to impress them upon his superiors. Fortunately, too, for us, Gen. S. G. French, in command at Petersburg, saw and appreciated the threat of the position, and immediately began the construction of a line of intrenchments about that city. These intrenchments, in 1864, defeated some attempts at surprise; and at last enabled Beauregard, with two divisions, to withstand the attack of Grant's whole army, between June 15 and 18 of that year.

My personal duties during the Seven Days were the supervision and distribution of our ammunition supplies. Our organized division supply trains and brigade wagons worked smoothly, and no scarcity was felt anywhere.

In addition to these duties, I was placed in charge of a balloon which had been manufactured in Savannah by Dr. Edward Cheves, and sent to Gen. Lee for use in reconnoitring the enemy's lines. It was made from silk of many patterns, varnished with gutta-percha car-springs dissolved in naphtha, and inflated at the Richmond Gas Works with ordinary city gas.

I saw the battle of Gaines Mill from it, and signalled information of the movement of Slocum's division across the Chickahominy to reënforce Porter. Ascensions were made daily, and when the enemy reached Malvern Hill, the inflated balloon would be carried down the river and ascensions made from the deck of a boat. Unfortunately, on July 4, the boat — the *Teaser*, a small armed tug — got aground below Malvern Hill on a falling tide, and a large Federal gunboat, the *Maritanza*, came up and captured both boat and balloon, the crew escaping.

We could never build another balloon, but my experience with this gave me a high idea of the possible efficiency of balloons in active campaigns. Especially did we find, too, that the balloons of the enemy forced upon us constant troublesome precautions in efforts to conceal our marches.

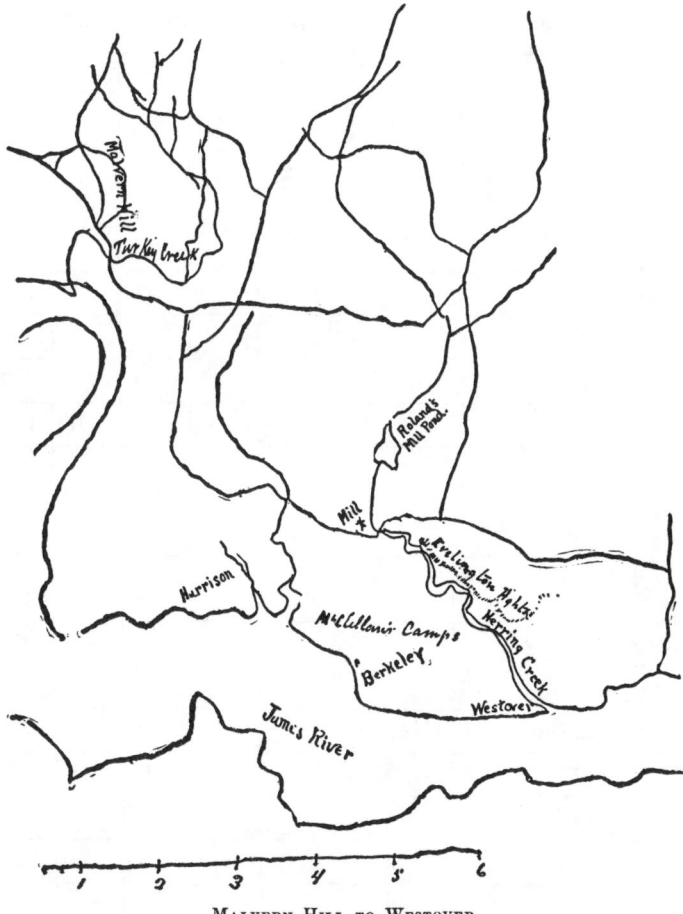

MALVERN HILL TO WESTOVER

As affording a bird's-eye view of our organization and of the forces engaged in the different actions, and the severity of the conflicts, a table of Confederate division casualties is attached, showing as accurately as can be determined, the losses of each command for each action. The total Federal losses in killed and wounded (excluding prisoners) is also approximately divided for the principal actions as nearly as records permit.

DIVISION CASUALTIES. SEVEN DAYS BEFORE RICHMOND

DIVISIONS	No. of Brigades	Mechanicsville	Gaines Mill	Savage Station	Frazier's Farm	Malvern Hill	Other Affairs	Totals
Whiting's Div.	2		1017			175		1192
Jackson's Div.	3		91			117		208
Lawton's Brig.	1		492			75		567
Ewell's Div.	4		764			223		987
D. H. Hill's Div.	5	586	1423			1743	15	3767
MAGRUDER'S CORPS — D. R. Jones's Div.	2					424	455	879
MAGRUDER'S CORPS — McLaws's Div.	2			357		315		672
MAGRUDER'S CORPS — Magruder's Div.	2			84		874	9	967
Longstreet's Div.	6		1883		2555			4438
Huger's Div.	3					1137	394	1531
A. P. Hill's Div.	6	764	2688		750	8		4210
Holmes's Div.	3					499	178	677
Pendleton's Art.							2	2
Stuart's Cav.							71	71
Totals 10 Divisions	39	1350	8358	441	3305	5590	1124	20168
Federal Losses (killed and wounded only)		361	4001	400	2034	2000	1000	9796

CHAPTER X

CEDAR MOUNTAIN

Recuperation. Gen. Pope Arrives. Gen. Halleck Arrives. McClellan Recalled. Lee Moves. Jackson Moves. Cedar Mountain. The Night Action. Jackson's Ruse. Casualties.

THE close of the Seven Days found both armies greatly in need of rest. Lincoln called upon the governors of the Northern States for 300,000 more men, and bounties, State and Federal, were offered to secure them rapidly. They were easily obtained, but a mistake was made in putting the recruits in the field. They were organized into entirely new regiments, which were generally hurried to the field after but little drilling and training. President Davis also called for conscripts, — all that could be gotten. No great number were obtained, for those arriving at the age of conscription usually volunteered in some selected regiment. Those who were conscripted were also distributed among veteran regiments to repair the losses of the campaign, and this was done as rapidly as the men could be gotten to the front. Although this method allowed no time for drill or training, yet it was far more effective in maintaining the strength of the army than the method pursued by the Federals.

During the short intermission from active operations, something was accomplished, too, to improve our organizations, though leaving us still greatly behind the example long before set us by the enemy. Longstreet and Jackson were still but major-generals commanding divisions, but each now habitually commanded other divisions besides his own, called a Wing, and the old divisions became known by the names of new commanders. Thus, Jackson's old division now became Taliaferro's, and Longstreet's division became Pickett's, while Longstreet and Jackson each commanded a Wing, so called.

It was not until another brief rest in October, after the battle

of Sharpsburg, that Longstreet and Jackson were made lieutenant-generals, and the whole army was definitely organized into
corps. Some improvement was also made in our armament by
the guns and rifled muskets captured during the Seven Days, and
my reserve ordnance train was enlarged. Lines of light earthworks were constructed, protecting Chaffin's Bluff batteries on
the James River, and stretching across the peninsula to connect
with the lines already built from the Chickahominy to the head
of White Oak Swamp.

Gen. D. H. Hill also constructed lines on the south side of the
James, protecting Drury's Bluff and Richmond from an advance
in that quarter; and Gen. French at Petersburg, as already
mentioned, threw lines around that city, from the river below to
the river above.

Just at the beginning of the Seven Days' Battles, President
Lincoln had called from the West Maj.-Gen. John Pope, and
placed him in command of the three separate armies of Frémont
and Banks, in the Valley of Virginia, and McDowell near Fredericksburg. The union of the three into one was a wise measure,
but the selection of a commander was as eminently unwise.
One from the army in Virginia, other things being equal, would
have possessed many advantages, and there was no lack of men of
far sounder reputation than Pope had borne among his comrades
in the old U. S. Army. He had spent some years in Texas
boring for artesian water on the Staked Plains, and making
oversanguine reports of his prospects of success. An army
song had summed up his reputation in a brief parody of some
well-known lines, "Hope told a flattering tale," as follows: —

> "Pope told a flattering tale,
>   Which proved to be bravado,
> About the streams which spout like ale
>   On the Llano Estacado."

Pope arrived early in July and began to concentrate and organize his army. A characteristic "flattering tale" is told in
an address to his troops, July 14, dated "Headquarters in the
Saddle": —

"Let us understand each other. I come to you from the West where
we have always seen the backs of our enemies; from an army whose busi-

ness it has been to seek the adversary, and beat him when he was found; whose policy has been attack and not defence. . . . I presume I have been called here to pursue the same system, and to lead you against the enemy. . . . Meantime, I desire you to dismiss from your minds certain phrases, which I am sorry to find so much in vogue amongst you. I hear constantly of 'taking strong positions and holding them'; of 'lines of retreat,' and of 'bases of supplies.' Let us discard such ideas. . . . Let us study the probable lines of retreat of our opponents and leave our own to take care of themselves. . . . Success and glory are in the advance. Disaster and shame lurk in the rear. . . ."

The arrogance of this address was not calculated to impress favorably officers of greater experience in actual warfare, who were now overslaughed by his promotion. McDowell would have been the fittest selection, but he and Banks, both seniors to Pope, submitted without a word; as did also Sumner, Franklin, Porter, Heintzelman, and all the major-generals of McClellan's army. But Frémont protested, asked to be relieved, and practically retired from active service.

Meanwhile, after the discomfiture of McClellan, Mr. Lincoln felt the want of a military advisor, and, on July 11, appointed Gen. Halleck commander-in-chief of all the armies of the United States, and summoned him to Washington City. Ropes's *Story of the Civil War* thus comments upon this appointment : —

"It is easy to see how this unfortunate selection came to be made: Halleck was at that time the most successful general in the Federal service; it was perfectly natural that he should be the choice of the President and Secretary of War, to whom his serious defects as a military man could not have become known. His appointment was also satisfactory to the public, for, as so much had been effected under his command in the West, he was generally credited with great strategic ability. . . . But both the people and the President were before long to find out how slender was Halleck's intellectual capacity, how entirely unmilitary was the cast of his mind, and how repugnant to his whole character was the assumption of any personal and direct control of an army in the field."

Halleck arrived in Washington and took charge on July 22. He found, awaiting for his decision, a grave problem. It was whether McClellan's army, now intrenched at Westover on the James, should be heavily reënforced and allowed to enter upon another active campaign from that point as a base, or whether it should abandon the James River entirely, and be brought back, by water, to unite with the army now under Pope, in front of Washington.

McClellan earnestly begged for reënforcements, and confidently predicted success if they were given him. He had begun to appreciate the strategic advantages of his position, and he was even proposing as his first movement the capture of Petersburg by a *coup-de-main*. This would not have been, at that time, a difficult operation. McClellan had 90,000 men available, for he could have even abandoned his position on the north side and used his whole force. As to its effect, it would probably have finally compelled the evacuation of Richmond, as it did in 1865. Had McClellan possessed enterprise and audacity, he would have waited neither for permission nor reënforcements, but have made the dash on his own responsibility as soon as he found that there was serious thought of recalling his army. All of this time, however, McClellan was still representing to his government that Lee had 200,000 men. If he really believed this, it is not strange that he kept closely within his intrenchments; but Mr. Ropes, the most careful historian of the war, asserts that neither McClellan nor Halleck believed this "preposterous story." McClellan told it, and stuck to it, trying to scare the administration into giving him unlimited reënforcements: but his real belief, Mr. Ropes thinks, is apparent in his offer to undertake the new campaign with only 20,000 reënforcements, raising his force to only 110,000. Mr. Ropes says that Halleck saw and appreciated McClellan's insincerity, but, wishing to have the army brought back, he affected to believe in the 200,000 men, and easily confounded McClellan's arguments by pointing out what such a force might do under such generals as Lee and Jackson.

Halleck had visited McClellan on the James soon after his arrival in Washington, and the matter was argued, pro and con, in correspondence afterward for some weeks.

McClellan ended with a strong appeal, pointing out that he could deliver his battle within 10 miles of Richmond, which was the heart of the Confederacy, while a victory 70 miles off might count for little. Halleck answered that it was unsafe to have a divided army in the face of Lee's force; that the location on the James River was very unhealthy in the fall months, and that most of McClellan's leading generals favored the withdrawal of the army. So orders were given, and the Federal army, on Aug. 14, began the evacuation of the only position from which it could soon have forced the evacuation of Richmond. They were only to find it again after two years' fighting, and the loss of over 100,000 men; and they would find it then, only by being defeated upon every other possible line of advance. The army was marched to Fortress Monroe, whence, as rapidly as boats could be furnished, it was carried up the Potomac to Acquia Creek or Alexandria. Thence, each corps, as fast as it arrived, was marched to join Pope's army, it being designed to concentrate everything behind the Rappahannock.

Now let us turn to Lee, and see how he met the difficulties of his situation, and what fortune attended his efforts. He realized that the immediate danger was that McClellan should be reenforced and renew his campaign from his new base. The first solicitude was to have McClellan's army recalled. Some early efforts were made to demoralize the transport vessels, on the James, by which the army was supplied. Light guns were sent to various points along the river, whence they could, as it were, ambush passing vessels and fire upon them. But the Federal gunboats had soon learned the danger points and how to protect transports passing them, and no serious result could be accomplished. There were, however, persistent rumors that the Confederates were constructing one or more ironclads at Richmond, which would soon come down the James and destroy the whole Federal fleet. The uneasiness caused in Washington by these rumors may have contributed to the result finally reached. But Lee could not afford to wait at Richmond for the enemy to make up his mind slowly. His only chance was to strike Pope's army before it could be joined by McClellan's. As early, therefore, as July 13, he had ordered Jackson, with Taliaferro's and Ewell's divisions, to Gordonsville, to oppose reported advances of Pope. The latter had, on July 14, ordered Gen. Hatch to seize Gordonsville, then held by only about 200 infantry and a few cavalry. Hatch, however, lost time by listening to false reports that the Confederates were near at hand, and by waiting to take infantry, artillery, and a wagon-train, along with the considerable cavalry force which Pope had intended should alone be used. It alone would have been ample, as Jackson's troops did not reach Gordonsville until July 19. Hatch's expedition, therefore, was a failure.

Jackson, on his arrival, was anxious to undertake some aggressive operation against Pope, but found his force — only about 12,000 men — inadequate to accomplish anything against Pope's 47,000; so he appealed to Lee for reënforcement. Not yet assured that McClellan would not soon resume the offensive, Lee hesitated; but, on July 27, ordered A. P. Hill's division, about 12,000 strong, to Gordonsville. Hill joined Jackson on Aug. 2. Meanwhile, Pope had received instructions from Halleck to make demonstrations toward Gordonsville, with the view of occupying Lee's attention, and preventing his interference with the contemplated withdrawal of McClellan's force from the Peninsula.

On Aug. 6, Pope began to cross his infantry over the Rappahannock to concentrate about Culpeper. With swift appreciation of the opportunity, Jackson, on the 7th, put his whole force in motion to fall upon that portion of the enemy which first reached Culpeper. Could he defeat one of Pope's three corps, and occupy that central position in time, he might deal with the other two in succession, as he had dealt with Shields and Frémont at Port Republic. His strategy was excellent, but it was defeated by his own logistics. On the 7th the march was but eight miles, having only been begun in the afternoon. On the 8th there were 20 miles to go to reach Culpeper, with the Rapidan and Robertson rivers to ford, the latter river being held by the Federal cavalry, about 12 miles in front of the town. The weather was intensely hot, and it could hardly be expected that the Confederates would make the march in time to give battle on the same day. It would have been, however, only an easy march to reach a point, so close to the enemy, that battle could be delivered at an early hour on the 9th, allowing time to reap the fruits of victory, if successful. But on the 8th, some little blunders and omissions in giving the orders to the three divisions utterly confounded the march, and the head of the column only made eight miles, and the rear of it but two.

In the first place, each division was allowed to take its own wagon-train behind it on the road, instead of concentrating all three into one train behind the whole force. In the next place, Ewell's division, which was to lead and be followed by Hill's, had its route changed without Hill's being informed. This led to delay on Hill's part; and to Jackson's division (now commanded by Winder) getting ahead. Winder presently found his line of march intersected by Ewell's. It was also charged that Hill showed little zeal, being offended that Jackson, with his usual reticence, had given him no information of his plans.

Lee, indeed, in a recent letter had given Jackson a hint that his reticence might be carried too far. He had said: —

"A. P. Hill you will, I think, find a good officer, with whom you can consult, and, by advising with your division commanders as to your movements, much trouble will be saved you in arranging details, and they can aid more intelligently."

The whole incident shows that our staff service was poorly organized, and not efficient in its operations. The result of all this delay was that it was about 3 P.M. on the 9th before Ewell's division on the right, and Winder's on the left, had formed line in front of Banks's corps, which had been encountered at Cedar Mountain, some seven miles south of Culpeper. Lawton's large brigade of Ewell's division and Gregg's of Hill's division, had been left behind to guard the wagon-trains against the enemy's superior force of cavalry. The remainder of Hill's division was not yet up, and, while waiting their arrival, 26 rifled guns were brought up by Jackson and opened upon the enemy's lines and batteries.

The left of Winder's division rested along the front edge of a considerable body of wood, which had not been thoroughly examined. Pope, in his report, asserts that Banks had been ordered to take a strong position and hold it, awaiting reënforcements, which were rapidly coming up. This should have been his play; but Pope had used expressions in orders, sent by his Chief of Cavalry, which Banks understood as permission to attack if the enemy were not in great force. Being, personally, both brave and aggressive, Banks thought the opportunity had arrived, and before Jackson was ready to advance, between 5 and 6 P.M., he attacked with his whole force.   The right of his line over-lapped the left of Winder's division, and taking it in flank and pressing vigorously, it entirely routed the left brigade under Garnett, and threw the whole division into much confusion. Winder himself had been killed by a cannon-shot in the pre-liminary artillery fighting.

Just at this juncture, however, Hill's division arrived upon the field, and not only restored the battle, but drove the enemy from the field and across Cedar Creek, a short distance in rear. By this time it was about dark, but Jackson was determined to lose no possible chance.   Favored by a moon but little past the full, he brought forward two fresh brigades, — Field's and Staf-ford's, and Pegram's battery, — crossed the creek, and continued the pursuit.

Banks's corps, however, had, in its retreat, met Ricketts's divi-sion of McDowell's corps, accompanied by Pope in person, and followed also by the leading troops of Sigel's corps.   About one and a half miles beyond Cedar Creek the Confederate advance found itself close in front of a strong line of battle, composed of Ricketts's four brigades, with four batteries of artillery.   Pegram's four guns were pushed to the front, and, at close canister range, opened upon the enemy.   They were replied to by a dozen guns, but continued the action until they were practically cut to pieces.   It was now nearly midnight, and Jackson, having learned from the cavalry of the capture of prisoners from Sigel's corps, was constrained to halt for the night.   By morning he found that the greater part of Pope's army was now united in his front, and that his opportunity to attack the enemy in de-tail had passed, — lost by the bad marching on the 8th.   He still, however, felt able to defeat them if they could be induced to attack him in position, as Pope was pledged to do in his order 75, so he withdrew his line across the creek, and occupied him-self in gleaning the battle-field of arms.   Pope showed too much wisdom to accept the gage of further battle.   Heavy reënforce-ments were coming to him, and it was as clearly his game to await their arrival as it had been Jackson's to anticipate it.   So, on the 11th, he sent in a flag of truce asking permission to bury his dead of the 9th, which were still within Jackson's lines. It was granted, until noon, and then extended until sundown.

On the 12th, finding that Pope would not be tempted to attack him there, he tried another ruse. He fell back from the battlefield, not only to the south side of the Rapidan, where he might easily have halted and maintained himself, but he continued his retreat through Orange C. H. and on to Gordonsville. He hoped that Pope would construe the move as a confession of weakness and would be inspired by it and his own boastings to follow. This strategy was very nearly successful. On Aug. 12, Pope, having heard that the reënforcements under Burnside would soon join him, wired Halleck that, on their arrival, he would cross the Rapidan and advance upon Louisa C. H. This would have given the Confederates the very opportunity desired. On Aug. 13, Lee had ordered Longstreet and Hood, with 12 brigades, to proceed by rail to Gordonsville, and, on the 14th, he also ordered up Anderson's division of infantry, three brigades, and Stuart's cavalry. On the 15th he went up in person and took the command.

The casualties at Cedar Mountain had been as follows: —

| Confederate: | killed 229, | wounded 1047, | missing 31, | total 1307 |
| Federal: | " 314, | " 1445, | " 622, | " 2381 |

The Confederate losses were distributed among nine brigades of infantry and one of cavalry, and were greatest in Garnett's and Taliaferro's, of Jackson's division, slightly over 300 in each. The Federal losses were in eight brigades of infantry and one of cavalry. Crawford's brigade lost 857, Geary's 465, Prince's 452, and Gordon's 344. The fighting upon Jackson's left, where Garnett's and Taliaferro's brigades were broken by the charge of Crawford's and Gordon's brigades, and the line reëstablished, by Branch's, Archer's, and Winder's brigades, was very desperate, as is shown by the casualties of some of the Federal regiments.[1]

---

[1] Gen. Williams, in his official report, says: —

"The 3d Wis., especially, fell under a partial flank fire from the underbrush, and woods, which swept its right companies with great destruction, and under which Lt.-Col. Crane fell pierced with several fatal wounds, and the regiment was obliged to give way. The enemy was, however, driven out of the open field by the other regiments and some distance into the woods,

An incident of the battle was a charge upon Taliaferro's brigade by two squadrons of the 1st Pa. Cav., under Maj. Falls, when the brigade, in some disorder, was pressing hard upon the retreat of the Federal infantry. The charge successfully rode through the Confederate skirmish-line, but was driven back by the fire of the line of battle with the loss of 93 men out of 164.

where, being strongly reënforced, their fire became overwhelming. No better proof of its terrific character can be given than the fact that of the three remaining regiments which continued the charge (28th N.Y., 46th Pa., and 5th Conn.) every field-officer and every adjutant was killed or disabled. In the 28th N.Y., every Company officer was killed or wounded; in the 26th Pa., all but five, and in the 5th Conn. all but eight. A combat more persistent or heroic can scarcely be found in the history of the war, but men, even of this unequalled heroism, could not withstand the overwhelming numbers of the enemy, especially when left without the encouragement and direction of officers."

CHAPTER XI

SECOND MANASSAS

The Situation, Aug. 15. Lee's Plan. How it Failed. A Federal Scouting Party. Pope Escapes. Stuart's Raid. Storm frustrates Efforts Lee plans his Move. Ropes's Criticism. Jackson's March. Aug. 26 Manassas Captured. Destruction of Stores. Pope's Move. Lee and Longstreet's March. Pope Blunders. Jackson's Move. Orders Captured. Johnson's Skirmish. Pope at a Loss. Ewell attacks King. Hard Fighting. Losses. Thoroughfare Gap. Flanking the Gap. The Opposing Forces. Sigel's Attack. Reno's and Kearny's Attack. Hooker's and Reno's Attack. Grover's Brigade. Porter's Corps. Pope *versus* Porter. Kearny and Reno Attack. Longstreet takes Position. Longstreet meets King. Pope is Misled. Lee awaits Attack. The Forces. The Lines. A Surprise. Longstreet comes in. The Henry House Hill. Night and Rain. No Pursuit. Centreville Turned. Affair at Ox Hill. Stevens and Kearny. Casualties. The Ammunition Supply.

GEN. LEE had arrived at Gordonsville early on Aug. 15, and taken command. On the 13th McClellan had abandoned his camp at Harrison's Landing and marched for Fortress Monroe. Lee now left at Richmond but two brigades of infantry to protect the city against cavalry raids, and took the rest of his army to the vicinity of Gordonsville for an aggressive campaign against Pope. He now occupied interior lines between McClellan and Pope, and it behooved him to crush Pope before McClellan's forces could join him. Lee understood this thoroughly, and Halleck and Pope understood it equally well; but Pope, perhaps inspired by his own boast that he was about to "seek the adversary and beat him when he was found," and tempted, also, by Jackson's retreat from Cedar Mountain, had decided to cross the Rapidan and advance upon Louisa C. H. Nothing could have suited Lee's plans better, but Halleck had not taken entire leave of his senses, and he no sooner heard of Pope's design to cross the Rapidan than he promptly forbade it. He also, in another letter, told Pope that he had much better be north of the Rappahannock. Lee's idea of the game the Federals should have played was to retreat to the north side of Bull Run.

Pope's army had now been reënforced by Burnside, and numbered about 52,000 men. Its left flank rested near Raccoon Ford of the Rapidan, some four miles east of Mitchell Station on the O. & A. R. R. His centre was at Cedar Mountain, and his right on Robertson's River, about five miles west of the railroad. He was, therefore, directly opposite Gordonsville, where Jackson's forces had arrived on the 13th.

About two miles below Rapidan Station was a high hill called Clark's Mountain, close to the Rapidan, and giving from its top an extensive view of the flat lands of Culpeper, across the river. A signal station was maintained there, and from it the white tents of the Federal camps, marking out their positions, were plainly visible. Spurs of Clark's Mountain, running parallel to the Rapidan, extended eastward down the river about three miles, to the vicinity of a ford called Somerville's, two miles above Raccoon Ford. Raccoon Ford was within ten miles of Culpeper C. H., almost as near it as the position of Pope's army.

Lee, on arriving about 8 A.M. on the 15th, and learning the details of the situation, lost no time. The topography gave him a beautiful opportunity to mass his army (now about 54,000 men) behind Clark's Mountain, to cross at Somerville Ford, fall upon Pope's left flank and sweep around it with a superior force, cutting off Pope's retreat to Washington. Probably at no time during the war was a more brilliant opportunity put so easily within his grasp. He appreciated it, and promptly issued the necessary orders on the very day of his arrival. His army, however, was not yet sufficiently well organized to be called a "military machine," or to be relied upon to carry out orders strictly. On the contrary, in some respects, it might be called a very "unmilitary" machine, as the history of the failure in this case will illustrate.

Lee, in his report, tells the story very briefly. He says, —

"The movement, as explained in the accompanying order, was appointed for Aug. 18, but the necessary preparations not having been completed, its execution was postponed until the 20th."

This postponement was the fatal act, for on the 18th the enemy discovered his danger, and in great haste put his army in motion to the rear and fell back behind the Rappahannock, during that day and the next.

The principal failure in the preparations was the non-arrival of Fitz-Lee's brigade of cavalry at the appointed rendezvous at Verdiersville, near Raccoon Ford, where it was to cross on the morning of the 18th to act upon the right flank of the army. Its commander had duly received orders from Stuart, but had taken the liberty to delay their execution for a day, not supposing that it would make any material difference. Stuart's report gives the following details: —

"On Aug. 16, 1862, in pursuance of the commanding general's secret instructions, I put this brigade (Fitz-Lee's) on the march for the vicinity of Raccoon Ford, near which point the army under Gen. Lee's command was rapidly concentrating. Gen. Fitzhugh Lee was directed by me to proceed the next day, from near Davenport's Bridge, opposite Beaver Dam, across to the vicinity of Raccoon Ford, where I promised to join him on that evening (17th). I proceeded on the cars directly to the commanding general, whom I found near Orange C. H."

After dark on the 17th Stuart arrived at Verdiersville with his staff, having ridden from Orange C. H., but to his surprise could find or hear nothing of Fitz-Lee's brigade. As it was highly important to communicate with it, he despatched a staff-officer on the road by which the brigade was expected, to find it. Unfortunately, he selected his adjutant-general, Maj. Fitzhugh, who carried Stuart's copy of Lee's order of the 15th, disclosing his plan.

This was careless practice, and some blame must, also, rest upon Stuart, for not having given his orders to Fitz-Lee so explicitly that the latter could neither misunderstand or disobey them. For the latter had deliberately marched on the 17th from near Davenport's Bridge to Louisa C. H. instead of to Verdiersville, as ordered. These three points are very nearly at the angles of an equilateral triangle, with sides of about 20 miles each. Taking his route by Louisa not only occupied two days, but so exhausted his horses that a third day was required to rest them before the proposed movement could be begun.

Fitz-Lee made no official report, but in his life of Gen. Lee refers to this occasion, as follows: —

"The brigade commander [Fitz-Lee] he [Stuart] had expected [at Verdiersville] did not understand from any instructions he had received that it was necessary to be at this point on that particular afternoon, and had marched a little out of his direct road in order to reach his wagons, and get from them a full supply of rations and ammunition."[1]

Such loose practices may occur a hundred times without any serious result, but once in a while the fate of campaigns will be changed by them, and this was such an occasion. A scouting party of Federal cavalry had been sent across Raccoon Ford on the evening of the 17th, and, in the darkness of the night, Maj. Fitzhugh, searching for the lost brigade, rode into it and was captured. His copy of Lee's order was taken from him, and on the 18th was delivered to Pope.

Meanwhile, Stuart and his staff had slept in the porch of a house at Verdiersville, and in the morning had been surprised by the Federal scouting party. All managed to escape, but the enemy secured Stuart's cloak and plumed hat. But the end of the matter was not yet. When no cavalry appeared at Verdiersville, as expected on the night of the 17th, Longstreet ordered two regiments of infantry to be put on picket on the road to Raccoon Ford. The order was brought to Toombs's brigade, when he was absent, visiting a neighboring brigadier. The senior colonel, however, sent out the regiments, and they were duly posted. Not long afterward Toombs, returning, came upon the regiments, and finding them to be a part of his brigade, ordered them back to camp, claiming that no orders should be obeyed from superior officers which did not come through himself. Thus it had happened that the Federal scouting party got within our lines unannounced. When these facts were developed, Longstreet's adjutant, in sword and sash, was sent to place Toombs in arrest. He was afterward ordered to Gordonsville and to confine himself to the limits of the town. After a few days, however, he sent an apology and was restored to duty, followed the army, overtook it, and rejoined his brigade, to their great delight, on Aug. 30, in the heat of the battle of Second Manassas.

[1] Fitz-Lee's *Lee*, p. 183.

When Lee learned of the absence of the cavalry, he at first proposed to defer the attack only a single day. Jackson is said to have urged that it would be best to make no delay at all, but to go ahead with the infantry. But the reports from the signal station on Clark's Mountain represented the enemy as quiet, and Lee decided to wait. Later, a telegraphic despatch from Fitzhugh Lee representing his animals as in bad condition, it was decided to postpone the movement until the 20th, and orders were issued accordingly.

Doubtless, Lee found it hard to believe that Pope, so soon after his boasting order, and still sooner after the "victory" he had claimed at Cedar Mountain, would now turn his back and fly without firing a shot; but, later on that day, there came reports of activity and stir among the enemy's camps, and on the 19th Lee and Longstreet, going up the mountain to see for themselves, saw Pope's whole army march away to the Rappahannock.

On the 20th Lee's advance took place, but although the march was rapidly made in hopes of overtaking some delayed portion of the enemy, the hopes proved vain.

On the north side of the Rappahannock, Pope found such advantages of position that, although for five precious days Lee sought diligently by feints and demonstrations to find a favorable opening, his efforts were vain. But to do nothing was to lose the campaign. By a bold raid of Stuart's, however, Lee now had the good luck to turn the tables and come into possession of Pope's private despatch book, with copies of his most important correspondence with Lincoln, Halleck, and others. Stuart had gotten Lee's permission to try to burn a railroad bridge over Cedar Run, near Catlett's Station, some 12 miles in rear of Pope's army. With about 1500 cavalry and two guns, he crossed the Rappahannock at Waterloo Bridge, above Pope's right flank, on Aug. 22, and pushed on through Warrenton toward Catlett's Station. A terrific rain-storm came on late in the afternoon, and in it the command captured the enemy's picket and surprised the Federal encampments. The night was memorable for black darkness, the time being just at the change of the moon. A negro recognized Stuart and volunteered to lead him to the camp of Pope's staff and baggage. A regiment under W. H. F. Lee raided this camp, while other regiments raided other camps in the vicinity, and a force was sent to burn the bridge. This was impossible on account of the rain, the structure being a two-story trestle. The party had no torpedoes, so a few axes were found and all damage possible was done with them, but it was not serious.

The storm which had prevented Stuart from burning the bridge and hastened his return, also nipped in the bud aggressive operations by both commanders. Jackson, on Lee's left, had crossed Early's brigade at Sulphur Springs, upon an old dam across the river, while his pioneers were repairing the broken bridge for a crossing in force. Pope, upon his own left, had designed to cross the Rappahannock and attack Lee's right flank. The freshet in the river not only called a halt upon both operations, but prevented all the Federal concentrations. Pope made a feeble effort to crush Early's brigade, but it was repulsed, and when a larger force had been brought up by the Federals, Early had withdrawn over the completed bridge.

Meanwhile, the information gained from Pope's correspondence showed Lee that his campaign was to be an utter failure, unless, within the next seven days, he could bring Pope to battle upon open ground. For, already, two of the corps of McClellan's army, the 3d and the 5th, and with Reynolds's Pa. Reserves, in all 20,000 men, were within two days of junction with Pope, and the 2d, 4th, and 6th, with Sturgis's division, and Cox's 7000 men from Kanawha, could not be more than five days later. Lee had but about 55,000 men. In two days Pope would have about 50,000, and in five days more he would have near 130,000. The situation was desperate, and it required a desperate remedy. Two divisions of infantry, — D. H. Hill's and McLaws's, — two brigades under Walker, and a brigade of cavalry under Hampton, which all together would raise Lee's force to 75,000, had been ordered up from Richmond, but could not be expected in time for the present emergency. Immediate action was necessary. It was taken with the quick decision characteristic of Lee.

Jackson, with three divisions of infantry (14 brigades about 22,000) and Stuart's cavalry (two brigades about 2000), set out in light marching order, with no trains but ordnance, ambulances, and a few wagons with cooking utensils, by a roundabout march of over 50 miles, to fall upon Pope's depot of supplies at Manassas Junction, 24 miles in Pope's rear, and only 26 miles from Alexandria. Lee, with Longstreet and about 30,000 men, would hold the line of the Rappahannock, and occupy Pope's attention, while Jackson was making his forced march. Lee's army, then, of 55,000, would be split in half, and Pope's army of about 80,000 would be about midway between the two halves. Any military student would pronounce such a situation absolutely ruinous to the divided army.

In his *History of the Civil War*, Mr. Ropes writes of Lee's strategy : —

" The disparity between Pope's force and that of Jackson is so enormous that it is impossible not to be amazed at the audacity of the confederate general, in thus risking an encounter in which the very existence of Jackson's command would be imperilled, and to ask what was the object which Gen. Lee considered as warranting such an extremely dangerous manœuvre. The answer is not an easy one. . . . We shall . . . only remark here that this move of Gen. Lee's in dividing his army, was an illustration of the daring, not to say hazardous, policy which he pursued in this summer of 1862."

The best answer is the one given by Lee himself, who is reported in Allan's *Army of Northern Virginia* to have said, in referring to some discussion of this matter, —

"Such criticism is obvious, but the disparity of force between the contending forces rendered the risks unavoidable."

It was scarcely 60 days since Ives, as has been told, stopped his horse in the road to say to me, —

"If there is a man in either army, head and shoulders above all others in audacity, that man is Lee, and you will live to see it."

There has been speculation whether this turning movement originated with Lee or Jackson. Lee's report only says, —

" In pursuance of the plan of operations determined upon, Jackson was directed on the 25th to cross above Waterloo," etc.

Jackson's report says, —

"Pursuing the instructions of the commanding general, I left Jeffersonton on the morning of the 25th," etc.

The most natural supposition would ascribe the plan to Lee. His own words would seem to confirm the supposition, and Jackson's form of expression to indorse it.

Col. Henderson, who would certainly assert a claim for Jackson, if it were possible, has written:[1] —

"It is only certain that we have record of few enterprises of greater daring than that which was there decided on; and no matter from whose brain it emanated, on Lee fell the burden of the responsibility. It is easy to conceive. It is less easy to execute, but to risk cause and country, name and reputation, on a single throw, and to abide the issue with unflinching heart, is the supreme exhibition of the soldier's fortitude."

Early on Aug. 25, Jackson set out upon what Henderson calls "his most famous march." He marched 26 miles that day, and bivouacked very late that night at Salem. His course was first northwest to Amissville, and thence about north to Salem. As his march was intended to be a surprise, it had been favored by the storm of the 23d. This tended to prevent large columns of dust, which so great a movement would surely have raised in dry weather. Considering the object of the march, it was a mistake to allow the infantry regiments to carry their banners displayed. For the country was moderately flat, and was dominated on the east by the Bull Run Mountains; upon which it was to be expected the enemy would have scouts and signal stations. This was actually the case, and the march of the column was observed by 8 A.M. on the 25th, and it was watched for 15 miles, and fair estimates were made of its strength from counting the regimental flags and the batteries. It was plainly seen that their immediate destination was Salem.

This information was promptly communicated to Pope, Halleck, and the leading generals, who began to guess what the movement meant. Naturally, no one guessed correctly; for the simple reason that no one could imagine that Lee would deliberately place his army in a position where Pope could deal with the two halves of it separately. It was correctly guessed that the troops marching to Salem were Jackson's, but Pope supposed them to be on their way to the Valley and probably covering the flank of Lee's main body, which might be on their left moving upon Front Royal.

[1] S. J. II., 124.

He has been justly blamed for not ordering a strong reconnoissance to develop the true state of affairs. His proper move
at the time, as, indeed, it had been for some days, was to fall back
with his whole army to Manassas. He would, perhaps, have done
this but that Halleck had ordered him to hold especially the
lower Rappahannock, covering Falmouth, and to "fight like the
devil."

On the 26th, Jackson marched at dawn, and now the head of his
column was turned to the east, and his men knew where they were
going. In front of them was Thoroughfare Gap, through the Bull
Run Mountains, which debouched upon the heart of the enemy's
territory, held by six times their numbers. A march of about
20 miles brought Jackson to Gainesville, on the Warrenton and
Alexandria pike, by mid-afternoon. Here he was overtaken
by Stuart with the cavalry. These had skirmished at Waterloo
Bridge all day of the 25th, and marched at 2 A.M. on the 26th
to follow Jackson's route. Near Salem, finding the roads blocked
by Jackson's artillery and trains, they had left the roads, and with
skilful guides had found passes through the Bull Run Mountains, without going through Thoroughfare Gap. Here Jackson,
instead of marching directly upon Manassas Junction, where
Pope's depot of supplies was located, took the road to Bristoe
Station, seven miles south of Manassas. There the railroad
was crossed by Broad Run. Jackson designed to destroy the
bridge and place a force in position to delay the enemy's approach, while he burned the supplies at Manassas. The head of
Ewell's column reached Bristoe about sunset, having marched
about 25 miles.

So far, during this whole day, no report of Jackson's march had
reached the Federals. Now, a train of empty cars, running the
gantlet of a hot fire and knocking some cross-ties off the track,
escaped going to Manassas, and gave the alarm. While Ewell's
division took position to hold off the enemy, Gen. Trimble
volunteered, with two regiments, the 21st Ga. and 21st
N.C., to march back and capture Manassas, before it could be
reënforced from Alexandria.

Proceeding cautiously in line of battle, it was nearly midnight
when these troops were fired upon with artillery from the Ma-

nassas works. Losing only 15 wounded, they charged the lines, and took them with eight guns. Our cavalry, following the movement, gathered 300 prisoners. Next morning Jackson came up with Taliaferro's and Hill's divisions at an early hour, and, about the same time, a Federal brigade, sent by rail from Alexandria, advanced from Bull Run in line of battle, expecting to drive off a raid of cavalry. Had the Confederates restrained their impatience, and permitted the enemy to approach, the whole brigade might have been captured. But their artillery could not resist the temptation to open upon the unsuspecting advance, and it retreated so rapidly that, although it was pursued for some miles, its whole loss was but 135 killed and wounded, and 204 prisoners. The Federal general, Taylor, was killed.

The Federal and sutler's supplies stored at Manassas presented a sight to the ragged and half-starved Confederates, such as they had never before imagined. Not only were there acres of warehouses filled to overflowing, but loaded cars covered about two miles of side-tracks, and great quantities of goods were stacked in regular order in the open fields, under tarpaulin covers. The supplies embraced everything eatable, drinkable, wearable, or usable, and in immense profusion. During the day, Jackson turned his men loose to feast and help themselves. At night, after astonishing their palates with real coffee, with cheese, sardines, and champagne, and improving their underwear, apparel, and footgear, and filling their haversacks, the torch was systematically applied. When Pope next day looked upon the ashes, he must have felt that it was bad advice, when he said, "Let us study the probable lines of retreat of our opponents and leave our own to take care of themselves."

Meanwhile, at Bristoe, Ewell had been unmolested until near three o'clock. About that time he was attacked by Hooker's division. This Pope had sent to develop the situation at Manassas, of which he was as yet not informed. Hooker had only about 5500 men, — less than Ewell had at hand, — but his attack was so vigorous that the latter, whose orders were not to bring on a general engagement, after an hour's fighting, withdrew across Broad Run (having fought on the south side) and marched to join Jackson at Manassas, without being followed.

Jackson had now accomplished the first object of his expedition — the destruction of the Manassas Depot. Pope would have to abandon his line on the Rappahannock, and would, of course, move at once to crush Jackson. A Napoleon, in his place, might have cut loose from his base and marched upon Richmond, leaving Lee to wreck his army on the fortified lines around Washington, but Pope was no Napoleon. When he realized the situation, however, his first orders were very judicious, a safer play if less brilliant than a Napoleonic advance upon Richmond would have been. He ordered the two corps of McDowell and Sigel, with Reynolds's division, about 40,000 men, to Gainesville. In support of them, to Greenwich, he sent Heintzelman with three divisions. Hooker was sent to Bristoe to attack Ewell, with Porter marching to support him. Banks, in the rear, protected the trains. The best part of all of these orders was the occupation of Gainesville with a strong force, for Gainesville was directly between Jackson and Longstreet. It behooved Pope to prevent any possible junction between these two, and now on the night of the 27th at Gainesville he held the key to the whole position.

But, unfortunately for Pope, as yet he had no conception that Lee, with Longstreet's corps, would be hurrying to throw himself into the lion's den by the side of Jackson. He seems to have thought that his effort should be to "bag Jackson," rather than to keep him from uniting with Lee.

Let us now turn to Lee and Longstreet. On the 26th, Jackson having about a day and a half the start, Longstreet's corps set out to follow. One division, Anderson's, of four brigades, was left at Sulphur Springs, in observation of the enemy, while the remaining 17 brigades, somewhat loosely organized into about five divisions, say 25,000 men, were put in motion to follow in Jackson's track. Lee rode with this command, and they bivouacked for the night near Orleans. At dawn on the 27th the march was resumed. He was delayed at Salem by some cavalry demonstrations from the direction of Warrenton, and, having no cavalry, he went into bivouac at White Plains, having marched about 18 miles.

I have already told of the course of events having been twice

modified in this campaign, by the commanders coming into possession of their rival's plans or orders, by virtue of some accident,
and there is yet to tell of other similar occurrences. Besides
these there was also a narrow escape from capture by Lee
himself. A Confederate quartermaster, on the morning of the
27th, was riding some distance ahead of Longstreet's column on
the march northward from Orleans. Approaching Salem, he suddenly came upon the head of a Federal squadron. He turned and
took to flight, and the squadron, breaking into a gallop, pursued
him.   Within a short distance the fugitive came upon
Lee with some ten or twelve staff-officers and couriers. He
yelled out as he approached, "The Federal cavalry are upon you,"
and almost at the same instant, the head of the galloping
squadron came into view, only a few hundred yards away. It
was a critical moment, but the staff-officers acted with good
judgment. Telling the general to ride rapidly to the rear, they
formed a line across the road and stood, proposing to delay the
Federals until Lee could gain a safe distance. This regular
formation deceived the enemy into the belief that it was the head
of a Confederate squadron. They halted, gazed for a while, and
then, wheeling about, turned back, never dreaming of the prize
so near.

On the night of the 27th, while Jackson is burning Manassas,
Lee and Longstreet are in bivouac at White Plains, 24 miles west
and beyond Thoroughfare Gap, while McDowell, Sigel, and Reynolds are about Gainsville, directly between them. In this situation, the game is in Pope's hands, but, as already said, instead
of trying to keep Lee and Jackson apart, his ambition is to make
short work of Jackson, who, he probably supposed, would fight in
the earthworks around Manassas. In some such belief, during
the night he issued further orders. All of his forces were ordered
to march upon Manassas at dawn on the 28th. This is the order
which lost Pope his campaign.

It is now time to return to Jackson. He knew that Lee and
Longstreet were coming, and his most obvious move, perhaps,
would have been to march for Thoroughfare Gap by some route
which would avoid McDowell at Gainesville. His movement,
however, had not been made solely to destroy the depot at

Manassas. That was but the first step necessary to get Pope out of his strong position. Now it was necessary to bring him to battle quickly, but in detail. His decision was a master-piece of strategy, unexcelled during the war, and the credit of it seems solely due to Jackson himself.

Soon after nightfall Taliaferro's division was started on the road toward Sudley's Ford of Bull Run, to cross the Warrenton turn-pike and bivouac in the woods north of Groveton. A. P. Hill's division was sent by the Blackburn's Ford road to Centreville. After midnight, Ewell, who had arrived from Bristoe and gotten some supplies, followed Hill across Bull Run. Then he turned up the stream, and made his way on the north side to the Stone Bridge. This he crossed and made a junction with Taliaferro's division. Hill remained at Centreville until about 10 A.M., when he moved down the Warrenton turnpike, also crossed at Stone Bridge, and, moving up toward Sudley, took position on Jack-son's left. His march and Ewell's were each about 14 miles. The wagon-trains all went with Taliaferro's division, which marched about nine miles. The sending of two divisions across Bull Run was doubtless to be in position to interpose if Pope attempted to move past him toward Alexandria. Perhaps, also, it had in it the idea of misleading the enemy, for it certainly had that desirable effect. It happened that a part of Stuart's cavalry, which was on that flank, during the morning raided Burke's Station on the railroad, only 12 miles from Alexandria. This, with the reported presence of Hill at Centreville, entirely misled Pope as to Jackson's true location.

Early on the 28th, two Federal couriers were captured, bearing important orders. Those of the first were from McDowell to Sigel, directing him to march to Manassas Junction. This order was taken to Jackson, and he seems to have interpreted the movement to mean that Pope was about to retreat to Alex-andria, for he at once sent orders to A. P. Hill, at Centreville, to move down to the fords of Bull Run to intercept the enemy. But, fortunately, the other captured courier bore orders from Pope to McDowell, ordering the formation of his line of battle for the next day on Manassas plains, and these orders, being brought to Hill, he appreciated that the enemy was not retreating and that it would be dangerous to separate his division from the other two. So, as has been told, about 10 A.M. he marched to join them.

Though it was Jackson's desire now to conceal his whereabouts until Longstreet was near, yet one of his brigadiers, Col. Johnson, came near, bringing the force which was now marching from Gainesville toward Manasses, down upon the right flank of Taliaferro's and Ewell's divisions. Johnson, with two guns, was on a high hill, a little out from Jackson's extreme right. He saw the head of a column, and skirmishers advancing, as he thought, upon his position. It was the head of Reynolds's division, on McDowell's left, straightening itself out for its prescribed march to Manassas, ten miles to the southeast. Johnson opened fire upon them with his guns. The enemy promptly deployed his column, advanced skirmishers, and brought into action a superior force of artillery, on which Johnson abandoned his hill and withdrew his small force to Jackson's lines. The enemy's skirmishers advanced and occupied the hill, but the Confederate force was now nowhere to be seen. So it was supposed that the affair was only a demonstration by some reconnoitring party, and, after caring for a few killed and wounded, the division marched for Manassas, where it was still supposed that Jackson was awaiting them.

The Federal marches were not rapid, and it was not until near noon that Pope himself arrived at Manassas, and found that Jackson had mysteriously vanished. He was utterly at a loss to guess where he had gone. His first supposition was that he had gone toward Leesburg, and he ordered McDowell to move to Gum Springs in pursuit. He soon countermanded that order, and hearing of Hill's having been at Centreville, and of the cavalry attack upon Burke's station, he ordered a general concentration of his troops at Centreville. This was his last order for that day, and all was now quiet for some hours. Jackson and his three divisions lay hidden in the woods within seven miles of the ruins of Manassas, until 5 P.M. At that hour King's division of McDowell's corps,—four brigades about 10,000 strong, with four batteries,—appeared upon the Warrenton pike, in front of Jackson's ambush, marching toward Centreville in pursuance of

Pope's order. King had been marching from Gainesville to Manassas, and Pope's orders had intercepted the march and changed its direction. Jackson, about a mile from the road, might have remained hidden and allowed King to pass. Had he known that, at that moment, Lee and Longstreet were still beyond Thoroughfare Gap, and that Ricketts's division of Mc-Dowell's corps was at the gap, one might suppose that he would hesitate to disclose himself. But if Pope was allowed to withdraw behind Bull Run, the result of the whole campaign would be merely to force Pope into an impregnable position. It was the fear of this which led Jackson to attack King immediately, even though he knew that it would draw upon him Pope's whole force.

Leaving Hill's division in position on his left (holding the road to Aldie by which he might retreat in case of emergency), Jackson formed a double line of battle, with Taliaferro's division on the right and Ewell's on the left. Taliaferro (W.B.) had in his front line from left to right the old Stonewall brigade, now under Baylor, and that of A. B. Taliaferro, and in rear the brigade of Starke. His fourth brigade under Bradley Johnson was detached and in observation near Groveton. Ewell had in his front line Lawton's and Trimble's brigades, and in his second Early's and Forno's,—in all about 8000 infantry. Orders were sent for 20 pieces of artillery, but owing to difficulties of the ground only two small batteries arrived in time to be engaged. These were isolated and could not be maintained against the superior metal of the enemy. King's division, not dreaming of the proximity of the enemy, was marching down the pike with only a small advanced guard and a few skirmishers in front. The brigades were in the following order: Hatch's, Gibbon's, Doubleday's, Patrick's.

The action which now ensued was somewhat remarkable in several features. It was fought principally by the brigadiers on each side. McDowell, in command of the Federal corps, was absent, having gone to find Pope and have a personal conference. The division commander, King, was absent, sick at Gainesville, only about two miles off. Ewell and Taliaferro (W.B.), the two Confederate major-generals, were both seriously wounded, Ewell losing his leg. Probably, for these reasons, less than a half of either force was brought into the brunt of the action. When this had developed itself, Jackson ordered Ewell's second line, Early and Forno, to turn the enemy's right flank. In the darkness, they were unable to make their way in time through the woods, and across the deep cuts and high fills of an unfinished railroad, stretching from near Sudley's Ford toward Gainesville. The fighting, meanwhile, had ceased. The notable part of this action was fought by Gibbon's brigade of three Wisconsin regiments, and one Indiana reënforced by two regiments of Doubleday's,—the 56th Pa. and the 76th N.Y.,—in all about 3000 men.   Opposed was Taliaferro's front line of two brigades (A. G. Taliaferro's on the right, and the Stonewall brigade, now only about 600 strong, under Baylor, on the left) with some help also from Ewell's front line of Lawton's brigade, and Trimble's. These troops were all veteran infantry, and it is to be noted that the decidedly smaller force of the Federals had never before been seriously engaged.   They had, indeed, the great aid and support of two excellent batteries, but their desperate infantry fight, attested by their losses, illustrates the high state of efficiency to which troops may be brought solely by drill and discipline. It may be a sort of mechanical valor which is imparted by long-trained obedience to military commands, but it has its advantages, even though there may be appreciable differences in it from the more personal courage inspired by a loved cause.

A good idea of this contest is given in the official report of Gen. W. B. Taliaferro :—

"At this time our lines were advanced from the woods in which they had been concealed to the open field. The troops moved forward with splendid gallantry and in most perfect order. Twice our lines were advanced until we had reached a farm-house and orchard on the right of our line, and were within 80 yards of a greatly superior force of the enemy. Here one of the most terrific conflicts that can be conceived of occurred. Our troops held the farm-house and one edge of the orchard, while the enemy held the orchard and the enclosure next to the turnpike. To our left there was no cover, and our men stood in the open field without cover of any kind. The enemy, although reënforced, never once attempted to advance upon our position, but withstood with great determination the terrible fire which our lines poured upon them. For two hours and a half, without an instant's cessation of the most deadly discharges of musketry, round shot and shell, both lines stood unmoved, neither advancing and neither broken or yielding until at last, about nine o'clock at night, the. enemy slowly and sullenly fell back and yielded the field to our victorious troops."

Separate returns for this action were made only for Lawton's and Trimble's brigades. Only partial statements for the other commands are found in the few official reports. Of many commands there are no reports, owing to the number of commanding officers who were killed or disabled in succeeding battles. The returns of Lawton's and Trimble's brigades are as follows: —

	KILLED		WOUNDED		MISSING	AGGREGATE
	OFFICERS	MEN	OFFICERS	MEN	MEN	
Lawton's	8	105	23	273	5	414
Trimble's	8	82	12	202	6	310
Total	16	187	35	375	11	724

The Stonewall brigade, out of its small force of 600 muskets, lost three colonels, two majors, and over 200 men, killed and wounded. Taliaferro's brigade lost a lieutenant-colonel and two majors. Its other casualties were probably about 100. Gibbon's brigade, out of 2300 men, lost about 750, and Doubleday's two regiments, about 800 strong, lost about 350. Hatch's brigade, from the front, and Patrick's from the rear, were not engaged, partly because of the length to which the marching column had been strung out upon the march, and partly, perhaps, because of the absence of Gen. King. But he came upon hearing of the action, and at 1 A.M. on the 29th, by his order, the division was put in motion for Manassas Junction. He thought himself in the presence of superior forces, and decided that it was best to get nearer to reënforcements.

It is now time to return to Lee and Longstreet, who bivouacked between White Plains and Thoroughfare Gap rather early in the afternoon of the 27th. Scouts sent ahead by Longstreet reported the Gap clear, and messages were received from Jackson that he was in ambush upon the Warrenton road. To make sure of the passage through Thoroughfare Gap, D. R. Jones's division was sent forward to occupy it. The Gap is a narrow pass, only 80 yards in width, bounded on the north by basaltic cliffs over 200 feet in height and on the south by steep hills, rocky, and covered with vines and undergrowth. A small force in possession could hold the pass against any front attack. As Jones's column drew near the Gap, officers riding ahead discovered the approach of a large Federal force. It was Ricketts's division, sent by McDowell upon his own responsibility, to prevent the advance of reënforcements to Jackson. It was a move which, quickly made and strongly backed, might have brought victory to the Federals.

Jones deployed the 9th Ga. of Anderson's brigade, and sent them through the Gap. They met and drove back the Federal pickets, until, meeting heavier forces with artillery, they were themselves driven into the Gap, where the whole brigade formed, and essayed to scale the mountain on the left. This was only possible at a few places, but the 1st Ga. succeeded and got into a good position, and repulsed with loss an attack by the enemy who came so near that some were killed by pistol fire of the officers.

Meanwhile, Benning, commanding Toombs's brigade, was ordered to occupy the mountain on the right of the pass. He started off at the double-quick, through a hot fire of artillery, and after a stiff climb occupied the crest just in time to repulse the enemy advancing upon it from the other side.

Sharp skirmishing took place until dark. Jones's division had no artillery, and it could only oppose the enemy's by selecting men armed with rifled muskets, and sending them as skirmishers to pick off the cannoneers and horses; yet this was done so successfully that the enemy's batteries were often compelled to move, and Ricketts speaks of his total losses as "severe." Jones's total casualties were "about 25."

One great disadvantage under which the whole Confederate army was still laboring at this period was that most of its arms were the old "calibre 69," smooth-bore musket, using the round ball with effective range of only about 200 yards. When Benning collected from two regiments all rifled muskets, he got only about 30 from the 20th Ga., and 10 or 12 from the 2d Ga.

When the enemy's heavy fire of artillery disclosed his force in front of the Gap, Longstreet at once took measures to turn the position. Hood, with his two brigades, was ordered to cross the mountain by a cattle trail a short distance to the north, and Wilcox's division of three brigades was ordered to force a passage, if necessary, through Hopewell Gap, three miles to the north.

Both of these flank movements were accomplished during the night, but Ricketts had decided not to wait. He had been so discouraged by his reception, that he scarcely waited until nightfall to start back to Gainesville; and at daylight next morning, having learned that King's division had fallen back to Manassas, Ricketts took the road to Bristoe.

The departure of the enemy from their front at dark on the 27th was observed by the Confederates, and on the morning of the 28th the remainder of Jones's division marched through the Gap, and was joined by Hood and Wilcox from their respective routes by the cattle trail and Hopewell Gap. By noon Lee and Longstreet had arrived at Gainesville, and connected with Jackson, and the second great step in Lee's strategy had been successfully accomplished. The third and last, also, by that time was in a fair way of accomplishment, for Pope, instead of concentrating his forces behind Bull Run, had taken the offensive, and had already begun his attack upon Jackson. Of that action it is now to tell.

Jackson's whereabouts had been disclosed to Pope by the attack upon King's division, but Pope failed to note that Jackson was the aggressor. He supposed that King had intercepted Jackson in an effort to escape through Thoroughfare Gap. His available forces, on the morning of the 29th, were as follows: —

On Bull Run, two miles east of Jackson, were Sigel's corps, three divisions, and Milroy's independent brigade, together about 11,000 strong, and Reynolds's division of Pa. Reserves, about 8000, with 14 batteries. At Centreville, seven miles to the northeast, were the three divisions of Hooker, Kearny, and Reno, about 18,000. About seven miles to the southeast at Manassas, and between there and Bristoe were the corps of McDowell and Porter, about 27,000,—in all about 64,000.

Jackson's forces, now about 18,000 infantry, with 40 guns, were formed along the unfinished railroad line, which stretched south from Sudley's Ford to the Warrenton pike, about three miles. Of this the two miles nearest Sudley were held in force; the rest by skirmishers, except that the right flank, on the Warrenton pike, was held by Early's and Forno's brigades of Ewell's division. The left of the line was held by A. P. Hill's strong division of six brigades. In front of the extreme left was wide, open ground for a half mile. Then came about a mile of wood from 200 to 600 yards wide, and then again the open, rolling fields. Hill's division was formed in three lines of battle, with 16 guns to command the open ground in his front.

Ewell's division, now under Lawton, held the centre, with the brigades of Lawton and Trimble, in two lines. Taliaferro's division, now commanded by Starke, held the right, formed in three lines of battle, with 24 guns massed to fire over the open ground in front.

Pope was not obliged to fight — certainly not to take the offensive. He might have withdrawn across Bull Run, and awaited the arrival, within two or three days, of Sumner's and Franklin's corps and Cox's division. If he did fight, he would have stood a fair chance of success, had he first massed his army, and concentrated its power in united effort, with reserves to follow up every success. But he was sure to lose if he allowed his divisions to fight in piecemeal.

As Jackson was forming his lines at sunrise, Sigel's and Reynolds's columns were visible, nearly two miles away, deploying for the attack. Sigel held the right, with three divisions, supported by Milroy's brigade. Reynolds held the left. The enemy's line was not parallel to Jackson's, their right being nearest to Jackson's left, and their left somewhat retired. About seven o'clock the enemy's batteries were brought forward and opened fire. Their skirmishers were advanced, and the lines of battle followed. On the right and the left of Groveton wood (the wood in front of Jackson's left centre), the Confederate batteries, having fair play, held back the enemy's advance. Opposite the wood the enemy encountered only skirmish fire, and they easily entered. But when they approached the Confederate line of battle and met its fire, the conflict was short and the Federals retreated, Gregg's brigade following them. Milroy's brigade came to their help, but Thomas's brigade came to Gregg's, and the Federals were driven completely through the wood and pursued by the Confederate fire as they retreated across the fields.

This much was over by 10.30 A.M. The best of Pope's opportunity would be lost by 1 P.M., for by that hour Longstreet's troops would be on hand. But now Reno and Kearny, from Centreville, were beginning to come upon the field, and Sigel, calling upon Reno for reënforcements, again made a desperate assault, which reached the Confederate line in such strength as to necessitate the calling up of Branch's brigade from Hill's third line. With this brigade the wood was again cleared and Sigel's divisions were practically put *hors du combat*. It was now about noon, and Pope, who had been at Centreville, not realizing the size of the affair near Groveton, arrived upon the field. He immediately organized a fresh attack with the three divisions of Kearny, Hooker, and Reno. Had he awaited their arrival before wrecking Sigel in vain efforts, his chances would have been better.

These three divisions made their assault about one o'clock. As before, the division on the extreme right, Kearny's, was held off by the 16 guns firing over the open ground on Jackson's left. The other two divisions came through the wood, and this time portions of the assaulting column actually crossed the railroad line, and fierce hand-to-hand fighting ensued, the brunt of it falling upon Field's and Thomas's brigades. Field was severely wounded; but Pender's brigade, from Hill's third line, joining in the mêlée, the Federals were again borne back, and again pursued, not only through the wood, but out into the open ground beyond, where Pender incautiously followed. Here he met a hot fire of artillery, and fell back to the woods.

On seeing his retreat, Grover's brigade of Hooker's division, being in reserve, was sent forward for a counterstroke. Advancing slowly through the wood, it gave a volley and then rushed the somewhat disorganized Confederate line, and carried a considerable space.   Had they had prompt and ample support, victory was within their grasp.

By this time, Longstreet's troops had connected with Jackson's extreme right, relieving the brigades of Early and Forno.   These had been brought from their isolated position on the right flank, and placed in the rear of the centre.   Jackson had seen Grover's advance, and now sent Forno's Louisianians and a regiment of Lawton's Georgians to the onset.   Johnson's and Starke's brigades were also brought to fire upon Grover's left flank.   So, caught in the whirlwind of fire which burst upon him in the high tide of his success, Grover was swept back across the line and out of the wood, and driven beyond the Warrenton pike, with a loss of one-fourth of his command.

Four determined assaults had now been made through the Groveton wood, and each had met with a bloody repulse.   At least 4000 Federals had fallen in them.   Not one attack had had any chance of success, for each had been made with too few men; but the continuous fighting from 7 A.M. until 4 P.M., had also thinned the Confederate lines, and had greatly reduced the ammunition supply of many of the brigades.   There was now a lull in the battle for a while, during which many Confederates collected cartridges from the bodies of the fallen.   On the right and left of the Groveton wood the fighting had been largely of artillery, or musketry, at long range, and there had been no actual collisions.

Pope had been very sanguine in the morning that he was about to "bag Jackson," and he was now unwilling to give up the effort, while the sun was still high above the horizon, and while he still had comparatively fresh troops.   Kearny's three brigades opposite the open ground on Hill's left, had had no close fighting, and Reno's two brigades were also in good condition. Besides these, he looked for help from Porter's corps, and from King's and Ricketts's divisions of McDowell's corps.   Ricketts could have been with him, but for his blunder in the morning, when he took the road to Bristoe on learning that King had fallen back to Manassas.   Thus, Jackson's attack upon King had produced the effect of keeping two divisions out of the next day's fight. As to Porter, there is much interesting history which can only be briefly summarized here.

Porter, in the Seven Days, had proved himself not only a hard fighter, but a skilful commander. He would have made a good leader of an army; but he had a low opinion of Pope, and, in his correspondence with brother officers about this period, did not conceal it. It so happened that, under Pope's orders, Porter's corps had that morning marched from Bristoe by Manassas for Gainesville. Now, at 4.30 P.M., supposing Porter in position at Gainesville, Pope sent him peremptory orders to immediately attack Jackson's right flank.

But Porter was not at Gainesville. When, about 11.30 A.M., he reached a little stream called Dawkins Branch, about three and a half miles short of Gainesville, he found Confederate cavalry in his front. He deployed a brigade in line of battle, and, advancing a strong skirmish-line, captured some of Longstreet's scouts. Meanwhile, clouds of dust, extending back 10 miles to Thoroughfare Gap, indicated that a large force was arriving at Gainesville. Stuart, to notify Jackson of his approach, had made some cavalry drag brush in the roads. Nevertheless, Porter prepared to force his way. He deployed his corps of two divisions in two lines, and advanced a brigade across the stream. King's division, which was marching in rear of Porter, closed up, but remained in column. About this time McDowell came upon the field and remonstrated with Porter, saying, "You are too far out; this is no place to fight a battle."

As McDowell ranked Porter, when their troops were together, McDowell was in command. Just before meeting Porter, he had learned that at 8.45 that morning 17 regiments of Confederate infantry and a battery had passed, marching down the Warrenton road toward Groveton. After some reconnoissance, McDowell decided to leave Porter where he was, and to take King back to a road by which he could reach the left flank of Reynolds's division, now engaged with Jackson's right. Ricketts's division, returning from its march to Bristoe, was now following King, but both divisions were exhausted by from 12 to 18 hours' marchings. When McDowell left, with King and Ricketts, Porter considered himself too weak to venture an attack upon the Confederates in his front. His force was only between 9000 and 10,000. He had no reënforcements at hand and he had in his front Longstreet's corps of nearly 25,000. His course was proper, and his threatening position practically neutralized an equal number of the Confederates, for D. R. Jones's division of three brigades, and Wilcox's of three, were each deployed and held in observation of Porter all the afternoon.

Pope, having sent his order to Porter to attack at 4.30, waited a half-hour to allow time for the message to reach Porter, and at five ordered Kearny and Reno with their five brigades to attack Jackson's left. To finish with Porter first: The 4.30 order did not reach him until about 6.30. He at once ordered his leading division, Morell's, to advance, but before the necessary arrangements could be made, darkness had come on, and he was compelled to abandon the idea of attacking. For this, and some other minor incidents, Pope, soon after the battle, preferred charges against Porter. He was tried, and on Jan. 10, 1863, was convicted of violations of articles of war, and sentenced to dismissal from the army, and to be disqualified from ever again holding office under the United States.

Thus was the Federal army deprived of the services of one among its officers of the very highest type. The ex-Federal Confederates who had known Porter considered this result as one of the best fruits of their victory. The gist of the charges against Porter lay in Pope's claim that Longstreet's troops had not reached Gainesville until late in the afternoon, and that Porter could have fallen upon Jackson's exposed right flank. After the war, when official reports of the Confederates were published, the actual facts became so notorious that, in 1878, the proceedings of the court were reviewed by a board appointed by the President. They found the facts and recommended the remission of Porter's sentence, though condemning the terms in which Porter had criticised Pope, in his correspondence above referred to. This report of the board was referred to Congress, which took no action. Finally on May 4, 1882, President Arthur remitted the sentence.

From this digression let us return to the attack at 5 P.M. on the 29th, by the two divisions of Kearny and Reno with their five brigades. Like the four preceding attacks, it is a predestined failure, for it is another case of a boy sent upon a man's errand. But, unlike the previous efforts, this gained a temporary success over the thin brigades of A. P. Hill, which had repelled all the preceding ones, and was now poorly supplied with ammunition. Here the thin lines were overrun by the superior numbers, in a very gallant and persistent attack. Hill's troops were forced back so far that Pope believed that Jackson's left "was doubled back upon his centre." He ordered King's division, which McDowell had now brought upon the field, to advance down the Pike and fall upon Jackson's right, where, too, he was momentarily expecting Porter to attack.

But Hill, though forced back for perhaps 300 yards, was not broken, and was still making a desperate fight, when, to his aid, came Early's and Lawton's brigades. The Federals were in disorder, and the fresh Confederate line had an easy victory, driving the enemy and pursuing them far across the railroad, before it could be halted and brought back. Meanwhile, King's division, though worn by its march to Manassas and back since 1 A.M. of the previous night, had advanced boldly down the Warrenton pike, stimulated by Pope's "flattering tale" that Jackson was "doubled back upon his centre."

Now we must take up the story of Longstreet's corps to explain the genesis of the sixth and last combat of the day. Like all the preceding, it, too, was made by an insufficient force. Longstreet, on his arrival, had formed his line, not in prolongation of Jackson's, but inclining forward, making a large obtuse angle. A few of his guns were pushed to the front, firing upon the left of Reynolds's line, and assisting Jackson's right in keeping Reynolds's from coming to close quarters. At the extreme right Jones's division was bent back, almost at right angles, to oppose a front to Porter's corps, and Wilcox's three brigades were held in reserve behind Jones.

Now that his army was again united, Lee was inclined to engage at once, but Longstreet asked to be allowed first to make a personal reconnoissance. After making one, occupying an hour, he reported adversely on account of the easy approach open on his right to large Federal forces reported to be at Manassas. Lee was not satisfied with this report, and recurred to the idea of attacking down the turnpike. It was now so late in the afternoon, however, that Longstreet suggested making only a reconnoissance in force, reserving the attack until dawn next morning, and to this Lee agreed.

Accordingly, Hood's and Evans's brigades were ordered to advance for the reconnoissance, and Wilcox's division was withdrawn from the rear of Jones, as a support to the movement.

Thus it happened that when King's division advanced, expecting to find Jackson in retreat, it met Longstreet advancing. The fight which ensued was prolonged until 9 P.M. It was fierce and bloody, but the first half-hour of it converted King's advance into a retreat. He. was pursued until he found refuge in the heavy lines holding the high ground about Pope's centre, with the loss of a gun, several flags, and some prisoners. Longstreet then withdrew his attacking brigades back to the ground from which they had advanced. It had happened also that, although Jackson had been entirely successful on the left, his victorious troops, being withdrawn from the pursuit, had not halted at the railroad cut, — their line during the day, — but had been carried back to a line a short distance in rear, selected by Jackson. Thus, on both flanks, the Federals, although defeated, were left during the night with deserted battle-fields in their front. They discovered the fact before midnight, and this discovery proved to Pope a fatal delusion and a snare. Had it been a deliberate ruse, it would have been a masterpiece. Pope thought it could have but one meaning — that the Confederates were retreating toward Thoroughfare Gap. At daybreak he had wired Halleck as follows : —

"We fought a terrific battle here yesterday, with combined forces of the enemy, which lasted with continuous firing from daylight until dark, by which time the enemy was driven from the field which we now occupy. The enemy is still in our front, but badly used up. We lost not less than 8000 killed and wounded, but from the appearance of the field, the enemy lost at least two to one. The news has just reached me from the front that the enemy is retreating toward the mountains."

Pope clearly believed this story on the insufficient evidence before him, and this error made him the aggressor next morning and cost him the battle, as we shall see.

The object of the Confederate advance on the afternoon of the 29th, as we have seen, was a reconnoissance preparatory to an attack at dawn, which Longstreet had suggested as better than one so late in the afternoon. Hood and Evans had been charged to examine the enemy's positions carefully, and to report as to the feasibility of the morning attack. About midnight reports were brought, by each, adverse to making it. Upon these reports Lee decided to stand his ground for the day, and see if the enemy would attack. If he did not, Lee proposed to inaugurate a fresh turning movement around Pope's right, during the night of the 30th. His force upon the field, including 2500 cavalry, was now nearly 50,000. Jackson, reduced by casualties, had about 17,000. Longstreet had, with R. H. Anderson, about 30,000.

Pope, at last, had united his whole army, except Banks's corps. This had hardly recovered from its so-called "victory" at Cedar Mountain, and was in charge of the wagon-trains about Bristoe. Before daylight orders had been sent withdrawing Porter from his isolated position on the extreme left, and bringing him around to the centre. And now Pope, believing his victory already half won, had massed, almost under his own eye, about 65,000 men and 28 batteries. Two corps, Sumner's and Franklin's, of the Army of the Potomac, and two extra divisions, Cox's and Sturgis's, — in all about 42,000, — were coming from Alexandria, 25 miles off, as fast as possible. With these, Pope would have about 107,000 in the field. Lee also had some reënforcements coming, and already at the Rappahannock River. They were the divisions of McLaws and D. H. Hill, each about 7000; Walker's division about 4000; Hampton's cavalry 1500, and Pendleton's reserve artillery 1000 — total 20,500.

Having telegraphed Halleck that the Confederates were retreating, Pope now began to set his army in battle array to press the retreat. Some hours were consumed, but they were well spent in forming his troops, thus avoiding the isolated efforts of the previous day, and arranging for a simultaneous attack along the whole line. Meanwhile, there was some artillery firing at rather long range by each side, and skirmishers in front were everywhere in easy range and sharply engaged.

The Federal line was short and strong. From its right on Bull Run in front of Jackson's left, to its left across the Warrenton pike, near Groveton, was less than three miles. Within this space were deployed about 20,000 infantry in the front line, and behind it 40,000 more were held in masses to be thrown where needed. Lee's line covered at least four miles. Jackson, on the left, had proved the strength of his unfinished railroad as a defensive line of battle, and had no wish to change. But, with his instinctive desire to mystify his opponent, he had withdrawn his men into the nearest woods and hollows, where he kept them carefully out of sight. He had had but one reënforcement from Longstreet's corps — a battalion of 18 guns under Col. S. D. Lee, which early that morning had taken position on his right flank, where it could support the fire of the large battery near his centre. Longstreet's line, as before said, was not a prolongation of Jackson's, but bent to the front — the two forming a rather flat crescent, its right flank overlapping Pope's left considerably. The Federal army made a finer display than was often seen on a battle-field in the war, being closely concentrated upon ground unusually open, and Pope, from one of the hills close in rear of the centre, viewed it with pride and confidence. Of his opponents he could see little but a few batteries, supported by little more than skirmishers; and he so firmly believed that Jackson was already retreating, that he would not be convinced by those of his officers who had had evidence of large forces near at hand, behind the Confederate skirmish-lines. A Federal who had been captured, and held a prisoner in the Confederate lines during the night, but who had escaped, reported that he had overheard Jackson's men say that they were going to join Longstreet. Porter had sent the man to Pope, with a message discrediting the story, and suggesting that he might have been deceived or sent as a ruse. Reynolds, on the left, had discovered that the Confederate line overlapped the Federal, and had had a narrow escape from capture. Ricketts had fought Longstreet at Thoroughfare Gap on the 28th and retreated before his advance; but the tale of the escaped prisoner was credited in preference to any other theory. About noon a swarm of skirmishers advanced along the whole Federal front, and were followed by the Federal line of battle, arrayed generally, three lines deep in front.

The Confederate artillery wasted but little fire on the skirmishers. When, however, the triple lines of battle revealed themselves, there happened something for which Pope was not prepared. Not only did every Confederate gun open a rapid fire, but above their roar could be heard the infantry bugles of Jackson's corps, and from the woods a wave of bayonets swept down to the unfinished railroad, and now Jackson and Longstreet were united, and Pope, with a force only 30 per cent superior, was committed to the attack. Possibly the Confederates may have flattered themselves that their victories in the six assaults made on the previous day would have diminished the ardor of the coming attack, but if so, they were to be disappointed. The value of discipline and training was again illustrated, and the battle which followed was scarcely surpassed for desperation upon either side in the war. The whole weight of the assault fell upon Jackson's corps. His men defended themselves with courage and the confidence inspired by their recent successes. When, at one point of the line, the ammunition ran low, men laid down muskets, and standing on the railroad embankment, made formidable missiles of an abundant outcrop of large pebbles. At length Pope's superior force produced such a pressure that Jackson called for assistance, and Lee ordered Longstreet to send a division of infantry. But Longstreet had discovered that the left flank of the attack upon Jackson had now advanced into the reëntrant angle between his front and Jackson's, so far that its lines of battle now presented their flanks and could be enfiladed. He believed that he could most quickly relieve Jackson by a severe enfilade fire of artillery.

Several batteries of artillery were rushed into a suitable position and opened upon the enemy's flank at easy range a raking fire which nothing could withstand. Within 15 minutes the aspect of the field was changed.

When Pope had first seen Jackson's corps disclose itself and re-occupy its defensive line along the unfinished railroad, he had very injudiciously withdrawn Reynolds's division from his extreme left and placed it in support of Porter's corps, although Milroy's corps, from among his masses in reserve, was equally available. In vain, now, were Reynolds and all his other reenforcements advanced to stem the tide of retreat across the open meadows, under the Confederate fire. Porter's triple lines had been practically merged into one, as the successive brigades came to the support of those in front. The merged forces were still pressing forward, and in close proximity to the Confederate line, when the flanking fire of the artillery opened, and quickly disorganized the attack. Jackson added to the confusion by advancing two brigades in a counter-stroke, and Pope's battle was lost. Unfortunately for Lee, Pope had not opened his battle early enough in the day to allow time for the Confederates to win a victory and to reap its full fruits. It was now about 4 P.M. when Lee, seeing the effects of Longstreet's fire, ordered his whole force to be advanced for a counter-stroke. Had the Confederate army been a well-organized force, able to bring quickly into play its full powers, much fruit might even yet have been gathered.

The objective point aimed at by Longstreet's advance was the plateau of the celebrated Henry house, upon which Jackson's brigade, "standing like a stone wall," had made his name immortal 13 months before.

Around this plateau the regulars and others of the best Federal troops, both of infantry, cavalry, and artillery, now made desperate stands, appreciating that its possession by the Confederates would cut off the Federal retreat across Bull Run, via the pike and the Stone Bridge. Their stand was also aided by two circumstances. First, Jackson's division, now greatly worn and reduced by their incessant fighting for three days, and having more exposed ground to advance over, were not able to push the enemy's retreat as rapidly in the counter-stroke as Longstreet could upon the right. Consequently Pope was able to bring over some reënforcements to his left flank from his right, and his artillery was able to take in flank those of Longstreet's forces which led the assault upon the Henry hill. Secondly, three of Longstreet's brigades were lost from his attack from looseness of organization. Wilcox's, Pryor's, and Featherstone's brigades had been called a division, and Wilcox ordered to command them as such. In the progress of the fighting, during the afternoon, Pryor's and Featherstone's brigades had become separated from Wilcox's, just when it was called for by Longstreet, and carried to assist the attack upon the Henry hill. The other two took some part upon the right flank of Jackson, but the weight of the division as a whole was lost. Drayton's brigade of D. R. Jones's division, also without orders, was taken by some un-authorized person to oppose a rumored advance of cavalry upon our right flank. The rumor proved to be unfounded, but the brigade was kept out of the action until the fighting was ter-minated by darkness.

Daylight was shortened by heavy clouds, and a rain which set in about dusk and continued during the night and much of the next day. Although the firing was kept up quite severely for some time after dark, the attack was practically over as soon as daylight was gone. For the irregular and disconnected lines, though with ample spirit and force to carry the position, had time permitted them to envelop it, were paralyzed by the danger of firing into each other in the darkness.

In the Federal army the confusion was very great, as troops and trains intermixed groped through the rain, and poured across the bridge and along the pike toward Centreville. There Franklin's corps had arrived about 6 P.M., only a few hours too late to have come upon the field and have saved the day. Upon this corps Pope ordered his whole army to concentrate.

An officer of the regular army, Capt. W. H. Powell, describing this night march, wrote in the *Century War Book*, as follows: —

" As we neared the bridge we came upon confusion. Men, singly and in detachments, were mingled with sutler's wagons, artillery caissons, supply wagons, and ambulances, each striving to get ahead of the other. Vehicles rushed through organized bodies, and broke the column into fragments. Little detachments gathered by the roadside, after crossing the bridge, crying out the numbers of their regiments as a guide to scat-tered comrades. And what a night it was! Dark, gloomy, and be-clouded by the volumes of smoke which had risen from the battle-field."

Had Longstreet pushed rifled guns to the front, upon the turn-pike, and fired at high elevations down its straight course, he might have landed shells in this retreating column as far as the Stone Bridge. This would probably have blocked the column and added much to the captured property. But the Confederates as yet had no artillery organization which could quickly appreciate and improve all the passing opportunities of a battle-field. Indeed, as before stated, the army was only a mass of divisions, associated by temporary assignments to Longstreet and Jackson, who were themselves only division commanders.

On the morning of the 31st, Lee lost no time in renewing his advance. As the position at Centreville was strong, and had been fortified by the Confederates in 1861, he ordered Jackson's corps to turn Centreville, crossing Bull Run at Sudley, and moving by the Little River turnpike upon Fairfax C. H. Stuart's cavalry were to precede Jackson. Longstreet was to glean the battle-field and then to follow Jackson. All progress was slow on account of the rain and mud. This was the third battle within 14 months which had been closely followed by heavy rain, — Bull Run, Malvern Hill, and Second Manassas. The theory took root that cannonading has rain-making virtue.

On the 31st Jackson, over wretched roads and through continued rain, advanced only about 10 miles, and bivouacked at Pleasant Valley on the Little River pike. Longstreet's advance reached Sudley Ford, and the care of the battle-field was left to the reënforcements from Richmond, which were now coming up. On Sept. 1, the march was resumed by Jackson at an early hour, and Longstreet followed over the same road. Pope, in a despatch to Halleck during the night, had reported his falling back to Centreville, but had still claimed a victory, saying: "The enemy is badly whipped and we shall do well enough. Do not be uneasy. We will hold our own here." Yet he had left 30 guns and 2000 wounded on the battle-field, and had ordered Banks at Bristoe Station, in charge of his trains, to destroy all supplies and to come to join him at Centreville, with his troops, by a night march. With Franklin's, Banks's, and Sumner's corps, which arrived early on the 31st, he had now 30,000 fresh men, but his delay at Centreville was limited to a single day. That evening the presence of Stuart's cavalry, shelling his trains near Fairfax C. H., became known, and next morning reports reached him of Jackson's corps on the Little River turnpike.

Finding his position again turned, Centreville was abandoned, and a new one ordered to be taken at Fairfax C. H. This move practically placed him beyond pursuit. His whole army was now united, and too close to its fortified lines to be again flanked out of position. And, although there was demoralization in some organizations, yet there were many excellent division and brigade commanders, leading veteran troops so well trained and disciplined that their fighting was of the highest type. An illustration of this took place late in the afternoon of the 1st. Jackson's corps, approaching the junction of the Little River and Warrenton pikes, had formed line of battle at Ox Hill, with A. P. Hill's division upon the right. Two of Hill's brigades, under Branch and Brockenbrough, were sent forward to develop the enemy, who were known to be near. A terrific thunder storm, with strong wind and blinding rain directly in their faces, came on just as this advance was being made. With this storm on their backs, Stevens's division of Reno's corps, the 9th, charged the approaching Confederates in front and flank, and drove them back in much confusion. The division making the charge had been engaged on both the 29th and 30th, and had been defeated on both days. Its fine behavior and hard fighting was the feature which makes this engagement notable. It was, under the circumstances, a useless affair. There was little chance of either side accomplishing any result beyond the killing of a few opponents, with probably equal loss to itself. Hill sent strong reënforcements to restore his battle, and Kearny's division of the 3d corps came to Stevens's assistance. Stevens was shot through the head. Kearny, riding into the Confederate lines in the dusk, was also shot dead, as he tried to escape capture by wheeling his horse and dashing off, leaning behind his horse's neck. The fighting on both sides was desperate and bloody, but the Federals were driven back. During the night, the whole Federal army was withdrawn from the vicinity of Fairfax, and took refuge within the fortified lines about Alexandria.

Stevens and Kearny were both prominent and distinguished

officers. The advantage to the Confederates of their being taken off, like the cashiering of Fitz-John Porter, was among the few fruits of their victory. Indeed, at the moment when Stevens fell, bearing the colors of a regiment which he had taken from the hands of a dying color-bearer, the authorities in Washington were about to supersede Pope, and place Stevens in command of the now united armies of Pope and McClellan. He had graduated at the head of Halleck's class at West Point in 1839, and Halleck was well acquainted with his military attainments. Both Stevens and Kearny were favorites in the old army, had served most creditably in Mexico, and both had been severely wounded in the capture of the city, Kearny losing his left arm. Kearny's body fell into the hands of the Confederates, and being recognized, it had been sent the next day, under a flag of truce, by Lee, into the Federal lines with a note to Pope, saying: —

" The body of Gen. Philip Kearny was brought from the field last night, and he was reported dead. I send it forward under a flag of truce, thinking the possession of his remains may be a consolation to his family."

This affair ended the battle. On the morning of Sept. 2 it was apparent that the enemy had escaped, and Lee allowed his whole army to lie in camp and have a little much-needed rest. While he had fallen short of destroying his greatly superior adversaries, he could yet look back with pride upon the record he had made within the 90 days since taking command on June 1. He had had the use of about 85,000 men, and the enemy had had the use, in all, of fully 200,000.

At the beginning, the enemy had been within six miles of Richmond. He was now driven within the fortifications of Washington, with a loss in the two campaigns of about 33,000 men, 82 guns, and 58,000 small-arms. Lee's own losses had been about 31,000 men and two guns.

The critics who had declared that he would never fight were forever silenced and pilloried in shame. In the last affair at Ox Hill, on Sept. 1, the casualties in A. P. Hill's corps were 39 killed and 267 wounded, and in Ewell's were 44 killed and 156 wounded, a total of 83 killed and 423 wounded; 506 total.

There were no reports in the Federal army of this particular affair, but probably the losses were not very unequal.

The losses of the two armies for the whole campaign are summarized as follows. No report was made of casualties in the Confederate cavalry, which were probably about 100.

CONFEDERATES	KILLED	WOUNDED	MISSING	TOTAL
Jackson's Corps	805	3547	35	4,387
Longstreet's Corps	663	4016	46	4,725
Total	1468	7563	81	9,112
FEDERALS	KILLED	WOUNDED	MISSING	TOTAL
Army of Virginia	929	4389	2787	8,105
Army of Potomac	600	3013	1151	4,728
Ninth Army Corps	204	1000	319	1,523
Kanawha Division	14	50	42	106
Total	1747	8452	4263	14,462

Thirty guns and over 20,000 small-arms were collected from the field.

My own share in this campaign was limited to keeping up the supply of the ammunition consumed. I had the satisfaction of seeing the organization and working of my department stand well the test of a severe campaign, and a considerable separation from its depots. Both in the artillery and infantry, the fighting was incessant and severe, but the supply of ammunition never failed, and, at the close of the campaign, without a day's delay, the army was prepared to undertake an even more distant and desperate adventure. When Lee moved from Gordonsville to cross the Rapidan, I was ordered to follow with my reserve ordnance train from near Richmond. I followed as rapidly as possible, but could not overtake the army until after Chantilly. Then I replenished all expenditures, so that the troops advanced into Maryland with everything full.

Thereafter I kept myself and train in close proximity to Lee's headquarters in all the movements, and, with my wagons running between our successive positions and Staunton, Va., we were able to meet all demands.

CHAPTER XII

BOONSBORO OR SOUTH MOUNTAIN, AND HARPER'S FERRY

Choice of Moves. Interior Lines. Policy of Invasion. Across the Potomac. Affairs in Washington. McClellan succeeds Pope. Lee's Proclamation. Organizations and Strength. Harper's Ferry Garrison. Orders No. 191. The Army Scatters. The Lost Order. Lee Warned. Battle of Boonsboro or South Mountain. Longstreet Arrives. The Retreat. Crampton's Gap. Franklin Attacks. Jackson before Harper's Ferry. Preparations for Assault. Bombardment and Surrender. Borrowed Wagons. Paroles and Colors. Casualties.

THE enemy having taken refuge within lines impregnable to assault, Lee had no alternative but to take the offensive elsewhere. He could not afford to sit down before Washington and await the enemy's pleasure.

There were two openings for offensive operations, each with some chances of success. The safest would have been to withdraw behind the Rappahannock, where he might occupy a strong line with one-half of his forces, under Jackson, while the other half, under himself and Longstreet, was sent by railroad to Chattanooga via Bristol. At the time, in Tennessee, the Confederates were conducting two campaigns aimed at Louisville; the design being to drive the Federals from Kentucky. Kirby Smith, with an army of about 15,000, from Knoxville, had opened the road through Cumberland Gap, and on Aug. 30 had won a victory over a Federal force at Richmond, Ky., and on Sept. 2 had occupied Lexington. Bragg, with about 30,000 men, from Chattanooga had moved northward up the Sequatchie Valley, and, crossing the Cumberland Mountains, was, on Sept. 5, at Sparta, Tenn., turning the Federal position at Murfreesboro, where Buell was in command with about 50,000 men.

Such a movement by Lee would have been utilizing our "Interior Lines," the one game in which the Confederacy had an advantage over the Federals. On a small scale it had been played both at Bull Run and in the Richmond campaign; the troops from the valley in both cases leaving the Federal armies opposite them, and quickly doubling on the point of attack.

Opportunities to do the same upon a larger scale were repeatedly offered between the Confederate armies before Richmond and those about Chattanooga. One had already occurred in the summer just passed. On May 30, Beauregard had evacuated Corinth with 52,000 men, and withdrawn to Tupelo, Miss. He was not followed, and the Federal army under Halleck of 100,000, was dispersed in different directions from Arkansas to Cumberland Gap. Beauregard was allowed two months of idleness and rest. It would have been possible to bring 20,000 of his veterans to Richmond by the 26th of June to reënforce Lee for the Seven Days' Campaign. With their assistance McClellan should have been destroyed. Then the Western troops could have returned, and, if necessary, carried large reënforcements with them. Now a second opportunity was offered for similar strategy. Others were offered later, as we shall see, whenever one of the Confederate armies, from any cause, was free from the prospect of an early attack by its opponent.

On this occasion, the joint campaign of Bragg and Smith in Kentucky, and the Maryland campaign, both failed. Had we utilized our interior lines, one of them at the least should have been made sure. It was hoped, indeed, when the campaigns were entered upon, that the Southern sympathies of the Marylanders and Kentuckians would cut real figures in the struggle by bringing thousands of recruits to the Confederates, but this hope proved vain in both cases. There had been already enough observation of the war to destroy its romance, and to make the most careless realize what a grave step one would take who shouldered a musket under the Starry Cross. Many sympathized with our cause, and wished us well. But few were willing to abandon homes and take sides before we had shown ourselves able to remain in their States for at least a few weeks.

And this, in the case of Maryland, was utterly out of the question for the simple reason that there was no railroad communication possible; and no army large enough to meet the Federal army, could support and supply itself by wagon-trains from Staunton, nearly 150 miles away, for any length of time. Whenever, therefore, we crossed the Potomac going northward, we were as certain to have to recross it coming southward, in a few weeks, as a stone thrown upward is certain to come down.

In a letter to President Davis, on Sept. 2, Lee gave as reasons

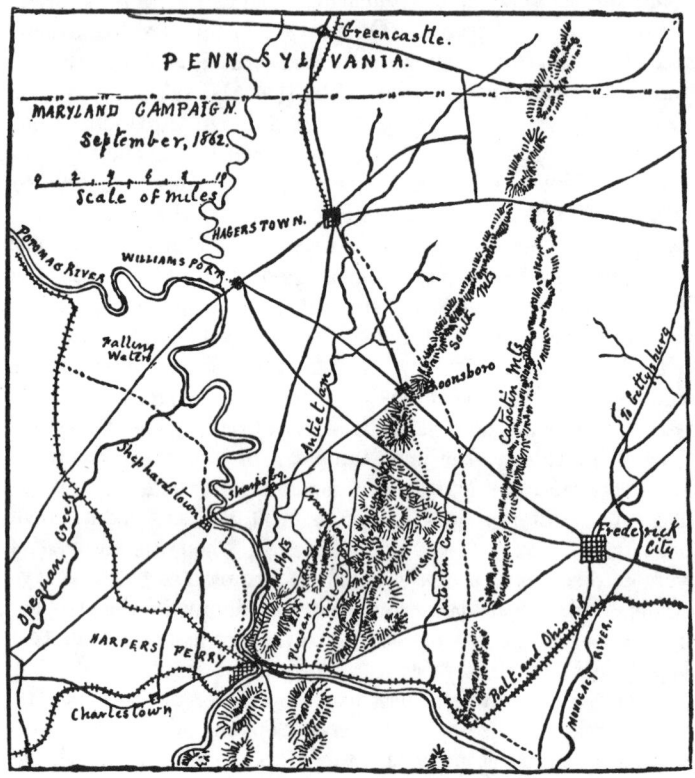

VICINITY OF HARPER'S FERRY

for the invasion of Maryland that it would relieve the Confederacy from the presence of hostile armies on her soil; and that the position of the army would be favorable for reaping the fruits of a victory, if one could be gained. Mr. Davis approved, and the campaign was made; but no victory was gained, nor is it easy to see where and how the chances of pursuit would have been improved, had it been.   Apparently Kentucky might have offered more favorable ones.

After a rest of a day, on Sept. 4, with Jackson in the lead, the army was put in motion for the fords of the Potomac, near Leesburg. With the reënforcements which had joined, Lee had now about 55,000 men, all in fine spirits and with their cartridge boxes full, but otherwise not in the best condition. The different divisions were still only associated, not formed, into corps, and in the matter of shoes, clothing, and food the army was, upon the whole, probably worse off during this brief campaign than it had ever been before or ever was again. About one-half of the small-arms were still the old smooth-bore muskets of short range, and our rifled cannon ammunition was always inferior in quality. The lack of shoes was deplorable, and barefooted men with bleeding feet were no uncommon sight. Of clothing, our supply was so poor that it seemed no wonder the Marylanders held aloof from our shabby ranks. For rations, we were indebted mostly to the fields of roasting ears, and to the apple orchards. Such diet does not compare with bacon and hardtack for long marches, and, before the campaign was over, the straggling from all causes assumed great proportions. Brigades were often reduced nearly to the size of regiments, and regiments to the size of companies. On Sept. 5 the army began to cross the Potomac, and on Sept. 7 the advance reached Frederick.

It is now to tell of events in Washington City. There was great alarm when Pope, with the combined armies of Virginia and the Potomac, fell back within the fortifications, almost in a state of rout. Col. Kelton of Halleck's staff, sent to find out the actual state of affairs, reported that there were 30,000 stragglers upon the roads. It was said that the money from the Treasury was being shipped to New York, and that an armed naval vessel, with steam up, was kept near at hand in the Potomac. Pope, making a virtue of necessity, applied to be relieved from command. There was no formal order relieving him until Sept. 5, when he was sent to the Northwest, where there were some Indian disturbances; but he was deprived of his army on Sept. 2, when McClellan was assigned to the defense of Washington, and the command of all the troops

engaged in it.   As this included the whole of both armies, Pope
was left without a man.   Yet neither Lincoln nor Halleck had
confidence in McClellan, and there was great reluctance to use
him.   Only the day before he had been instructed that he "had
nothing to do with the troops engaged in active operations under Gen. Pope, but that his command was limited to the immediate garrison of Washington."   At that time Pope himself
had already been adjudged incompetent, and the decision would
surely have been made to place Stevens in command had he been
alive.

But the death of Stevens, and the disorderly retreat of Pope's
forces within the fortifications, had demoralized the government.
McClellan alone was supposed to have the confidence of the
army.   It was the day of his triumph, and one of humiliation
to both Lincoln and Halleck.

Yet McClellan was out of place.   He would have been an
excellent chief of staff, but was unfit for the command of an
army.   He was as utterly without audacity, as Lee was full of it.
His one fine quality was his ability to organize and discipline.
He constructed a superb machine, which, being once constructed, would fight a battle with skill and courage if only let
alone.   McClellan, during the Seven Days, let it alone, absenting
himself as if by instinct.   Never but at the battle of Sharpsburg
was he present on any field, and his presence, by keeping Porter's
corps out of the action, made a drawn fight of what would otherwise have been a Federal victory, as will duly appear.

So now, Sept. 2, while Lee's army is resting on the field of
Ox Hill, McClellan begins to reorganize the 120,000 troops at
his disposal within the lines of Washington.   It is quick and
easy work, for his own old army composes two-thirds of it.
By Sept. 7, when Lee's army is concentrated about Frederick,
McClellan had six corps in the field, holding a line covering
Washington.

Lee, perhaps unfortunately, was not then seeking an action.
He had issued a proclamation to the people of Maryland, and for
a few days he wished to observe its effect.   It told the Marylanders, briefly, that the liberty of free choice between the
Union and the Confederacy had been denied them by the United

States, and that he had come to assist them in regaining their rights, and would respect their decision. It took but a short while to show that very few had any interest in the matter. When our troops forded the Potomac, the bands playing "Maryland, my Maryland," there was great enthusiasm, but it was confined to the invaders. The invaded were conspicuously absent, attending to their daily occupations, and evidently not ambitious to offer their fertile and prosperous fields for the movements and conflicts of armies.

I think the only real effect of that proclamation was subjective, or upon Gen. Lee himself. Necessarily, in it he was compelled to appear as a deliverer who had come to free the Marylanders from a yoke. A few days later, as will be seen, there was an opportunity for him to avoid a great risk of grave disaster by withdrawal into Virginia, without serious loss of men or impairment of prestige, and with richer booty in prisoners, guns, and ammunition than he had ever gathered from a battle-field.

In his decision to stand his ground and fight, his attitude as deliverer probably had a large share.

The organization and strength of the two armies is given on pages 226 and 227. As before noted, the Confederate organization into corps was slowly developing. What is here given is what was reached at the close of the campaign. In its earlier stages, there was much independence of action by some divisions. This independent communication with headquarters, it will presently be seen, resulted in a mishap — the loss of an order of prime importance to the issues of the campaign. It is but an illustration of how gravest results hang on care in most trifling details.

It was Lee's plan to draw the Federal army away from Washington before delivering battle. To do this he contemplated an advance into Pennsylvania west of the Blue Ridge. This plan was frustrated by the Federal forces at Harper's Ferry and Martinsburg, continuing to hold their positions after Lee had crossed into Maryland. As they were exposed to capture, he had expected them to withdraw. McClellan had desired to withdraw them, but Halleck objected that there was then no way by which Miles could withdraw. McClellan then suggested that Miles should cross the river and occupy Maryland Heights, where he

ORGANIZATION, ARMY OF NORTHERN VIRGINIA, SEPT., 1862

CORPS	DIVISIONS	BRIGADES	BATTS.
1st Corps Longstreet's	McLaws	Kershaw, Semmes, Cobb, Barksdale	5
	Anderson, R. H	Wilcox, Armistead, Mahone, Pryor, Featherstone, Wright	4
	Jones, D. R.	Toombs, Drayton, Garnett, Kemper, Jenkins, Anderson, G. T.	4
	Walker, J. G.	Walker, J. G. Ransom	2
	Evans	Evans, Hood, Law	3
	Reserve Artillery	Washington Artillery, Lee's Battalion	10
Total 1st Corps	5 Divisions	21 Brigades, 28 Batteries, 112 Guns	28
2d Corps Jackson's	Ewell	Lawton, Trimble, Early, Hays	7
	Hill, A. P.	Branch, Archer, Gregg, Pender, Field, Thomas	7
	Jackson	Winder, Jones, J. K., Taliaferro, Starke	6
	Hill, D. H.	Ripley, Garland, Rodes, Anderson, G. B. Colquitt	4
Total 2d Corps	4 Divisions	19 Brigades, 24 Batteries, 100 Guns	24
Artillery	Pendleton	Pendleton's Reserve, 58 Guns	12
Cavalry	Stuart	Hampton, Lee F., Robertson, 14 Guns	3
Aggregate	2 Corps, 10 Divisions	43 Brigades, 284 Guns, 55,000 Men	67

ORGANIZATION, ARMY OF THE POTOMAC, SEPT. 17, 1862

CORPS	DIVISIONS	BRIGADES	BATTS.
1st Corps Hooker	King	Phelps, Doubleday, Patrick, Gibbon	4
	Ricketts	Duryea, Christian, Hartsuff	2
	Meade	Seymour, Magilton, Gallagher	4
2d Corps Sumner	Richardson	Caldwell, Meagher, Brooke	2
	Sedgwick	Gorman, Howard, Dana	2
	French	Kimball, Morris, Weber	3
5th Corps Porter	Morell	Barnes, Griffin, Stockton	3
	Sykes	Buchanan, Lovell, Warren	3
	Humphreys	Humphreys, Tyler, Allabach	2
6th Corps Franklin	Slocum	Torbert, Bartlett, Newton	4
	Smith, W. F.	Hancock, Brooks, Irwin	3
	Couch	Devens, Howe, Cochrane	4
9th Corps Burnside	Willcox, O. B.	Christ, Welsh	2
	Sturgis	Nagle, Ferrero	2
	Rodman	Fairchild, Harland	1
	Cox	Scammon, Crook	3
12 Corps Mansfield	Williams	Crawford, Gordon	3
	Greene	Tyndale, Stainrook, Goodrich	4
Cavalry	Pleasanton	Whiting, Farnsworth, Rush, McReynolds, Davis	4
Aggregate	6 Corps, 19 Divisions	54 Brigades, 300 Guns, 97,000 Men	55

could defend himself, but the suggestion was not adopted by
Miles, who felt himself obliged by his orders to hold the village
itself.   As Lee could not advance freely into Pennsylvania with
Miles's force so close in his rear, he determined to capture the
Harper's Ferry garrison.   Discussing the matter with Longstreet, the latter advised against it, saying that it would require
a wide separation of our divisions, with rivers between them,
which would be dangerous so near the enemy.   Lee, however,
believed that it was possible to capture Harper's Ferry and reunite his army before McClellan could fully apprehend his plans.

As Jackson took the same view, the enterprise was committed
to him, and a carefully drawn order was prepared, "No. 191,"
detailing the march of each division.   Jackson, with his corps (except D. H. Hill's division) was ordered via Williamsport to
drive the Federals from Martinsburg into Harper's Ferry, which
he would then attack from the south.   Walker's division was
to cross the Potomac below Harper's Ferry and occupy Loudon
Heights.   McLaws, with his own and Anderson's divisions, was
to move by the most direct route and possess himself of Maryland
Heights, overlooking Harper's Ferry, whence he could with
artillery, and even with musketry, command the town.

Longstreet, with the two divisions of D. R. Jones and Evans,
was to march to Boonsboro and await the return of the forces
from Harper's Ferry.   Finally, D. H. Hill's division was to act
as rear-guard at Turner's Gap in South Mountain.

On Sept. 10, the army marched at daylight.   On the road
Longstreet was ordered to continue his movement to Hagerstown, while D. H. Hill, leaving two brigades in Turner's Gap,
came on to Boonsboro.   This change was caused by the collection of a force of Pennsylvania militia at Chambersburg.   It was
not formidable, as the regiments refused to leave the State, yet
its formation materially affected the course of events.   For it
will be seen that this separation of Longstreet by 13 miles from
D. H. Hill, caused the loss of the position at Turner's Gap.   The
loss of that gap brought on at Sharpsburg the battle which would
otherwise have probably been fought upon the mountain.

Meanwhile, there had occurred the mishap already referred to,
which gave to McClellan an opportunity rarely presented to a

general.   An official copy of Lee's order No. 191, addressed to
D. H. Hill, fell into McClellan's hands on Sept. 13 soon after
his arrival at Frederick.

The incident occurred from our unsettled organization.   D. H.
Hill's division had been attached to Jackson's command upon its
crossing the Potomac.   No order should have issued from Lee's
office for Hill.   Jackson so understood it, and, with his usual
cautious habit, on receipt of the order, with his own hand made a
copy for Hill, and sent it.   This copy Hill received and carefully
preserved, and produced it after the war, when the matter was
first inquired into.   But Lee's office had also prepared an official
copy for Hill, and this copy serving as a wrapper to three cigars
was picked up by a private soldier of the 12th corps in an
abandoned camp near Frederick.   When found, it was promptly
carried to McClellan, reaching him before noon on the 13th.   Its
importance was recognized, and its authenticity proved by the
fact that the different Confederate divisions had all pursued the
roads assigned them in the order.   Already McClellan had learned
of the crossing of the Potomac by Walker at Point of Rocks, and
by Jackson at Williamsport, but he had not understood the
object.   There had been fear that it might mean a dash at the
lines about Alexandria.   Now the whole situation was explained.
Lee and Longstreet with only 14 brigades were about Boonsboro.
McLaws and Anderson with 10 brigades were between Harper's
Ferry and Crampton's Gap, eight miles south of Turner's Gap.
Jackson, with 14 brigades, was southwest of Harper's Ferry, and
Walker, with two brigades, was southeast of it, across the
Shenandoah.   By all the maxims of strategy Lee had put it
in the power of McClellan to destroy his army.   He had not only
divided his force into four parts and scattered them, with rivers
and mountains between, but he had scattered more than was
necessary.   There was no need to place Longstreet as far away
even as Boonsboro.   A safer movement would have been to
unite Longstreet with McLaws and Anderson at Crampton's Gap,
that it might be more securely held, and the capture of Maryland
Heights be expedited, and that the distances separating his
forces should be the least possible.

McClellan's opportunity was obvious.   It was to take quick

advantage of the separation and move in between the parts. Then to overwhelm each in detail. This could be done by forcing the bulk of his army through Crampton's Gap. This move would have the further advantage of most speedily relieving Harper's Ferry. But just as Pope had lost his campaign by moving directly upon Jackson, as he supposed, at Manassas Junction, instead of upon Gainesville, where he would have been between Jackson and Lee, here McClellan lost his campaign by moving directly after Lee upon Turner's Gap. Even that he did with deliberation strangely out of place for the occasion. By night marches, over good roads with a good moon, he might have attacked and carried both Turner's and Crampton's gaps by sunrise on the 14th, for each was then held by only cavalry and a single brigade of infantry.

Fortunately for Lee, a citizen of Frederick whose sympathies were with the Confederate cause, was accidentally present at McClellan's headquarters during the afternoon of the 13th and heard expressions of gratification at the finding of the order, and learned of directions being given for a vigorous advance the next morning. With full appreciation of its importance he made his way through the Federal lines, and brought the information, after dark, to Stuart, who at once sent it on to Lee, then in camp at Hagerstown. Four brigades of Hill's division were at different points, from two to five miles west of Turner's Pass. They were ordered back, and barely arrived in time to save it from being seized by the enemy. Meanwhile, too, Jones's and Evans's divisions were ordered to march in the morning to reenforce Hill, and Lee and Longstreet returned with them to Turner's Gap.

It was between three and four o'clock when they reached the scene of action, after an oppressively hot and dusty march of 14 miles. There were eight brigades in the column, Toombs being left at Hagerstown to protect the trains. Hill had already had severe fighting. Turner's Pass was flanked upon each side by secondary passes within a mile, through each of which roads reached the crest, and cross-roads connected both with the main pike. On the right Garland's brigade had been attacked at 7 A.M. by a superior force; Gen. Garland, an officer of great promise, had been killed, and his brigade driven back in confusion, but the enemy did not follow up, and Anderson's brigade arrived in time to hold the position. D. H. Hill never failed to get good fighting out of his veteran division, and from 7 A.M. to 3 P.M., without support, he held the Gap successfully. But two corps of the enemy, the 1st and 9th, comprising 18 brigades and 18 batteries, were attacking it and gradually outflanking Hill's positions. By 3 P.M. they had occupied ground on the Confederate left which assured their final success in spite of all that could be accomplished by the eight tired brigades newly arrived. These, however, began to climb the hills from the west in support of Hill's five brigades, now much reduced by their long conflict. Hill, in his report, says : —

" Had Longstreet's division been with mine at daylight in the morning, the Yankees would have been disastrously repulsed, but they had gained important positions before the arrival of reënforcements. These came up, after a long, hurried, and exhausting march, to defend localities of which they were ignorant, and to fight a foe flushed with partial success and already holding key points to farther advance. Had our forces never been separated, the battle of Sharpsburg never would have been fought."

On the arrival of the head of Longstreet's column, Evans was sent to the left to support Rodes, and Kemper, Jenkins, and Picketts were sent to the right at the foot of the mountain, by a rough road, to meet a force of the enemy said to be crossing the mountain in that direction. After marching a mile and a half, the report having been found to be erroneous, they were called to hasten to the top of the mountain by obscure by-roads and across fields, and on reaching the top they were at once sharply engaged. Longstreet writes : —

"They were put in as they arrived to try to cover the right of Rodes and Evans, and fill the intervening space to the turnpike. As they marched the men dropped along the road as rapidly as if under severe skirmish. So manifest was it that nature was exhausted that no one urged them to get up and try to keep their ranks."

Before their ranks could be formed they were under fire, and the action was kept up until darkness finally called its truce upon the field.

At this time both Lee and Jackson were disabled, and com-

pelled to ride in ambulances.   On Aug. 31, Lee, in reconnoitring Pope's lines, had dismounted, and was holding his
horse by the bridle when an alarm of Federal cavalry had
startled the party, and the general's horse had jerked him to the
ground, fracturing some of the bones of his right hand.   It now
was carried in a sling, and he could not handle his reins.   Jackson
at Frederick had been presented with a fine horse, but the animal
was not well broken and had reared up and fallen over, bruising
him so that he, too, was an invalid.

Lee was now halted at the foot of the mountain, and thither
Longstreet and Hill repaired as the firing ceased.   Hill made a
report of the situation.   Darkness had saved the Confederate
line from serious disaster.   The tired troops and trains could
not be allowed to rest, but must at once be put in motion to the
rear.   At first Lee designated Keedysville as the point at which
the troops would halt; but later news reached him that the
enemy had also gotten possession of Crampton's Gap and he
changed the order, and directed that the new position should be
at Sharpsburg, behind the Antietam River, distant from Turner's
Gap about 10 miles.   D. H. Hill's troops were first withdrawn,
and were followed by the rest of the infantry and artillery.
Fitz-Lee's brigade of cavalry and Hood's and Whiting's brigades
of infantry acted as rear-guard to the column.

My reserve ordnance train, of about 80 wagons, had accompanied Lee's headquarters to Hagerstown, and had also followed
the march back to Boonsboro.   I was now ordered to cross the
Potomac at Williamsport, and go thence to Shepherdstown,
where I should leave the train and come in person to Sharpsburg.   The moon was rising as I started, and about daylight I
forded the Potomac, unaware of having had a narrow escape
from capture, with my train, by Gregg's brigade of cavalry.   This
brigade had escaped that night from Harper's Ferry, and crossed
our line of retreat from Boonsboro.   It had captured and destroyed the reserve ordnance train, of 45 wagons of Longstreet's
corps.

It is now necessary to describe what took place at Crampton's
Gap, where McClellan should have gone in person, as that position was the key-point of the whole situation.   Only Franklin's

corps of nine brigades was sent there.   They might have marched
on the 13th from their position, three miles east of Jefferson, but
did not until the 14th.   Having only about 10 miles to go, they
arrived in the forenoon, and at once deployed and formed for
attack.   The Gap offered fairly good positions for defence of its
eastern outlet, had there been troops enough to hold its flanks;
but the task imposed upon McLaws, with his four brigades and
Anderson's six, was beyond his strength.   To protect his own
rear, and to prevent the escape from Harper's Ferry of the 13,000
men to be besieged there, while he captured the heights above
them and cannonaded them into a surrender, it was essential
that he should occupy Pleasant Valley.   This lay between the
Blue Ridge (here called South Mountain) on the east, and Elk
Ridge (or Maryland Heights) on the west.   The protection of
his rear required him to hold in force Crampton's Gap in the
Blue Ridge, and to observe Brownsville Gap, about a mile south
of it, and also Solomon's Gap in Elk Ridge opposite on the west.
At Weverton, where the Potomac breaks through the Blue
Ridge, five miles from Crampton's, he had to protect against an
advance from the direction of Washington, and at Sandy Hook,
where the road from Harper's Ferry comes around South Mountain into Pleasant Valley, he had to guard against an attack by
the whole garrison of Harper's Ferry.   Besides this, he had to
send a force along Elk Ridge strong enough to defeat the intrenched brigade which held the extremity, overlooking Harper's
Ferry, and to hold it while his guns bombarded the town.   There
was thus one point to be attacked, two others to be observed,
and three to be defended against large forces.   The two most
important points, — Crampton's Gap and Sandy Hook, — were
over five miles apart.   Considering the proximity of the immense
Federal force, McLaws and Anderson were within the lion's
mouth, and that they ever got out of it was no less due to good
management, than it was to good luck on their part, and mismanagement by the enemy.

Holding Crampton's Gap were only Munford's cavalry and
Mahone's brigade of infantry, under Parham.   Cobb's brigade
and part of Semmes's were near in reserve.   From noon on the
14th until near five o'clock there was sharp skirmishing and

artillery fire, while the enemy deployed Slocum's division on his right and Smith's on his left. Having, by then, gotten the measure of their enemy, and deployed lines which outflanked him upon both sides, a handsome charge was made by four brigades, — Bartlett's, Newton's, Torbert's, and Brooke's. Of course, there could be no effective resistance. The whole Confederate line was overwhelmed and driven back in confusion. The reserve endeavored to rally the fugitives, but the small force — only about 2200 men in all — were so far outflanked by the Federal lines that no stand could be held until darkness put an end to the Federal pursuit, the whole Gap being now in their possession.

The battle was well contested, as shown by the losses inflicted upon the enemy, 531 killed and wounded. The Confederates were fortunate to get off with a loss as reported by Franklin of only 400 prisoners and 450 killed and wounded left upon the field, and a single gun.

In the scattered condition of McLaws's command, he was now in great danger. His one chance of safety was in an early surrender of Harper's Ferry to afford him an outlet for escape. He acted promptly and with good judgment. Drawing the brigades of Kershaw, Wilcox, and Barksdale from the forces on South Mountain, with the remnants of Semmes, Cobb, and Mahone, he threw a line of battle across Pleasant Valley about a mile and a half below Crampton's Gap, with its left flank upon Elk Ridge, and its right upon South Mountain. Here he made a bold front on the morning of the 15th against Franklin and his whole corps. Of course, Franklin, about 12,000 strong, could have run over him, and was under orders, too, to do so. Franklin was preparing to undertake the work, when, about eight o'clock, heavy firing which had been going on for over two hours at Harper's Ferry, suddenly ceased. Franklin correctly interpreted this to mean that Miles, at Harper's Ferry, had surrendered, and he abandoned his proposed attack. This was a gross blunder. It lost an easy opportunity to defeat six of Lee's brigades. One can but wonder if McClellan had communicated to Franklin a copy of Lee's order No. 191, for, with the knowledge of the situation given by that order, it seems impossible that the latter could have remained idle so near a divided enemy for two whole days, as he now did on the 15th and 16th, receiving, meanwhile, no orders from McClellan.

McClellan either did not himself appreciate the value of the opportunity chance had given him, or did not choose to let Halleck know it. His letters to them seem vague and non-committal. He cannot be held blameless for Franklin's small performance in view of the opportunity.

Let us now turn to Harper's Ferry. Jackson, with his three divisions under Jones, Lawton, and A. P. Hill, marching from Frederick on Sept. 10, had much the longest march to make, about 62 miles, nearly double those of McLaws and Walker. He made it, however, in good time, his marches being on the 10th, 14 miles; on the 11th, 20 miles; on the 12th, 16 miles; and on the 13th by 11 A.M., 12 miles, which brought him to the Harper's Ferry pickets. The other commands reached their destinations about the same time, and the next morning, signal parties opened wigwag communication between all.

McLaws had had some fighting to get in position on South Mountain, for it had been held by a brigade and two batteries under Col. Ford. Ford did not make a good defence and was afterward court-martialled and dismissed.

During the forenoon of the 14th, Walker, on Loudon Heights, reported six rifled guns in position, but Jackson ordered him not to open fire until McLaws was ready   Jackson, before opening fire, intended to demand a surrender, and to allow time for non-combatants to be removed. Before this could be done, however, the sounds of battle at Turner's and Crampton's gaps admonished him of the importance of hours, and, about 4 P.M., McLaws being prepared, a heavy cannonade was opened and kept up during the rest of the afternoon. Its effect, however, was more moral than physical. The rifled ammunition of the Confederates was decidedly inferior to that of the enemy, many of their shells failing to burst, or bursting prematurely, or tumbling; and even the smooth-bore shells often burst near the guns. The part of the town near the rivers was within effective range of McLaws and Walker, but Bolivar Heights, where the most of the Federal force was located, was beyond it.

Meanwhile, Jackson arranged a direct assault upon Bolivar Heights. Ten of Walker's rifles were brought across the Shenandoah, about four miles above the town, and found good positions to take in rear the Federal left from spurs near the river. A. P. Hill's infantry, on Jackson's right, worked down the river bank over ground the Federals had thought impassable, and found lodgment in rear of the Federal line; and Hill's artillery established several batteries on the very ridge held by the Federals, and in easy range. On the left, near the Potomac, Jones's division drove off Federal outposts and also established batteries in effective range on commanding hills.

Opposite the centre, Ewell's division under Lawton was moved up near the works, and its smooth-bores posted for direct fire. All was ready by the morning of the 15th, and Jackson had the game in his hands. The Federals, indeed, were naturally depressed. Their affair on Maryland Heights, with McLaws, had been discouraging, and now they saw guns being posted to command all of their positions. Col. Davis, with about 1200 cavalry, got permission to make his escape during the night. The road to Sharpsburg, on the north bank of the river, was unguarded, save by a picket some four miles out. The cavalry crossed on the pontoon bridge and made its escape, riding by the picket at a gallop in the moonlight. On their march to Hagerstown they had the luck to meet Longstreet's reserve ordnance train, as already told, and burned 45 wagons of ammunition. This train had a guard, but, unfortunately, it was concentrated at the rear, where alone was danger apprehended.

Before sunrise on the 15th, Jackson opened all his guns from seven points, and prepared to storm the Federal lines after a severe cannonade. His new positions gave effective enfilade fire at fair ranges. Lt. Binney, of Miles's staff, writes in his journal: —

" We are surrounded by enemy's batteries; they open from Loudon Mountain and Loudon farm, Maryland Heights, Charlestown road, Shepherdstown road. Nothing could stand before such a raking cannonade. Col. Miles was everywhere, exposing himself to danger with the bravest, encouraging his artillerists, and met with many narrow escapes from the bursting shells of the enemy. At 8 A.M. our battery officers report their ammunition exhausted.   Gen. White meets Col. Miles on the crest of heights and consults. . . .   The white flag is exhibited, the artillery stops firing for about 15 minutes, when the enemy again open with a terrific cannonade. . . .   Col. Miles and Lt. Binney, aide-de-camp, started down the eastern slope of the heights, where every inch of ground is being torn up by the enemy's fire.   Col. Miles took Lt. Binney's hand and remarked, ' Well, Mr. Binney, we have done our duty, but where can McClellan be ?   The rebels have opened on us again ! What do they mean ?'   Immediately after a shell passed us, striking and exploding immediately behind us, a piece of which tore the flesh entirely from his left calf, and a small piece cutting his right calf slightly.   Lt. Binney immediately tied his handkerchief above the knee and called for assistance, put him in a blanket, and, obtaining six men, dragged him to an ambulance and sent word to Gen. White."

Col. Miles only survived for a day.   A military commission which reported upon the circumstances of the surrender severely criticised it as premature.   It may be said, however, that the immediate necessity for surrender was, not to escape the fire of the artillery, which was so much in evidence, but the charge of the infantry which was about to follow.

The actual casualties of the Federals were 217.   The total number surrendered was about 12,500.   Jackson, in his official report, says : —

"In an hour the enemy's fire seemed to be silenced, and the batteries of Gen. Hill were ordered to cease their fire, which was the signal for storming the works.   Gen. Pender had commenced his advance, when the enemy again opening, Pegram and Crenshaw moved forward their batteries, and poured a rapid fire into the enemy.   The white flag was now displayed, and, shortly afterward, Gen. White (the commanding officer, Col. D. S. Miles having been mortally wounded), with a garrison of about 11,000 men, surrendered as prisoners of war.   Under this capitulation we took possession of 73 pieces of artillery, some 13,000 small-arms, and other stores.   Liberal terms were granted to Gen. White and the officers under his command in the surrender, which, I regret to say, do not seem from subsequent events to have been properly appreciated by their Government."

It is interesting to inquire why this criticism?   The official reports contain two documents which may explain.   The first is a letter from Gen. White to Gen. D. Tyler at Annapolis, as follows:[1] —

[1] O. R. 27, 801.

"GENERAL: I have the honor to state that, after capitulating at Harper's Ferry, I was allowed by Gen. A. P. Hill, commanding at that post the forces of the enemy, some 24 wagons for the transportation of officers' baggage, after my pledge to return them to the enemy's lines. I respectfully request, therefore, that the quartermaster be directed to forward them back."

Tyler, however, instead of returning them, forwarded White's letter to Halleck's office, calling it a "strange arrangement," and asks "shall the wagons be returned, and how?" What Tyler saw "strange" in it is not clear; but the tone of the letter suggests that difficulty was made, which is confirmed by Hill's report that "the wagons which were loaned to carry off the private baggage of the officers were not returned for nearly two months, and not until repeated calls had been made for them."

The second document, by Lt. Bacon, adjutant of D'Utassy's brigade, concerns the paroling of the Federals.[1]

A difference arose between Col. D'Utassy and Gen. Branch, in charge of the details, as to the meaning of the words "will not serve against the Confederate States until regularly exchanged." A pass to the brigade, allowing it to cross the bridge, was refused until the matter was adjusted. D'Utassy claimed that they might go West and serve against the Indians. The question was referred to Gen. A. P. Hill who refused to admit that understanding. This was about 9 P.M. About 6 A.M. Lt. Bacon reports that he —

"handed the muster-rolls to Gen. Hill at his headquarters and asked a pass for the brigade. Hill asked if the brigade was paroled. I replied, evasively, 'I thought so.' He then sat down and wrote a pass, upon which we immediately crossed the river, thus giving them the slip.

"Upon the announcement of the surrender, Col. D'Utassy ordered the colors of all the regiments of our brigade to be conveyed to his headquarters. This was done, and two hours were spent in removing the various colors from their staffs and packing them in the Colonel's private trunk. The Adjutant General of Gen. Gregg made several demands on me for the colors, where I was engaged on the hill turning over the arms. I informed him that they had been sent to our brigade headquarters. He left, but shortly returned, saying that he could not find them. I said I regretted it but could not aid him, that he must see my

[1] O. R. 27, 552.

Colonel. These flags are now in my Colonel's private trunks in this city. These are the simple facts which on my honor as a gentleman I certify to."

A military commission which investigated found nothing that called for censure in these matters, and *per contra* had a complaint of its own, as follows: —

"During the week previous to the evacuation of Maryland Heights a Lt. Rouse of the 12th Va. Cav., who had been engaged in a raid upon a train from Harper's Ferry to Winchester a short time before, was captured and brought into Harper's Ferry. He escaped while on the way to the hospital, he pretending to be sick, but was retaken. He was paroled, but returned in command of some rebel cavalry on the morning of the surrender. The attention of Gen. A. P. Hill was called to the fact that Lt. Rouse was a paroled prisoner, but no attention was paid to it. Lt. Rouse, on being spoken to about it, laughed at the idea of observing his parole."

The casualties of the campaign are shown in the following table: —

CASUALTIES, SIEGE OF HARPER'S FERRY, SEPT. 13–15, 1862

	KILLED	WOUNDED	MISSING	TOTAL
Sept. 13. McLaws's Div., Md. Hgts.	35	178		213
" 14. " " , Crampton's Gap	62	208	479	749
" 14. Mahone's Brig., Crampton's Gap	8	92	127	227
" 14–15. A. P. Hill's Div., Bol. Hgts.	3	66		69
" 14–15. Walker's " , Loudon "	1	4		5
Aggregate	109	548	606	1,263
Total Fed., Crampton's Gap	115	416	2	533
" " , Harper's Ferry	44	173	12,520	12,737
Aggregate	159	589	12,522	13,270

The casualties given in Mahone's brigade include those of the battle of Sharpsburg, which was not reported separately. No reports were made by the Confederate cavalry.

The Confederate casualties at Boonsboro are not reported separately, except Rodes's brigade, which reports: killed 61, wounded 151, missing 204, total 522. It was most severely

engaged of any, except, possibly, Garland's, which was routed
when he was killed. Garland's losses for the whole campaign
are given as: killed 86, wounded 440, total 526.

Livermore's *Numbers and Losses in the Civil War* estimates
the totals for the two armies at South Mountain, as follows: —

	FORCE ENGAGED	KILLED	WOUNDED	MISSING	TOTAL
Confederates	17,852	325	1560	800	2685
Federals	28,480	325	1403	85	1831

CHAPTER XIII

SHARPSBURG OR ANTIETAM

McLaws and Jackson Recalled. The Ordnance Train. The Question of
giving Battle. Confederate Straggling. Ropes's Comments. McClel-
lan's Pursuit. Lee's Line of Battle. Battle of Hooker's Corps. Hood's
Counter-stroke. On Jackson's Left. Battle of Mansfield's Corps.
Battle of Sumner's Corps. Sedgwick Ambuscaded. The Artillery
Fighting. Fourth Attack Prepared. French's Advance. Swinton's Ac-
count. The Bloody Lane. Franklin is Halted. Both Sides Exhausted.
Pleasanton and Porter. Burnside Advances. Toombs's Good Defence.
The Bridge Carried. The Advance upon Sharpsburg. A. P. Hill's
Counter-stroke. Lee in Council. Sept. 18. Faulty position of Fed-
eral Cavalry. The Pursuit. The Counter-stroke. Captured Ordnance
Stores. Casualties.

THE surrender of Harper's Ferry had come in the very nick of
time for the Confederates. Fortunately for them, Franklin at
Crampton's Gap, as already told, interpreted the cessation of
firing as an indication that there was now no use in his attacking
the enemy in his front. For orders were on the way from Lee
summoning McLaws to —

"withdraw immediately from your position on Maryland Heights and
join us here. If you cannot get off any other way, you must cross the
mountain. The utmost despatch is required."

Jackson, too, had been urgently summoned. As soon as the
terms of capitulation were agreed upon, he ordered Hill to su-
perintend the paroling of the Federals, cooked two days' rations,
and set out, with his own and Walker's divisions, at 1 A.M., for
Sharpsburg, distant 17 miles. By a rapid night march he arrived
early on the 16th, having forded the Potomac at daylight, at
Boteler's Ford near Shepherdstown. McLaws extricated himself from Pleasant Valley by coming into Harper's Ferry. Here
he was much delayed in crossing the pontoon bridge with his
trains and getting through the crowded streets. It was after

241

dark on the 16th when his tired and hungry troops bivouacked within two miles of Shepherdstown.

At midnight, summoned by Lee, he marched again, and, crossing the ford before daylight, the head of his column reported to Lee about sunrise on the 17th.   A. P. Hill's division was detained in Harper's Ferry until the morning of the 17th.   He marched at 7.30 A.M. with five brigades, leaving Thomas's to look after the captured property, to remove which Jackson had requested Lee to send his chief quartermaster and ordnance officer.

Thus it happened that, when I arrived at Shepherdstown, about noon on the 16th, with my ordnance train, and rode across the river and reported to Lee, I was ordered to collect all empty wagons and go to Harper's Ferry and take charge of the surrendered ammunition; bringing back to Sharpsburg all suiting our calibres, and sending to Winchester whatever we could not use in the field.   The prospect of this addition to our supply was grateful, for the expenditures had been something, at Boonsboro, Crampton's Gap, and Harper's Ferry; and the loss of the 45 loads, burned by the cavalry, had been a severe blow at such a distance from our base at Culpeper.   I was soon on my way back, and encamped that night with many wagons not far from Harper's Ferry.

It had been easily within Lee's power, all day on the 15th, to cross the river into Virginia, without loss, and to reunite his scattered divisions and collect his multitude of stragglers behind the Potomac.   The more that one studies the situation, the more amazed he must be at the audacity which deliberately sought a pitched battle in the open field, without a yard of earthworks, against a better-equipped army of double his force, and with a river close behind him, to be crossed by a single ford, peculiarly bad and exposed, in case he had to retreat.   A defeat would certainly involve the utter destruction of his army.   At Manassas, at Ox Hill, and even at Boonsboro and Crampton's Gap, he had had recent evidence that there was in the Federal army, and, especially in the Army of the Potomac, no lack of veteran troops, well organized, well led, and capable of strong offence and stubborn defence.   Let us analyze the conditions, and balance roughly the pros and the cons.

The actual number which McClellan brought upon the field of Sharpsburg during the battle, he states at 87,164. Besides these, Couch's and Humphrey's divisions, 14,000 men, were within a day's march and arrived, on the 18th, in time for use either in defeat or victory.

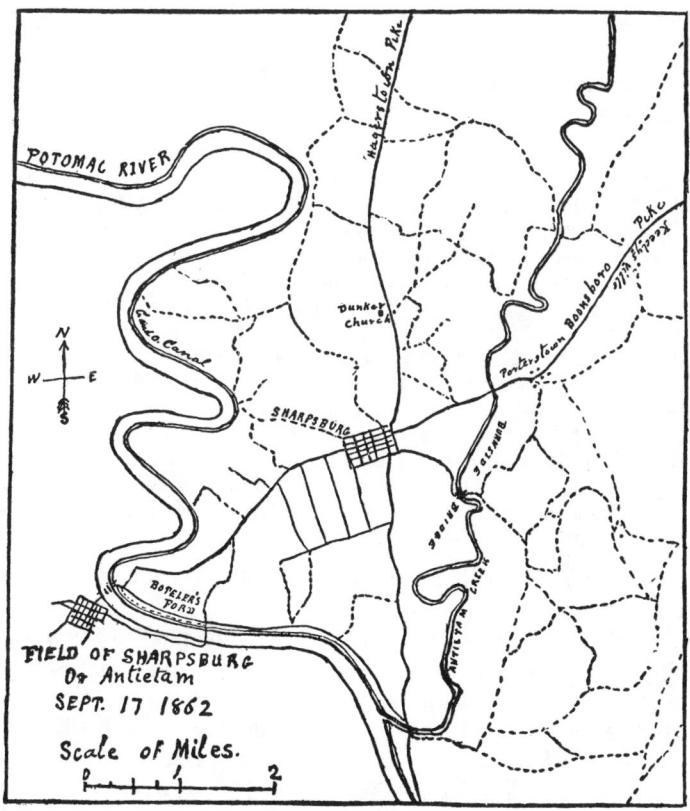

FIELD OF SHARPSBURG

Lee's force should have been about 55,000 men; but we have already referred to the enormous amount of straggling, caused by poor discipline, lack of shoes, and hard marches, on the insufficient diet of green corn and apples. That the effects were not unknown to Lee is shown by the following extracts from his letters to President Davis.

On Sept. 13, from Hagerstown, he wrote:[1] —

"Our great embarrassment is the reduction of our ranks by straggling, which it seems impossible to prevent with our present regimental officers. Our ranks are very much diminished, — I fear from a third to one-half of our original numbers, — though I have reason to hope our casualties in battle will not exceed 5000 men."[2]

After the battle of Sharpsburg, on Sept. 21, he wrote more fully, as follows: —

"A great many men belonging to the army never entered Maryland at all; many returned after getting there, while others who crossed the river kept aloof. The stream has not lessened since crossing the Potomac, though the cavalry has been constantly employed in endeavoring to arrest it. . . . Some immediate legislation, in my opinion, is required, and the most summary punishment should be authorized. It ought to be construed into desertion in face of the enemy, and thus brought under the Rules and Articles of War.

"To give you an idea of its extent, in some brigades, I will mention that on the morning after the battle of the 17th, Gen. Evans reported to me on the field, where he was holding the front position, that he had but 120 of his brigade present, and that the next brigade to his, that of Gen. Garnett, consisted of but 100 men. Gen. Pendleton reported that the brigades of Gens. Lawton and Armistead, left to guard the ford at Shepherdstown, together contained but 600 men. This is a woful condition of affairs."

Lawton's brigade had been the largest in the army, and it had carried into action at Gaines Mill, on June 27, 3500 men. It has seemed incredible to many writers that the small forces mentioned in many of the official reports, as engaged at Sharpsburg, could be correctly stated; but I am satisfied from my own observations at the time that the following estimate by Col. Walter H. Taylor, Gen. Lee's adjutant, is essentially correct.

Col. Taylor, in his book *Four Years with Lee*, writes: —

"The following recapitulation is established upon indisputable and contemporaneous authority, being nothing less than the testimony of the commanding officers, as shown by their official reports made at the time.

[1] O. R. 28, 606.
[2] His losses at Second Manassas were actually 9112.

Longstreet's Command	6,262	(9 Brigades).
Jackson's Command	5,000	(8 Brigades).
D. H. Hill's Division	3,000	(5 Brigades).
R. H. Anderson's Division	3,500	(6 Brigades).
A. P. Hill's Division	3,400	(5 Brigades).
McLaws's Division	2,893	(4 Brigades).
J. G. Walker's Division	3,200	(2 Brigades).
Total Effective Infantry	27,255	(39 Brigades).

"I cannot verify the estimate made for the cavalry and artillery, viz. 8000, but I am sure it is rather excessive than the reverse. This would make Gen. Lee's entire strength 35,255."

It must be noted, also, that the Federal equipment was far superior to that of the Confederates. Not only was their artillery more numerous and with a greater proportion of 20-pounder rifles and 12-pounder guns (as against 10-pounder rifles and six-pounder guns of the Confederates) and with better qualities of projectiles and fuses, but their infantry was almost entirely supplied with rifled muskets, while the Confederate infantry carried about 30 per cent of smooth-bore muskets.

Per contra. There is a single item, but it is an important one. Not only did McClellan bring upon the field his 87,176 well-equipped men, against Lee's 35,255 ragged and poorly equipped; but he brought *himself* also. Perhaps the anticipation of that fact encouraged Lee to risk the odds, and if so, the event justified his judgment. McClellan not only fought his battle in detail, engaging not more than two of his six corps simultaneously, but he held two of them out of the battle almost entirely, — Porter's 5th corps with 19,586 men, and Franklin's 6th with 12,300. The total casualties, in these two corps, 31,886 strong, were but 109 in the 5th corps and 439 in the 6th, — less than were experienced in many single brigades. So when the proper deduction is made from the Federal forces for McClellan's presence; and a fair allowance for the disadvantage of the Federals in having to take the offensive, all that would otherwise seem incredible about the battle disappears; and it is seen to be both natural and reasonable that the game should result in a draw. For the *fighting* was of about 47,000 Federals attacking 35,000 Confederates, under Lee, Jackson, and Longstreet, in a fairly good defensive position.

Next to the comparative forces of the combatants the most important feature of the situation was the topography of the battle-field which Lee had chosen. It was a fairly good one for defence as positions go in a well-settled agricultural country, but it was by no means as strong as it is often said to be. The line was somewhat over three miles long, from its left flank on the Potomac to its right at Burnside's Bridge across the Antietam. Its left flank had an excellent position for defence against cavalry, and it was held by Stuart's cavalry and artillery successfully against the Federal cavalry which was opposed to it. Thence, running southeast about a mile, generally behind fences and across open ground, it crossed the Hagerstown pike, and became parallel to it and about a quarter of a mile in front of it. At this point the Antietam is about a mile away to the eastward, winding its way a little west of south. After holding these courses for about a mile and a half the turnpike reaches Sharpsburg, the line of battle here being a fourth of a mile in front of the village, and a half-mile in rear of the river. Here the pike and the line turn more to the east and unite at Burnside's Bridge about a mile away. This bridge is over two miles above the junction of the Antietam with the Potomac. This flank was the weakest part of the line, for the river below was crossable by infantry at several points, and the flank was, therefore, practically "in the air."

A strong feature of our centre was that the Antietam cut in half the ground over which the enemy must manœuvre, and would more or less embarrass any infantry attack upon it; but, *per contra*, there were two ugly features: (1) The country is a rolling one and the hills near the stream are often quite steep, thus giving the enemy fairly close approach under cover. (2) Our whole line except the cavalry on the left was within range of the enemy's rifle-guns planted along the high ridges east of the Antietam, beyond the effective range of our guns. Thence, perfectly safe themselves, they practised upon us at leisure all day. Hunt, the Federal chief of artillery, describes the location of 10 heavy batteries of the reserve artillery, and says: —

"They overlooked the enemy and swept most of the ground between them and our troops. They were well served, especially the guns of Benjamin's battery. Their field of fire was extensive, and they were usefully employed all day and so constantly that the supply of ammunition for the 20-pounders ran short."

As to how our artillery fared in opposition, we may judge from a remark made to me two months later by Col. S. D. Lee, upon my being transferred to the artillery service: "Pray that you may never see another Sharpsburg. Sharpsburg was Artillery Hell."

D. H. Hill, in his report, says that he had nearly 50 guns available, and writes: —

"Positions were selected for as many of these guns as could be used, but all the ground in my front was commanded by the long-range artillery of the Yankees, on the other side of the Antietam, which concentrated their fire upon every gun that opened and soon disabled it."

Whatever the advantages or disadvantages of the field, there was one feature of it which should have been conclusive against giving battle there. That feature was the Potomac River. We were backed up against it, within two miles, and there was no bridge and but a single ford accessible, and that a bad one, rocky and deep. On the Maryland side, a mile of hilltops, some of them beyond the Antietam, offered sites for rifled guns to rake the ford and entirely cut off any retreat, should we meet with a reverse. This single feature of the field should have been conclusive against giving battle there. I believe that Lee would never have done so, had he ever before crossed the ford in person. Briefly, the most sanguine hope which Lee could reasonably entertain, with his inferior force, was to fight a drawn battle, and then safely withdraw what was left of his army. Against it he risked its utter destruction, which would have been the speedy end of the Confederacy. Ropes, the best critic and the best-informed writer upon the war, comments as follows upon the situation at this time.[1]

"This decision, to stand and fight at Sharpsburg, which Gen. Lee took on the evening of Sept. 14, just after his troops had been driven from the South Mountain passes, is, beyond controversy, one of the bold-

[1] Ropes, 2, 349.

est and most hazardous decisions in his whole military career. In truth, it is so bold and so hazardous that one is bewildered that he should even have thought seriously of making it. Nearly the whole force which he had on the north bank of the Potomac had been engaged that afternoon, in an unsuccessful attempt to hold a defensive position, and it had been badly beaten. . . . Of his two principal lieutenants, one, Longstreet, was opposed to this perilous course. Jackson, however, was, as we know, in favor of making a stand at Sharpsburg."

From a careful study of all the reports upon both sides, not only of the text but between the lines, I believe that the course of Lee was largely influenced by the hope, and that of McClellan by the fear, of events whose improbability surpassed that of an earthquake. To McClellan they evidently seemed, however, easily possible. So much so, that in explaining why he did not renew the battle on Sept. 18th, he was not ashamed to give frank expression to his fear as follows: " At that critical juncture, I should have had a narrow view of the condition of the country, had I been willing to hazard another battle with less than an absolute assurance of success. At that moment, Virginia ost, Washington menaced, Maryland invaded, the national cause could afford no risk of defeat. One battle lost and almost all would have been lost. Lee's army might then have marched as it pleased on Washington, Baltimore, Philadelphia, or New York."

If McClellan entertained such fears at the close of the battle, must it not have been these fears which made his coming to the battle so slow and deliberate as to allow Lee even superfluous time to make his escape if he wished? Considering the rare opportunity which chance had given him for brilliant and decisive work, he displayed little ambition to be at it, and his conduct was more suggestive of providing a bridge for a flying enemy.

Lee's hopes were by no means so exaggerated as McClellan's fears. He counted upon no hope from Maryland, until his own army should have demonstrated its ability to maintain itself within the state. He hardly hoped for more than " to detain the enemy upon the northern frontier until the approach of winter should render his advance into Virginia difficult, if not impracticable." But he did entertain hopes of a decisive victory here on a field more remote from a safe place of refuge for the enemy than his victories of the Seven Days and of 2d Manassas had been. The hope would have been reasonable had his army been larger and his armament better, but under all the circumstances and conditions it was as improbable of realization as the chance of an earthquake would have been. He did, indeed, win a complete victory over all the infantry which the enemy engaged, but their position was more favorable to prevent his making a counter-stroke than was his to resist their attack. Their heavy guns across the Antietam gave him protection, just as at Fredericksburg the Federal artillery on the Stafford heights, afterward in two battles, safely covered the Federal infantry on the opposite shore.

Briefly, Lee took a great risk for no chance of gain except the killing of some thousands of his enemy with the loss of, perhaps, two-thirds as many of his own men. That was a losing game for the Confederacy. Its supply of men was limited; that of the enemy was not. That was not war! Yet now, who would have it otherwise? History must be history and could not afford to lose this battle from its records. For the nation is immortal and will forever prize and cherish the record made that day by both sides, as actors in the boldest and the bloodiest battle ever fought upon this continent.

Longstreet and D. H. Hill, after their night march from Boonsboro, took line of battle in front of Sharpsburg early on the morning of Sept. 15. During the morning the news of the surrender of Harper's Ferry was received, and gave a different complexion to the whole situation. Until that time Lee had contemplated crossing the river at Shepherdstown, and he had directed Jackson to move to that vicinity to cover the crossing; but Jackson replied that he could bring his divisions over to Sharpsburg, upon which he was ordered to do so.[1]

On the morning of the 15th McClellan in person started in pursuit of Lee from Turner's Gap with four corps, — the 1st, 2d, 5th, and 12th, — comprising 33 brigades of infantry. After a march of about seven miles he found Lee, with the 14 brigades under Longstreet and D. H. Hill, in line of battle in front of

[1] Ropes, 2, 348.

Sharpsburg about noon. They scarcely numbered 10,000 infantry, and McClellan must have known that all the remainder of Lee's army was concentrated about Harper's Ferry. He could never wish for a fairer chance to crush an adversary, but he did nothing that afternoon or the next morning. During the 16th he was joined by the 9th corps, and at 7.30 P.M. he ordered two divisions of the 6th corps from Pleasant Valley, under Franklin, to join him next day, while the 3d division under Couch was ordered to occupy Maryland Heights; for what useful purpose it is hard to divine.

Meanwhile, his plan of battle had been formed. It was to send the 1st, 2d, and 12th corps, over 30,000 men, across the Antietam above the Confederate lines, to turn their left flank, while the 9th corps under Burnside, about 10,000, should attack their right at Burnside Bridge as soon as things looked favorable above. The 5th and 6th corps, Porter and Franklin, would be in reserve opposite our centre with 31,339 infantry and artillery besides a considerable force of cavalry and horse artillery. The plan was not a good one, involving as it did a piecemeal beginning. The three corps to attack the Confederate left should have been under one commander, and should have moved together. Instead, the 1st corps, under Hooker, was started about 2 P.M. on the 16th; the 12th corps, under Mansfield, not until 11.30 P.M. The 2d corps, under Sumner, was ordered to be ready to march an hour before daylight. It was ready, but received no orders. After daylight, the battle having opened and the firing become heavy, Sumner rode to McClellan's headquarters to ask for orders, and waited an hour or more without being able to see him. Orders to advance finally reached him at 7.30 A.M.   The sun had risen at 5.45 and Hooker had become engaged soon after daylight, probably about five o'clock. Sumner had some distance to march, and was only able to get into action after 10 A.M. By this time, as we shall see, Hooker and Mansfield had been wrecked, and Sumner's wreck soon followed.

When Lee formed his line on the 16th, Jackson's two divisions held the left, between the Hagerstown pike and Stuart's cavalry, which held a road nearer the river. Hood's two brigades had their left upon the pike, and on their right D. H. Hill's division formed a curve by which the line swept around parallel to the pike. Longstreet, with Jones's division and Evans's brigade, extended the line to the Burnside bridge. Walker's division was in reserve behind the extreme right flank. McLaws's, Anderson's, and A. P. Hill's divisions had not yet arrived. Some artillery duelling across the Antietam took place, but the first infantry affair occurred late in the afternoon, when Hooker's corps came in contact with Hood's pickets. Hooker's orders were to attack. It is hard to believe that McClellan deliberately sent a single corps so far away from prompt support to attack Lee's whole army in position, and had daylight lasted, Hooker would probably have been overwhelmed that afternoon. McClellan had ridden with Hooker in the beginning of his march, and Hooker had called his attention to the hazard of sending him so far upon such a serious errand. It was probably this remonstrance of Hooker's which moved McClellan to send Mansfield at 11.30 P.M. and to order Sumner to be ready to move an hour before daylight. The time of these orders is much more suggestive of a gradually developed plan, than of one formulated beforehand, and it resulted in four extensive combats instead of in one great battle.

The engagement in the afternoon between Hood and Hooker's advance was quite sharp, Hood advancing Law's brigade to the support of his skirmishers and driving back until dark the enemy's advance. In this affair Col. Liddell of 11th Miss. and Col. McNeil of the 1st Pa. (Bucktail) Rifles, both distinguished and promising officers, fell mortally wounded. The fighting ceased at dark, and pickets were established on each side, in such close proximity that they could hear each other's voices. About nine a light rain began to fall and continued most of the night. When all was quiet Hood's brigades were withdrawn to cook rations, they having been without food, but one half ration of meat, for three days. Their positions were filled by Lawton's and Trimble's brigades, of Lawton's division (which were in reserve near Jackson's line), with Hays's brigade in support.

At early dawn the fight was renewed, and Hooker's three fine divisions advanced in columns of brigades in line. Doubleday on the right, Ricketts on the left, and Meade in reserve close behind, — 10 brigades with 10 batteries. The fighting even before sunrise had become very severe. In his official report, Hooker gives the following incident: —

"We had not proceeded far before I discovered that a heavy force of the enemy had taken possession of a corn-field (I have since learned about a 30-acre field) in my immediate front, and from the sun's rays falling on their bayonets projecting above the corn, could see that the field was filled with the enemy with arms in their hands, standing apparently at a 'support arms.' Instructions were immediately given for the assemblage of all my spare batteries near at hand, of which, I think, there were five or six, to spring into battery on the right of this field and to open with canister at once. In the time I am writing every stalk of corn in the northern and greater part of the field was cut as closely as could have been done with a knife, and the slain lay in rows, precisely as they had stood in their ranks a few moments before. It was never my fortune to witness a more bloody, dismal battle-field. Those that escaped fled in the opposite direction from our advance, and sought refuge behind the trees, fences, and stone ledges nearly on a line with the Dunker Church, as there was no resisting this torrent of death-dealing missives."

This attack fell principally upon Lawton's and Hays's brigades extending from the Hagerstown pike through the corn-field to the right. Trimble's brigade, on their right, connected with D. H. Hill's division. Hays's brigade had also just been brought up in rear of Lawton's as a support. Across the pike, Doubleday's division had, at the same time, made a furious attack upon the old Jackson division under J. R. Jones. This division, though of four brigades, was one of the smallest in the army, Jones reporting that it went into action with only 1600 men. Its position, on the extreme left, was exposed to the view of, and enfiladed and taken in reverse by, the enemy's rifle batteries, across the Antietam, at a range of about 3000 yards. Hooker's troops were well handled; both his infantry and artillery and the full fighting power of his whole corps was soon brought into play and skilfully applied. The Confederate resistance was desperate, and the slaughter upon both sides great; Lawton and J. R. Jones were both borne off wounded within an hour. Jones was succeeded by Starke of Louisiana, who "soon after fell pierced by three balls and survived but a few moments." Col. Douglas, commanding Lawton's brigade, was killed, and five out of six regimental commanders, the brigade losing 554 killed and wounded out of 1150.

Hays's brigade lost 323 out of 550, including all of his staff and every regimental commander. In Trimble's brigade, Col. Walker, commanding the brigade, was wounded, with one of his staff, and the brigade lost three out of four regimental commanders and 228 men out of 700 present.

Early's, the remaining brigade of Ewell's division, had been sent about dawn to the extreme left, as a support to Stuart's cavalry, which occupied a position whence our artillery could annoy the flank of Hooker's attack. When Lawton was wounded, Early and his brigade were sent for. Leaving the 13th Va., numbering less than 100 men, with Stuart, at his request, Early started back toward the position where he had left the other brigades of the division, but soon came upon Cols. Grigsby and Stafford, with about 300 men, who were the remnant of J. R. Jones's division. He learned that Lawton and Hays had also been driven back with great losses, and that only a handful were left, who were probably not in condition to go into action again.

The 10 brigades of Hooker had carried the whole line held in their front by the seven brigades which they had struck, with such losses of men and officers, as practically to put the Confederate brigades out of action for the day, and to make a great gap in Lee's line from Early's brigade on the left to D. H. Hill's line upon the right. In this gap was Hooker's corps, badly shaken by the desperate resistance which it had overcome, but with the 12th corps just arriving to its support.

Not far in their front were Hood's two unfortunate brigades who had not yet gotten their last night's suppers. When the fighting ceased the night before, Hood, moved by the hunger of his men, had gone to Lee and asked for two brigades to take his place in the line of battle for the night, that he might have time to cook. Lee had answered that he would gladly send them, but that he had none available. He suggested, however, that Hood should see Jackson. Hood rode a long time in search of Jackson, and at last found him alone, asleep on the ground at the root of a tree. Jackson at once gave the orders which had put Lawton's and Trimble's brigades in the place of Hood and Law, and also sent Hays in support of Lawton; but he had exacted from Hood a promise that he would come instantly, when called to support the line. Hood then rode to find his wagons and bring up the rations, but the darkness caused such delay that it was already dawn, and the sound of battle was heard in front before many of the men had time to do more than to prepare their dough. No meat had been issued for several days, and only reduced rations of flour. Soon afterward, a staff-officer of Lawton's dashed up with the message, "Gen. Lawton's compliments, and will you come at once to his support." "To arms" was instantly sounded, and the lines formed and marched to the front, leaving the half-cooked dough in camp. Near the Dunker Church they passed Lawton, being borne to the rear on a litter, and here Hood found Hays with about 40 men, whom he had rallied, but all out of ammunition. He suggested to Hays to withdraw and collect his men, and replenish ammunition. He then launched his two brigades, about 2000 men, under Wofford and Law, through the bloody corn-field, already thickly strewn with dead and dying. Hood's brigades had made the successful charge at Gaines Mill, which broke through Porter's intrenched line, but he wrote in his report that here he "witnessed the most terrific clash of arms, by far, that has occurred during the war." Hooker was wounded, and the enemy was driven back so far as to be forced to abandon some of his guns.

Meanwhile, Early's brigade on his left, in the long body of woods called the West Woods, on the left of the Hagerstown pike, was able to hold the enemy at bay and to protect Stuart's flank. When Early left with Stuart but one small regiment of infantry, Stuart withdrew from his advanced position to a hill a little nearer our line. Here he had 13 pieces of artillery, and was able to greatly annoy the Federal infantry near the Hagerstown pike. On Hood's right the battle had been held by three brigades, which D. H. Hill had had near at hand and in reserve, — Colquitt's, Ripley's, and Garland's, the last now under MacRae. On Hood's left, Lee had sent Walker's two brigades and the Ga. brigade of G. T. Anderson, of D. R. Jones's division, which he had withdrawn from his right flank, opposite the Burnside bridge.

Mansfield's 12th corps had reënforced Hooker just in time

to save the 1st corps from being routed by the counter-stroke, given so heavily by Hood and his reënforcements. Hooker's corps had now lost 2590 men and was practically put out of action. Meade succeeded to the command of the corps, when Hooker was wounded, and he withdrew from the field to a commanding ridge about a mile in rear, where he endeavored to collect the remnants, and on which he now established a battery of 30 guns. In his official report, McClellan says that the 1st corps —

"was for the time much scattered and somewhat demoralized," and that "there were but 6729 men present on the 18th, whereas, on the morning of the 22d, there were 13,093 present for duty in the same corps, showing that previous to and during the battle, 6364 men were separated from their commands."

The defeat of Hooker's corps may be considered as ending the first affair of the day, but the ending of that, and the beginning of the second, with Mansfield's 12th corps, somewhat overlapped each other in occurrence. Mansfield had but two divisions —Williams's with two brigades and Greene's with three. These troops had composed Banks's army in the Valley and under Pope. The fight which now followed can scarcely be told in detail. It was one continuous exchange of heavy musketry and artillery at quarters sometimes as near as fifty yards or less, sometimes in woods and sometimes in the open ground; sometimes receding and again advancing. Action and reaction, in such affairs, are usually not very unequal, and six of the nine Confederate brigades now conducting it (MacRae, Ripley, Colquitt, Law, Wofford, and Early) had exhausted a part of their strength upon Hooker. After nearly two hours of this heavy fighting, with ammunition nearly gone and supplied principally with cartridges obtained from the dead and wounded, — with ranks reduced to skeletons, — the gap which Hooker had originally opened again yawned, even more widely, and Greene's division had entered it and was in possession of the Dunker Church and a portion of the woods near it.

But the 12th corps had now, itself, lost all of its aggressiveness, and was glad to pause and await reënforcement. Mansfield had been killed early in the action, and his corps now under Williams

had sustained a loss of 1746 men out of 8000. Williams's division
had suffered so severely that it was withdrawn to the rear to rest
and replenish ammunition. Here may be said to end in a draw
the second affair. The combatants upon both sides were worn
out to frazzles, and the firing had ceased entirely. The remnant of Hood's division was also withdrawn to replenish ammunition. The Tex. brigade under Wofford had lost 548 men
out of 864 carried into action. The 1st Tex. regiment had lost
45 killed, 141 wounded, and 12 missing from 227. Law's brigade
had lost 454.

But this truce was of short duration.   From the northwest
heavy masses of blue, and from the south long lines of gray, were
marching rapidly toward the fields, already so thickly strewn
with killed and wounded. A third encounter equally desperate
and bloody was now to take place over the bodies of slain and
wounded, friends and foes. At 7.20 A.M. Sumner had, at last,
received his needlessly delayed orders to advance. If his nine
brigades of veterans had been put into action along with Mansfield's five, they would have made decisive work upon Lee's left
flank, and have opened the road to Porter's corps to attack his
centre. Here McClellan threw away another one of his many
chances for a decisive victory, though it was by no means his
last.

The march of Sumner's columns could be seen from commanding points upon the Confederate lines, and movement was
also seen in Porter's corps, suggestive of preparation for assault;
several of his battalions crossing the Boonsboro bridge and coming to the support of his cavalry and horse artillery. Meanwhile,
Lee was sending to the front his last reserves — McLaws's and
R. H. Anderson's divisions — which had marched from Harper's
Ferry at 3 P.M. on the 16th, and arrived near Sharpsburg soon
after sunrise. These troops had had hard marching in withdrawing from Pleasant Valley and passing through Sharpsburg,
and, on arrival, were allowed a rest of about an hour. By that
time it was seen that Sumner's attack was imminent, and they
were ordered to the front. R. H. Anderson's six brigades,
about 3600 strong, were sent to D. H. Hill's division. But
Armistead's brigade was presently withdrawn and added to

McLaws's division. McLaws's four brigades, about 3000 strong, were directed to the woods behind the Dunker Church, under the guidance of Hood, who was acquainted with the ground.

At the time of this lull in the firing, it was, perhaps, a little after nine o'clock. Sumner had been impatient at the three hours' delay imposed upon his corps, and, as he listened to the tremendous musketry and artillery of the two first combats, he doubtless recalled the field of Seven Pines, where he had arrived in time to save the battle. His corps had not fought at 2d Manassas, and consequently it was large, numbering in its nine brigades over 17,000 men. It came upon the field led by Sedgwick's three brigades in column of brigade front. Sumner rode with this division. French's and Richardson's divisions followed *in echelon* to the left and rear. Before the Committee on the Conduct of the War, Sumner afterward testified as follows: —

"On going upon the field I found that Hooker's corps had been dispersed and routed. I passed him some distance in the rear where he had been carried wounded, but I saw nothing of his corps at all, as I was advancing with my command on the field. There were some troops lying down on the left, which I took to belong to Mansfield's command. In the meantime Mansfield had been killed, and a portion of his corps (formerly Banks's), had been thrown into confusion."

The troops of the 12th corps which Sumner saw lying down were the remains of Greene's division, about the Dunker Church, and it were better for Sumner had they not held ground so far in front of their general line. For Sumner did not realize that he was now within the Confederate lines, and he continued his advance into the woods, leaving the church and Greene's forces on his left. The formation of his division was in too close order to be safely brought under fire. He should have taken greater intervals between his brigades. It is said that they were only between 50 and 100 feet apart.[1]

[1] When troops are in masses, only the outside men can fire. The outside men are comparatively few, and hence the mass is weak for either offence or defence, until it can deploy into lines from which every individual can fire freely to the front. Hence troops, once broken, become almost helpless, and unable to defend themselves. As lines can only fire efficiently squarely to the front, or very nearly so, they also are helpless against fire coming from the flanks. Flank fire, too, is naturally of the most concentrated and fatal character, and troops exposed to it are quickly broken and helpless.

In this formation he pushed through the rather open woods with occasional rocky ledges, and passed, without being aware of it, Early's brigade upon his right with the remnants of Jones's division under Grigsby and Stafford; and on his left, he passed the remnants of Walker's two brigades, who were holding in front of Greene's troops about the church. Early, himself unseen by reason of a ridge between them, moved down parallel to Sedgwick's march, leaving Grisby and Stafford behind, to hold his rear against some troops *in echelon* behind Sedgwick's right, who seemed disposed to follow. As soon as Early passed the ridge which had concealed him, he opened fire upon the flank of Sedgwick's column. This was in such close formation that it could not deploy an opposing front. Just at this time the head of the column emerged from the woods on the far side, and found itself presenting its left front angle to McLaws's division, which was deploying from column into line of battle within close range. Sedgwick had practically marched into an ambuscade.

McLaws opened fire quickly from a front of a brigade and a half. The remaining brigades came into line at double-quick and soon poured a terrific fire, taking Sedgwick's column so obliquely that it could not be effectively replied to. At the same time the remnants of Walker's two brigades lined up against the left flank of the column, now almost helpless between converging fires.

It has rarely happened that heavier losses have been incurred more rapidly. Sedgwick himself was wounded, with Dana, one of his brigadiers, and the losses of the division were 2210. It is stated by Ropes that Sedgwick's loss was all suffered "in a very few minutes." In endeavoring to meet the flank fires, the rear brigade was ordered to face about. Fortunately, this order was understood by the brigade to mean a rearward march which was soon begun, and was hastily followed by the other brigades. The Confederates followed in pursuit, and once more the tide of battle swept across the ghastly corn-field, and the adjacent open ground between the Dunkard or West wood, and an East wood about 700 yards east of its northern end. Some of the brigades of D. H. Hill's left joined in the counter-stroke, and the Federals were driven to the shelter of their strong line of artillery in front of the North wood, which bounded the open fields to the northward. McLaws pushed his assault much too far, for his numbers were too light to hope for any great result, and the favorable ground enabled the enemy's artillery to punish severely all open exposures. Thus, McLaws lost 1103 out of 2893 carried into action in his four brigades, — Kershaw's, Semmes's, Barksdale's, and Cobb's, — an average of 39 per cent. These losses occurred mostly in the pursuit after Sedgwick, and mostly befell within two hours. At the same time that Sedgwick was driven back, Greene's men about the Dunker Church were also forced back to the Federal guns, leaving the Confederate line practically the same that it had been in the morning, although now held only by scattered fragments and almost entirely destitute of artillery.

In each of these three affairs the division batteries had been effectively fought against the enemy's infantry, but gradually they had nearly all been put out of action. As an illustration of their experiences, and of the condition of our line at this time, McLaws, in his report, says: —

"Capt. Read's battery had been placed in position on the right of the woods which we had entered, and did most excellent service, but it was exposed to such a severe fire Gen. Kershaw ordered it back, after losing 14 officers and men and 16 horses. Another battery, Capt. Carlton's, which I had ordered into position in the woods in front of Gen. Ransom's brigade, was so severely cut up in a short time by the direct and cross-fire of numerous batteries, that I ordered it to retire. . . ."

This finished the third affair of the day, though there were still upon the field Sumner's two other large divisions to be reckoned with, equal in strength to the whole of the 12th corps; and, in addition, there could be seen across the Antietam, but moving to support the attack upon our left, the 6th corps under Franklin. It was plain that a fourth and even more terrible struggle was to come, but it befell principally over new ground bordering the scene of the previous fighting upon the east, and extending southward. Here the division of D. H. Hill held the salient east of the Hagerstown pike where our line of battle changed direction and became parallel to the pike. The ground was open and moderately rolling and had but one good feature for defence.

This was a sunken road, an excellent thing when it has the right direction, perpendicular to the enemy's line of approach, but a dangerous trap if the enemy·can obtain an enfilading position. The salient outline here involved this danger.

In the second affair of the day, as has been told, D. H. Hill had sent three of his five brigades forward to support the flank of Hood's attack, and these brigades (Colquitt's, Ripley's, and Garland's) had remained holding advanced ground about the Roulette house, a few hundred yards in front of the sunken road before referred to. Here they had already suffered severe losses.

When Sedgwick's division was driven back and hardly pressed, Sumner had sent word to French and Richardson to attack, in order to make a diversion. From his position *in echelon*, on Sedgwick's left and rear, French soon came into collision with D. H. Hill's advanced brigades. These made a stubborn defence for a while, but their front was narrow and on its exposed right flank was Garland's brigade, which, on the 14th, had been routed and badly cut up at Turner's Gap. Hill reports: —

"Garland's brigade (Col. MacRae commanding), had been much demoralized by the fight on South Mountain, but the men advanced with alacrity, secured a good position, and were fighting bravely when Capt. Thompson, 5th N.C., cried out, 'They are flanking us.' This cry spread like an electric shock along the ranks, bringing up vivid recollections of the flank fire at South Mountain. In a moment they broke and fled to the rear; Col. MacRae, though wounded, remained on the field all day and succeeded in gathering up some stragglers and personally rendered much efficient service. The 23d N.C. of this brigade was brought off by the gallant Lt.-Col. Johnston and posted by my orders in the old road already described. Ripley's brigade had united with Walker's and fallen back with it behind the ridge to the left of this road and near to it. We had now lost all the ground wrested from the enemy, and were occupying the position held in the morning; but three of my brigades had been broken and much demoralized, and all of the artillery had been withdrawn from my front."

Out of 10 field-officers in Colquitt's brigade, which had fought after the giving way of Garland's brigade until its ranks were nearly mingled with the enemy's, four were killed and six wounded.

Hill now had left in the sunken road only two of his original

five brigades, — G. B. Anderson, comparatively fresh, and Rodes
who had been severely engaged at Boonsboro, losing one-third of
his force.   Here Hill received the united attacks of both French's
and Richardson's divisions, and for some time successfully
repulsed them.   He was aided by R. H. Anderson's division —
"some three or four thousand men," Hill reports, which had
taken position in his rear.   Anderson was soon severely wounded,
and no one seems to have exercised active command of the
division after he left the field, nor are any reports published of
the division or any of its brigades or regiments, except the
casualties.   These, in the five brigades of Wilcox, Mahone,
Pryor, Featherstone, and Wright, amounted to 1430 killed,
wounded, and missing, — over one-third of the force engaged.
    Swinton describes the conflict at this period, as follows: —

"The action here was of a very animated nature, for Hill, being reenforced by the division of Anderson, assumed a vigorous offensive, and
endeavored to seize a piece of high ground on the Union left with the view
of turning that flank.   This manœuvre was, however, frustrated by the
skill and promptitude of Col. Cross of the 5th N.H., Caldwell's brigade,
who, detecting the danger, moved his regiments toward the menaced point.
Between his command and the Confederate force there then ensued a
spirited contest, each endeavoring to reach the high ground, and both
delivering their fire as they marched in parallel lines by the flank.   The
effort to flank on the right was handsomely checked by Brooke, French,
and Barlow — the latter of whom changing front, with his two regiments,
obliquely to the right, poured in a rapid fire, compelling the surrender of
300 prisoners with two standards."

When this fighting had lasted perhaps an hour, the Federals
had gradually brought in the whole of French's and Richardson's
divisions, and extended their lines.   At last they reached a
position from which a portion of the sunken lane could be
enfiladed.   This being reported to Rodes by the Lt.-Col. of the
6th Ala., he was directed to throw his right wing back and
out of the road.   Rodes reports: —

"Instead of executing the order he moved briskly to the rear of the
regiment and gave the command, 'Sixth Alabama about face; forward
march.'   Maj. Hobson of the 5th, seeing this, asked if the order was intended for the whole brigade.   He said, 'Yes,' and thereupon the 5th
and the other troops on their left retreated.   I did not see their retrograde

movement until it was too late to rally them; and for this reason: Just as I was moving on I heard a shot strike Lt. Berney, Aide, who was immediately behind me. Wheeling around, I found him falling, and that he had been struck in the face. He found that he could walk, after I raised him. . . . As I turned to the brigade I was struck heavily by a piece of shell on the thigh. At first I thought that the wound was serious, but, finding upon examination that it was slight, I turned toward the brigade, when I discovered it, without visible cause to me, retreating in confusion. I hastened to intercept it at the Hagerstown road. I found though that with the exception of a few men, . . . not more than 40 in all, the brigade had disappeared from this portion of the field. This small number, together with some Mississippians and North Carolinians, about 150 in all, I rallied and stationed behind a small ridge leading from the Hagerstown road."

When, by this misunderstanding between Rodes and Lt.-Col. Lightfoot, Rodes's brigade abandoned this sunken road, — ever since known as "The Bloody Lane," — Lee's army was ruined and the end of the Confederacy was in sight. Even the rank and file in the 5th corps, looking on from across the Antietam, saw and appreciated the situation. "Now is the time" was a general comment. McClellan, from his headquarters at the Fry house, looked on, but he did not come and he issued no order. The gap left by Rodes was speedily filled by the encouraged Federals, and now the whole lane was enfiladed, and the slaughter which took place in it strewed it with dead and wounded, probably as thickly as has ever been seen in this country. G. B. Anderson's brigade, next on the left, attempted to stay the tide, but Anderson was killed, and, in the rout which followed, the supporting troops of R. H. Anderson's division were involved, and only small squads of stragglers could be rallied at scattered points in the rear. The Confederates had, however, exacted severe penalties from French and Richardson. Neither suffered to quite the extent that Sedgwick had done, though each of them lost heavily and Sumner himself had much of his ardor cooled. Richardson lost 1165, and was himself mortally wounded. French lost 1750.

But the danger to the Confederates now lay in the presence on the field of Franklin, with Slocum's and Smith's divisions of the 6th corps of about 6000 each, fine troops and well commanded. Franklin, too, was anxious to attack. Already he had sent one brigade, Irwin's, to the relief of Greene, when he was pursued out of the Dunkard woods, and this brigade found work enough to do to suffer 342 casualties. Another brigade, Hancock's, though not seriously engaged, —

"formed as support to two of Gen. Sumner's batteries, then severely pressed by the enemy, drove away his skirmishers who had already advanced close to the batteries, and occupied some buildings and fences in front of his position. This brigade was the means of saving the two batteries."

But, just as Franklin was about to attack, Sumner met him, and, being the ranking officer, he ordered the attack postponed. Meanwhile, however, under the personal direction of Richardson himself and of Barlow commanding two regiments in Caldwell's brigade, the battle was kept up by the troops already engaged, who were encouraged by their recent success and were quite disposed to follow it up. But there were no fighters in the Confederate army capable of more desperate and pertinacious defence than Longstreet and D. H. Hill. The latter's official report thus briefly summarizes what followed : —

"Col. Bennett of the 14th, and Maj. Sellers of the 30th N.C. regiment rallied a portion of their men. There were no troops near to hold the centre except a few hundred rallied from various brigades. The Yankees crossed the old road which we had occupied in the morning and occupied a corn-field and orchard in advance of it. They had now got within a few hundred yards of the hill which commanded Sharpsburg, and our rear. Affairs looked very critical. I found a battery concealed in a corn-field, and ordered it to move out and open upon the Yankee columns. This proved to be Boyce's S.C. battery. It moved out most gallantly, although exposed to a direct and reverse fire from the long-range artillery across the Antietam. A caisson exploded, but the battery unlimbered, and with grape and canister drove the enemy back. [Boyce fired 70 rounds of canister, and lost 19 men and 15 horses.] I was now satisfied that the Yankees were so demoralized that a single regiment of fresh men could drive the whole of them in our front across the Antietam.

"I got up about 200 men who said they would advance to the attack if I would lead them. We met, however, with a warm reception, and the little command was broken and dispersed. Maj. Hobson and Lt. I. M. Goff of the 5th Ala. acquitted themselves handsomely in this charge. Col. Alfred Iverson, 20th N.C., Col. D. H. Christie, 23d N.C., Capt. Garret, 5th N.C., Adjt. J. M. Taylor and Lt. Isaac E. Pearce of the same regiment had gathered up about 200 men, and I sent them to the right to attack the Yankees in flank. They drove them back a short distance, but were in turn repulsed. These two attacks, however, had a most happy effect. The Yankees were completely deceived by their boldness, and induced to believe that there was a large force in our centre. They made no further attempt to pierce our centre."

These details give an instructive lesson in the value of pertinacity; Longstreet with his staff helped man two guns of the Washington Artillery and materially aided in the result.

While Richardson's advance was still being pushed, Pleasanton advanced about three brigades of cavalry and four batteries across the Antietam, by the Boonsboro bridge. The batteries crowned the hills upon our side and opened fire, supported by the cavalry, and by a regiment of regulars deployed as skirmishers. Presently the line was reënforced by three more batteries of the 5th corps and Buchanan's brigade of regulars. These troops felt of our line quite heavily, the pressure coming upon Evans's brigade and parts of the brigades of Wilcox, Featherstone, and Pryor of R. H. Anderson's division, and G. T. Anderson of D. R. Jones's division. D. H. Hill, himself on foot (having had three horses killed under him during the morning) and carrying a musket, led some of these troops which he had rallied. S. D. Lee's battalion of artillery was also now back upon the field with ammunition replenished, and this demonstration was presently driven back under cover of the hills bordering the Antietam.

Pleasanton, who appreciated the opportunity, called for reënforcements, but McClellan had started on a visit to his right flank, and had ordered two brigades of regulars of the 5th corps to follow him. The absence of these brigades prevented Porter from complying with Pleasanton's request. So his demonstration was abandoned, and his troops and artillery were withdrawn, having suffered something over 100 casualties.

When McClellan reached the field on his right, he conferred with Sumner and Franklin. The latter urged a renewal of the attack, but Sumner advised against it, and McClellan took his advice. Franklin was ordered simply to stand on the defensive. The two brigades of regulars brought over from the centre were marched back. Thus, McClellan's expedition to the right at a critical time saved the shattered Confederate lines from two assaults by fresh troops, on their left and on their centre, just at the time when Burnside was beginning to get in serious work upon their right. The battle was now practically finished upon the Federal right and centre, and finished in a draw. We may now turn to their left.

In his final report, dated Aug. 4, 1863, McClellan writes that he sent an order to Burnside to carry the bridge in front of him at 8 A.M., but in his preliminary report, Oct. 15, 1862, he says the order was communicated at 10 A.M. Burnside's report, dated Sept. 30, gives the same hour. Gen. Cox, who had charge of the initial operations, in his report, dated Sept. 23, gives the hour as 9 A.M., and all the circumstantial evidence bears this out as correct. The immediate defence of the bridge was made by Toombs with the 2d, 20th, and 56th Ga. regiments, about 600 men, supported by Richardson's, Eshleman's, and Eubank's batteries. His infantry was partially covered by a thin wood, but the ground, sloping toward the stream, gave little shelter from the enemy's fire.

Burnside's corps comprised four divisions of two brigades each, averaging about 1500 men to each brigade. Rodman's division was sent to the extreme left, to make its attack upon a ford a half mile below the bridge, where a reëntrant angle gave the Federals a strong attack. There was here only a Confederate picket.

The other Federal divisions were under cover opposite the bridge, with abundant artillery on the hills. When the orders to attack were received, the artillery fire, of which there had been some all the morning, was redoubled, and skirmishers were pushed forward close to the stream. Crook's brigade was directed to approach as nearly as possible, unobserved, and then to make a dash for the bridge. But Crook missed his direction, and when he came near the stream he found himself somewhat above the bridge, and under such a heavy fire that he could not approach closer. He took what cover he could get and opened fire on the Confederate position. So the first Federal effort was a failure.

A second effort was soon organized to be made by Sturgis's division. Sturgis sent two regiments from Nagle's brigade, covered by the fire of the rest of this brigade and of Ferrero's brigade. Their hot reception by Toombs's Georgians checked the advance before they could reach the bridge, and the second effort was also a failure.

Meanwhile, more urgent orders from McClellan were coming to Burnside, and being reiterated by him to his subordinates as the battle upon the Federal right grew more desperate. Of course, Toombs's three regiments and three batteries, fighting without intrenchments, and in the open country along the Antietam, could not hope to do more than merely to delay four divisions with eight or ten batteries. By this time the enemy had discovered all our weak points, and their own strong ones, and Toombs's ammunition was getting low, for he could not replenish under the enemy's fire. Moreover, Rodman's division had already driven off the picket force at the ford below, and Toombs knew that it would soon appear in his rear. He had, however, not only saved three precious hours, but he had put up a fight which had so exhausted, both the energy and ammunition of his adversary, as to entail upon them the loss of three hours more, before they would be across the bridge and prepared to begin their attack on our right.

During all these six hours, A. P. Hill would be marching rapidly. It was said that on this march he stimulated laggards with the point of his dress sword. For his third attack, Cox took two regiments, marching by the flank, side by side. The regiment on the right was left in front; and the one on the left was right in front. Crook, too, organized five companies of the 28th O. to cross at a ford opposite his position, a short distance above the bridge. About 1 P.M. the charge was made. Toombs knew that his game was played, and all that remained to make it a perfect success was to safely withdraw his men. He did this with combined skill and good luck. He gave the enemy a farewell volley, ran safely to the rear, replenished his ammunition, got together parts of his brigade which had been detached, and took an active part in the final assault of the day, which drove the enemy to cover in the valley of the Antietam.

Rodman had gotten over, practically without opposition, before the charge upon the bridge, and Crook had carried the ford above the bridge, at the same time with the charge. The losses on either side in this affair are not given; but the total killed and wounded for the whole day, in the three Georgia regiments, was 217, about 38 per cent. But they had saved the day, for, while the Federals were crossing the Antietam, A. P. Hill forded the Potomac.

Having crossed the bridge, Burnside's first task was to secure his possession of it, against any counter-stroke, by bringing over a number of batteries. With these he crowned the adjacent heights, while his infantry deployed under their crests. Meanwhile came urgent orders from McClellan to press his advance. But the three brigades of Nagle, Ferrero, and Crook, which had been engaged, reported their ammunition as nearly exhausted. Sturgis also reported Nagle and Ferrero as too exhausted physically to be fit for an immediate advance. On this Willcox's division, with an ammunition train, was ordered across the creek, and Willcox relieved Sturgis in the advance. These arrangements just consumed the time remaining in which an advance could have been opposed only with four of Jones's brigades, under Drayton, Garnett, Walker, and Kemper, and the fragments of earlier battles which could be rallied in the rear.

Wilcox's division formed the right wing of the line of battle, and Rodman's the left; Cox's division gave Crook's brigade to support Willcox, and Scammon's to support Rodman, while Sturgis in reserve held the heights near the bridge. At 4 P.M. the advance was made in handsome style, somewhat to the right oblique, so as to envelop the village of Sharpsburg. In front of this village it struck Jones's four brigades, which had been held all day unengaged, but exposed to the enemy's rifle fire across the Antietam. Though now scarcely numbering 2000 men, they made a desperate fight, as the casualties upon both sides attest; but the long Federal lines gradually overlapped their narrow fronts and the Federal progress, though slow, was sure. The Confederates hurried to oppose them with all the artillery and the fragments of infantry which could be drawn from their left, many of those going being already wounded. Before the advancing troops of A. P. Hill appeared upon the scene, the leading Federals had crossed the brook running east from the town into the Antietam, and were well up on the slope of Cemetery Hill, while others occupied the eastern part of the village.

It had been about 3 P.M., when A. P. Hill coming up from the ford with his five brigades, had first reported in person to Lee. Getting information as to localities from D. R. Jones, he formed three brigades on the right of Jones and advanced to the attack. The other two brigades (Pender and Brockenbrough) were placed on his extreme right looking to a road coming from across the Antietam at its mouth. One of his batteries, under McIntosh, which had been sent ahead to the relief of Jones, had been left unsupported as Jones was driven back. The guns had fired canister until the enemy's line was within 60 yards, when the limbers and caissons were withdrawn, leaving the guns in the hands of the enemy.

Meantime, in the enemy's oblique advance a gap had opened between Willcox on the right and Rodman on the left, now become the rear. In fact, the movement had converted the line into a formation of brigades *in echelon*, and the interval between Willcox and Rodman had widened as Willcox, over less exposed ground, had advanced more rapidly. Now, having gained a foothold on the edge of Sharpsburg, he had stopped his advance to bring up his ammunition wagons.

Rodman had found the enemy extending to his left and was passing, on his extreme left, some fields of high corn, which cut off his view upon that flank. The four Confederate brigades advanced to the attack in the order from the left, — Toombs, Archer, Branch, and Gregg, — not in a continuous line, but with intervals of from 100 to 300 yards between them, which enabled them to overlap both of the Federal flanks.

Gregg's brigade on the right, having replenished their tattered wardrobes from the blue Federal uniforms captured at Harper's Ferry, were at first mistaken for friends, and approached to close quarters through the high corn before they opened fire. The weight of the attack fell upon the three brigades under Rodman, say 4500 men. The Confederates probably numbered 2700, but the attack was furious, and, enveloping both flanks, it was successful from the first. Rodman was killed early in its progress. Among the Confederates, Branch was killed and Gregg wounded. McIntosh's guns were recaptured, and the whole Federal line, although resisting, was forced back toward the Antietam. Cox at once ordered forward Sturgis's division, to support the line, and also sent orders to Willcox to withdraw his three brigades from the vicinity of Sharpsburg to the place where his division had formed, under cover near the river. With the assistance of Sturgis the Confederate pursuit was finally checked, but not until all the ground over which the enemy had advanced had been recovered, and the approach of night had at last put an end to the battle.

As darkness enveloped the scene, the Confederates, worn and exhausted by eight days of marching and fighting, dropped down where they stood to sleep and could scarcely be roused even to eat the cooked rations brought up from their camps in the rear.

When all was quiet, the division commanders met where Lee had taken his position on the road near the village, and made their separate reports of the condition of their commands.

Without exception all reported heavy losses and the men exhausted, and all considered it necessary to withdraw from the field during the night. Lee, alone, was in no wise moved. He had read McClellan's inmost soul and knew he was not to be feared. Without a word of explanation or asking advice from either Jackson or Longstreet or any one else, he directed all to collect their stragglers, strengthen their lines, and be prepared to renew the battle in the morning.

When the morning dawned, disclosing the opposing skirmishers in easy range, and the hostile guns nowhere out of range, but no shot being fired on either side, the Confederates drew long breaths of relief. Many men already half understood McClellan, but Lee alone had read him thoroughly and speculated boldly upon the knowledge. Indeed, when the advancing hours of the forenoon had made it certain that McClellan did not intend to attack that day, Lee recurred to a proposed plan of the day before to turn McClellan's right, and he abandoned it reluctantly only after careful reconnoissance by Col. S. D. Lee, on learning of the peculiar strength and heavy preparation of the enemy at that point.

Now there was nothing left to do but to recross into Virginia. That afternoon the orders were given and the trains were started. Soon after dark the movement of the troops began, and when the sun was two hours high on the morning of the 19th, everything was safely across. Gen. Walker, in an account of the battle in *Battles and Leaders of the Civil War*, writes: —

"Detained in superintending the removal of a number of the wounded of my division, I was among the last to cross the Potomac. As I rode into the river I passed Gen. Lee sitting on his horse in the stream, watching the crossing of wagons and artillery. Returning my greeting, he inquired as to what was still behind. There was nothing but the wagons containing my wounded, and a battery of artillery, and I told him so. 'Thank God,' I heard him say, as I rode on."

In offering battle on the 18th Lee had everything to lose and nothing to gain; McClellan, on the contrary, in accepting battle, would have had everything to gain both for himself and his cause, and nothing to lose. He had 24,000 men who had not been seriously engaged, and 12,000 more near enough to come into the battle before noon. Couch's division, 6000 strong, recalled from its useless expedition to Maryland Heights, rejoined the army early in the morning on the 18th, and Meade's division, 6000 strong, arrived by 11 A.M. It is strange but true that, with 36,000 fresh men at hand, neither McClellan nor any of his six corps commanders, except Franklin, approved the idea of an attack. Ropes says that Franklin alone —

"recognized the importance of the high ground held by Stuart and desired to begin by driving him and his artillery from it."

This point was indeed one of the key-points of Lee's line, but the dominant feature of the whole situation was the fact that Lee was fighting with his back to a river, which he could not have crossed under fire. McClellan fought with a safe retreat assured to him, in case of disaster, by the Antietam in his front and the powerful artillery on the hills behind it. The battle-field is unique, among the fields of the war, in offering all the prizes to the Federals and all the risks to the Confederates. To McClellan it was the opportunity of a lifetime.

One other feature of this battle is worthy of special note as unique. McClellan concentrated his powerful cavalry and horse-artillery force, not upon either flank, and especially not upon his left flank where were great opportunities for it, but at his centre, where it would have been in the way of his infantry, and where the ground was much cut up with fences and cultivation. On his right it might have been able to drive Stuart from his commanding hill. On his left, from which direction he should have expected Jackson's troops, it might have crossed the bridge over the Antietam near its mouth. Where it was, it was superfluous.

When, on the morning of the 19th, it was discovered that Lee had retreated, a brigade of cavalry was ordered in pursuit and was soon followed by Porter's corps. I have before, in the account of the battle of Malvern Hill, spoken of our reserve artillery under the command of Pendleton, and not attached to any division. It had been left in Richmond, when Lee with Jackson and Longstreet advanced against Pope. After McClellan was withdrawn from the James, it marched with D. H. Hill's division, and joined the army in Maryland on Sept. 8. On the 10th and 11th it marched to Hagerstown, with Longstreet's corps, and on the 14th returned with it to Boonsboro. That night, when the army was put in motion for Sharpsburg, Pendleton was ordered to take the reserve artillery across the Potomac at Williamsport, and distribute it to guard the fords of the Potomac at that point, and below to Shepherdstown. Hence it happened that on the morning of the 19th the hills on the Virginia side of Boteler's Ford were being held by 15 light rifle guns, and 19 smooth-bores of Pendleton's reserve, while 10 other smooth-bores were held close by.

In his advance to the river Pleasanton's cavalry picked up 167 stragglers, one abandoned gun, and one color. When he approached the river he was opened upon by Pendleton's artillery. Gibson's, Tidball's, and Robertson's batteries of horse artillery, 18 guns, went into action and replied so effectively as to silence most of the Confederate guns and also to run off all camps and wagon-trains in sight near the river.

After two hours of this, the Federal cavalry and its artillery were relieved by the arrival of the 5th corps, by which the affair was kept up until night. The canal bank along the river on the Maryland side served the purpose of a parapet, and enabled the enemy to aid their artillery fire with a heavy fire of musketry against the Confederate guns and sharp-shooters on the Virginia side, where there was but little cover. During the afternoon this combined fire compelled the abandonment of several guns. Seeing this, the 4th Mich. forded the stream and took possession of four of them. After dark this regiment was withdrawn, but early on the 20th Porter started to cross the two divisions of Morell and Sykes, and a brigade of cavalry.

Meanwhile, Pendleton during the night had found Lee and reported, and Lee had ordered Jackson to send back his nearest division. This was A. P. Hill's. Fortunately, Hill moved early, and, forming in two lines of battle, he approached the ford before Porter had gotten more than a half of his men across. Porter, informed that a large force was approaching, decided to withdraw, and did so with but little loss. One regiment, however, the 118th Pa., was thrown into confusion and driven over a steep descent and across the river under fire, losing 269 men. The total losses reported by the Federals for this affair were 363. A. P. Hill reported 30 killed and 231 wounded. Pendleton reported three killed and four wounded of his reserve artillery.

I have already told of my being sent on the 16th to Harper's Ferry to remove the captured ordnance stores and to bring what was available for use to Sharpsburg. I sent to Winchester 49 field-pieces and 24 mountain howitzers, and quite a lot of artillery ammunition not suitable for our calibres. Of what was suitable the supply was small, except of canister. There was also a fair amount of small-arm ammunition. Much of it had been brought from the depots, and unloaded along Miles's intrenchments, ready for use. While gathering this in the afternoon from Bolivar Heights, I could see the smoke of the conflict and the incessant bursting in the air of shells and shrapnel over the field where Burnside made his advance and was beaten back by A. P. Hill. I could not tell how the fight was going, but at that time no Confederate expected anything less than victory. I was until late at night despatching wagons to Winchester, and to the ford near the battle-field. I finished the work next morning, and returned to the vicinity of the ford in the afternoon. Here I found orders to await the army, which would recross the river that night, and here the next morning we received a liberal shelling from the enemy's horse batteries across the river, which perforated some of our wagons, but did no other harm.

The Confederate casualties by brigades are given below from the War Records as far as they appear. Also, in a second table, the Federal casualties are distributed among the different actions.

CONFEDERATE CASUALTIES. MARYLAND CAMPAIGN

BRIGADES		KILLED	WOUNDED	MISSING	TOTAL
McLaws's Div.	Kershaw	107	455	6	568
	Semmes	56	274	43	373
	Cobb	76	318	452	846
	Barksdale	35	272	4	311
	Total	274	1319	505	2098
R. H. Anderson's Div.	Wilcox	34	181	29	244
	Armistead	5	29	1	35
	Mahone	8	92	127	227
	Pryor	48	285	49	382
	Featherstone	45	238	36	319
	Wright	32	192	34	258
	Total	172	1017	276	1465
D. R. Jones's Div.	Toombs	16	122	22	160
	Drayton	82	280	179	541
	Garnett	30	199	32	261
	Jenkins	27	196	12	235
	Kemper	15	102	27	144
	Anderson, Geo. T.	8	80	6	94
	Total	178	979	278	1435
Walker's Div.	Manning	140	684	93	917
	Ransom	41	141	4	186
	Total	181	825	97	1103
Hood's Div.	Wofford	69	417	62	548
	Law	53	390	25	468
	Artillery	4	19		23
	Total	126	826	87	1039
Evans's Brigade		40	185	65	290
S. D. Lee's Art.		11	75		86
Washington Art.		4	28	2	34
Agg. Longstreet's Corps		986	5254	1310	7550

Brigades		Killed	Wounded	Missing	Total
		986	5254	1310	7550
Ewell's Div.	Lawton	106	447	21	574
	Trimble	27	203	8	238
	Early	18	167	9	194
	Hays	45	289	2	336
	Total	196	1106	40	1342
A. P. Hill's Div.	Branch	24	154	4	182
	Archer	22	161		183
	Gregg	38	188	2	228
	Pender	12	103		115
	Field [1]				
	Thomas [2]				
	Total	96	606	6	708
J. R. Jones's Div.	Winder	11	77		88
	Johnson, B. T. [3]	36	116		152
	Taliaferro	41	132		173
	Starke	81	189	17	287
	Total	169	514	17	700
D. H. Hill's Div.	Ripley	110	506	124	740
	Garland	46	210	187	443
	Rodes	111	289	225	625
	Anderson	64	299	202	565
	Colquitt	129	518	184	831
	Hill's Art.	4	30	3	37
	Total	464	1852	925	3241
Reserve Artillery		3	4		7
Cavalry		10	45	6	61
Agg. Jackson's Corps		938	4127	994	6059
Grand Aggregate Confed.		1924	9381	2304	13,609

[1] Field's not engaged.

[2] Thomas's brigade absent.

[3] Johnson made no brigade report, but losses have been estimated to conform to the division report.

FEDERAL CASUALTIES. MARYLAND CAMPAIGN

	KILLED	WOUNDED	MISSING	TOTAL
Cavalry Affairs, Sept. 3–20	12	52	20	84
Boonsboro or South Mountain,Sept.14	325	1,403	85	1,813
Crampton's Pass, Sept. 14	113	418	2	533
Harper's Ferry, Sept. 14–15	44	173	12,347	12,564
Sharpsburg, Sept. 16–18	2,708	9,549	753	12,410
Shepherdstown Ford, Sept. 20	71	161	131	363
Grand Aggregate, Federal	3,273	11,756	13,338	27,767

The casualties among general and field-officers were unusually heavy. Among the Federals' commanding corps were Reno and Mansfield killed, and Hooker wounded. Commanding Divisions or Brigades were, killed: Richardson, Rodman, Goodrich, and Miles. Among the wounded were Hatch, Hartsuff, Sedgwick, Crawford, Dana, Weber, Wainwright, Gallagher, Barlow, and Tyndale.

Among the Confederate generals were, killed: Garland, G. B. Anderson, Branch, Starke, and Douglas. Among the wounded were Lawton, R. H. Anderson, Wright, Ripley, J. R. Jones, and MacRae.

CHAPTER XIV

FALL OF 1862

Political Situation. Lincoln orders Advance. A Confederate Raid. Lincoln Dissatisfied. Condition of Confederates. Reorganization. Lee moves to Culpeper. McClellan succeeded by Burnside. Plan of Campaign Changed. Burnside's Strength. Lee's Strength. Sumner at Falmouth. Non-arrival of Pontoons. Surrender Demanded. Earthworks Erected. Jackson Arrives. Burnside's Plan. Marye's Hill. Building the Bridges. The Bombardment. The Crossing Made. Dec. 12. The Plan Changed. Jackson's Line. Franklin Advances. Gibbon supports Meade. Meade strikes Gregg. The Counter-stroke. Jackson's Proposed Attack. Casualties. On the Federal Right. The Formations. French and Hancock Charge. Howard Charges. Sturgis Charges. Sunken Road Reënforced. Griffin's Charge. Humphreys's First Charge. Humphreys's Second Charge. Humphreys's Report. Tyler's Report. Getty's Charge. Hawkins's Account. A Federal Conference. Dec. 14, Sharp-shooting. Dec. 15, Burnside Retreats. Flag of Truce. Casualties. New Plans. The Mud March. Burnside Relieved.

AFTER the battle of Sharpsburg, rest, reorganization, and supplies were badly needed by both armies, and, as the initiative was now McClellan's, he determined not to move until he was thoroughly prepared. Lincoln had two months before drawn up his Emancipation Proclamation and was waiting for a victory to produce a favorable state of feeling for its issuance. Sharpsburg was now claimed as a victory, and, on Sept. 22, the Proclamation was issued, freeing all slaves in any State which should be in rebellion on the coming Jan. 1. This was supposed to be a war measure, though nothing could have been more void of effect than it proved. McClellan did not approve of the Proclamation, and he let his sentiments on the subject be known, although he issued a very proper order to the army, deprecating political discussion. His attitude, however, alienated him from the administration, and the party in power in Washington.

A few days after the battle, Lincoln had visited the army, and, on parting from McClellan, had expressed himself as entirely satisfied, and had told McClellan that he should not be forced to advance until he was ready. But when two weeks had passed, during which great quantities of supplies of all kinds were rushed to the army by every channel, McClellan on Oct. 7 received instructions to " cross the Potomac and give battle to the enemy, or drive him south. The army must move now while the roads are good."

On receipt of this, McClellan conferred with his chief quartermaster, who thought that sufficient supplies would be on hand within three days. Meanwhile, on Oct. 10 a fresh trouble arose. Stuart with 1800 cavalry and Pelham's battery had been sent by Lee upon a raid. Fording the Potomac, some 15 miles above Williamsport, at dawn on the 10th, by dark Stuart reached Chambersburg, where he burned a machine-shop, many loaded cars, and a supply depot, paroled 285 sick and wounded Federals, and gathered about 500 horses. Next morning he moved to Emmitsburg, and thence below the mouth of the Monocacy, where he recrossed the Potomac, on the forenoon of the 12th. The distance travelled had been 126 miles, of which the last 80 from Chambersburg were accomplished without a halt.

An epidemic of foot-and-mouth disease was prevailing at this time among the enemy's cavalry,[1] and the desperate efforts to intercept Stuart, made with reduced forces, put much of it out of condition for active service until they could get some rest and several thousand fresh horses. Pleasanton had made a march of 55 miles in 24 hours, part of the distance across the mountains by very bad roads, and Averill's brigade had travelled 200 miles in four days. Stuart's loss was but one man wounded, and his conduct of the expedition was excellent. Yet the raid risked a great deal in proportion to the results accomplished. It might easily have happened that the whole command should be captured. But the incident contributed largely to McClellan's delay, and to the growing dissatisfaction of the government with his conduct.[2]

[1] The same disease, "sore tongue and soft hoof," was complained of by Lee on Nov. 7 to the Sec. of War, as affecting his cavalry.

[2] This was the second occasion, within four months, on which Stuart had ridden entirely around McClellan's army. Col. R. B. Irwin tells of the effect

Mr. Lincoln had allowed McClellan to decide whether his advance should be up the Shenandoah Valley, or east of the Blue Ridge, but expressed a preference for the latter route.

McClellan, however, had decided to take the Valley route, for fear of Lee's advancing into Md. and Pa. if it was left uncovered. Both Lincoln and Halleck thought his fears groundless and his caution excessive. Neither of them believed the Confederate army to be as immense as McClellan reported, and both knew that if the Federals needed supplies the Confederates needed them much more. In Lincoln's practical style, he often made pertinent suggestions to McClellan and would sometimes mingle with them a touch of sarcasm. He wrote that if Lee " should cut in between the Army of the Potomac and Washington, McClellan would have nothing to do but to attack him in the rear." Soon after Stuart's raid, he suggested that " if the enemy had more occupation south of the river, his cavalry would not be so likely to make raids north of it." And on Oct. 25, he telegraphed McClellan in reply to a despatch about sore-tongued and fatigued horses, " Will you pardon me for asking what the horses of your army have done, since the battle of Antietam, that fatigues anything?"

On Oct. 26, McClellan put his army in motion, 19 days after his receipt of the President's order. By this time he was willing to adopt the line of advance east of the Blue Ridge, as the stage of water in the Potomac River now made all fords impracticable. The crossing was made at Berlin, about 10 miles below Harper's Ferry. Pontoon bridges were laid, and the army crossed over rather leisurely, the last of it, Franklin's corps, on Nov. 1 and 2.

We will now return to the Confederates, who, since Sharpsburg, have been resting and recuperating between Winchester and Bunker Hill.

---

of this raid on the mind of President Lincoln, in the following anecdote: —

"When the President seemed in unusually high spirits and was conversing freely, some one (I think De Kay) suddenly asked, 'Mr. President, what about McClellan?' Without looking at his questioner, the President drew a ring upon the deck with a stick or umbrella, and said quietly, 'When I was a boy we used to play a game, three times round and out. Stuart has been around him twice; if he goes around him once more, gentlemen, McClellan will be out.'"

Our base of supplies was now Staunton, more than 100 miles distant, but over fairly good roads. Our trains were actively at work, bringing ammunition, food, and clothing, and gradually our condition approached the normal. But the supply, even of wagons, was limited, and, as late as Oct. 20, 55 were wanted for the reserve ordnance train of Longstreet's corps, and 41 for that of Jackson.

Meanwhile, as important as reëquipment, a thorough reorganization took place, and at last we became an army rather than a collection of brigades, divisions, and batteries. In Oct. Longstreet and Jackson were made lieutenant-generals, and major-generals and brigadiers were promoted and our 1st and 2d army corps were formed, following the example of the Federals nearly a year before.

The formation of our batteries into battalions was also carried forward, but rather slowly. A large proportion of our guns were but 6-Pr. and 12-Pr. howitzers, which the enemy had now discarded as too light. There are no returns showing our different varieties of small-arms, but that we still had men armed with flintlocks is shown by the return of 13 picked up on the field after the battle of Fredericksburg.

The organization, when completed, stood as follows, the strength being given from the returns of Nov. 20, 1862.

ORGANIZATION OF ARMY OF NORTHERN VA., NOV., 1862

1ST CORPS, LONGSTREET'S		
DIVISION	BRIGADES AND ARTILLERY	PRESENT FOR DUTY
McLaws's	Kershaw's, Barksdale's, Cobb's, Semmes's, Cabell's Battalion Artillery, 4 Batteries, 18 Guns	7,898
Anderson's	Wilcox's, Mahone's, Featherstone's, Wright's, Perry's Unorganized Artillery, 4 Batteries, 18 Guns	7,639
Pickett's	Garnett's, Kemper's, Armistead's, Jenkins's, Corse's Unorganized Artillery, 3 Batteries, 14 Guns	7,567
Total		23,104

1st Corps, Longstreet's (Continued)		
DIVISION	BRIGADES AND ARTILLERY	PRESENT FOR DUTY
Hood's	Total carried forward	23,104
	Law's, Robertson's, Anderson's, Benning's	7,334
	Unorganized Artillery, 3 Batteries, 14 Guns	
Walker's	Ransom's, Cooke's, No Artillery	3,855
Reserve Artillery	Alexander's Battalion. 6 Batteries, 26 Guns	623
	Washington Artillery. 4 Batteries, 9 Guns	
Total	5 Divisions, 20 Brigades	
	24 Batteries, 99 Guns	29,916

2d Corps, Jackson's		
Ewell's	Lawton's, Early's, Trimble's, Hays's, Latimer's Battalion	7,716
	6 Batteries, 26 Guns	
D. H. Hill's	Rodes's, Dole's, Colquitt's, Iverson's, Ramseur's	6,944
	H. P. Jones's Battalion, 5 Batteries, 22 Guns	
A. P. Hill's	Field's, Gregg's, Thomas's, Lane's, Archer's, Pender's	11,554
	Walker's Battalion, 7 Batteries, 28 Guns	
Taliaferro's	Paxton's, J. R. Jones's, Warren's, Pendleton's	5,478
	Brockenbrough's Battalion, 5 Batteries, 22 Guns	
Total	4 Divisions, 18 Brigades, 23 Batteries, 98 Guns	31,692
Stuart's Cavalry	Brigades, Hampton's, Lee F., Lee, W. H. F., Jones's, W. E.; Pelham's Artillery	9,146
	5 Batteries, 22 Guns	
Pendleton's Reserve Artillery	Brown's Battalion, 6 Batteries	718
	Cutt's Battalion, 3 Batteries	
	Nelson's Battalion, 3 Batteries	
	Total 36 Guns	
Aggregate	38 Brigades Infantry, 4 Brigades Cavalry, 63 Batteries, 255 Guns	71,472

On Oct. 27 Lee moved with Longstreet's corps and Pendleton's reserve arty. toward the eastern slope of the Blue Ridge. My reserve ordnance train moved on the 29th via Nineveh, Front Royal, Chester Gap, Gaines's Cross-roads and Sperryville, and encamped at Culpeper on Nov. 4. Lee, in person, had already arrived there. A few days after I was placed in command of the battalion of artillery which had been commanded by Col. S. D. Lee, who was now promoted brigadier-general and sent to Vicksburg. My successor as chief of ordnance was Col. Briscoe G. Baldwin, who served with great success until the surrender at Appomattox.

Meanwhile, an important event was on foot. We have seen the lack of cordiality between McClellan and the President, and the growth of mistrust of the former's intention to prosecute the active offensive campaign desired. On Oct. 27 he had telegraphed the President urging the necessity of filling the old regiments with drafted men " before taking them into action again." The tone of his letters had long been unsatisfactory, and this expression kindled into flame the growing suspicion that he was simply preparing new excuses for delay. Immediately on reading the message Lincoln showed himself ready to meet the issue by wiring back : —

Now I ask a distinct answer to the question, "Is it your purpose not to go into action again until the men now being drafted in the States are incorporated into the old regiments?"

McClellan read between the lines the threat conveyed, and backed squarely down. He promptly explained that the offensive despatch was the inadvertence of an aid, and promised to " push forward as rapidly as possible and endeavor to meet the enemy." Indeed, the Confederates noted, during the next week, the unwonted vigor of his advance. There were constant sharp skirmishes, and the enemy got possession of the two lower gaps in the Blue Ridge, Snicker's and Ashby's, and held the outlet of Manassas Gap. McClellan's headquarters were advanced to Rectortown. His cavalry occupied Warrenton, and it was evident that he would soon cross the Rappahannock. Then, suddenly, his activity ceased, and from Nov. 9 to the 17th, the Federal army laid quietly in its camps. His backdown had come too late. He had been removed from the command on Nov. 7, and Burnside substituted in his place.

McClellan's promises of Oct. 27 might have satisfied President Lincoln, but there were strong influences now determined upon a change, and which wanted not only the head of McClellan, but that of Porter. On Nov. 5 the President wrote an order authorizing Halleck, in his own discretion, to relieve McClellan, and to place Burnside in command of the army. Porter was also to be relieved from the command of the 5th corps, and to be succeeded by Hooker.

On the same date these formal orders were prepared and signed by Halleck, but they were not promulgated for two days.

The designation of Burnside to succeed McClellan was a great surprise to old army circles, both in the Federal and Confederate armies; and was, perhaps, an unpleasant one to Burnside himself. He was popular, but not greatly esteemed as a general. He had commanded a brigade at the first battle of Bull Run, but had in no way risen above, even if he reached, the average of the brigade commanders. He had later had the luck to command the expedition to the N.C. Sounds, where his overwhelming force easily overcame the slight resistance that it met. This gained him the prestige, in newspapers and political circles, of successful independent command. As commander of a corps, he was one of the four next in line for promotion — Burnside, Hooker, Sumner, and Franklin.

The older officers dreaded Hooker's appointment. By many he was thought utterly unfit, though a brave man and a hard fighter. Moved by the wishes of his friends, Burnside was brought to accept the command rather than see it go to Hooker.

McClellan was not unprepared for the blow, and he met it gracefully and did all in his power to commend his successor to the confidence of the army. He had not, however, anticipated that he was to be relegated to private life, but had supposed that he would be transferred to some command in the West. But no other command was ever offered him. A few days later Burnside submitted to the President his plan for the campaign, and it was approved, though reluctantly. McClellan's plan had been to interpose between Lee's divided forces. Already he was not far from such a position. From Longstreet's corps to Jackson's was over 40 miles by the roads across the mountains, and McClellan's forces were within 20 miles of either. But Lee could have delayed a march upon either, and, by falling back, might unite his two corps, behind the Robertson River, before accepting battle.

This had been Lee's plan, if the threat of Jackson's position upon the Federal flank should fail to prevent their advance.

Burnside's organization was as follows: —

GRAND DIVS.	CORPS	DIVISIONS	BRIGADES	ARTILLERY
Right Grand Division	2d Corps Couch	Hancock Howard French	Caldwell, Meagher, Zook Sully, Owen, Hall, Kimball, Palmer, Andrews	8 Batteries
Sumner	9th Corps Willcox	Sturgis Getty	Poe, Christ, Leasure Nagle, Ferrero Hawkins, Harland	6 Batteries
Centre Grand Division	3d Corps Stoneman	Birney Sickles Whipple	Robinson, Ward, Berry Carr, Hall, Revere Piatt, Carroll	9 Batteries
Hooker	5th Corps Butterfield	Griffin Sykes Humphreys	Barnes, Sweitzer, Stockton Buchanan, Andrew, Warren Tyler, Allabach	8 Batteries
Left Grand Division	1st Corps Reynolds	Doubleday Gibbon Meade	Phelps,Rogers,Gavin, Meredith Root, Lyle, Taylor Sinclair, Magilton, Jackson	11 Batteries
Franklin	6th Corps W.F.Smith	Brooks Howe Newton	Torbert, Cake, Russell Pratt, Whiting, Vinton Cochrane, Devens, Rowley	11 Batteries
	6 Corps	18 Divisions	51 Brigades	53 Batteries

Burnside began his campaign with a blunder. He adopted Richmond as his objective, instead of Lee's army. The latter was within a day's march of him, and its wings were separated by two days' march. Here was an opportunity for a skilful commander, but Burnside decided to make Fredericksburg a base, and to move thence upon Richmond. On Nov. 15, he turned his back upon Lee and marched for Fredericksburg. Meanwhile, he had made some important changes in his organization, by the formation of three grand divisions out of his six corps in order to lessen the routine duties of his office.[1]

Besides the troops shown above, the right grand division comprised two brigades of cavalry and a battery, and each of the others, one brigade of cavalry and a battery. There was also an artillery reserve of 12 batteries, an engineer brigade with the pontoon train, and an escort and a provost guard of infantry and cavalry.

On Dec. 10, the return of the army showed "present for duty," as follows: —

Right Grand Division, Sumner . . . 31,659
Centre Grand Division, Hooker . . . 40,396
Left   Grand Division Franklin . . 46,897 . . 118,952
The Artillery comprised 374 guns.

Besides these troops there were two corps, the 11th, with 15,562 present for duty, under Sigel; and the 12th, with 12,162, under Slocum, which Burnside called his reserve grand division. These troops, under command of Sigel, were on the march to Fredericksburg, but they did not arrive until after the battle.

Besides these, there were 51,970 holding the line of the Potomac above Washington, and the fortified lines about the city and Alexandria, with 284 guns of position, and 120 field-pieces. Thus, all together, there were available for use against Lee and to protect the capital, 198,546 men and about 900 guns.

On the same day, Dec. 10, Lee's return showed his present for duty, by divisions, as follows: —

[1] This organization was not kept up by Burnside's immediate successors, but under Grant in 1864 something equivalent was developed in separate armies and in large corps.

1st Corps, Longstreet	Strength	2d Corps, Jackson	Strength
Anderson's Division	7,639	Ewell's Division	7,716
Hood's Division	7,334	A. P. Hill's Division	11,554
McLaws's Division	7,898	D. H. Hill's Division	8,944
Pickett's Division	7,567	Jackson's Division	5,005
Ransom's Division	3,855	Reserve Artillery	473
Reserve Artillery	623		
		Total 2d Corps	33,692
Total 1st Corps	34,886	Total two Corps	68,578

Adding Pendleton's reserve artillery, 718, Stuart's cavalry, 9146, and 41 general staff, we have Lee's aggregate, 78,483, and about 250 guns. This was practically the largest army which Lee ever had in the field. Possibly, during the Seven Days, more troops were near Richmond, but, being organized only in divisions, or in independent brigades and batteries, and thus less easy to handle, they constituted a much less powerful army.

As before stated, on Nov. 15, Burnside commenced his movement upon Fredericksburg, Sumner's grand division leading the way. Already his cavalry had made reconnoissances which had attracted attention, and Lee, on the 15th, had sent a regiment of cavalry, one of infantry, and a battery to reënforce four companies of infantry and a battery already at Fredericksburg. Orders were also sent to destroy the railroad from Fredericksburg to Acquia Creek. On the 17th it was learned that gunboats and transports had entered Acquia Creek, on which W. H. F. Lee's brigade of cavalry was despatched in that direction, and Stuart was ordered to force a crossing of the Rappahannock and reconnoitre toward Warrenton. This was done on the 18th, and the enemy's general movement was discovered. A part of Longstreet's corps was put in motion on the 18th, and the remainder followed next day.

Sumner's corps arrived at Falmouth on the 17th, and an artillery duel ensued, across the river, rashly provoked by the Confederates, who had orders to oppose any force attempting to cross. It really came near inducing the enemy to cross, though under orders from Burnside not to do so. For under the superior metal of the Federals, the Confederate gunners were driven from their guns. There was a ford in the vicinity, and the temptation was strong to come over for them, but the existence of orders prevented its being done.

For Burnside had feared that Lee would overwhelm any small force which should cross before he was prepared to support it. Lincoln and Halleck, indeed, had only consented to the movement via Fredericksburg with the understanding that the army should possess itself of the heights opposite the town by crossing the river above and coming down. Burnside had deliberately changed this plan, after starting on the march. After the battle, his personal responsibility for the changed result was brought home to him unpleasantly.

Swinton asserts that Burnside —

"did not favor operating against Richmond by the overland route, but had his mind turned toward a repetition of McClellan's movement to the Peninsula; and in determining to march to Fredericksburg he cherished the hope of being able to winter there upon an easy base of supplies, and in the spring embarking his army for the James River."

The three weeks' delay between his arrival and his crossing the river suggests the lack of definite plans. At first the delay was attributed to the non-arrival of pontoon trains. These trains had been ordered on Nov. 6 from Rectortown to Washington City. This order failed to reach Berlin until the 12th.

Sumner was anxious to cross, and asked Burnside if he might do so without waiting for pontoons, "if he could find a ford." He had found the ford before he made the request, but Burnside's inclinations were adverse to a battle and he could not be beguiled.

So the small Confederate force held the town until the 20th, when Longstreet arrived with McLaws's division, and was followed the next day by the remainder of the corps.

On the 21st Sumner sent a formal demand for the surrender of the town, basing it upon the statement that his troops had been fired upon from under cover of the houses, and that mills and manufactories in the town were furnishing provisions and clothing to the enemy. He demanded an answer by 5 P.M., and said that if the surrender was not immediate at nine next morning, he would shell the town, the intermediate 16 hours being allowed for the removal of women and children.

This note, only received by the Mayor at 4.40 P.M., was referred to Longstreet, who authorized a reply to be made that the city would not be used for the purposes complained of, but that the Federals could only occupy the town by force of arms. Mayor Slaughter pointed out that the civil authorities had not been responsible for the firing which had been done, and, further, that during the night it would be impossible to remove the noncombatants. During the night Sumner sent word that in consideration of the pledges made, and, in view of the short time remaining for the removal of women and children, the batteries would not open as had been proposed.

But the letter left it to be inferred that the purpose to shell was only postponed, and Lee, who had now arrived, advised the citizens to vacate the town. This advice was followed by the greater part of the population. It was pitiable to see the refugees endeavoring to remove their possessions and encamping in the woods and fields, for miles around, during the unusually cold weather which soon followed.

This incident is responsible for the existence of most of the earthworks, which, at the time of the battle, contributed largely to the repulse of the enemy's assaults upon Marye's Hill. Great sympathy, of course, was felt for the citizens, and Lee, immediately after his arrival, ordered batteries to be erected, from which the enemy's positions, upon the hills commanding the town from the north, could be replied to by our rifled guns, in case of their shelling the town. Lee at first had not intended to give battle at Fredericksburg, but had proposed after delaying the enemy to fall back behind the North Anna River, and to deliver his battle there. Both he and Jackson objected to the position at Fredericksburg that the river, with the commanding positions on the north bank, could always afford a safe retreat to a beaten enemy, as the Antietam had done at Sharpsburg. This was undoubtedly true, as was soon afterward proved when the battle took place. At the North Anna the enemy, if defeated, might be successfully pursued and some fruits of victory be gathered.

But the position at Fredericksburg soon began to show its

good points, and as the country behind the Rappahannock was able to supply some subsistence which would otherwise be lost, it was decided to give battle at Fredericksburg, against Jackson's protest.

Burnside's pontoons arrived on Nov. 25. By this time a few earthworks showed upon the Confederate hills, and led him to delay, and to reconnoitre the river for a flank movement. Above Fredericksburg the country was hilly and wooded. The river was narrow, and there were several fords. These features would have made a crossing easy to accomplish by a surprise. Below the town the river widened, and the country opened. Yet Burnside adopted that flank for his movement, and began his preparations to cross at Skinker's Neck, 12 miles below Fredericksburg, where the river was over 1000 feet wide.

Lee discovered his preparations, and as Jackson's corps had arrived from the Valley about Nov. 29, it was moved to the right, and observed the river as far as Port Royal, 18 miles below. Jackson had not left Winchester until Nov. 22, five days after Sumner's arrival at Falmouth. His troops had marched 150 miles in 10 days, but Lee and Jackson had both presumed largely on Burnside's want of enterprise in allowing, for even a few days, 150 miles to separate the two corps. Lee had given no express orders to Jackson, but as late as Nov. 19, had written him to remain in the Valley as long as his presence embarrassed the enemy, but to keep in view that the two corps must be united in order to give battle.

The Federal army was supplied with balloons. McClellan had used them on the Peninsula, but during Pope's campaign, and in Md., they had not been seen, although the open character of the country would have often exposed and embarrassed the most important movements of the Confederates, had balloonists been on the lookout. Now, the balloons reconnoitring the country about Skinker's Neck, discovered Jackson's camps, and Burnside knew that his designs were disclosed. The discovery suggested an alternate piece of strategy. If he could cross at Fredericksburg, and rapidly push a force around Lee's right at Hamilton's Crossing, he might interpose between the forces about Skinker's Neck and those in front of Fredericksburg. The press-

ure upon him to fight was great, and on Dec. 10 the orders
were issued for a crossing that night. The programme was as
follows: —

Two bridges were to be thrown across the river at the upper
end of the town, one bridge at the lower end, and two about a
mile below the town. Where the bridges were in pairs, one was
for the use of artillery and one for infantry. The pontoon trains
were to arrive opposite the chosen sites at 3 A.M., and unload the
boats and material. By daylight this was to be finished and the
boats placed in the river. The bridges were then to be built in
from two to three hours. In length they would be from 400 to
440 feet. The weather was unusually cold, the thermometer
being 24 degrees above zero. The ice in the river was about an
inch thick. The bridges would be concealed from Confederate
fire by the town. On the north bank, 179 Federal guns were
put in position during the night, to cover the crossing, and it
was believed that they could instantly silence any musketry fire
from the opposite bank.

There had been ample time for the construction of formidable
earthworks and abattis, had Lee originally intended to receive
battle there. Probably 30 pits had been made, each for a single
gun, but in few places had any protection for infantry been
provided, except upon the river bank in front of the town. This
portion of the line was under charge of McLaws, who had carefully located every sharp-shooter with reference to his protection and his communications. Elsewhere there was little preparation of any sort.

There was, however, one natural feature which proved of great
value. The Confederate line occupied a range of low hills nearly
parallel to the river and a few hundred yards back from the
town. The Telegraph road, sunken from three to five feet
below the surface, skirted the bottom of these hills for about
800 yards, until it reached the valley of Hazel Run, into which
it turned. This sunken road was made part of the line of battle
for McLaws's infantry. It not only formed a parapet invisible
to the enemy until its defenders rose to fire over it, but it afforded
ample space for several ranks to load and fire, and still have
room behind them for free communication along the line. In

easy canister range, nine guns on the hills above could fire over the heads of the infantry. This position was known as Marye's Hill.

The crossing had been expected for some days, and orders given for two signal guns, whenever it was attempted. On the 10th Burnside's army was ordered to cook three days' rations, and the news was quickly conveyed to Lee, being shouted across the river to one of our pickets. At 2 A.M., the pickets reported that pontoon trains could be heard on the opposite bank, and at 4.30 A.M. the building of the bridges commenced. The signal guns were fired about 5 A.M., and the different brigades and batteries, already alert, quickly took positions in the early dawn. The day was calm and clear except for a peculiar smoky haze or dry fog which now prevailed in the forenoons for several days. In the early hours it limited vision to a range of scarcely 100 yards, but, as the sun rose higher, it faded and disappeared by noon.

The sharp-shooters along the river front had reserved their fire until after the discharge of the signal guns. They then opened upon the bridge builders, who could now be dimly seen, and soon drove them off the bridges with some loss. A heavy fire of infantry and artillery was opened in reply, upon the Confederate rifle-pits, under which they became silent. After a half-hour's fire, the bridge builders made a fresh attempt; but their appearance provoked fresh volleys from Barksdale, whose brigade was holding the city, and again the bridges were cleared. Several efforts of this sort were made during the morning, all resulting similarly, and the casualties in the Engineer brigade, which had the work in charge, ran up to near 50.

At the site selected for Franklin's crossing about a mile below the city, there was no opposition, for there was no shelter for even a Confederate skirmish-line. The bridges here were finished by 11 A.M. Franklin, however, was ordered not to cross until the resistance at the town had been overcome. Here, by 11 A.M., the Engineer brigade had abandoned the task of building bridges under fire. When this state of affairs was reported to Burnside, he ordered every gun in range of the city to fire 50 rounds into it. Probably 100 guns responded, and the spectacle which was now presented from the Confederate hilltops was one of the most magnificent and impressive in the whole course of the war.

The city, except its steeples, was still veiled in the mist which had settled in the valleys. Above it and in it incessantly showed the round white clouds of bursting shells, and out of its midst there soon rose three or four columns of dense black smoke from houses set on fire by the explosions. The atmosphere was so perfectly calm and still that the smoke rose vertically in great pillars for several hundred feet before spreading outward in black sheets. The opposite bank of the river, for two miles to the right and left, was crowned at frequent intervals with blazing batteries, canopied in clouds of white smoke.

Beyond these, the dark blue masses of over 100,000 infantry in compact columns, and numberless parks of white-topped wagons and ambulances massed in orderly ranks, all awaited the completion of the bridges. The earth shook with the thunder of the guns, and, high above all, a thousand feet in the air, hung two immense balloons. The scene gave impressive ideas of the disciplined power of a great army, and of the vast resources of the nation which had sent it forth.

Under cover of this storm of shell, the Federal bridge builders again ventured upon their bridges and tried to extend them, but the artillery fire had been at random into the town, and not carefully aimed at the locations of the sharp-shooters. Consequently, these had not been much affected, and presently the faint cracks of their rifles could be heard, between the reports of the guns. The contrast in sound was great, but the rifle fire was so effective that, again, the bridges were deserted. Indeed, the promiscuous fire of bombardments seldom accomplishes any result. Carnot, in his *Defence of Strong Places*, says that they "are resorted to when effective means are lacking." No citizen was reported injured, though many left the town only after firing began in the morning, and some remained during the whole occupation by the Federals.

Presently Gen. Hunt, chief of artillery, suggested an expedient. There were 10 pontoon boats in the water along the north shore. On the southern shore the sharp-shooters, a little back from the high brink of the river, could only see the farther half of its

width. Hunt proposed that troops should make a rush and fill
the boats. These should then be rowed rapidly across to the
shelter of the opposite shore, where the men could disembark
under cover. A lodgment once made, other troops could follow,
until a force was accumulated which could capture the rifle-pits.

This sensible course, which should have been the one first
adopted in the morning, under cover of the fog, was now tried.
Four regiments, the 7th Mich., the 19th and 20th Mass., and the
89th N.Y., volunteered for the crossing. The first boats suffered
some casualties, but were soon safe under shelter of the bank.
Other instalments followed, and the Confederates, appreciating
that their game was up, and that the bridges below the town
were already available, began to withdraw. The pontoniers
now returned to their work, and the bridges were completed.
Some skirmishing took place in the streets, and a few were cut
off and captured. But the defence had practically gained the
entire day, for although a division of the 6th corps crossed in
the afternoon, it was subsequently recalled, all but one brigade,
left to guard the bridge-heads during the night.

This delay robbed Burnside's strategy of its only merit. It
had been his hope to find Lee's army somewhat dispersed, as
indeed it had been; D. H. Hill's and Early's divisions having
been at Skinker's Neck and Port Royal, 12 to 22 miles away.
But they were recalled on the 12th and reached the field on the
morning of the 13th after hard marching. The casualties suffered
by the Confederates engaged in this defence were 224 killed and
wounded and 105 missing. Of the Federal losses, separate reports were made only of the Engineer brigade, engaged upon the
bridge work. This lost 50 killed and wounded, and Hancock
reported the loss of 150 in two regiments which had supported
the Engineers.

The night was quite cold, the thermometer falling to 26 degrees.
While this is not extreme for this latitude and season, it caused
great suffering among the troops from the South, generally thinly
clad, and for some months far from railroad transportation.
Especially was this the case on the picket-lines where fires were
forbidden. Kershaw reported it "a night of such intense cold as
to cause the death of one man, and to disable temporarily others."

The whole of the 12th was occupied in crossing two grand divisions. Sumner crossed the 2d and the 9th corps by the upper bridges and occupied the town. Franklin crossed the 1st and 6th corps by the lower bridges and occupied the plain as far out as the Bowling Green road, a half mile from the river, and the same distance in front of the wooded range of hills occupied by Jackson's corps. Much has been said of the strength of the Confederate position upon the hills overlooking the plateau of the valley, with its sunken road in front of Marye's Hill. The Federal position was even a stronger one, against any attack by the Confederates. The dominating hills and plateaus of the north bank, with its concave bend at Falmouth and unlimited positions for artillery, protected by the wet ditch, as it were, of the river in front, practically constituted a fortress, with the plains of the south bank as its glacis. The Bowling Green road, along their middle, running between high banks on each side, made a powerful advanced work, and the low bluffs near the river made a second line. The Confederate line, also concave in its general shape and dominating the plains between, was strong against assaults in front, but neither flank was secure against being turned. Its right especially was in the air at Hamilton's Crossing, and Burnside planned to attack this flank.

Franklin's grand division had been strengthened for that purpose by three divisions assigned to his support. One of them, Burns's, of the 9th corps, was already across the Rappahannock and on the left of Sumner, separated from Franklin's right only by Deep Run, across which bridges had been laid. The other two were Sickles's and Birney's divisions of the 3d corps, of Hooker's grand division, which was still upon the north side, but close to the bridges, in readiness to cross. With these troops, Franklin had nearly 60,000 men. During the afternoon of the 12th, Franklin had urged that these two divisions should be brought over during the night, and that preparations should be made for an advance at daylight. Burnside promised to order it, but the order was not given until the next morning.

He apparently lacked confidence in himself and shrank back from his own plans as the moment of execution drew near. Franklin had been informed that Burnside would give the final

order which should put his force in motion.   About 7 A.M. on
the 13th an order came, but it was not at all the order expected.
It made no reference to the plans of the day before, but ordered
Franklin to "keep his whole command in position for a rapid
movement down the old Richmond road."   Then he was to
"send out, at once, a division, at least, to seize, if possible, the
height near Capt. Hamilton's on this side of the Massaponax,
taking care to keep it well supported and its line of retreat open."

The order went on to tell Franklin what Sumner was to be
doing at the same time.   He was also to send "a division or more
up the Plank road to its intersection with the Telegraph road,
where they will divide with the view of seizing the heights on
both of these roads."   Then the order set forth what he hoped
to accomplish.   "Holding these two heights, he hopes will
compel the enemy to evacuate the whole ridge between them."
It is enough to say that this change from a single attack with
full force upon our right, to two weak and isolated attacks on
the right and left, lost the battle.   Being ordered to send "at
least a division," Franklin designated the 1st corps under
Reynolds for the attack upon the height at Hamilton's Crossing.
Meade's division was to lead, closely followed and supported by
Gibbon; Doubleday's was to protect the left flank of the advance, which was threatened by Stuart's artillery.   Franklin
would have also sent a portion of the 6th corps, but it had been
placed in position for the attack first planned, and time would
have been lost by a change.

The Confederate right flank was not well prepared to stand
the coming shock in view of the long warning it had had.   The
fact was that Jackson's troops had been in observation of the
river below, and had only arrived upon the field on the 12th.
Previously this flank had been held only by Hood's division, and
during its stay, little probability of attack had been foreseen.
Consequently, Hood made but two works of preparation.   On
the edge of the woods, overlooking the railroad, a trench had
been dug long enough to hold a brigade and a half; and through
the thick wood 500 yards in the rear, a road had been cleared,
affording communication behind the general line which occupied
the wooded hills.

On the 12th A. P. Hill was placed in front, to cover about a mile and a half of line with his six brigades. On the extreme right he posted 14 guns, and supported them with half of Brockenbrough's brigade. No other position for artillery offered along the front until the left of the division was reached. Here 12 guns were advanced north of the railroad, and 21 more were placed upon a low, open hill, south of the road some 200 yards to the left and rear, supported by Pender's brigade. The wooded hills between these positions were held by the four remaining brigades, but no two of them connected with each other. On the right, the other half of Brockenbrough's and Archer's brigade occupied the trenches which had been built by Hood. Archer's left rested on a swampy portion of the wood overgrown with underbrush, and it had carelessly been assumed to be impassable. Maj. Von Borcke, a German officer on Stuart's staff, had suggested felling it, but it was not thought worth while. On the far side of this swamp, Lane's brigade took up the line; the gap between it and Archer's being about 500 yards.

Beyond Lane was another considerable gap to his left and rear, where Pender's brigade was supporting the 12 and 21 guns before referred to. Behind Lane, about 400 yards, was Thomas's brigade. The remaining brigade of the division, Gregg's, was placed in the military road opposite the swamp and gap between Archer and Lane.

If we call this disposition of Hill's troops one of two lines, a third line was formed by the divisions of Early and Taliaferro — Early on the right—a short distance in rear, and a fourth one by the division of D. H. Hill in rear of that. Burnside was losing one of the advantages of his superior force by concentrating it upon too short a front. He was hemmed in on the left by Massaponax Creek, and was confined to a front attack. With only a mile and a half to defend and with about 30,000 infantry in hand, covered by the woods from accurate artillery fire, Jackson was very strong. With this understanding of the positions and forces the result might have been predicted. The faulty disposition of A. P. Hill's division, with two gaps in his front line, would surely allow to the enemy a temporary success. But the strong reserves close at hand were enough to restore the battle, and even induce a counter-stroke. The counter-stroke, however, must be driven back with loss when it ventures out into the plain. With this foregone result of the game set forth, we may now briefly describe the moves by which it was played on the left, before taking up the independent battle to be fought out during the whole afternoon by the Federal right.

During the night of the 12th, the ground was frozen, and the movements of artillery could be plainly heard through the fog, even before dawn brought the music of bands and commands of officers all strangely muffled but clearly audible in the still air. We were now about to measure our strength with the largest and best-equipped army that had ever stood upon a battle-field in America. But our own army was better organized and stronger than ever before, and now, finding itself concentrated at exactly the right moment, it was as confident and elated as if the victory had already been won.

About 10 A.M., the gradual clearing of the mist began to reveal the plain, and the Federal skirmishers and guns began to feel for our positions. Our own guns took little or no part in this preliminary firing, saving themselves for the approach of the hostile infantry. This was not long delayed, Meade's division of three brigades taking the lead, supported by Gibbon's division, a little in rear on its right flank, and Doubleday's on its left. Some delay ensued in their crossing the Bowling Green road, owing to the hedges and ditches lining it, which had to be made passable for the artillery, and here the Confederates first took the aggressive. From across the Massaponax "the gallant Pelham," as he was called by Lee in his report to Richmond for the day, opened an enfilading fire upon the Federal lines with two guns which he had advanced within easy range. Meade replied with 12 guns, and one of Doubleday's batteries assisted. Pelham frequently changed his position, but kept up his fire for nearly an hour until ordered by Jackson to withdraw, one gun having been disabled.

The advance was now resumed until within easy range, when a furious cannonade was opened upon the Confederate line, and maintained for nearly an hour. To this our guns made little reply, but both the artillery and infantry, concealed in the woods, suffered a good many casualties.

It was now about 11.30 A.M., and Meade's infantry again advanced and were soon within 800 yards of the Confederate batteries. These opened with the 47 guns in position upon the two flanks, and eight more sent out from Pendleton's reserve to Pelham. Under this fire the Federal advance was checked, and portions of the line, which received the brunt of it, were driven back. Meanwhile, fresh guns were added to the Federal line. The artillery duel raged for over an hour, when the Confederate fire ceased, the enemy's infantry being no longer in sight, and the Confederate guns low in ammunition.

Upon this check, Gibbon's division was sent to Meade's support and formed in column of brigades on Meade's right flank. Meade had two brigades in his front line, and his remaining brigade in a second line in close support. Doubleday's division was moved up nearer behind Meade's left, and engaged with Stuart's skirmishers and artillery across the Massaponax. Birney's and Newton's divisions of the 3d and 6th corps were also sent forward to the Bowling Green road to support the attack, which Meade, at 1 P.M., was about to renew with Gibbon on his right. So the assault had a front of three brigades, and was three lines deep behind the right brigade; two lines deep behind the centre brigade, and only one line deep on the left.

The Confederate artillery fire at once reopened, but in weaker force than before, owing to its losses and expenditures, and the attacking forces were soon within musket range. Crashes of infantry now swelled the roar to the proportions of a great battle, mingling with a similar tumult which had now broken out in front of Fredericksburg. The battle was now on in its full force at two points, nearly five miles apart. Franklin's part in it was of the shortest duration, and will be first told.

Gibbon's division on Meade's right overlapped the left flank of Lane's brigade, and came in front of the 33 guns on A. P. Hill's left. The 12 in advance had to be withdrawn to escape capture, but Gibbon's three brigades were able to do no more than to fight their way up to the railroad with the loss of 1267 men; the two foremost brigades being successively broken and reënforced by the brigade following.

On Meade's extreme left, his 3d brigade, under Gen. C. F. Jackson, found the artillery fire from the 14-gun battery on Hill's right so effective that it abandoned the direct advance, and, inclining to the right, it moved behind Meade's other brigades and took part in their fight, which has now to be described.

The marshy woods before referred to, which filled the wide gap between Archer and Lane, extended in a long triangle to the front across the railroad. The march of Meade's division brought its right brigade into this wood, where the men found themselves free from the Confederate artillery fire. Not only were they hidden from view, but they were too far to the left for the guns on the right flank, and too far to the right for the guns on the left flank. It was this immunity from fire which brought C. F. Jackson's brigade into the woods, and thus formed Meade's division into a column of three brigades. This column, without firing a shot or meeting a picket, made its way entirely through the woods, until it fell upon Archer's left flank and Lane's right flank, turning each, and capturing about 300 prisoners. Archer's men were so taken by surprise that some of his troops were caught with their arms stacked. Two regiments were quickly routed, and it was said that they were fired on as they retreated by their own comrades, who believed them to be deserting their posts without cause.

But the other regiments of Archer's brigade held firmly, repulsing the enemy by the help of the troops on their right. Lane's brigade, attacked in front by Gibbon's division and its right flank turned by Meade's through the unoccupied gap, was forced back in the woods, until Thomas's brigade came to its support. This soon restored the line. Of Meade's three brigades, the leading one was drawn into these separate fights upon each flank, while the second brigade continued to push forward. In this way it advanced unseen and unmolested for 500 yards, when it came upon the brigade of Gregg at rest in the so-called military road. Meade immediately opened a hot fire. Gregg could not realize that a Federal brigade could be so far within our lines. He rushed in front of Orr's regiment, beating up the muskets of men who were firing and calling out that they were firing on friends, until he fell mortally wounded. This was the culmination of the Federal attack, and its collapse came quickly.

Orr's regiment was broken, but the rest of the brigade stood firm, and changed front to meet the Federal advance. The latter were already in confusion when Lawton's brigade came to reënforce Gregg, and the enemy was driven back rapidly. Hoke's brigade was also sent to the assistance of Archer, and Early's brigade to support Lane and Thomas. The whole Federal advance was driven from the woods and pursued out into the plain. The troops of Archer, Lane, and Thomas, or portions of them, joined in the counter-stroke, and the whole of both Meade's and Gibbon's divisions were involved and carried along with the retreat. But there was no adequate debouchment from the dense woods for rapid advance, and when the Confederates, disorganized by the pursuit, met the fresh troops of the enemy, the advance was checked, and, unpursued, it fell back to the line of the railroad. Indeed, the whole advance beyond the railroad had been unwise. Its only result would surely be the loss of the most daring of the pursuers. And the loss of such men from a brigade is like the loss of temper from a blade.[1]

The Federals made no further effort on their left during the day, and distant sharp-shooting, with intermittent artillery, was

[1] In illustration, I quote from the report of Col. Evans, commanding Lawton's brigade, as follows: —

"I cannot forbear to mention in terms of unqualified praise the heroism of Capt. E. P. Lawton, Asst. Adjt.-Gen. of the brigade, from the beginning of the advance until near the close of the fight, when he received a dangerous wound, and was unavoidably left in the open plain where he fell. Cheering on the men, leading this regiment, or restoring the line of another, encouraging officers, he was everywhere along the whole line, the bravest among the brave. Just as the four regiments emerged from the neck of woods referred to, his horse was shot under him, and, in falling, so far disabled him that thousands, less ardent or determined, would have felt justified in leaving the field; but limping on he rejoined the line again in their advance toward the battery, but soon received the wound with which he fell."

The wound unfortunately proved mortal. Gen. Burnside, a few days later, generously returned the body to the Confederate lines, giving it an escort of honor from the hospital across the river.

now the only activity until near sundown, which occurred about 4.45.

Burnside, at 1 P.M., had sent orders to Franklin to attack with the 6th corps on the right of Gibbon, and at 2 P.M. had repeated the order urgently and explicitly. But about this time Meade and Gibbon were driven back, and pursued, and put so completely out of action that fresh divisions had to replace them. When his left had been made secure, Franklin thought it too late to organize a fresh attack.

Jackson had noted within the Federal lines movements of troops and artillery with which they were preparing themselves to resist further attack. He had misinterpreted them, and supposed them to be preparations for a renewed assault. His appetite for battle had not been satisfied, and seeing the heavy force at the enemy's disposal, he could not believe that they would be content with an affair of only two or three divisions. He accordingly waited to receive the expected assault, and finally, when it did not materialize, he determined to take the offensive himself. Apparently, he did not yet fully appreciate that the enemy's position was practically a citadel. But he fortunately discovered it in time. While his assault was being prepared, he had indulged in some preliminary cannonading, which had put the enemy fully on the alert. In his official report, he writes: —

"In order to guard against disaster the infantry was to be preceded by artillery, and the movement postponed until later in the evening, so that, if compelled to retire, it would be under the cover of night. Owing to unexpected delays the movement could not be gotten ready until late in the evening. The first gun had hardly moved forward from the wood 100 yards when the enemy's artillery reopened, and so completely swept our front as to satisfy me that the proposed movement should be abandoned."

A. P. Hill's division, which bore the brunt of the fighting on the 13th, out of 11,000, lost 2122 men. Early's, which came to his support, lost 932 out of 7500. The other divisions lost less than 200 each, principally from the heavy artillery fire which the enemy threw into the woods. Meade's division, out of 5000, lost 1853, and Gibbon lost 1267. So the casualties of the two fighting divisions on each side were nearly balanced; the Confederate loss being 3054 out of about 18,500 engaged, and the Federal, 3120 out of about 10,000 engaged.

We will now take up affairs at Fredericksburg. In his plans on the 12th, Burnside had not proposed a direct attack from the town, but on the 13th, as already told, had directed Sumner to prepare to assault Marye's Hill with at least two divisions, but

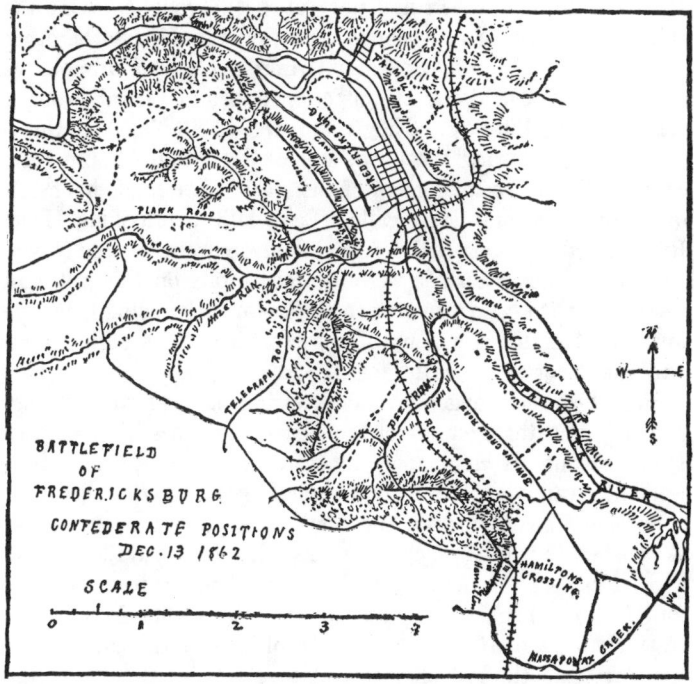

he was not to advance until Burnside gave the order. At first he proposed to give it only when Franklin had gotten possession of the hill at Hamilton's Crossing; but about 10.30, becoming impatient, he delayed no longer.

The selection of the point of attack immediately opposite the town was perhaps influenced by the shelter afforded the troops within the town. But it was a fatal mistake. The most obvious, and the proper attack for the Federal right, was one turning the Confederate left along the very edge of the river above Falmouth, supported by artillery on the north bank which could enfilade and take in reverse the Confederate left flank. This attack is indicated by the concave north bank of the river, and it offered the easiest proposition to the Federals of the whole topography.

Sumner's grand division numbered about 27,000 on the field. Hooker's grand division had not yet been brought across the river, except the two divisions supporting Franklin. The other four (Whipple of the 3d corps, and Griffin, Sykes, and Humphreys of the 5th) were held near the upper bridges, and were all brought across during the day. They numbered about 26,000. Burnside's position during the battle was at the Phillips house, on a commanding hill a mile north of the river. Lee made his headquarters on a hill, since called Lee's Hill, overlooking Hazel Run and the eastern half of the field in front of the town. Two 30-Pr. Parrott rifles were located in pits on this hill, and were used with good effect upon the enemy advancing from the lower part of the town, until one exploded at its 39th round, and the other at its 54th.

Here Lee and Longstreet stood during most of the fighting, and it is told that, on one of the Federal repulses from Marye's Hill, Lee put his hand upon Longstreet's arm and said, "It is well that war is so terrible, or we would grow too fond of it."

Sumner's advance from the town began about noon. With skirmishers in front, French moved his brigades by parallel streets, and, crossing on bridges the little canal (about 20 feet wide and four feet deep) some 300 yards from the town, they formed successively for the attack in a considerable sheltered area, between the canal and the low bluff of a plateau which extended to the front some 400 to 500 yards from the sunken road at the foot of Marye's Hill.

The three brigades of French formed in the order — Kimball, Andrews, Palmer. In close support came Hancock with Zook, Meagher, and Caldwell. Howard's division was also brought out from the town as a further support. There was no special difficulty in coming from the town and getting under cover in the sheltered area above described, although it was done under fire of our artillery. The real trouble would lie in advancing about 400 yards across the plateau to the sunken road. There was no intervening abattis or ditch, but there were some small houses, gardens, and fences, affording some shelter, but breaking the continuity of the ranks. These two divisions numbered about 9000 men.

The front line of the Confederate defence was held by three Ga. regiments in the sunken Telegraph road, the 18th, 24th, and Philip's legion of Cobb's brigade. The 24th N.C. of Ransom's held an infantry trench, which extended from the Telegraph to the Plank road.

On the crest of the hill above the road were four 12-Pr. guns, two 12-Pr. howitzers, and three 10-Pr. rifles, comprising the three batteries of the New Orleans Washington artillery under Col. Walton. On the left of the Plank road were four guns of Maurin's battery, in pits, and, at Stansbury's house, Parker's battery of Alexander's battalion, with four guns, found positions during the afternoon to fire upon the enemy's right flank. His left flank was also partially exposed to the fire of the two Parrotts on Lee's Hill. The infantry in the sunken road and ditch numbered at the commencement of the action only about 2000; but in support behind Marye's Hill were about 7000 more, most of whom were brought into action later.

As each of the six brigades at short intervals was advanced over the crest of the plateau, it met the Confederate fire. Kimball's brigade led, and no brigade during the day advanced farther, and but few as far. But he was wounded, and his brigade repulsed with a loss of 520 men within 20 minutes. Andrew's brigade followed, and was likewise driven back with the loss of 342. Palmer, who came next, lost 291. The whole loss of the division (including its artillery which fired from the edge of the town) was 1160. About this time Ransom, seeing preparations for further attack, reënforced his line by Cooke's brigade. The 27th N.C. took position in the sunken road, and the 15th, 46th, and 48th occupied the crest of the hill, giving a second tier of infantry fire.

The remnants of French's division, extending to right and left, took shelter in slight undulations and kept up fire both at

the Confederate guns and infantry. Hancock's division soon
followed French's and with a similar experience, but more prolonged and bloody. His leading brigade, Zook's, lost 527. The
second, Meagher's, lost 545, and the third, Caldwell's, lost 952.
The loss of the division was 2032. The battle at this point had
developed into a fearful example of successive attacks by small
forces; the same vicious game which had lost 2d Manassas and
Sharpsburg. But Burnside was now obstinate, and was ordering in fresh troops upon each of his two battle-fields. The turn
of Howard's division came next. He had been at first directed
to attack upon his right of the Plank road, and was preparing to
do so, when Hancock called for supports, and Howard was
diverted to the same field. His leading brigade, Owen's, did
not push its assault so far as to be broken by the Confederate fire,
but lay down where it could find a little cover. It was able here
to hold its position until relieved after nightfall. His losses
were 258. Howard's second brigade was Hall's, which was sent
upon its charge somewhat to the right of the ground covered by
the preceding charges. He was broken, rallied, charged again,
and was again driven back, when he also found shelter, halted his
command, and held on until night, having lost 515 men.

Howard's third brigade was Sully's, which was kept in reserve,
and two regiments sent to reënforce Owens, and one to Hall.
The losses in this brigade reached 122. Howard's entire loss
was 914. Couch's whole corps had now been practically wrecked
with a loss of 4114 men, in fighting eight separate battles with
his nine brigades, against a force not half his size, all within
four hours.

Next to the left of Couch's corps was the 9th, under Willcox.
Sturgis's division of two brigades was on its right, occupying the
lower portion of the city. Next came Getty's division of two
brigades under cover of the bluffs at the mouth of Hazel Run.
Burns's division of three brigades on the left connected with
Franklin at Deep Run, and was under his orders. During the
day Burns went across Deep Run to Franklin's support.

When French's division was advanced, Sturgis was ordered to
support it upon its left. He threw forward Dickenson's battery
and Ferrero's brigade. The battery received a heavy fire from

guns on and near Lee's Hill, and was soon disabled and with-drawn, Dickenson being killed. Ferrero advanced from the lower part of the city to the left of the ground over which French and Hancock had fought. He did not have the canal to cross, as it terminated near the railroad. He met a severe fire, however, and finding depressions of ground in which his troops could get cover, his brigade occupied them for the rest of the day and fired from 60 to 200 rounds per man at the Confederate lines and batteries.

Sturgis's second brigade, under Nagle, about an hour later, was ordered to support Sturgis's on the left. After some delay in crossing ravines, this brigade also found cover somewhat to Ferrero's rear, which it occupied and joined in the fire upon the Confederate lines until dark.

Ferrero's casualties were 491 and Nagle's 500. About 3 P.M., Ferrero having asked for reënforcements, and Griffin's division having reported as support to the 9th corps, Barnes's brigade, of that division, was sent in over the same ground that Ferrero had traversed. This brigade also made a gallant advance, but finally took cover with the loss of 500.

Meanwhile, Whipple's division of the 3d corps, of two brigades, which had been placed at the upper end of the town to guard the right flank, having no enemy close in front, sent Carroll's brigade to support Sturgis. Griffin placed Sweitzer's brigade on the right of Carroll, and sent forward the two brigades sup-porting them with Stockton's brigade, the last of his division.

This charge of Griffin's was the eleventh separate effort made up to this time. But the infantry fire met was now being con-stantly increased, the Telegraph road affording the opportunity. Cobb had been killed and Cooke, soon after, severely wounded early in the affair. On the latter event, Kershaw with his bri-gade was ordered up, and about the same time, Ransom brought up the remaining three regiments of his brigade. Some of these troops doubled upon those already in the sunken road, until there were six ranks. These were effectively handled by Ker-shaw in person. Others took the best partial cover they could find about the top and slopes of the hill, whence their fire con-tributed to that from the sunken road. There the six ranks fired successive volleys from each rank, with only a few seconds' intervals. A regiment from Jenkins's brigade was also advanced down the right bank of Hazel Run, reënforcing a company of sharp-shooters which had been doing fine service all day upon the enemy's flanks.

Under this increased fire Griffin's charge differed but little in its results from those immediately preceding it. The men advanced as far as they could find some partial protection, and there they lay down. Carroll's brigade here lost 118; Sweitzer's 222; and Stockton's 201. It was now nearly four o'clock and there came a comparative lull in the conflict. But Hooker was under orders to attack with his whole force, and he had yet intact Humphreys's and Sykes's divisions of the 5th corps. Even before Griffin's charge, Hooker had looked at the field, and become so convinced that the Confederate line could not be carried, that he had sent an aid to Burnside to say that he advised against attack. The answer came that the attack must be made. Hooker, however, considered it a duty to his troops to make a fuller explanation, and endeavored to dissuade Burnside from what he was sure would be a hopeless effort. Burnside still insisted that the position must be carried before night.

Hooker, accordingly, returned and began to prepare for the attack by advancing as many batteries as could be located on the edge of the town, and even sending two, Hazard's and Frank's, across the canal, where they opened with a range of less than 300 yards.

While these preparations were going on, the troops holding the hollows and undulations in front, where they had found shelter when the charges had been repulsed, reported that the Confederates were withdrawing from their positions. This report was quickly spread and reached Couch, who said to Humphreys, "Hancock reports the enemy is falling back. Now is the time for you to go in." [1]

[1] This false impression doubtless arose from seeing the nine guns on the crest of Marye's Hill limber up, and leave the hill. When the lull in the firing occurred, Walton had requested Alexander's battalion to relieve his guns, which had nearly exhausted their ammunition. Nine fresh guns were quickly moved up. Walton's guns were withdrawn to give clear roads, and the reliefs replaced them at a gallop. These movements were seen by the enemy and thought to be the beginning of a retreat.

Humphreys's division was composed of two brigades, Allabach's and Tyler's, and it went into action 4500 strong.   It
was already under urgent orders to attack.   Allabach's brigade
was in front, and Tyler's in motion to get upon its right flank.

Now, without waiting for Tyler, Humphreys ordered Allabach to advance, and, throwing themselves in front, he and
Allabach led the charge.   In about 200 yards they reached the
continuous line now formed of the fragments of the preceding
charges, lying down where they could find cover.   Here, in spite
of all their efforts, Allabach's troops also lay down and began
to fire.   Humphreys could now see the Confederate line, and
appreciated that it was so covered that fire against it was of little
effect.   With some difficulty and delay he succeeded in checking the fire of his men, got them on their feet, and again started
to advance.   Up to this point his line had had partial cover, but
now for 150 yards there was none.   They advanced for 50 yards
and then broke, a part stopping with the line of remnants, and
the remainder were rallied near the canal.

Tyler's brigade after a little delay was formed in a double line
of battle on the left of Allabach's position.   It had first moved
to the right, but there met enfilading fire of artillery, and it was
withdrawn to the left.   Humphreys joined it and ordered the
charge to be made with the bayonet alone, and that the men
should pass directly over the line of those lying down.

Meanwhile, as sundown approached, Burnside's orders had
grown urgent that the position should be carried before dark.
Getty's division of the 9th corps, two brigades, from the left on
Hazel Run, was ordered to assault, but no steps were taken to
have it simultaneous with that of Humphreys.

Had there been time, Humphreys, from his experience with
Allabach, would have preferred to first clear his path of the line
of men lying down, already spoken of.   Not only were they
physically much in the way, but even more were they a moral
obstacle.   A repulsed line, which is not ready to join in a fresh
assault, does not at all like a new line to pass over it, for it seems
a reflection upon their courage.   They are apt to do all they can
to discourage and obstruct the newcomers, and the latter cannot fail to appreciate that an advance, leaving a large force

behind, is very liable to receive fire from the rear, intended to go over their heads, but likely to land a good many bullets in their backs. And, even if this does not happen, a false alarm of "fire from the rear," is almost sure to occur.

Under the conditions confronting him, Humphreys's charge was utterly hopeless, and should never have been made. But it illustrated a high type of disciplined valor, and, but for the men lying down, might have crossed bayonets with the Confederates. The six ranks of seasoned veterans in the road, however, could scarcely have been overcome by those who would arrive.

With all its officers in front, led by Humphreys and Tyler, and with a loud hurrah, which was a signal to our guns on the hill to put in rapid work from full chests of canister, Tyler's brigade now made a rapid advance under what, in his official report, Humphreys called "the heaviest fire yet opened, which poured upon it from the moment it first rose from the ravine." They came in two lines, quite close together, and without firing a shot. A more beautiful charge is not recorded in the annals of the Army of the Potomac.

Its experiences, as told in the official reports both of Humphreys and Tyler, are instructive. Humphreys writes: —

"As the brigade reached the masses of men referred to, every effort was made by the latter to prevent our advance. They called to our men not to go forward, and some attempted to prevent by force their doing so. The effect upon my command was what I apprehended.... The line was somewhat disordered, and, in part, was forced to fall into a column, but still advanced rapidly. The fire of the enemy's musketry and artillery, furious as it was before, now became still hotter. The stone wall was a sheet of flame that enveloped the head and flanks of the column. Officers and men were falling rapidly, and the head of the column was at length brought to a stand when close up to the wall. Up to this time not a shot had been fired by the column, but now some firing began. It lasted but a minute, when, in spite of all our efforts, the column turned and began to retire slowly. I attempted to rally the brigade behind the natural embankment, so often mentioned, but the united efforts of Gen. Tyler, myself, our staffs, and the other officers could not arrest the retiring mass. My efforts were the less effective, since I was again dismounted, my second horse having been killed under me. . . . Our loss in both brigades was heavy, exceeding 1000 in killed and wounded, including in the number

officers of high rank.   The greater part of the loss occurred during the brief
time they were charging and retiring, which scarcely occupied more than
10 or 15 minutes for each brigade."

Tyler's report says: —

"The brigade moved forward, in as good order as the muddy condition
of the ground on the left of my line would admit, until we came upon a
body of officers and men lying flat upon the ground in front of the brick
house, and along the slight elevation on its right and left.   Upon our approach the officers commanded halt, flourishing their swords as they
lay, while a number of their men tried to intimidate our troops by crying
out that we would be slaughtered, etc.   An effort was made to get them out
of the way, but failed, and we marched over them.   When we were within
a very short distance of the enemy's line, a fire was opened on our rear,
wounding a few of my most valuable officers, and, I regret to say, killing
some of our men.   Instantaneously the cry ran along our lines that we
were being fired into from the rear.   The column halted, receiving at the
same time a terrible fire from the enemy.   Orders for the moment were
forgotten, and a fire from our whole line was immediately returned.   Another cry passed along the line, that we were being fired upon from the rear,
when our brave men, after giving the enemy several volleys, fell back."

Besides suffering from the infantry fire of their own men in the
rear, the Federal column, or portions of it, also believed that
the Federal artillery above Falmouth, which kept up a constant
long-range fire with their heavy rifles upon the Confederate
position, had mistaken localities and was landing its projectiles
in the Federal ranks.   Couch writes of this charge of Humphreys's division, as follows, in the *Century Magazine:* —

"The musketry fire was very heavy and the artillery fire was simply
terrible.   I sent word several times to our artillery on the right of Falmouth that they were firing into us and were tearing our men to pieces.
I thought they had made a mistake in the range, but I learned later that
the fire came from the guns of the enemy on their extreme left."

This fire came from Parker's battery, of my battalion, located
near the Stansbury house.   The losses in Allabach's brigade were
officially reported as 562, and those in Tyler's as 454.

The attacks by these brigades were the twelfth and thirteenth
separate charges of the day, and there was still one to follow.

Getty's division, comprising Hawkins's and Harland's brigades,
received orders to attack about the same time that Humphreys
was arranging his attack.   Being near the mouth of Hazel Run,

they had farther to advance before reaching the field, and only arrived upon it after Tyler was repulsed. They had not been engaged during the day, but had suffered some casualties from premature explosions of Federal shell fired from the hills across the river. Hawkins's brigade led, advancing by right of companies as far as the railroad, where the brigade line was reformed and a fresh start taken, directed at the southern extremity of Marye's Hill. Harland's brigade was to follow in similar formation.

In view of the lateness of the hour, this charge was even more hopeless than any of the preceding. Hawkins had protested against it before starting, but the orders were explicit. By the time that the division crossed the railroad, it was so dark that distinct vision was limited to a few hundred feet. The first portion of the march was unobserved by the Confederates, and the line rapidly advanced until it came to marshy ground, through which ran a ditch to Hazel Run. Here they opened fire, and their position was defined to the Confederates by the flashes of their muskets, and infantry and artillery replied from Marye's Hill, from across Hazel Run, and from guns upon Lee's Hill. They crossed the ditch, however, and had advanced quite close to the sunken road, when suddenly the infantry in it opened fire, and, at the same time, fire was opened upon them from the right and rear by the line of Federals lying down, in front of whom their advance from the left had brought them. Hawkins thus describes the scene : —

"When the brigade arrived at this cut [ditch] it received an enfilading fire from the enemy's artillery and infantry, but, notwithstanding, the plateau on the other side was gained, the left of the line advancing till within about 10 yards of a stone wall, behind which a heavy infantry force of the enemy was concealed, which opened an increased artillery and infantry fire, and, in addition to this, the brigade received the fire of the 83d Pa. Volunteers and of the 20th Me. Volunteers who were on the left of Gen. Couch's line, which our right had overlapped. This firing from all quarters, and from all directions, I should think, lasted about seven minutes, when I succeeded in stopping it and then discovered that the greatest confusion existed. Everybody, from the smallest drummer boy up, seemed to be shouting to the full of his capacity. After considerable exertion, comparative quiet and order were restored, and the command re-formed along the canal cut [ditch]. I then reported to you for further orders, and you ordered the command withdrawn, and placed in its former position in the town."

Getty not only showed good judgment in withdrawing Hawkins's brigade on the first opportunity, but he had done even better with Harland's brigade, for he halted it near the railroad, and did not permit it to participate in the charge. Sykes's division was also held in reserve on the edge of the town, behind Humphreys, and at 11 P.M. was sent across the canal, where it relieved the remnants of all of the brigades which had made their advances from that quarter.

The Confederate fire soon ceased when the flashes of the enemy's guns no longer gave targets. The losses in Hawkins's brigade had been 255, in Harland's they were 41.

Among the Confederates, no one conceived that the battle was over, for less than half our army had been engaged, only four out of nine divisions. It was not thought possible that Burnside would confess defeat by retreating.

Burnside himself, however, was far from having given up the battle, and, though many prominent officers advised against it, he determined to renew the attack at dawn. He proposed to form the whole 9th corps into a column of regiments and to lead it in person upon Marye's Hill.

He came across the river after the fighting ceased, gave the necessary orders, and returned to the Phillips house about 1 A.M. He found there waiting for him Hawkins, who had made the last charge, and who had now come at the request of Willcox, Humphreys, Meade, Getty, and others to protest against the proposed attack, and to give information about the situation, which it was supposed that Burnside did not possess. A long conference ensued in the presence of Sumner, Hooker, and Franklin, the commanders of the three grand divisions. On their unanimous advice, verbal orders were sent countermanding the proposed assault. Before these could be delivered, many preparatory movements were under way. And while they were in progress, a courier bearing orders which disclosed Burnside's plan, becoming lost in the darkness, wandered up to our picket-line. He was captured, and his orders were found and taken to Longstreet and Lee. Notice was at once sent along our lines, with instructions to extend and strengthen our intrenchments, and to make all necessary preparations of ammunition, water, and provisions, which was vigorously set about with no suspicion that Burnside would disappoint us.

So on the 14th, when, at dawn, the Confederates stood to arms, they looked and listened in vain for signs of the fresh assaults which the captured order had led them to expect. About 10 o'clock, the morning fog began to lighten, and a vicious sharp-shooting sprang up. Sykes's regulars were now in our front, and the guns from the Stafford hills kept up a slow target practice at our lines, to which we made no reply.

The day passed without serious hostilities. During the afternoon some of their shells prematurely exploding, caused orders to be issued not to fire any more at our position about Marye's Hill.

During the night of the 14th, we received ammunition from Richmond, and Longstreet authorized a moderate fire on the 15th, to suppress the sharp-shooting. During the night, also, we had located two guns on our left where they could enfilade the sheltered position, in front of the canal, from which the Federal attacks had come.

So, on the 15th, our position was agreeably improved. A few shots, raking the depressions in which the enemy had so far found shelter, routed the picket reserves. A single shot into a loopholed brick tannery on the Plank road, silenced it, and for the rest of the day nothing annoyed us, and we worked openly at our defences.

The night of the 15th was dark and rainy, with high wind from the south, preventing us from hearing noises from the enemy's direction. During the night Burnside safely withdrew across the river. Commencing his movement at 7 P.M., his whole enormous force was across in 12 hours of a stormy night. It was a great feat, and its successful performance, unmolested, under our guns, reflects badly upon the vigilance of the Confederates. It should have been suspected, discovered by scouts, and vigorously attacked with artillery.

On the morning of the 15th, both Hooker on the right and Franklin on the left had applied to Burnside for permission to send a flag of truce and recover the wounded in their respective fronts. It seems that Hooker's request was refused, for no flag was here shown. But on Franklin's front an informal arrangement was made by which all picket firing ceased, and the Federal ambulances and burial parties were allowed to remove the dead and wounded in front of our pickets, and our own men brought forward and delivered those who had fallen within our lines. On the 16th, when the city was evacuated, very few of the wounded who had fallen on the 13th in front of the town were found alive.

The Federal guns were, generally, still in position on the hills on the north side, and a few spiteful shells were thrown by them in the early hours, but, before noon, the pickets of both sides were peacefully reëstablished.

The whole action resolved itself into two separate offensive battles by the Federals, one on their right and one on their left, with some unimportant skirmishing in the centre. The forces present or near at hand on each field, and the losses, may be divided about as follows: —

		FEDERAL RIGHT ATTACK	FEDERAL CENTRE SKIRMISH	FEDERAL LEFT ATTACK	AGGREGATE
Federal	Forces	51,623	13,735	39,337	104,695
	Losses	7,817	383	4,447	12,647
Confederate	Forces	20,043	14,901	43,569	78,513
	Losses	1,589	305	3,415	5,309

Whatever may be said of Burnside's strategy or tactics, he was not deficient in moral courage. Although well aware that most of his generals were in a despondent mood, he determined within a very few days to make a fresh effort. He had his cavalry reconnoitre the river below Fredericksburg, and then decided to cross in that direction.

On Dec. 26 he ordered three days' cooked rations, and 10 days' rations in the wagons, with beef cattle, forage, and ammunition, all to be prepared to move at 12 hours' notice. His cavalry advance was already in motion for a raid within the Confederate lines, when he received a message from President Lincoln forbidding any movement without his being previously informed. This interference broke up his plan. Some of the generals had communicated it to the President with adverse criticisms.

Not discouraged, however, he soon devised another, and, doubtless, a better one. He proposed to cross the river at Banks Ford, only about four miles above Fredericksburg, making at the same time demonstrations at several points, both above and below. His losses at Fredericksburg had been more than repaired by the arrival within reach of the 11th and 12th army corps, some 30,000 strong, under Sigel. There had been good weather since the battle and the roads were in fair order. He had visited Washington and sought the approval of the President and War Department, but had found them reluctant to give it, being influenced by the general distrust of Burnside's ability among the principal officers of his army.

To bring the matter to an issue, Burnside tendered his resignation, to be accepted "in case it was not deemed advisable for him to cross the river." He then returned and hurried his preparation. On Jan. 20, he put his army in motion. Positions for 184 guns had been selected, covering the approaches to the points chosen for crossing, and roads had been found and opened as secretly as possible. But, nevertheless, the Federal activity had been noted, especially at Banks and United States fords, and, on the 19th, Lee sent a brigade to strengthen our pickets there. As the distances were not great from the Federal camps before Fredericksburg to the positions about Banks Ford, most of their guns were able to reach their positions by the night of the 20th. About dark on that day, a violent rainstorm set in, which continued all that night and the two following days. The pontoon trains in rear of the guns had farther to go, and were unwieldy to handle. Many troops and trains were still far from their destinations, and now every road became a deep quagmire, and even small streams were impassable torrents. Although desperate efforts were made all during the night to get the pontoons to the river, when morning dawned, not enough for a single bridge had arrived, and five bridges were required.

Swinton writes of the situation, as follows: —

"It would have been judicious in Gen. Burnside to have promptly abandoned a situation that was now hopeless. But it was a characteristic of that general's mind (a characteristic that might be good or bad according to the direction it took) never to turn back when he had once put his hand to the plough; and it had already, more than once, been seen that the more hopeless the enterprise, the greater his pertinacity. The night's rain had made deplorable havoc with the roads, but Herculean efforts were made to bring pontoons enough into position to build a bridge or two withal. Double and triple teams of mules were harnessed to each boat, but it was in vain. Long stout ropes were then attached to the teams, and a hundred and fifty men put to the task on each. The effort was but little more successful. Floundering through the mire for a few feet, the gang of Lilliputians, with their huge ribbed Gulliver, were forced to give over, breathless. Night arrived, but the pontoons could not be gotten up, and the enemy's pickets, discovering what was going on, jocularly shouted their intention to 'come over to-morrow and help build the bridges.'

"Morning dawned upon another day of rain and storm. The ground had gone from bad to worse, and now showed such a spectacle as might be presented by the elemental wrecks of another deluge. An indescribable chaos of pontoons, vehicles, and artillery encumbered all the roads — supply wagons upset by the roadside, guns stalled in the mud, ammunition trains mired by the way, and hundreds of horses and mules buried in the liquid muck. The army, in fact, was embargoed. It was no longer a question of how to go forward — it was a question of how to get back. The three days' rations, brought on the persons of the men, were exhausted, and the supply trains could not be moved up. To aid the return, all the available force was put to work to corduroy the rotten roads. Next morning the army floundered and staggered back to the old camps, and so ended a movement that will always live, in the recollection of the army, as the 'Mud March,' and which remains a striking exemplification of the enormous difficulties incident to winter campaigning in Va."

Burnside's plan had been a good one, and his army, with the 11th and 12th corps, had numbered on Jan. 20, 152,516 present for duty, besides 45,239 in the defences of Washington. But for the rain-storm — the "Act of God" — he certainly had reasonable ground to hope for success. But he was not disposed to lay the whole blame upon the storm. He had been greatly dissatisfied with Franklin, and his conduct of his command, at the battle of Fredericksburg, and he now keenly resented hostile criticisms which had injured him in estimation of the President.

From the scene of the Mud March he went direct to Washington, with an order in his pocket for the President to approve, or else to accept, his resignation. He made the issue boldly, first with Hooker, and next with Franklin, and his principal officers. The proposed order dismissed from the army Hooker, Brooks, and Newton, commanding divisions, and Cochrane, commanding a brigade in the 6th corps; and it relieved from further duty with the army, Franklin, Smith, commanding the 6th corps, Sturgis, commanding a division, and Ferrero, a brigade in it, and Taylor, Franklin's Asst. Adjt.-Gen.

Lincoln felt kindly to Burnside and respected him, but he had now more confidence in Hooker, who had won the sobriquet of "Fighting Joe," and much general popularity, both in the army and in the newspapers, with his fine bearing and frank manners. So Lincoln met the issue and suppressed the order, relieved Burnside from the command, and gave it to Hooker on Jan. 25. None of the other proscribed officers were disturbed, except Franklin, who was placed on waiting orders and afterward transferred to La.

CHAPTER XV

CHANCELLORSVILLE

Winter Quarters. Rations Reduced. Hays's Louisiana Brigade. Officers' Servants. Hooker's Reorganization. Confederate Organization. Hooker's Plan of Attack. Lee's Proposed Aggressive. Hooker Crosses. Hooker's Fatal Mistake. Lee's Prompt Action. The Wilderness. Hooker Advances. Lee's Advance. Hooker Retreats. Hooker Intrenches. Lee Reconnoitres. Lee's Plan of Attack. Jackson's March. The Movement Discovered. Sickles Advances. Jackson Deploys. Jackson Attacks. Colquitt's Blunder. Dowdall's Tavern. Casualties. At Hooker's Headquarters. Defensive Measures. Jackson Pauses. A Cannonade. Wounding of Jackson. Stuart in Command. Formation for Attack. Sickles's Midnight Attack. Hooker's Interior Line. Hooker abandons Hazel Grove. Stuart Attacks. Assaults Repulsed. Hazel Grove Guns. Federals Withdraw. Lee and Stuart Meet. Sedgwick's Advance. Wilcox on Taylor's Hill. Assaults Renewed. Early falls Back. Salem Church. Casualties. Early's Division. Lee organizes an Attack. Sedgwick driven Across.

Soon after the battle of Fredericksburg, Lee placed his army in winter quarters. Jackson was extended along the river, below the town, as far as Port Royal, his own headquarters being at a hunting lodge on the lawn of a Mr. Corbin, at Moss Neck, 11 miles below Fredericksburg. Longstreet was encamped from a little above Fredericksburg to Massaponax Creek. Lee established his headquarters in a camp a short distance in rear of Hamilton's Crossing. Most of the artillery was sent back to the North Anna River for convenience of supply. My own battalion occupied a wood at Mt. Carmel church, five miles north of Hanover Junction, the horses being sheltered in an adjoining pine thicket. On the occasion of Burnside's Mud March, we marched about halfway to Fredericksburg, but were then allowed to return. The infantry generally did not leave their camps, as there was nowhere any fighting.

Although so near to Richmond, the army was inadequately clothed, shod, and fed, in spite of Lee's earnest efforts. As far back as April 28, 1862, the meat ration had been reduced from 12 to 8 ounces, and a small extra allowance of flour (two ounces) was given. It was claimed that but for this reduction, the supply of meat would not have held out throughout the fall. On Jan. 23, 1863, a further reduction was ordered, by the commissary-general, to four ounces of salt meat with one-fifth of a pound of sugar. Lee wrote of the situation on March 27 : —

"The men are cheerful, and I receive but few complaints, still I do not consider it enough to maintain them in health and vigor, and I fear they will be unable to endure the hardships of the approaching campaign. Symptoms of scurvy are appearing among them, and, to supply the place of vegetables, each regiment is directed to send a daily detail to gather sassafras buds, wild onions, garlic, lamb's quarter, and poke sprouts; but for so large an army the supply obtained is very small."

Some idea of the situation is given in the following extracts from a letter of a staff-officer of Hays's La. brigade to his representative in Congress : —

"Among 1500 men reported for duty there are 400 totally without covering of any kind for their feet. These men, of course, can render no effective service, as it is impossible for them to keep up with the column in a march over frozen ground. There are a large number of men who have not a single blanket. There are some without a particle of underclothing, having neither shirts, drawers, nor socks, while overcoats, from their rarity, are objects of curiosity.

"The 5th regiment is unable to drill for want of shoes. The 8th regiment will soon be unfit for duty from the same cause; and indeed, when shoes are supplied, the men will be unable to wear them for a long while, such is the horrible condition of their feet from long exposure.

"This destitution, in the way of clothing, is not compensated by close shelter or abundant food, for the troops have no tents, and are almost totally unprovided with cooking utensils for the petty rations they receive. . . .

"Troops from other States are supplied, indeed, in a great degree by individual contributions from their homes, while we of Louisiana have received nothing whatever, since the fall of New Orleans, with the exception, I believe, of a company of the 9th regiment."

Troops from the more distant States suffered many more privations, both in food and clothing, than those near home.

Some of the State governments also did much toward the clothing of their own troops, and private families, too, sent largely both of food and clothing to their members in the armies.

Without such help, Confederate officers would often have suffered for food. Early in the war, officers received no rations, but were allowed to purchase from the commissaries, for themselves and servants. But as rations became scarce, the privilege of purchase was taken away, and a ration was given each officer. Nothing, however, was allowed for a servant. Thereafter, officers had to divide with their servants and supply the deficiency as best they could.

Personally, my mess received constant supplies of bacon and peas from our country homes in S.C. and Ga., and other articles giving the most nourishment in the least space.

Our scarcities were due entirely to insufficient railroad transportation. Before the war, our roads had but a light traffic. They were now loaded with a very heavy one, and as cars, engines, and rails wore out, they could not be replaced. When complaint was made to the commissary-general of insufficient supplies, he would answer, "Stop running passenger trains, and I can run more freight trains and supply you."

The great need of rations for the coming summer led the War Dept. to send Longstreet with two divisions for a campaign in the vicinity of Suffolk. Its object was to collect forage and provisions from counties near the Federal lines. The campaign was not initiated by Lee, and he thought that one division would have been sufficient, as the result showed. For the little fighting done was unnecessary, being initiated by the Confederates. And, although Lee at Chancellorsville repulsed Hooker's attack, it was poor policy to take the risk of battle against enormous odds, with one-fourth of his infantry absent.

As might have been expected, under the difficult circumstances attending our transportation either by wagon or by rail, Pickett's and Hood's divisions could not be gotten back in time for the battle, and our victory was the product of lucky accident combined with sublime audacity, desperate fighting, and heavy losses.

Hooker proved himself a good organizer. When placed in command, the army was much discouraged and desertions were numerous. Hooker abolished the grand divisions; devised a system of furloughs as a check to desertion; improved the transportation and supply departments, and organized his cavalry into a corps. In addition, he instituted the system of badges, showing at a glance the corps and division to which the wearer belonged. It was simply a piece of flannel, sewed on the top of the cap, whose shape designated the corps, and its color the division. A circle indicated the 1st corps; a trefoil the 2d; a lozenge the 3d; a Maltese cross the 5th; a Latin cross the 6th; a crescent the 11th; and a star the 12th. These shapes cut from red flannel were worn by the 1st divisions; from white flannel by the 2d; from blue flannel by the 3d, and from green flannel by the 4th divisions, should there be so many. Discipline, drill, and instruction were well maintained, supplies of all kinds abundantly furnished. The spirit of the men revived with the consciousness of their immense superiority in numbers and equipment, and it was with good show of reason that Hooker spoke of his army when it took the field, as "the finest army on the planet." His organization was as follows, with the strength of each corps present for "duty equipped" on April 30.

CORPS	DIVISIONS	BRIGADES	ARTILLERY	
			Batts.	Guns
1st Reynolds 16,908	Wadsworth Robinson Doubleday	Phelps, Cutler, Paul, Meredith Root, Baxter, Leonard Rowley, Stone	10	52
2d Couch 16,893	Hancock Gibbon French	Caldwell, Meagher, Zook, Brook Sully, Owen, Hall Carroll, Hays, MacGregor	8	48
3d Sickles 18,721	Birney Berry Whipple	Graham, Ward, Hayman Carr, Revere, Mott Franklin, Bowman, Berdan	9	54
5th Meade 15,724	Griffin Sykes Humphreys	Barnes, McQuade, Stockton Ayres, Burbank, O'Rorke Tyler, Allabach	8	42
6th Sedgwick 23,667	Brooks Howe Newton Burnham	Brown, Bartlett, Russell Grant, Neill Shaler, Brown, Wheaton Burnham	9	54

Corps	Divisions	Brigades	Artillery	
			Batts.	Guns
11th Howard 12,977	Devens Von Steinwehr Schurz	Von Gilsa, McLean Buschbeck, Barlow Schimmelpfennig, Krzyzanowski	6	36
12th Slocum 13,450	Williams Geary	Knipe, Ross, Ruger Candy, Kane, Greene	5	28
Cavalry Stoneman 11,544	Pleasonton Averell Gregg Reserve Brig.	Davis, Devin Sargent, McIntosh Kilpatrick, Wyndham Buford	5	22
1,610 2,217		Artillery Reserve Provost Guard	12 2	58 10

8 Corps, 23 Divisions, 64 Brigades, 133,711 Men, 74 Batteries, 404 Guns

The nearest Confederate return is for March 21. It is not entirely complete for the artillery and cavalry, but, estimating for them, Lee's organization and strength at that date was as follows:

1st Corps, Longstreet's, March 31, 1863

Divisions	Strength	Brigades	Batts.	Guns
Anderson's	8,232	Wilcox, Wright, Mahone, Posey, Perry	4	18
McLaws's	8,567 850	Wofford, Semmes, Kershaw, Barksdale Corps' Reserve Artillery	4 10	18 36
2 Divisions	17,649	9 Brigades	18	72

2d Corps, Jackson's

A. P. Hill's	10,400	Heth, Thomas, Lane, McGowans, Archer, Pender	6	26
Rodes's	9,632	Rodes, Colquitt, Ramseur, Doles, Iverson	4	18
Early's	8,243	Gordon, Hoke, Smith, Hays	4	18
Colston's	6,629 900	Paxton, Jones, Warren, Nichols Corps' Reserve Artillery	4 9	18 83
4 Divisions	35,795	19 Brigades	27	118
	600	General Reserve Artillery	6	26

CAVALRY				
DIVISIONS	STRENGTH	BRIGADES	BATTS.	GUNS
Stuart	2,400	Fitzhugh Lee, W. H. F. Lee	3	12

2 Corps, 7 Divisions, 30 Brigades, 56,444 Men, 54 Batteries, 228 Guns

Allowing for about 3500 reënforcements during the month of April, Lee's whole force was about 60,000, of whom some 57,000 were infantry and artillery. Of these arms Hooker had about 122,000.

Each commander planned to take the initiative. Hooker knew that he had double Lee's infantry, and great superiority in artillery, and he desired only to get at Lee away from breastworks. On April 13 he ordered Stoneman's cavalry upon a raid to Lee's rear, which expedition was to be the opening of his campaign. A rain-storm on the 14th, lasting 36 hours, halted the movement, after its leading brigade had forded the Rappahannock. The brigade was recalled, having to swim horses across the fast-rising river, and two weeks elapsed before the movement could be renewed. It was intended that Stoneman should destroy the railroads, which would force Lee to retreat. Stoneman should then harass and delay him as he fell back, pursued by Hooker.

Lee's proposed campaign was another invasion; this time of Pa. He could neither attack Hooker, nor even threaten his rear across the Rappahannock. But he could again sweep the Valley and cross the Potomac; and beyond, both Lee and Jackson imagined great possibilities.[1] Three months later the opportunity offered, and Lee put it to the test; but his great lieutenant, Jackson, was no longer at the head of his 2d corps.

On April 29, Lee found himself anticipated by Hooker's having, the night before, laid pontoon bridges across the Rappahannock, below Deep Run, at the site of Franklin's crossing in

[1] Between Jan. and April, 1863, Jackson had his chief engineer, Maj. Hotchkiss, prepare a remarkable map of the country from Winchester to the Susquehanna, compiled from county maps of Md., Va., and Pa. It was on a large scale, and noted farmhouses, with names of occupants. It was used by Lee on the Gettysburg campaign, and has been reproduced on smaller scale in the O. R. Atlas, Plate CXVI.

Dec. Hooker had commenced his movement, on the 27th, by going with the 5th, 11th, and 12th corps to cross the Rappahannock at Kelly's Ford, above the mouth of the Rapidan, 27 miles from Fredericksburg. A picket, at this point, was driven off, a pontoon bridge laid, and the whole force, about 42,000 men, was across the river on the 29th, when the 6th corps, under Sedgwick, was crossing in front of Jackson. Hooker immediately pushed his force by two roads from Kelly's to Germanna and Ely's fords of the Rapidan — about 11 miles off, and, on arriving, the troops forded, although the water was nearly shoulder deep. The fording was kept up all night by light of large bonfires, and the next morning the march to Chancellorsville, six miles away, was resumed.

Meanwhile, two divisions of the 2d corps had moved up from Fredericksburg to United States Ford, where they laid a pontoon bridge about noon on the 30th. By 9 P.M. they had crossed and united with the 5th, 11th, and 12th corps at Chancellorsville. No resistance had been encountered anywhere, but that of picket forces. Hooker, in 84 hours, had covered about 45 miles, crossing two rivers, and had established a force of 54,000 infantry and artillery upon Lee's flank at Chancellorsville.[1] Hooker was naturally elated at his success, and issued an order to his troops, congratulating them, and announcing that now —

" the enemy must either ingloriously fly, or come out from behind his defences, and give us battle on our own ground, where certain destruction awaits him."

And, indeed, if a general may ever be justified in enumerating his poultry while the process of incubation is incomplete, this might be an occasion. He was on the left flank and rear of Lee's only strong position with a force fully equal to Lee's, while another equal force threatened Lee's right. And somewhere in Lee's rear — between him and Richmond — was Stoneman with 10,000 sabres, opposed only by two regiments of cavalry,

[1] Hooker's men carried eight days' rations. Three days' full rations, cooked, were in the haversacks; five days' bread and groceries in the knapsacks, and five days' beef on the hoof. The total weight carried by each man, including 60 rounds of ammunition, was 45 pounds. But few wagons were brought across the Rappahannock. Most of the reserve ammunition was carried by pack mules, coupled in pairs and driven in trains.

tearing up the railroads and waiting to fall upon Lee's flank when he essayed the retreat which Hooker confidently expected to see. He had said to those about him that evening: —

"The rebel army is now the legitimate property of the Army of the Potomac. They may as well pack up their haversacks and make for Richmond, and I shall be after them."

But Hooker had made one mistake, and it was to cost him dearly. He had sent off, with Stoneman, his entire cavalry force, except one brigade. This proved insufficient to keep him informed of the Confederate movements, even though their efforts were supplemented by many signal officers with lookouts and field telegraphs, and by two balloons.

It was during the morning of the 30th, that Lee learned that Hooker had divided his army, and that one-half of it was already at Chancellorsville, while most of the remainder was in his front. By all the rules of war, one-half or the other should be at once attacked, and as Sedgwick's was the nearest, and Lee's whole force was already concentrated, Jackson at first proposed to attack Sedgwick. Lee, however, thought the position impregnable, and Jackson, after careful reconnoissance, came to the same conclusion. Orders were then at once prepared to march and attack Hooker before he could move from Chancellorsville. Early with his division, Barksdale's brigade, Pendleton's artillery reserve, and the Washington artillery, in all about 10,000 men, were left to hold the lines before Fredericksburg. These covered about six miles, and the force averaged about one man to each yard, and nine guns to each mile. About midnight on the 30th, Jackson marched from Hamilton's Crossing with his three remaining divisions, under A. P. Hill, Rodes, and Colston. He was joined on the road in the morning by Lee with the remaining brigades of McLaws, and by Anderson's division, and Alexander's battalion of artillery.

Jackson's three divisions numbered about 25,000, Anderson's division about 8000, and three brigades of McLaws about 6000. Thus, Lee had in hand nearly 40,000 men, with which to attack Hooker at Chancellorsville, where Hooker now had four corps — the 3d, 5th, 11th, and 12th — and two divisions of the 2d; a total effective of about 72,000 infantry and artillery, and was intrenching himself.

Chancellorsville was situated about a mile within the limits of a tract called the Wilderness. It stretched some 12 or 14 miles westward along the Rapidan and was some 8 or 10 miles in breadth.

The original forest had been cut for charcoal many years before, and replaced by thick and tangled smaller growth. A few clearings were scattered at intervals, and a few small creeks drained it. Chancellorsville was merely a brick residence at an important junction of roads, with a considerable clearing on the west. Three roads ran toward Fredericksburg: the old Turnpike most directly; the Plank road to its right, but uniting with the Turnpike at Tabernacle Church—about halfway; the River road to the left, by a roundabout course passing near Banks Ford of the Rappahannock.

Hooker's line of battle ran from Chancellorsville, about two miles northeastward to the Rappahannock, covering United States Ford. Westward it covered the Plank road for about three miles, ending in a short offset northward. Intrenchment was quickly done by cutting abattis, or an entanglement, in front, and throwing up slight parapets, or piling breastworks of logs. About 11 A.M., however, Hooker prepared to resume his advance, and ordered the 5th and 12th corps to move out on the three roads toward Fredericksburg and establish a line in the open country beyond the Wilderness. Griffin's and Humphreys's divisions of the 5th were sent down the River road, on the left, Sykes's division down the Turnpike in the centre, and the 12th corps, under Slocum, down the Plank road on the right.

Meanwhile, Lee and Jackson disposed Anderson's division for an advance, covering both the Pike and the Plank roads. Wilcox's and Mahone's brigades, with Jordan's battery of Alexander's battalion, moved upon the former; Wright's, Perry's, and Posey's brigades, with the remainder of Alexander's battalion, on the latter. McLaws's division moved by the Pike, and Lee, with Jackson's three divisions, followed the Plank road. Thus the two armies were marching toward each other on these two roads, while on the River road two of the Federal divisions were

marching toward Banks Ford, which was at this time unde-
fended, although some intrenchments had been erected there.
The possession of Banks Ford by Hooker would shorten the distance between Chancellorsville and his left wing under Sedgwick, by several miles.

The advancing forces first came into collision on the Pike.
Sharp fighting followed, Semmes's brigade coming up on the
left of Mahone and bearing the brunt of it against Sykes's
regulars.   Sykes's orders had been, however, only to advance
to the first ridge beyond the forest, and he maintained his
position there, though menaced by the extension of the Confederate lines beyond his flank, until orders were received from
Hooker to withdraw to the original position within the forest.
Similar orders were also sent to Slocum on the Plank road,
and to Griffin and Humphreys who had advanced, nearly five
miles down the River road, entirely unopposed, and who were
within sight of Banks Ford when the orders for the counter-
march reached them.   Slocum's corps had not become seriously
engaged, but its skirmishers had been driven in and its right flank
threatened by Wright's brigade.   This advanced upon the line
of an unfinished railroad, which, starting from Fredericksburg,
ran through the Wilderness generally a mile or two south of the
Plank road.

Up to the moment of the withdrawal of his troops, Hooker's
campaign had been well planned and well managed, and its
culmination was now at hand in the open field—as he had desired.   He could scarcely hope for more propitious circumstances,
and, by all the rules of the game, a victory was now within his
grasp.   His lieutenants received the order to fall back with surprise and regret.   The advance, upon both the Plank road and
the Pike, had cleared the forest and reached fairly good positions.   An officer was sent to Hooker to explain and request
permission to remain, but he returned in a half-hour, with
the orders repeated.

Hooker has been severely blamed for these orders, subverting
all the carefully prepared plans only published to the army that
morning.   It is interesting to learn the cause.   Reports from
the balloons and signal officers had informed him of the march

of a force toward Chancellorsville, estimated at two corps. Rumors had also been brought by deserters, the night before, that Hood's division had rejoined Lee, coming from Suffolk, but Hooker's information from Fortress Monroe should have shown that to be impossible. There is no sign of any hesitation upon his part until 2 P.M. At that hour he wired Butterfield, his chief of staff, at Falmouth: —

"From character of information have suspended attack. The enemy may attack me,—I will try it. Tell Sedgwick to keep a sharp lookout, and attack if he can succeed."

This despatch makes clear Hooker's mind. He realized from the rapid manner of Lee's approach, and from the sounds of battle already heard, both on the Pike and the Plank road, that Lee meant to attack. He had confidently expected Lee to retreat without a battle, and finding him, instead, so quick to take the aggressive, he lost his nerve and wished himself back on the line he had taken around Chancellorsville, where he would enjoy the great advantage of acting upon the defensive. He had seen in Dec. the enormous advantage which even slight breastworks could confer, and now he saw the chance of having his battle a defensive one behind intrenchments. It was surely the safest game to play, and Hooker is fully justified in electing to play it. No remonstrances shook his confidence in the least. He said to Couch, —

"It is all right, Couch, I have got Lee just where I want him. He must fight me on my own ground."

Orders were given to intrench, and work was at once begun with abundance of men and tools, and it was pushed during most of the night. Couch says, —

"At 2 A.M. the corps commanders reported to Gen. Hooker that their positions could be held; at least so said Couch, Slocum, and Howard."

Indeed, no better field fortification can be desired than what it was the quickest to build in the Wilderness. A wide belt of dense small growth could be soon felled in front of shallow ditches, with earth and log breastworks. Any charging line is brought to a halt by the entanglement, and held under close fire of musketry and canister, while the surrounding forest prevents the enemy from finding positions to use his own artillery.

So the corps commanders, responsible only for the front of their own lines, might truly report that their positions could be held. Yet the line, as a whole, may have a weak feature. This was the case here. Its right flank "rested in the air," and was not even covered by a curtain of cavalry.

Hooker, however, was not entirely blind to this weakness of his line. He inspected it early next morning, May 2, and ordered changes and enjoined vigilance which might have saved him from the surprise of the afternoon, had he not, like Pope in his campaign of the previous fall, failed to fathom the boldness of Lee's designs even after discovering the Confederate movements.

Lee appreciated that Hooker's withdrawal into the Wilderness was not forced, but to fortify and concentrate. He could, therefore, lose no time in finding how and where he might attack. Until nightfall the skirmishes were pushed forward everywhere, in order to locate the exact position of the enemy.

The result is briefly given in Lee's report, as follows: —

"The enemy had assumed a position of great natural strength, surrounded on all sides by a dense forest, filled with a tangled undergrowth, in the midst of which breastworks of logs had been constructed, with trees felled in front so as to form an almost impenetrable abattis. His artillery swept the few narrow roads by which his position could be approached from the front, and commanded the adjacent woods."

Hooker had, indeed, manœuvred Lee out of his position without a battle. There was now nothing left but to attack the greatly superior force in the impregnable position, or to attempt a retreat already dangerously delayed. But presently there came some more cheerful news. Fitzhugh Lee, who held the extreme left of our cavalry, had also reconnoitred the enemy, and had discovered that his right flank was in the air.

The one chance left to Lee was to pass undiscovered entirely across the enemy's front and turn his right flank. The enterprise was of great difficulty and hazard. To try it and fail meant destruction. For the army, already divided, must now be further subdivided, and the largest fraction placed in a position whence retreat would be impossible. Only a very sanguine man could even hope that 15 brigades, with over 100 guns, could make a march of 14 miles around Hooker's enormous army without being discovered. The chance, too, must be taken of aggressive action by the enemy at Fredericksburg or Banks Ford, even if Hooker himself did nothing during the eight hours in which the flanking force would be out of position in a long defile through the forest.

But no risks appalled the heart of Lee, either of odds, or position, or of both combined. His supreme faith in his army was only equalled by the faith of his army in him. The decision to attack was quickly made and preparations begun. Wilcox's brigade was ordered to Banks Ford to hold the position. This precaution was well taken, for after midnight of the 1st, Hooker ordered Reynolds's corps to leave Sedgwick and join the army at Chancellorsville. Reynolds started at sunrise and marched by Banks Ford, where he expected to find a bridge. But, as has been told, Griffin's and Humphreys's divisions, after being within sight on the afternoon of the 1st, had been recalled. Wilcox, at dawn on the 2d, had occupied the trenches. So Reynolds, arriving after sunrise and seeing Confederates in possession, continued his march on the north side, and crossed at United States Ford.

Anderson's four remaining brigades, with McLaws's three, were ordered to intrench during the night. Jackson, with his three divisions, his own artillery, and Alexander's battalion of Longstreet's corps, were assigned to make the march through the Wilderness and turn Hooker's right.

Lee himself would remain with McLaws's and Anderson's troops, and occupy the enemy while the long march was made. Cheering was forbidden, and stringent measures taken to keep the column closed. Fitz-Lee, with his cavalry, would precede the infantry and cover the flank. Two hours after sunrise, Lee, standing by the roadside, watched the head of the column march by, and exchanged with Jackson the last few words ever to pass between them. Rodes's division led the column, Colston's division followed, and A. P. Hill's brought up the rear.

The sun rose on May 2 a few minutes after five, and set at

6.50 P.M. The moon was full that night. The march led by a cross-roads near the Catherine Furnace, thence southward for over a mile and then southwestward for two miles before turning west and striking the Brock road within another mile. At the cross-roads, the line of march was nearest the Federal lines and was most exposed. Here the 23d Ga. regiment of Colquitt's brigade, Rodes's division, was left to cover the rear.

When the line of march reached the Brock road, it turned southward for about a mile, and then, almost doubling back upon itself, it took a woods road running a trifle west of north, nearly parallel to the Brock road itself, and coming back into it about three miles north of the point at which it was first entered. This made a route two miles longer than would have been made by turning northward when the Brock road was first reached. And as this part of the road was farthest of all from the enemy (over three miles), and in the densest woods, it would seem that two miles might have been saved, had there been time and opportunity for reconnoissance.

Where the Brock road crossed the Plank road, the column halted, while Fitz-Lee took Jackson to the front to a point whence he could see the Federal lines, with arms stacked, in bivouac behind their intrenchments, and utterly unconscious of the proximity of an enemy. Until that moment it had been uncertain exactly where Jackson would attack. But he now saw that by following the Brock road about two miles farther he would get upon the old turnpike, beyond the enemy's flank, and could take it in the rear. So the march was at once resumed to reach that position. But Paxton's brigade of Colston's division was here detached and placed with the cavalry, in observation on the Plank road, and did not rejoin its division until near midnight.

The head of the column made about two and a half miles an hour, the rear about one and a half, for in spite of all efforts the column lost distance. During the day there were three halts for rest of perhaps twenty minutes each. There were no vehicles except the artillery, ambulances, and ammunition wagons. These, marching each behind its division, made the column 10 miles in length, of which the infantry occupied over six. The head, marching at about 6 A.M., reached the deploying point on the turnpike by 4 P.M. The distance had proven greater than anticipated, and time was now of priceless value.

Meanwhile the movement, though misunderstood, had been detected by the enemy.[1] About a mile southwest of Chancellorsville was a settlement called Hazel Grove, on a cleared ridge. From this ridge, about 8 A.M., Birney, of Sickles's corps, discovered a column of infantry, trains, and artillery passing his front. He brought up a battery and opened on the train at a range of 1600 yards, throwing it into much confusion, and compelling it to find other routes around the exposed point. Jackson sent a battery to reply and check the enemy from advancing. Sickles came to Birney's position and observed Jackson's column. His official report says: —

"This continuous column — infantry, artillery, trains, and ambulances — was observed for three hours, moving apparently in a southerly direction toward Orange C. H., on the O. & A. R. R. or Louisa C. H. on the Va. Cen. The movement indicated a retreat on Gordonsville, or an attack upon our right flank — perhaps both, for if the attack failed, the retreat would be continued.

"I hastened to report these movements, through staff-officers, to the general-in-chief, . . . to Maj.-Gen. Howard and also to Maj.-Gen. Slocum, inviting their coöperation in case the general-in-chief should authorize me to follow up the enemy and attack his columns. At noon I received orders to advance cautiously toward the road followed by the enemy, and attack his columns."

Sickles advanced Birney's division, which engaged an outpost on the flank and captured a regiment, the 23d Ga. The two rear brigades, under Thomas and Archer, with Brown's battalion of artillery, were halted for an hour in observation, but were not engaged, and then followed on after the column. They were only able to overtake it, however, after night.

It was about 4 P.M. when the head of Jackson's column began its deployment on both sides of the Plank road, beyond Hooker's right, in the tangled forest; and it was nearly 6 P.M. when eight

[1] Jackson's celebrated march around Pope had also been discovered by the enemy as soon as it was begun, but had also been misunderstood — doubtless for a similar reason. No one could conceive that Lee would deliberately plan so unwise a move as this was conceived to be — dividing his army under the enemy's nose.

of the 12 brigades now in his column, had formed in two lines of battle, and one of the remaining four in a third line.

Meanwhile Sickles, though now unopposed in front, had brought up Whipple's division of his own corps, and, having asked for reënforcements, had also received Barlow's brigade from the right flank of the 11th corps, Williams's division of the 12th corps, and three regiments of cavalry and some horse artillery under Pleasonton. Posey's brigade held the left flank of Lee's line of battle in Hooker's front, while Jackson conducted the flanking movement. Posey had a strong force of skirmishers in front, which became hotly engaged with the left flank of Sickles's advance, when it engaged Jackson's rear-guard. While bringing up their reënforcements, the Federals made several efforts to carry Posey's position, but were always repulsed. Sickles then planned to outflank and surround it, but he had been so slow that, before he was ready to act, Jackson had attacked, and Sickles was hastily recalled.

Otherwise there might have been a strange spectacle. Sickles might have routed Anderson at the same time that Jackson was routing Howard. For he was on Anderson's flank with over 20,000 infantry, a brigade of cavalry, and some horse artillery. He wandered off, however, to the south and west, for miles, where there was no enemy before him.

Along the front of Lee's line the six brigades present of Anderson's and McLaws's divisions, aided by their artillery, had spent the day in more or less active skirmishing and cannonading with the enemy. Where the enemy showed a disposition to advance, the Confederates were well satisfied to lie quiet and repel them, as on the left in front of Posey. But on the Confederate right the Federal skirmish-line, under Col. Miles, being strongly posted and showing no disposition to advance, it was wise to be moderately aggressive and keep the enemy in hopes of an attack. Kershaw and Semmes did this handsomely throughout the day, though the threat of Sickles's movements caused Lee to draw his troops to his left, and reduce his right to less than a full line.

About 6 P.M., the sun being then about one hour high, Jackson gave the signal to Rodes to move forward. His brigades were in the following order from left to right: Iverson, O'Neal, Doles, and Colquitt, with Ramseur's brigade 100 yards in rear of Colquitt on the right. Colston's three brigades formed in line with Ramseur, and in the following order from the left: Nichols, Jones, Warren. About half of each division was on each side of the pike, and two Napoleons of Breathed's horse artillery stood in the pike ready to follow the skirmishers. Two hundred yards behind Colston, A. P. Hill had deployed Pender on the left of the pike. Lane, McGowan, and Heth were coming in column down the pike. Archer and Thomas were following, but some miles behind. Jackson had made his play so far with fair success, and he now stood ready with over 20,000 men to surprise Howard's 13,000. He was sure of an important victory, but the fruits to be reaped from it would be limited for two reasons.

1st. Two brigades were some hours behind, for Archer, without orders, had taken them to protect the rear. 2d. There were now but two hours of daylight left, and only in daylight can the fruits of victories be gathered. The question is suggested whether or not time had been anywhere lost unnecessarily. It would seem that 12 hours should not be needed to march 14 miles and form 20,000 men in line of battle. Briefly, it may be said, that with good broad roads, or with troops formed, ready to march at the word, and disciplined to take mud holes and obstructions without loss of distance, two hours could have been saved. But none of these conditions existed. Especially was time lost in the morning in getting the column formed.

Rodes reports it about 8 A.M. before the start was made. Further on, his report notes, "a delay was caused by an endeavor on our part to entrap some Federal cavalry." There may have been, during the morning, lack of appreciation of the value, even of the minutes, in an enterprise of the character now on foot, and an inadequate idea of the distance to be covered.

Some time was also lost in deploying Pender's brigade in the third line just before the charge was ordered. It would have saved a half-hour of great value to have ordered the charge as soon as the 2d line was formed, and allowed A. P. Hill's division to follow Rodes and Colston in column from the first, as they actually did at last. For, after advancing some distance through the tangled undergrowth, Pender's brigade was brought back to the road and placed at the head of the column for the rest of the advance.

It was nearly 6 P.M. when the signal for the advance was given by a bugle, and taken up and repeated for each brigade by bugles to the right and left through the woods. But the sounds seem to have been smothered in the forest, for the Federal reports make no mention of them. Their first intimation of anything unusual was given by wild turkeys, foxes, and deer, startled by the long lines of infantry and driven through the Federal camps. Then came shots from the Federal pickets, and then the guns on the turnpike opened and were soon followed by Confederate volleys and yells, impressing upon the enemy the fact that an overwhelming force had surprised them. Nevertheless, a gallant effort at resistance was made. The extreme right of the Federals was held by Von Gilsa's brigade of four regiments, about 1400 strong, which was formed, a half facing south and half facing west. They stood to fire three volleys, but by that time the Confederate lines were enveloping their flanks, and enfilade and reverse fire was being opened upon them. Only prompt flight could save the brigade from annihilation. After the third volley the brigade very wisely took to its heels and made its escape with a loss of 264 killed, wounded, and captured. Two guns with Von Gilsa were also captured. The next brigade to the left, McLean's, endeavored to change front. But it did not take long for the stern facts of the situation to become clear to every man of the brigade. As the canister fire of the Confederate guns was added to the enfilade fire of the Confederate infantry, this brigade also dissolved into a mass of fugitives, and two more guns, serving with them, were captured. But that they had fought well is shown by their losses, which were 692 out of about 2500. The division commander and four out of five regimental commanders were killed or wounded.

For a while, now, the fight degenerated into a foot race. Howard's original force of 13,000 had been reduced to 10,000 by the sending off of Barlow's large brigade. Of the 10,000, in a half-hour 4000 had been routed. The Confederates, recognizing the importance of pushing the pursuit, exerted themselves to the utmost. The lines broke into the double-quick wherever the ground was favorable, stopping only to fire at fugitives, or when completely out of breath. The horse artillery kept nearly abreast, and directed its fire principally at the Federal batteries which endeavored to cover the retreat. Some of these were fought gallantly, and some were overrun and captured. More might have been, and more prisoners taken, but for a blunder by Colquitt. His brigade was on the right of the front line, and its advance was least obstructed either by woods or the enemy. It could have moved most rapidly, and might have narrowed the enemy's avenue of escape.

Jackson's instructions had been explicit. Rodes's report says :—

"Each brigade commander received positive instructions which were well understood. The whole line was to push ahead from the beginning, keeping the road for its guide. . . . Under no circumstances was there to be any pause in the advance."

Ramseur's brigade was ordered to move in rear of Colquitt's and to support it. Colquitt, early in the advance, halted to investigate a rumor of a body of the enemy on his right flank, which proved to be a small party of cavalry. He delayed so that neither his brigade or Ramseur's rejoined the line until late at night.

Thus two brigades, by disregard of instructions and without need, were kept entirely out of action during the whole afternoon. So it happened that five of Jackson's 15 brigades (Thomas, Archer, Paxton, Colquitt and Ramseur) were missing from his line of battle during the whole afternoon, and, as A. P. Hill's four remaining brigades were not deployed until after dark, only six brigades were in the attack and pursuit of the 11th corps: to wit, Rodes, Doles, and Iverson of Rodes's division, and Jones, Warren, and Nichols of Colston's division. The great advantage of the Confederates lay in their being able to bring the centre of their line of battle against the flank of the enemy's line. This overwhelmed the two right brigades in a very short while, as we have seen, and the line pushed rapidly on, hoping to overwhelm the succeeding brigades likewise, one at a time.

The next division was Schurz's of two brigades, in line of battle along the Plank road, with two batteries which took positions and fired on the approaching Confederates. Schurz endeavored to form at right angles to their approach, but the mass of fugitives with wagons, ambulances, beef cattle, etc., entirely overwhelmed some of his regiments, and only two or three isolated ones were able to march in good order, and, facing about, to fire from time to time at their pursuers.

Next, at Dowdall's tavern, was a line of rifle-pits at right angles to the Plank road, and already occupied by Buschbeck's brigade of Von Steinwehr's division, the last of Howard's corps — its companion brigade, Barlow's, being away with Sickles. Three or four batteries were here established upon the line, and to it were rallied numbers of fugitives. At last an organized resistance was prepared. When the Confederates approached, in very scattered shape, they met a severe fire, and the advance was checked. Had Colquitt here been on the Confederate right with his and Ramseur's brigades, an opportunity was offered for a large capture. It might have been accomplished by the force at hand with a little delay. But they were already flushed with victory and would not be denied. After a sharp fight of perhaps 20 minutes, Colston's second line merged into the first, and the two lines pushed forward everywhere. The Federal artillery foresaw the end and fled, five guns being too late and captured. Buschbeck followed in fairly good order, but preceded by a stampede of troops and trains, principally down the Plank road, though a part diverged to the left by a road to the White House, called the Bullock road.

The casualties in Schurz's division were 919. In Buschbeck's brigade were 483. The total loss of Howard's corps was: killed,

	KILLED	WOUNDED	MISSING	TOTAL
Schimmelpfennig	84	215	120	419
Krzyzanowski	45	277	178	500
Buschbeck's	26	229	228	483
Total	155	721	526	1402

217; wounded, 1221; missing, 974; total, 2412; only about 20 per cent of the corps.

It was a very trifling loss, compared with what it might

have been had all of Jackson's troops been upon the field, and had his orders been strictly observed.

The casualties of the Confederates are not known, their returns consolidating all separate actions together.

Much undeserved obloquy was heaped upon the 11th corps for their enforced retreat. No troops could have acted differently. All of their fighting was of one brigade at a time against six. With the capture of the Buschbeck position, the fighting of the day practically ceased. The Confederate troops were at the limit of exhaustion and disorganization. Daylight was fading fast, and commands badly intermingled. The pursuit was kept up, however, for some distance, although the enemy was no longer in sight. A few hundred yards beyond the Buschbeck position, the Plank road entered a large body of forest, closing on both sides of the road for nearly a mile before the open Chancellorsville plateau is reached. At the entrance of the wood a single Federal gun, with a small escort, was formed as a rearguard, and followed the retreat to Chancellorsville without seeing any pursuers.

A notable case of acoustic shadows occurred during this action. Sickles, some two and a half miles away, heard nothing of the attack upon Howard until word was brought him, which he at first refused to believe. At 6.30 P.M., Hooker sat on the veranda of the Chancellorsville house in entire confidence that Lee was retreating to Gordonsville and that Sickles was "among his trains." Faint sounds of distant cannonading were at first supposed to come from Sickles. Presently, an aid looking down the road with his glass suddenly shouted, "My God! here they come." All sprang to their horses and, riding down the road, met, in a half-mile, the fugitive rabble of Howard's corps, and learned that Jackson, with half of Lee's army, had routed the Federal flank. Had there been some hours of daylight, Hooker's position would have been critical. For Lee and Jackson were now less than two miles apart, and between them were of infantry less than two divisions; Geary's of the 12th corps in front of Lee, and two brigades of Berry's of the 3d, near the path of Jackson.

But darkness puts an embargo upon offensive operations in a

wooded country. Troops may be marched during the night, where there is no opposition, but the experiences of this occasion will illustrate the difficulty of fighting, even when the moon is at its best. The night restored to the Federals nearly all the advantages lost during the day. Hooker acted promptly and judiciously. Urgent recalls were sent for Sickles and his entire force. His advance had gone two miles to the front and was preparing to bivouac, when orders overtook it. It did not reach the field until after 10 P.M.

The force first available against Jackson was the artillery of the 12th corps, for which a fine position was offered along the western brow of the Chancellorsville plateau, south of the Plank road. This position was known as Fairview, and it now became the key-point of the battle. In front of it the open ground extended about 600 yards to the edge of the forest. A small stream, between moderate banks at the foot of the plateau, offered shelter for a strong line of infantry in front of the guns. Here, within an hour, was established a powerful battery of 34 guns, and during the night all were protected by parapets. The position was essentially like the Confederate position at Marye's Hill before Fredericksburg, but on a larger scale. The forest in front offered no single position for a Confederate gun.

Only from one point could it be assailed by artillery. Across the stream in front, about 1000 yards obliquely to the left, was the small settlement called Hazel Grove, occupying some high open fields, from which, as has been told, Birney had that morning discovered Jackson's march. Hazel Grove offered excellent positions for attacking the Fairview lines, but Hazel Grove was itself within the Federal lines, and, about sundown, was occupied by a few cavalry with some artillery of the 3d corps, and some miscellaneous trains.[1]

---

[1] Two small collisions had occurred just before the close of the fighting between some of these troops and small bodies of Jackson's men still making their way forward. The 8th Pa. Cav. had been ordered to Howard, and at the Plank road it suddenly met a column of infantry in pursuit of Howard's fugitives. The cavalry received a volley emptying about 30 saddles and turning the regiment back. Meanwhile, about 200 of Doles's brigade, under Col. Winn of the 4th Ga., had stampeded the trains at Hazel

The only Federal infantry near at hand when the fugitives reached Chancellorsville were Carr's and Revere's brigades of Berry's division of the 3d corps. These brigades were formed in line of battle in the forest north of the Plank road, with their left resting on the guns at Fairview. Here they promptly set to work to intrench themselves in the forest across the Plank road, and to cut an abattis in front. They were soon reënforced by Hays's brigade of French's division of the 2d corps, and later by Mott's, the remaining brigade of Berry's division, which had been guarding bridges at United States Ford.

Meanwhile, as darkness fell, the Confederate pursuit died out upon entering the forest beyond the open lands about Dowdall's tavern. The cessation was not voluntary on Jackson's part, but it was necessary that Rodes's and Colston's divisions should be re-formed, and that Hill's division should take the lead. It had followed the pursuit, marching in column, and was in good order and comparatively fresh. The other divisions were broken, mingled, and exhausted, and several brigades were far behind. During the long pause in the advance, while Hill's brigades filed into the woods to the right and left, and the disorganized brigades were withdrawn to re-form, Jackson impatiently supervised and urged forward the movements. It is possible that he proposed to push his attack down the Bullock road which, a short distance ahead, diverged to the left, toward the river, instead of following the Plank road to Chancellorsville, as he had said to Hill: "Press them, Hill! Press them! Cut them off from United States Ford." It would, however, have

Grove, and had been heavily cannonaded by the Federal batteries. They had, however, found shelter and suffered no loss. The affairs were insignificant, and are only referred to here because absurd exaggerations of Pleasonton's Federal reports have been accepted by many reputable authors. A Federal writer, Col. A. C. Hamlin, historian of the 11th corps, has published the fullest and most accurate account yet produced of the history of that evening, including the wounding of Stonewall Jackson, from either Confederate or Federal sources. He made many visits to the field in company with the most prominent living actors, and has carefully compared the official reports, both of Federal and Confederate officers. No future student of this battle can afford to be ignorant of his story. — *The Battle of Chancellorsville.* By A. C. Hamlin, historian, 11th Army Corps. Bangor, Me. Published by the author, 1896.

been an error to make such a diversion, for the attack would have met an overwhelming force. Its only hope of success was to reunite with Lee at Chancellorsville with the least delay. Meanwhile, partaking of the impatience of Jackson, his chief of artillery, Col. Crutchfield, pushed some guns forward on the Plank road, and opened a random fire down it toward Chancellorsville, now less than a mile away.

It was an unwise move, for it provoked a terrific response from the 34 guns now in position upon Fairview plateau. The Plank road was now crowded with troops and artillery in column, and the woods near it were full of the reorganizing brigades. Under such a fire, even in the dim light of the rising moon, great confusion soon resulted, and although actual casualities were few, it became necessary to discontinue our fire before order could be restored and the formation of the line of battle be resumed.

Lane's N.C. brigade was at the head of Hill's division. One regiment, the 33d, was deployed and sent some 200 yards ahead as skirmishers, and the other four formed line of battle with the centre on the Plank road in the following order from left to right: 28th, 18th, 37th, 7th. The Bullock road here diverged to the left, toward United States Ford, but the enemy was evidently close in front, and Jackson said to Lane, "Push right ahead, Lane. Right ahead."

While the formation was still in progress, Jackson, followed by several staff-officers and couriers, rode slowly forward upon an old road, called the Mountain road, which left the Bullock to its left near the Plank road, and ran parallel to the latter, about 80 yards distant, toward Chancellorsville.[1]

Up this road the party advanced for 100 or 200 yards, but not passing the 33d N.C. skirmish-line. They then halted and listened for a while to the axes of the Federals, cutting abattis in the forest ahead. Beyond the Plank road, the Federal troops who had been off with Sickles were now returning, and were slowly working their way to reoccupy some breastworks which

[1] Most accounts have stated that this ride was *along the Plank road*, but careful investigation by Col. Hamlin, and the testimony of the most competent living witnesses, make it clear that this ride, and the shooting of Jackson, both took place *in the Mountain road*, which is now almost obliterated by the forest.

CHANCELLORSVILLE   341

had been built the night before in the forest south of the Plank
road. Between their skirmishers and those of the 33d N.C. on their
side of the Plank road, there suddenly began some firing. The
fire spread rapidly in both directions, along the picket-lines, and
was presently taken up by Federal regiments and lines of
battle in the rear. Jackson, at the head of his party, was
slowly retracing his way back to his line of battle, when this
volley firing began. Maj. Barry, on the left of the 18th N.C.,
seeing through the trees by the moonlight a group of horsemen
moving toward his line, ordered his left wing to fire. Two of
the party were killed, and Jackson received three balls; one in
the right hand, one through the left wrist and hand, and one
shattering the left arm between shoulder and elbow.

The reins were dropped, and the horse, turning from the fire,
ran into overhanging limbs which nearly unhorsed him; but,
recovering the rein, he guided into the Plank road where Capt.
Wilbourn of his staff helped him off. Meanwhile, the enemy
had advanced guns to their skirmish-line, and presently began to
sweep the Plank road with shell and canister. A litter was
brought and Jackson placed in it, but a bearer was shot, and
Jackson fell heavily on his wounded side. With great difficulty he was finally gotten to an ambulance, which already held
his chief of artillery, Col. Crutchfield, with a shattered leg.

During the night Jackson's left arm was amputated, and the
next day he was taken in an ambulance via Spottsylvania, to a
small house called Chandler's, near Guinea Station. For a few
days his recovery was expected, but pneumonia supervened, and
he died on May 10. In his last moments his mind wandered,
and he was again upon the battle-field giving orders to his
troops: "Order A. P. Hill to prepare for action. Pass the infantry to the front. Tell Maj. Hawks —" There was a pause
for some moments, and then, calmly, the last words, "Let us
pass over the river, and rest under the shade of the trees."

Jackson's fall left A. P. Hill in command, but Hill was himself
soon disabled by a fragment of shell, and sent for Stuart. Rodes
ranked Stuart, but the latter was not only best known to the
army, but was of great popularity, and Rodes cheerfully acquiesced. His whole career, until his death at Winchester, Sept.

19, '64, was brilliant, and justifies the belief that he would have proven a competent commander, but, as will be seen, Stuart's conduct, upon this occasion, was notably fine. A little before dark, Stuart, with Jackson's consent, had taken his cavalry and a regiment of infantry and started to attack the camps and trains of the enemy near Ely's Ford. He had reached their vicinity and was forming for the assault, when one of Jackson's staff brought the message of recall. He ordered the command to fire three volleys into the nearest camp and then to withdraw, while he rode rapidly back—about five miles—and took command between 10 and 11 P.M.

There was but one course to take — to make during the night such preparation as was possible, and, at dawn, to renew the attack and endeavor to break through the enemy's line and unite with Lee at Chancellorsville. The wounding of Crutchfield had left me the senior artillery officer present, and I was sent for, and directed to reconnoitre, and to post before dawn as many guns as could be used. I spent the night in reconnoissance and, beside the Plank road, could find but one outlet through the forest, a cleared vista some 200 yards long and 25 wide, through a dense pine thicket, opening upon a cleared plateau held by the enemy. This plateau afterward proved to be the Hazel Grove position, and I concentrated near it several batteries. In his *Life of Stuart*, Maj. McClellan, his adjutant, writes: —

"Col. Alexander's reconnoissance convinced Stuart that Hazel Grove was the key to the Federal line, and to this part of the field Stuart directed a large share of his personal attention on the morning of the 3d."

One of Jackson's engineers was sent by a long detour and found Lee before daylight and explained to him Stuart's position and plans, that he might, during the action, extend his left and seek a connection with our right. During the night, the brigades in rear rejoined, and the three divisions were formed for the attack in the morning, with Hill's division in front, Colston's in a second line, and Rodes's in a third.

Two brigades on Hill's right were placed obliquely to the rear, to present a front toward that flank. The positions of the different brigades are roughly shown thus: —

Thomas	Pender			Lane		
			Heth		McGowan	
						Archer
Nichols	Paxton	Plank Road		Warren	Jones	
Iverson	Rodes			Ramseur,	Doles,	Colquitt

When Hooker found that the Confederate attack had come to a standstill in front of the Fairview line, with Sickles near Hazel Grove upon its right flank, he ordered Sickles to move forward by the moonlight, and attack. Birney's division, in two lines with supporting columns, about midnight, advanced from Hazel Grove upon the forest south of the Plank road and in front of the Fairview position. The left wing of this force grazed the skirmishers of McGowan and struck the right flank of Lane's brigade, of which two and a half regiments became sharply engaged. But the whole Federal advance glanced off, as it were, and, changing its direction, it turned toward the Federal line in front of Fairview, where it approached the position of Knipe's and Ruger's brigades of Williams's division of the 12th corps.

Hearing their noisy approach, and believing them to be Confederates, the Fairview guns and infantry opened fire upon the woods, while the approaching lines were still so distant that they were unable to locate their assailants, and supposed the fire to come from the Confederate line. And now for a long time, for one or perhaps two hours, the Confederates listened to a succession of furious combats in the forest in their front, accompanied by heavy shelling of the woods, volleys of musketry, and a great deal of cheering. Our pickets and skirmish-lines were forced sometimes to lie down or seek protection of trees from random bullets, but we had no other part in it. It extended northward sometimes even across the Plank road. And the official reports of many Federal officers give glowing accounts of the repulse of desperate Confederate attacks, and even of the capture of Confederate guns. These stories were founded on the finding of some Federal guns, which had been abandoned in one of the stampedes of the afternoon.

Col. Hamlin's book, above referred to, says: —

"Some of the reports of this midnight encounter are missing, and their publication will throw much light on the details. On the Federal side it was undoubtedly a mixed-up mess, and some of the regiments complain of being fired into from the front and from both flanks. . . . At all events, after reading the reports of Gen. Sickles at the time, and his statement a year afterward to Congress . . . the brilliant array of gallant troops in the moonlight . . . the bold attack . . . the quick return of one of the columns to be stopped by the bayonets of the 63d Pa. . . . the advance of the other column deflecting to the right, until it met Gen. Slocum in person . . . certainly there is occasion for a slight smile on the part of the reader. And this smile may be lengthened on reading the story of Gen. De Trobriand, who was a participator, or the account left by Col. Underwood of the 23d Mass., who returned from the depths of the wilderness in time to witness and describe the ludicrous scene."

Hooker had little cause for apprehension after darkness had come to his relief, yet the shock to his overconfidence had been so severe that his only new dispositions were defensive. Yet he had over 60,000 fresh troops present, while Lee had on the east but about 16,000 and on the west about 24,000.

His first care was to order the intrenchment of an interior line, upon which he could fall back in case Stuart forced his way through to a junction with Lee. A short line was quickly selected, of great natural strength, behind Hunting Run on the west, and behind Mineral Spring Run on the east, with both flanks resting on the river and covering his bridges. This line will be more fully described and referred to later. It took in the White House, some three-fourths of a mile in the rear of Chancellorsville, and was probably the strongest field intrenchment ever built in Va. Next, Hooker sent orders to Sedgwick at 9 P.M., as follows: —

"The major-general, commanding, directs that you cross the Rappahannock at Fredericksburg on receipt of this order, and at once take up your line of march on the Chancellorsville road until you connect with him, and will attack and destroy any force you may fall in with on your road.

"You will leave all your trains behind, except pack trains of your ammunition, and march to be in the vicinity of the general at daylight. You will probably fall upon the rear of the forces commanded by Gen. Lee, and between you and the major-general, commanding, he expects to use him up. Send word to Gen. Gibbon to take possession of Fredericksburg. Be sure not to fail."

These orders were good, and would have insured victory, had they been carried out. And Hooker took a further precaution, most desirable whenever important orders are issued. He despatched a competent staff-officer, Gen. Warren, his chief engineer, to supervise their execution. Unfortunately for him, however, under the conditions it proved impossible to execute the orders within the time set, as will be told later. Here it is only necessary to note that Sedgwick was never able to get near Chancellorsville.

Even as the field stood, with or without the arrival of Sedgwick, the battle was still Hooker's, had he fought where he stood. But about dawn he made the fatal mistake of recalling Sickles from the Hazel Grove position, which he was holding with Whipple's and Birney's divisions, and five batteries. There has rarely been a more gratuitous gift of a battle-field. Sickles had a good position and force enough to hold it, even without reenforcements, though ample reënforcements were available. The Federal line was longer and overlapped ours on its right, and our only opportunity to use artillery was through the narrow vista above referred to, which was scarcely sufficient for four guns, and had but a very restricted view.

Had Stuart's attack been delayed a little longer, our right flank might have marched out upon Hazel Grove plateau without firing a shot. A Federal battery, supported by two regiments, had been designated as a rear-guard, and it alone occupied the plateau when our advance was made, though the rear of the retiring column was still near.

Stuart's men, when the lines were finally formed, got from two to three hours' rest before dawn. About that time, cooked rations were brought up. Before the distribution, however, was finished, Archer's and McGowan's brigades were moved forward, from their retired positions as the right flank, to straighten the line. They soon came upon a picket-line of the enemy, and sharp firing began. Stuart, without waiting further, ordered the whole line to the attack.

Archer's brigade, about 1400 strong, in advancing through the pine thickets, drifted to the right, and gradually opened a gap between it and McGowan's brigade, emerging from the forest alone, and in front of the enemy's rear-guard. A sharp action ensued, while Archer extended his right and threatened the enemy's rear, forcing the battery to retreat. He then charged and captured 100 prisoners, and forced the abandonment of four of the guns.

He attempted to push his advance much farther, but was checked by the fire of the enemy's artillery and of the rear brigade, Graham's, of Sickles's column. After two efforts, realizing that his force was too small, and leaving one of his captured guns, he fell back to Hazel Grove ridge, about 6.30 A.M. This was now being occupied rapidly by our guns. Thus, so easily that we did not at once realize its great value, we gained space for our batteries, where we soon found that we could enfilade the enemy's adjacent lines.

Meanwhile, the first assault had been made along the whole line by Hill's division. The enemy's advanced line crossed the Plank road and was held by Williams's division of the 12th corps, Berry's of the 3d corps, and Hays's brigade of the 2d corps. In rear of the front line was a second line near the edge of the forest. Across the small stream and along the edge of the elevated plateau, their artillery had been strongly intrenched during the night, making a third line. The two divisions from Hazel Grove, with their four batteries, were brought up in rear of the forces already holding the front to the west. This whole front from north to south was scarcely a mile and a quarter long. It was defended by about 25,000 men, and it was being attacked by about an equal number. The Confederates, however, had the hot end of the affair, in having to take the aggressive and advance upon breastworks protected by abattis and intrenched guns.

In his first assault, however, Hill's division, now commanded by Heth, after a terrific exchange of musketry, succeeded in driving the Federals from the whole of their front line. They followed the retreating enemy, and attacked the second line, where the resistance became more strenuous. On the extreme right, Archer's brigade had now fallen back to Hazel Grove, where it remained, supporting the guns now taking position there. This left McGowan's flank uncovered, and a Federal force attacked it, and drove it back to the captured line. This uncovered Lane's brigade, and it was also forced to fall back. On the left of the Plank road, the advance of Thomas beyond the enemy's first line met both a stronger second line and a flank attack, his left being in the air. After an hour's hard fighting, the whole line was forced back to the captured breastworks, with severe losses. It was clear that extreme efforts would be needed to drive the enemy from his position. Stuart ordered 30 additional guns to Hazel Grove, and brought forward both the second and third lines, putting in at once his last reserves. It would be useless to follow in detail the desperate fighting which now ensued and was kept up for some hours. The Federal guns on the Fairview heights were able to fire over the heads of two lines of infantry, and other batteries aided from the new position in which Hooker had now established the 1st, 2d, and 5th corps. This was so near on our left that Carroll's and McGregor's brigades of the 2d corps, with artillery, were sent forward to attack our flank, and were only repulsed after such fighting that they lost 367 men. With the aid of our second and third lines, fresh assaults were made on both sides of the Plank road, and now the enemy's second lines were carried. But his reserves were called upon, and again our lines were driven back, and countercharges south of the road again penetrated the gap between McGowan and Archer. Paxton's brigade was brought across from the north and restored the situation at a critical moment, Paxton, however, being killed. Some of our brigades were now nearly fought out, the three divisions being often massed in one, and the men could only be moved by much example on the part of their officers. Stuart himself was conspicuous in this, and was everywhere encouraging the troops with his magnetic presence and bearing, and singing as he rode along the lines, "Old Joe Hooker, won't you come out the Wilderness." There can be no doubt that his personal conduct had great influence in sustaining the courage of the men so that when, at last, our artillery had begun to shake the Federals' lines, there was still the spirit to traverse the bloody ground for the fourth time and storm the Fairview batteries.

Guns had been brought to Hazel Grove from all the battalions on the field—Pegram's, Carter's, Jones's, McIntosh's, and Alexander's. Perhaps 50 guns in all were employed here, but less than 40 at any one time, as guns were occasionally relieved, or sent to the rear to refill. Their field of fire was extensive, being an oblique on both the enemy's artillery and infantry. Some ground having been gained on the Plank road, Cols. Jones and Carter had also been able to establish 10 rifle guns there, which enfiladed the Plank road as far as the Chancellorsville house.

About nine o'clock, the Federal artillery fire was perceptibly diminished. Many of their guns were running short of ammunition, and fresh ammunition was not supplied. Sickles asked for it, and for reënforcements, but none were sent. It would seem that Hooker preferred to lose the Chancellorsville plateau entirely, and fall back into his new position, which was like a citadel close at hand, rather than risk fighting outside of it.

At Stuart's last charge, the Federal lines yielded with but moderate resistance. The guns in the Fairview intrenchments abandoned them, and fell back to the vicinity of the Chancellorsville house.

The guns at Hazel Grove moved forward across the valley and occupied the deserted Federal positions, here making connection with Anderson's division which Lee was extending to his left to meet them. They were soon joined by Jordan's battery of my own battalion, which had been serving with Anderson.

The enemy, driven out of their fortified lines, attempted to make a stand near the Chancellorsville house, but it was a brief one. There were no breastworks here to give shelter, and their position was now so contracted that our guns from three directions crossed their fire upon it. Hooker, in the porch of the Chancellorsville house, was put *hors de combat* for two or three hours by a piece of brick torn from a pillar by a cannon-shot. No one took command in his place, and for a while the army was without a head. Meanwhile, McLaws and Anderson had seen the enemy withdrawing from their fronts and pressed forward at the same time that Stuart's infantry crowned the plateau from the west. Some prisoners were cut off and captured on each flank, and a few guns also fell into our hands, but, as a whole, the enemy's withdrawal was orderly and well managed, and with less loss than might have been expected. One sad feature of the occasion was that the woods on the north of the road were set on fire by shells, and the dry leaves spread the fire rapidly, although the trees and undergrowth did not burn. Efforts were made to remove the wounded, but the rapid spread of the fire prevented, and some of the wounded of both armies were burned.

About 10 A.M., Lee, advancing with McLaws's division, met Stuart with Jackson's corps near the site of the Chancellorsville house, now only a smoking ruin, for our shells had set it on fire. It was, doubtless, a proud moment to Lee, as it was to the troops who greeted him with enthusiastic cheering.

Lee, by no means, intended the battle to end here. Both infantry and artillery were ordered to replenish ammunition and renew the assault, but there came news from the rear, which forced a change of programme. Sedgwick's corps had broken through the flimsy line in front of it, and was now moving up the Plank road. With all his audacity Lee could not venture to attack five corps intrenched in his front, while Sedgwick came up in his rear.

The story of events at Chancellorsville must now pause, as the action there paused, while that is told of Sedgwick's venture against Lee's rear.

Hooker had sent urgent orders the night before to Sedgwick to come to his help, and a staff-officer, Warren, to supervise their execution. But Sedgwick, though already on the south side of the river, which Hooker did not seem to know, was three miles below Fredericksburg, near the scene of Franklin's crossing in Dec. He had been under orders to advance toward Richmond on the Bowling Green road, and had disposed his troops accordingly.

To advance up the Plank road, it was necessary to march to Fredericksburg and force the Confederate lines on Marye's Hill. These lines were held from Taylor's Hill to the Howison house, about three miles, by only two brigades, Barksdale's and Hays's, with a small amount of artillery. The regiments were strung out in single rank, the men sometimes yards apart, and with

wide intervals at many places between regiments. On Marye's
Hill, two regiments, the 18th and 21st Miss., with six guns of the
Washington Arty. and two under Lt. Brown of Alexander's
Bat., were distributed from the Plank road to Hazel Creek,
about a half-mile.

Sedgwick had marched at midnight with a good moon, but
his progress was slow, for the Confederate pickets annoyed it.
By daylight he was in Fredericksburg, and his batteries from
both banks of the river and from the edge of the town opened
on the Confederates. Sedgwick had been informed by Hooker
that the Confederate force left at Fredericksburg was very small,
and, without delay, he sent forward four regiments from Whea-
ton's and Shaler's brigades to charge the works in front of Marye's
Hill. It was sending a boy on a man's errand. The Confederate infantry reserved its fire until the enemy were within
40 yards, when they opened and quickly drove them back.
A second assault was made, but with similar result. Sedgwick
was now convinced that a heavy force confronted him, and he
waited for Gibbon's division of the 2d corps. This had just
crossed from Falmouth, and it made an effort upon the extreme
Confederate left. It proved futile on account of the canal along
the front at that part of the field, which was defended by three
regiments of Hays's brigade of Early's division, hurried there
by Early on seeing the enemy's preparations.

Soon afterward, Wilcox's brigade came to the scene from
Banks Ford, where it had been in observation on the 2d. At
dawn on the 3d, Wilcox noted that the enemy's pickets on the
north side were wearing haversacks, and correctly guessed that
the forces opposite were leaving for Chancellorsville. He was
preparing to march in the same direction, when a messenger
brought word of the advance of Gibbon's division. Thereupon leaving a picket of 50 men and two guns in observation at
Banks Ford, Wilcox marched to Taylor's Hill.

About 10 A.M., Gibbon having reported that an attack on our
extreme left was impracticable, and Howe's division, making no
progress east of Hazel Run, Sedgwick had no recourse but to
renew his attack upon Marye's Hill by main force. He accordingly
prepared a much stronger assault than that of the morning.

Newton's division, supported by Burnham's brigade, was to attack Marye's Hill, while Howe's division assaulted Lee's Hill beyond Hazel Run.

This force numbered about 14,000 men, with an abundant artillery. Across Hazel Creek were seven guns of Cutt's and Cabell's battalions, and the two remaining regiments of Barksdale's brigade and one La. of Hays's brigade.

About 11 A.M., both Newton and Howe renewed the assault. Newton advanced rapidly through the fire of the few Confederate guns, but recoiled soon after the infantry opened, although Barksdale's line was so thin that it scarcely averaged a man to five feet of parapet. Some of the Federal regiments, however, suffered severely, and a number of killed and wounded were left near the Confederate line.

This, by a strange piece of good nature on the part of one of our best officers, proved our undoing. When Newton's line was beaten back, the firing on both sides nearly ceased, and some Federal officer sent forward a flag of truce. No Federal report mentions this incident. The flag was probably sent by only a brigade commander, for the fighting, by Howe's division, across Hazel Run, was kept up without cessation. Col. Griffin of the 18th Miss. received the flag. The officer bearing it asked to be allowed to remove his dead and wounded in Griffin's front. Without referring to his brigade commander, Griffin granted the request, and, still more thoughtlessly, allowed his own men to show themselves while the wounded were being delivered. The enemy, to their great surprise, discovered what a small force was in their front.

They lost little time in taking advantage of the information. The action was reopened, and now a charge was made with a rush, and the enemy swarmed over our works. The Mississippians had no chance to escape, but fought with butts of guns and bayonets, and were mostly captured, with the loss of about 100 killed and wounded. The casualties in Newton's division and Burnham's brigade, in the whole battle, were about 1200, of which probably 900 fell in this affair. All of the guns on the hill were captured, Brown's section last of all, firing until surrounded.

Meanwhile, Howe's division had a full mile to traverse before reaching the Confederate lines. Instead of a charge, their progress was a slow advance under cover of heavy artillery fire. Before they reached the Confederate line, Newton's division had made its second charge and was in possession of Marye's Hill. Thereupon, Early, who was in command, ordered the withdrawal of his whole division, and the formation of a new line of battle across the Telegraph road, about two miles in the rear. Here he concentrated Gordon's, Hoke's, and Smith's brigades, with the remnants of Barksdale's. Hays's brigade had been cut off with Wilcox, and these two brigades were in position to delay Sedgwick in advancing upon the Plank road toward Chancellorsville. But Hays, under orders from Early, crossed the Plank road before Sedgwick had made any advance. Wilcox then took position with four guns across the Plank road, and delayed the enemy's advance as much as possible, while he fell back slowly to Salem Church, where he had been notified that McLaws would meet him with reënforcements. He reached this point about 3 P.M., meeting there Wofford's, Semmes's, Kershaw's, and Mahone's brigades, under McLaws. The five brigades rapidly formed a single line of battle across the Plank road. Wilcox's brigade held the centre, with the 14th and 11th Ala. on the left of the Plank road, and the 10th and 8th on the right. The 9th Ala. was in reserve a short distance in rear of the 10th. Four guns were posted across the Plank road, and a company of infantry was put in Salem Church, and one in a schoolhouse a short distance in front. Kershaw's brigade was on the right of Wilcox, and Wofford on right of Kershaw; Semmes's brigade was on Wilcox's left, and Mahone's brigade was on the left of Semmes.

In front of the line of battle stretched a fringe of dense young wood, some 200 yards wide, and beyond that, for perhaps a half-mile, were open fields, which extended with a few interruptions on each side of the Plank road back to Fredericksburg, about four miles. Sedgwick had been delayed over four hours in traversing that distance.

About 4.30 P.M., Sedgwick established a battery 1000 yards in front of Wilcox, and opened fire. The Confederate artillery was nearly out of ammunition, and after a few rounds it was withdrawn. Encouraged by this, the Federals now sent forward Brooks's divison, formed across the road in two lines, with Newton's division in the same formation upon Brooks's right.

Now ensued one of the most brilliant and important of the minor affairs of the war. McLaws had reached the field and assumed the command, but credit is also due to Wilcox, who had delayed many times his number for several hours, and gained time for reënforcements to arrive.

The story of the battle may be told very briefly. North of the road, opposite the 14th and 11th Ala., was Torbert's Jersey brigade under Brown, in a double line. On the south, opposite the 8th, 9th, and 10th Ala., was Bartlett's brigade, one of the best in the Federal army, which boasted that it had never been repulsed, and had never failed to hold any position it was ordered to occupy.

The strength of the Confederate position consisted in the thick undergrowth which completely hid their lines, lying down on the crest of a slight ridge in rear of the woods. These were held by skirmishers during the enemy's approach across the open. When the artillery was withdrawn, it left a gap of about 50 yards between the 11th Ala., on the left of the road and the 10th on the right. Bartlett's brigade advanced gallantly through the severe skirmish fire, fought through the strip of woods, drove the company from the church, and cut off the one in the schoolhouse. Pushing on and overlapping the left of the 10th Ala., they enfiladed it, broke its line, and drove it back in confusion. The 8th Ala., under Lt.-Col. Herbert, on the right of the 10th, however, did not break, but threw back its three left companies, and brought an enfilade fire on the enemy's further advance. The 9th Ala., being in reserve a little in rear of the 10th, rose from the ground, and, giving the enemy a volley, charged them and drove them back.

Brown's brigade, on the opposite side of the road, had a wider body of woods to cross, and had not advanced as far as Bartlett. But when Bartlett was driven back, Wilcox's whole brigade joined in the counter-stroke. Bartlett's first line was followed so rapidly that the prisoners in the schoolhouse were liberated, and the rush of the fugitives and the quick pursuit overwhelmed the second line, giving it no chance to make a stand.

Across the Plank road, Semmes's two right regiments, the 10th and 51st Ga., joined the 14th and 11th Ala., and these four regiments, meeting the Jersey brigade in the woods, drove it back in such a direction that the fugitives from each side of the Plank road converged upon the road. The Confederates in pursuit said that they had never had such crowds to fire upon. The pursuit was dangerously prolonged, but fortunately the enemy contented himself by checking it, and the Confederates then slowly withdrew. Long-range firing, however, was kept up until night.

Bartlett's brigade reported a loss in this attack of 580 officers and men out of less than 1500 men. Brown's brigade reported a loss of 511. Brooks, commanding the division, said in his official report : —

"In this brief but sanguinary conflict this division lost nearly 1500 officers and men. Col. H. W. Brown, commanding the Jersey brigade, was severely wounded; and Col. Collet, 1st N.J., Col. G. W. Town, and Lt.-Col. Hall, 95th Pa., were killed."

Wilcox's brigade lost 75 killed, 372 wounded, and 48 missing, a total of 495. The losses of Semmes's brigade are included with the campaign losses. One of its regiments, however, the 10th Ga., reports for this day: 21 killed, 102 wounded, and 5 missing, a total of 128 out of 230 present. In the morning at Chancellorsville, this regiment had received the surrender of the 27th Conn., which had been on picket and was cut off by the capture of Chancellorsville. During this charge it also captured over 100 prisoners. While this action was going on, Early had formed line of battle to resist an advance of the enemy upon the Telegraph road, and was bringing up his extreme right from Hamilton's Crossing. It was about night when his whole division was concentrated.

The enemy was holding Gibbon's entire division idle in Fredericksburg, guarding the pontoon bridges to Falmouth. Had Gibbon moved up on Sedgwick's flank to Banks Ford, his division would have counted for something in the next day's affairs. His force was just what Sedgwick needed to enable him to hold his ground.

Returning now to Chancellorsville, we have to note a movement which involved an unfortunate Confederate delay on the next day — a delay which enabled Sedgwick's corps to escape scot-free from a position which should have cost him all his artillery and half his men. The River road, from Chancellorsville to Fredericksburg via Banks Ford, was left unoccupied when Hooker took refuge in his fortified lines on the morning of the 3d. Anderson, with his three remaining brigades, — Wright's, Perry's, and Posey's,—was sent at 4 P.M. to watch that road, and threaten the enemy upon that flank. Two hours after sunrise on the 4th, Heth arrived with three brigades to relieve Anderson, who was now ordered to proceed to Salem Church, about six miles, and report to McLaws, which he did about noon. This sending Anderson to reënforce McLaws might have been done the afternoon before. He would then have been on hand at the earliest hour for the joint attack upon Sedgwick, on the 4th, which is now to be described.

The events of the morning of the 4th had been as follows: No communication had been received by Sedgwick from Hooker, and he was still under orders to come to Chancellorsville. But at an early hour, movements of Early's troops were discovered in his rear, and, instead of advancing, Sedgwick had deployed Howe's division perpendicular to the Plank road facing to his rear, and stretching to the river above Banks Ford, where pontoon bridges had been laid the afternoon before. Sedgwick's scouts had reported that "a column of the enemy, 15,000 strong, coming from the direction of Richmond, had occupied the heights of Fredericksburg, cutting him off from the town." He at once abandoned all idea of taking the aggressive, and only wished himself safely across the river. But he did not dare to attempt a crossing, except under cover of night. His lines were too long, and were weak in plan, as they faced in three directions, —east, south, and west. But he dared not venture a change, for fear of precipitating an attack. When at last he received a despatch from Hooker, its noncommittal advice was not encouraging. It said: —

"Everything snug here. We contracted the lines a little and repulsed the last assault with ease. Gen. Hooker wishes them to attack him tomorrow, if they will. He does not desire you to attack them again in force, unless he attacks him at the same time. He says you are too

far away for him to direct.   Look well to the safety of your corps, and keep
up communication with Gen. Benham at Banks Ford and Fredericksburg.
You can go to either place if you think it best to cross.   Banks Ford would
bring you in supporting distance of the main body, and would be better
than falling back to Fredericksburg."

A little later Hooker sent another message, urging Sedgwick, if
possible, to hold a position on the south bank, to which Sedgwick replied: —

"The enemy threatens me strongly on two fronts.   My position is bad
for such attack.   It was assumed for attack, not for defence.   It is not
improbable that the bridges at Banks Ford may be sacrificed.   Can you
help me strongly if I am attacked?"

No answer to this inquiry appears, and Sedgwick stood on the
defensive, awaiting nightfall.   Meanwhile, early in the morning,
Early's division, with Barksdale's brigade, had moved down upon
Marye's Hill, which they found held by a picket force only, and
easily occupied.   An advance was attempted into Fredericksburg, but it was found with barricades across the streets held by
one of Gibbon's brigades, supported by two other brigades and a
number of guns on the north bank.   Early then sent to communicate with McLaws and endeavor to arrange a joint attack upon
Sedgwick, but received information that Anderson's division was
coming, and was himself sent for to meet Lee.

Before leaving Chancellorsville that morning, Lee had examined
Hooker's lines with the view of assaulting at once, but their
strength made it imprudent to do so while Sedgwick was still
south of the river.   So he next set out to dispose of Sedgwick,
that he might then concentrate his whole force to attack Hooker.

Probably no man ever commanded an army and, at the same
time, so entirely commanded himself, as Lee.   This morning was
almost the only occasion on which I ever saw him out of humor.
It was when waiting the arrival of Anderson, with his three
brigades from the River road, after being relieved by Heth.
Anderson was in no way to blame for the delay, but he should
have been relieved the afternoon before, which would have
let him move during the night.

Some delay was inevitable, as Sedgwick's peculiar rectangular
formation was not readily understood.   It was about three

miles in extent, and occupied high ground, with a wide, open valley
in its front, forcing a development of our line of nearly six miles
to cover its three fronts.   An entire day would have been none
too much to devote to the attack, if the fruits of victory were to
be reaped.   Although Lee urged all possible speed, it was 6 P.M.
when the advance commenced.   Sunset was at seven.   Darkness fell before the lines could be gotten into close action.   In
the dusk, two of Early's brigades, Hoke's and Hays's, fired into
each other by mistake, and were thrown into confusion.   Both
had to be withdrawn and re-formed.   The enemy was, however,
forced back to the vicinity of Banks Ford, and had there then
been daylight to bring up our batteries, there might have been
large captures.   Upon McLaws's front, ranges were marked by
daylight for firing upon Banks Ford and some guns were kept
firing all night.   But all that was possible amounted only to
annoyance.   It was again illustrated that afternoon attacks
seldom reap any fruits of victory.

It was with great elation on the morning of the 5th, that our
guns fired the last shots across the Rappahannock at Sedgwick's retreating columns.   But orders, soon received from headquarters, indicated that our commander was not yet satisfied.
Early's division and Barksdale's brigade were directed to remain
in observation at Banks Ford and Fredericksburg, — which
had also been evacuated by Gibbon's division during the
previous night, — while all the rest of the army was ordered
to return to the front of Hooker's lines near Chancellorsville,
which Lee intended to assault on the morrow with his whole
force.

What was known of the enemy's position gave assurance that
the task would be the heaviest which we had ever undertaken.
Hooker now had his entire army concentrated, and, allowing
for his losses, must have had fully 90,000 men to defend about
five miles of breastworks.   These he had had 48 hours to prepare,
with all the advantages for defence which the Wilderness offered.
Lee would scarcely be able to bring into action 35,000 under all
the disadvantages imposed by the Wilderness upon the offensive
and by two streams which on the southeast and northwest covered three-fourths of the enemy's front.   Behind these streams

both flanks rested securely upon the river. The attack would have to be made everywhere squarely in front, and our artillery would be unable to render any efficient help. When, upon the 6th, we found the lines deserted and the enemy gone, our engineers were amazed at the strength and completeness of the enemy's intrenchments. Impenetrable abattis covered the entire front, and the crest everywhere carried head-logs under which the men could fire as through loopholes. In rear, separate structures were provided for officers, with protected outlooks, whence they could see and direct without exposure.

Four of Hooker's corps had suffered casualties averaging 20 per cent, but three, the 1st, 2d, and 5th, had scarcely been engaged. It must be conceded that Lee never in his life took a more audacious resolve than when he determined to assault Hooker's intrenchments. And it is the highest possible compliment to the army commanded by Lee to say that there were two persons concerned who believed that, in spite of all the odds, it would have been victorious. These two persons were Gens. Lee and Hooker. For Hooker was already hurrying his preparations to retreat during the coming night. Clearly, this decision was the mistake of his life.

During the afternoon of the 5th, there came on one of the remarkable storms which on many occasions closely followed severe engagements. The rainfall was unusually heavy and continued long after dark, converting roads into quagmires, rivulets into torrents, and causing great discomfort to man and beast. But its occurrence was advantageous to the Confederates, as it prevented their pressing upon the enemy's impregnable line, and it hurried the efforts of the Federals to cross the river, as rapidly rising waters overflowed the approaches to their bridges. Before the rain, I had found positions for several guns close upon the river-bank, partly around a bend below the Federal left, giving an oblique fire upon some of their batteries. During the night we constructed pits, and, at early dawn, were putting the guns in them, when we were suddenly fired upon by guns square upon our own flank and across the river. A lieutenant had his ankle smashed, some horses were killed, and some dismounted limber chests were exploded, before all could be gotten under cover in the pits. From these we could make no reply, as they faced Hooker's lines, and we could only lie close and wait for more daylight. This revealed that the enemy had abandoned his works during the night and recrossed the river. To retaliate I brought up seven other guns, under cover of a wood, and engaged the enemy for a half-hour, inflicting "some loss in killed and wounded," as reported by Gen. Hunt, with no further loss to ourselves, but the wheel of a gun. Finding by then that the battle was over and no enemy left on our side of the river, the guns were gradually withdrawn and camps were sought in another severe rain-storm, which came up about 5 P.M. and lasted far into the night.[1]

The battle made by Stuart on the 3d, has rarely been surpassed, measured either by the strength of the lines carried or by the casualties suffered in so brief a period. In Colston's division four brigades lost eight brigade commanders, three killed and five disabled. Three out of six of the division staff fell. In Pender's brigade of Heth's division, six out of ten field-officers were killed or wounded. Our brigades rarely came to the field 2000 strong, and casualties of 600 to a brigade were rarely reached even in battles prolonged over a day. Here within six hours, five of the 15 brigades lost over 600 in killed and wounded each: Lane's N.C. brigade losing 786; Colston's N.C. and Va. losing 726; Pender's N.C., 693.

The battle of Chickamauga is generally called the bloodiest of modern battles. The losses given by Livermore are 22 per cent in the Federal army and 25 per cent in the Confederate, in two days' fighting. Jackson's three divisions had a paper strength of 26,661, and their losses were 7158, about 27 per cent. They were, doubtless, over 30 per cent of the force actually engaged. The losses in the 3d and 12th Federal corps, which composed the principal part of our opponents, were less, as they fought behind breastworks. Their strength on paper was 32,171. Their losses were 4703, being about 15

---

[1] A reminiscence of that night is the finding of our camp in the heaviest of the rain and blackest of the darkness by a lost ambulance carrying a Virginian colonel, whose leg had been amputated on the field. He was taken out and fed, slept on the crowded floor of our tent, and next morning was started for a hospital in fine spirits in spite of his maimed condition.

per cent of the paper strength and probably 18 per cent of the actual.

Had Gen. Lee been present on the left, during the Sunday morning attack, and seen Stuart's energy and efficiency in handling his reserves, inspiring the men by his contagious spirit, and in the coöperation of artillery, with the infantry, he might have rewarded Stuart on the spot by promoting him to the now vacant command of Jackson's corps. Ewell, who did succeed Jackson, was always loved and admired, but he was not always equal to his opportunities, as we shall see at Gettysburg. Stuart's qualities were just what were needed, for he was young, he was not maimed, and he had boldness, persistence, and magnetism in very high degree. Lee once said that he would have won Gettysburg, had he had Jackson with him. Who so worthy to succeed Jackson as the man who had successfully replaced him on his last and greatest field?

CONFEDERATE CASUALTIES

COMMANDS	KILLED	WOUNDED	MISSING	TOTAL	STREN.
S.C. Kershaw's Brig.	12	90	2	104	
Miss. Barksdale's "	43	208	341	592	
Ga. Semmes's "	85	492	26	603	
Ga. Wofford's "	74	479	9	562	
Cabell's Battn. A	5	21	2	28	
McLaws's Div.	219	1,290	380	1,889	8,800
Ala. Wilcox's Brig.	72	372	91	535	
Va. Mahone's "	24	134	97	255	
Miss. Posey's "	41	184	65	290	
Ga. Wright's "	25	271		296	
Fla. Perry's "	21	88		109	
Anderson's Div.	183	1,049	215	1,485	8,500
Washington Arty.	4	8	33	45	
Alexander's "	6	35	21	62	
Hardaway's "	1	12		13	
Total Res. "	11	55	54	120	
Total 1st Corps	413	2,394	687	3,494	

CONFEDERATE CASUALTIES (*Continued*)

	COMMANDS	KILLED	WOUNDED	MISSING	TOTAL	STREN.
	Hd. Qrs., 2d Corps	2	3		5	
	Hd. Qrs., 1st Div.	2	2		4	
Va.	Heth's Brig.	44	259		303	
S.C.	McGowan's " [1]	46	402	7	455	
Ga.	Thomas's "	21	156		177	
N.C.	Lane's "	161	626	121	908	
Ala.	Archer's "	44	305	16	365	
N.C.	Pender's "	116	577	68	761	
	A. P. Hill's Div.	436	2,330	212	2,978	10,400
Ala.	Rodes's Brig.	90	538	188	816	
Ga.	Doles's "	66	343	28	437	
Ga.	Colquitt's "	9	128	312	449	
N.C.	Iverson's "	67	330	73	470	
N.C.	Ramseur's "	151	529	108	788	
	Rodes's Div.	383	1,868	709	2,960	9,600
Ga.	Gordon's Brig. [1]	16	145		161	
Va.	Smith's " [1]	11	75		86	
N.C.	Hoke's " [1]	35	195		230	
La.	Hays's " [1]	63	306		369	
	Early's Rept. adds	11	117	500	628	
	Early's Div.	136	838	500	1,474	8,200
Va.	Paxton's Brig. [1]	54	430		484	
"	Garnett's " [1]	52	420		472	
N.C.	Colston's (Va.)	128	594	80	802	
La.	Nicholls's [1]	47	266		313	
	Colston's Div.	281	1,710	80	2,071	6,600
	Artillery, 2d Corps	26	124			150
	Total 2d Corps	1,262	6,870	1,501	9,633	35,800
	Lee, F., Cav. Brig.	4	7		11	
	Pelham's Arty.	4	6	8	18	
	Grand Total	1,683	9,277	2,196	13,156	56,444

[1] From Report of Surgeon Guild, excluding slightly wounded and missing.

FEDERAL CASUALTIES

COMMANDS	KILLED	WOUNDED	MISSING	TOTAL	STRENGTH
Reynolds's Div.	1	15	2	18	
Robinson's "	7	42	6	55	
Doubleday's "	1	23	38	62	
Total 1st Corps	9	80	46	135	16,908
Hancock's Div.	78	445	601	1,124	
French's "	63	506	119	688	
Two Divs. 2d Corps	141	951	720	1,812	16,893
Birney's Div.	119	925	563	1,607	
Berry's "	148	1,037	244	1,429	
Whipple's "	111	682	289	1,082	
Total 3d Corps	378	2,644	1,096	4,118	18,721
Griffin's Div.	17	108	13	138	
Sykes's "	27	167	91	285	
Humphreys's "	25	197	55	277	
Total 5th Corps	69	472	159	700	15,724
Deven's Div.	61	477	432	970	
Steinwehr's "	27	248	244	519	
Schurz's "	129	496	298	923	
Total 11th Corps	217	1,221	974	2,412	12,927
Williams's Div.	135	801	676	1,612	
Geary's "	125	637	444	1,206	
Total 12th Corps	260	1,441	1,121	2,822	13,450
Deven's Brig. Cav.	8	35	98	141	
Total about Chancellors-ville	1,081	6,844	4,214	12,140	
Gibbon's Div., 2d Corps	8	90	12	110	
Brooks's " 6th "	203	923	366	1,492	
Howe's " 6th "	91	697	502	1,290	
Newton's " 6th "	98	605	307	1,010	
Burnham's " 6th "	93	395	310	798	
Total 6th Corps	485	2,620	1,485	4,590	23,667
Total about Fredericksburg	493	2,710	1,497	4,700	
Grand Total	1,574	9,554	5,711	16,804	

CHAPTER XVI

GETTYSBURG: THE FIRST DAY

A PAUSE of four weeks after the battle of Chancellorsville to
prepare for an aggressive counter-stroke, was, perhaps, the period
of highest tide in *Confederate hopes* among all the vicissitudes
of the war. The campaign which ensued, culminating at Gettysburg, is generally accepted as the turning-point of Confederate
fortunes. I think it may be held that each summer campaign
in Va. marked a Confederate crisis. That is to say, that defeat in any one of them would have been followed by the collapse of its government, within less than another 12 months,
while a victory would assure it only of that much of life. More
than that was impossible as long as the war spirit ruled the
North, and this was certainly the case in 1863.

A year later, however, there did come a period of very great
Federal discouragement, due to a succession of severe losses.
At the same time, there occurred a crisis in the military situation,
which threatened an ignominious termination to Grant's campaign, the greatest campaign of the war. This was saved by a
brilliant piece of Federal strategy, which is to be told of in due
course. In it will be found the real crisis — the story of the
passing of the last hope of Confederate success. It was not

lost upon any field of battle, either of offence or of defence. It was a victory of strategy and not one of arms.

It was now for Lee to take the offensive — a rôle appealing strongly to his disposition. The defensive was to invite the enemy to accumulate his resources to the point at which their very weight would crush us. But, for a brief period, we enjoyed a choice of the field of action. It was a fatal mistake that in this choice we failed to utilize the single advantage in the game of war, which the Confederacy enjoyed.

We occupied the "Interior Lines," and could reënforce from one flank to the other, across our country, more quickly than the enemy could discover and follow our movements by round-about routes. Only by such transfers of her armies could the South ever hope to face her adversaries with superior, or even with equal, numbers — by demanding double duty of her regiments, fighting battles with them alternately in the east and in the west. In Lee we had a leader of phenomenal ability, could this policy have been once adopted under his direction. Here in May, 1863, was presented a rare opportunity to inaugurate what might be called an "Army on Wheels" within the Confederate lines, as distinguished from an Army of Invasion beyond them. The situation was this. Grant was investing Vicksburg with 60,000 men, and we were threatened with the loss of the Mississippi River, and of 30,000 men at Vicksburg under Pemberton. At Jackson, Miss., Johnston, with scarcely 24,000 men, was looking on and begging vainly for reënforcements.

At Murfreesboro, Tenn., Bragg, with about 45,000 Confederates, confronted Rosecrans with about 84,000. Neither felt strong enough for the aggressive, and the whole spring and summer passed idly. At Knoxville were about 5000 Confederates under Buckner, and there were also scattered brigades in southwest Va. and eastern N.C., from which reënforcements might be drawn. In this state of affairs, Longstreet, with Hood's and Pickett's divisions, arrived in Petersburg, under orders to rejoin Lee at Fredericksburg. Hooker had just been driven across the Rappahannock, and his army was soon to lose largely from the expiration of terms of service of many regiments.

Nothing aggressive was probable from him for many weeks.

Longstreet's veteran divisions, about 13,000 strong, could have been placed on the cars at Petersburg and hurried out to Bragg, via Lynchburg and Knoxville.   Johnston's 25,000 from Jackson, and Buckner's 5000 from Knoxville, could have met them.   With these accessions, and with Lee in command, Rosecrans might have been defeated, and an advance made into Ky., threatening Louisville and Cincinnati.   If anything could have caused Grant's recall from Vicksburg, it would have been this.   Surely the chances of success were greater, and of disaster less, than those involved in our crossing the bridgeless Potomac, into the heart of the enemy's country, where ammunition and supplies must come by wagons from Staunton, nearly 200 miles, over roads exposed to raids of the enemy from either the east or the west. In this position, a drawn battle, or even a victory, would still leave us compelled soon to find our way back across the Potomac.

Longstreet [1] tells of his having suggested to Secretary Seddon such a campaign against Rosecrans, and he also suggested it to Lee on his arrival at Fredericksburg.   Mr. Seddon thought Grant could not be drawn from Vicksburg even by a Confederate advance upon the Ohio River.   To this Longstreet answered that Grant was a soldier and must obey orders if popular alarm forced the government to recall him.   At that time Davis was sanguine of foreign intervention, and the Emperor Napoleon was permitting a French firm to build some formidable ironclads for the Confederate navy.   These might have accomplished some results, had not the issue of the Gettysburg campaign induced the Emperor to withdraw his consent to their delivery.

Lee recognized the strong features of the proposed strategy, and took a day or two to consider it.   But he finally decided upon an invasion of Pa.   He was averse to leaving Va. himself, and also to any division of his army.   Both he and Jackson, ever since the failure of the Md. campaign, had longed to try it once more, and Jackson had had prepared during the winter and spring the remarkable map, already mentioned (p. 322), covering the whole scene of the coming campaign.   In the discussion with Longstreet, it was assumed that the strategy of the

---

[1] *Manassas to Appomattox*, p. 327.

campaign should be such as would force the enemy to attack our army in position. Jackson had once said, and it was ever afterward an article of our steadfast faith and confidence, "We sometimes fail to drive the enemy from position, but they always fail to drive us."

Lee fully appreciated the over-anxiety of the enemy for the safety of Washington, and proposed, for this occasion, a special feature, which he hoped would play upon and exaggerate these fears. Two of Pickett's five brigades had been temporarily left, — Jenkins's at Petersburg, and Corse's at Hanover Junction. Lee proposed that when his column of invasion crossed the Potomac, these two brigades, reënforced by whatever could be drawn from lower Virginia and the Carolinas, should form a column commanded by Beauregard, who should come from Charleston for the purpose. This column, with some parade of its intention, should advance from Culpeper and threaten Washington. Hooker's army would have been drawn by Lee north of the Potomac. The prestige of Beauregard's name would doubtless exaggerate the numbers in his command, and Lee hoped that the sudden danger might lead the enemy to call troops from the West, particularly if his army could win a battle north of the Potomac. The weak feature was that Lee did not have under his own control the troops which he desired to move. Davis had, indeed, proposed to him to control all troops on the Atlantic slope; but Lee insisted even on being relieved of the department south of the James, under D. H. Hill. He did not take the War Dept. into his confidence at first, hoping to accomplish his purpose by gradual suggestion and request. The process was too slow, and the result was unfortunate. Only on June 23 from Berryville, Va., did he fully explain to the President his wishes. On the 25th, from Williamsport, he followed the matter up with two letters, urging "the organization of an army, even in effigy, under Beauregard, at Culpeper C. H." Meanwhile, some demonstrations by the enemy from the York River had excited apprehensions at Richmond, and neither Corse's or Jenkins's brigades were sent forward, as had been planned.

A reply was despatched on June 29, saying, —

"This is the first intimation the President has had that such a plan was ever in contemplation, and, taking all things into consideration, he cannot see how it can by any possibility be carried into effect."

Explaining the difficulty of protecting the railroads near Richmond, the letter even suggested that Lee spare some of his own force to better protect his own communications. This caution was not excessive. The messenger carrying this letter to Lee was captured on July 2, by a raid upon our rear, and, its importance being recognized, it was hurried to Meade and delivered to him on the field of Gettysburg at 4.10 A.M. on July 4. At that hour there was some uncertainty in the Union councils as to their best policy. The facts given in the captured letter of the difficulties of the Confederates, and the impossibility of Lee's receiving any reënforcements, doubtless increased Meade's confidence in all his later movements. The letter was considered of such importance that the officer who brought it, Capt. Ulric Dahlgren, was complimented and promoted.

In May our army was reorganized into three corps, each comprising three divisions of infantry, generally of four brigades each, and five battalions of artillery, averaging 16 guns each. Ewell succeeded Jackson in command of the 2d corps, and A. P. Hill took command of the new 3d corps. He had been an excellent division commander, and done conspicuous fighting and marching in the previous campaigns.[1] It has already been said that Stuart would have made a more active and efficient corps commander than Ewell.

[1] D. H. Hill also had strong claims for promotion. He had done as much hard fighting as any other general, and had also displayed great ability in holding his men to their work by supervision and example. But at this time he was not with the army, and was in command of the important department south of the James. He was a North Carolinian, and was very acceptable to the State authorities, who objected if too many North Carolinians were taken to Va., leaving N.C. exposed to Federal raids. There was an earnestness about D. H. Hill's fighting which was like Jackson's at its best. Had opportunity come to him, he must have won greater fame. His individuality may be briefly illustrated by an official indorsement placed upon the application of a soldier to be transferred from the infantry to the band.

"Respectfully forwarded, disapproved. Shooters are more needed than tooters."

Reorganized, the army stood as follows: —

1st Corps. Longstreet

Divisions	Strength	Brigade Commander	Batts.	Guns
McLaws	7,311	Kershaw, Barksdale, Semmes, Wofford		
Pickett	5,200	Garnett, Kemper, Armistead		
Hood	7,720	Law, Robertson, Anderson, G. T. Benning		
Arty. Battns.	1,000	Cabell, Dearing, Henry, Walton, Alexander	21	84
Totals	21,231	11 Brigades, 5 Battns. Arty.	21	84

2d Corps. Ewell

Early	6,943	Hays, Smith, Hoke, Gordon		
Johnson	5,564	Stuart, Walker, Nichols, Jones		
Rodes	8,454	Daniel, Doles, Iverson, Ramseur, O'Neal		
Arty. Battns.	1,000	Jones, Latimer, Carter, Brown, Nelson.	21	84
Totals	21,961	13 Brigades, 5 Battns. Arty.	21	84

3d Corps. A. P. Hill

Anderson	7,440	Wilcox, Wright, Mahone, Perry, Posey		
Heth	7,500	Pettigrew, Brockenbrough, Archer, Davis		
Pender	6,800	Perrin, Lane, Thomas, Scales		
Arty. Battns.	1,000	Lane, Garnett, Poague, McIntosh, Pegram	20	80
Totals	22,740	13 Brigades, 5 Battns. Arty.	20	80
	65,932	3 Corps, 9 Divisions, 37 Brigades, 15 Battns. Arty.	62	248
Stuart	10,292	Hampton, Robertson, Jones, F. Lee, Jenkins, W. H. F. Lee		
Cavalry		Imboden		
		1 Battn. Arty.	6	24
Totals	10,292	1 Division, 7 Brigades	6	24
Aggregate	76,224	3 Corps, 10 Divisions, 44 Brigades, 16 Battns. Arty.	68	272

The figures given are the returns of the "Officers and men present for duty" on May 31.   No later return was made before the battle.

Similarly, for the Federal army, the table below gives the "Officers and men present for duty" on June 30, the last return before the battle.   To arrive at the forces actually engaged, deductions must be made from these figures in both armies for sick, guards, and details.   This deduction Livermore averages at seven per cent for Infantry and Artillery and 15 per cent for Cavalry.

ARMY OF THE POTOMAC.   PRESENT FOR DUTY, JUNE 30, '63

Corps Strength	Divisions	Brigades	Artillery	
			Batts.	Guns
1st Corps Reynolds 10,355	Wadsworth Robinson Rowley	Meredith, Cutler Paul, Baxter Biddle, Stone, Stannard	 5	 23
2d Corps Hancock 13,056	Caldwell Gibbon Hays	Cross, Kelley, Zook, Brook Harrow, Webb, Hall Carroll, Smyth, Willard	 5	 24
3d Corps Sickles 12,630	Birney Humphreys	Graham, Ward, De Trobriand Carr, Brewster, Burling	 5	 30
5th Corps Sykes 12,211	Barnes Ayres Crawford	Tilton, Sweitzer, Vincent Day, Burbank, Weed McCandless, Fisher	 5	 26
6th Corps Sedgwick 15,710	Wright Howe Newton	Torbert, Bartlett, Russell Grant, Neill Shaler, Eustis, Wheaton	 8	 48
11th Corps Howard 10,576	Barlow Steinwehr Schurz	Von Gilsa, Ames Coster, Smith Schimmelpfennig, Krzyzan- owski	 5	 26
12th Corps Slocum 8,597	Williams Geary	McDougall, Lockwood, Ru- ger Candy, Cobham, Greene	 4	 20
2,568	Tyler	Artillery Reserve	21	110

Corps Strength	Divisions	Brigades	Artillery	
2,580		Engineers, Provost Guard's Escorts		
100,283	7 Corps, 19 Divisions, 51 Brigades, Infantry and Artillery		58	312
Cavalry Corps Pleasonton 14,973	Buford Gregg, D. Kilpatrick	Gamble, Devin, Merritt McIntosh, Huey, Gregg, J. Farnsworth, Custer	9	50
115,256	8 Corps, 22 Divisions, 59 Brigades		67	362

The Confederate infantry by this time were about nine-tenths armed with the rifled musket, muzzle loading, mostly of calibre .58, but some of calibre .54. Their artillery was now, also, all organized into battalions, usually of four-gun batteries each. Each corps had five of these battalions. One of these served with each of the three divisions, and the remaining two constituted a corps reserve, under command of the senior artillery officer, who began to be called, and to act, as chief of artillery of the corps.

The general artillery reserve, which had been commanded by Pendleton, was broken up, on the organization of the 3d corps, and it was never reëstablished. Pendleton, however, was retained as chief of artillery. It is worthy of note that this artillery organization of a few batteries with each division, and a reserve with each corps, but with no general reserve for the army, was the first of the kind ever adopted by any foreign army, and that it was subsequently copied by Prussia and Austria after 1866, and by France after 1870, and later by England. But, although our reserve under Pendleton had never found the opportunity to render much service, its being discontinued was due to our poverty of guns, not to dissatisfaction with the system. And the fine service at Gettysburg by the Federal reserve of 110 guns, under Hunt, would seem to demonstrate the advantage of such an organization in every large army.

On Wednesday, June 3, Lee began the delicate operation of

manœuvring Hooker out of his position behind the Rappahannock by a movement of the 1st and 2d corps toward Culpeper. Hood and McLaws marched on the 3d, Rodes on the 4th, and Early and Johnson on the 5th. Longstreet's reserve — the Washington Artillery with eight guns, and my own with 26 — marched on the 3d. On the 5th, the enemy, having discovered that something was on foot, crossed a small force over the Rappahannock, at the old position near the mouth of Deep Run. On this, Lee ordered Ewell's corps to halt and await developments. But on the 6th he became satisfied that nothing serious was intended, and Ewell was ordered to proceed. In the afternoon, Lee himself left Fredericksburg for Culpeper. Hill's corps now stood alone in front of Hooker's entire army.

Meanwhile, Hooker had sent Buford's and Gregg's divisions of cavalry, supported by Russell's and Ames's brigades of infantry, to attack Stuart's camps near the Rappahannock. A severe cavalry battle resulted on the 9th, near Brandy Station. The enemy's attack was a surprise, and the isolated Confederate brigades, first encountered, were so roughly handled that help was called for from the infantry and artillery. My own battalion and an infantry force were sent to the field, but reached it too late. The enemy, having obtained the information which was the object of his expedition, withdrew across the Rappahannock under cover of his infantry brigades, with loss of three guns and 907 men. Stuart's loss was 485.

On June 10, Ewell's corps left Culpeper for the Valley. Rodes moved to Berryville, while Early and Johnson advanced upon Winchester, and, on the 13th and 14th, drove Milroy's forces into the city. Preparations were made to storm the fortified line at dawn on the 15th, an enterprise which might easily have been disastrous, had they been well defended. But Milroy saw his communications threatened, and did not wait for the attack. About dawn, his retreating forces were struck in the flank near Stephenson's depot by Steuart's and the Stonewall brigade, and were routed with the loss of about 2400 men and 23 guns. Rodes's division, going by Berryville, had driven the enemy from that point on the 13th, and on the 14th had captured Martinsburg late in the afternoon, taking five guns and many stores. Most of the enemy escaped under cover of darkness, though the pursuit was pushed until late at night. On the 15th, starting at 10 A.M., Rodes reached Williamsport at dark and at once crossed three brigades and three batteries over the Potomac. The marches made by Ewell's whole corps in this swoop upon Milroy, and the fruits of victory secured, compare well with the work of the same corps under Jackson 13 months before. Early and Johnson, advancing upon Winchester, made 70 miles in three days. Rodes speaks of his march to Williamsport as —

"the most trying march we had yet had; most trying because of the intense heat, the character of the road (stony and dusty) and the increased number of barefooted men in the command."

He goes on to say : —

"It was not until this day that the troops began to exhibit unmistakable signs of exhaustion, and that stragglers could be found in the line of march, and even then none but absolutely worn-out men fell out of the line. The whole march from Culpeper to Williamsport, which was an extremely rapid one, was executed in a manner highly creditable to the officers and men of the division. A halt at Williamsport was absolutely necessary from the condition of the feet of the unshod men. Very many of these gallant fellows were still marching in ranks with feet bruised, bleeding, and swollen."

Of the fruits gathered by the victory, Lee reports, —

"More than 4000 prisoners, about 30 pieces of artillery, 250 wagons, 400 horses, 20 ambulances, and a lot of ammunition, etc."

Besides these captures of military material, large quantities of cattle, provisions, and supplies of all kinds useful to the army were now to be collected in the fertile farming country, into which the army had penetrated.

Stringent orders were issued, forbidding the taking of private property except by duly authorized officers, giving formal receipts in all cases, that the owners might have no difficulty in establishing claims and receiving payment at fair prices.

On June 13, as Ewell's corps approached Winchester, Longstreet being at Culpeper, and Hill still opposite Fredericksburg, Hooker put his army in motion from Falmouth for Manassas. Before Lee began his movement, Hooker had anticipated it, and had proposed in that event to cross the Rappahannock and interpose between Lee's flanks. It was, doubtless, his proper move, and would have forced Lee to recall Longstreet and Ewell and have broken up his campaign. But it had been decided, soon after the battle of Chancellorsville, in a council between Mr. Lincoln, Halleck, and Stanton, that Hooker should never again be intrusted with the conduct of a battle. He could not be at once removed on account of the support of politicians who desired to have Secretary Chase succeed Mr. Lincoln as President. This party, with the active aid of Chase, had placed Hooker in his position by turning the scale in his favor, when the choice was between Hooker and Meade, as successor to Burnside. They still supported Hooker strongly, and a dead-lock was only averted by Chase's friends consenting to a change of the commander *in case Hooker should voluntarily resign.*

The secret of Chase's interest lay in the fact that Hooker had pledged himself not to become a candidate for the Presidency, should he win a great victory.

Meanwhile, as he was not to be allowed to fight, both Halleck and Lincoln refused his sensible proposition to cross the Rappahannock, and Lincoln wrote him the oft-quoted advice, —

"not to be entangled on the river, like an ox jumped half over a fence, and liable to be torn by dogs, front and rear, without a fair chance to gore one way or kick another."

Now that Lee's army was stretched out over a line more than 100 miles long, even Lincoln saw that a wonderful opportunity was flaunted in the face of the Federals. He now wrote to Hooker in quite a different spirit: —

"If the head of Lee's army is at Martinsburg, and the tail of it on the Plank road between Fredericksburg and Chancellorsville, the animal must be very slim somewhere. Could you not break him?"

Hooker would have only been too glad to try, but Stanton and Halleck were on guard over him, and practically the Army of the Potomac was bound hand and foot, and Lee was free to work his own will, unmolested, until Hooker should be forced to tender his resignation.

Hooker's movement toward Manassas was at once followed by

Hill's marching for Culpeper on the 14th, and, on the 15th, Longstreet marched from Culpeper to take position east of the Blue Ridge, while Hill passed in his rear and crossed the mountains to Winchester via Front Royal. When Hill was safely in the Valley, Longstreet also entered through Ashby's and Snicker's gaps, and about the 20th the two corps were united.

The cavalry had acted as a screen in front of Longstreet during this advance, and, in this duty, had severe encounters with the enemy at Aldie, Middleburg, and Upperville, losing in them over 500 in killed, wounded, and missing.

About June 22, as Hill and Longstreet drew near the Potomac, ready to cross, Stuart made to Lee a very unwise proposition, which Lee more unwisely entertained. It was destined to have an unfortunate influence on the campaign. Stuart thus refers to the matter in his official report : —

"I submitted to the commanding general the plan of leaving a brigade or so in my present front, passing through Hopewell or some other gap in the Bull Run Mountains, attain the enemy's rear, passing between his main body and Washington, and cross into Md., joining our army north of the Potomac.

"The commanding general wrote authorizing this move, if I thought it practicable, and also what instructions should be given the two brigades left in front of the enemy. He also notified me that one column would move via Gettysburg, and the other via Carlisle, toward the Susquehanna, and directed me, after crossing, to proceed with all despatch to join the right (Early) of the army in Pa."

In view of the issues at stake, and of the fact that already he had been deprived of two promised brigades (Corse's and Jenkins's), it was unwise even to contemplate sending three brigades of cavalry upon such distant service. When one compares the small beneficial results of raids, even when successful, with the risks here involved, it is hard to understand how Lee could have given his consent.

Hooker's Chancellorsville campaign had been lost by the absence of his cavalry, and Lee's Gettysburg campaign was similarly compromised. Lee, however, acquiesced, only attaching the condition that Longstreet could spare the cavalry from his front, and approved the adventure. Longstreet, thus sud-

denly called on to decide the question, seems not to have appreciated its importance, for he decided it on the imaginary ground
that "the passage of the Potomac by our rear would, in a measure,
disclose our plans."

Accordingly, about midnight of June 24, Stuart, with Hampton's, W. H. F. Lee's, and Fitz-Lee's brigades, six guns, and
some ambulances, marched from Salem, for the Potomac River.
Making a circuit by Brentsville, Wolf Run shoals, Fairfax
C. H., and Dranesville, he crossed the Potomac at Rowser's
Ford at midnight of the 27th, about 80 miles by the route
travelled. The ford was barely passable. The water came on
the saddles of the horses and entirely submerged the artillery
carriages. These were emptied and the ammunition carried
across by hand. Here the Chesapeake and Ohio Canal was cut.
Next morning at Rockville, a train of wagons eight miles long
was captured, and 400 prisoners were taken and paroled. In
saving a large number of wagons, instead of burning them, and
in delaying 12 hours to parole his prisoners, instead of bringing
along the officers and letting the men go, Stuart committed fatal
blunders. The Federal authorities refused to recognize the paroles
(though they were given at the earnest solicitation of the captured officers), and all the paroled were at once returned to duty.
The delay caused to subsequent marches by the long wagon-train,
and the embarrassment of protecting it, was responsible for the
loss of time which made, on the whole, a sad failure of the expedition. On the 29th, the Baltimore and Ohio R.R. was crossed
and torn up at Hood's Mills. At Westminster about 5 P.M., a
squadron of Federal cavalry was routed, and the head of the
column bivouacked that night midway between Westminster and
Littletown. Had it here followed the direct road, via Littletown
to Gettysburg, only about 16 miles away, it could have occupied
Gettysburg before 11 A.M. on the 30th, where it would have
found itself in good position in front of Lee's army, then concentrating at Cashtown. It might, however, have had a severe
fight with Buford's two brigades of cavalry, which arrived in the
afternoon, just in time to anticipate Pettigrew's brigade of
Heth's division, which had been directed to visit Gettysburg in
quest of shoes.

This incident will be referred to again. It is mentioned here only to show how near Stuart's expedition came to a happy issue on June 30. Had it done so, Lee's army would have occupied some strong position between Cashtown and Gettysburg, and the onus of attack would have been upon the Federals, as had been the plan of the campaign.

But his orders led Stuart toward the Susquehanna, so he proceeded north to Hanover, which was reached at 10 A.M. on the 30th. Here he had a sharp skirmish with Kilpatrick's cavalry. Hampered by his 125 captured wagons, he turned squarely to the right, and, making a detour by Jefferson, he reached Dover on the morning of July 1, crossing during the night the road on which Early's division had marched on the 30th from York to Heidlersburg. Here he learned that Early had gone toward Shippensburg. Stuart was practically lost, and had to guess in which direction he should go to find Lee's army. Lee was now beginning the battle of Gettysburg, 25 miles off to the southwest. Stuart's report says: —

"After as little rest as was compatible with the exhausted condition of the command, I pushed on for Carlisle [25 miles to the northwest], where I hoped to find a portion of our army."

He arrived before Carlisle in the afternoon. His rations were now entirely exhausted. He desired to levy a contribution, but learned that a considerable force of militia was ambushed in the town, "with a view to entrap him on his entrance." He invested the town, threw in some shells, and burned the United States Cavalry barracks. "The whereabouts of our army," he says, "was still a mystery, but during the night I received a despatch from Lee that the army was at Gettysburg [about 30 miles south] and had been engaged this day." The investment was abandoned, and the column headed for Gettysburg, where it arrived that afternoon "just in time to thwart a movement of the enemy's cavalry upon our rear." . . .

The expedition had occupied eight days, and had traversed in that time about 250 miles. Meanwhile, Lee had been exceedingly impatient. When Stuart, at last, reported in person, late in the afternoon of the 2d, although Lee said only, "Well, General, you are here at last," his manner implied rebuke, and it was so understood by Stuart.

He, however, is scarcely to be blamed for suggesting the raid. Had he wasted no time paroling prisoners and saving wagons, his raid might have been successful, as raids go, for his whole casualties were but 89 killed, wounded, and missing. But the venture was a strategic mistake, for it resulted in the battle's being one of chance collision, with the Confederates taking the offensive, whereas the plan of the campaign had been to fight a defensive battle.

Hill crossed the Potomac at Shepherdstown on June 23, and Longstreet began crossing at Williamsport on the 24th. Hooker was not far behind, for he crossed at Edward's Ferry on the 25th and 26th, and moved to the vicinity of Frederick. Here he threatened Lee's rear through the South Mountain passes, if he moved north, and, at the same time, covered Washington. Hooker had, meanwhile, been placed in command of the troops at Washington (some 26,000 men), and at Harper's Ferry, where there were about 11,000. It was a wise order, but under the policy of not allowing Hooker to fight, it was but a sham, as he soon discovered. He attempted to draw 15,000 men from the Washington lines, as his whole army was now in front of the city, but Halleck refused to allow it. He then proposed to throw a strong force across the mountains upon Lee's rear, and, for this purpose, he ordered the 11,000 under French at Harper's Ferry to unite with the 12th corps, which was to lead the movement. Again Halleck interposed. He refused the troops on the absurd ground that "Maryland Heights have always been regarded as an important point to be held by us, and much labor and expense has been incurred in fortifying them."

Hooker appealed in vain to Stanton and Lincoln, pointing out the folly of holding so large a force idle. Then Hooker realized that he had lost the support of the government, and tendered his resignation June 27. It was just what Stanton and Halleck had been seeking, and was no sooner received than accepted, and prompt measures adopted to relieve him, lest the armies should come into collision with Hooker still in command.

Meade succeeded Hooker. He was an excellent fighter, but

too lacking in audacity for a good commanding general. He was also of cross and quarrelsome disposition, and unpopular with his leading officers.

Duplicate orders, relieving Hooker and installing Meade, were sent that afternoon by Hardie, Stanton's chief of staff. He delivered the order to Meade about midnight, while Hooker was still in ignorance how his proffered resignation was being received. Meade protested, and begged to be excused in favor of Reynolds, who was the favorite of the army. But he was compelled to accompany Hardie on a ride to Hooker's quarters, some miles away, to deliver the order superseding him. Hooker had hoped for a different outcome. He acquiesced gracefully, but the scene was a painful one.

Meanwhile, Lee, with Longstreet and Hill, had reached Chambersburg and bivouacked in its neighborhood from June 27 to the 29th. The Federal army had now been across the Potomac for three days, but Lee was not yet informed, and he now became anxious to hear from his cavalry. An additional large brigade coming from W. Va., under Imboden, should have joined him here, but it had not yet arrived. It had been delayed in its approach by destroying the Chesapeake and Ohio Canal about Hancock. A very essential part, also, of Stuart's proposed programme had not been carried out.

This was that two of his five brigades should cross into Md. with Lee and continue on his right flank, to screen it and observe the enemy. Longstreet had specially directed Stuart to let Hampton's brigade be one of these, with Hampton in command of both. This was not convenient, and Stuart had left Robertson's and Jones's brigades, with Robertson in command. Also, he had failed to make Robertson understand what was expected of him. The result was that Robertson and his two brigades remained in Va. until brought over by Lee's order on July 2.[1]

To gain information, Stuart had designed to have two efficient scouts operating within the enemy's line, but accident had

[1] This failure to carry out Lee's orders indicates a staff insufficient to keep him in touch with what was taking place. A notable feature of the coming battle will be found in the number of important events which seemed to happen without any control for the Commander-in-Chief.

prevented in both cases. Mosby, one of them, had failed to reach Stuart, at his crossing of the Potomac, owing to an enforced change of Stuart's line of march. Stringfellow, the other, had been captured. Lee, therefore, on June 28, still believed that Hooker's army had not yet crossed the Potomac, and, to hurry Hooker up, he issued orders for an advance, the next day, of all his forces upon Harrisburg.

But there was still one scout, Harrison, within the Federal lines. Longstreet had despatched him from Culpeper, three weeks before, to go into Washington and remain until he had important information to communicate.

With good judgment and good fortune he appeared about midnight on the 28th, with the news that Hooker had crossed the Potomac, and had been superseded by Meade. He was also able to give the approximate locations of five of Meade's seven corps, three being near Frederick and two near the base of South Mountain.

This news caused an immediate change in Lee's plans. He was specially anxious to hold Meade east of the Blue Ridge, and not have him come into the Valley behind us — the movement which Hooker had brought on his own resignation by seeking to make. To forestall this, Lee's plan had long been formed to concentrate his own army somewhere between Cashtown and Gettysburg, in a strong position where it would threaten at once Washington, Baltimore, and Philadelphia. The enemy, he hoped, would then be forced to attack him. His report states that, —

"the march toward Gettysburg was conducted more slowly than it would have been had the movements of the Federal army been known."

Accordingly, on the 29th, orders were sent, countermanding those of the day before and directing movements which would concentrate the three corps at Cashtown, eight miles west of Gettysburg. There was no urgency about the orders, which indicates that Lee had not yet selected any particular site for his coming battle. Meade, however, very soon after taking command on the 28th, had selected a position, Parr's Ridge, behind Pipe Creek, on the divide between the waters of the Potomac and Chesapeake Bay. Here he, too, hoped to fight on the

defensive. It would have been safe play, but not so brilliant as
what Hooker had proposed, or as what Lee himself had used
with Pope in Aug., 1862.

On June 29, Hill moved Heth's division from Fayetteville to
Cashtown, about 10 miles. Heth heard that shoes could be
purchased in Gettysburg, and, with Hill's permission, authorized
Pettigrew's brigade to go there next day and get them. On the
30th, Pender's division followed Heth's from Fayetteville to
Cashtown, and was followed by Longstreet with Hood and
McLaws from Chambersburg as far as Greenwood, about 11 miles.
Here they bivouacked about 2 P.M. Lee accompanied this march,
and also bivouacked at Greenwood. Pickett's division was left
at Chambersburg to guard the rear until Imboden's cavalry
should arrive, and Law's brigade was detached from Hood's
division and sent to New Guilford C. H., a few miles south
of Fayetteville, until Robertson's cavalry should relieve it. On
the 30th, Ewell's corps, having received the orders from Lee,
also marched toward Cashtown, the place of rendezvous.

Meanwhile, Pettigrew, on approaching Gettysburg, found
Buford's cavalry just occupying it, upon which he withdrew
about five miles and bivouacked.

Previously, everything had moved favorably for the Confederates' strategy. Now, Stuart was still unheard from, Robertson and Imboden were still behind, and four brigades of infantry
were detained waiting for them. Lee knew approximately the
enemy's position, however, and his own three corps were converging by easy marches upon Cashtown, near which village he
proposed to select his ground and await an attack.

Meade's army was equally near Pipe Creek, where he hoped to
be able to play the same game. But a chance collision suddenly
precipitated a battle, unforeseen and undesired by either party.

Hill's report describes how it began : —

"On arriving at Cashtown, Heth, who had sent forward Pettigrew's
brigade to Gettysburg, reported that Pettigrew had encountered the enemy
at Gettysburg (principally cavalry), but in what force he could not determine. A courier was then despatched with this information for the
general commanding, and with orders to start Anderson early. Also to
Ewell informing him, and that I intended to advance the next morning,
and discover what was in my front."

Thus Hill's movement to Gettysburg was made of his own motion, and with knowledge that he would find the enemy's cavalry in possession. Ewell was informed of it. Lee's orders were to avoid bringing on an action.

Like Stuart's raid, Hill's venture is another illustration of an important event allowed to happen without supervision. Lee's first intimation of danger of collision was his hearing Hill's guns at Gettysburg. He was much disturbed by it, not wishing to fight without the presence of his cavalry to gather fruit in case of victory.

On July 1, of his nine divisions, Pickett's was in bivouac at Chambersburg. The other eight, except Law's brigade, were all in motion toward Gettysburg, Ewell having at an early hour ordered Rodes and Early to diverge to that point from the roads they were pursuing, toward Cashtown. Unfortunately, six of the divisions, and the trains and the reserve artillery of all three corps, were concentrated upon the turnpike from Fayetteville to Gettysburg. Anderson's division, followed by the 3d corps trains, had started soon after daylight from Fayetteville. Here they had halted, but Lee, passing, had ordered them on to Gettysburg, following Heth and Pender, who had marched from Cashtown at 5 A.M., and become engaged at Gettysburg about 10.

Soon after Anderson had passed Greenwood, Hood and McLaws were starting to follow, when they encountered Johnson's division of the 2d corps cutting in from the left, with the trains and reserve artillery of that corps. Lee, who was riding with Longstreet at the head of his infantry, directed that he should halt until these had all passed. This column occupied about 14 miles of road, and it delayed Longstreet's infantry until 4 P.M. In the morning, Longstreet's orders had been only to go as far as Cashtown, but later orders were sent for all troops to come to Gettysburg.

It was now the fourth day since Meade had relieved Hooker. Harper's Ferry had been evacuated. Of its 11,000 troops, 7000 under French were brought to Frederick, and 4000 escorted to Washington the artillery and stores of the post.

Meade knew that Ewell's corps was between York and Carlisle, and, on the 29th, put his whole army in motion in that direction, encamping that night on a line extending from Emmitsburg to Westminster. On the 30th, his advanced corps moved forward within a few miles of Gettysburg on his left, to Littletown in the centre, and toward Manchester on his right.

He now found that Lee was withdrawing and concentrating near Cashtown. He wrongly ascribed this to his own advance from Frederick, and published orders on the 30th, saying: —

"The General believes he has relieved Harrisburg and Philadelphia, and now desires to look to his own army, and assume position for offensive or defensive, as occasion requires, or rest to the troops. It is not his desire to wear the troops out by excessive fatigue and marches, and thus unfit them for the work they will be called upon to perform."

In fact, Lee did not know that Meade had moved at all, and his own movement eastward was really inspired by apprehension for his own communications, aroused by Hooker's action before he had been superseded.

Although Meade had selected his proposed line of battle behind Pipe Creek, and now announced his intention to rest his troops, he still, on the 1st, ordered a further advance of each of his seven corps, as follows: The 5th corps was ordered to Hanover; the 6th corps to Manchester; the 12th corps to Two Taverns; the 3d corps to Emmitsburg, and the 1st and 11th corps to Gettysburg.

These advances were not intended to bring on a battle, but to cover the position selected, allowing space in front to delay the enemy's approach and give time for preparation. The instructions to Reynolds, who was in command on the left, were not to bring on a general engagement.

But, though both Meade and Lee had cautioned their lieutenants to this effect, it was precipitated by Hill's initiative and Reynolds's willing concurrence. In the first collision of the day, Reynolds's leading division, by good handling, got decidedly the best of the affair, giving the Federals quite a taste of victory. Lee had been very uneasy as the roar of the distant battle increased, but when, later, the arrival of Ewell had turned the scale, and he, reaching the field, saw the Federals routed and prisoners taken by the thousand, it became simply impossible for him to hold

back his hand.   And not only impossible, but then unwise, for
a great opportunity was undoubtedly before him.   He ordered
it seized "if possible," and for the rest of the afternoon rested in
the belief that efforts were being made, being misled by Ewell's
not informing him that the pursuit had been abandoned before
his orders to push it were given.

The course of the battle had been as follows: About 10 A.M.,
the advance of Heth's division became engaged with Buford's
cavalry, between one and two miles in front of Gettysburg.
Buford, with his horse artillery, sought to detain the enemy until
Reynolds's corps (seven brigades), which he knew was approaching, could come to his assistance.   By 11 o'clock, however, he was forced to withdraw to the left, where he took
position, and during the rest of the day protected the left flank
of the Federals.   As Buford withdrew, Wadsworth's two brigades
became engaged with Davis and Archer.

Davis, on the left, overlapped Cutler on the Federal right and,
of course, soon drove back his right wing along with Hall's
battery, all of which were withdrawn without severe loss.   But,
on the Confederate right, Archer's brigade was overlapped by
Meredith's, which struck it on the flank and captured Archer
and several hundred prisoners.   This blow to Archer relieved
Cutler's brigade, which, changing front to its left, was able to
cut off and capture two regiments of Davis's brigade which had
advanced in pursuit of Cutler's right, and taken position in the
cut of an unfinished railroad north of the Chambersburg Pike.

Almost at the moment of his victory, however, Reynolds was
killed.   He was an excellent soldier and was well known to have
been the choice of the army to replace Hooker.

Meanwhile, Cutler was now reënforced by Rowley's division
of the same corps, which extended its line farther to the right.
Robinson's division also approached and was held in reserve
near by.   Later, as the engagement grew more severe, it was
also put into the battle.

Meanwhile, Hill had formed Pender's division in line of battle
in rear of Heth, but it was held in reserve for some time, as
Heth about noon received a reënforcement by the arrival of
Rodes's division, on his left flank, coming in from Middletown.

About the same time, also, the head of the 11th corps, under Howard, arrived at Gettysburg, and Howard succeeded Reynolds in command of the field.   He halted Steinwehr's division, two brigades, on Cemetery Hill, as a reserve, and advanced Schurz and Barlow to the front.   With these he formed line to cover the approaches from the north as far east as Rock Creek.   This disposition was bad.   The force was small for so long a line, and its right flank was in the air near the Heidlersburg road, by which Early was now drawing near.

For a while, however, the Federal forces were superior in numbers at the actual points of contact, where only Rodes's and Heth's divisions were yet engaged.   And, whether from discipline or from the inspiration of home, the fighting done by the Federal brigades was of the best type.   At this period some Confederate brigades were seriously crippled.   Heth's division, which had already suffered severely in Archer's and Davis's brigades, now lost heavily in Pettigrew's by a musketry combat at very close quarters.   It won the affair, but the brigade was scarcely a half brigade for the rest of the battle.

Iverson's brigade was exposed to a severe flank fire and lost three regiments.   In his report, Iverson says : —

"When I saw a white handkerchief raised, and my line of battle still lying down in position, I characterized the surrender as disgraceful.   But when I found afterward that 500 of my men were left lying dead and wounded on a line as straight as a dress parade, I exonerated the survivors and claim for the brigade that they nobly fought and died without a man running to the rear."

It is needless to detail the fighting when Early's division advanced upon the right of the 11th corps; and when Pender reënforced Heth against the 1st corps.   The enemy was forced back, and an advance of the Confederate line swept forward into the city.   About 5000 prisoners were captured, and fugitives could be seen in disorganized masses passing over the hills in the rear.

It was now about three o'clock.[1]

[1] The time and the condition of affairs are given in Hancock's report, as follows: "At 3 P.M. I arrived at Gettysburg and assumed the command. At this time the 1st and the 11th corps were retiring through the town, closely

Sunset was about 7.30, twilight was long, and the moon was full. There was daylight enough, and force enough at hand, to follow the pursuit and at least to carry Cemetery Hill, from which one of the two reserve brigades, Coster's, had been withdrawn.

Soon after two o'clock, Lee had arrived on Seminary Ridge, and seen the defeat of the enemy and their retreat over Cemetery Hill. His first impulse was to have the pursuit pushed and he sent his Adjt.-Col. W. H. Taylor, to instruct Ewell accordingly. Unfortunately, he took no steps to see that the order was obeyed. Taylor gives the following account: —

"Gen. Lee witnessed the flight of the Federals through Gettysburg and up the hills beyond. He then directed me to go to Gen. Ewell, and to say to him that from the position which he occupied, he could see the enemy retreating over those hills without organization and in great confusion, that it was only necessary to press 'those people' in order to secure possession of the heights, and that, if possible, he wished him to do this.

"In obedience to these instructions I proceeded immediately to Gen. Ewell, and delivered the order of Gen. Lee, and after receiving from him some message for the commanding general in regard to the prisoners captured, returned to the latter and reported that his order had been delivered. Gen. Ewell did not express any objection or indicate the existence of any impediment to the execution of the orders conveyed to him, but left the impression upon my mind that they would be executed. . . . "[1]

After reading this circumstantial statement, it is hard to understand Ewell's conduct. Not only did he fail to renew the pursuit which he had previously stopped, but, by apparent

pursued by the enemy. The cavalry of Buford was occupying a firm position on the plain to the left of Gettysburg, covering the rear of the retreating corps. The 3d corps had not yet arrived from Emmitsburg. Orders were at once given to establish a line of battle on Cemetery Hill with skirmishers occupying that part of the town immediately in our front. The position just on the southern edge, overlooking the town and commanding the Emmitsburg and Taneytown roads and the Baltimore Turnpike, was already partially occupied on my arrival by direction of Gen. Howard. Some difficulty was experienced in forming the troops of the 11th corps, but by vigorous efforts a sufficiently formidable line was established to deter the enemy from any serious assault on the position."

It will presently appear that the enemy was not deterred by the Federal line, but was halted by Ewell without orders, and was deliberately kept halted even after orders to attack "if possible" had arrived, and remained halted all the rest of the afternoon.

[1] *Four Years with Lee*, p. 95.

acquiescence and sending messages about prisoners captured, he seems to have intentionally misled Lee into the belief that his orders were being obeyed, while the rare opportunity slipped rapidly away. There could not be a more striking illustration, either of the danger of giving any important orders in *any conditional form*, or of failing to follow up all such orders with *some* supervision. When the firing gradually died out instead of being renewed, Lee took no action.

Meanwhile, Johnson's division, closely followed by Anderson's, had reached the field, and was ordered by Ewell to pass the town and occupy Culp's Hill, a half-mile to the east. Ewell's report says : —

"Before Johnson could get up, the enemy was reported moving to out-flank our extreme left, and I could see what seemed to be his skirmishers in that direction."

The skirmishers turned out to be our own men. Before this was discovered, it was sunset, and the hill about that time was occupied by Wadsworth's Federal division. Ewell, however, was not informed of this, and was again about to despatch Johnson on his errand when orders arrived from Lee to draw his corps to the right. He rode to see Lee and persuaded him to let the expedition be made. It was a most unfortunate decision, as will presently appear, for it fatally extended Lee's left flank. About midnight, Johnson's division was moved around the base of Culp's Hill and a reconnoitring party ascended, but found the enemy in possession. No one ordered the division to be carried back to the right, where it could have been of much service in subsequent operations, and where Lee had intended it to be. It was far too weak to attack the strong position of the enemy on Culp's Hill, and its communication with the rest of the army was long, roundabout, and exposed to the enemy's view. But *the division was allowed to remain until the end of the battle, and, as long as it remained absent, the task before the remainder of the army was beyond its strength.*

During the afternoon, Longstreet had joined Lee on Seminary Ridge overlooking the town, and had noted the position being taken by the enemy. He had said to Lee : " We could not call the enemy to a position better suited to our plans. We have only to file around his left and secure good ground between him and his capital."

To his surprise, Lee had answered, " If he is there to-morrow, I shall attack him."

Longstreet replied, " If he is there to-morrow, it will be because he wants you to attack him."

Later in the afternoon Lee rode forward to arrange a renewal of the attack upon Cemetery Hill from the town at daylight next morning. He held a long conference with Ewell, Early, and Rodes, who urged, instead, that Longstreet should attack the enemy's left flank. No one of those present had more than a very vague idea of the character and features of the enemy's line, and it is therefore not surprising that this advice, though very plausible in view of the success of former flank movements, was here the worst possible.

The enemy's line, though taken hurriedly upon the natural ridges overlooking the open country, which nearly surrounded it, was unique both in character and strength. In plan it nearly resembled a fish-hook, with its convexity toward us, forcing upon our line a similar shape with the concavity toward them. Their lines were the interior and shorter, being scarcely three miles in length, giving ability to reënforce at any point by short cuts across the interior area. Our exterior lines were about five miles in length, and to move from point to point required long, roundabout marches, often exposed to the enemy's view. Their force would allow 25,000 infantry and 100 guns for each mile of line. Ours would allow but 13,000 infantry and 50 guns per mile. Their flanks were at once unassailable and unturnable. Their left, which was the top of the fish-hook shank, rested on Big and Little Round Top mountains; and their right, which was the "point" of the "fish-hook," was on Culp's Hill over Rock Creek. Both flanks presented precipitous and rocky fronts, screened from artillery fire by forest growth, and the convexity of the line was such that the two flanks approached and each was able to reënforce the other. The shank of the fish-hook ran north, nearly straight, for about two miles from Little Round Top to Cemetery Hill, where the bend began. The bend was not uniform and regular, but presented a sharp salient at the north, and on the east a deep reëntrant around which the line swept to reach Culp's Hill, and pass around it nearly in an S.

This salient upon Cemetery Hill offered *the only hopeful point of attack upon the enemy's entire line,* as will more fully appear in the accounts of the different efforts made at various places during the battle. It would be too much to say that an attack here on the morning of July 2 *would have succeeded.* But it is not at all too much to say that no other attack was possible at that time which would have had near as good chance of success, yet it was deliberately discarded, and Lee's conference closed with the understanding among all those present that Longstreet should attack in the morning upon the enemy's left. It was this which gave rise to the mistaken charges made after Lee's death that Longstreet had disobeyed orders in not attacking early on the 2d.

No orders whatever were given Longstreet that night. Before sunset, he had ridden back from his interview with Lee to meet his troops, who, about 4 P.M., marched from near Greenwood with orders to come to Gettysburg, 17 miles. About midnight they bivouacked four miles from the field. Marching again at dawn on the 2d, they arrived near the field between 6 and 8 A.M. His reserve artillery (the Washington artillery and Alexander's battalion), which was ordered to follow the infantry from Greenwood at midnight, was much detained upon the road by passing trains, and did not reach the field until 9 A.M.

Law's brigade of Hood's division, recalled from New Guilford C. H., did not rejoin its division until noon on the 2d, having marched at 3 A.M., and covered by that time about 20 miles. Pickett's division was also upon the road, having marched from Chambersburg at 2 A.M. It made 22 miles and encamped within three miles of Gettysburg at 4 P.M., reporting its presence to Lee.

The most important occurrence of the evening had been Meade's wise decision to abandon his plan of offering battle behind Pipe Creek, and to concentrate upon the position at Gettysburg, which Hancock had recommended. He was most anxious to fight upon the defensive, and he knew that Lee, having a taste of victory, was not one to recoil from further offensive efforts. So, although reports during the afternoon had been discouraging, the march of all the corps had been hastened to find the defensive battle-field; and their arrivals upon it had been about as follows: —

Geary's division of the 12th corps had arrived about 6 P.M. and was placed on the left of the Federal line by Hancock. Williams's division of the same corps bivouacked near Rock Creek Bridge that night.

The advance of the 3d corps came upon the field about sunset. During the night, or early in the morning, the entire corps arrived.

The 2d corps, having come from Taneytown, also reached the field soon after nightfall, and was all at hand in the morning.

The 5th corps, marching from Hanover at 7 P.M., arrived on the field, 14 miles, at 8 A.M. on the 2d.

The 6th corps, from the Union right at Manchester, arrived about 2 P.M., after a march of about 32 miles in 17 hours.

At 8 A.M. of the 2d, therefore, practically the whole of both armies was upon the field except Pickett's division and Law's brigade of the Confederates, and the 6th corps of the Federals.

CHAPTER XVII

GETTYSBURG: SECOND DAY

The Situation. Lee decides to Attack. The Attack to be on our Right. Longstreet's Flank March. Sickles's Advance. Meade foresees Sickles's Defeat. Progressive Type of Battle. Hood proposes Flank Movement. Formation and Opening. Hood's Front Line. Fight on Little Round Top. Hood's Second Line. McLaws badly Needed. Kershaw and Semmes. Artillery Fighting. Barksdale and Wofford. Anderson's Division. Wilcox's Brigade. Wilcox asks Help. Why No Help was Given. Lang's Brigade. Wright's Brigade. Wright carries the Stone Wall. Wright's Retreat. Reënforcements for Sickles. Ayres's Division. Confederate Situation. The Artillery Engaged. Ten More Brigades in Sight. Crawford's Advance. Ewell's Coöperation. The Afternoon Cannonade. Johnson's Assault. Early's Attack. Federal Account. Rodes's Failure to Advance. Rodes's New Position. Rodes's Summary, Second Day.

LONGSTREET, riding ahead of his approaching troops, met Lee upon Seminary Ridge about dawn on July 2. Daylight disclosed the enemy in his position overlooking the town, and it was apparent that he was intrenched and was offering us the privilege of taking the offensive. Lee was far from disposed to decline the offer. Col. Long, of his staff, reports that he advised Lee during the night, —

"At present only two or three corps of the enemy are up, and it seems best to attack before they are greatly strengthened."

But, as a matter of fact, 43 of the 51 Federal brigades of infantry were upon the ground at 8 A.M. and occupying the strong position already described. Four of Lee's 37 infantry brigades were absent; four more (Johnson's division), were out of position east of Culp's Hill, and the lack of cavalry required the use of part of his remaining infantry upon each flank to protect from surprise. When, at nine o'clock, the arrival of Longstreet's reserve artillery was reported, it must be admitted that there was little to be hoped for from any immediate attack then possible.

Lee however had decided to make one. He had said to Hood soon after the latter's arrival: "The enemy is here. If we don't whip him he will whip us." He had sent staff-officers to each flank and was awaiting their reports. Longstreet's only suggestion had been a turning movement, and taking a position threatening the enemy's rear. Lee seems to have doubted that this would force the enemy to attack. He feared being manœuvred out of position, and perhaps forced back across the Potomac without any opportunity of fighting. It was a reasonable fear, now that the Federal army had drawn near, and could much restrict his foraging for supplies. This was a risk inseparable from campaigns of invasion, and it evidently seemed a much greater one now, than when the campaign was being decided upon. Not fully appreciating the strength of the enemy's position, and misled by the hope that a large fraction of the Federal army was out of reach, Lee had determined to strike, and only hesitated as to the best point to attack. About nine o'clock, he rode to the left and conferred again with Ewell and Early, who again discouraged attack in their own front, and urged that it be by Longstreet on the right. About 10 he returned, and presently received the report from Long and Pendleton who had reconnoitred on the right.

About 11 A.M., his orders were issued. Anderson's division of Hill's corps was directed to extend Hill's line upon Seminary Ridge to the right, while Longstreet with Hood's and McLaws's divisions should make a flank march to the right and pass beyond the enemy's flank, which seemed to extend along the Emmitsburg road. Forming then at right angles to this road, the attack was to sweep down the enemy's line from their left, being taken up successively by the brigades of Anderson's division as they were reached. Ewell's corps, holding the extreme left, was to attack the enemy's right on hearing Longstreet's guns. Longstreet was directed, in his march, to avoid exposing it to the view of a Federal signal station on Little Round Top Mountain.

Meanwhile, on the arrival of Longstreet's reserve artillery in the vicinity of the field, I had been placed in charge of all the artillery of his corps, and directed to reconnoitre the enemy's left and to move some of the battalions to that part of the field.

This had been done by noon, when three battalions, — my own, Cabell's and Henry's—were located in the valley of Willoughby Run awaiting the arrival of the infantry. Riding back presently to learn the cause of their non-arrival, the head of the infantry column was found halted, where its road became exposed to the Federal view, while messages were sent to Longstreet, and the guide sought a new route. The exposed point had been easily avoided by our artillery, by turning out through a meadow, but after some delay there came orders to the infantry to counter-march and take a road via "Black Horse Tavern." This in-cident delayed the opening of the battle nearly two hours. It is notable, both as illustrating the contingencies attending move-ments over unfamiliar ground, and also the annoyance which may be caused an enemy by the use of balloons to overlook his territory. It hardly seems probable, however, that in this instance the delay influenced the result of the battle. The same may be said, too, of a preliminary delay in Longstreet's begin-ning his march to the left after Lee's order at 11 A.M. Long-street's official report says, —

"Fearing that my force was too weak to venture to make an attack, I delayed until Gen. Law's brigade joined its division."

The history of the battle seems to justify this delay (Longstreet calls it 30 minutes), as without Law's brigade our first attack must have been dangerously weak.

Meanwhile, an important change had occurred in the enemy's position. Until noon, their main line had run nearly due south from Cemetery Hill to Little Round Top, while a strong skir-mish-line only was held upon the Emmitsburg Pike, for about a mile from Cemetery Hill, to a cross-road at the Peach Orchard. About noon, the movements of the Confederates toward the Fed-eral left were noted, and Sickles, whose corps held that flank, sent forward from the Peach Orchard a small reconnoitring force. It encountered Wilcox's brigade, and was driven back with severe loss, but not before it had discovered the approach of Long-street's column. This being reported to Sickles, he unwisely ordered an advance of his whole corps to hold the ground about the Peach Orchard. He probably had in mind the advantage given the Confederates at Chancellorsville in allowing them the occupation of the Hazel Grove plateau. But it was, nevertheless, bad tactics. It exchanged strong ground for weak, and gave the Confederates an opportunity not otherwise possible. They would be quite sure to crush the isolated 3d corps. If their attack was properly organized and conducted, it might become possible to rush and carry the Federal main line in the pursuit of the fugitives.

Meade, however, having seen Hooker's movement, at once visited the ground, and, after conferring with Sickles, ordered his return to his original position. Before the movement could be begun, however, Longstreet's guns had opened, and it was unwise to attempt a withdrawal under fire. Meade saw the danger, and with military foresight prepared to meet it with every available man. There was not during the war a finer example of efficient command than that displayed by Meade on this occasion. He immediately began to bring to the scene reënforcements, both of infantry and artillery, from every corps and from every part of his line. As will be seen in the account of the fighting, he had engaged, or in hand on the field, fully 40,000 men by the time that Longstreet's assault was repulsed.

On the other hand, it must be said that the management of the battle on the Confederate side during this afternoon was conspicuously bad. The fighting was superb. But there appears to have been little supervision, and there was entire failure everywhere to conform to the original plan of the battle, as it had been indicated by Lee. Offensive battles are always more difficult of control than defensive, and there were two special difficulties on this occasion. First, was the great extent of the Confederate lines, about five miles — and their awkward shape, making intercommunication slow and difficult. Second, was the type or character of the attack ordered; which may be called the echelon, or progressive type, as distinguished from the simultaneous. The latter should be the type for any battle in the afternoon. Battles begun by one command and to be taken up successively by others, are always much prolonged. We had used this method on four occasions,—at Seven Pines, Gaines Mill, Frazier's Farm or

Glendale, and Malvern Hill, — and always with poor success. Our effort this afternoon will be seen to be a monumental failure. General instructions were given to each corps commander, but much was left to their discretion in carrying them out. More than one fell short in performance.

It was about 3 P.M. when Hood's division, in the advance, crossed the Emmitsburg road about 1000 yards south of the Peach Orchard. The enemy's artillery had opened upon us as soon as our approach was discovered, and we presently replied. Hood's division crossed the road and formed in two lines, Robertson and Law in front, with Law on the right; Anderson and Benning 200 yards in rear, with Benning on the right.

While this formation was taking place, scouts reported that Big Round Top Mountain was unoccupied and that an open farm road around it led to unguarded supply trains and hospitals. Hood and Law earnestly urged upon Longstreet that instead of making the direct attack, he should pass around the 3d corps, seize Big Round Top, and fall upon the trains. Longstreet replied that Lee had ordered the direct attack, and it must be made without delay.

It is not likely that the movement proposed by Hood would have accomplished much. Already our line was dangerously extended, and to have pushed one or two divisions past the 3d corps and around the mountain would have invited their destruction. Had our army been more united and able to follow up the move in force, it might have proved a successful one. Not by assaulting the enemy in his chosen position where his whole army stood, as it were, in a circle back to back, but by threatening his communications while covering our own. It might easily have resulted in our being able to secure a position which would force the enemy to take the aggressive. Had Johnson's division been brought back from its isolated position, and had Lee been present to hear the report brought by Hood's scouts, the whole subsequent history of the battle might have been changed.

Meanwhile, McLaws's division had been formed, west of and parallel to the Emmitsburg road, with Kershaw on the right supported by Semmes, and Barksdale on the left supported by Wofford. In front of Kershaw, Cabell's battalion of artillery was engaged with 18 guns; and in front of Barksdale were 18 of my own battalion. Ten guns, also of Henry's battalion, were engaged across the Emmitsburg road. The remaining 8 guns of my own battalion were held close by, to follow the infantry promptly in any advance, and the Washington artillery with 10 guns, by Longstreet's order, were held in reserve in rear.

Thus, about 3.45 P.M., 36 guns were in action against the Peach Orchard, and the enemy's adjacent lines and 10 guns against the enemy's left. The ranges were generally between 500 and 700 yards. After this cannonade had continued for perhaps 30 minutes, Hood received the order to advance.

Following the initiative prescribed by Lee, Longstreet, Hood, and McLaws all made progressive attacks. Hood at first advanced only his front line. McLaws was about to advance upon Hood's left very soon after, when Longstreet halted him. He was held back for about an hour, during which Hood's second line was sent in, and both lines suffered severely. Then McLaws advanced both lines of his right wing, Kershaw and Semmes; and, after a further interval of at least 20 minutes (long enough to cause severe loss to Kershaw's exposed left), Barksdale and Wofford followed. There were thus four partial attacks of two brigades each, requiring at least an hour and a half to be gotten into action; where one advance by the eight brigades would have won a quicker victory with far less loss.

When Hood's first line commenced the advance, Law, on the right, overlapped the Federal left. On the left Robertson was greatly overlapped by the Federal line. Law, obliquing still farther to his right, hoping to turn the Federal flank, a gap opened between Robertson and himself. The 4th and 5th Tex., on Robertson's right, trying to dress upon Law, were drawn entirely away from Robertson, and attached themselves to Law's brigade. This brigade became divided, in the rough ground it traversed, into two bodies. The two regiments on the right, the 15th and 47th Ala. with a few of the 4th and 5th Tex., swung still farther to the right, meeting no enemy, and, crossing Plum Run, they ascended the side of Big Round Top. Then, wheeling to the left, they crossed the depression between Big and Little Round Top and finally found the enemy in position on the top of the latter. Quite a sharp action ensued, which may be described here, out of its order in time, as it was entirely isolated.

Three companies of the 47th Ala. were detached and left on picket at the foot of the mountain. The remaining force was but about 500 men under the command of Col. Oates of the 15th Ala. The mountain had been partially occupied in the morning by the 3d corps, but was vacated when they moved to the front. About 4 P.M., Gen. Warren, seeing the deployment of our lines, had brought up Vincent's brigade of Barnes's division of the 5th corps. Swinton has written that a foot-race occurred for the commanding position, and that a desperate hand-to-hand fight with bayonets and clubbed muskets took place for a half-hour between "Hood's Texans" and Vincent's men.

None of the official reports on either side are consistent with this story. There was some sharp fighting and Vincent was killed, but Oates's small and isolated force was soon outflanked and compelled to retreat to the foot of the mountain. It was not pursued, and, at the foot, it built breastworks of rocks which it held all night and part of the next day. The total casualties reported for the battle by the 15th Ala. were: 17 killed, 54 wounded, and 90 missing, total 161. Maj. Campbell of the 47th reported "about one-third of his whole number of men were killed and wounded." The losses of Vincent's brigade for the battle were 352.

Hood's front line had, meanwhile, been reduced, by Oates's divergence to Big Round Top, to less than seven regiments in two isolated bodies. Law, on the right, had the 4th, 44th, and 48th Ala., and parts of the 4th and 5th Tex. Robertson, on the left, had only the 1st Tex. and 3d Ark. His left flank, too, was in the air, and was much overlapped by the Federal line. It could make no progress, but maintained a position under very severe fire of artillery and infantry, which, within the first half-hour, severely wounded Hood. Law succeeded to the command of the division.

His part of the brigade had made more progress, but already reënforcements sent by Meade were reaching the enemy and Law's advance was checked. He ordered in the second line, using Benning's brigade to reënforce his own, and Anderson to extend Robertson on his left. Law thus describes the advance of his reënforced line in an article in *Battles and Leaders*: —

"The ground was rough and difficult, broken by rocks and boulders, which rendered an orderly advance impossible. Sometimes the Federals would hold one side of the huge boulders on the slopes until the Confederates occupied the other. In some cases my men, with reckless daring, mounted to the top of the large rocks in order to get a better view and to deliver their fire with greater effect. . . .

"In less than an hour from the time we advanced to the attack, the hill by Devil's Den, opposite our centre, was taken with three pieces of the artillery that had occupied it. The remaining piece was run down the opposite slope by the gunners, and escaped capture."

During all this time, however, McLaws's division was standing idle, though Barksdale was begging to be allowed to charge, and McLaws was awaiting Longstreet's order. Even when prolonged by Anderson's Georgians, the Texans' line was still so overlapped by the Federals that it could not advance. Law, placing his two brigades on the defensive on the captured hill, now came to the left and made a strong appeal to Kershaw for help. This was referred to McLaws and probably to Longstreet, for now the order was given for the advance of Kershaw supported by Semmes. But, by some unaccountable lack of appreciation of the situation, Barksdale, Wofford, and all the brigades of Anderson's division are still left idle spectators of the combat, while Hood's division is wearing itself out against superior numbers in strong position. Lee seems not to have been near. This was unfortunate, for his whole field of battle had been waiting all day and was still waiting for Longstreet's battle to be developed; and here it was being begun, in the progressive manner which had been ordered, but with unwise deliberation. Longstreet, of course, is responsible, but every commanding officer takes great risks when he leaves such important movements without supervision. It was especially unfortunate in this case, because advancing Kershaw without advancing Barksdale would expose Kershaw to enfilade by the troops whom Barksdale would easily drive off. Few battle-fields can furnish examples of worse tactics.

Kershaw was put in motion by a signal. Cabell's guns, in his front, were ordered to pause in their firing, and then to fire three guns in rapid succession. At the signal the men leaped the wall in their front and were promptly aligned by their company officers. Kershaw writes, in *Battles and Leaders:* —

"The brigade moved off at the word with great steadiness and precision, followed by Semmes with equal promptness. Longstreet accompanied me in this advance on foot as far as the Emmitsburg road. All the field and staff officers were dismounted on account of the many obstacles in the way.

"When we were about the Emmitsburg road I heard Barksdale's drums beat the assembly and knew then that I should have no immediate support on my left about to be squarely presented to the heavy force of infantry and artillery at and in rear of the Peach Orchard."

As such a position would be speedily ruinous, Kershaw directed the three regiments on his left to wheel to the left and to charge the batteries in rear of the Orchard, while with the right wing he continued the movement to the aid of Hood's division. Thus this brigade was also separated into two parts. Kershaw moved with the right wing, and presently, finding his right regiment, the 7th S.C., beginning to overlap one on its left, he halted his line and ordered the 7th to move by the right flank. By some misunderstanding the order was shouted to the left, and was overheard by the left wing, who supposed it was an order for themselves to move by the right flank.

Kershaw's narrative continues: —

"After passing the building at Rose's, the charge of the left wing was no longer visible from my position, but the movement was reported to have been magnificently conducted until the cannoneers had left their guns and the caissons were moving off, when the order was given by some unauthorized person to 'move by the right flank,' and was immediately obeyed by the men. The Federals returned to their guns and opened on these doomed regiments a raking fire of grape and canister at short distance which proved most disastrous, and for a time destroyed their usefulness. Hundreds of the bravest and best men of Carolina fell victims of this fatal blunder."

Meanwhile our own artillery fire had been kept up without intermission for what seemed more than two hours, though I know of no one who timed it. The range was very close, and the ground we occupied gave little shelter except at few points for the limbers and caissons. Our losses both of men and horses were the severest the batteries ever suffered in so short a time during the war. Moody's battery had four 24-Pr. howitzers and two 12-Pr. guns on a rocky slope, and the labor of running the guns up after each recoil presently became so exhausting that, with Barksdale's permission, eight volunteers from a Miss. regiment were gotten to help the cannoneers. Two of this detachment were killed and three severely wounded. Fickling's battery of four 12-Pr. howitzers had two of them dismounted, and forty cannoneers killed or wounded.

At last the 10 guns of Jordan and Woolfolk which had been held in reserve were sent for, but just as they arrived Barksdale's brigade made its advance, and was soon followed by Wofford's, which Longstreet also accompanied in person. While the infantry was passing, my four batteries, which had been engaged in the cannonade, were gotten ready, and the whole six followed the charge of the infantry, and came into action in and about the Peach Orchard.[1]

Barksdale's brigade advanced directly upon the Peach Orchard. Wofford's inclined somewhat to the right and went to the assistance of Kershaw and Semmes, striking the flank of the Federals opposing them. The enemy was driven back with severe loss and followed across the Wheat Field and on to the slopes of Little Round Top. Barksdale had made an equal advance upon our left. But by this time the reënforcements which Meade was hurrying from every part of the Federal line began to swarm around our mixed-up brigades. Barksdale was killed, Semmes mortally wounded, and our lines were slowly forced back. Another partial attack had spent its energy upon a task impossible for so small a force.

Under the orders, Anderson's division was to take up the attack next after McLaws, so that the delay in starting Barksdale delayed also Wilcox's brigade on his left. Wilcox's report states that "the cannonading continued until 6.20 P.M. when McLaws's

---

[1] As we advanced we saw a number of prisoners being sent to the rear, passing a rail fence across our path. Maj. Dearing, commanding the battalion attached to Pickett's division was with us, and he shouted an order to the prisoners to "move those rails." Never was an order executed with more alacrity. Every prisoner seemed to seize a rail, and the fence disappeared as if by magic.

troops advanced to the attack." There was again much delay, due to the fact that Wilcox had not been previously located at the position from which his charge should be made. This required a flank movement to the left of 400 or 500 yards over ground obstructed by stone and plank fences. The 8th Ala. was even hurried into the charge in column of fours. Proper preparation of the line during the long delay might have saved much time and permitted Wilcox's brigade to cover Barksdale's exposed left.

Wilcox made a brilliant charge, and was soon followed *in echelon* on the left by Perry's brigade under Lang, and Lang was similarly followed by Wright's brigade. These two charges followed with the least delay of any during the affair. But each brigade was formed in a single line and without support, each advanced with its left flank in the air, intervals of time and space intervened even between these attacks, and each was finally and separately repulsed with severe loss. The two remaining brigades of the division, Posey's and Mahone's, were withheld from the assault. I will describe briefly the action of each brigade.

Wilcox first encountered skirmishers in front of the Emmitsburg pike with a line of infantry and batteries along the pike. These fell back before his musketry fire, leaving in the road two guns whose horses had been killed. Beyond the pike the ground sloped gradually some 600 yards to a ravine fringed with small trees in rocky ground. Beyond the ground rose rapidly some 200 yards to a ridge, crowned with numerous batteries and held by the enemy in force. Wilcox's report gives his strength as about 1200, and thus describes his advance : —

"When my command crossed the pike and began to descend the slope they were exposed to an artillery fire from numerous pieces both from the front and from either flank. Before reaching the ravine at the foot of the slope two lines of infantry were met and broken, and driven pell-mell across the ravine. A second battery of six pieces here fell into our hands. From the batteries on the ridge above referred to, grape and canister were poured into our ranks. This stronghold of the enemy, together with his batteries, were almost won when still another line of infantry descended the slope in our front, at a double quick, to the support of their fleeing comrades, and for the defence of the batteries.

"Seeing this contest so unequal I despatched my adjutant-general to the division commander to ask that support be sent to my men, but no support came. Three several times did this last of the enemy's lines attempt to drive my men back and were as often repulsed. This struggle at the foot of the hill on which were the enemy's batteries, though so unequal, was continued for some 30 minutes. With a second supporting line the heights could have been carried. Without support on either my right or my left my men were withdrawn to prevent their entire destruction or capture. The enemy did not pursue, but my men retired under a heavy artillery fire, and returned to their original position in the line, and bivouacked for the night, pickets being left on the pike. . . . In the engagement of this day I regret to report a loss of 577 men killed, wounded, and missing."

Soon after this battle a newspaper correspondent, " P. W. A.," described Wilcox's charge and his sending in vain to Anderson for reënforcements, and stated that Anderson had Posey's and Mahone's brigades idle, and that the battle was lost for lack of their support. Anderson replied, admitting the facts, but stating that he was under orders from Hill to hold two brigades in reserve, and that when Wilcox's call for help was received he was unable to find Hill and refer the matter to him.

Next on Wilcox's left was our lone Fla. brigade, Perry's, now under Lang. It had but three small regiments, and mustered about 700 bayonets. Lang reports as follows: —

"At 6 P.M., Wilcox having begun to advance I moved forward, being met at the crest of the first hill with a murderous fire of grape, canister, and musketry. Moving forward at the double quick, the enemy fell back beyond their artillery, where they were attempting to rally, when we reached the crest of the second hill. Seeing this the men opened a galling fire upon them, thickly strewing the ground with their killed and wounded. This threw them into confusion when we charged them with a yell, and they broke and fled into the woods and breastworks beyond, leaving four or five pieces of cannon in my front, carrying off, however, most of the horses and limbers.

"Following them rapidly I arrived behind a small eminence at the foot of the heights, where, the brigade having become much scattered, I halted for the purpose of re-forming, and allowing the men to catch their breath before the final assault upon the heights.

"While re-forming, an aid from the right informed me that a heavy force had advanced upon Wilcox's brigade and was forcing it back. At the same time a heavy fire of musketry was poured upon my brigade from the woods 50 yards in front, which was gallantly met and handsomely replied

to by my men.   A few moments later another messenger from the right
informed me that Wilcox had fallen back and the enemy was then some
distance in rear of my right flank.   Going to the right I discovered that the
enemy had passed me more than 100 yards and were attempting to surround me.   I immediately ordered my men back to the road some 300
yards to the rear.   Arriving there I found there was no cover under which
to rally and continued to fall back, rallying and re-forming upon the line
from which we started. . . .   In this charge the brigade lost about 300
killed, wounded, and missing."

Next came Wright's Ga. brigade about 1800 strong.   Wright,
in his report, describes the ground over which his advance was
to be made, the distance to be traversed under fire increasing
toward the left.

"I was compelled to pass for more than a mile across an open plain,
intersected by numerous post and rail fences, and swept by the enemy's
artillery, posted along the Emmitsburg road, and upon the crest of the
heights a little south of Cemetery Hill."

He noted that Posey's brigade upon his left was not advancing,
and fearing that with his left flank in the air he would be involved
in serious difficulty, he sent an aid to Anderson with a message
on the subject.   Anderson ordered Posey to send forward two
regiments as skirmishers.   Later Posey speaks of supporting
his skirmishers with his remaining regiments; but as his casualties in the whole campaign were but 12 killed and 71 wounded,
evidently his brigade was not seriously engaged, and the whole
attack was allowed to terminate with that of Wright.   Neither
Hill nor Anderson give any explanation.   Hill had still unengaged and close at hand Mahone's brigade and Heth's division in
reserve.

Wright's report is of special interest as his advance was over
the same ground covered the next day by the charge of Pickett's
division.   His report thus describes it after he had carried the
enemy's advanced line, capturing several guns, crossed the
pike, and approached the stone wall marking Pickett's farthest
advance in his charge on the 3d.

"We were now within less than 100 yards of the crest of the heights,
which were lined with artillery, supported by a strong body of infantry
under protection of a stone fence.   My men, by a well-directed fire, soon
drove the cannoneers from their guns, and leaping over the fence charged

up to the top of the crest, and drove the enemy's infantry into a rocky gorge on the eastern slope of the heights, and some 80 or 100 yards in rear of the enemy's batteries.

"We were now complete masters of the field, having gained the key, as it were, of the enemy's whole line.   Unfortunately, just as we had carried the enemy's last and strongest position, it was discovered that the brigade upon our right had not only not advanced across the turnpike, but had actually given way and was rapidly falling back to the rear, while on our left we were entirely unprotected, the brigade ordered to our support having failed to advance. . . .

"We were now in a critical condition.   The enemy's converging lines were rapidly closing upon our rear; a few moments more and we would be completely surrounded; still no support could be seen coming to our assistance, and with painful hearts we abandoned our captured guns, faced about, and prepared to cut our way through the closing lines in our rear. This was effected in tolerable order, but with immense loss.   The enemy rushed to his abandoned guns as soon as we began to retire and poured a severe fire of grape and canister into our thinned ranks as we retired slowly down the slope into the valley below. I continued to fall back until I reached a slight depression a few hundred yards in advance of our skirmish line of the morning, when I halted, re-formed my brigade, and awaited the further pursuit of the enemy. . . .

"In this charge my loss was very severe, amounting to 688 in killed, wounded, and missing, including many valuable officers.   I have not the slightest doubt that I should have been able to have maintained my position on the heights and secured the captured artillery if there had been a protecting force on my left, or if the brigade on my right had not been forced to retire.   We captured over 20 pieces of artillery, all of which we were compelled to abandon."

Is there anywhere a sadder story of the war than this?   In all the reports of all the battles of the war there is no one more eloquent of fine conduct, but of poor handling of splendid troops. And presently we shall see in sharp contrast, in the Federal army, during this same afternoon, perhaps the best example which the war produced of active supervision and efficient handling of a large force on the defensive.

This action of Wright's ended Longstreet's battle of the afternoon.   Three of Anderson's five brigades had attacked in progressive order and in single lines.   They had been defeated and driven back, one at a time, in the order of their advance.   No better demonstration could be asked of the evils of progressive attacks.   The three brigades could just as easily have attacked simultaneously with McLaws, and several other brigades of Hill's corps could have supported and advanced with them. The temporary success of each brigade in a single and isolated line puts it beyond doubt that such an attack would have had better result.

It has been told that Meade, being on the left with Sickles at the time of Longstreet's attack, had at once begun to bring up reënforcements. It is interesting to note the number thus brought forward before the fighting ceased at dark.

The first help sent Sickles, when his six brigades were attacked by Longstreet's eight, was Barnes's division of the 5th corps, three brigades, — Tilton's, Sweitzer's, and Vincent's. Vincent fought Oates on Little Round Top and repulsed him, Vincent, however, being killed. Tilton and Sweitzer attacked Law and Anderson, but were themselves soon driven back.

The losses of this division were: Vincent's, 352; Tilton's, 125; Sweitzer's, 427; total, 904. As Barnes retreated, Caldwell's division of the 2d corps came up, with four brigades under Cross, Kelley, Zook, and Brook. The battle seesawed, but Caldwell was driven back with the loss of half his division. Cross and Zook were killed and Brook wounded. The brigade losses were: Cross, 330; Kelley, 198; Brook, 389; Zook, 358; total, 1275.

While Caldwell was in the stress of action, Sykes advanced Ayres's division of three brigades, sending Weed to the left to the aid of Vincent; and the two brigades of regulars, under Day and Burbank, to the left of Caldwell's division. Here their right was exposed by the retreat of Caldwell, and they were compelled to cut their way back to the main Federal line upon the crest of the ridge, closely pursued and severely punished by the Confederates. Weed, supporting Vincent at a critical juncture, had been himself killed. Between Weed and Vincent, however, Oates's force had been driven to the base of the mountain, where it remained unpursued. Day and Burbank, when driven back, formed upon Weed's left upon the crest. Weed's losses were 200; Day's, 382; Burbank's, 447; total, 1029.

Most of this fighting was taking place about midway between Little Round Top, which was the left flank of the Federal line, and the Peach Orchard on the Emmitsburg road. In the disputed arena was a wheat field nearly surrounded by woods on the west of Plum Run, here running south through marshy ground. The tide of battle rolled back and forth across this field several times, and when Ayres's regulars were driven back and pursued, Sykes ordered forward his last division, Crawford's, called the Pa. Reserves, two brigades under McCandless and Fisher. Crawford formed in two lines, the second massed on the first, and his report thus describes the scene as he approached it: —

"Our troops in front, after a determined resistance, unable to withstand the force of the enemy, fell back, and some finally gave way. The plain to my front was covered with fugitives from all divisions, who rushed through my lines and along the road to the rear. Fragments of regiments came in disorder, and without their arms, and for a moment all seemed lost. The enemy's skirmishers had reached the foot of the rocky ridge (Little Round Top) and his columns were following rapidly."

One is tempted to pause for a moment to contemplate the really hopeless situation of the Confederate battle. Already Sickles's six brigades had been reënforced by 10 brigades which had been defeated one, two, or three at a time, with losses to the reënforcements alone of 3108 men and five generals. The eight Confederate brigades had themselves suffered terribly and lost four generals. All had marched fully 20 miles within 24 hours, and the attack, much of it through woods and over rugged ground, had mingled commands and broken ranks. Infantry can never deliver their normal amount of fire except in regular ranks, shoulder to shoulder. When ranks are broken the men interfere with and mask each other. To say nothing of probable need of ammunition at this stage of the action, one must recognize that now, as the 11th and 12th brigades of the Federal reënforcements approach, the Confederate need of at least a fresh division is great. There are not only no reënforcements on the way, but none within two miles.

Both Hill and Ewell have orders to coöperate with Longstreet's battle, but they are limiting their coöperation to ineffective cannonading of the enemy's intrenchments in their front, while the enemy is stripping these of infantry and marching fresh divisions to concentrate upon Hood and McLaws, and the three brigades of Wilcox, Perry, and Wright, which had supported them. But when these had carried the lines in their front (Carr's, Brewster's, and Burling's brigades of the 3d corps), Hancock had brought up Harrow's and Hall's brigades of Gibbon's division; and Willard's of Hays's division. One at a time, the three Confederate brigades were driven back with losses, already stated, amounting to 1565 men. The six Federal brigades had lost as follows: Harrow's, 768; Hall's, 377; Willard's, 714, Willard being killed; Carr's, 790; Brewster's, 778; Burling's, 513; total, 3940.[1]

It would be tedious to attempt to follow the artillery reënforcements which came to the aid of Sickles's corps, but Hunt, Chief of Artillery, in his report, mentions 11 batteries with 60 guns being engaged from his general reserve. In addition to these the 2d, 3d, and 5th corps had 80 guns engaged. Against these 140 guns, Longstreet had but 62 guns on the field, and Anderson's division but seven. The artillery on both sides suffered severely in men and horses. A number of Federal batteries were captured, and held temporarily, but only two or three guns could be brought off the field. Hunt's report says : —

"The batteries were exposed to heavy front and enfilading fires and suffered terribly, but as rapidly as any were disabled they were retired and replaced by others."

Besides the reënforcements of 12 brigades already mentioned (including Crawford's Pa. reserves), Meade had followed them with Robinson's and Doubleday's divisions of the 1st corps, five brigades (taken from the lines in front of Hill's corps), and with Williams's division, three brigades of the 12th corps. Two more brigades, Candy's and Cobham's, of Geary's division of the 12th corps, were also withdrawn from the intrenchments upon Culp's Hill, and ordered to the left, but they missed their road and did not reach the scene of action in time. These withdrawals left of the 12th corps but a single brigade, Greene's, holding the intrenchments upon Culp's Hill in front of Johnson's division of Ewell's corps, who had been all day under

---

[1] The Federal losses stated are from the official returns which include the losses of all three days, but most of the brigades mentioned suffered the greater part of their losses during the afternoon of the 2d.

orders to attack at the sound of Longstreet's guns. What they did will be told presently.

All of these reënforcements did not become engaged. A part of Stannard's brigade recaptured six of the Federal guns, which the Confederates had overrun but could not remove. Part of Lockwood's brigade of the 12th corps, who were raw troops, were led into action by Meade in person, and also retook a captured battery. Most of these reënforcements came into view upon the crest, from the lower slopes of which Crawford's division now advanced in a counter-stroke to the Confederate charge which had routed and pursued Ayres's division. The mere sight of the long lines and solid blue masses which appeared to the Confederates as they cleared the woods and scanned the opposite slopes, was calculated to paralyze the advance. Ten fresh brigades were in position before them, besides the remnants of the 13 brigades which had been driven back. About 75 guns were in action supporting this huge force. To this day there survive stories showing how the Confederates were impressed by this tremendous display. One, still told by guides at Gettysburg, is that a cry was heard in the Confederate ranks, "Have we got all creation to whip?" And another of the time was that the Federal commander was heard to give his orders: "Attention, Universe! Nations into line! By Kingdom! — Right wheel."

Fortunately for the Confederates, the Federal counter-stroke was confined to a very moderate advance by Crawford's division. Our disorganized lines made a show of resistance, but it only led to the loss of perhaps 200 prisoners from Anderson's brigade, which unwisely prolonged its fire. The enemy, however, only advanced to the eastern edge of the Wheat Field, and the Confederates retreated no farther than the western edge. From those positions the firing was kept up until darkness brought a welcome end. For in our worn-out condition and isolated position we were in a very dangerous situation. Had Meade now ordered an advance he would have found Longstreet's left flank in the air, and the whole line of McLaws's and Hood's divisions much exhausted and but poorly supplied with ammunition. The ground on the left was open and the moon was full. There was certainly a great opportunity offered the

Federal commander, with his large force of fresh troops in hand near the field, and only needing the word to go.

It is now time to see how Lee's orders were being interpreted and carried out upon the left. The official reports are a painful record of insufficient comprehension of orders and inefficient attempts at execution, by officers each able to shift the blame of failure upon other shoulders than his own. Between the lines the apparent absence of supervision excites constant wonder. But everywhere that the troops fought their conduct was admirable.

Ewell, as before told, was ordered to attack with Johnson's division when he heard the sound of Longstreet's guns. Ewell says that later his instructions were modified into "making a diversion," but Lee's report does not recognize such modification. Ewell interpreted his orders as calling only for a cannonade. It must be admitted that any serious attack by Johnson would have been suicidal. The enemy's lines were of exceptional strength, which is noted in the Federal reports. Ruger, for instance, thus describes the position of his division.

"Breastworks were immediately constructed of logs, rocks, and earth along the whole line, and at the gap in the line caused by the swale, so as to give cross fire in front of gap. In rear of breastworks of 1st brigade, about 75 yards and nearly parallel therewith, was a stone wall, behind which the second line of the brigade was placed. In front of the line of the 3d brigade Rock Creek was from four to six feet deep, with muddy bottom, caused by a dam near the turnpike. The whole position was covered with rocks. . . ."

Added to these difficulties was the fact that there was but a single position where the Confederates could plant guns to fire upon this line, and that an inferior one, giving little shelter and exposed to an enfilade fire. It was so contracted that with difficulty 14 guns were crowded upon it, within about 1000 yards of the enemy. It might have been foreseen that this battery, exposed to the fire of double its number of guns, would soon be put out of action. That was what happened: its commander, an especially gallant "Boy Major," Latimer (under 21 years), being killed. Besides these guns Ewell's diversion embraced six rifles, in rear of Latimer at a range of 2000 yards;

and 12 more, on Seminary Ridge to the left of Hill's artillery at a range much over a mile. Hill's artillery comprised 55 guns on Seminary Ridge. So the whole assistance given to Longstreet's attack between 4 P.M. and darkness by the other two corps was confined to an artillery duel by 32 guns of Ewell and 55 of Hill, mostly at extreme ranges. But the value of this duel as assistance to Longstreet was absolutely nothing, for it did not prevent the enemy from withdrawing troops from every corps in his line to repel our assault.

This cannonading was maintained for about two hours, after which it gradually diminished until dark. Meanwhile, about six o'clock, Ewell had sent orders to each of his division commanders to attack the enemy's lines in his front. This involved for Johnson an attack upon Culp's Hill. The division had not been pushed close to the hill in preparation for an assault, although one had been contemplated all day. It now had a full mile to advance and Rock Creek had to be crossed. This could only be done at few places and involved much delay. Only three of Johnson's four brigades moved to the attack. His official report says : —

"I then advanced my infantry to the assault of the enemy's strong position — a rugged and rocky mountain, heavily timbered and difficult of ascent; a natural fortification rendered more formidable by deep intrenchments and thick abattis — Jones's brigade in advance, followed by Nichols's and Steuart's. Gen. Walker was directed to follow, but reporting to me that the enemy were advancing upon him, from their right, he was ordered to repulse them as soon as possible. . . . Gen. Walker did not arrive in time to participate in the assault that night.

"By the time my other brigades had crossed Rock Creek and reached the base of the mountain, it was dark. His skirmishers were driven in, and the attack made with great vigor and spirit. It was as successful as could have been expected under the circumstances. Steuart's brigade, on the left, carried a line of breastworks which ran perpendicular to the enemy's main line, captured a number of prisoners and a stand of colors, and the whole line advanced to within short range and kept up a heavy fire until late in the night."

As has been told, the whole of the 12th corps had been withdrawn from the lines except Greene's brigade. This brigade was being extended when its advance was met by Steuart, who got possession only of empty trenches. Johnson's other brigades found the trenches in front of their approach held by Greene's thin line, but in the darkness of the woods, the steep and rocky ground, and the abattis and obstructions in front, Johnson's line was halted at irregular distances, and the attack resolved itself into a random and ineffective musketry fire. Nothing more was possible. And even had they found more trenches vacant and occupied them, Meade could at will concentrate ample force to drive them out. The more one studies the situation, the more strange it seems that Lee abandoned his first purpose to withdraw Johnson from his false position.

Early's attack is next to be described. It, too, was isolated, inadequate, and unsupported. It necessarily failed. Both attacks were in progress at the same time, but Longstreet's, which they were intended to support, had already ceased. Like Johnson's division, Early was also short of one brigade, Smith's having been sent to guard the rear from the direction of York. Gordon also was not engaged, as Early soon realized that the attack was an isolated one and would be quickly repulsed.

Early's report gives the following details : —

". . . As soon as Johnson became warmly engaged, which was a little before dusk, I ordered Hays and Avery to advance and carry the works on the height in front. These troops advanced in gallant style to the attack, passing over the ridge in front of them under a heavy artillery fire, and then crossing a hollow between that and Cemetery Hill and moving up this hill in the face of at least two lines of infantry posted behind stone and plank fences; but these they drove back, and passing over all obstacles they reached the crest of the hill and entered the enemy's breastworks crowning it, getting possession of one or two batteries.

"But no attack was made on the immediate right, as was expected, and not meeting with support from that quarter, these brigades could not hold the position they had attained, because a very heavy force of the enemy was turned against them from that part of the line which the divisions on the right were to have attacked, and these brigades had, therefore, to fall back, which they did with comparatively slight loss, considering the nature of the ground over which they had to pass, and the immense odds opposed to them, and Hays's brigade brought off four stands of captured colors. Gen. Rodes did not advance for reasons given in his report."

The maps show that Hays's brigade on the right had only

about 500 yards to advance over ground exposed to the enemy's fire. Avery's brigade on the left had a somewhat greater distance. Hays reports his casualties in this affair as 181. Avery was killed. The casualties of his brigade for the three days were 345, of which at least two-thirds were suffered in this charge.

Howard's report gives the story from the Federal side: —

"The attack was so sudden and violent that the infantry in front of Ames was giving way. In fact, at one moment the enemy had gotten within the batteries. A request for assistance had already gone to headquarters, so that promptly a brigade of the 2d corps under Col. Carroll moved to Ames's right, deployed, and went into position just in time to check the enemy's advance. At Wiedrich's battery, Gen. Ames, by extraordinary exertions, arrested a panic, and the men with sponge staffs and bayonets forced the enemy back. At this time he received support from Gen. Schurz. Effective assistance was also rendered at this time by a portion of Gen. Steinwehr's command at points where the enemy was breaking through. This furious onset was met and withstood at every point, and lasted less than an hour."

It only remains to show why Rodes failed to coöperate with Early and Johnson as Ewell had ordered. The fault was with Ewell himself. We have already seen that he had allowed Johnson's division to remain all day so far from the position which he was to attack that, when ordered to advance, darkness fell upon him before he could reach it. Similarly Ewell had allowed both of his other divisions to locate themselves far out of reach of the places where they were likely to be needed. Of his own motion, however, Early had advanced half of his division at dawn to the Federal skirmish line, and these two brigades were ready to advance when ordered.

Rodes had remained about the northwestern edge of the town, near where the fighting of the first day had ended, and was still there when the orders came to attack. He was already preparing to advance, having seen both infantry and artillery withdrawn by the enemy from his front to resist Longstreet's pressure upon their left. But his location was so unfortunate that, in spite of this warning, both Johnson's and Early's attacks were begun and finished before Rodes had reached the enemy's skirmish line.

Finding then his opportunity gone he wisely desisted. But

as Lee and his staff during the morning had visited Ewell's lines, it is strange that such faulty locations escaped notice and correction. Rodes's report not only shows the badness of his original position, but tells of an excellent one for the attack, which so far had entirely escaped the recognition of any Confederate reconnoitring officer. His report says: —

"Having to draw my troops out of town by the flank, change the direction of the line of battle, and then to traverse a distance of 1200 to 1400 yards, while Gen. Early had to move only half that distance without change of front, the result was that before I drove the enemy's skirmishers in, Gen. Early had attacked and been compelled to withdraw. . . . But instead of falling back to the original line, I caused the front line to assume a strong position in the plain to the right of the town along the hollow of an old road-bed. This position was much nearer the enemy, was clear of the town, and was one from which I could readily attack without confusion."

Rodes's description of his new position is of special interest. Taken in connection with his statement of the distance to be traversed by Early's charge, it shows the existence of far more favorable ground for an attack upon Cemetery Hill than is to be found elsewhere upon the Federal line of battle from Culp's Hill to Little Round Top. It was open to our occupation from the afternoon of the first day, when Ewell stopped the pursuit, and it must ever remain a grave reflection upon the Confederate conduct of the battle that the weakest part of the Federal position was the only portion which was not attacked. It will be more fully described in the account of the action on the 3d.

Thus ended the second day, and one is tempted to say that thus ended the battle of Gettysburg. For of the third day it must be said, as was said of the charge of the Six Hundred at Balaklava, "Magnificent, but not War!"

The first day had been won by 17 Confederate brigades of infantry attacking 13 Federal. The victory was fruitless because Ewell stopped the pursuit in full tide.

On the second day, Longstreet, with 11 brigades, in seven piecemeal attacks, drives back six Federal brigades, which, being gradually reënforced by 18 fresh brigades, check the Confederate advance, and recover part of the lost ground, before night ends the conflict.   Coöperative attacks by Ewell and Hill, ordered by Lee, fail to be effective because both Ewell and Hill had failed to have their divisions in proper positions for the charge long before the moment arrived, although each had had ample time.

CHAPTER XVIII

GETTYSBURG: THIRD DAY

The Plan of the Day. Johnson Reënforced. Johnson's Battle. Lee joins Longstreet. A Discussion. The Decision. The Neglected Opportunity. Posting the Guns. Artillery of Other Corps. Infantry Formation. Hill's Cannonade. The Nine Howitzers. Note from Longstreet. Talk with Wright. Cannonade Opens. Pickett called for. Pickett and Longstreet. Pickett Appears. The Repulse. Lee on the Field. The Afternoon. Nelson's Enfilade. Advances from Peach Orchard.

IN his official report Lee writes: —

"The result of the (second) day's operations induced the belief that with proper concert of action, and with the increased support that the positions gained on the right would enable the artillery to render the columns, we should ultimately succeed, and it was accordingly determined to continue the attack. The general plan was unchanged. Longstreet, reënforced by Pickett's three brigades, was to attack the next morning, and Ewell was ordered to assault the enemy's right at the same time. The latter during the night reënforced Johnson with two brigades from Rodes's and one from Early's division."

This statement shows that the strongest features of the enemy's position were not yet apprehended. These were the ability of the enemy to concentrate their whole force upon any point attacked; and the impregnable character of the two Federal flanks. The two brigades sent from Rodes to reënforce Johnson were taken from the new position discovered by him early in the evening and already referred to, not only as the most favorable, but as practically the only position from which the Federal line could have been attacked with any hope of success. The brigade sent from Early was sent from a force which could have effectively coöperated with an attack by Rodes. The effect of sending the three brigades was to emasculate the centre of our line and to concentrate seven brigades where they were utterly useless. Before proceeding, however, we may best here give briefly the outcome of Johnson's battle.

He had been ordered by Ewell to attack at daylight, under the impression that Longstreet would attack at the same hour. In fact, however, Longstreet received no orders during the night, and the troops required for his attack could not be gotten into their positions before noon. Johnson, however, was himself attacked by the enemy at daylight at a point where he was still holding the trenches he had found abandoned the night before. He repulsed the Federal assault and attempted to follow the fugitives, but was repulsed. Heavy firing was kept up from behind rocks, trees, and parapets until near noon. Rumors of movements of the enemy upon his left, which afterward proved to be false, then led him to withdraw to the base of the hill where he remained unmolested until night, when he was at last recalled to the west of the town. His losses were about 1873, showing that the fighting was severe.

Lee's headquarters were beyond the Chambersburg pike, about four miles by road from the scene of battle on our right. During the night the Washington artillery was brought up and disposed with the rest of Longstreet's guns about the Peach Orchard, with the intention of resuming the battle in the morning. During the night Longstreet had sent scouts in search of a way by which he might turn the enemy's left and believed he had found one with some promise of success. Soon after sunrise, while Longstreet awaited the arrival of Pickett's division with Dearing's battalion of artillery, intending then to extend his right, Lee joined him and proposed an assault upon the enemy's left centre by Longstreet's three divisions.

Longstreet demurred, and, as had occurred on the day before, some time was spent in discussion and examination. Although the opposing lines were in full view and easy range of each other, neither seemed anxious to begin an action. The enemy's guns were generally behind breastworks on the high hills and ridges with ample covering in rear for their horses and caissons. Ours, posted before daylight, stood exposed on gently rolling ground about the Peach Orchard and vicinity. The enemy fired occasional shots, but not enough to force us to reply, and we were but too glad to be able to reserve our ammunition for more important work.

Longstreet pointed out to Lee the enemy's position on the Round Tops and the danger of withdrawing Hood and McLaws from our right flank, which would be necessary if they were to take part in the attack upon the enemy's left centre. Lee recognized the necessity and substituted six brigades from Hill's corps. His report says : —

"Longstreet was delayed by a force occupying the high rocky hills on the enemy's extreme left, from which his troops could be attacked in reverse as they advanced. His operations had been embarrassed the day previous from the same cause and he now deemed it necessary to defend his flank and rear by the divisions of Hood and McLaws. He was, therefore, reënforced by Heth's division and two of Pender's brigades to the command of which Trimble was assigned."[1]

Longstreet further objected that the enemy's artillery on the "high rocky hills" would enfilade the lines assaulting the left centre. Col. Long, of Lee's staff, in his *Memoirs of Lee*, writes : —

"This objection was answered by Col. Long who said that the guns on Round Top could be suppressed by our batteries. This point being settled, the attack was ordered and Longstreet was directed to carry it out."

Longstreet, in his *Manassas to Appomattox*, describing the same conversation, gives further detail as follows : —

"I asked the strength of the column. He (Lee) stated, 15,000. Opinion was then expressed that the 15,000 men who could make successful assault over that field had never been arrayed for battle ; but he was impatient of listening and tired of talking, and nothing was left but to proceed."

It seems remarkable that the assumption of Col. Long so easily passed unchallenged that Confederate guns in open and inferior positions could "suppress" Federal artillery fortified upon commanding ridges. Our artillery equipment was usually admitted to be inferior to the enemy's in numbers, calibres and quality of ammunition. Moreover, here, the point selected and the method of the attack would certainly have been chosen for us by the enemy had they had the choice. Comparatively the

---

[1] Pender had been mortally wounded in the artillery duel of Hill's corps during the afternoon of the 2d.

weakest portion of their line was Cemetery Hill, and the point of greatest interest in connection with this battle is the story of our entire failure to recognize this fact. The narrative may therefore pause while this neglected opportunity is pointed out.

There was one single advantage conferred by our exterior lines, and but one, in exchange for many disadvantages. They gave us the opportunity to select positions for our guns which could enfilade the opposing lines of the enemy. Enfilading fire is so effective that no troops can submit to it long. Illustrations of this fact were not wanting in the events of this day. What has been called the shank of the Federal fish-hook, extending south from the bend at Cemetery Hill toward Little Round Top, was subject to enfilade fire from the town and its flanks and suburbs. That liability should have caused special examination by our staff and artillery officers, to discover other conditions which might favor an assault. There were and are others still easily recognizable on the ground. The salient angle is acute and weak, and within about 500 yards of its west face is the sheltered position occupied by Rodes the night of July 2d, which has already been mentioned.

From nowhere else was there so short and unobstructed an approach to the Federal line, and one so free from flank fire. On the northeast, at but little greater distance, was the position whence Early's two brigades the evening before had successfully carried the east face of the same salient. Within the edge of the town between these two positions was abundant opportunity to accumulate troops and to establish guns at close ranges.

As long as Gettysburg stands and the contour of its hills remains unchanged, students of the battle-field must decide that Lee's most promising attack from first to last was upon Cemetery Hill, by concentrated artillery fire from the north and assaults from the nearest sheltered ground between the west and northeast.

That this was not realized at the time is doubtless partly due to the scarcity of trained staff and reconnoitring officers, and partly to the fact that Ewell had discontinued and withdrawn the pursuit on the afternoon of the 1st, when it was about to undertake this position. Hence the enemy's pickets were not driven closely into their lines, and the vicinity was not carefully examined. Not a single gun was established within a thousand yards, nor was a position selected which enfiladed the lines in question.

Quite by accident, during the cannonade preceding Pickett's charge, Nelson's battalion of Ewell's corps fired a few rounds from a position which did enfilade with great effect part of the 11th corps upon Cemetery Hill, but the fire ceased on being sharply replied to. Briefly the one weak spot of the enemy's line and the one advantage possessed by ours were never apprehended.

In addition to the six brigades of Hill's corps assigned to Longstreet for his column of assault, one more, Wilcox of Anderson's division, was later added, making ten brigades in all, of which only three were Longstreet's and seven were Hill's. I was directed by Longstreet to post all of his artillery for a preliminary cannonade, and then to take a position whence I could best observe the effect of our fire, and determine the proper moment to give the signal to Pickett to advance. The signal for the opening of the cannonade would be given by Longstreet himself after the infantry brigades were all in position.

A clump of trees in the enemy's line was pointed out to me as the proposed point of our attack, which I was incorrectly told was the cemetery of the town, and about 9 A.M. I began to revise our line and post it for the cannonade. The enemy very strangely interfered with only an occasional cannon-shot, to none of which did we now reply, for it was easily in their power to drive us to cover or to exhaust our ammunition before our infantry column could be formed. I can only account for their allowing our visible preparations to be completed by supposing that they appreciated in what a trap we would find ourselves. Of Longstreet's 83 guns, 8 were left on our extreme right to cover our flank, and the remaining 75 were posted in an irregular line about 1300 yards long, beginning in the Peach Orchard and ending near the northeast corner of the Spangler wood.

While so engaged, Gen. Pendleton offered me the use of nine 12-Pr. howitzers of Hill's corps, saying that that corps could not use guns of such short range. I gladly accepted and went to receive the guns under command of Maj. Richardson. I placed them under cover close in rear of the forming column with orders to remain until sent for, intending to take them with the column when it advanced.

A few hundred yards to left and rear of my line began the artillery of the 3d corps under Col. Walker. It comprised 60 guns, extending on Seminary Ridge as far as the Hagerstown road, and two Whitworth rifles located nearly a mile farther north on the same ridge. In this interval were located 20 rifle guns of the 2d corps under Col. Carter. Four more rifles of the same corps under Capt. Graham were located about one and a half miles northeast of Cemetery Hill. These 24 guns of the 2d corps were ordered to fire only solid shot as their fuses were unreliable.

There remained unemployed of the 2d corps 25 rifles and 16 Napoleons, and of the 3d corps, fifteen 12-Pr. howitzers. It is notable that of the 84 guns of the 2d and 3d corps to be engaged, 80 were in the same line *parallel to the position of the enemy and 56 guns stood idle.* It was a phenomenal oversight not to place these guns, and many beside, in and near the town to enfilade the "shank of the fish-hook" and cross fire with the guns from the west.

The Federal guns in position on their lines at the commencement of the cannonade were 166, and during it 10 batteries were brought up from their reserves, raising the number engaged to 220 against 172 used upon our side during the same time.

The formation of our infantry lines consumed a long time, and the formation used was not one suited for such a heavy task. Six brigades, say 10,000 men, were in the first line. Three brigades only were in the second line — very much shorter on the left. It followed about 200 yards in rear of the first. The remaining brigade, Wilcox's, posted in rear of the right of the column, was not put in motion with the column, and being ordered forward 20 minutes or more later, was much too late to be of any assistance whatever. Both flanks of the assaulting column were in the air and the left without any support in the rear. It was sure to crumble away rapidly under fire. The arrangement may be represented thus: —

Brockenbrough, Davis, McGowan, Archer, Garnett, Kemper,
Lane, Scales, Armistead,
Wilcox.

No formation, however, could have been successful and the light one doubtless suffered fewer casualties than one more compact and deeper would have had.

A little before noon there sprung up upon our left a violent cannonade which was prolonged for fully a half-hour, and has often been supposed to be a part of that ordered to precede Pickett's charge. It began between skirmishers in front of Hill's corps over the occupation of a house. Hill's artillery first took part in it, it was said, by his order. It was most unwise, as it consumed uselessly a large amount of his ammunition, the lack of which was much felt in the subsequent fighting. Not a single gun of our corps fired a shot, nor did the enemy in our front.

When the firing died out, entire quiet settled upon the field, extending even to the skirmishers in front, and also to the enemy's rear; whence behind their lines opposing us we had heard all the morning the noise of Johnson's combats.

My 75 guns had all been carefully located and made ready for an hour, while the infantry brigades were still not yet in their proper positions, and I was waiting for the signal to come from Longstreet, when it occurred to me to send for the nine howitzers under Richardson, that they might lead in the advance for a few hundred yards before coming into action. Only after the cannonade had opened did I learn that the guns had been removed and could not be found. It afterward appeared that Pendleton had withdrawn four of the guns, and that Richardson with the other five, finding himself in the line of the Federal fire during Hill's cannonade, had moved off to find cover. I made no complaint, believing that had these guns gone forward with the infantry they must have been left upon the field and perhaps have attracted a counter-stroke after the repulse of Pickett's charge.

Meanwhile, some half-hour or more before the cannonade began, I was startled by the receipt of a note from Longstreet as follows : —

"Colonel: If the artillery fire does not have the effect to drive off the enemy or greatly demoralize him, so as to make our effort pretty certain, I would prefer that you should not advise Pickett to make the charge. I shall rely a great deal upon your judgment to determine the matter and shall expect you to let Gen. Pickett know when the moment offers."

Until that moment, though I fully recognized the strength of the enemy's position, I had not doubted that we would carry it, in my confidence that Lee was ordering it. But here was a proposition that *I* should decide the question. Overwhelming reasons against the assault at once seemed to stare me in the face. Gen. Wright of Anderson's division was standing with me. I showed him the letter and expressed my views. He advised me to write them to Longstreet, which I did as follows:—

"General: I will only be able to judge of the effect of our fire on the enemy by his return fire, as his infantry is little exposed to view and the smoke will obscure the field. If, as I infer from your note, there is any alternative to this attack, it should be carefully considered before opening our fire, for it will take all the artillery ammunition we have left to test this one, and if result is unfavorable we will have none left for another effort. And even if this is entirely successful, it can only be so at a very bloody cost."

To this note, Longstreet soon replied as follows: —

"Colonel: The intention is to advance the infantry if the artillery has the desired effect of driving the enemy's off, or having other effect such as to warrant us in making the attack. When that moment arrives advise Gen. Pickett and of course advance such artillery as you can use in aiding the attack."

Evidently the cannonade was to be allowed to begin. Then the responsibility would be upon me to decide whether or not Pickett should charge. If not, we must return to Va. to replenish ammunition, and the campaign would be a failure. I knew that our guns could not drive off the enemy, but I had a vague hope that with Ewell's and Hill's coöperation something might happen, though I knew little either of their positions, their opportunities, or their orders.

I asked Wright: "What do you think of it? Is it as hard to get there as it looks?" He answered: "The trouble is not in going there. I went there with my brigade yesterday. There is a place where you can get breath and re-form. The trouble is to stay there after you get there, for the whole Yankee army is there in a bunch."

I failed to fully appreciate all that this might mean. The question seemed merely one of support, which was peculiarly the province of Gen. Lee. I had seen several of Hill's brigades forming to support Pickett, and had heard a rumor that Lee had spoken of a united attack by the whole army. I determined to see Pickett and get an idea of his feelings. I did so, and finding him both cheerful and sanguine, I felt that if the artillery fire opened, Pickett must make the charge; but that Longstreet should know my views, so I wrote him as follows: —

"General: When our fire is at its best, I will advise Gen. Pickett to advance."

It must have been with bitter disappointment that Longstreet saw the failure of his hope to avert a useless slaughter, for he was fully convinced of its hopelessness. Yet even he could have scarcely realized, until the event showed, how entirely unprepared were Hill and Ewell to render aid to his assault and to take prompt advantage of even temporary success. None of their guns had been posted with a view to coöperative fire, nor to follow the charge, and much of their ammunition had been prematurely wasted. And although Pickett's assault, when made, actually carried the enemy's guns, nowhere was there the slightest preparation to come to his assistance. The burden of the whole task fell upon the 10 brigades employed. The other 27 brigades and 56 fresh guns were but widely scattered spectators.

It was just 1 P.M. by my watch when the signal guns were fired and the cannonade opened. The enemy replied rather slowly at first, though soon with increasing rapidity. Having determined that Pickett should charge, I felt impatient to launch him as soon as I could see that our fire was accomplishing anything. I guessed that a half-hour would elapse between my sending him the order and his column reaching close quarters. I dared not presume on using more ammunition than one hour's firing would consume, for we were far from supplies and had already fought for two days. So I determined to send Pickett the order at the very first favorable sign and not later than after 30 minutes' firing.

At the end of 20 minutes no favorable development had occurred. More guns had been added to the Federal line than at the beginning, and its whole length, about two miles, was blazing like a volcano. It seemed madness to order a column in the middle of a hot July day to undertake an advance of three-fourths of a mile over open ground against the centre of that line.

But something had to be done. I wrote the following note and despatched it to Pickett at 1.25 : —

"General: If you are to advance at all, you must come at once or we will not be able to support you as we ought. But the enemy's fire has not slackened materially and there are still 18 guns firing from the cemetery."

I had hardly sent this note when there was a decided falling off in the enemy's fire, and as I watched I saw other guns limbered up and withdrawn. We frequently withdrew from fighting Federal guns in order to save our ammunition for their infantry. The enemy had never heretofore practised such economy. After waiting a few minutes and seeing that no fresh guns replaced those withdrawn, I felt sure that the enemy was feeling the punishment, and at 1.40 I sent a note to Pickett as follows : —

"For God's sake come quick. The 18 guns have gone. Come quick or my ammunition will not let me support you properly."

This was followed by two verbal messages to the same effect by an officer and sergeant from the nearest guns. The 18 guns had occupied the point at which our charge was to be directed. I had been incorrectly told it was the cemetery. Soon only a few scattered Federal guns were in action, and still Pickett's line had not come forward, though scarcely 300 yards behind my guns.

I afterward learned what had followed the sending of my first note. It reached Pickett in Longstreet's presence. He read it and handed it to Longstreet. Longstreet read and stood silent. Pickett said, "General, shall I advance?" Longstreet knew that it must be done, but was unwilling to speak the words. He turned in his saddle and looked away. Pickett saluted and said, "I am going to move forward, sir," and galloped off.

Longstreet, leaving his staff, rode out alone and joined me on the left flank of the guns. It was doubtless 1.50 or later, but I did not look at my watch again. I had grown very impatient to see Pickett, fearing ammunition would run short, when Longstreet joined me. I explained the situation. He spoke sharply, — "Go and stop Pickett where he is and replenish your ammunition." I answered: "We can't do that, sir. The train has but little. It would take an hour to distribute it, and meanwhile the enemy would improve the time."

Longstreet seemed to stand irresolute (we were both dismounted) and then spoke slowly and with great emotion: "I do not want to make this charge. I do not see how it can succeed. I would not make it now but that Gen. Lee has ordered it and is expecting it."

I felt that he was inviting a word of acquiescence on my part and that if given he would again order, "Stop Pickett where he is." But I was too conscious of my own youth and inexperience to express any opinion not directly asked. So I remained silent while Longstreet fought his battle out alone and obeyed his orders.

The suspense was brief and was ended by the emergence from the wood behind us of Garnett riding in front of his brigade. I had served on the Plains with him and Armistead in 1858, and I now met him for the first time since Longstreet's Suffolk campaign. He saluted and I mounted and rode with him while his brigade swept through our guns. Then I rode down the line of guns, asking what each gun had left. Many had canister only. These and all having but few shell were ordered to stand fast. Those with a moderate amount of suitable ammunition were ordered to limber up and advance.

During the cannonade the reserve ordnance train had been moved from the position first occupied, and caissons sent to it had not returned. Only about one gun in four could be ordered forward from the centre, but from the right Maj. Haskell took five from Garden's and Flanner's batteries, and Maj. Eshleman, of the Washington artillery, sent four somewhat to Haskell's left.

Returning to the centre I joined the few guns advancing from the batteries there, and moved forward to a swell of ground just west of the Emmitsburg road, whence we opened upon troops advancing to attack the right flank of Pickett's division. Eshleman and Haskell to the left front of the Peach Orchard soon also opened fire. The charging brigades were now close in front of the Federal lines and the musketry was heavy.

As we watched, we saw them close in upon the enemy in smoke and dust, and we ceased firing and waited the result. It was soon manifest in a gradual diminution of the fire and in a stream of fugitives coming to the rear pursued by some fire but not as much, it seemed to me, as might have been expected.

After perhaps 20 minutes, during which the firing had about ceased, to my surprise there came forward from the rear Wilcox's fine Ala. brigade, which had been with us at Chancellorsville, and, just 60 days before, had won the affair at Salem Church. It had been sent to reënforce Pickett, but was not *in the column.* Now, when all was over, the single brigade was moving forward alone, and there was no one there with authority to halt it. They were about 1200 strong and on their left were about 250, the remnant of Perry's Fla. brigade. It was at once both absurd and tragic.

They advanced several hundred yards beyond our guns, under a sharp fire. Then they halted and opened fire from some undergrowth and brushwood along a small ravine. Federal infantry soon moved out to attack their left, when Perry fell back past our guns; Wilcox moved by his right flank and making a circuit regained our lines at the Peach Orchard. His loss in this charge was 204 killed and wounded. Perry's loss was about proportional, with some prisoners in addition.

While Wilcox's brigade was making its charge, Gen. Lee rode up and joined me. He was entirely alone, which could scarcely have happened except by design on his part. We were not firing, but holding position to prevent pursuit by the enemy. I have no doubt that Lee was apprehensive of this, and had come to the front to help rally the fugitives if that happened. He remained with us perhaps an hour and spoke to nearly every man who passed, using expressions such as: " Don't be discouraged." "It was my fault this time." " Form your ranks again when you get under cover." "All good men must hold together now."

I had with me as an aid, Lt. Colston, ordnance officer of my battalion. At one time loud cheering was heard in the Federal lines and Lee asked Colston to ride to the front and find out the cause. Colston's horse was unused to the spur and, balking, Colston had a stick handed him and used it. Lee said: "Oh, don't do that. I once had a foolish horse and I found gentle measures so much the best." Colston presently reported that the Federals were cheering an officer riding along their line. Lee remarked that he had thought it possible that Johnson's division in the Federal rear might have gained some success. Evidently he was not yet informed that Johnson, about noon, had withdrawn to a defensive position. Kemper was brought by on a litter. Lee rode up and said, "General, I hope you are not badly hurt." Kemper replied, "Yes, General, I'm afraid they have got me this time." Lee pressed his hand, saying: "I trust not! I trust not." Col. Fremantle, of her Majesty's Coldstream Guards, had also joined the party. We sat on horseback on the slope behind the guns where we could see over the crest, but the group of horses was not visible to the enemy.

When all the fugitives had passed and there was still no sign of counter-stroke, Lee rode off. I continued to hold my line of guns with few changes until after dark. There were some advances by Federal skirmish lines, which we kept in check with our guns, sometimes having to use canister sharply. But the Federal guns did not interfere, for which we were duly grateful.

During the afternoon I quietly withdrew guns, one at a time, sending them to be refitted, and by 10 o'clock our whole line had been retired about to the position from which the attack began on the 2d.

Now that we have reached the turning-point of our campaign, we may revert to some incidents of note in the progress of the battle.

In speaking of our neglect to enfilade the Federal lines, it was stated that quite by accident a few rounds were fired during the cannonade which happened to enfilade a part of Cemetery Hill. In the *Philadelphia Weekly Times* of May 31, 1877, Col. Osborne, Chief of Artillery, 11th corps, describes the cannonade, in which he commanded "a little over 60 guns," and mentions this incident as follows: —

"The fire from our west front had progressed 15 to 20 minutes when several guns opened on us from the ridge beyond East Cemetery Hill. The line of fire from these last batteries, and the line of fire from the batteries on our west front, were such as to leave the town between the two lines of fire. These last guns opened directly on the right flank of my line of batteries. The gunners got our range at almost the first shot.

"Passing low over Wainwright's guns they caught us square in flank and with the elevation perfect. It was admirable shooting. They raked the whole line of batteries, killed and wounded the men and horses, and blew up the caissons rapidly. I saw one shell go through six horses standing broadside.

"To meet this new fire I drew from the batteries facing west the 20-lb. Parrott battery of Capt. Taft, and wheeling it half round to the right brought it to bear on them. I also drew from the reserve one battery and placed it in position on Taft's right. . . .

"Fortunately for us these batteries, placed in the new line, at once secured the exact range of their immediate adversaries. In a few minutes the enemy's fire almost ceased, and when it again opened, and while the fire was progressing, it was irregular and wild. They did not again get our range as they had it before we replied."

Gen. Howard in the *Atlantic Monthly*, July, 1876, writing of this occasion, says, "One regiment of Steinwehr's was fearfully cut to pieces with a shell." It doubtless received an enfilading shot from the firing here described.

The official reports enable us to identify this firing as done at a range of 2500 yards by three rifled guns of Milledge's battery of Nelson's battalion of Ewell's reserve artillery. Nelson had three batteries carrying 13 guns, and the 48 rounds fired by Milledge were the only shots fired by the battalion during the campaign. It was not, however, Nelson's fault, but his superior's. His report says: —

"About 12 M. I was ordered to draw the attention of the enemy's batteries from our infantry, in connection with Capt. Graham, commanding Rockbridge artillery, and fired about 20 or 25 rounds from a point to the left and somewhat in advance of Capt. Graham's position. On Friday night I encamped about one-half mile in rear of my position on that day."

The Ordnance report of the 2d corps identifies the guns and gives the rounds fired as 48.

Mention has been made of the five guns advanced by Maj. Haskell from the Peach Orchard, and the four from the Washington artillery a little to their left. These guns moved so far outside of Pickett's charge that they were able to fire obliquely upon the Federals opposing it. Haskell on the extreme right was even able to enfilade portions of the Federal reënforcements The fighting here was almost hand to hand. The following account is given by Col. Rice of the 19th Mass.:[1] —

"The men in gray were doing all that was possible to keep off the mixed bodies of men, who were moving upon them swiftly and without hesitation, keeping up so close and continuous a fire that at last its effects became terrible. . . . The grove was fairly jammed with Pickett's men, in all positions, lying and kneeling. Back from the edge were many standing and firing over those in front. By the side of several who were firing, lying down or kneeling, were others with their hands up in token of surrender. In particular I noticed two men, not a musket length away, one aiming so that I could look into his musket barrel; the other, lying on his back, coolly ramming home a cartridge. A little farther on was one on his knees waving something white in both hands. Every foot of ground was occupied by men engaged in mortal combat who were in every possible position which can be taken while under arms or lying wounded or dead.

"A Confederate battery near the Peach Orchard commenced firing. A cannon-shot tore a horrible passage through the dense crowd of men in blue, who were gathering outside the trees. Instantly another shot followed and fairly cut a road through the mass. . . ."

The official report of Col. Abbott of the 20th Mass. thus describes the same scene: —

"The enemy poured in a severe musketry fire, and at the clump of trees they burst also several shells, so that our loss was very heavy, more than half the enlisted men of the regiment being killed or disabled, while there remained but three out of 13 officers. . . ."

The enfilading shots described by Col. Rice doubtless came from the batteries under command of Maj. Haskell. No official report was made, but I quote from a personal letter of Maj. Haskell some years later: —

[1] B. & L. 387.

"Just before Pickett's division charged, you rode up and after inquiring what ammunition I had, you ordered me to move forward with five guns, part of which were taken from each battery. We advanced about 300 to 500 yards when I saw a large mass of infantry to our left front beginning to deploy, apparently to strike the right flank of Pickett's division. I at once opened fire on this infantry, which almost immediately scattered or withdrew, unmasking a large number of guns. Gen. Hunt told me after the war there were over 20. In a very few minutes these guns had disabled several of mine, killing and wounding quite a number of men and horses. Our ammunition being exhausted, I ordered such guns as could be moved to withdraw, ordering Garden and Flanner to return as quickly as possible with litters for the wounded, and teams and limbers for the disabled guns. This they did, getting everything out."

The four guns under Capt. Miller and Lt. Battle fared nearly as badly. Maj. Eshleman, seeing that they were being rapidly cut up, withdrew them; but two of the guns, three of the teams, a Lt., and several men were put *hors de combat* in the movement.

But one official report from Pickett's division has been published, that of Garnett's brigade, by Maj. C. S. Peyton, 19th Va., who was the only field officer of the division not killed or wounded. Pickett wrote a report which reflected unjustly upon the brigades of Hill's corps, among which the break first occurred. Lee returned the report, asking Pickett to modify it, which Pickett delayed and finally neglected to do. I quote from Peyton's report, dated July 9, as follows: —

"Notwithstanding the long and severe marches made by the troops of this brigade, they reached the field about 9 A.M. in high spirits and in good condition. At about 12 M. we were ordered to take position behind the crest of the hill, on which the artillery under Col. Alexander was planted, where we lay during the most terrific cannonading, which opened at 1.30 P.M., and was kept up without intermission for one hour.

"During the shelling we lost about 20 killed and wounded. Among the killed was Lt.-Col. Ellis of the 19th Va. . . . At 2.30 P.M. the artillery fire having to some extent abated, the order to advance was given, first by Gen. Pickett in person, and repeated by Gen. Garnett with promptness, apparent cheerfulness, and alacrity. The brigade moved forward at quick time. The ground was open, but little broken, and from 800 to 1000 yards from the crest whence we started to the enemy's line. The brigade moved in good order, keeping up its line almost perfectly, notwithstanding it had to climb three high post and rail fences, behind the last of which the enemy's skirmishers were first met, and immediately driven in. Moving on, we soon met the advanced line of the enemy, lying concealed in the grass on the slope about 100 yards in front of his second line, which consisted of a stone wall, about breast high, running nearly parallel to and about 30 paces from the crest of the hill which was lined with their artillery.

"The first line referred to above, after offering some resistance, was completely routed, and driven in confusion back to the stone wall. Here we captured some prisoners, which were ordered to the rear without a guard. Having routed the enemy here, Gen. Garnett ordered the brigade forward, which it promptly obeyed, loading and firing as it advanced.

"Up to this time we had suffered but little from the enemy's batteries, which apparently had been much crippled previous to our advance, with the exception of one posted on the mountain, about one mile to our right, which enfiladed nearly our entire line with fearful effect, sometimes as many as 10 men being killed and wounded by the bursting of a single shell. From the point it had first routed the enemy, the brigade moved rapidly toward the stone wall, under a galling fire both from artillery and infantry, the artillery using grape and canister. We were now within about 75 paces of the wall, unsupported on the right and left. Gen. Kemper being some 50 or 60 yards behind and to the right, and Gen. Armistead coming up in our rear.

"Gen. Kemper's line was discovered to be lapping on ours, when, deeming it advisable to have the line extended on the right, to prevent being flanked, a staff officer rode back to the general to request him to incline to the right. Gen. Kemper not being present (perhaps wounded at the time), Capt. Fry of his staff immediately began his exertions to carry out the request, but in consequence of the eagerness of the men in pressing forward, it was impossible to have the order carried out.

"Our line, much shattered, still kept up the advance until within about 20 paces of the wall, when, for a moment, it recoiled under the terrific fire that poured into our ranks both from their batteries and from their sheltered infantry. At this moment Gen. Kemper came up on the right and Gen. Armistead in rear, when the three lines, joining in concert, rushed forward with unyielding determination and an apparent spirit of laudable rivalry to plant the Southern banner on the walls of the enemy. His strongest and last lines were instantly gained; the Confederate battle flag waved over his defences, and the fighting over the wall became hand to hand and of the most desperate character; but, more than half having already fallen, our line was found too weak to rout the enemy.

"We hoped for a support on the left (which had started simultaneously with ourselves), but hoped in vain. Yet a small remnant remained in desperate struggle, receiving a fire in front, on the right and on the left, many even climbing over the wall, and fighting the enemy in his own trenches until entirely surrounded; and those who were not killed or wounded were captured, with the exception of about 300 who came off slowly, but greatly scattered, the identity of every regiment being entirely lost, and every regimental commander killed or wounded.

"The brigade went into action with 1287 men and about 140 officers, as shown by the report of the previous evening, and sustained a loss, as the list of casualties will show, of 941 killed, wounded, and missing, and it is feared, from all the information received, that the majority (those reported missing) are either killed or wounded. . . .

"There was scarcely an officer or man in the command whose attention was not attracted by the cool and handsome bearing of Gen. Garnett, who, totally devoid of excitement or rashness, rode immediately in rear of his advancing line, endeavoring by his personal efforts, and by the aid of his staff, to keep his line well closed and dressed. He was shot from his horse while near the centre of the brigade, within about 25 paces of the stone wall. . . .

"The conduct of Capt. M. P. Spessard of the 28th Va. was particularly conspicuous. His son fell mortally wounded at his side; he stopped but for a moment to look on his dying son, gave him his canteen of water, and pressed on, with his company, to the wall, which he climbed, and fought the enemy with his sword in their own trenches until his sword was wrested from his hands by two Yankees; he finally made his escape in safety."

All accounts of the charge agree that its failure began when the advance had covered about half the distance to the Federal line. At that point the left flank of Pettigrew began to crumble away and the crumbling extended along the line to the right as they continued to advance until two-thirds of the line was gone, before the remainder, beginning at Fry's brigade, was finally absorbed in the collision with the enemy. That result was inevitable. Under the conditions it should have been foreseen.

The Federal line on our left overlapped our line by nearly a half-mile. It was crowded with guns, and their oblique fire upon the unsupported left could be endured but for a short period, particularly, as several fences crossed their line of advance, causing constant disturbance of their ranks. The artillery of the 3d corps, firing from Seminary Ridge, which had been vainly expected to silence this portion of the enemy's line, was now itself practically silent, on account of its imprudent expenditure in the duel about 11 A.M. Lee's report says : —

"Our artillery, having nearly exhausted their ammunition in the protracted cannonade that preceded the advance of the infantry, were unable to reply or render the necessary support to the attacking party.

Owing to this fact, which was unknown to me when the assault took place, the enemy was enabled to throw a strong force of infantry against our left, already wavering under a concentrated fire of artillery from the ridge in front and from Cemetery Hill on the left. It finally gave way, and the right, after penetrating the enemy's lines, entering his advanced works and capturing some of his artillery, was attacked simultaneously in front and on both flanks, and driven back with heavy loss."

Evidently the reliance for the support of our left flank had been the fire of the 82 guns from Seminary Ridge. It was as oversanguine as that expressed by Col. Long in the morning conference on the right, and it failed to note that the enemy might hold guns in reserve. This was done on the present occasion. Hunt, the Federal chief of artillery, had withdrawn many guns to await the charge which he knew was coming.

The crumbling away of Pettigrew's left precipitated the advance of Wilcox. Pickett, who was riding with his staff in rear of his division, saw that the brigades on the left were breaking and sent two aides to endeavor to rally them, which they were unable to do. A third was sent at the same moment to Longstreet to say that the position in front would be taken, but that reënforcements would be required to hold it. Longstreet, in reply, directed Pickett to order up Wilcox, and Pickett sent three messengers in succession to be sure that the order was promptly acted upon. As the fugitives from Pettigrew's division came back, Wright's brigade of Anderson's division was moved forward a few hundred yards to cover their retreat. Later, after Wilcox had fallen back, by Lee's order, Wright was moved across to the rear in support of Wilcox, in case the enemy should make an advance, which at times seemed probable during the entire afternoon.

It must be ever held a colossal mistake that Meade did not organize a counter-stroke as soon as he discovered that the Confederate attack had been repulsed. He lost here an opportunity as great as McClellan lost at Sharpsburg. Our ammunition was so low, and our diminished forces were, at the moment, so widely dispersed along our unwisely extended line, that an advance by a single fresh corps, the 6th, for instance, could have cut us in two. Meade might at least have felt that he had nothing to lose and everything to gain by making the effort.

Longstreet felt that the lines held by Hood and McLaws were unwisely advanced for the changed conditions, and, during the afternoon, he quietly withdrew these divisions to the rear of the Emmitsburg road.   During the process of the withdrawal, the enemy advanced McCandless's brigade of the 5th corps into the neutral ground between the lines, where it accidentally encountered the 15th Ga. of Benning's brigade.   This by mistake had been marched to the front, when it was intended to be moved to the rear.   The regiment, though only numbering about 250, took a position and opened fire, expecting reënforcements. It was quickly outflanked and only with difficulty and by severe fighting did it extricate itself, losing 101 men.

During the morning there were cavalry affairs upon each of our flanks. Upon our left, Stuart advanced, and a severe combat ensued with Gregg's division and Custer's brigade. The result was a draw, each side claiming what it held at the close as a victory.   Upon our right, Kilpatrick reports that at 8 A.M. he received orders, —

"to move to the left of the Federal line and attack the enemy's right and rear with his whole command [Custer's and Farnsworth's brigades], and the regular brigade [Merritt's]."

By some mistake, surely a fortunate one for the Confederates, Custer's brigade had already been sent to Gregg's division, on the other flank. Our right was at first merely picketed by 100 cavalry on the extreme flank, while, nearer the position of our infantry, was a strong line of skirmishers with Bachman's and Reilly's batteries in support.

Had Kilpatrick come with three brigades upon our right flank, he could not have failed to discover an immense opportunity open to him.   Behind the mask of our videttes were wide fields stretching along the valleys of Willoughby Run and Marsh Creek for miles to the north and west, containing all our trains practically unguarded.   The bulk of our cavalry was engaging Gregg's division about two miles east of Gettysburg. Once through our skirmish line, Kilpatrick would have had great scope before any adequate force could be brought against him.   As it was, we had a narrow escape.   Merritt's dismounted men had found the flank of our videttes, and were driving them rapidly to the rear, when Anderson's brigade was brought to the rescue, and Merritt was driven back.

Meanwhile, Kilpatrick had ordered Farnsworth to charge through our long line of infantry pickets extending from the Emmitsburg road to the right flank of our infantry line on the lower slope of Big Round Top. Farnsworth at first remonstrated, but then made the charge gallantly, with about 300 men of the 1st W. Va. and the 1st Vt. They rode through the Texan skirmish line, but found themselves surrounded with no escape but to make a circuit and return, broken into squads by the fire of infantry and artillery, and by the natural obstacles of the ground. Farnsworth fell with five mortal wounds. The total killed and wounded in the charge were 65.[1]

The report of the Federal chief of artillery gives interesting details. The supply of ammunition carried with that army was 270 rounds per gun. The Confederate army carried for the campaign about 150 rounds per gun.

Hunt reports an expenditure in action of 32,781 rounds, an average of 106 per gun for 310 guns, excluding the cavalry. Ewell's corps reports 5851 rounds expended, and Hill's corps 7112 rounds. No report was made of Longstreet's ammunition, but his 83 guns were all engaged, while Ewell and Hill each engaged only 65. Ewell averaged about 90 rounds per gun engaged, and Hill about 110. Longstreet's 83 guns doubtless averaged as much as Hill's, which would make about 9000 for the battle. This gives an aggregate for the army of about 22,000, or 103 rounds per gun for 213 guns engaged, excluding cavalry. The killed and wounded (not including the missing) in the Federal reserve artillery, 108 guns all engaged, numbered 230, an average per gun of 2.1. In Longstreet's corps the total was 271, for 83 guns, an average per gun of 2.6. In

_____

[1] Confederate eye-witnesses declared that Farnsworth, having fallen mortally wounded, was summoned to surrender, but refused and shot himself. His shoulder-straps and papers were brought into our lines and the story told by reliable witnesses during the afternoon. Federal accounts, however, claim that the wounded officer who shot himself was not Farnsworth but a Capt. Cushman who was left for dead on the field, but recovered and was killed in a later battle.

Ewell's the total was 132, and average per gun engaged 2. In Hill's the total was 128 and average per gun engaged 2. The destruction of artillery horses was very great, but figures are given only for Hill's corps. This reported 190 killed in action, 80 captured, 187 abandoned on the road, and 200 condemned as broken down; a total of 627 lost in the campaign, with 77 guns. Serving the 26 guns of Alexander's battalion, 138 men and 116 horses, or over 5 men and 4 horses per gun, were killed or wounded. The greater part of this loss was from artillery fire, and its severity shows that the ground occupied was unfavorable and afforded little shelter.

An anxious inventory of the ammunition left on hand was made during that afternoon, and much relief was felt that "enough for one day's fight" was found.

During the afternoon of the 3d, Lee determined upon immediate retreat to Va. Such an end to our invasion had, indeed, been inevitable from its beginning, but the difficulties were now greatly increased. Fortunately, Meade was not in aggressive mood, and Lee decided to give his trains one day's start of his troops. Many Federal writers have sought to excuse Meade's failures to improve the opportunities offered him, one after the other, on the 3d, 4th, and 5th, and 11th, 12th, and 13th of July. It is needless to balance pros and cons. An axiom of the game of war is to attack whenever a large stake may be won by success, and but small loss incurred by repulse. Then the game is worth the candle, and the game must be played. It is the hardest of all games to a general new to the responsibility of chief command.

Under cover of the night, Lee took a defensive line upon Seminary Ridge with its right flank retired to Willoughby Run. Here he stood all day of the 4th, apparently inviting attack, but fortunate in remaining unmolested.

Imboden's cavalry had joined him on the 3d, 2100 strong, with a six-gun battery. During the night of the 3d, Imboden had been directed to organize most of our vehicles into a single train, and to conduct it without a halt to Williamsport. Here it would stop only to feed, and would then ford the Potomac and move without a halt to Winchester. Imboden's force, with a few more guns, would guard the front and flanks of the column, which would be about 17 miles long. A brigade of Stuart's cavalry, with a battery, would guard the rear. Lee's medical director was charged to see that all the wounded who could bear the journey were carried in the empty wagons and ambulances.

What this journey was to mean to the wounded, none seem to have imagined before starting, or they would have greatly preferred to become prisoners. Every vehicle appeared to be loaded to its capacity.

It was about 4 P.M. on the 4th before the head of the train was put in motion from Cashtown. Meanwhile, what would have seemed a visitation of the wrath of God had come upon us, had we not preferred the theory which has been previously referred to, that storms may be generated by heavy firings. Now there came suddenly, out of the clear sky of the day before, one of the heaviest rainfalls I have ever seen. Probably four inches of water fell within 12 hours, and it was sure to make the Potomac unfordable for a week. Imboden, in *Battles and Leaders*, gives the following description: —

"Shortly after noon on the 4th, the very windows of heaven seemed to have opened. The rain fell in blinding sheets, the meadows were soon overflowed, and fences gave way before the raging streams. During the storm, wagons, ambulances, and artillery carriages by hundreds — nay, by thousands — were assembling in the fields along the road from Gettysburg to Cashtown in one confused and apparently inextricable mass. As the afternoon wore on, there was no abatement of the storm. Canvas was no protection against its fury, and the wounded men, lying upon the naked boards of the wagon-bodies were drenched, horses and mules were blinded and maddened by the wind and water, and became almost unmanageable."

My personal recollections of the occasion are vivid. About 5 P.M., my somewhat battered battalion drew into a meadow adjoining the Fairfield Pike with orders to watch the passing column of troops and take its place in the column immediately behind the 3d corps, when it passed. This might be, we were told, in an hour or two. There was good grass in the meadow and the horses needed food, but the need to move promptly when the time came prevented unhitching. By good fortune, four of us got possession of an old door, upon which we could sit, laying it flat on a knoll some 50 yards from the road. On that door we sat or lay in the rain all night, every half-hour taking turns in walking out to the road to see what command was passing. At daylight the rain ceased to fall, but the sky remained threatening. About 6 A.M., we took our place in the column, and marched 19 hours until 1 A.M. that night. Then we bivouacked until four near Monterey Springs on the Blue Ridge. We then marched again for 14 hours, and bivouacked about 6 P.M. two or three miles beyond Hagerstown. Ewell's corps, moving behind ours, did not leave the vicinity of Gettysburg until about noon on the 5th.

The wagon-train under Imboden moved on roads to our right, via Greenwood to Williamsport. It made better speed than our column of infantry and artillery, but at a cost of human suffering which it is terrible to contemplate. Some of the wounded were taken from the wagons dead at Williamsport, and many who were expected to recover died from the effects of the journey. Among these, it was said, were Gens. Pender and Semmes, neither of whom had been thought mortally wounded.

Imboden gives a harrowing account of the movement of the train, as follows: —

"After dark I set out from Cashtown to gain the head of the column during the night. My orders had been peremptory that there should be no halt for any cause whatever. If an accident should happen to any vehicle, it was immediately to be put out of the road and abandoned. The column moved rapidly, considering the rough roads and the darkness, and from almost every wagon issued heart-rending wails of agony. For four hours I hurried forward on my way to the front, and in all that time I was never out of hearing of the groans and cries of the wounded and dying. Scarcely one in a hundred had received adequate surgical aid, owing to the demands on the hard-working surgeons from still worse cases which had to be left behind. Many of the wounded in the wagons had been without food for 36 hours. Their torn and bloody clothing, matted and hardened, was rasping the tender, inflamed, and still oozing wounds. Very few of the wagons had even a layer of straw in them and all were without springs. The road was rough and rocky from the heavy washings of the preceding day. The jolting was enough to have killed strong men if long exposed to it."

"From nearly every wagon as the teams trotted on, urged by whip and shout, came such cries and shrieks as these: —

"'Oh God! Why can't I die!'

"'My God! Will no one have mercy and kill me!'

"'Stop! Oh! for God's sake stop just for one minute; take me out and leave me to die by the roadside.'

"'I am dying! I am dying! My poor wife, my dear children! What will become of you?' . . .

"No help could be rendered to any of the sufferers. No heed could be given to any of their appeals. Mercy and duty to the many forbade the loss of a moment in the vain effort then and there to comply with the prayers of the few. On! On! We *must* move on. The storm continued, and the darkness was appalling. There was no time to fill even a canteen of water for a dying man, for, except the drivers and the guards, all were wounded and utterly helpless in that vast procession of misery."

When daylight came, the head of the column had reached Greencastle, having traversed about 30 miles, and it still had 15 to go to reach Williamsport. Here began a succession of small attacks of the long train by citizens, and small detachments of Federal cavalry, scouting in the country. At one point some citizens cut the spokes of a dozen wagons, but a guard sent back, arrested and took them off as prisoners of war. At another point about a hundred wagons were captured. The head of the column reached Williamsport in the afternoon and during the night the balance came up. Here it met two regiments of Johnson's division, returning from Staunton, where they had escorted the prisoners taken at Winchester on the advance.

Imboden required every family in the town to cook provisions for the wounded, under pain of having its kitchen occupied. The river was in flood and impassable except by two small ferry-boats. Next morning he learned of the approach of five Federal brigades of cavalry — about 7000 men, with 18 guns. The flanks of the city fortunately rested upon creeks, leaving only the north front to be defended. He armed about 800 teamsters and convalescents, and with the two regiments of infantry and his dismounted cavalry he marched about so as to create the impression of a large force. He put in the line all of his guns and brought over some ammunition in the ferry-boats. A sharp fight ensued, the teamsters acquitting themselves handsomely. The enemy was driven back and held off until the approach of Stuart's cavalry in the afternoon caused the Federal cavalry to withdraw.

As a precaution against such freshets, Lee had maintained a pontoon bridge at Falling Waters. But it was weakly guarded, and on June 5, a small raiding party, sent by French from Frederick, had broken it, and destroyed some of its boats, fortunately not all. The retreat of the army was, therefore, brought to a standstill just when 48 hours more would have placed it beyond pursuit. We were already nearly out of provisions, and now the army was about to be penned upon the river bank, and subjected to an attack at his leisure by Meade.

All diligence was used to relieve the situation. The ferry-boats were in use by day and by night carrying over, first, our wounded, and next 5000 Federal prisoners brought from Gettysburg. These were safely escorted on to Staunton by Imboden with a single regiment of infantry. Warehouses upon the canal were torn down, and from the timber new pontoon boats were being built to repair the bridge at Falling Waters.

Meanwhile, the engineers selected and fortified a line of battle upon which we would make a last stand. A fairly good line was found with its right flank on the Potomac near Downsville, passing by St. James College and resting its left on the Conococheague. Longstreet's corps held its right flank, Hill the centre, and Ewell the left. On the 10th, Meade was approaching rapidly, driving in our advanced guards. An unfortunate affair occurred at Funkstown, where Anderson's Ga. brigade, called upon to assist our cavalry, was so badly directed by them that a Federal battery enfiladed the line, and a battery of our own horse artillery by mistake also fired into it. The brigade suffered 126 casualties.

On the 11th, the army was ordered into position upon the selected line, Lee in person overlooking the placing of Longstreet's corps. I never before, and never afterward, saw him as I thought visibly anxious over an approaching action; but I did upon this occasion. No one can say what might have been the result of a Federal attack, for, although our supply of ammunition was low, we were on the defensive, and the temper of the troops was excellent for a desperate resistance.

Meade's report indicates easy acquiescence in our retreat from Gettysburg. While the 6th corps followed us to the vicinity of Fairfield on the 5th, picking up stragglers, the rest of the army remained on the battle-field for two days, "employed in succoring the wounded and burying the dead."

A third day was lost "halting a day at Middletown to procure necessary supplies and to bring up the trains." Under ordinary circumstances Lee might now have been across the Potomac, but there were further rains on the 7th and 8th, and Lee's escape was exceedingly narrow.

On the 13th, both his bridge and the ford near Williamsport were passable, and orders were issued to make the crossing during that night. The river had fallen to a stage barely permitting infantry to ford, but about dark it again began to rise. Ewell's corps was ordered to cross by the ford. Longstreet, followed by Hill, was to cross by the pontoon bridge. Caissons were ordered to start from the lines at 5 P.M., the infantry and artillery at dark.

Meade might have attacked on the 12th but contented himself with reconnoissance. As a result of the reconnoissance of the 12th, he assembled his corps commanders and proposed a demonstration in force on the 13th by the whole army, to be converted into an attack if any opening was found.

The opinion of a majority of his leading officers was so adverse to the proposition that Meade allowed himself to be persuaded, thus giving Lee the last day needed. Later in the day he repented and issued orders for a general advance on the 14th. It was made just a day too late. Lee had left only two guns stalled in the mud, and a few hundred stragglers broken down by the night march, short in distance, but rarely equalled for its discomfort and fatigue.

Another rain-storm had set in before dusk, and it kept up nearly all night. It was the dark period of the moon and the blackness of the night was phenomenal. The route to the bridge was over small farm roads, rough, narrow, and hilly. Already from the incessant rains they were in bad condition, and now, under the long procession of heavy wheels, churning in the mud, they became canals of slush in which many vehicles were hopelessly stalled.

My command, between sunset and sunrise, was only able to cover about three miles — seldom moving more than a few yards at a time. Large bonfires on the banks were kept up to light the entrance upon the bridge, but in spite of them a wagon loaded with wounded ran off into the river. After daylight the weather cleared and better progress was made, the last of Hill's corps crossing about 1 P.M. During the morning it was followed by the enemy who skirmished with our rear-guard and picked up stragglers.

In one of these skirmishes, a small body of Federal cavalry was allowed to approach within 200 yards of Heth's division under Pettigrew, who supposed them to be our own cavalry bringing up the rear. These, however, had passed without giving notice that they were the last. A Maj. Weber, of the 6th Mich. Cav., seeing but a small portion of the Confederate line, charged it with about 40 men. Weber was killed and ninetenths of his command shot down, but one of a few pistol-shots which they fired gave a mortal wound to Gen. Pettigrew. He had been wounded in the hand on the 3d, and was unable to manage his horse, which reared and fell with him. In the act of rising, the fatal shot struck him.

Ewell's corps reached Williamsport by the Hagerstown turnpike and commenced fording the river by midnight. The artillery with an escort of one brigade was sent to cross the pontoon bridge. Rodes's report describes the fording of the Potomac, as follows: —

"My division waded the river just above the aqueduct over the mouth of the Conococheague; the operation was a perilous one. It was very dark, raining, and excessively muddy. The men had to wade through the aqueduct, down the steep bank of soft and slippery mud, in which numbers lost their shoes and down in which many fell. The water was cold, deep, and rising, the lights on either side of the river were dim, just affording enough light to mark the places of entrance and exit. The cartridge boxes of the men had to be placed around their necks; some small men had to be carried over by their comrades; the water was up to the armpits of a full-sized man.

"All the circumstances attending this crossing combined to make it an affair, not only involving great hardship, but one of great danger to the men and company officers; but be it said to the honor of these brave fellows, they encountered it not only promptly but actually with cheers and laughter.

"We crossed without loss except of some 25,000 or 30,000 rounds of ammunition unavoidably wetted and spoiled. After crossing, I marched a short distance beyond Falling Waters and then bivouacked; and there ended the Pa. campaign."

It is not necessary to follow the march of the army from the Potomac via Front Royal and Culpeper to the line of the Rapidan, which it finally occupied. It is notable that Lee had not proposed to entirely withdraw from an aggressive attitude when he crossed the Potomac. His report states that he intended to cross the Blue Ridge into Loudon Co., where he might oppose Meade's crossing into Va., but that the Shenandoah was found to be impassable. While waiting for it to subside, the enemy crossed below and seized the passes he had designed to use.

Not only this, but Meade also moved along the eastern slope, threatening to cut Lee off from Gordonsville and the railroad. Longstreet was pushed ahead and barely succeeded in crossing the Shenandoah in time to prevent the enemy from occupying Manassas and Chester gaps, through which Longstreet moved to Culpeper by July 24. Hill's corps soon followed, and Ewell, moving farther up the valley, crossed at Thornton's Gap. All were finally united behind the Rapidan on Aug. 4, while the cavalry, under Stuart, held Culpeper, and the enemy held the line of the Rappahannock.

The following tables of casualties furnish the best comparative indications of the amount of fighting which fell to the lot of different organizations. It is notable that six Confederate brigades were not severely engaged, and the 6th Federal corps was scarcely engaged at all. The totals given are from the official returns of both armies, but the Confederate returns are known to be very incomplete. The best estimate of actual Confederate losses has been made by Livermore in *Numbers and Losses in the Civil War*. It is about 50 per cent greater for the killed and wounded, and is attached hereto.

CONFEDERATE CASUALTIES. GETTYSBURG. APPROXIMATE

BY BRIGADES

COMMANDS	KILLED	WOUNDED	MISSING	TOTAL
Kershaw	115	483	32	630
Semmes	55	284	91	430
Barksdale	105	550	92	747
Wofford	30	192	112	334
Cabell's Arty.	8	29		37
McLaws's Div.	313	1538	327	2,178
Garnett	78	324	539	941
Armistead	88	460	643	1,191
Kemper	58	356	317	731
Dearing's Arty.	8	17		25
Pickett's Div.	232	1,157	1,499	2,888
Law	74	276	146	496
Anderson, G. T.	105	512	54	671
Robertson	84	393	120	597
Benning	76	299	122	497
Henry's Arty.	4	23		27
Hood's Div.	343	1,504	442	2,289
Alexander's Arty.	19	114	6	139
Washington Arty.	3	26	16	45
Reserve Arty.	22	140	22	184
Aggregate 1st Corps	910	4,339	2,290	7,539
Hays	36	201	76	313
Hoke	35	216	94	345
Smith	12	113	17	142
Gordon	71	270	39	380
Jones's Arty.	2	6		8
Early's Div.	156	806	226	1,188
Steuart	83	409	190	682
Nichols	43	309	36	388
Stonewall	35	208	87	330
Jones	58	302	61	421
Latimer's Arty.	10	40		50
Johnson's Div.	229	1,269	375	1,873

CONFEDERATE CASUALTIES. GETTYSBURG. APPROXIMATE

By Brigades

COMMANDS	KILLED	WOUNDED	MISSING	TOTAL
Daniel	165	635	116	916
Iverson	130	328	308	820
Doles	24	124	31	179
Ramseur	23	122	32	177
O'Neal	73	430	193	696
Carter's Arty.	6	35	24	65
Rodes's Div.	421	1,728	704	2,853
Brown's Arty.	3	19		22
Nelson's Arty.				
Reserve Arty.	3	19		22
2d Corps	809	3,823	1,305	5,937
Wilcox	51	469	257	777
Mahone	8	55	39	102
Wright	40	295	333	668
Perry	33	217	205	455
Posey	12	71		83
Lane's Arty.	3	21	6	30
Anderson's Div.	147	1,128	840	2,115
Pettigrew	190	915		1,105
Brockenbrough	25	123		148
Archer	16	144	517	677
Davis	180	717		897
Garnett's Arty.		5	17	22
Heth's Div.	411	1,905	534	2,850
Perrin	100	477		577
Lane	41	348		389
Thomas	16	136		152
Scales	102	323	110	535
Poague's Arty.	2	24	6	32
Pender's Div.	262	1,312	116	1,690
McIntosh's Arty.	7	25		32
Pegram's Arty.	10	37	1	48
Reserve Arty.	17	62	1	6,735
3d Corps	837	4,407	1,491	6,735

CONFEDERATE CASUALTIES. GETTYSBURG. APPROXIMATE

By Brigades

COMMANDS	KILLED	WOUNDED	MISSING	TOTAL
Hampton	17	58	16	91
Lee, F.	5	16	29	50
Lee, W. H. F.	2	26	13	41
Jones	12	40	6	58
Jenkins's Arty.				
Total Cavalry	36	140	64	240
Aggregate	2,592	12,709	5,150	20,451
Livermore's Estimate	3,903	18,735	5,425	28,063

FEDERAL CASUALTIES. GETTYSBURG

By Divisions

COMMANDS	KILLED	WOUNDED	MISSING	TOTAL
Wadsworth	299	1,229	627	2,155
Robinson	91	616	983	1,690
Rowley	265	1,296	541	2,103
Wainwright's Arty.	9	86	11	106
1st Corps	666	3,131	2,162	6,059
Caldwell	187	880	208	1,275
Gibbon	344	1,212	101	1,647
Hays	238	987	66	1,291
Hazard's Arty.	27	119	3	149
2d Corps	797	3,194	378	4,369
Birney	271	1,384	356	2,011
Humphreys	314	1,562	216	2,092
Randolph's Arty.	8	81	17	106
3d Corps	593	3,029	589	4,211
Barnes	167	594	142	904
Ayres	164	802	63	1,029
Crawford	26	181	3	210
Martin	8	33	2	43
5th Corps	365	1,611	211	2,187

FEDERAL CASUALTIES. GETTYSBURG

By Divisions

COMMANDS	KILLED	WOUNDED	MISSING	TOTAL
Wright	1	17		18
Howe	2	12	2	16
Newton	20	148	28	196
Tompkins's Arty.	4	8		12
6th Corps	27	185	30	242
Barlow	122	677	507	1,306
Steinwehr	107	507	332	946
Schurz	133	684	659	1,476
Osborn's Arty.	7	53	9	69
11th Corps	369	1,922	1,510	3,801
Williams	96	406	31	533
Geary	108	397	35	540
Muhlenberg's Arty.		9		9
12th Corps	214	812	66	1,082
Arty. Reserve	43	187	12	242
Gen. Hd. Qrs.		4		4
Cavalry	91	354	407	852
Aggregate	3,155	14,529	5,365	23,049

CHAPTER XIX

HAVING rested at Culpeper from July 24 to 31, and then
crossed the Rapidan to Orange C. H., where we could receive
supplies by rail, Lee's army now recuperated rapidly from its
exhaustion by the campaign of Gettysburg. There remained
nearly five months of open weather before winter. The prospects of the Confederacy had been sadly altered by our failures
at Gettysburg and Vicksburg. Grant would now be able to
bring against us in Ga. Rosecrans reënforced by the army which
had taken Vicksburg. To remain idle was to give the enemy
time to do this. Once more the necessity was upon us to devise
some offensive which might bring on a battle with approximately
equal chances. Lee, accordingly, urged forward the building up
of his own army with the design of an early aggressive movement
against Meade. It must be admitted that the opportunity for
such was slight. The enemy's fortified lines about Alexandria
were too near; as was proven later, when in Nov. an advance
was actually attempted.

But the Confederacy still held unimpaired the advantage of the
"Interior Lines," already spoken of as open to them in May,
and then urged by Longstreet both upon Secretary Seddon and
Lee. These still offered the sole opportunity ever presented the
South for a great strategic victory. Already, however, move-

ments of the enemy were on foot which, in a few weeks, would enable them to close the shorter route from Richmond to Chattanooga via Knoxville, and leave us only the much longer and less favorable line via Weldon, Wilmington, and Augusta. Unfortunately, no one but Longstreet seems to have appreciated this, and he was very slow in again taking up the matter and urging it.

It resulted that the movement, when attempted, was too late to utilize the short Knoxville line and that only five small brigades of infantry were transferred to the west in time to take any part in the hard-fought battle of Chickamauga. This was consequently but another bloody and fruitless victory to be followed by a terrible defeat in a few weeks when the enemy's reënforcements had joined. It is first to tell of the dilatory consideration and slow acceptance of the proposed strategy, which should have been decided upon even before Lee's army was again south of the Potomac, and every subsequent movement planned to facilitate it.

It was not until about Aug. 15, two weeks after the army was safe behind the Rapidan, that Longstreet again called the attention of Sec'y Seddon to the tremendous threatenings of the situation, and pointed out the one hope of escape which he could suggest. There seems to have been no reply. A few days later, in conversation with Lee, Longstreet again expressed his views. Lee was unwilling to consider going west in person, but approved the sending of Longstreet, and even spoke of his being given independent command there, if the War Department could be brought to approve.

About Aug. 23, Lee was called to Richmond, and was detained there by President Davis for nearly two weeks. During this time, consent was given that Longstreet should go to reënforce Bragg against Rosecrans, but with only Hood's and McLaws's divisions, nine brigades, and my battalion of 26 guns. It was proposed to send this force from Louisa C. H. by rail to Chattanooga, via Bristol and Knoxville, a distance of but 540 miles, and it was hoped that the movement could be made within four days.

There was too little appreciation of the importance of time in the enterprise proposed, and it was not until Sept. 9 that the first train came to Louisa C. H. to begin the transportation.

On that day 2000 Confederates under Gen. Frazier, who had been unwisely held at Cumberland Gap and allowed to be surrounded by a superior force, surrendered without a fight. Already Burnside had occupied Knoxville, leaving us only the long line via Petersburg, Wilmington, Augusta, and Atlanta, about 925 miles, with imperfect connections through some cities and some changes of gauge. The infantry was given precedence, and my battalion was marched to Petersburg, where it took trains about 4 P.M., Thursday, Sept. 17. At 2 A.M., Sunday, the 20th, we reached Wilmington, 225 miles in 58 hours. Here we changed cars and ferried the river, leaving at 2 P.M. The battle of Chickamauga was being fought upon the 19th and 20th, only five of our nine brigades having arrived in time to participate. We reached Kingsville, S.C., 192 miles in 28 hours, changed trains in six hours, and got to Augusta, 140 miles, at 2 P.M. on Tuesday, the 22d. Leaving Augusta at 7 P.M., we reached Atlanta, 171 miles, at 2 P.M., Wednesday. Leaving at 4 A.M., Thursday, we were carried 115 miles and landed at Ringgold Station, 12 miles from the battle-field, at 2 A.M. on Friday, Sept. 25. Our journey by rail had been 843 miles and had consumed seven days and 10 hours, or 178 hours. It could scarcely be considered rapid transit, yet under the circumstances it was really a very creditable feat for our railroad service under the attendant circumstances. We found ourselves restricted to the use of one long roundabout line of single-track road of light construction, much of it of the "stringer track" of those days, a 16-pound rail on stringers, with very moderate equipment and of different gauges, for the entire service at the time of a great battle of the principal armies of the Confederacy. The task would have taxed a double-tracked road with modern equipment.

Its *efficient* performance was simply impossible, and the incomplete success we were able to obtain by getting five brigades of Longstreet's infantry upon the field, without any of his artillery, shows the soundness of our strategy, and is an earnest of what might have been accomplished, had a campaign upon our short interior lines been inaugurated in May, under Lee in person, instead of the unfortunate invasion of Pa. Indeed, it must be said of the battle itself, that the force upon the field was ample to have reaped the full fruits of victory, had its management been judicious. The story of the details, presently to be told, is but another story of excellent fighting made vain by inefficient handling of an army hastily brought together, poorly organized, and badly commanded.

It will be seen that the battle was opened by two divisions attacking the whole army of the enemy in a fortified position, the attack being made in a single line without supports at hand. They are defeated and put out of action for the day. Two more divisions try and fare little better. A fifth, in reserve, sends in one brigade without result; four are not engaged. The morning is gone and the battle of the Right Wing is over. That of the Left Wing has scarcely begun. It advances, finds by accident a gap in the enemy's line, and drives off three divisions of the enemy. The left wing fights the rest of the enemy's army (three-fourths of it) until near dark, when both wings unite and drive the enemy off the field; darkness covering his retreat. It is the old familiar story of piecemeal attacks.

On the arrival of Longstreet, Bragg's army would comprise five corps and a reserve division, organized as shown below. No exact returns of the total "present for duty" exist, but instead are given Livermore's estimates of the "Effective Strength." [1]

ARMY OF TENN., GEN. BRAGG, SEPT. 19–20, 1863

CORPS	DIVISIONS	BRIGADES	BATTERIES
Polk	Cheatham	Jackson, Smith, Maney, Wright, Strahl	5
	Hindman	Anderson, Deas, Manigault	3
Hill, D. H.	Cleburne	Wood, Polk, Deshler	3
	Breckenridge	Helm, Adams, Stovall	4
Walker	Gist	Colquitt, Ector, Wilson	2
	Liddell	Govan, Walthall	2
Buckner	Stewart	Bate, Brown, Clayton	4
	Preston	Gracie, Trigg, Kelly	3

[1] Livermore's *Numbers and Losses in Civil War*, p. 105.

ARMY OF TENN., GEN. BRAGG, SEPT. 19–20, 1863

CORPS	DIVISIONS	BRIGADES	BATTERIES
Res. Div.	Johnson	Gregg, McNair, Fulton	2
Longstreet	McLaws	Kershaw, Humphreys, *Wofford,*[1] *Bryan* [1]	
	Hood	Law, Robertson, Benning, *Jenkins,*[1] *Anderson* [1]	
Res. Arty.	Batteries	Williams, 4; Robertson, 5; *Alexander,* 6 [1]	9

Total Inf. and Arty., 33 Brigades, 174 Guns.   Effective total 52,066

Wheeler Cavalry	Wharton	O'Rews, Harrison	1
	Martin	Morgan, Russell	1
Forrest Cavalry	Armstrong	Wheeler, Dibbfell	2
	Pegram	Davidson, Scott	2

Total Cavalry, 8 Brigades, 24 Guns.   Effective total, 14,260

Unlike the armies in Va., which had never considered themselves defeated, our Western army had never gained a decided victory.   Naturally, therefore, Lee enjoyed both the affection and confidence of his men, while there was an absence of much sentiment toward Bragg.   It did not, however, at all affect the quality of the fighting, as shown by the casualties suffered at Chickamauga, which were 25 per cent by the Confederates in killed and wounded, exclusive of the missing.

Neither in armament, equipment, or organization was the Western army in even nearly as good shape as the Army of Northern Virginia.   About one-third of the infantry was still armed only with the smooth-bore musket, calibre .69.   Only a few batteries of the artillery were formed into battalions, and their ammunition was all of inferior quality.

Much has been said in the accounts of prior battles of the insufficient and unskilled staff service in the Army of Northern Virginia, even after many active campaigns.   The Western armies generally had had far less opportunities to learn from

[1] Names in italics arrived too late for the battle.

experience, and fewer resigned ex-army officers from the old U. S. Army among them, to organize and train their raw material. Several of Bragg's divisions had been recently brought together and were strangers to each other. Nearly all were unfamiliar with the country in which they found themselves, which was unusually wooded and hilly. Bragg, himself, was lacking in quick appreciation of features of topography.

The organization of the Federal army, with its strength present for duty before the battle, is given below, and also Livermore's estimate of the "Effective Strength."

ARMY OF THE CUMBERLAND, GEN. ROSECRANS, SEPT. 19–20, '63

CORPS	DIVISIONS	BRIGADES	BATTERIES
14th Thomas Pres. 22,758	Baird Negley Brannon Reynolds	Scribner, Starkweather, King Beatty, Stanley, Sirwell Connell, Croxton, Van Derveer Wilder, King, Turchin	3 3 3 3
20th McCook Pres. 13,372	Davis Johnson Sheridan	Post, Carlin, Heg Willich, Dodge, Baldwin Lytle, Laiboldt, Bradley	3 3 3
21st Crittenden Pres. 14,190	Wood Palmer Van Cleve	Buell, Wagner, Harker Cruft, Hazen, Grose Beatty, Dick, Barnes	3 4 3
Reserve Granger Pres. 5,489	Steedman	Whitaker, Mitchell, McCook	3

Total Inf. and Art., 33 Brigades, 204 Guns, Pres. 53,919. Effective 50,144

Cavalry Mitchell	McCook Crook	Campbell, Ray, Watkins Minty, Long	1 1

Total Cavalry, 5 Brigades, 30 Guns, Pres. 9,504. Effective 8,078.

Comparing the two armies, we see that while Bragg's "Effective total" (66,326) is largely greater than Rosecrans (58,222), it is due to Bragg's excess in cavalry (6182), which arm had little opportunity in the battle upon either side. Of infantry and artillery, Rosecrans had an excess of 1853 men and 30 guns, besides the superiority of his small-arms and rifled artillery over the inferior equipment of the Confederates. It is well recognized that the defensive rôle is the least hazardous, and, on this campaign, Rosecrans, although on the strategic offensive, gladly seized the tactical defensive when Bragg incautiously gave him the privilege.

Bragg's daily experience in the handling of his army should have warned him that it was not a military machine which could be relied upon to execute orders strictly, or to be alert to seize passing opportunities, and it is safe to say that its power for offence was scarcely 50 per cent of what the same force would have developed upon the defensive.

The position at Chattanooga held by Bragg at the beginning of the campaign was entirely untenable, as Rosecrans's line of approach, along the Nashville and Chattanooga R.R., reaching the Tennessee River at Stevenson, threatened Bragg's communications for 40 miles south, and he was forced to fall back without a battle and take position where he might guard his communications. He withdrew from Chattanooga on Sept. 8, and, moving south about 22 miles, disposed his forces in the vicinity of Lafayette and held the gaps in Pigeon Mountain, a spur of the great plateau of Lookout Mountain, running northeast, with McLemore's Cove between the two. Rosecrans was misled by Bragg's easy abandonment of Chattanooga into the belief that his retreat would be continued at least as far as Dalton, and perhaps to Rome. So, with little delay or caution, the Federal troops were pushed forward in rapid pursuit.

As the country was semi-mountainous, well wooded, and but sparsely settled, neither commander proved able to keep himself fully informed of his adversary's movements. Each lost, therefore, possible opportunities of attacking isolated portions of his adversary with a superior force.

The most important of these was lost by Bragg, who, on Sept. 10 and 11, might have crushed, in McLemore's Cove, parts of Thomas's and McCook's corps. Orders were issued for attacks, but there was no supervision of the necessary preparatory movements, and various obstacles intervened, until the enemy discovered his danger and made his escape. Bragg, in his official report, placed the principal blame for this failure upon Gen. Hindman, and preferred charges against him, which, upon further investigation, he subsequently withdrew. There can be no doubt that upon this occasion an opportunity was lost to the Confederates which might have won the campaign. But the loss was due entirely to the misfortune of inadequate organization, and lack of the trained staff, which alone can make an efficient army of any assemblage of troops. Of course, rumors of the sending of Longstreet with two divisions to reënforce Bragg, were sure to, and did, reach the enemy by many channels and from many sources. Even from the lines along the Rapidan, there were deserters and negro servants who were well informed about all considerable movements. At Richmond and Petersburg, at Wilmington, Charleston, and Atlanta, the enemy, doubtless, maintained spies, and the coming of the reënforcements from Lee was no secret among Bragg's brigades, even long before their arrival. One would suppose, too, that the wisdom of such strategy would be so apparent that it would be easily guessed, on hearing that any movement was on foot. It is, therefore, worthy of note that the Federal War Department, where reports and rumors from all sources were brought together and studied, even as late as Sept. 11, was inclined to believe that Bragg was reënforcing Lee. It was not convinced to the contrary until Sept. 15. Before that, Rosecrans had discovered the proximity of Bragg's army and had hastened to concentrate his scattered divisions, some of which, mistaking the roads, made marches of 50 miles. The concentration took place in the valley of Chickamauga Creek, about 12 miles south of Chattanooga on the western slope of Missionary Ridge.

Bragg, meanwhile, realizing something of his opportunities, made more than one effort to strike in detail some of the nearest Federal divisions, but was unable to succeed. It was only on the night of the 17th that he finally issued an order for an advance in force upon the next day. Having waited so long, he had best have waited longer. Already he had given Rosecrans just the time needed to concentrate his entire army. Even a day sooner might have caught portions of it out of position and much exposed, but when the action opened on the 19th, not only was the whole Federal army in hand, but most of it had fairly well intrenched itself.

There was now no reason to hasten an attack, and there were two reasons for delay. First, by taking a threatening position, and using his superior force of cavalry upon Rosecrans's rear, he might have forced the Federals to attack; and Bragg's army, as has been said, was twice as powerful for defence as for offence. Second, he was now receiving reënforcements, averaging nearly a brigade a day. On the 19th, only Hood with three of Longstreet's veteran brigades had reached the field. Longstreet, in person with two more, arrived in time to take part on the 20th. McLaws with four more brigades of infantry and 26 guns of the reserve artillery were close behind, and were enough to have turned the evenly balanced scale in the battle.

On Sept. 15, Rosecrans's army was west of the Chickamauga, and had its right extended south beyond the left of Bragg's army. Bragg's right, at the same time, east of the Chickamauga extended north beyond Rosecrans's left. Either army, changing front to its left, might thus have turned the other's flank with great advantage, but neither was quite prepared to act promptly. Rosecrans, however, on the 17th, appreciated his own danger and began to extend his left and to draw down his right, practically moving his whole army to the left. This movement was continued during the night of the 18th and on the morning of the 19th. Before Bragg was prepared to open his attack, Rosecrans's left had occupied the strong ground chosen for it to rest upon, on Kelley's farm, about nine miles south of Chattanooga. From this point, the line extended to the Chickamauga at Lee and Gordon's Mill, about four miles, with the divisions in the following order from left to right: —

Brannon, Baird, Reynolds, Palmer, Van Cleve, Wood, with Negley's division in reserve, and the three divisions of McCook's corps — Davis, Johnson, and Sheridan — massed near Crawfish Spring, near by on the right. At Rossville, six miles from Chattanooga and about three north of Kelley's farm, was Granger's reserve corps, of three brigades, holding the very important gap at that point in Missionary Ridge.

Bragg's order of battle was of the progressive or echelon type, and prescribed that the attack should be begun by his right column under Hood, which should cross at Reed's Bridge, and, turning to the left oblique, should sweep up the Chickamauga and be reënforced as it proceeded by Walker's and Buckner's corps, crossing by Alexander's Bridge and Tedford's Ford. Meanwhile Polk, at Lee and Gordon's Mill, should press the enemy, bearing to the right where resistance was met, until a crossing was made at or between the mill and Dalton's or Tedford's Ford. Hill's corps would watch the left flank and cross and attack the enemy's right if he attempted to reënforce his centre. The cavalry would protect the flanks, Wheeler on the left and Forrest on the right. Cooking was ordered to be done at the trains, and cooked rations forwarded to the troops.

This order seems simple, well conceived, and apparently as well adapted to surrounding conditions as it could have been made, but its execution, as will be seen, departed widely from the course prescribed.

The right column under Hood, charged with the opening of the battle, was composed of three brigades of Hood's and three of Bushrod Johnson's. In reaching their assigned positions, there was much delay to all of the columns, due to the bad and narrow roads through the forest, and, in addition, Hood's column was opposed by the enemy's cavalry, and had a preliminary skirmish at Pea Vine Church. At Reed's Bridge, and also at Alexander's, it was necessary to force the crossing, and both bridges were so injured by the enemy that fords somewhere in the vicinity had to be used to cross the stream. These delays consumed the whole of the 18th, and, at nightfall, Hood's six brigades and Walker's five bivouacked on the west side of the Chickamauga about a mile and a half in front of the Rossville and Lafayette road, upon which Rosecrans began to arrive and take position before daylight on the 19th. Buckner's corps, at Tedford's Ford, having been directed to delay until Hood and Walker were across, had, after a slight skirmish, gotten possession of both banks of the river at Tedford's, and also at Dalton's, a half-mile to the left. Polk's corps and Hill's occupied the day in moving from the vicinity of Lafayette to their prescribed positions opposite the enemy's right. At dawn on the 19th, the division of Buckner began crossing at Tedford's and Dalton's, but, before they were ready to attack, the initiative was seized by the Federals, under the impression that only a single Confederate brigade was in front of them. Croxton's brigade, supported by the other two brigades of Brannan's division, was ordered to advance. This brought on the battle, which was waged all day with severe losses on each side, but with material success on neither. The entire Federal army was engaged, except two brigades. Of the Confederates, the brigades of Anderson, Deas, Manigault, Helm, Adams, Stovall, Gracie, Trigg, Kelley, Kershaw, and Humphreys were not engaged. The fighting was desultory and without concert of action. From 7 A.M. until noon, there was a gap of about two miles between the 14th and 21st Federal corps, which, had the Confederates discovered it, might have given them the victory.

The fighting was kept up until dark. Longstreet arrived on the field at 11 P.M., having arrived at Catoosa Station about four, and ridden without a guide, narrowly missing riding into the enemy. The battle was ordered to be renewed at daylight, but under a different organization. The army was now divided into two wings, the right under Polk, and the left under Longstreet. To Polk's wing was assigned Cheatham's division of his corps, and the corps of Hill and Walker, with the cavalry under Forrest on the right. To Longstreet, Bragg gave the division of Hindman of Polk's corps, Johnson's division, Buckner's corps, and the five brigades of Hood's and McLaws's divisions, with the cavalry under Wheeler on the left. This organization was adopted, because the troops were already approximately in the positions assigned, but it involved further subdivision of the command without any increase of staff, and led to an unfortunate delay of some hours in opening the battle.

This was to be begun by Hill's corps at daylight. Sunrise was at 5.45. The orders were given by Bragg to Polk about midnight, but never reached Hill until 7.30 in the morning. The locations of the different commanders were not known to each other. When the orders to attack arrived, there were essential preparations still to be made, as the troops were not in position, and two hours were consumed in getting them even approximately so. These hours were very precious to the enemy. All

during the night, the noise of his axes had been heard felling trees
and building breastworks of logs, and this work was kept up
until the Federal left, under Thomas, occupied a veritable
citadel, from which assaults by infantry alone could scarcely
dislodge him.

His divisions were in the following order from left to right:
Baird of the 14th corps, Johnson of the 20th, Palmer of the 21st,
Reynolds of the 14th. These divisions occupied the breastworks
above described, which ran north and south and were terminated
at each end by wings extending well to the rear. Next on the
right was Brannan's division of the 14th, and then Negley's, of
the same. Then came Sheridan and Davis of the 20th, and then
Wood and Van Cleve of the 21st in reserve.

At 9.30 A.M., Breckenridge moved to the attack and was soon
followed by Cleburne. These two divisions were unfortunately
placed in a single line and without any supports in the rear. They
advanced in the following order from right to left: Adams,
Stovall, Helm, Polk, Wood, Deshler. The two right brigades of
Adams and Stovall were found to entirely overlap the enemy's
line, and they pushed on slowly, and gradually swung to the left
and came into collision with the retired portion of the enemy's
line. Meanwhile, the centre of Helm's brigade had struck the
enemy's fortified line, and, after a severe fight in which Helm was
killed, it was repulsed. The brigades of Adams and Stovall
were now entirely isolated, but maintained their aggressive until
Adams was himself wounded and captured, when they were withdrawn, and the three brigades cut no further figure in the battle
until late in the afternoon. Had Cleburne's division been behind
this division in support, or even had their advance been simultaneous, there might have been a different story to tell.

Its three brigades — Polk, Wood, and Deshler — were also in
single line and advanced a little after the repulse of Helm.
Polk and the right flank of Wood's met the same fire which had
repulsed Helm. Wood and Deshler advanced farther before
they received it, but they were all driven back with heavy losses,
which included Deshler himself. The contest was kept up for
a long time, and was reënforced by the five brigades of Walker's
division, who were brought up from the rear and put in at

various points without making any serious impression. These brigades constituted the whole command of Polk in charge of the right wing, except the division of Cheatham which contained five brigades. Why neither Bragg or Polk put them in until after 6 P.M. is not explained. One would imagine that they would have been called upon before giving up the whole plan of the battle, which was now done. Originally, it had been designed to break the left flank of the enemy and then sweep him to the right. Now the effort will be to break the right flank and sweep to the left. And in this the right wing of the army will take no more part than the left wing has taken in the battle of the morning, and Cheatham's division will practically take none at all.

About 11 A.M., Bragg, finding the attack on the enemy's left making no progress, sent a staff-officer down the lines with orders to every division commander to move upon the enemy immediately. The order was first delivered to Stewart's division of Buckner's corps. This formed two lines deep and two brigades front, with the aid of Wood's brigade of Cleburne's division on its right. The four brigades, Brown and Wood followed by Clayton and Bate, advanced together. The enemy were driven by this charge some 200 yards and lost a battery of guns, but here the impulse was gone and the advance stopped. Meanwhile, Longstreet had appealed to Bragg for permission to attack with his entire wing, and, consent being given, had formed Johnson's division with Fulton and McNair in front, with Gregg in the second line, and with Hood's division in a third line. Hindman's division formed on the left, and about 11.30 a general advance was essayed. Preston's division was in reserve on the extreme left.

It is now time to look in the Federal ranks and see what was taking place there. Although the attack was only made at 9.30, and by only 12 brigades, and was resisted by Thomas with 12 brigades in fortified lines, yet, at 10.10 A.M., we find Garfield, Rosecrans's adjutant, writing to McCook to be prepared to support the left flank, "at all hazards even if the right is drawn wholly to the present left." At 10.30 he called for help, and Sheridan's division was ordered to him. At 10.45, upon a further call, Van Cleve's division was also ordered to support him "with all despatch." Negley's division had withdrawn from its position in line to support Baird, and had been replaced by Wood's division, making the order of the divisions: Baird, Johnson, Palmer, Reynolds, Brannan, Wood, Davis, Sheridan. About this time another message from Thomas reached Rosecrans that he was heavily pressed, and the aide who brought it informed Rosecrans that "Brannan was out of line and Reynolds's right was exposed." On this Rosecrans dictated a message to Wood: —

"The general commanding directs that you close up on Reynolds as fast as possible and support him."

This order changed the issue of the battle. Reynolds's division was slightly echeloned with Brannan's, but no one other than Reynolds considered it worthy of note. When Wood obeyed his order and reached the ground, Brannan was found to already occupy it, and Thomas sent Wood on to the support of Baird. Reynolds had blundered in his complaint, and Rosecrans had blundered in acting on it without reference to Thomas.

On receipt of the order, Wood, leaving his skirmishers in front, started his division at a double-quick to the left, passing in rear of Brannan's division to reach the right of Reynolds. He had advanced but little more than a brigade length when Johnson's Confederate division, supported by Hood and Hindman, burst through the forest in front and fell upon the movement. Had this movement of Wood's division been foreseen by the Confederates and prepared for, it could not have happened more opportunely for them. Longstreet has been given great credit for it, which, however, he never claimed. It was entirely accidental and unforeseen, but in a very brief period it threw the entire left flank of the enemy in a panic.

Longstreet's advance cut off the rear of Buell's brigade of Wood's division, and two brigades of Sheridan's advancing to fill the gap being opened behind Wood. These brigades did not make enough resistance to check the Confederates, whose triple lines could be seen advancing and who now followed the fugitives. Hindman's brigades, diverging to the left, routed the division of Davis and captured 27 guns and over 1000 prisoners. Rosecrans, McCook, and Crittenden were all caught and involved in the confusion of a retreat which soon became a panic. It was not, however, pursued and might have halted and been re-formed within a mile of the field without seeing the enemy. The retreat, however, was continued to Chattanooga. A severe check was sustained by Manigault, who attacked Wilder's brigade. This brigade had two regiments armed with Spencer repeating rifles, and the 29th Ill. serving with it on this occasion, carried the same arm. They occupied a very favorable position on a steep ridge and their fire at close quarters was very severe and drove back the first advance. Then, finding themselves isolated, they presently withdrew from the field.

About this time, Longstreet was sent for by Bragg, who was some distance in rear of Longstreet's present position. The change in the order of battle was explained to Bragg and the route of two divisions of the enemy, and he was requested to draw the forces from the right wing to unite with the left, and move behind Thomas, where a gap of great extent had been opened, and drive him out of his fortified position. Bragg, however, was discouraged, and said "there was no fight left in the right wing." Cheatham's division had not been engaged.

Longstreet's account of the interview states: —

"He [Bragg] did not wait, nor did he express approval or disapproval of the operations of the left wing, but rode for his headquarters at Reed's bridge. There was nothing for the left wing to do but to work along as best it could."

A pause in the fighting now ensued, which the Federals employed in forming a new line for their centre and right with the troops remaining on the field, — Baird, Johnson, Palmer, and Reynolds, — whose positions had not been changed, and Brannan, with fragments of Wood, Negley, and Van Cleve. With these troops a short and very strong line was formed scarcely a mile in extent from right to left, and occupying favorable ground in the forest which gave it protection from artillery fire. In plan the right wing of this line covered two reëntrant angles located on commanding ridges, from which they were able to deliver a plunging fire by volley, the ranks alternating with little exposure.   During the afternoon they were reënforced by two brigades of Granger's division coming up from Rossville. Practically about two-thirds of the army, say 30,000 men under Thomas, here held together in a strong position and stood practically back to back, while he repelled a series of desperate charges by the brigades of Anderson, Deas and Manigault, Gracie, Trigg and Kelley, Gregg, McNair and Fulton; and the five brigades of Longstreet, Kershaw, Humphreys, Law, Robertson and Benning, about 25,000.   Not more than half of these brigades were engaged at any one time.   The bayonet was sometimes used, and men were killed with clubbed muskets.   This was kept up from 2 to 6 P.M., during which time the infantry fire was incessant and tremendous.   About 5 P.M. Longstreet succeeded in getting 11 guns under Williams into position, whence their fire could take in flank and rear the positions of Thomas's four left divisions; but the distance was about 900 yards, and the effect was not immediate.

About 6 P.M. the Confederates on the right flank, who had lain quiet since noon, recovering from their severe punishment in the morning, prepared to make a general advance.   About the same time, Thomas had taken warning from the artillery fire now coming in on his flank and rear and made preparations to withdraw his command.   He had also received orders from Rosecrans to withdraw to Rossville, but had delayed to execute them until the last moment.   It had now come, and had he delayed longer his losses would have been great.   As it was, they were comparatively light.   At some points there were severe struggles and at others there was little resistance, but everywhere his lines were occupied and the triumphant Confederates celebrated their victory with such cheering as is said never to have been heard before.

The table of casualties shows the heaviest percentages of the war.   Deducting the missing, many of whom were prisoners, and also the losses of the cavalry, which were light, the killed and wounded among the infantry and artillery were 14,871 out of 47,520, or over 31 per cent among the Confederates.

CASUALTIES ARMY OF TENN., CHICKAMAUGA, SEPT. 19–20, 1863

CORPS AND DIVISION	BRIGADE	KILLED	WOUNDED	MISSING	TOTAL	STRENGTH
Polk Cheatham	Jackson	55	430	5	490	1,405
	Smith	40	260	7	307	1,200
	Maney	54	315	15	384	1,177
	Wright	44	400	43	483	1,252
	Strahl	19	203	28	250	1,149
	Total	212	1,608	99	1,919	6,183
Polk Hindman	Anderson	80	454	24	558	1,865
	Deas	123	578	28	729	1,942
	Manigault	66	426	47	539	1,914
	Total	269	1,458	99	1,826	5,621
Hill Cleburne	Wood	96	680	2	778	Not giv.
	Polk	52	493	2	547	"
	Deshler	56	366	2	424	1,783
	Total	204	1,539	6	1,749	5,115
Hill Breckenridge	Helm	63	408	35	506	1,485
	Adams	66	269	84	429	1,314
	Stovall	37	232	46	305	970
	Total	166	909	165	1,240	3,769
Walker Gist	Colquitt	49	251	36	336	Not giv.
	Ector	59	239	138	436	"
	Wilson	99	426	80	605	"
	Total	207	916	254	1,377	5,000
Walker Liddell	Govan	73	502	283	858	Not giv.
	Walthall	61	531	196	788	"
	Total	134	1,033	479	1,646	3,175
Buckner Stewart	Bate	63	530	11	604	1,316
	Brown	50	427	4	481	1,412
	Clayton	86	518	15	619	1,446
	Total	199	1,475	30	1,704	4,174
Buckner Preston	Gracie	90	576	2	668	2,128
	Trigg	46	231	4	281	1,536
	Kelly	66	241	3	310	1,136
	Total	202	1,048	9	1,259	4,800

CASUALTIES ARMY OF TENN., CHICKAMAUGA, SEPT. 19–20, 1863

Corps and Division	Brigade	Killed	Wounded	Missing	Total	Strength
Johnson's	Gregg	113	447	17	577	1,436
Reserve	McNair	67	320	54	441	1,291
	Fulton	28	271	74	373	956
	Total	208	1,038	145	1,391	3,683
Longstreet	Law	61	329		390	Not giv.
Hood	Robertson	78	457	35	570	"
	Benning	46	436	6	488	"
	Kershaw	68	419	1	488	"
	Humphreys	20	132		152	"
	Total	273	1,773	4	2,088	6,000
Total Polk's Corps		481	3,066	198	3,745	11,804
Total Hill's Corps		370	2,448	171	2,989	8,884
Total Walker's Corps		341	1,949	733	3,023	8,175
Total Buckner's Corps		401	2,523	39	2,963	8,974
Total Johnson's Div.		208	1,038	145	1,391	3,683
Total Longstreet's Corps		273	1,773	42	2,088	6,000
Total Inf. and Arty.		2,074	12,797	1,328	16,199	47,520
Total Cavalry					250	14,260

CASUALTIES ARMY OF THE CUMBERLAND, CHICKAMAUGA, SEPT. 19–20, 1863

Corps	Division	Killed	Wounded	Missing	Total	Strength
14th	1st	181	794	1,202	2,177	
Corps	2d	66	430	295	791	
Thomas	3d	325	1,652	214	2,191	
	4th	93	685	176	954	
Total	14th Corps	665	3,561	1,888	6,114	22,758
20th	1st	124	720	405	1,349	
Corps	2d	148	940	554	1,642	
McCook	3d	151	939	276	1,366	
Total	20th Corps	423	2,699	1,235	4,357	13,372
21st	1st	132	744	194	1,070	
Corps	2d	134	1,031	203	1,368	
Crittenden	3d	56	604	302	962	
Total	21st Corps	322	2,382	699	3,403	14,190
Reserve	Granger	215	976	631	1,822	5,479
Total Inf. and Arty.		1,625	9,618	4,453	15,696	55,799
Total Cavalry		32	136	300	468	9,842

Among the Federal infantry and artillery the killed and wounded were 11,243 out of 55,799, or an average of about 21 per cent. No returns are given of the Confederate losses in the cavalry, but they were very light in the Federal cavalry, only 32 killed and 136 wounded, and there is no reason to suppose them any heavier among the Confederates. Apparently the forest paralyzed the cavalry of both armies.

Very many of the reports of the Confederate brigadiers state the number of men engaged, and these statements, excluding cooking details, ambulance men, and stragglers, are more exact than the official returns, and are used in estimating the percentages of killed and wounded. In Gist's and Hood's divisions only no figures are given, and here estimates have been made in round numbers.

There is much discrepancy in the reports of the two commanders as to the guns, small arms, and prisoners taken. Bragg reports 51 guns and 15,000 stand of small-arms. Rosecrans admits but 36 guns and 8450 small-arms, which is more probably correct. The Confederates were in the habit of exchanging their inferior guns and small-arms on the field for the better ones of the enemy, leaving the old in their places. Some of these found on the field were by mistake assumed to be captured. A list of the 51 reported captured is given in the reports with the manufacturers' marks, and of these 15 appear as of Confederate make. Of prisoners, Bragg reports 8000, while Rosecrans admits but 4750. No accurate returns were made of the prisoners captured. The numbers were largely guesswork, the same prisoners being often claimed by more than one command. There is no reason to doubt the accuracy of Rosecrans's report. It gives, also, some interesting statistics of the ammunition expended which was but 7325 rounds of artillery and 2,650,000 of infantry. The wooded character of the field is shown in the comparatively small amount of artillery ammunition which is said to have been "12,625 less than was expended at Stone River," and is less than one-fourth of the Federal expenditure at Gettysburg.

On the morning of the 21st the army under Thomas was in position on Missionary Ridge, about Rossville, five miles in rear of the field of the day before. Here it took position and awaited attack all day, but none was made. Longstreet reports that he advised crossing the Tennessee River and moving upon Rosecrans's communications, and that Bragg approved and ordered Polk's wing to take the lead, while his wing cared for the wounded and policed the field. The army, however, was in such confusion and need of ammunition that it was dark before the rear of Polk's corps was stretched out upon the road, and Longstreet's march was postponed until the 22d. During the night Thomas withdrew into the city, which was already partially fortified, and was now easily made impregnable.

Bragg followed on the 22d and took position in front of him, Longstreet's scheme of moving across the Tennessee River on Rosecrans's communications he deemed impracticable and dropped it. The town was not invested closely, but position was taken on Missionary Ridge and Lookout Mountain, about three miles out, with the intention of compelling the evacuation of Chattanooga by cutting it off from its base of supplies at Stevenson, Ala.

The shortest and best road came via Jasper, crossed the river at Kelley's Ferry, and, recrossing at Brown's Ferry, found itself directly opposite Chattanooga on the north side of the river, about 40 miles from Stevenson. But this road could not be used. Below Kelley's Ferry it skirted the river and was commanded by small-arms from the south side. This compelled the enemy to cross Walden's Ridge to get by, adding many miles to their journey over exceedingly rough country.

The importance of holding strongly the country between the two ferries, Kelley's and Browns's, seems never to have been appreciated by either Bragg or Longstreet, who had charge of the left wing of the army. The duty was confided to a single small brigade, Law's, of Hood's division, which was sent around the toe of Lookout Mountain for the purpose. A full division at least should have guarded so important a point, and one so exposed.[1]

---

[1] It was about this time that Gen. W. F. Smith, known in the U. S. Army as "Baldy" Smith, was assigned to the Federal army, as chief engineer. He superintended the execution of the skilful strategic moves, previously designed by Rosecrans, by which the blockade of Chattanooga was broken. Also those by which Grant on Nov. 25 so easily, and with such little loss, routed Bragg at Chattanooga.

The opportunity to blockade the wagon traffic was not at once understood by the Confederates, and it was Oct. 11 before it was fully enforced. After that date wagons were often eight days in bringing a load from Stevenson, and reduced rations were issued to the Federals. Wheeler's cavalry in a raid had destroyed most of the transportation of the 14th corps, but was itself nearly destroyed by the opportunity of plundering the wagons. Couriers reported that "from Bridgeport to the foot of the mountains the mud is up to the horses' bellies." On the 6th Rosecrans reported "the possession of the river is a *sine qua non* to the holding of Chattanooga." Reconnoissances and preparations were made, and on the night of the 27th a flotilla of pontoons, carrying about 1500 men under Hazen, was floated down and landed at Brown's Ferry. On the north side a force was marched by land to meet them, and a pontoon bridge was built. By morning a brigade with artillery was established and fortifying itself in a strong position on the southern bank. Before Bragg could concentrate enough to attack them, Hooker appeared, coming from Bridgeport, with the 11th and 12th corps of the Army of the Potomac. These had been hurried out to reënforce Rosecrans, when the Federals realized that Longstreet had reënforced Bragg.

This, of course, put an end to the contemplated attack, but, with very questionable judgment, Bragg ordered a night attack upon a portion of Geary's division of the 12th corps (about 1500 strong with four guns), which had encamped at a point called Wauhatchie. This was about three miles from Brown's Ferry, where Hooker, with the remainder of his force, had united with the force under Hazen.

THE BATTLE OF WAUHATCHIE

Night attacks are specially valuable against troops who have been defeated and are retreating. They are of little value under any other circumstances. The war, too, had now reached a stage where men had become impossible to replace in the Confederate ranks. Nothing could be more injudicious than to sacrifice them, even for a success, which would have no effect upon the campaign.

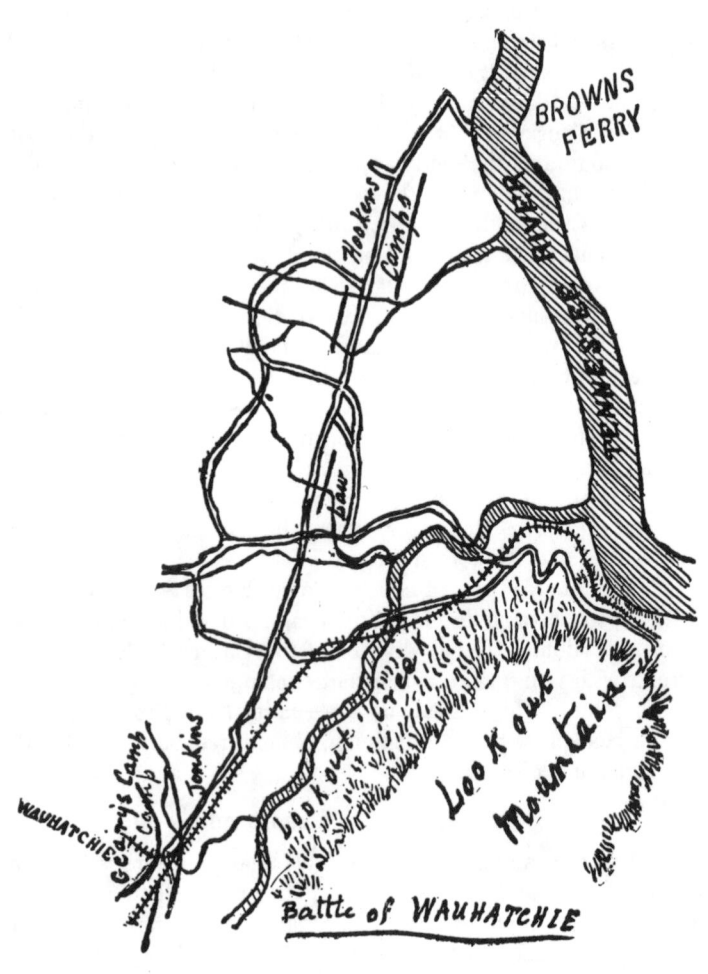

Battle of WAUHATCHIE

That was the case in this instance. Near at hand, the Federals had double or treble the force of the Confederates, and the camp to be attacked was two miles within the Federal lines. The attack must be made, the fruit of it be gathered, and withdrawal accomplished before the light of dawn; for with the dawn, or even before it, an overwhelming force of the enemy would cut off the withdrawal.

The only troops available for the attack were four brigades of Hood's division, under Jenkins, which had been brought around the high toe of Lookout Mountain. This road was exposed to batteries on the north side of the river and could only be used at night. Three of the brigades, Law, Benning, and Robertson, had suffered severely, both at Gettysburg and Chickamauga, and scarcely averaged 700 men each. These brigades were ordered to cross Lookout Creek, and seize the road between Hooker's camp near Brown's Ferry and the camp of Geary to be attacked. The remaining brigade was Jenkins's own, now under Bratton, and was about 1800 strong.

Law, with two regiments, had opposed Hazen's landing on the 27th, and skirmished on the 28th with the advance of the 11th and 12th corps under Hooker, but had now withdrawn across Lookout Creek. From the mountains above, a fine view was afforded of the valley with Hooker's camp at the north end, and Geary's three miles behind it. Jenkins had been summoned before sundown to view it and get some idea of the topography. He returned after dark and joining Law discussed the enterprise, which Law strongly advised against. The orders, however, were peremptory and there was no superior at hand to appeal to. The moon was about full, and soon after dark Law moved with his brigade across the bridge and, after some time spent in exploration, took position on a ridge nearly parallel to the road between Brown's Ferry and Wauhatchie, and some 50 to 150 yards distant. It was about two miles below the camp of Geary's division, and less than a mile above the encampments of the 11th and 12th corps. The Texas brigade reporting to Law, he placed two of its regiments on his left and one on his right, and sent the 4th regiment to hold the bridge in his rear. Benning's brigade was sent to ambush the road farther ahead.

This effort to hold the road against efforts to reënforce Geary might have been much more effective had Law thrown his brigades boldly across the road, with perhaps two brigades in his front line supported by the third in a second line. He probably failed to adopt this policy only because he was too conscious of his weakness. His retreat was more assured and easier from the position which he took. And, in view of the risks attendant on the venture, and the small chances of success, it may have been the more prudent course.

In the placing of Law's command there had been a few picket shots about 10 o'clock, which had caused Geary's command to be put under arms and to be unusually alert. Soon after midnight their own picket challenged and was shot down, upon which the camp was alarmed, all lights extinguished, and the troops formed in line. The weather was somewhat cloudy, making the moonlight fitful. Jenkins endeavored to restrain his men from firing as they deployed before the camp, but it was in vain, and gradually the regiments extending on each side overlapped the Federal line and awaited an attack on the Federal rear by Lt.-Col. T. M. Logan, with a force of sharp-shooters, who had passed around to the rear. Their attack was to be a signal for a general charge. About an hour had now elapsed.

It was just at this juncture that Jenkins gave orders to withdraw. Law had notified him that the enemy had passed his position, which was a mistake. The road had been open all the while, but no troops had passed. On the opening of the attack upon Geary there had been a general alarm in all the camps below, and several brigades had been ordered to go to his relief. The first brigade passing Law's ambush received volleys which, in the darkness, did little harm but threw their lines into confusion. Forming then parallel to the road, the Federals charged Law's position, but were at first repulsed. Re-forming, and extending their lines, Steinwehr's division made a second attempt, but Smith's brigade, which struck Law's front, was again repulsed with heavy loss. The men, however, did not on this occasion fall back to the foot of the hill, but rallied in the darkness of the woods, near at hand, until a part of the 136th N.Y., which had overlapped Law's front, had appeared in his rear. The attack being then renewed was successful all along the line, and Law fell back toward the bridge, not being pursued. Robertson, who had had eight casualties, and Benning, who had had none, also withdrew, as the retreat of Law compelled.

Meantime, in the confusion of the night a column of two Federal brigades, ordered to go direct to Geary's help, had halted without orders, and was overlooked for nearly two hours. Owing to this oversight, and the non-pursuit of Law, both he and Jenkins were able to cross the bridge before daylight.

No artillery was used by the Confederates, but Knaps's battery of four guns, with Geary, was severely engaged at close quarters, expending 224 rounds and losing 3 killed and 19 wounded.

Geary's total casualties were : —

34 killed, 174 wounded, 8 missing: total 216.

These all occurred in Greene's and Cobham's brigades about 1600 strong. The Federal casualties in the brigades opposing Law were : —

45 killed, 150 wounded, 7 missing: total 204.

These occurred principally in Tyndale's and Orland Smith's brigades. The aggregate was 420. The Confederate casualties reported are as follows : —

Law: 3 killed, 19 wounded, 30 missing: total 52.
Jenkins: 31 killed, 286 wounded, 39 missing: total 356. Aggregate 408.

The character of the attack by Jenkins's brigade, and of the defence by Greene's and Cobham's, aided by the battery, had been excellent. The casualties were heavy, and included many officers distinguished among their comrades for conduct. Nothing less could have been expected, and nothing materially more could be hoped for, and such considerations should have forbidden this adventure. The guarding of the rear by Law proved a success, though due to a Federal mistake, not to his disposition. Only about half his force was engaged. It repulsed two attacks, but was swept away by the third. The enemy, however, made no advance and a free road, left open until after daylight, provided an escape for all four brigades from one of the most foolhardy adventures of the war. A Court of Inquiry in the 11th corps was held, which found that Krzyzanowski's brigade had halted without authority and against the orders of the division commander, when under orders to go to Geary's assistance.

These operations left Rosecrans with free communications by the shortest and best roads, and at liberty to receive all the reënforcements coming to him. Besides the 11th and 12th corps, under Hooker, already near at hand, it was known that Grant was bringing up a large force under Sherman from Memphis, and it was clear that within 30 days a force would be concentrated against us sufficient to overwhelm us. Rosecrans had now converted Chattanooga into a citadel, impregnable to assault by storm, within which he could confidently await the accumulation of whatever force was needed.

The burden of the attack was upon us. We must promptly take the aggressive, and meet and defeat, either Grant and Sherman approaching from the west, or Burnside, near at hand and threatening on the east, and be able then to reconcentrate our army against the other adversaries. President Davis had recently paid a visit to the army, which, it was known, was dissatisfied with Bragg as a commander, but after some investigation had decided to sustain him. Bragg, accordingly, had the decision of the question what should be done.

On Nov. 3 he issued orders for Longstreet's corps, with Wheeler's cavalry, to attack Burnside's corps at Knoxville, which was to be assailed at the same time by a force of perhaps 4000 men under Ransom, coming from southwest Virginia. With the remainder of his army, Bragg proposed to hold his present lines, in front of Chattanooga, during the absence of Longstreet's division. As these lines occupied a concave front of fully eight miles against an enemy concentrated within four, they were necessarily weak and unable to quickly reënforce threatened points. Longstreet pointed out their disadvantages and urged a withdrawal of the remainder of the army to a strong defensive position behind the Chickamauga River, and that his own force for the attack of Burnside at Knoxville should be increased to 20,000 men, to insure quick and easy work, and save any dependence upon the hypothetical force from south-west Virginia. Bragg, however, overruled all suggestions, and Longstreet was put in motion on Nov. 4 for Knoxville, with Wheeler's two divisions (four brigades) of cavalry.

The result was what might have been expected, and we may anticipate and record it, briefly, before following Longstreet in his adventure against Knoxville.

THE BATTLE OF CHATTANOOGA OR MISSIONARY RIDGE

On Oct. 22 Grant had reached Chattanooga and superseded Rosecrans. By Nov. 20 he had concentrated at Chattanooga about 65,000 infantry and artillery present for duty, and provided siege artillery for the forts about Chattanooga. Bragg, meanwhile, had further reduced his force by sending Bushrod Johnson with two brigades, 2500 men, to Knoxville, who joined Longstreet just too late to be of any service. This had reduced his force to about 40,000 infantry present for duty, greatly handicapped by their position in the long concave exterior line. On Nov. 22 Grant took the aggressive and set on foot attacks upon Bragg's extreme right and left flanks. On the morning of the 24th Hooker turned the extreme left flank at Wauhatchie, in the valley of Lookout Creek, by climbing the slope of Lookout Mountain to the foot of the palisade. This palisade is a precipice dividing the top of the mountain from the slopes forming its toe. These were held by one brigade of Bragg's infantry who were advanced some distance down the slope. Advancing along the foot of the precipice he took the Confederate positions on the toe of the mountain in reverse. They were also exposed to artillery fire from the front across the river and were thus surely driven out, about as fast as Hooker's men could pick their way along the steep slopes at the foot of the precipice, which bounded the mountain on the west.

Ten miles away on the right flank, Chickamauga Creek emptied into the Tennessee by two mouths, and, in the eastern mouth of the creek, Grant had concealed a number of pontoons, and behind the hills north of the river was Sherman with over three divisions. On the morning of Nov. 24 a bridge was built across the

Tennessee and 12,000 men were brought across and made a lodgment on the east end of Missionary Ridge, before Bragg was aware of it.

At sunrise, on the 25th, both Hooker and Sherman were ordered to attack.   When Hooker advanced it was discovered that during the night of the 24th, the Confederate forces had abandoned Lookout Mountain and withdrawn all of their men across Chattanooga Creek, burning the bridge.   Hooker followed in pursuit with three divisions, Osterhaus's, Cruft's, and Geary's, about 10,000 men.   About four hours were lost in rebuilding the bridge.   Beyond it, only a feeble resistance was developed near Rossville on the western extremity of Missionary Ridge by two regiments of Stewart's division.   Stevenson's division, which had held Lookout Mountain, had been transferred during the night to the extreme right to oppose Sherman.   Hooker placed Osterhaus on the right of the ridge, Cruft on the ridge (which being narrow he occupied with three lines), and Geary on the left or front of the ridge.   In this formation he advanced almost unopposed and with slight loss until he connected about sundown with Johnson's division of the 14th corps, which had formed a part of Thomas's attack upon the centre in the afternoon, as will presently be described.

Sherman had had the entire day of the 24th practically unmolested to establish himself on the northern extremity of Missionary Ridge, and reënforcements from Chattanooga had reached him in the afternoon.   Soon after sunrise on the 25th he moved to the attack.   A wide depression in the ridge separated the portion of it which he occupied from that held by Bragg.   Here, during the afternoon and night, Hardee had intrenched Cleburne's division and prepared to make a desperate stand.   Sherman's men, fresh from Vicksburg, attacked with great vigor, and being repulsed, renewed the attack several times with no better success.   Sherman, in his report, denies that they were repulsed, but says: —

"Not so.   The real attacking columns of Gen. Corse, Col. Loomis, and Gen. Smith were not repulsed.   They engaged in a close struggle all day, persistently, stubbornly, and well."

This is one way of stating it.   Their charges were all driven back, with losses more or less severe, to the nearest places affording cover. From these they kept up musketry fire, with little loss or execution, all the rest of the day. Some reënforcements sent on the flanks did similarly, and before three o'clock in the afternoon Sherman's whole force had been fought to a standstill, and Cleburne held his position intact and with very little fighting the rest of the day.

But Grant's third attack, the one upon the centre, was yet to be made. It was to be upon Missionary Ridge and the topography requires some description. The ridge is here an average of some 200 feet high, with steep slopes, averaging on each side fully 500 yards wide. Many ravines and swales intersect the surface, which had been wooded but was now recently cleared, leaving many stumps. When the position was first occupied, a line of breastworks had been built at the foot of the slopes, between one and a half and two miles from the Federal lines. Later some unfinished breastworks were erected halfway up the hill.

The Confederate engineers now seemed at a loss to decide exactly where to make their final stand, and only at the last did they decide to make it at the proper place, at the top of the hill. But with it they made the fatal mistake of dividing their forces, already too small, and putting one-half in their skirmish line, at the bottom of the hill, and the other half at the top. Very few of the Confederate reports of this battle have been preserved, but many interesting details are given in papers, left by Gen. Manigault of S.C., who commanded a brigade in Hindman's division. The construction of the works was only begun on the 23d, with a very insufficient supply of tools. The ground was hard and rocky, and when the assault was made on the 25th, the trenches were but half completed, and only afforded protection to the lower part of the body. The Confederate engineer who laid it out had orders to locate the line upon the highest ground, and blindly obeyed. At many places this left numerous approaches, up ravines and swales, entirely covered from the fire of the breastworks. Manigault persuaded the engineer, who complained of having too much to do, to allow him to lay out his own line, and at such places he located the line below the crest so as to sweep the whole approach. Brigades to the right and left did not do this, and there were many places where an assaulting column could approach within a short distance without receiving any fire.

The fatal mistake of dividing the force seems to have been decided on during the night of the 24th, for it was not done until the morning of the 25th. One-half of each brigade was then sent to the line at the foot of the hill, and the remainder to the line at the top. This disposition of forces was made in all the troops on the ridge, and the number available gave, in each position, only a single rank, with the men about one pace apart. Private instructions were given the superior officers, if attacked by more than a single line of battle, to await the enemy's approach within 200 yards, then to deliver their fire, and retire to the works above. This was an injudicious order, as will be seen—impracticable of successful execution after the enemy had gotten that near in such large force.

About noon the enemy began to form in masses in front of our centre, about two miles away. About two o'clock these masses deployed and formed two lines of battle, with a front of at least two and a half miles. After completing their arrangements these moved within a mile of our lower works and halted. Behind these two lines a reserve force, apparently equal in number to one of them, was disposed at intervals in close columns of regiments, and followed them some 300 yards in rear. The whole array was preceded by a powerful line of skirmishers deployed at half distances. One could not but be struck with the order and regularity of the movements and the ease with which the Federals preserved their lines. The sight was a grand and impressive one, the like of which had never been seen before by any one who witnessed it.

Manigault writes : —

"I felt no fear for the result, even though the arrangements to repel the attack were not such as I liked, neither did I know at the time that a column of the enemy was at that moment on our left flank and rear, or that our army numbered so few men. I think, however, that I noticed some nervousness among my men as they beheld this grand military spectacle, and I heard remarks which showed that some uneasiness existed, and that they magnified the host in their view to at least double their number."

The reference made to the "column of the enemy at that moment on our left flank and rear" is to the three divisions under Hooker, advancing from Rossville on both sides of Missionary Ridge. They were due to reach the field about sundown.

For some time after the last halt of the enemy there was an ominous silence over the whole field, except for an occasional distant cannon-shot. Sherman's battle, from one to two miles to the right, had been fought out. Hooker was marching cautiously unopposed, and, by a sort of tacit understanding, even the skirmishers in front paused in contemplation of the coming storm.

The attack on the Confederate centre was assigned to Thomas, who had been in readiness all the morning, but was still delayed by Grant, who hesitated to order it until either Sherman had turned our right flank or Hooker had turned our left. Hooker was delayed and does not seem to have been heard from. Sherman had been fought to a standstill; but thinking that he saw reënforcements moving from the Confederate centre against Sherman, Grant directed Thomas to give the signal. It was a dozen guns, fired by the enemy, and was followed by the opening of their whole line, and soon after by our own guns from Missionary Ridge directed at the dark masses of their troops. The effect of a plunging fire, however, from our high elevation, was distinctly less than it would have been upon a plain, and when the enemy's lines were set in motion, which soon followed, it was apparent, at a glance, that our artillery was utterly inadequate to the task of stopping the great force before us.

Meanwhile one-half of the whole Confederate force was under secret orders to retreat when the enemy arrived within 200 yards, and the enemy's generals were themselves under orders from Grant not to advance beyond our skirmish line. Manigault thus describes what took place: —

"When the enemy had arrived within about 200 yards our men gave their volley, and a well-directed and fatal one it proved, but then followed a scene of confusion rarely witnessed, and only equalled at a later hour on that day. The order had been issued to retire, but many did not hear it, owing to the reports of their own pieces and the deafening roar of artillery. Others supposed their comrades flying and refused to do likewise. Some

feared to retire up the hill, exposed to a heavy fire in their rear, feeling
certain, as their movements must be slow, that they would be killed or
wounded before reaching their friends above. All order was lost, and each
striving to save himself took the shortest direction for the summit. The
enemy seeing the confusion and retreat moved up their first line at a
double quick and came over the breastworks, but I could see some of
our brave fellows firing into the enemy's faces and at last falling overpowered. . . .

"The troops from below at last reached the works exhausted and
breathless, the greater portion so demoralized that they rushed to the rear
to place the ridge itself between them and the enemy. It required the utmost efforts of myself and other officers to prevent this, which we finally
succeeded in doing. Many fell, broken down from over-exertion, and
became deathly sick or fainted. I noticed some instances of slight hem-
orrhage, and it was fifteen minutes before the nervous systems of those
men were so restored as to be able to draw a trigger with steadiness."

In the meantime, Grant had observed the battle from his
commanding position in the rear. As above said, he thought he
had seen Bragg detaching troops from his centre, opposite
Thomas, and sending them to reënforce the right opposite
Sherman, and many Federal reports, ever since, have fallen into
the same error. But all are wrong. Sherman had been fought
to a standstill, and Cleburne had no need for reënforcements.
Also, Thomas's preparations could be seen too plainly. So the
elaborate strategy, which had sent Sherman to turn Bragg's
right, came to naught at the fighting point. Grant had seen,
with much satisfaction, the Confederate lower line of intrenchments in the possession of his forces. But, as he looked, he was
surprised to see, at a number of points, that his men had not
halted as he had ordered, but were beginning to climb the slope
and advance against the fortified line at the crest. He asked
angrily: "Who ordered those men up the hill?" and, when all
present disclaimed it, said: "Some one will suffer for it, if it
turns out badly." But the men themselves, having reached the
designated position, were able to take a more practical view of
it than the general himself at a distance.

It would be impossible for the troops to remain in the new
position under the fire of the Confederate line at the top of the
hill. There was nothing to do but to follow the fugitives and
endeavor to mingle with them. As the pursuers advanced, they

soon appreciated the fact that the ravines and swales afforded more or less protection from fire, and the whole line soon divided and concentrated itself on about six separate lines of advance. Not one of these was on the front held by Manigault's brigade. Every attempted advance here had been met with fire, before which it either fell back to cover, or disappeared to the right or left.   Next on the left was Patton Anderson's brigade of Mississippians, and next on the right was Deas's brigade of Alabamians. A large number of Federals soon found shelter behind some overhanging rocks in Deas's front within 20 yards of his line of battle. Manigault turned a gun upon them and they were driven from view, but beyond a turn of the rock, they got a lodgment in large numbers, so that the division commander called for and took Manigault's largest regiment to reënforce Deas.

Meanwhile an officer from the left reported that the enemy had broken the Miss. brigade, and, going to the left to get a view, Manigault saw the Federals in possession of the Miss. battery and the brigade retreating in disorder.   The Federals soon turned the captured guns upon his line, enfilading a portion of it, and about the same time the Alabamians on the right also gave way.   His own men on the flanks were still fighting well, but the centre, the part being enfiladed, even now wavering, would soon melt away.

A ridge some 500 yards to the rear offered favorable ground for a rally, and, seeing that all was lost and to check the fugitives impossible, he commanded a retreat, directing the officers to rally the men upon that ridge.   A rapid run-for-it was successfully made, with some loss under a heavy fire, but about two-thirds of what was left of the brigade were rallied on the ridge, and were soon joined by the remnants of the Ala. and Miss. brigades.   Manigault saved two of his guns, but two were captured.   The enemy seemed contented with his success and did not pursue, and the firing ceased all along the line except at the extreme right, where Cleburne and the troops opposing Sherman still held their ground until withdrawn after dark.

Considering how utterly the centre of his line was routed, Bragg made a surprisingly good retreat, the enemy not pursuing vigorously.   Bragg crossed the Chickamauga that night, de-

stroying the bridges behind him.   On the 26th, he retreated to
Ringgold, where on the 27th he repulsed a pursuing force which
then retired.   The army then withdrew to Dalton, where, five
days later, Bragg, at his own request, was relieved of the command.   He lost his campaign primarily when he allowed Rosecrans to reopen the short line of his communications.   Sending
Longstreet to Knoxville while holding such advanced lines cannot be excused or palliated.   It was a monumental failure to
appreciate the glaring weakness of his position.   His men never
really fought except against Sherman on his extreme right, and
there they were victorious and retreated unmolested after night.
He was simply marched out from his position on Lookout, and
he would have been also marched off of Missionary Ridge by
Hooker, had not Grant grown impatient.   The unwise division
of his forces had put it in Grant's power to defeat him by marching with at least 50 per cent less than the usual fighting.

Bragg's casualties were but 361 killed and 2160 wounded,
about the average of a single corps or one-sixth of those at
Chickamauga.   But he lost 40 guns.   Grant's losses were also
but small, on Lookout Mountain and on Missionary Ridge.
They were heaviest where Sherman attacked Cleburne's and
Breckenridge's divisions, but even there where the fighting was
prolonged most of the day, there were no such casualties as there
had been at Chickamauga.

Grant's total was 753 killed, 4722 wounded, 349 missing.
Total 5824.

Livermore estimates the forces engaged on each side as follows : —

Effective Federal infantry and artillery, ...   56,359.
Effective Confederate infantry and artillery, ...   40,929.

THE KNOXVILLE CAMPAIGN

On Nov. 3, as has been told, Longstreet was ordered to
march against Burnside in E. Tenn., with McLaws's and Hood's
divisions of infantry, Alexander's and Leyden's battalions of
artillery (of 23 and 12 guns) and five brigades of cavalry under
Wheeler with 12 guns.   This force numbered about 15,000, of
which about 5000 were cavalry and 10,000 infantry and artillery.

Coöperation was promised from southwest Va. by a force of about 4000 under Ransom, but it was too late in starting, and its infantry and artillery only reached Longstreet on his retreat northward after the siege of Knoxville.

It was designed to move Longstreet by rail from Chattanooga to Sweetwater, Tenn., within 40 miles of Knoxville. This, it was hoped, could be easily done by the 7th or 8th. The artillery and McLaws's division were marched to Tyner's Station on Nov. 4, and Hood's division to the tunnel through Missionary Ridge on the night of the 5th. Trains, however, could only be furnished to carry them to Sweetwater by the 12th, and it was the night of the 14th before a pontoon bridge could be thrown across the river at Huff's Ferry near London, and the advance upon Knoxville, 29 miles off, actively undertaken. The men and guns of my own battalion were carried on a train of flat cars on the 10th, the train taking over 12 hours to make the 60 miles. The cannoneers were required to pump water for the engine and to cut up fence rails for fuel along the route, and the horses were driven by the roads.

The forces of Burnside at Knoxville consisted of four small divisions, two of the 9th corps, and two of the 23d, about 12,000 infantry and artillery and 8500 cavalry. The cavalry, during the coming siege, for the most part held the south side of the river, where they erected strong works on the commanding hills and were little molested, as our own cavalry was generally kept on the north bank on our left flank. Burnside was ordered not to oppose Longstreet's advance, but to retreat before him and draw him on, as far as possible from Chattanooga. On Sunday, Nov. 15, Longstreet crossed and advanced as far as Lenoirs; Burnside falling back, skirmishing. On the 16th, an effort was made to bring him to battle at Campbell's Station, but only a skirmish resulted, in which the Federal loss was 31 killed, 211 wounded, and 76 missing, and the Confederates 22 killed, 152 wounded. Burnside withdrew into Knoxville that night and Longstreet followed and drew up before it on Nov. 17. On the 18th, the outposts were driven in and close reconnoissances made, in which the Federal Gen. Sanders was killed. He had been recently promoted, was an officer of much promise, and a

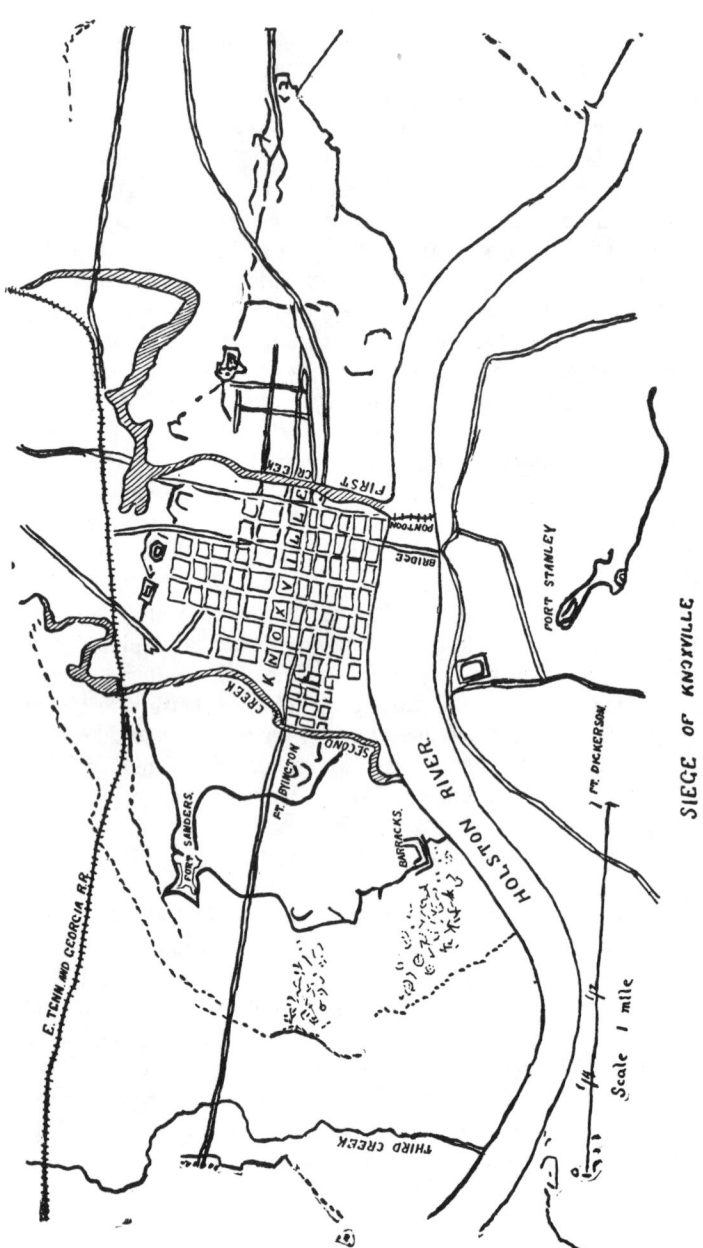

SIEGE OF KNOXVILLE

relative of President Davis.   The reconnoissances developed the
enemy holding a very strong defensive line with but a single
weak point.   This was the northwest salient angle where their
north and south line, running perpendicular to the river below
the town, made a right angle and turning to the east ran parallel
with the river to the northeast of the town.   There it rested,
behind an extensive inundation of First Creek, upon a strong
enclosed work on Temperance Hill, mounting 12 guns, with
outlying works upon Mabry's and Flint Hills.

These had been built, with several other works, during the
prior Confederate occupation, and one, enclosing three sides of a
rectangle about 125 by 95 feet with bastion fronts, the rear being
open, had been nearly completed at the northwest salient angle
above referred to.   This was now called Fort Sanders, after the
general killed on the 18th, and every exertion was used to complete and strengthen it, all able-bodied inhabitants of the town
being impressed, both white and black, to aid in labor upon the
fortifications.   The Confederate engineer who laid out this work
had injudiciously turned the salient angle of its northwest bastion
directly toward the valley of Third Creek, just at the point where
this valley allowed an approach, within 120 yards, completely
covered from the fire of the fort.   A convex crest of the valley
curved from this point to the east and south, and sheltered a
large territory, affording space for many brigades to be held
completely under cover, within distances of from 150 to 400
yards of the enemy's intrenchments.   These conditions made it
the most favorable point for attack, and, indeed, the only one
at all favorable north of the river.

A third of the enemy's northern front was protected by inundations of First and Second creeks, across which his guns had
open sweep for a mile.   To make a large circuit, and turn it,
would be to abandon our communications with our base of supplies.   An attack upon either of his short flanks running back
to the river would be enfiladed from the south bank.   Two
strong enclosed works, Fort Comstock and Battery Wiltsie,
covered the only approach between the inundations.

The theory of Longstreet's expedition was that he should take
a much superior force and make short work of it.   In fact, we

had an inferior force of infantry and artillery, until after the arrival of Johnson's and Gracie's brigades, which will be referred to presently. The cavalry on neither side took any part in the siege operations. We had now to take the offensive which made the task harder, but yet we seem to have stood a fair chance to carry Fort Sanders had we made an attack with all our force soon after our arrival. But every day of delay added to the strength of the enemy's breastworks, and in a very few days he had an interior line which might have successfully resisted, even had Fort Sanders been captured. It is now to tell how the 10 days were consumed which were allowed to intervene before the attack. By that time a second line had been constructed which might or might not have survived the loss of the first.

The 20th saw our own line finished with batteries erected to repel any offensive movements of the enemy, and, incidentally, enfilade some of the lines of Fort Sanders, which was already recognized as the most feasible point of attack. Had the advantage of an early attack been fully realized, it might have been organized and delivered on the 21st, or at latest by the 22d. But on that day one of our staff-officers, who had crossed the Holston River on our right flank and reconnoitred the country, had found it possible to locate a battery upon a high hill close to the river, giving an advantageous line of fire upon Fort Sanders at a distance of 2400 yards.

Longstreet directed this to be done, and the attack postponed for it. A flat boat and some wire were procured, a ferry fixed up, Law's and Robertson's brigades of infantry and Parker's rifle battery was crossed, and, by working all night of the 24th, it was possible by noon of the 25th to report as ready to open an enfilade fire on Fort Sanders. But the loss of this time and the transfer of this infantry and artillery to the south side of the river were both ill-advised. Our rifle ammunition was defective in quality, our supply of it was quite limited, and the range was too great for effective work under such conditions.

Longstreet felt too the need of the two brigades sent across the river, and, hearing of the coming of Bushrod Johnson's and Gracie's brigades, he decided to await their arrival expected the night of the 26th. They brought an effective force of about

2600 men, but they did not actually arrive until the night of the 28th, and were not able to render any service.

That night Longstreet was joined by Gen. Leadbetter, Bragg's Chief Engineer, who had been at Knoxville during the Confederate occupation, and being the oldest military engineer in the Confederate service, was supposed to be the most efficient. He was a graduate of West Point of 1836, the class ahead of Bragg's. Coming to Longstreet, as he did, with the prestige of being on the staff of the commanding-general, and especially charged with the decision of all questions of military engineering, it is perhaps not strange that Longstreet was quick to adopt his suggestions, and these, it will be seen, robbed him of most of his few remaining chances of victory.

On Thursday, the 26th, the attack having already been postponed to await the arrival of Johnson's brigades, Leadbetter and Longstreet rode on a reconnoissance around the enemy's entire position. Leadbetter pronounced Fort Sanders to be assailable, but expressed a preference for an attack upon Mabry's Hill. This was the enemy's extreme right flank, and was undoubtedly the strongest portion of his whole line, besides being the farthest removed and the most inaccessible. In fact our own pickets had been advanced but little beyond Second Creek, and Leadbetter's opinion was based upon very imperfect and distant views.

It was therefore determined to drive in the enemy's pickets, and make a better reconnoissance on Friday, the 27th. Meanwhile, so certain was Leadbetter of the advantage of a change in the point of attack, that Parker's battery was ordered to be withdrawn from the south side of the Holston on Thursday night. On Friday the cavalry was called on to drive in the enemy's pickets, and Longstreet and Leadbetter, accompanied by the leading generals, made a thorough reconnoissance of our left flank. The attack upon Mabry's Hill was unanimously pronounced impossible, Leadbetter himself concurring. On the way back the party stopped opposite Fort Sanders, and while watching it with glasses, saw a man cross the ditch in front of the northwest salient, showing the depth of it at that point as less than five feet. This encouraged a hope that the ditch of the fort would not be found a formidable obstacle, and as there was now no alternative, and Leadbetter was urgent against further delay, the attack was ordered at noon on the 28th, this time being necessary to return Parker's battery to its enfilading position on the south side, whence Leadbetter had had it withdrawn the night before.

At noon the next day all was ready, but the day was rainy, and very unfavorable for artillery practice, so Longstreet again decided to postpone the attack until the next morning, the 29th.

Some howitzers had been raised upon skids, so as to permit fire with small charges at high elevations, as mortars, in order to probe behind the parapets of the fort. It had been ordered that the opening of these mortars should be the signal for the advance of a large number of skirmishers, who should occupy the enemy's rifle pits within 120 to 250 yards of the fort, enveloping completely its north and west fronts and keeping down the fire, either from its embrasures or parapets. After some practice by the mortars and the sharpshooters, the mortars would suspend, and allow the rifled guns and others to fire to get their ranges. When all had gotten ranges, a rapid fire by both guns and mortars, 34 in all, would begin, concentrated upon the fort as long as seemed necessary. Its cessation would be the signal for the advance of the storming force of two brigades, in columns of regiments, supported by adjacent brigades upon the flanks. If the passage of the ditch was found difficult, the pioneers with spade and picks were expected to rapidly cut small steps in the slopes which would enable the men to swarm over. The sharpshooters and the storming column itself could be relied upon to keep down the fire of the fort on the men in the ditches while this was being done.

The garrison of the fort, as afterward shown, did not exceed 220, including the artillery, and could be overpowered as quickly as they could be reached. It is now to show how all preparations were thrown away and all advantages sacrificed for the illusive merits of a night attack, decided upon by Longstreet after dark on the 28th. Leadbetter was spending the night with him, but whether he suggested or acquiesced was never disclosed.

About 9 P.M. that night I received notice that the plan of attack would be changed and that neither the rifles across the river, the howitzers rigged as mortars, nor any other of the 34 guns arranged to fire on the fort would be used, except to fire a signal. Several days had been spent in preparation for a cannonade, with all our guns concentrated on the small area enclosed by the fort, and now it was all to be given up as well as all to be hoped for from the fire by daylight of a half mile of sharpshooters within from 120 to 250 yards. The fort had no embrasure on its west front and its fire would have to be over the parapets and much exposed.

The advance was intended to be a surprise, and the signal guns were ordered to be fired just before dawn, that the approach of the column might not be visible. There was little time for consultation for it was ordered that at moon rise, about 10 P.M., the enemy's picket line should be taken and occupied by our sharpshooters, and the troops should be under arms.

Soon after 10 P.M., there was a general advance by our picket lines on both sides of Fort Sanders, and after some two hours of sharp fighting, 50 or 60 prisoners had been taken, the enemy's pit occupied, and they did not have out a picket 20 yards from the fort. Lt. Benjamin, commanding, feeling sure that the attack would be at daylight, required every man to sleep at his post, and one in every four to keep awake as a sentry. During the night an occasional gun was fired with canister or shell at random from the fort. Federal accounts state that our own artillery was also fired during the night, but this is a mistake. Our own troops were being moved and would have been endangered by such a fire.

At the earliest sign of light in eastern sky, three successive guns fired from different batteries gave the signal to the sharpshooters to open fire and for the storming columns to advance. Their shells were visible like meteors in the air and they exploded high above the fort. For a few minutes about a dozen guns poured a hot fire on the fort and into the angle of the lines behind it. This was intended only to encourage the storming columns, and was discontinued in a few minutes. At once the sharpshooters opened their fire upon the parapet, and orders were given the storming columns to move. It had been intended that these should be formed close behind the sharpshooters, within 150 to 200 yards of the fort, but in the darkness this had not been done. The columns each had several hundred yards to go and Johnson's and Gracie's brigades, ordered up in support, had from 800 to 1000.

The storming column was composed of Wofford's Ga. brigade, four regiments, under Col. Ruff on the left, and of two regiments of Humphreys's Miss., and three of Bryan's Ga. brigade on the right. Anderson's Ga. brigade was ordered to support the storming column on the left by an attack on the lines beyond the fort on that side. As the two columns advanced on converging lines, they presently ran into an entanglement of telegraph wires stretched between stumps which threw down the leading files and caused a little delay. But these were soon torn away and with very little loss. Two or three shots each were fired from a barbette gun in the salient, and from an embrasure in the northeast bastion, but with the arrival of the men at the ditch the artillery fire was silenced. The two columns were soon found to have converged in the darkness too much, and being already deep columns, one of four lines and one of five, they simply coalesced in the darkness into a mass whose officers could no longer separate or distinguish their own men. To this mass was presently added Anderson's brigade, ordered to carry the breastworks east of the fort. Through some mistake, some minutes later, they came in from the left, in two lines, where already nine lines were crowding each other. The ditch was found to be from four to eight feet deep, and about twelve feet in width, without any berm at the top of the counterscarp, and with steep sides rendered slippery by freezing weather and the rain of the previous day. Yet many officers and men were able to cross the ditch and scale the parapet, but not in such numbers as to overcome the 150 infantry defending the fort with fine tenacity. A few shells were lighted by Lt. Benjamin and thrown by hand into the ditch as hand grenades, and axes and billets of wood were thrown over the parapets. Lt. Cumming, Adj. of the 16th Ga., made his way through an embrasure with a dozen men, but the party was captured inside. Col. Thomas of the same regiment was killed in the ditch as was also Col. McElroy of the 13th Miss.   Lt.-Col. Fizer of the 17th lost his arm on the parapet and Col. Ruff, commanding Wofford's brigade, was killed on the counterscarp.

Meanwhile fully 20 minutes elapsed and daylight began to make things dimly visible.   Nearly 200 men had gotten into the ditch and not finding it easy to advance, now preferred to surrender.   The fire from the fort had ceased except an occasional musket fired over the parapet exposing only a hand of the man holding it.   But at a point 500 yards to the south of the fort, an offset 200 yards long, running nearly west from the Federal breastworks, gave a fair enfilade fire upon the crowd of men along the counterscarp of the west front of the fort, and from this point the increasing daylight was bringing a fire which rapidly multiplied the casualties.

Longstreet, about this time, was advancing with the brigades of Johnson and Gracie, with those of Jenkins and Benning upon the left, when he received an exaggerated report of the wire entanglement which had been first encountered.   Without a second thought Longstreet ordered the recall.   Johnson begged to be allowed to go on, as also did Jenkins, but Longstreet, giving full faith to the report, forbade.

It is certain that after a little delay the attack would have been renewed, being preceded by a cannonade, and with a storming column provided with tools to cut steps in the scarp and parapet.   But within a half-hour a staff officer of Ransom's arrived with a telegram from President Davis, by way of Bristol, Va., telling of Bragg's defeat on Missionary Ridge on the 25th, and ordering Longstreet to march to join Bragg at Dalton. Vague rumors of this had reached Longstreet the night before, but had not been credited, and had rather confirmed his intention to attack.

Very soon after this Burnside sent out a flag and offered us a truce to remove our dead and wounded, which Longstreet accepted, — all thought of renewal of the attack being abandoned. The truce was later extended until dark, Longstreet at first proposing to retreat southward at night to join Bragg, but during the day messages arrived from that direction, and we learned of the approach of a force under Sherman to relieve Burnside, and that our road to Dalton was closed.

The roads through upper Ga. were deemed impracticable for an army and destitute of supplies, so it was determined to retreat toward southwest Va. But, in order to relieve the pressure upon Bragg as far as we could, Longstreet determined to maintain a threatening position before Knoxville until the approaching Federal reënforcements were within a day's march. This was done and on the night of Dec. 4, in a severe rainstorm, the retreat began. During the night and next morning we made 18 miles and encamped at Blain's Cross Roads, where we met Ransom's artillery and infantry coming to help us in the attack upon Knoxville, but nearly three weeks late.

Having retreated nearly to Rogersville, 65 miles, by the 9th, on the 14th we returned to Bean Station to attack a force under Parke which had followed us from Knoxville. Sending two brigades of cavalry on the flanks to cut off the enemy's retreat, Longstreet advanced his whole force directly on Bean Station. The enemy's skirmishers were met about three miles in front with artillery, but were driven in by Gracie's brigade. Gracie was wounded in the skirmish. The Federal line was formed just in rear of the town, with a large hotel building on the edge of the town strongly held by sharpshooters, firing from loopholes in the second and third stories. Parker's battery was advanced within 350 yards of the hotel, which was soon charged by Gracie's brigade and taken possession of. Meanwhile Kershaw's brigade had turned the left flank of the enemy's line and four more batteries had been advanced to close ranges, when it was found that the enemy was withdrawing in the dusk which was now rapidly obscuring the field. The day was a short one and cloudy, the infantry had marched 16 miles over bad roads, and Longstreet feared that in the darkness his troops might fire into each other. The enemy were mainly cavalry, under Shackelford, and pursuit at night by our infantry would be bootless. So the artillery held its fire and the infantry went into bivouac. The affair had been bloody for its duration and our side had the worst of it.

The casualties in Gracie's brigade   162
In Johnson's they were   60

And in other commands they were . . . 68 290
The Federals report in 13 regiments total 115

It is needless to give further details of the retreat. The campaign had been one of much hardship. Some facts may be given showing how poorly we were provided, even with prime necessities, though we were in our own country. We were so deficient in horseshoes that on the advance to Knoxville we stripped the shoes and saved the nails from all dead horses, killing for the purpose all wounded and broken-down animals, both our own and those left behind by the enemy. During the siege, the river brought down a number of dead animals thrown in within the town. We watched for these, took them out, and stripped their feet of shoes and nails. Our men were nearly as badly off for foot gear as our animals. I have seen bloody stains left on frozen ground where our infantry had passed. In the artillery we took the shoes from the feet of the drivers to give to the cannoneers who had to march. Our rations were also frequently not even the reduced rations now issued to the whole army. Corn, unground, was often the only ration.

Longstreet's retreat was now continued without serious engagement to Morristown and later to Greenville, where he wintered, and rejoined Lee at Gordonsville, Va., in the spring.

The following table gives the Confederate casualties of the campaign. Those of the unfortunate assault on Fort Sanders, badly begun, suspended by mistake, and never concluded, are shown separately below.

RETURN OF CASUALTIES, LONGSTREET'S CORPS,
NOV. 14 TO DEC. 4, 1863

DIVISION	BRIGADE	KILLED	WOUNDED	MISSING	TOTAL	DATE
Hood's	Jenkins	22	109	5	136	Nov. 4 to Dec. 5
"	Benning	1	5		6	Nov. 4 to Dec. 5
"	Robertson	9	18	6	33	Nov. 4 to Dec. 5
"	Law	15	69	8	92	Nov. 4 to Dec. 5
"	Anderson	3	57		60	Nov. 17 and 18
"	Anderson	33	129	25	187	Nov. 29
Total Hood's Division		83	387	44	514	

Division	Brigade	Killed	Wounded	Missing	Total	Date
McLaws's	Wofford	48	121	81	250	Nov. 4 to Dec. 5
"	Bryan	27	121	64	212	Nov. 4 to Dec. 5
"	Humphreys		18		18	Nov. 4 to Dec. 5
"	Humphreys	21	87	56	164	Nov. 29
"	Kershaw	19	116	3	138	Nov. 17 and 18
Total McLaws's Division		115	463	204	782	
Aggregate		198	850	248	1296	

Loss in the assault on Fort Sanders, Nov. 29: killed, 129; wounded, 458; missing, 226; total, 813, included in the above.

RETURN OF CASUALTIES, BURNSIDE'S COMMAND, NOV. 14 TO DEC. 4, 1863

Division	Brigade	Killed	Wounded	Missing	Total
9th Corps 1st Div.	Morrison	5	19	6	30
	Christ	15	25	24	64
	Humphreys	18	102	46	166
	Artillery		2		2
	Total	38	148	76	262
9th Corps 2d Div.	Sigfried	5	27	32	64
	Schall	4	7	3	14
	Artillery		1		1
	Total	9	35	35	79
Total 9th Corps		47	183	111	341
23d Corps 2d Div.	Chapin		13	6	19
23d Corps 3d Div.	Hascall	2	15	7	24
23d Corps 3d Div.	Cameron	9	97	2	108
Total 23d Corps		11	125	15	151
Cavalry. Total 4 Brigs.		34	85	80	199
Aggregate		92	383	206	681

CHAPTER XX

Battle of the Wilderness

Review. Lee's Force. Situation. Longstreet's Position. Longstreet's
March. Ewell's Advance. Ewell's Fight.

Lee honored our return to his command with a review. It
was the only one ever held, after the one in the Shenandoah Valley,
in Oct., 1862. He was not given to parades merely for show.
Now, doubtless, he felt and reciprocated the stirrings of affection in
the hearts of his men, inseparable from our return from bloody
Chickamauga, upon the eve of what all felt must be the struggle
to a finish, and no one who was present can ever forget the
occasion.

It took place in a cleared valley with broad pastures, in which
our two divisions of infantry, with my old battalion of artillery,
could be deployed, not far from Mechanicsburg, where we were
encamped some six or eight miles south of Gordonsville.

It is now over 40 years, but in imagination I can see to-day
the large square gate-posts, without gate or fence, for troops
had been everywhere in that vicinity, marking where a country
road led out of a tall oak wood upon an open knoll in front of
the centre of our long double lines. And as the well-remembered
figure of Lee upon Traveller, at the head of his staff, rides between the posts and comes out upon the ground, the bugle sounds
a signal, the guns thunder out a salute, Lee reins up Traveller
and bares his good gray head and looks at us, and we give the
"rebel yell" and shout and cry and wave our flags and look at
him once more.

For a wave of sentiment — something like what came a year
later at Appomattox when he rode back from his meeting with
Grant — seemed to sweep over the field. All felt the bond
which held them together. There was no speaking, but the
effect was as of a military sacrament.

Dr. Boggs, a S.C. chaplain riding with the staff, said to Col. Venable, Lee's aid, "Does not it make the General proud to see how these men love him?" Venable answered, "Not proud. It awes him." He rode along our lines close enough to look into our faces and then we marched in review and went back to our camps.

ARMY OF THE POTOMAC, MAY 4, 1864

2D CORPS. HANCOCK					
DIVISIONS	BRIGADES				ARTILLERY
Barlow	Miles	Smyth	Frank	Brooke	Tidball
Gibbon	Webb	Owen	Carroll		10 Batts.
Birney	Ward	Hayes			60 Guns
Mott	McAllester	Brewster			

5TH CORPS. WARREN					
Griffin	Ayres	Sweitzer	Bartlett		Wainwright
Robinson	Leonard	Baxter	Dennison		9 Batts.
Crawford	McCandless	Fisher			54 Guns
Wadsworth	Cutler	Rice	Stone		

6TH CORPS. SEDGWICK, WRIGHT					
Wright	Brown	Russell	Upton	Shaler	Tompkins
Getty	Wheaton	Grant	Neill	Eustis	9 Batts.
Ricketts	Morris	Seymour			54 Guns

9TH CORPS. BURNSIDE, PARKE					
Stevenson	Carruth	Leasure			Edwards
Potter	Bliss	Griffin			14 Batts.
Willcox	Hartranft	Christ			84 Guns
Ferrero	Sigfried	Thomas			

RESERVE ARTILLERY. HUNT	
	26 Batts.
	106 Guns

CAVALRY. SHERIDAN					
Torbert	Custer	Devin		Res.Brig.	
Gregg,D.M.	Davies	Gregg, J. I.		Merritt	
Wilson	Bryan	Chapman			

ARMY OF NORTHERN VIRGINIA, MAY, 1864

1ST CORPS. LONGSTREET, ANDERSON

DIVISIONS	BRIGADES				ARTILLERY
Kershaw Field	Henagan Jenkins	Wofford Anderson	Humphreys Law Benning	Bryan Gregg	Alexander 54 Guns

2D CORPS. EWELL, EARLY

Early Johnson Rodes	Hays Walker, Jr. Daniel	Pegram Steuart Ramseur	Gordon Jones Doles	Johnston Stafford Battle	Long 70 Guns

3D CORPS. HILL

Anderson, R. H. Heth Wilcox	Perrin Davis Lane	Mahone Kirkland McGowan	Harris Cooke Scales	Wright Perry Walker, H. A. Archer Thomas	Walker, L. 80 Guns

CAVALRY. STUART, HAMPTON

Hampton Lee, F. Lee, W. H. F.	Young Lomax Chambliss	Rosser Wickham Gordon	Butler	Chew 20 Guns

Our narrative may pause for a bird's-eye view of the situation. In all previous campaigns there had been "intermission for refreshment" between our battles, in which the armies would replenish and recruit before initiating new strategy leading up to a new collision — usually under a new Federal leader. Now from May 5, when battle was joined in the Wilderness until April 9, 1865, when Lee surrendered at Appomattox, there was scarcely a day when the armies were not under each other's fire.

Grant decided beforehand not to exchange prisoners. This added much to the suffering to be endured on both sides. It may be condoned as tending to shorten the war, but the way in which it was done savored more of the "sharp trick" than of Grant's usual dignity and frankness of character. We had, perhaps unwisely, "outlawed" Butler, and Grant's trick consisted in making him "Commissioner for exchange of prisoners" in hopes that we would decline to hold communication with him. When we swallowed our pride and offered exchanges, pretences were found to still refuse.

The campaign against us was practically to be one of extermination, and it was to be conducted by four separate armies and as much of the navy as could be used in the James River.

First. Grant had four corps — the 2d, 5th, 6th, and 9th — and a large force of cavalry. His returns show 102,869 present for duty with 242 guns. Besides, there was a siege-train being prepared of 106 guns and mortars, among which were six 100-Pr. rifles. This train came into service in May and June. The cavalry were all armed with Spencer carbines, the first magazine guns ever used by the army. They fully doubled the efficiency of the cavalry against ours with only muzzle-loaders. Wilder's mounted infantry had had them at Chickamauga, and their value on that occasion has been told. Brigades of them soon began to appear among the Federal infantry, as will appear hereafter. It was useless to capture these guns, as we could not supply the brass cartridges required.

Second. In the Shenandoah Valley, Sigel was preparing a force of about 15,000 men with 40 guns, which was to move upon Staunton.

Third. From W. Va., Crook also was to move upon Staunton with about 9000 men and 24 guns. When Crook and Sigel had united, they were to move upon Lynchburg and thence upon Richmond.

Fourth. Butler, at Fortress Monroe, was organizing the Army of the James, to move upon Richmond by its south bank. It would be escorted by four monitors, a fleet of gunboats, and a large collection of ferry-boats and river craft of every description. These would facilitate all movements by water. His force comprised the 10th and 18th corps and Kautz's cavalry, 30,000 men with 79 guns, of which about 5000 were cavalry. Besides these four armies, there were, near Washington, about 40,000 troops which were used for reënforcements during the next two months, besides a constant stream of recruits from all over the North, stimulated by bounties now being paid of a thousand dollars per man, and, early in July, Grant also brought around from New Orleans the 19th corps, about 12,000 men.

There were no returns of Longstreet's corps after his return from E. Tenn., but he gives as a "liberal estimate," 10,000 men. The return of the rest of the Army of Northern Virginia, on April 20, was as follows: —

Ewell's Corps	.	.	.	.	.	17,079
Hill's Corps	.	.	.	.	.	22,199
Artillery	.	.	.	.	.	4,854
Cavalry	.	.	.	.	.	8,497
Miscellaneous	.	.	.	.	.	1,355 . 53,984

Adding 10,000 for Longstreet, Lee's total force was about 64,000, and he had about 274 guns. Against the armies of Sigel and Crook, Breckenridge was able to muster in the Valley and in the S. W. Va., about 9000 men and 24 guns.

To meet Butler, Beauregard brought to Petersburg, from various points in the South, troops which he organized into four divisions, comprising about 22,000 infantry, 2000 cavalry, and about 50 guns. These included Pickett's division of Longstreet's corps, say 5000 men, which rejoined Longstreet about June 1, and Johnson's brigade of Early's division, which was returned to the division on May 6.

To recapitulate, the forces under Grant's command were about 156,000 men and those under Lee's were about 95,000.

Grant had been urged by some of his advisers to transfer his army to the James, and to make his advance upon Richmond by that line, by which he could approach within 20 miles without the loss of a man. But he wisely held that his objective was Lee's army, and that it could most easily be reached in a half day's march from his camps at Culpeper.

A word about our position, where Longstreet's corps was to await Grant's opening the campaign. It was at Mechanicsburg, about six miles south of Gordonsville. Lee was fully aware that Grant's first move would be an attempt to turn his right flank, which would bring him through the Wilderness, and had decided to attack him *en route.* Ewell's corps, from its camps in winter quarters, could reach Grant's probable route by a march of 18 miles. Hill's corps was farther to the left and would have about 28 miles to go. Longstreet's, from Mechanicsburg, would have a somewhat later start and 30 miles in an air line, which proved to be 42 by the country roads, used to avoid interference with Hill's route.

The first day would offer us the best chances, as Grant would have no breastworks and could use little artillery in the Wilderness. What proved a drawn battle, begun by three divisions, reënforced by two after six hours, and by three more after 18 hours, might have had a different result if begun by five and reënforced by two after six hours, and only one left (Anderson's) to come in after 18 hours. This might have been the history, if Longstreet's corps had been located a few miles north of Louisa C. H., instead of at Mechanicsburg.

Maj.-Gen. Field had now been assigned to the command of Hood's division and Kershaw had been promoted to the command of McLaws's.   I had been made Chief of Artillery of the corps, and the two battalions, Cabell's and Henry's (now Haskell's), which had been left in Va. when we went to Chickamauga, rejoined us. Col. Frank Huger succeeded to the command of my old battalion.

It was near midday on May 4, when the news came that Grant was crossing the Rapidan at Ely's and Germanna fords, with orders from Lee to march to Todd's Tavern on the Brock road, the road by which Jackson on May 2, 1863, had turned Hooker's position. At 4 P.M., we were on the way, with orders to march all night, only stopping to feed and water. We kept it up until near sundown the next day, when the two divisions went into bivouac near Craig's meeting-house, on the Carthapin road, having travelled about 36 miles. We were ordered to cook, eat, and rest until 1 A.M., and then start for Todd's Tavern. Before starting, orders came from Lee to come across to the Plank road at Parker's store, about six miles. There was a good moon, about 11 days old. At a fork in the road, our leading division took the wrong road and lost about its length in distance, while the other lost none. It resulted that at Parker's store, where we took the broad, straight Plank road, the heads of the two sets of fours came together, and the two columns, eight abreast, filled the road.

The story may now pause, to tell what had already taken place. Grant's effort was to pass our flank and get between us and Richmond.   He had started after thorough preparation at midnight on the 3d, and in 18 hours had put most of his force with its artillery and fighting trains across the river, using five pontoon bridges.   He had made about 12 miles, and might have made a few miles more, but preferred to encamp on the night of the 4th in close order and wait for the 9th corps, which, with the great bulk of the ordnance and subsistence trains, was still behind. This had been the most critical day, and, to Grant's relief, it closed without Lee's having made an appearance.   The swiftness of a concentration is only that of its most distant part, and Ewell had been ordered to march slowly down the Turnpike, and let Hill, coming down the Plank road, get abreast of him, and both were directed not to bring on a general engagement until Longstreet's arrival.

So Ewell encamped the night of the 4th at Locust Grove, five miles from Wilderness Tavern, the centre of Grant's line. Hill's advanced division, Heth, encamped at Mine Run, about 13 miles from his battle-field of the next day.

On the 5th, Grant moved early, intending to take a line from Locust Grove to Parker's store.   But at 7 A.M., the 5th corps met Ewell's corps within two miles of Wilderness Tavern.   Ewell had his whole corps with him, about 17,000 men.   Grant, guessing that the rest of our army was not up, thought to whip it in detail and concentrated upon it the whole of the 5th corps, about 24,000, and over half of the 6th, say 12,000.

It did, indeed, seem that Ewell had ventured rashly and had put his head in the lion's mouth, for the ground around Lacy's, where Grant made his headquarters, a half-mile southwest from Wilderness Tavern, was open, affording opportunity for artillery and free communication for movement of troops, and Ewell had no intrenchments and was strung out upon the road.   It is not surprising that as Grant's different divisions deployed, and attacked from different directions, in the early part of the fighting, some of the Confederate brigades were thrown into temporary confusion.

But by eleven o'clock, Ewell was all up and had taken a line in the forest which he was able to maintain all day and until darkness ended the fighting. He had even captured two 24-Pr. howitzers in a counter-charge, and, during the night, he managed to intrench himself. Gens. J. M. Jones and Stafford had both been killed and Pegram severely wounded.

Hill, on the 5th, had met the enemy's cavalry at Parker's store, and, driving them before him, had pushed down the Plank road. Meanwhile, when Grant had discovered Ewell in his front and attacked with the 5th, and part of the 6th, corps, he had halted the 2d corps on the Brock road, on which it had been marching, and had ordered the remainder of the 6th to advance up the Plank road that they might come upon the flank of Ewell. As the latter already had enough to occupy him, it was well that Hill, about noon, encountered the skirmishers of the 6th. Having orders not to bring on an action until the arrival of Longstreet, and having only Heth's division present, Hill halted and formed line of battle, but did not attack.

Grant, however, was promptly notified of Heth's arrival, and, knowing that Longstreet, having to come from beyond Gordonsville, could not arrive that day, he redoubled his efforts to destroy both Hill and Ewell before night. So Hancock with the whole of the 2d corps, 28,000, and the smaller half of the 6th, say 10,000 men, was ordered to attack Hill's two divisions, Heth and Wilcox, of about 7000 each.

Hancock, though ordered to lose no time, delayed for an hour or two in order to complete some intrenchments already started along the Brock road, so as to have something to fall back upon in case of disaster. This delay was of great value to Hill, enabling him to partially select and prepare his ground. This day, May 5, was Grant's day, full of golden opportunities. May 4 would have been Lee's day, had he prearranged his camps so as to enable him to concentrate his army more promptly where he knew that Grant would cross. The 6th, after Longstreet's arrival, would belong to the chapter of accidents. Grant seems to have himself appreciated this, and to have continually urged his battle faster than his army could make the speed.

Hill's line of battle was square across the Plank road, with one brigade on the left and three on the right. On the left, the line ran through a clearing now grown up in broom-grass and small pines, and containing a house known as the Widow Tabb's. Some artillery, under Poague, was stationed here, and Lee and Hill made the clearing their headquarters. Wilcox's division, soon arriving, was posted on Hill's left flank, extending back obliquely in the direction of Ewell's battle, but with a gap of at least a mile between. At last, at 4.15 P.M., the sun setting at seven, Hancock, having built strong breastworks for his whole line along the Brock road, joined Getty's division of the 6th corps, already skirmishing for an hour with Hill, and put the whole weight of his corps into an attack upon Heth. Hill soon found that Wilcox's line was not assailed, and that it was necessary to bring it to the support of Heth. At first Wilcox passed to the front and made some charges, but finally fell back, and the two divisions were practically merged into one line, which fought lying down.

There was never more desperate fighting than now ensued, and continued until about 8 P.M., when darkness terminated the battle. Fortunately for Hill, the dense forest prevented his men from realizing the enormous odds against him, or, like Bragg's men on Missionary Ridge, they might have become demoralized by the sight. Night did not terminate the fighting any sooner than Hill wished. His ammunition was low, his lines disarranged, often disconnected, and some even facing in different directions. Besides the danger impending from Hancock on his front and right, a greater one threatened Hill on his left.

Warren, while fighting Ewell, had seen Wilcox in his temporary location and had seen his withdrawal to go to Heth's aid. He sent Wadsworth's division and Baxter's brigade, about 8000 men, to move in that direction and attack Hill's flank. Darkness overtook Wadsworth at Hill's skirmish line and he halted and bivouacked, ready to attack in the morning.

During the night, Grant had been joined by Burnside's 9th

corps, 24,000 strong, comprised in four divisions, one of which was of negroes. This was left to guard the trains. Two of the white divisions, Potter and Willcox, supported by the 3d, Stevenson's, were sent to penetrate the gap between Hill and Ewell, now over a mile in extent.

Long before day, Hill could hear the enemy forming in the woods near at hand. Nothing was done in the way of preparation or of intrenchment during the night, as the men expected to be relieved by Longstreet's two divisions in the morning. Meanwhile, Grant had been misled into a serious blunder by false information, curiously like what had been imposed upon Hooker in the Chancellorsville campaign. By the stories of prisoners he was led to believe, just as Hooker had been, that Pickett's division had arrived, and he ordered Hancock to withdraw Barlow's division from the force about to attack Heth, and post it on his left, on the Brock road, in anticipation of Pickett's expected appearance. There happened to be near that point the grading of an unfinished railroad, designed to run from Fredericksburg to Orange C. H., and here passing through the Wilderness a little south of it, and nearly parallel to the Plank road. It offered a great opportunity to turn the flank of either of the lines about to be engaged near that road. Fortunately for us, Barlow did not utilize it, but left the opportunity to Longstreet.

Punctually at 5 A.M. on the 6th, Warren and Sedgwick attacked Ewell and Hancock, with Wadsworth and Getty, attacked Hill. A short story can be made of the attack upon Ewell. He had strengthened his lines during the night and gotten in more of his artillery. The attacks upon him were fierce and bloody, but were all repulsed. For six hours they were renewed frequently, but by 11 A.M. the fight was all out of the assailants, and for the rest of the day they were satisfied to lie behind their breastworks and keep up a more or less noisy, but harmless, fire upon the Confederates in theirs. Late in the afternoon, however, an attack was made upon an exposed flank of the 6th corps by Gordon, of Early's division, which will be described later. But, of all the chapter of accidents affecting the Confederate fortunes, scarcely one was more unfortunate for them than what was then disclosed. The opportunity for this attack, which might have been fatal to Grant's campaign, had lain open all day, uninvestigated by Ewell and Early, although both were notified of it, and begged to verify it.

Hancock's attack upon Hill opened with every promise of success. Birney's, Mott's, and Getty's divisions advanced simultaneously upon Heth and Wilcox, who made a strong resistance until Wadsworth's division and Baxter's brigade struck them upon the left flank, and Hancock's left overlapped and turned their right. With both flanks broken, they were rapidly rolled up toward the centre, and the men, appreciating that their position was no longer tenable, fell back from both flanks into the Plank road, and came pouring down the road past the open field near the Tabb house, where Lee stood among the small and scattered pines. Seeing McGowan pass, Lee rode up and said: "My God! Gen. McGowan, is this splendid brigade of yours running like a flock of geese?" McGowan answered: "General, the men are not whipped. They only want a place to form, and they will fight as well as ever they did."

Meanwhile, as already told, Longstreet's double column had turned into the Plank road, at Parker's store, about five o'clock with about three miles to go. Longstreet and staff rode at the head of the column, which filled the whole road. As we drew near the Tabb house, we met what seemed to be an orderly body of troops marching in the opposite direction, who parted, taking the woods on each side and giving us the road. Presently an excited staff-officer appeared, trying to stop them, who, being asked why, answered, — "They are running, d—n them." Soon bullets began to whistle down the road, and Longstreet ordered the leading brigades forward into line on each side. Gregg, Benning, and Law, under Field, took the left. Kennedy, Humphreys, and Bryan, under Kershaw, took the right. Some of the bullets were coming across the road from the right, their direction showing that the enemy was about to pass around our flank.

Poague's guns opened fire, and Lee, seeing the Texas brigade passing, rode to place himself at its head. The men, recognizing him and his intention, shouted, "Go back! Lee to the rear," and a Texan Major caught his horse by the bridle and stopped him. He was assured that the men did not need any leading, and would soon restore the battle. Some one, about that time, pointed out Longstreet, and Lee was taken to him.

The Federals had now advanced over a mile through the tangled forest and were necessarily in much disorder. Both sides were fighting without intrenchments, and the Federals were everywhere being pushed slowly back with severe loss. Gregg and Benning, on the left, bore the brunt of the action. Both were small brigades and their casualties were heavy. Benning was severely wounded. The losses of the brigades cannot be given. But few reports were made after the commencement of this campaign, and there are only a small number of these which state the casualties.

The news of Longstreet's presence was soon conveyed to Meade and Grant, and reënforcements were sent Hancock, while Sedgwick and Warren were ordered to press their attacks. Getty was wounded and his division was withdrawn. Stevenson's division, the reserve of the 9th corps, was ordered to the left, and Barlow, on the extreme left, was directed to attack Hill's right. Barlow, however, only sent one brigade, Frank's, having been misled by the approach from his left of a body of Federal convalescents who were at first taken for Pickett's division. He also attributed to Pickett some very rapid fire heard on the left, where Sheridan, with his Spencer carbines, had attacked Stuart, by Grant's orders, but had been repulsed. Willcox's and Potter's divisions of Burnside's corps, sent to penetrate the gap between Hill and Ewell, were urged forward, and a staff-officer sent to guide them, but they did not come into action until two o'clock, before which time the ground had been occupied by Heth and Wilcox, who were able to repel their assault when it was made. With the aid of these reënforcements, the Confederate advance was brought to a standstill and the firing gradually ceased. Engineer troops were brought up, and the Federals began improving and extending their lines.

Meanwhile, about 8 A.M., Anderson's division of Hill's corps had arrived on the field, and also Lee's Chief Engineer, Gen. M. L. Smith. He had been sent to search for an opportunity to turn the enemy's left. Of course, he soon found the unfinished railroad, and about 10 A.M., he reported it to Longstreet. Four

brigades were promptly formed for a flank attack to be conducted by Col. Sorrel, Longstreet's Adj.-Gen. They were
G. B. Anderson of Field's division, Wofford of Kershaw's,
Mahone of Anderson's (R. H.), and Davis of Heth's. This attack
was to be at once followed by a general advance of all Longstreet's force, which included Jenkins's large brigade and four
others of Anderson's division, which had not yet fired a shot.

Sorrel moved the four brigades by the flank to the unfinished
railroad, where they faced to the left, and, about 11 A.M., they
advanced upon the Federal line, striking it in flank and rear.
The success of the movement was complete. Brigade after
brigade was routed and rolled up. Hancock, noted for his
power and influence with his men on such occasions, endeavored
in vain to stay the panic, but was unable to do so, and, con-
sulting with Birney, he decided to abandon all in front and
endeavor to reëstablish his line upon the Brock road. Here he
had, the day before, sacrificed valuable time to intrench a line
which might now serve him as a refuge. The panic had extended
even across the Plank road where Wadsworth had been killed
and Baxter wounded, when their troops were routed.

This was Longstreet's great opportunity. Nearly the whole
of Grant's army had been first fought to a standstill, and now
four brigades, with little loss by a lucky movement, had utterly
routed about two full corps in the Wilderness, where it was
almost impossible to rally broken troops. Longstreet, with five
more fresh brigades, was close at hand, fully prepared to join
the victorious four and to be aided by the brigades which had
relieved Heth and Wilcox in the morning in a supreme effort
to follow up the fugitives, and to drive them into the Rapidan.
When Smith had directed Sorrel's column on its turning expedition, he had been given a small party and directed to find a way
across the Brock road which would turn Hancock's extreme
left. He had now returned and reported one found. He was
asked to conduct the flanking brigades and handle them as the
ranking officer. He was a fine tactician, a skilful engineer, and
had been noted for gallantry in the defence of Vicksburg, where
he had been chief engineer. He was a native of N.Y. and a
graduate of West Point of the class of 1838.

When Sorrel's flanking brigades reached the Plank road, some crossing in the attack and pursuit of Wadsworth, and some in line, a little ways in the woods on the right, whence they fired on the fugitives down the road, he rode back to where Longstreet, Smith, Field, Kershaw, and others stood at the head of Jenkins's brigade, in column in the road, ready to be launched in the pursuit. He made his report, which was of an ideal success, as had already been made known by the progress of the musketry. It may be imagined how rapidly the news was spread down the ranks and with what alacrity was heard the order to advance.

Meanwhile, the 12th Va., of Mahone's brigade, had crossed the Plank road in the pursuit of Wadsworth and gotten ahead of the other regiments, detained by a fire in the woods across their path. It was now returning to find its brigade, which was in line near the road, and had, only a short while before, been firing at Wadsworth fugitives. The 12th, on the left of the road, was mistaken in the woods for an advance of the enemy, and fire was opened on it by the other regiments, just as the head of the column was about to pass, and it rode into the fire. Jenkins had just before ridden close to Longstreet to offer congratulations, and had said: "I feel happy. I had felt despair of our cause for some months, but am relieved. I feel assured we will put the enemy back across the Rapidan before night."

Jenkins and Longstreet were both struck, the former mortally, dying within two hours; the latter in the throat, passing out behind the right shoulder. Capt. Doby, and Bowen, an orderly of Kershaw's staff, were killed. Jenkins's brigade levelled to return the fire, but Kershaw shouted "F-r-i-e-n-d-s," and arms were recovered, and the men lay down without firing a shot. The 12th Va. had also lain down.

Longstreet at once summoned Field, the senior officer present, to take the command and to press the pursuit, one column the direct attack, the other to turn the position along the Brock road. Before Field, however, had taken command, Gen. R. H. Anderson, his senior, arrived, and Lee soon after came up.

Longstreet writes that the plans, orders, and opportunity were explained to Lee, but the woods concealed everything except the troops along the road, and Lee did not care to handle broken lines, and ordered a formation for parallel battle.

This consumed so much time that it was 4.15 P.M. when the attack was renewed by Field's and Anderson's divisions, excepting Law's and Perry's brigades. Gen. Humphreys, in his account of this campaign, says of this attack, " Could it have been made early in the day and followed up, it would have had important consequences." Earlier in the day, it might have been made by three divisions, and would have found the enemy already retreating. Now he had had four hours to reform in intrenchments and strengthen them. Grant had himself given orders to renew his attack upon us at 6 P.M. Our attack at 4.15 so reduced the Federal ammunition, and their ordnance wagons were so far in the rear, that the attack was given up. As it was, Jenkins's brigade, under Bratton, after a half-hour's attack, drove off Ward's brigade and a portion of Mott's division, and planted their colors upon the intrenchments. But there were no reënforcements and the enemy had a second fortified line full of troops, so Bratton was at last forced to withdraw with severe loss. His attack, and his final repulse by Carroll, were both highly complimented by Hancock. Under all the circumstances, the renewal of the attack at the late hour, and without Kershaw's division, was unwise. It was certain to cost many lives, the chances of success were not good, and, even had they been, the lateness of the hour would have interfered with gathering the fruit of victory.

The fire in the woods, which had started during Mahone's attack, had continued to burn, and some of the wounded perished in it. It had reached Hancock's log breastworks, and a part of them were on fire at the time of our afternoon assault, with which it materially interfered.

It only remains to complete the record of the day's misfortunes with a brief account of Gordon's attack upon the right of the 6th corps, commenced a little before sundown, although the existence of the opportunity for it, as already mentioned, had been discovered by scouts and reported to Gordon by 9 A.M. Gordon had verified it by personal observation and reported it to his division commander, Early, and urged an attack. Early had adopted a theory that Grant would have Burnside's 9th corps in support of the right of the 6th. In vain Gordon answered that observation showed it was not there, and in vain he appealed to Ewell, the corps commander, to verify it. Early's personality dominated Ewell's to such an extent that Ewell not only sustained him in his theory, but would neither go and see or refer the important question to Lee. And so the matter remained during all the hours and all the vicissitudes of the day, until about 5.30 P.M., when Lee, who had been occupied until then on the right, and wondered at the strange silence on his left, rode up and asked, "Cannot something be done on this flank to relieve the pressure on our right?"

Ewell, Early, and Gordon all happened to be present. Gordon's proposal was mentioned, and Early vigorously combated it. Lee listened in grim silence to his reasons for non-action, and answered only with direct orders to Gordon to proceed immediately to make the attack, taking one other brigade, Johnson's, to support his attack.

Strange to say, the situation had not changed. The attack took place just as the sun sank in the west. It was as immediately and brilliantly successful as Longstreet's flank attack with four brigades at eleven o'clock had been; but now darkness intervened to save Grant's army as effectually as had the bullet which disabled Longstreet. Two brigades, Seymour's and Shaler's, were completely routed, the brigadiers and several hundred men being captured. Gordon's casualties were very small and a large proportion of them were from a cross-fire of our own men upon the flanking party, as it swept down the Federal line in front of the Confederate line of battle in the twilight. Darkness, of course, soon put an end to the possibility of fighting, and the Federals, during the night, fell back and occupied an entirely new line in the rear. Early, during the war, never admitted that the 9th corps was not on the right and rear of the 6th, but the publication of the official records shows that it was employed entirely in other parts of the field.

There are no Confederate returns for 112, out of 183, regiments. The Federal casualties for the two days were: —

Killed, 2246; wounded, 12,037; missing, 3383; total, 18,366.

Livermore estimates that in proportion to the numbers engaged, the Confederate losses could not have been any less than the Federal, which, estimating only the killed and wounded, were 14,283 or 127 per 1000 men engaged. The numbers engaged, Livermore estimates as : —

Federals	101,895
Confederate	61,025

and the corresponding Confederate loss would be 7750. The Confederates had: killed, Gens. J. M. Jones and L. A. Stafford, and wounded, Longstreet, Pegram, Benning, and Perry. The Federals had, wounded, Gens. Carroll and Baxter.

Gen. Humphreys writes of this battle : —

"I have gone into more detail because it may serve to show what difficulties were encountered by the forces engaged in it, owing to the character of the field on which it took place. . . . So far as I know, no great battle ever took place before on such ground. But little of the combatants could be seen, and its progress was known to the senses chiefly by the rising and falling sounds of a vast musketry fire that continually swept along the lines of battle many miles in length, sounds which at times approached the sublime."

SPOTTSYLVANIA

My command had not been engaged in the Wilderness. When the battle began, on the 6th, I was ordered to halt all the artillery at Parker's store, and it remained there until in the afternoon of the 7th, when it was started for Spottsylvania C. H. When Grant made no attack on the morning of the 7th, and, in the afternoon, his trains were seen moving toward our right, Lee correctly guessed that his design was to turn our right. Late in the afternoon, Lee ordered Anderson, who had succeeded Longstreet in command of the 1st corps, to march at night for Spottsylvania. It was to be a foot-race to see who could first occupy the ground, and the advantages seemed to be with Grant, who had ordered Meade to start his trains at 3 P.M., so as to clear the roads, and to establish one corps at the court-house, one at the cross-roads known as the Blockhouse, and one at Todd's Tavern. The troops were to march at 8.30 P.M., and they had about 12 miles to go. It was in the dark of the moon.

We had about 15 miles to go, and, on arrival, only two divisions to oppose to the three corps. Fitz-Lee's cavalry, however, was on the road in front of Spottsylvania, and Hampton's defended Corbin's Bridge on the Catharpin road, by which the enemy might have interfered with our march. Our cavalry had cut down trees to blockade the roads, and they defended their blockades so well that the enemy's cavalry could not force them in the night, but had to wait for daylight.

The enemy enjoyed a great advantage in having the initiative. Lee could not know until after daylight in the morning whether Grant's entire army had left his front or not. In any event, our two divisions could have no reënforcements during the greater part of the day. Thanks to the good work of Hampton's division at Corbin's Bridge, we passed that danger point safely. Our artillery, from Parker's store, came by the Shady Grove road, and about daylight we joined the two divisions of infantry near the Po River, where the column halted for an hour to rest and eat breakfast, expecting this to be a busy day. For already we could hear the beginning of some fighting two miles to our left, indicating that the Federal columns were finding our cavalry in their way.

The Federals, however, were sure that they had won the race. Mr. Dana, Asst. Sec. of War, who was with Grant at the time, wrote of it afterward, as follows: —

"I remember distinctly the sensation in the ranks when the rumor first went around that our position was south of Lee's. It was the morning of May 8. The night before, the army had made a forced march on Spottsylvania C. H. There was no indication the next morning that Lee had moved in any direction. As the army began to realize that we were moving south, and, at that moment were probably much nearer Richmond than was our enemy, the spirits of both officers and men rose to the highest pitch of animation. On every hand I heard the cry 'On to Richmond.'"

Our little halt for breakfast, greatly needed by both men and animals after the night march, about exhausted all the margin by which we had won the race. About 7 A.M., we reached a cross-road, where stood the peculiar looking house, called the Blockhouse, built of squared logs. Here we met pressing

appeals for help from two directions. From Spottsylvania
C. H., one and a half miles in front, Rosser's brigade reported
itself as being driven by Wilson's division of cavalry, coming
from the direction of Fredericksburg. From the road to the
left, which crossed the Brock road on the Spindler farm one
mile away, Fitz-Lee reported himself as heavily pressed by
Warren's corps of infantry, and the increasing musketry fire
told that the situation was fast growing critical. The two leading brigades, Kennedy and Humphreys of Kershaw's division,
were at once filed to the left and hurried to the relief of Fitz-
Lee's cavalry. The other brigades of the same division, Wofford
and Bryan, went on ahead to the aid of Rosser. Haskell's
battalion of artillery went with Kershaw and Humphreys. Fitz-
Lee was defending some slight rail breastworks on the edge of a
dense pine thicket, overlooking a large open area, and the infantry quickly relieved the men with carbines behind the rails.
The latter, unobserved, were withdrawn to the rear through the
thicket, mounted and taken by Lee to the aid of Rosser.

Kennedy and Humphreys had hardly gotten into position
when they were charged by the three brigades of Robinson's
division of the 5th corps. Each brigade was formed in column
of regiments, four lines deep. Two brigades formed the first
line, and the third brigade the second line. Warren had told
them, the prisoners afterward stated, that there was only
cavalry behind the rail breastworks, who had no bayonets, and
could not stand close quarters. They actually did charge home
to the rails, and a bayonet fight took place across them; but
though superior in numbers, the Federals were repulsed, leaving
the ground strewn with dead and wounded, Robinson being
among the latter. Haskell's guns took part in the repulse and
did fine service, losing a captain, Potts, killed.

Field's division now came up to Kershaw's support and
extended his line to the left. Huger's battalion took position
in the edge of the pine thicket where the cavalry had stood,
and Cabell's battalion was held in reserve. Wilson's cavalry,
having held Spottsylvania C. H. for two hours, was withdrawn
by Sheridan, as Rosser, reënforced by Fitz-Lee, was moving upon
him. Wofford and Bryan now rejoined Field.

Meanwhile, after the repulse of Robinson's division, Griffin's division made two assaults. The first met about the same fate as Robinson. The second did not come so far, but secured positions to our right, where they could find cover from 300 to 400 yards away, and began to intrench. Crawford's division next came up to Griffin's left and extended his intrenchment, only exchanging rather distant fire with ours. Wadsworth's, the last division, now under Cutler, next made an attack upon our left, driving in our pickets and establishing a line prolonging Griffin's to his right. It was now about midday, and Warren's corps had been fought to a standstill.

About this time, Meade ordered Sedgwick to reënforce Warren with his whole corps and join him in an attack upon our two divisions, which was to be "immediate and vigorous." It was scarcely done as ordered, for it was not made until five o'clock; it was but a partial attack, and it was nowhere successful. The time required to form troops for an attack can seldom be exactly fixed, and here it was said that the ground was new to every one and the troops were tired with an all-night march.

The attack was made, however, by so large a force, that it overlapped our line on its right, which might have proved a very serious matter. As luck would have it, however, Crawford's division, the overlapping part which entered the woods beyond our extreme right about dusk, ran into Rodes's division of Ewell's corps, just arriving on the field, after an all-day march from the Wilderness, nearly exhausted by the heat, dust, and the smoke of the fires still burning there. Rodes promptly drove Crawford back to his place in the Federal line, and then forming his division on the right of Kershaw, he proceeded to intrench. Johnson's division formed on his right and Early's division, now under Gordon, in reserve. The fighting along the lines lasted until dark. During it, nearly every gun in our corps had been engaged, and was now assigned to some position, either on the line or behind, where it could fire over. Now at night, all were intrenching themselves, and we made our bivouac near the Blockhouse.

Hill's corps, now under Early, Hill being sick, had remained all day of the 8th guarding the movement of our trains from the Wilderness. On the 9th, it followed the other corps to Spottsylvania and took position on Ewell's right, except Mahone's division (formerly Anderson's), which was formed on the left of Field, overlooking the Po. The day was taken as a much-needed day of rest by the Federals, in which we cheerfully acquiesced. The sharpshooting, however, was active upon both sides. One of our sharpshooters killed Gen. Sedgwick at a range of about 700 yards from the pine thicket on the Brock road. He was succeeded by Wright in the command of the 6th corps.

The day was largely devoted to improving our breastworks, an art in which we were much behind our adversaries. Our equipment with intrenching tools was always far below our requirements, and in emergencies the men habitually loosened the ground with bayonets, and scooped it up with tin cups. The line was laid out generally by those who built it. The Federals had a large force, perhaps 2500 men, of engineer troops and heavy artillery regiments, habitually employed in building and improving their intrenchments under the direction of engineer officers. They were more valuable than an equal number of regular troops, and should be a part of the equipment of every army.

Sheridan, on the 8th, had been ordered to concentrate his cavalry, move against Stuart, and then upon our communications, and when his supplies were exhausted, to proceed to the James River, renew his supplies, and return to the army.

Burnside's corps arrived on the 9th by the Fredericksburg road and began intrenching opposite Hill, whose lines covered the court-house on our right. He had encountered some dismounted cavalry whom he mistook for a brigade of Longstreet's infantry, and so reported it to Grant. This misled Grant into the belief that Lee was moving in the direction of Fredericksburg, and he ordered Hancock immediately to cross the Po, move down it and recross by the Shady Grove road, thus turning our left flank. Hancock at once put three divisions to cross simultaneously at three different points. The farthest up-stream met a stubborn resistance from dismounted cavalry, but it was presently driven off by those who had crossed below, where the second effort had met little resistance, and the third none.

Pontoon bridges were immediately thrown at all three places, and the troops were pushed down-stream, hoping to secure the Shady Grove road bridge. Darkness, however, soon forced a halt, but some of the men reached the river and found it not fordable. At early dawn, Hancock reconnoitred, but found Mahone's brigade on the opposite bank too strongly posted to be attacked. Further reconnoissances were being made, when, about 10 A.M., Hancock was ordered to send two divisions of his three back across the Po to take part in an assault ordered in the afternoon at five. Gibbon and Birney were accordingly withdrawn, leaving Barlow's division alone on the south side.

Meanwhile, when Hancock crossed the Po on the afternoon of the 9th, Lee had ordered Heth's division from his extreme right to the extreme left, with orders to cross below our lines, and, coming up, to strike Hancock's three divisions on the flank. Heth had crossed the Po, some distance below our left flank, on the morning of the 10th, and turned to the right, hunting for Hancock's flank. It was fortunate for him that he had made so wide a circuit that he did not find it until after Hancock, with his two divisions, had been withdrawn to the north side, for Barlow's four brigades alone largely outnumbered him with only three, and Barlow could have been quickly reënforced. Heth would otherwise have lost much of his division, as its retreat across the Po would have been difficult.

As it was, Heth made two spirited charges upon two of Barlow's brigades drawn up behind the crest of a ridge, with the others supporting in the rear. Both charges were repulsed with severe loss, but meanwhile, a fire breaking out in the woods in rear, Meade ordered Barlow withdrawn. This was done with the loss of one gun, wedged between trees by the horses, who were stampeded by the fire. In withdrawing, Barlow suffered severely from the artillery across the Po, which swept the plain over which he reached the bridge. Some of the wounded perished in the fire. Gen. H. H. Walker of Heth's division was severely wounded. It had been a mistake to send Hancock across the Po at such a late hour in the afternoon. Night intervened before he could accomplish anything, and it disclosed his plan. Next day he abandoned it before discovering that Heth was in his power. At night Heth was returned to the right flank.

Heavy shelling of the 1st corps lines had been kept up all the morning, and in the afternoon three assaults were made at different points. One against Field's division had been ordered at 5 P.M., but at 3.30 Warren thought the opportunity for attack so favorable that he made it without further delay. In full uniform, he attacked the lines held by Field's division with Cutler's and Crawford's divisions and Webb's and Carroll's brigades, approaching through dense thickets which hid him from view until at quite close quarters. But our guns had been placed to flank these thickets and riddled them with canister as the enemy passed through. They emerged in bad order and unable to form under close musketry, and were repulsed with severe losses, among them Gen. Rice, mortally wounded. A few only succeeded in gaining our works, where their covered approach had been closest, but they were killed or captured.

Not satisfied with this effort, Hancock tried a second assault at 7 P.M., with Birney's and Gibbon's divisions, supported by part of the 5th corps, but it was also repulsed with severe loss to the enemy and with very trifling loss to us. Glancing back over the sequence of events, it appears that Burnside's mistaking dismounted cavalry for Longstreet's infantry on the 9th, was a most fortunate one for Lee. For it led to Grant's prematurely sending Hancock across the Po and then withdrawing him. Had he continued on that flank and perhaps been reënforced by Warren, it is hard to see how he could have failed to defeat Heth and completely turn Lee's flank, and get upon his communications which now ran to Louisa C. H.

While these affairs were going on upon our left, a carefully planned and partially successful effort was being made near our centre. In the hasty extension of our line to the eastward in the afternoon of the 8th, Ewell, to keep on high ground, had changed direction and gone a mile north; then, making a right-angled salient, had returned within three-fourths of a mile of the point of departure before resuming his eastward course. There resulted a great salient a mile long, reaching out toward the enemy and ending in the point afterward known as the "Bloody

Angle." It was a piece of bad engineering and certain to invite
an attack as soon as the enemy understood it.

This it required a few days for them to do, for our sharp-
shooters prevented any close reconnoissance. Meanwhile, however, our men found that the sides of the salient angle were enfiladed by the musketry fire of the enemy's sharpshooters coming
over the parapets, and, for protection, traverses were erected
every few yards along them. On the 10th, all the features
of this salient had not been understood, but on its western
face the enemy had found a place where a large force could
approach within 200 yards of our intrenchments, entirely unobserved, and would have but that distance under fire to enter
them. It was here that the carefully planned effort was made
at 5 P.M.

The assault was made under Col. Upton commanding a brigade in Russell's division of the 6th corps. He was a graduate
of West Point of the class of '61, and had already shown himself distinguished as a tactician and a leader of troops. His
command included three brigades, comprising 12 regiments which
were formed in four lines. No commands were given while
moving into position. All had bayonets fixed and guns loaded,
but only the front line had them capped. On reaching our
works, the 1st line would divide, half going to the right and half
to the left, to sweep in each direction. The 2d line would halt
at the works and open fire to the front. The 3d would lie
down behind the 2d, and the 4th would lie down at the edge of
the wood, whence they charged, and awaited the result. In the
charge, all officers would constantly repeat the shout "forward,"
and the men would rush forward with eyes on the ground they
were traversing.

The attack fell upon Doles's Ga. brigade of Rodes's division,
and Upton thus describes how the charge was met: —

"Here occurred a deadly hand-to-hand conflict. The enemy sitting in
their pits with pieces upright, loaded, and with bayonets fixed ready to im-
pale the first who should leap over, absolutely refused to yield the ground.
The first of our men who tried to surmount the works fell pierced through
the head by musket balls. Others, seeing the fate of their comrades, held
their pieces at arm's-length and fired downward, while others, poising their

pieces vertically, hurled them down upon their enemy, pinning them to the ground. . . . Numbers prevailed and like a resistless wave the column poured over the works, quickly putting *hors de combat* those who resisted, and sending to the rear those who surrendered."

Mott's division was to have supported Upton on the left, but it did not appear. It seems that this division was formed for the attack where our batteries had a view of it, and that when it attempted to advance, at the signal for the charge, it found itself the target of a severe artillery fire, under which the brigades broke and fell back to the foot of the hill. Meanwhile, the Confederate brigades on the right and left had promptly attacked Upton upon both flanks, and Battle's brigade, brought up from the rear, attacked him in front. He brought up his fourth line in vain in a hard fight, and was finally driven back with loss, which he states as "about 1000 in killed, wounded, and prisoners," probably about 20 per cent of his command. Ewell's official report of the affair, dated Richmond, March 20, 1865, says : —

"The enemy was driven from our works, leaving 100 dead within them and a large number in front. Our loss, as near as I can tell, was 650, of whom 350 were prisoners."

The total losses of the Federals for the day were estimated at 4100, and included Gen. Stevenson of Burnside's corps killed by a sharpshooter.

Grant believed that the failure of Mott's division to advance had caused Upton's defeat upon the 10th, and on the 11th he planned a much more powerful attack to be made by the whole of the 2d and the 9th corps. In preparation for this, the corps commanders were ordered to ascertain the least force which could hold their lines, and leave the remainder available for service elsewhere. They were also directed to press their skirmishers forward so as to allow close reconnoissance of our works. Later, he determined upon the salient already described, and afterward known as the "Bloody Angle," as the point of attack. On our lines the day was one of bitter sharpshooting and angry artillery practice. Meanwhile, all movements of the enemy were carefully watched for indications of his plans, and one was reported from which Lee derived the impression that he was preparing to make a flank march to our left.

Hancock had sent Miles to reconnoitre across the Po in the direction of Todd's Tavern. Only two regiments were sent, and they returned in the evening, but our report had exaggerated the numbers and undue importance was attached to the incident. Early had also reported indications of movements to the left. Lee believed that Grant was preparing for another flank march to be attempted during the night, and orders were sent to each chief of artillery to withdraw at sundown all of his guns which were in lines close to the enemy, so that if it became necessary to move during the night, the withdrawal of the guns would not be heard. Mahone's division was still upon Field's left, and Lee also ordered it, with two brigades of Wilcox, to make a night march and occupy Shady Grove before daylight.

During the night, it was discovered that the movement to the left had been unimportant (it was supposed to have been a feint, but it was not) so that Mahone was recalled, and now he, with Wilcox's two brigades, were returned to Hill's corps. The order to the chiefs of artillery, however, was not recalled, and consequently 22 guns of Page's and Cutshaw's battalions were, about sundown, withdrawn from the position about to be attacked. It was a fatal mistake, as will presently appear.

On the line of Longstreet's corps, I had ventured to accomplish the intent of the order without literal compliance with its terms. I had visited every battery and had its ammunition chests mounted (they were usually dismounted, and the chests placed under cover in the pits) and the carriages so placed and the roads so prepared that we could withdraw easily and without noise. Our guns all remained in position on the lines.

It was in the dark of the moon, and heavy rain was falling as the Federals began to move soon after nightfall. It was after midnight when they reached the ground where they were to form. Hancock's formation is interesting, but it failed from an over-concentration of force.

HANCOCK'S FORMATION FOR CHARGE, MAY 12, 1864

BARLOW'S DIV.

BROOKS'S BRIG.   MILES'S BRIG.   BIRNEY'S DIV.

↑   ↑   ↑

SMYTH'S BRIG.   BROWN'S BRIG.   MOTT'S DIV.

↑   ↑   ↑

GIBBON'S DIV.

↑

Did not follow until advance struck the works.

At Gettysburg, our formation for Pickett's charge (which was too light) was in two lines supported at a little distance by a part of a third. Upton's charge, on the 10th, was in four lines, and was at first successful, but was finally repulsed. Hancock seemed anxious to make sure, and formed Barlow's division in two lines of two brigades each, "closed in mass." This gave a column at least 10 ranks (or 20 men) deep. Barlow had open ground to advance over. On his right, Birney had a marsh and then a thick wood of low pines, until quite near the enemy. He was in two lines followed by Mott in one. In rear of all stood Gibbon's division deployed. All officers were dismounted, and the division and brigade commanders and their staffs marched in the centre between the lines. The intervals between the ranks in Barlow's division were all so small that, soon after the advance began, the intervals were lost and the division became a solid mass.

Grant had ordered the charge at 4 A.M., but, owing to fog, Hancock delayed until 4.35. As it began to grow light, the order was given to charge. The men moved at first quietly and slowly, but about the time when the Confederate pickets fired, they broke into a run and there was some cheering. The distance to

our works was about 1200 yards. The Confederates had heard
the noise of the column being formed, and urgent calls had been
sent for the return of the 22 guns which had garnished our parapets the day before, but had been withdrawn about sundown, as
already told. They were now coming back through the woods
in two long lines under Page and Cutshaw. The two leading
guns were in time to unlimber, and, between them, fired three
rounds into the Federal masses before they were surrounded.
All the column, except the two rear guns, was captured. Had
they been in their places, it is quite certain that the charge would
not have been successful. Nowhere else, in the whole history
of the war, was such a target, so large, so dense, so vulnerable,
ever presented to so large a force of artillery. Ranks had
already been lost in the crowd and officers could neither show
example or exercise authority. A few discharges would have
made of it a mob which could not have been rallied.   There was
a thick abattis of felled trees in front and " chevaux de frise "
which, Barlow says, "would have been very difficult to get through
under a cool fire." For the mob, which his division would have
soon formed, there would have been no escape but flight, with
phenomenal loss for the time exposed to fire. As it was, our
infantry had time to fire only two or three hurried rounds, when
the enemy were upon them. Perhaps one-third escaped, but
about two-thirds were captured, among them being Maj.-Gen.
Johnston and Brig.-Gen. Steuart. Of the 22 guns, 18 were captured at once. Two more were abandoned between the lines,
where our men were able to use them against the enemy during
the day, but the enemy got them during the night.

Thus, the first Federal operation of the day was a great success,
so far as guns and prisoners were concerned; but the tactics
used were so faulty that they practically so embarrassed all the
future operations, as to prevent any further fruit from the victory, although the whole force of the army was brought to bear.
The enemy, in possession of the salient and the captured guns,
pursued the fugitives and turned some of the captured guns upon
them. But the fugitives, falling back, soon met reënforcements
coming from the brigades of Johnston and Gordon on the right,
and from Daniel and Ramseur on the left, who attacked them

with great spirit. The pursuers were utterly disorganized, as, indeed, was almost the whole of Hancock's corps, and there was
scarcely room within the salient to organize and re-form the lines.

Efforts were being made by Barlow when the well-organized
Confederate brigades began to push back the disorganized pursuers and recover some of the ground which had been lost. It
was reported to Grant that Hancock was being checked and
eight brigades of the 6th corps were ordered to reënforce him.
They charged in with cheers and were added to the troops already much too crowded in the confined space. This was about
8 A.M.

Meanwhile, Burnside had been ordered at 5 A.M. to assault
A. P. Hill's lines on our right. He had sent Potter's division
against Lane's, our extreme brigade on that flank. Potter carried the line and captured two guns. Lane re-formed his brigade
in some old breastworks, which enfiladed those Potter had taken,
drove him out, and recaptured the guns. Wilcox sent two brigades to Lane's help, but they were not needed and were sent
back.

About 8 A.M., Burnside was ordered to move to his left and
connect with Hancock's line, which he did by 9.15. Willcox's
division of the 9th was now ordered to attack Heth's line, at a
favorable point where a pine thicket allowed a close approach
under cover. While his attack was in progress, he was struck
on his left flank by Lane's and Weisiger's brigades of Hill's corps,
who had been sent out by Early to endeavor to relieve the pressure at the salient. Lane claimed to have captured a battery,
but was unable to take it off. Willcox was helped by Crittenden's
division, and skirmishing and heavy artillery firing was kept up
all day without material result.

To return now to the Angle where eight brigades of the 6th
corps had arrived about 8 A.M. The determined counter attacks
of Ewell's brigades had cleared the space within the breastworks
and compelled the enemy to confine themselves to the outside
slopes of the parapet or the interior of a few enclosures along its
inside slopes made by joining the ends of the traverses, which
were only 10 or 12 feet apart, and built up of logs. Every available foot of cover was occupied, and outside of the parapets the

men stood from 20 to 40 deep. Those in rear would pass guns to some in front, who would fire almost as rapidly as if they had breech-loaders. Fortunately, much of the fire was without aim or nothing could have lived before it. The entire forest in its front was killed, logs were whipped into basket stuff. An oak tree, 22 inches in diameter, whose trunk is still preserved in Washington, was cut down entirely by musketry fire, disabling several men in the 1st S.C. regiment, by its fall. Ammunition was supplied liberally from the rear and many men fired over 300 rounds. The bodies of the wounded and slain of both sides who had fallen in the earlier attacks were shot to pieces and mangled beyond any recognition.

In the meantime, Lee had brought up three brigades of Hill's corps (Perrin's, and Harris's of Mahone's division and McGowan of Wilcox's), and Grant added two brigades of Ricketts's division and three of Cutler's to the 19 brigades already engaged. He also brought up artillery on the two flanks outside the salient to rake the prolongations of the parapet held by the Federals. In their reserve artillery were eight 24-Pr. Cochorn mortars, and these, too, were brought and effectively used to drop shells behind the Confederate parapets. Across the throat of the Angle, our line was covered from view by the wood. Lee's only opportunity for attack was along the west parapet, where the traverses were close together, as already told. Here the Confederates never relaxed their efforts and succeeded in getting possession of nearly all of them up to the salient. Many were shot and stabbed through the crevices of the logs. Perrin was killed and McGowan severely wounded. In his report, the latter writes as follows : —

"In getting into this trench, we had to pass through a terrific fire. . . . We found in the trenches Gen. Harris, and what remained of his gallant brigade, and they (Mississippians and Carolinians), mingled together, made one of the most gallant and stubborn defences recorded in history. These two brigades remained there, holding our line without reënforcements, without food, water, or rest, under a storm of balls, which did not intermit one instant of time, for 18 hours. The trenches on the right of the Bloody Angle ran with blood and had to be cleared of the dead bodies more than once. . . . The loss in my brigade was very heavy, being in the aggregate 451. . . . Our men lay on one side of the breastwork and the enemy on the other, and in many cases men were pulled over. It is believed we captured as many prisoners as we lost."

We pass now to the left, to Longstreet's front opposite Warren. At dawn, Warren had opened all his guns and pressed forward his skirmishers, hoping soon to see us sending forces to our right, to meet Hancock's victorious advance. But Hancock had overdone his effort, as has been seen, and his advance had been brief. Our guns were all behind their parapets and firing slowly in reply to the enemy. Warren saw no encouragement to attempt an attack, so he waited. At 9.15, Grant ordered him "to attack at once, at all hazards and with his whole force if necessary." At 10 A.M., we saw Warren's men advance over the open ground where they had first assaulted us on the 8th. By common consent, infantry and artillery reserved their fire until his line was within 100 yards. Then both opened, and the line was quickly driven back with heavy loss to them, and but little to ourselves. They fell back to their right out of our sight in a hollow. We followed their disappearance with a random fire of artillery down the hollow, which Bratton's skirmishers reported enfiladed them and caused much loss. But, being random fire, it was presently discontinued to save ammunition. Soon there broke out in the hollow a furious fusillade for which we could find no explanation, unless they were firing on each other by mistake. This seemed unlikely when it was kept up for over two hours, a great roar of musketry. Bratton, in his report, says: —

"It seemed a heavy battle and we had nothing to do with it. Skirmishers from the 1st and 5th (S.C.) regiments were ordered up to the crest to discover what it meant.

"They found them lying behind the crest, firing at what did not clearly appear, but they (the skirmishers), with great gallantry, charged them with a yell, routed, and put the whole mass to flight most precipitate and headlong, capturing some 40 prisoners. In their haste and panic a multitude of them ran across an open space and gave our battery and my line of battle on the right a shot at them, the skirmishers, too. We kept up a most effective fire on them, and that field also was thickly dotted with their dead and wounded."

I can find no mention of this episode in any Federal report

beyond statements in the itineraries of Griffin's and Cutler's divisions that they were engaged, Griffin three and Cutler four hours, on the morning of the 12th. Can it be that two Federal divisions fought each other for nearly that time and that every reference to it in the official reports has been carefully suppressed? It seems so. Warren's account of the attack gives suspiciously few details, not even noting the divisions engaged. Here is the whole of it: —

"I also again assailed the enemy's intrenchments, suffering heavy loss but failing to get in. The enemy's direct and flank fire was too destructive. Lost very heavily."

It hardly seems likely that so much loss could have been incurred from their very brief exposure to *our* fire. Longstreet's official diary describes the action only as two violent assaults between nine and ten, on a part of Field's line. Gen. B. G. Humphreys's book throws no light on the subject beyond the following footnote: —

"I was overlooking the right of the army and gave the order for the assaults there to cease as soon as I was satisfied they could not succeed; and directed the transfer of the troops to the centre for the attack there."

What, then, prolonged the engagements of Griffin and Cutler between three and four hours, of which no one gives any details?

Immediately after this failure of Warren to break our line, his whole force was transferred to the Angle, except Crawford's division of two brigades, and Kitching's and Denison's brigades. This added 8 brigades to the 24 already massed there, and artillery was also brought to bear from every spot, near and far, which offered a location. It had been intended to use Warren's corps in a fresh attack upon the Angle, but after some preparation it was wisely abandoned. Lee had brought up Humphreys's brigade from Kershaw's, and Bratton's from Field's division. We had also contributed Cabell's Art'y Batt'n to strengthen the force holding the line across the gorge, and it was practically impregnable. As night approached, several Federal brigades were designated to keep up the fire upon our lines all night. It was faithfully done, at least until 1 A.M., about which time, under cover of the darkness, we withdrew to the gorge line, leaving to the enemy the intrenchments which had been so well defended all day. It had been necessary in the morning to retake them from Hancock's first assault, and to hold them until Lee could close the gorge. Afterward, he could not withdraw the force with which he had done it until nightfall, though there was no longer any value in the lines they held.

The military lesson to be learned from the failure of Hancock's assault (for it was a failure to get only 20 guns and perhaps 4000 prisoners for such a gigantic effort) is, that there is a maximum limit to the force which can be advantageously used in any locality, and a superfluity may paralyze all efforts. Here there was a great superfluity.

The Federal losses for the 12th are given by Humphreys as : —

Killed and wounded	6,020	
Missing	800	6,820

The Federal Gens. Wright, Webb, and Carroll were wounded. The Confederate losses, Humphreys estimates as between 4000 and 5000 killed and wounded and 4000 prisoners. We had: Gens. Daniel and Perrin killed; James A. Walker, R. D. Johnston, McGowan, and Ramseur severely wounded; Edward Johnson and George A. Steuart captured. One feature of the occasion which added to the hardship and suffering on both sides was the rain which fell almost incessantly for two nights and a day. Mr. Dana gives the following account of a visit to the Angle on the 13th : —

"All around us the underbrush and trees had been riddled and burnt. The ground was thick with dead and wounded men, among whom the relief corps was at work. The earth, which was soft from the heavy rains we had been having both before and during the battle, had been trampled by the fighting thousands of men until it was soft like hasty pudding. As we stood there looking silently down at it, of a sudden the leg of a man was lifted up from the pool and the mud dripped off his boot. It was so unexpected, so horrible, that for a moment we were stunned. Then we pulled ourselves together and called to some soldiers near by to rescue the owner of the leg. They pulled him out with but little trouble and discovered that he was not dead, only wounded. He was taken to the hospital where he will get well, I believe."

As might have been expected, May 13 was comparatively a day of rest. The only record in my note-book is of the Federal

wounded in front of our lines, who had been left on the ground
since the 8th.   Some were still alive, and we had noticed one who
had occasionally raised himself to nearly a sitting posture.   To-
day he was trying to knock himself in the head with the butt of
his musket, making several feeble efforts.   Grant only consented to ask a flag of truce for the wounded some days after
Cold Harbor on June 3.   On more than one occasion, the wounded
Federals had been burnt by fires in the woods.

On the 14th, we found the enemy gone from our front, but none
of the wounded were now found alive.   The man who had tried
the day before to kill himself was found to belong to the Maryland
brigade.   He had been partially stripped and was most elaborately
tattooed.   At night, Field's division was transferred from our
left flank to the extreme right, where we found Warren's corps
already in front of us, having been transferred the night before.

We did not know it at the time, but it afterward appeared that
Grant had designed another great battle for us this morning.
Only the fearful roads, due to the recent rains, and the exhaustion of his men had forced him to abandon the effort.   On the
11th, he had sent his famous despatch that he would "fight it
out on this line if it takes all the summer."

On the night of the 13th, the moon was young, the night foggy,
rainy, and intensely dark.   The 5th and 6th corps were ordered
to march by farm roads, passing in rear of the 2d and 9th, cross
the Ny, move through fields to the Fredericksburg road, on it
recross the Ny, form on Burnside's left, and attack our right
flank at 4 A.M. on the 14th.   The 2d corps and the 9th were to
be ready, and, when ordered, to join in the attack upon our
whole line.   Though every precaution had been taken to mark
the way with bonfires and men posted along the route, Warren
only arrived on time with about 4000 men.   The rain had put
out the fires and the men had lost their way and floundered in
the mud, until they were so broken and scattered that they could
not be gotten into condition for operations that day, and the
proposed attack was abandoned.   We had doubtless had a
narrow escape from serious trouble.   With ordinary weather the
distance was not great, and both the 5th and 6th corps could
have surprised our flank at dawn in the morning.   Our in-

trenchments on that flank did not then extend much beyond the court-house.

At 10 o'clock at night of the 14th came orders for our headquarters and Kershaw's division to follow Field to the right flank. There we extended our line to the right, covering Snell's Bridge over the Po. The enemy occupied himself with building defensive lines which did not follow ours toward the Po, but turned eastward and bent back toward the northeast, designed to be held by a reduced force, while he concentrated for another effort to break our line in the gorge of the salient, where he had been checked on the 12th. It had been suggested to Grant by Wright and Humphreys that, after the lapse of a few days, his movement to the left and concentration there would have caused Lee to weaken his left, and afford a favorable opportunity to surprise our Bloody Angle position again.

By the 17th, his works were strong enough to be held by Warren with the 5th corps, and the 2d and 6th were ordered to pass around the 9th during the night, and the three corps to attack in conjunction at dawn, while Warren's corps coöperated with the artillery from the Federal left. The attack seemed to promise well. Three corps of infantry were to make it, and the artillery of four were to support it. It would fall wholly on Ewell's corps, reduced by capture of Johnson's division on the 12th; its artillery only supplemented by a few guns of Hill's corps. It proved, however, an utter failure. The infantry was so slow in finding its way through the woods, behind which the line lay, that it was nearly 8 A.M. when it found itself in sight of our line through an opening in the woods. Twenty-nine guns opened upon it. Gibbon's and Barlow's division, which had been in the assaulting column on the 12th, again led the assault in lines of brigades, a much more effective formation than the column closed in mass, which presented itself on the 12th. They advanced over the same ground they had then traversed, and it is reported that the stench, which arose from the unburied dead, "was so sickening and terrible that many of the officers and men were made deathly sick from it." But our guns, which had been absent before, were now in position. Already, before they emerged from the wood, they were much shaken, and some of the brigades were driven back entirely by the artillery fire, our guns giving little attention to their artillery but confining their fire to the infantry. Only a few of these approached our abattis. None penetrated it, and the first attack was never renewed. About 10 A.M., Meade ordered the attack discontinued, and the troops withdrawn. Few of our infantry were engaged and none of them heavily for any length of time, the whole affair being decided by the artillery of the 2d and 3d corps. McParlin, Medical Director, reports of this affair : —

"Five hundred and fifty-two wounded were the result, and the character of the wounds were unusually severe, a large proportion being caused by shell and canister."

Our own loss was very trifling.

Grant, on the 19th, was preparing to move Hancock at night on the road to Richmond and had issued the order about noon. In the afternoon, he was interrupted in his preparations by the appearance of Ewell with his corps, about 6000 men, in his rear. Lee had suspected that Grant was beginning a flanking movement, and had directed Ewell to demonstrate against him to find out. Ewell obtained leave, instead, to move around his right, hoping to accomplish the result with less loss, as Grant's position in our front was strongly intrenched. By a circuitous route and roads impassable for artillery, he took his infantry far around the enemy and crossed the Ny in their rear, near the camp of Tyler's large division and Kitching's larger brigade. Here Ewell occupied a very critical position. He was so slow in realizing this and beginning his retreat that Ramseur, fearing that further delay would cause disaster, charged the enemy. Having driven them a short distance, he retreated, and, taking a position in rear with Pegram, the two were able to delay the enemy until darkness covered a withdrawal. Hancock and Warren both hurried reënforcements to Tyler, and Ewell made a lucky escape. His loss in this venture was severe for the time engaged, being about 900 killed, wounded, and missing, or 15 per cent of his whole force. It would have cost less and have risked much less to have made a demonstration in front. The Federal loss was estimated at 1100.

The two battles of the Wilderness and Spottsylvania may be

considered as parts of the one great battle of *"Grant and Lee,"* begun in the Wilderness on May 5, 1864, and terminated only at Appomattox on April 9, 1865. During all this time the two armies were locked as if in a mortal embrace. Only by night could they shift positions. Firing by day was almost incessant. The consumption of men was far in excess of anything ever known before. The killed and wounded of the Federals in the Wilderness and Spottsylvania had been 28,202, and with 4,225 missing, the total loss had been 33,110.

The Confederate losses can never be accurately known for any of the battles, from now until the close of the war, as few reports could be made in such active campaigns. Livermore's estimates give 17,250 for the same battles, the missing not included.

THE NORTH ANNA AND COLD HARBOR

After the signal failure on the 18th of his second venture at the Bloody Angle, Grant seems to have exhausted the possibilities on the Spottsylvania lines, and for his next effort he decided to lay a snare for Lee. It was thought that if Hancock's corps was sent off about 20 miles on the line of the Fredericksburg R.R., that Lee would be tempted to attack it and endeavor to crush it while isolated. Grant, having every preparation made for a rapid march, might follow and attack Lee before he could intrench himself. Hancock, accordingly, marched at nightfall on the 20th, and, by midday of the 21st, Barlow had crossed the Mattapony and began to intrench at Milford Station, the rest of the 2d corps following. Next morning, the 5th corps marched about 10 A.M., and the 6th and 9th followed later in the day.

Lee never knew of the trap set for him. When he was informed of Hancock's appearance at Milford by signal stations and cavalry detachments, he supposed it to be an effort to pass him on the flank. Little time was wasted. Wilcox drove in the 6th corps skirmishers in an effort to find out what was going on, and Ewell was moved at once across the Po, on the right, and about noon was started to Hanover Junction. Longstreet followed him at night, and Hill moved at the same time by a parallel road. Longstreet marched all night and until about noon on the 22d, when we bivouacked on the south side of the North Anna about 30 miles from the camps we had left, and within a mile of the Junction. Hill, who had now returned to duty, crossed the North Anna about 10 miles above us on the 22d, and moved down next morning.

The lure set for Lee had failed of its object. To make the effort, Hancock had been sent by a route about nine miles longer than the most direct from Grant's left to Hanover Junction, which was only 25 miles, and three miles shorter than Lee's shortest. Having the additional advantage of the initiative, it was doubtless an error on Grant's part to undertake it. On the 22d, it was learned that all three of Lee's corps had passed the night before, and the Federal corps were now all directed to follow.

At Hanover Junction, Lee received his first reënforcements, about 9000 men. On May 15, Breckenridge had severely defeated Sigel at New Market, in the Valley, and driven him south of Cedar Creek, allowing Lee to bring down Breckenridge with two brigades of infantry, about 2500 men. Beauregard, on May 16, had also defeated Butler at Drury's Bluff, allowing Lee to send for Pickett's division, about 5000 men. Hoke's brigade, about 1200 strong, was also brought from Petersburg and assigned to Early's division. Gordon was promoted and assigned to the remnant of Johnson's division, to which also his own brigade under Evans was now transferred from Early.

We had taken position behind the North Anna, but had not yet selected a line of battle or started any intrenchments, when early in the afternoon, the enemy appeared north of the river, and opened fire with artillery upon two slight bridge-head works at the north ends of the railroad bridge and the Telegraph road bridge, which had been constructed to repel raiders a year before. We brought up guns and replied, but ravines on the north side allowed covered approaches to both bridge-heads, and both were captured with some prisoners. We held, however, the south end of the railroad bridge, until after dark, and burned it.

Hancock's corps had approached along the railroad and the Telegraph road. Burnside's corps, next on his right, was directed on the Ox Ford, a crossing about two miles above the

railroad. The 5th corps came to the river at Jericho Mills, four
miles above the railroad, and, finding no enemy opposing, a
pontoon bridge was laid and the whole corps was crossed by
4.30 P.M.   Meanwhile, at Ox Ford, Burnside had found the
south bank held in such force that it was not deemed prudent
to attack. The 6th corps was held in reserve on the north bank.

Finding himself at Jericho Mills in the vicinity of Hill's corps.
Warren had formed line of battle in very favorable position,
He was able to cover his front with the edge of a wood concealing
his actual line.   His left rested on the river, which made a large
concave bend in his rear and again drew near his right, with open
ground upon that flank commanded by the artillery.   But the
rare opportunity of an isolated corps unintrenched was here
offered, and Hill hastened to attack it.

About 6 P.M., he fell upon Griffin in the centre, and Cutler on the
right, who had not fully formed their lines.   Cutler was broken
and pursued, but the artillery on that flank was able to save the
situation and Hill was finally repulsed.   The casualties were
about equal, perhaps 1500 on each side.

During the night, Lee had selected and intrenched an excellent
line, in fact, it was too good, for it defeated its object, as the
enemy never dared to attack.   It rested on the river from a half-
mile above the bridge to the Ox Ford, and thence, leaving the
North Anna, it ran across the narrow peninsula one and a half
miles to Little River, where its left rested.   Returning to the
centre, on the North Anna above the bridge, the line ran southeast across a large bend of the river and rested on its right three
miles below, near the site of Morris's Bridge.   In front of us, the
enemy formed with the 5th and 6th corps before our left flank,
and with the 2d and part of the 9th before our right flank.   Their
two wings, both south of the river, were unable to communicate
without crossing the river twice.   This peculiar situation could
not fail to suggest unusual opportunities to each commander.

Burnside was first ordered to attack and carry Ox Ford, which
would at once unite their wings and divide ours.   But Burnside
pronounced the task impossible, and did not attempt it.   Hancock on his left, and Warren on his right, each advanced skirmishers and felt our lines, but both reported against any attack.

Lee, at this time, happened to be very much indisposed and confined to his tent. But he was exceedingly anxious, with the reenforcements which he had received, to improve the slightest opportunity to give Grant a severe blow. This seemed a rare occasion where he might fall upon Hancock's and Potter's division of the 9th before they could be assisted by the other corps. He said to his staff: "We must strike them. We must never let them pass us again."

But it happened that the country occupied by the Federal lines upon both flanks, and especially on their left, was flat and open, allowing full use of their artillery, and their intrenchments were very strong. Probably it was wisely held by our subordinates that no successful attack could be made, and at night on May 26, Grant removed the temptation, ere Lee had recovered from his illness, by moving for the Pamunkey.

On May 24, Sheridan had rejoined from his expedition to the James, on which he had done some damage to the two railroads, entering Richmond from the north, and burned some rolling stock and stores, but had made no impression on the campaign. I think it quite probable, however, that had Sheridan's cavalry been with the army, Grant would not have tried his vain stratagem of placing Hancock as a lure at Milford, but, with his aid, have endeavored to anticipate us at Hanover Junction. So I think this raid should be classed as a blunder, like Pleasonton's at Chancellorsville and Stuart's at Gettysburg. Our most serious loss in connection with it had been the death of our brilliant cavalry leader, Maj.-Gen. J. E. B. Stuart, who was killed at Yellow Tavern, near Richmond, on May 11. As before said, I have always believed that Lee should have made him the successor of Stonewall Jackson when the latter was killed at Chancellorsville.

Grant's total casualties in the North Anna lines, May 23 to 27, are given as : —

Killed 22, wounded 1460, missing 290, total 1973.

The Confederate losses were probably about the same.

On the 26th, Grant, at noon, started Sheridan and the pontoon trains to cross the Pamunkey River at Hanover Town. After dark the infantry moved, and by next morning his whole army had vanished, except cavalry pickets at the sites where the bridges had stood. The movement of the enemy was not discovered until the morning of the 27th. The rough sketch map represents the essentials of the position.

The army was put in motion without delay, crossing the South Anna on the railroad bridges and, after a march of 15 miles, we encamped that night near Half Sink. The next morning, we

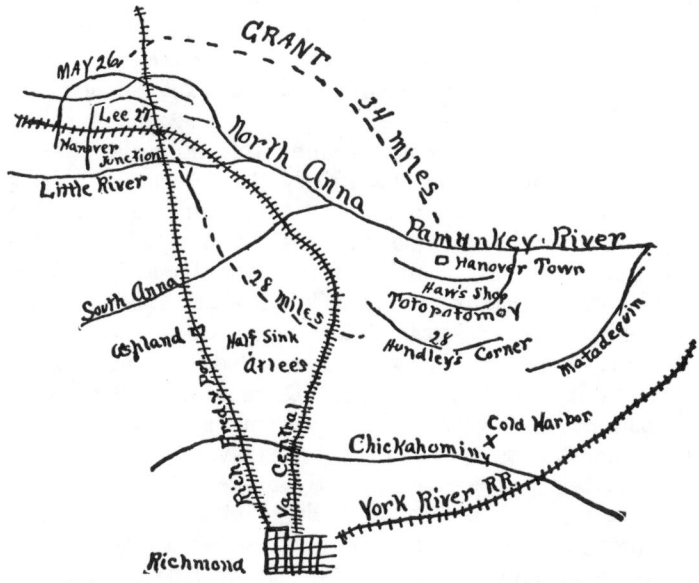

moved about 13 miles and found ourselves near the Totopotomoy, with Grant just arriving on the opposite side. Sheridan's cavalry was in his front, and under orders to make a demonstration toward Richmond. Hampton, with his own and Fitz-Lee's divisions, and Butler's brigade of cavalry, recently arrived from S.C., were attacked by Gregg's and Torbert's divisions, with Merritt's reserve brigade at Haw's Shop. The battle was fiercely contested all day, but the enemy had the great advantage of the Spencer magazine carbine, and, late in the after-noon, they drove Hampton back.

Ewell's health at this time required him to surrender the command of his corps permanently to Early, who was succeeded by Ramseur, promoted.

On Sunday, the 29th, Grant ordered the 6th, 2d, and 5th corps, in that order from his right to left, to reconnoitre in their fronts and locate our lines, the 9th corps being held in reserve. The 6th corps found only the cavalry on our left flank. The other two found our pickets on the Totopotomoy, and, at an average distance of a thousand yards behind, our line was rapidly intrenching. Some sharp skirmishing occurred during the next three days, the enemy crossing the Totopotomoy and intrenching opposite to us.

In many of the Federal accounts, it is assumed that Lee's attitude at this period was strictly the defensive. Perhaps it should have been, but all who were near him recognized that never in the war was he so ready to attack upon the slightest opportunity. An instance occurred on May 30, of which I was a spectator. A half-mile in front of our line we could see Bethesda Church, an important junction point, well within the enemy's territory, and sure to be included within his lines, rapidly being extended to his left. Down a long, straight road, we had seen their cavalry all the morning, and, about noon, a brigade of infantry appeared. Immediately, Lee ordered Early to send a brigade to attack it. Early selected Pegram's brigade, commanded by Gen. Edward Willis, a brilliant young officer, just promoted from the 12th Ga., who had been a cadet at West Point at the beginning of the war. He had been a personal friend and I saw his brigade start on its errand with apprehension of disaster, for it was evident that a hornets' nest would be stirred up. The Federal brigade was quickly routed and pursued, but the pursuers soon encountered a division with its artillery and were repulsed with severe loss. It had "made a resolute attack," as stated by Humphreys, and lost Willis and two of his colonels, killed.

Meanwhile, Butler having been defeated, and, as said by Grant, "bottled" at Bermuda Hundreds, Grant decided to draw from him two divisions of the 10th and one of the 18th corps, under command of W. F. Smith, with which to give Lee a surprise. The orders had been given on May 22, the troops to be brought by water down the James and up the York. On May 30, the transports bearing them began to arrive at the White House, and to disembark about 16,000 infantry, whose coming was not known to Lee. But he, having the reënforcements which joined him at Hanover Junction, about 9000, and receiving now Hoke's division, which had come over from Drury's Bluff, about 6000, and being disappointed at Grant's failure to attack his lines on the Totopotomoy, had himself planned a grand stroke for June 1.

The cavalry of the two armies had been heavily engaged for two days near Cold Harbor, and Hoke's division was in that neighborhood. Lee proposed to extend Longstreet's corps to join it, and, attacking early, to sweep to his left behind Grant's lines, taking them in flank, while Hill and Ewell pressed them in front. He did not even yet suspect the presence of Smith's troops, and it was with high hopes of a great victory on the 1st that Longstreet's corps, under Anderson, with all its artillery, marched to the vicinity of Cold Harbor, during the night of May 31.

Grant had, meanwhile, determined to send two corps to seize Cold Harbor on the 1st. Torbert, the evening before, with his dismounted troopers and magazine carbines, had repulsed a severe attack by Fitz-Lee, but, anticipating attack by Hoke's infantry in the morning, he had begun to withdraw during the night. He received orders, however, to hold the position at all hazards, on which he returned, and devoted the night to intrenching his position. The 6th corps, from the extreme Federal right, was put in motion that night for Cold Harbor, having about 15 miles to go. Smith, with 10,000 men and 16 guns, already on the march from White House to join Grant, had also been ordered during the night to Cold Harbor. A mistake in the order took him first to New Castle Ferry on the Pamunkey, and it was only at 4 P.M. of the 1st that he joined at Cold Harbor the 6th corps, the head of which had reached the ground about 10 A.M. after a fatiguing all-night march. It is plain, then, that here a rare opportunity had been offered the Confederates.

With Hoke's large division on its right flank, Longstreet's corps should have been able to quickly clear the way of three brigades of cavalry. It would have had then the opportunity to meet the 6th corps scattered along the road for many miles and in an exhausted condition. Unfortunately, Hoke's brigade had not been put under Anderson's command, so neither felt full responsibility. It only formed in line, but did not attack the cavalry breastworks, reporting them as too strong. Kershaw made an attack about 6 A.M., but only put into it two brigades. The enemy, with their magazine carbines behind intrenchments, repulsed two assaults with severe loss, and then the turning enterprise was abandoned. Lee was not upon the ground in the early hours of the day, and Longstreet was absent, wounded. No effort worthy the name was used to carry out Lee's plan of attack, nor were the favorable conditions appreciated, although they might have been, as only cavalry was found in our front. Hoke's division should have been used to turn their flank and get among their dismounts.

While Kershaw made his attack, the remainder of the long column halted in the road, expecting the march to be presently resumed. But when the delay was prolonged, and a few random bullets from the front began to reach the line, without any general instructions, the men here and there began to dig dirt with their bayonets and pile it with their tin cups to get a little cover. Others followed suit, and gradually the whole column was at work intrenching the line along which they had halted. Gradually it became known that the enemy were accumulating in our front, and then, as the country was generally flat, orders were given to close up the column and adopt its line as the line of battle, distributing our guns upon it at suitable points. Our intrenchments were scarcely more than a good beginning, a line of knee-deep trench with the earth thrown in front. It was entirely without abattis or obstruction in front, except at a point on our picket line where a small entanglement had been left by our cavalry. Meanwhile, Grant, under the mistaken idea that Lee was afraid to fight in the open, was urging an early attack before Lee had time to fortify. But it was 1 P.M. before the whole of the 6th corps was up, and it was 6 P.M. before Smith's command was in position.

In the 6th corps, each brigade was formed in column of regiments, with the brigade on the extreme left refused. The 18th corps was formed in columns of brigades, with the extreme right refused. So the columns of the 18th were three ranks deep, and those of the 6th averaged four. The Confederate formation was but a single rank behind their breastwork, which, as has been described, was the work of but a few hours, almost without intrenching tools. There was also in it a gap of something over 50 yards, where a wooded and tangled ravine and small stream separated Hoke's and Kershaw's divisions.

A rough sketch will illustrate:—

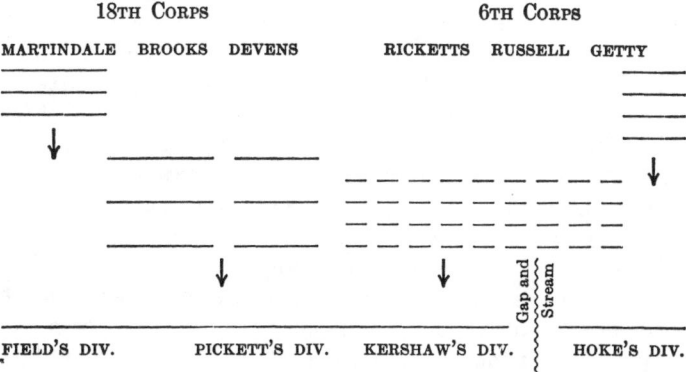

The distance between the lines was about 1400 yards, and our pickets were about 300 yards in our front. About 6 P.M., we had ceased to expect an attack that evening, when a sudden increase of fire on the picket line and the opening of artillery stopped our digging and called all to arms. Soon a perfect tornado of fire broke out in front of Hoke and Kershaw, and extended, but not heavily, to Pickett's front. It soon appeared that at all points but one the enemy's advance had been checked by our fire, without its reaching our line of battle. This was at the 50-yard gap which had been carelessly left between Hoke and

Kershaw. Here a body of wood, fronting on our line for about 200 yards, extended quite a distance toward the enemy, allowing their approach free from observation, until they had actually passed through the gap and were in our rear. This they did in such numbers that they were able to turn to the right and left and possess themselves of a small portion on each flank, capturing a few hundred prisoners.

As there were no reserves, Hunton's brigade from Pickett's division, and Gregg's from Field's, were hurried to the spot and checked the enemy, recovered the portion taken from Hoke, and connected the broken ends by a horseshoe some 200 yards in length. At all other points the enemy stopped at what was practically our picket line and intrenched themselves. Darkness put an end to the fighting. The Federal loss was about 2650. The Confederate was evidently less, as the enemy only came to close quarters near the gap in the line.

Grant felt encouraged by his partial success, and, believing that he had inserted the small end of a wedge, prepared to drive it home. Lee was practically fighting with a river at his back. It was only the Chickahominy, but could his army be routed, Grant could surely inflict severe losses upon it before Lee could retreat over the few available roads. The 2d corps, on Grant's right, was ordered during the night to march around 9th and 5th and reënforce the 6th, which was ordered to the attack at dawn. But it was the dark of the moon, and the night march proved slow and exhausting; the 18th corps was also short of ammunition, so the attack was postponed, at first until 5 P.M. The 5th corps, on June 2, was ordered to draw in its right flank, and extend its left past the front of Field's and Pickett's, to unite with Smith; and the 9th corps was ordered to be massed in rear of the 5th and to support it in the general attack. This was now again postponed until 4.30 A.M., on the 3d, to allow a full night's rest and ample preparation.

Lee, meanwhile, was no less busy. When he found in the morning that the 2d corps had gone from his front, he had no doubt of its destination, and marching Breckenridge's, Wilcox's, and Mahone's divisions past our rear, he extended Hoke's line to the Chickahominy. He also sent Fitz-Lee's division of cavalry across the river to observe and picket the south side. Early, he directed to cross the lines which had been deserted by the 2d corps and to sweep down to the right on the flank of the 5th. This movement captured the skirmish line of the 9th corps which had marched off not long before, and some of that of the 5th which was being shifted to its left, but by that time Warren had changed front to oppose it and received assistance from the 9th corps, and Early's advance was checked. The fighting lasted until night, and Gen. Doles of Rodes's division, a very valuable officer, was killed. Had Early had enough men to give his movement force, it might have had important results.

On our front the sharpshooting and artillery practice were incessant. In fact, as a diversion in favor of Early, I was ordered to be aggressive with the artillery, and on Field's line Huger's battalion was put out in front of the works to get enfilading fires. In front of Pickett and Kershaw, the enemy's intrenchments were within good range, and their accuracy of fire was such as to disable gun carriages through the embrasures by cutting their spokes. A Napoleon gun of Cabell's was placed in a pit at the end of Kershaw's line (where it was broken the night before), ammunition for it being passed up by hand along the line for several hundred yards. The country was so flat that at few points could the line be safely approached from the rear.

A better horseshoe connection around the gap between Kershaw and Hoke was built to replace the temporary one of the night before; and our intrenchments everywhere got all the work we were able to put upon them, but were still quite imperfect.

Grant received to-day a reënforcement of 3000 infantry and 2000 cavalry under Gen. Cesnola, from Port Royal. They were sent to join Wilson's cavalry upon our left, and were ordered to join in the attack upon Early next morning in flank and rear, while Warren and Burnside attacked in front.

No long description of this carefully planned battle is necessary. Of course, it came off punctually to the minute. For among Grant's great and rare qualities was his ability to make his battles keep their schedule times. One may almost say also, "Of course, we repulsed him everywhere." For it was still true, as Stonewall Jackson had said of the Army of Northern Virginia, "We sometimes fail to drive the enemy from positions. They always fail to drive us." In that respect our army singularly resembled the famous "One-Horse Shay." We held together wonderfully until all our parts, worn out together, failed together at Appomattox. Naturally, as the attack had been on the largest possible scale, the repulse was unusually severe and bloody; and ,the roar of the battle, while it lasted, probably exceeded even that of the combats in the Wilderness, which Humphreys described as often approaching the sublime. It broke forth, mingled with vast cheering, in the stillness of early dawn, but it was no surprise. For over an hour the men in the trenches had been alert at hearing in front muffled commands and smothered movements. The Napoleon of Cabell's in the pit at the end of Kershaw's broken line, which had been supplied with ammunition the day before by passing it from hand to hand along the line, was to be withdrawn to the angle where the new horseshoe joined our old line, and the trench in front of its new position was abandoned. The necessary work was only finished at the approach of dawn, and, in whispers, the gunners and infantry supports rolled it back by hand, leaving the trench empty behind them. It was safely located at the embrasure prepared for it, enfilading the deserted trench, and double-shotted with canister, but a few minutes before the cheering enemy, who here had not 100 yards to advance through thin woods, swarmed over the parapet to find the trench deserted, into which they leaped, and to receive the double canister and the musketry and artillery of the new line as they paused wondering at our disappearance.

The sound of the battle reached Richmond, and men came out on the streets to listen to it. Some houses were prepared for an unusual influx of wounded, but few came. Richmond listened calmly, for it had confidence in the One-Horse Shay.

The brunt of the action lasted about an hour, though at isolated places attacks were renewed, or more or less distant fire was kept up until after noon. As a general thing, the assaults were checked at about 50 yards from our lines, but at two or three points leading officers were killed on or very near our parapets.

At one point only was our parapet carried.   There a hurried location in front of Barlow's division permitted him to approach,
under complete shelter from fire of our line of battle, within 75
yards.   Here a rush captured three guns and some few hundred
prisoners, but Finnegan's brigade soon recaptured the guns
and drove out the enemy.

Grant had authorized Meade, about 7 A.M., to discontinue all
assaults which seemed unpromising, but Meade continued to
urge renewed efforts until 1.30 P.M.   Each of the principal corps
complained repeatedly of cross-fires of artillery which swept
through the ranks "from the right of Smith to the left of Hancock," as reported by Humphreys.   Again he states, —

"The assault of the 2d corps could not be renewed unless the enemy's
enfilading artillery fire could be silenced."

Of the 6th corps he writes: —

"During all this time, besides the direct fire, there was an enfilade
artillery fire that swept through the ranks from the right to the left."

And of the 18th corps: —

"The fire from the right came from a part of the enemy's works against
which no part of our attack was directed, and Gen. Smith was unable to
keep it down with his artillery."

The artillery so complained of was mostly Huger's battalion
of 24 guns, which held the line between Pickett's and Field's
divisions and was, some of it, used in front of the breastworks.

Swinton narrates that some hours after the failure of the first
assault, Meade sent instructions to each corps commander to
renew the attack without reference to the troops on his right or
left; that the order descended through the wonted channels, but
was not obeyed — "the immobile lines pronounced a verdict
against further slaughter."

As so told, an entirely erroneous impression is here created.   No
such silent defiance of orders occurred, or anything like it.   But
there were, doubtless, in the situation described above, occasions
when there was delay in obedience until artillery could be sent
to suppress the hostile guns.   This might be distorted in the
telling and so originate such stories.

At dusk, heavy firing of musketry and artillery broke out at

two or three points, and presently died away.   Each side believed
it had been attacked and had repulsed an assault.   The actual
fact was that each was putting out pickets for the night and had
drawn the other's fire in false alarm.   I have not mentioned
them before, but, throughout the campaign, whenever the lines
were close together, there was likely to be heavy firing of musketry and artillery breaking out in the night, which was afterward reported to be a night attack repulsed.   Every one of
them upon both sides was but a false alarm.   The only actual
night attack of the war of which I know was the battle of Wauhatchie near Chattanooga, Oct. 28, '63.

The Federal casualties are given for June 1–3 as 9948.   As the
losses on the 1st were approximately estimated at 2650, those
on the 3d were approximately 7300.   The loss of officers killed and
wounded was particularly heavy.   The total casualties of the
campaign since crossing the Pamunkey were 14,129.

The Confederate losses on the 3d were never reported, but are
known to have been small.   The *Confederate Medical and Surgical History of the War* gives 1200 wounded and 500 missing
from June 1 to 12.   This, Humphreys estimates, represents about
1500 killed and wounded, which may be taken as a maximum.
Besides the general officers already mentioned as having been
killed and wounded during the campaign, there were also wounded
Gen. Kirkland of Heth's division and Lane of Wilcox's.   Also, on
the 3d of June, were wounded Law of Field's division and Finnegan of Mahone's.

There now ensued on Grant's part several days of indecision,
while he debated what to do next.   Meanwhile, to keep up
appearances, regular approaches were suggested in the orders,
and, at one point in our front, they broke ground at night a
short distance in front of their line of battle and attempted the
construction of a battery.   Having no Coehorn mortars, we improvised mortar fire with howitzers, and the battery was never
completed.   But, during this whole interval, a terrible fire of
sharpshooters was maintained upon both sides, which made life
in our cramped and insufficient trenches almost unsupportable.
Scarcely anywhere in them could one stand erect without being
exposed to a sharpshooter.   Head logs and loopholes built up

of sandbags on the parapets, gave accuracy to the fire. By watching, all the low points on the enemy's line, where men would be exposed in moving about, soon became known. The sharp shooters would then lie with guns already aimed, ready to draw the trigger at the slightest glimpse.

To shield themselves from the midsummer sun, our men were accustomed to invert their muskets, sticking the bayonets in the ground, and letting the hammers of four guns pinch the four corners of a blanket, under which the four men might crowd and get some shelter from the direct midday blaze. To visit the guns scattered all along the lines, one must crouch under the blankets and step over the men, who, in the summer of 1864, were far from being free of insect pests. Points where one could get out to the rear were fully a half-mile apart, and between brigades and regiments there would often be a gap of a few feet or a few yards which the enemy's sharpshooters were usually watching with their fingers on the triggers.

In the Federal lines their intrenchments were deeper and broader, and with abundant zigzag approaches from the rear. Their force was ample to permit frequent reliefs, while we had none. Yet they suffered proportionately. Gibbon's single division reported 280 officers and men killed and wounded by sharpshooters between the 3d of June and the 12th.

Humphreys thus describes the conditions in the Federal army, which had both men and supplies in profusion : —

"The labor in making the approaches and strengthening the intrenchments was hard. The men in the advance part of the lines, which were some miles in length, had to lie close in narrow trenches; with no water, except a little to drink, and that of the worst kind, being from surface drainage; they were exposed to great heat during the day; they had but little sleep; their cooking was of the rudest character. For over a month the army had had no vegetables. . . . Dead mules and horses and offal were scattered all over the country, and between the lines were dead bodies of both parties lying unburied in a burning sun. The country was low and marshy in character. The exhausting effect of all this began to show itself, and sickness of malarial character increased largely. Every effort was made to correct this. Large quantities of vegetables were brought up to the army, and a more stringent police enforced."

Meanwhile, Lee made two efforts to take the offensive against

Grant's right flank and rear. On the 6th, he sent Early on the north of Matadequin Creek, and on the 7th he made an attempt south of the same. In each case swamps were found intervening, which prevented anything being accomplished.

A few days after the battle, while Grant was still in his state of indecision and the make believe of siege operations was going on, Halleck suggested to him the investment of Richmond on the north bank of the James. It was seriously considered, as offering greater security to Washington, but finally rejected.

On June 5, Hunter, in the Valley, who had succeeded Milroy, defeated Jones, who had succeeded Breckenridge. As soon as Lee learned of this, he ordered Breckenridge to return and take with him the troops he had brought to Lee at Hanover Junction. On June 12, he took the bold move of detaching Early's whole corps and sending it to the Valley, by way of Charlottesville. It was ordered to attack Hunter in rear, and, having disposed of him and united with Breckenridge, to move down the Valley, cross the Potomac, and threaten Washington. It is probable that in deciding upon this line of strategy, Lee was influenced by hopes that strong demonstrations against Washington might recall Grant's army for its protection, as had so often happened before. If so, however, the hope now proved vain. Grant's force proved ample to detach enough to protect Washington and still prosecute his campaign before Petersburg. If Early could be spared, it might have been wiser to have sent him to Johnston's army in Ga.

CHAPTER XXI

THE MOVEMENT AGAINST PETERSBURG

The Crisis of the War. High Price of Gold. Difficulty of recruiting in the North. Grant crosses the James and moves on Petersburg. Hancock's Corps Delayed. Movements of Lee. Beauregard's Defence. Fighting of June 16 and 18. Success of Grant's Strategy.

IT is now time to describe Grant's movement against Petersburg which, I think, more than any battle or other incident, constituted what may be called the Crisis of the War. Possibly the South never had any real chance of success from the first, and the actual crisis was past when she fired the first gun. But, though the North was immensely her superior in all the resources of war, the South was able to win many hard-fought battles, and her armies to cherish the hope, as year after year elapsed, that the desperation of her resistance might exact such a price in blood and treasure as would exhaust the enthusiasm of her adversary. Certainly, at no other period was there such depression among the people at home, in the army, in the field, or among the officials of the government in Washington. The expenses of the war were nearly $4,000,000 a day. Gold was at a high premium and advancing rapidly. It went from 168 in May to 285 in July.

The following table shows the fluctuations for each month of 1864:—

MONTH	DAY	HIGHEST	DAY	LOWEST
Jan.	19	$159\frac{3}{8}$	6	$151\frac{1}{2}$
Feb.	16	161	27	$157\frac{1}{8}$
March	26	$169\frac{3}{4}$	1	159
April	26	$186\frac{1}{4}$	4	$166\frac{1}{4}$
May	27	190	10	168
June	30	250	8	193
July	11	285	1	222
Aug.	5	$261\frac{3}{4}$	30	$231\frac{1}{2}$
Sept.	2	$254\frac{1}{2}$	30	191
Oct.	31	$227\frac{3}{4}$	3	189
Nov.	8	260	18	210
Dec.	7	243	18	$212\frac{3}{4}$

Enlisting had almost ceased, although stimulated by enormous bounties. A thousand dollars per man was the ordinary price, and single regiments would sometimes take from their counties 1000 men, and draw a million dollars in bounties the day of their muster. There was growing bitterness in political circles in view of the approaching presidential election. The terrible lists of casualties in battle were daily bringing mourning and distress to every hamlet in the country.

Swinton (p. 494) writes of this period as follows: —

"War is sustained quite as much by the moral energy of a people as by its material resources; and the former must be active to bring out and make available the latter. . . . For armies are things visible and formal, circumscribed by time and space, but the soul of war is a power unseen, bound up with the interests, convictions, passions of men. Now so gloomy was the outlook after the action on the Chickahominy, and to such a degree, by consequence, had the public mind become relaxed, that there was at this time great danger of a collapse of the war.[1]

"Had not success come elsewhere to brighten the horizon, it would have been difficult to have raised new forces to recruit the Army of the Potomac, which, shaken in its structure, its valor quenched in blood, and thousands of its ablest officers killed and wounded, was the Army of the Potomac no more."

It was under these circumstances that Grant made his first move after the week of indecision which followed the battle of Cold Harbor. The most natural movement, and the one which Lee expected, was that he would merely cross the Chickahominy and take position on the north bank of the James at Malvern Hill, adjoining Butler on the south bank at Bermuda Hundreds. This would unite the two armies at the nearest point to Richmond, and they would have the aid of the monitors on the river in a direct advance. But Grant determined to cross the James at Wilcox's Landing, 10 miles below City Point, and entirely out of Lee's observation, and to move thence directly upon Petersburg with his whole army. He would thus pass in rear of Butler and attack the extreme right flank of the Confederate line, which, it was certain, would now be held by only a small

[1] The archives of the State Department, when one day made public, will show how deeply the government was affected by the want of military success and to what resolutions the Executive had in consequence come.

force. It involved the performance of a feat in transportation which had never been equalled, and might well be considered impossible, without days of delay.

It was all accomplished, as will be seen, without mishap, and in such an incredibly short time that Lee refused for three days to believe it. During these three days, June 15, 16, and 17, Grant's whole army was arriving at and attacking Petersburg, which was defended at first only by Beauregard with about 2500 men. Lee, with Longstreet's and Hill's corps, for the same three days, lay idle in the woods on the north side, only replacing some of Beauregard's troops taken to Petersburg from in front of Butler.

But for this, Longstreet's corps might have manned the intrenchments of Petersburg, when Grant's troops first appeared before them, and it is not too much to claim that his defeat would have been not less bloody and disastrous than was the one at Cold Harbor. For, while the intrenchments at Cold Harbor were the poorest and slightest in which we ever fought, the Petersburg lines had been built a year before, and were of the best character, with some guns of position mounted and all the forest in front cleared away to give range to the artillery.

This, then, was really the nearest approach to "a crisis" which occurred during the war, as will more fully appear as we follow the details. Instead of "success elsewhere," Grant here escaped a second defeat more bloody and more overwhelming than any preceding. Thus the last, and perhaps the best, chances of Confederate success were not lost in the repulse at Gettysburg, nor in any combat of arms. They were lost during three days of lying in camp, believing that Grant was hemmed in by the broad part of the James below City Point, and had nowhere to go but to come and attack us. The entire credit for the strategy belongs, I believe, to Grant, though possibly it may be shared by Meade's chief of staff, Humphreys, whose modest narrative makes no reference to the subject.

On Saturday, June 11, the 5th corps was moved down the Chickahominy, about 10 miles to the vicinity of Bottom's Bridge. The next night it crossed on two pontoon bridges, and, inclining to the right, it took position east of Riddle's Shop, where it

intrenched to cover the passage of the other corps. All of the
other corps moved at the same time. The 2d corps crossed at
the same bridge and marched to Wilcox Landing on the James.
The 6th and 9th corps crossed the Chickahominy at Jones's
Bridge and marched to the same place; the 18th corps, under
Smith, was sent back to the White House, where it took transports for City Point, and was landed there the night of the 14th.
Here it was joined by Kautz's cavalry, about 2400 strong, and
by Hink's colored division, 3700, making in all about 16,000 men,
who were ordered to march at dawn on the 15th for Petersburg,
about eight miles, which they were to attack. Here we may
leave them for a while.

Hancock's 2d corps reached Wilcox's Landing at 6 P.M. on
Monday, the 13th, after an all-night march of about 30 miles.
The 5th corps, under Warren, held its position covering the
passage of other corps until night of the 13th, when it followed
Hancock and reached Wilcox's Landing the next noon. The
cavalry and infantry had had some sharp skirmishing, and reported their casualties as 300 killed and wounded. The 6th and
9th corps, whose marches had been from 5 to 10 miles longer
than Hancock's, arrived in the afternoon of the 14th.

During the 14th, the transports, which had brought the 18th
corps around from the White House to City Point, were employed in ferrying Hancock across the James. By the morning
of the 15th, his whole corps was across, with most of its artillery,
and at 10.30 A.M., it set out for Petersburg, following Smith who
had gone from City Point for the same destination about sunrise.
Hancock had about 20,000 men, and about 16 miles to go. All
the complicated movements involved in this manœuvre, and in
the capture of Petersburg at which it was aimed, had been as
usual well thought out, and covered in the orders and instructions to the different commanders, *with a single exception.*

This exception was very serious in its results, as it postponed
the capture of Petersburg for over nine months. It had its rise
in the division of command and responsibility between the co-
operating armies. This, in its turn, had arisen from the political
necessity of placing Butler in command of the Army of the
James. Smith's corps was a part of that army, and Grant,

feeling that secrecy was essential to success, visited Butler on the 14th, and at his quarters prepared the orders for Smith's advance and attack on Petersburg the next day. When he returned to the Army of the Potomac, he failed to notify Meade of the hour of Smith's march, and other details, and Meade, of course, did not inform Hancock. It resulted that Hancock was not ordered to march until 10.30 A.M., when he might just as easily have marched at sunrise, and he was directed by a route an hour or two longer than one he might have used. Finally, he came upon the field at Petersburg after dark, when he might have arrived in time to unite in Smith's assault.

Meanwhile, the 5th, 6th, and 9th corps on the banks of the James, awaited the construction of the greatest bridge which the world has seen since the days of Xerxes. At the point selected, the river was 2100 feet wide, 90 feet deep, and had a rise and fall of tide of 4 feet, giving very strong currents. A draw was necessary for the passage of vessels. The approaches having been prepared on each side, construction was begun at 4 P.M., on the 14th, by Maj. Duane, simultaneously at both ends. In eight hours the bridge was finished, and the artillery and trains of the 9th, 5th, and 6th corps began to cross in the order named, that being the order in which the corps would follow. For 48 hours, without cessation, the column poured across, and at midnight on the 16th Grant's entire army was south of the James.

Let us now turn to Lee. On the morning of the 13th, finding the enemy gone, he at once put his army in motion, crossed the Chickahominy, and that afternoon took position between White Oak Swamp and Malvern Hill. Hoke's division went on to Drury's Bluff. His cavalry came in contact with Wilson's cavalry, and also with Warren's infantry, which had intrenched itself on the Long Bridge road not far in front of his position. Some sharp skirmishing took place, as shown by Warren's report of 300 casualties. The presence of Warren was taken as assurance that Grant's army was about to advance on the north side of the James, and Warren's withdrawal at dark, discovered the next day, was supposed to mean only a drawing nearer to Butler's position, where the narrowness of the river would permit the easy establishment of pontoon bridges. On the 14th, a staff-officer of Beauregard's came over from Petersburg to lay before Lee the defenceless position of that city, and to beg for reënforcements. Lee consented that Beauregard should take Hoke's division, which had already gone to Drury's Bluff, but would not consent to weaken Longstreet or Hill, who were near Riddle's Shop. Hoke was accordingly started for Petersburg early on the 15th, with 18 miles to go. His leading brigade, Hagood's, was picked up by railroad trains and reached Petersburg about sunset, the rest of the division arriving about 9 P.M. Until Hoke came, the whole force at Petersburg consisted of Wise's brigade of infantry "not more than 1200 strong," two small regiments "of cavalry under Dearing." "Some light artillery with 22 pieces . . . besides a few men manning three or four heavy guns in position." [1]

Besides these, there were some old men and boys, called Local Reserves, who on June 9 under Col. F. H. Archer, a veteran of Mexico, and Gen. R. E. Colston, disabled at Chancellorsville, had acted with great gallantry in repelling a raid by Kautz's cavalry. The total gross of all arms is given as 2738.

After Beauregard's staff-officer had left him, Lee gave orders to our corps to march the next morning, the 15th, to Drury's Bluff. About sunrise, we broke camps and took the road, but there was a demonstration of the enemy's cavalry about Malvern Hill and we were halted to learn what it meant. About midday, the report came that the enemy had fallen back, but our march was not resumed, and we later returned to our bivouacs.

On the 16th, the 1st corps headquarters, with Pickett's and Field's divisions, were hurried across the pontoon bridge at Drury's Bluff and down to the Bermuda Hundreds lines, which had been held by Bushrod Johnson's division, but had been abandoned the night of the 15th when Beauregard had withdrawn it for the defence of Petersburg. Kershaw's division followed us only as far as Drury's Bluff, and was halted there. We reached the ground in time to drive off one of Butler's brigades which had come out to the railroad and begun to tear it up. We drove this brigade back very nearly into their original

[1] Roman's *Beauregard*, II., 229.

lines, and, on the next afternoon, the 17th, a charge of Pickett's division entirely regained our lines which had been abandoned by Bushrod Johnson.

During these three days, the 15th, 16th, and 17th, Beauregard, while defending Petersburg, with great skill and tenacity, had repeatedly reported to Lee the arrival of Grant's army at Petersburg, and begged for reënforcements. Lee's replies were as follows : —

"June 16, 10.30 A.M. I do not know the position of Grant's army and cannot strip the north bank of troops."

"June 17, 12 M. Until I can get more definite information of Grant's movements, I do not think it prudent to draw more troops to this side of the river."

On this day, Grant's entire force being now on the field, his attacks were urged with increasing vigor, and at 6.40 P.M. Beauregard telegraphed Lee as follows : —

"The increasing number of the enemy in my front, and inadequacy of my force to defend the already too much extended lines, will compel me to fall back within a shorter one, which I will attempt to-night. This I shall hold as long as practicable, but, without reënforcements, I may have to evacuate the city very shortly. In that event I shall retire in the direction of Drury's Bluff, defending the crossing of Appomattox River and Swift Creek."

After the receipt of this despatch, Kershaw's division was ordered to proceed during the night to Bermuda Hundreds, and a little later the order was extended to continue the march to Petersburg. The fighting on Beauregard's lines lasted until nearly midnight. But when it was over, and the transfer of his troops to their new line was fairly under way, he began to take more radical measures to convince Lee of the situation. He sent three of his staff, one after the other, within two hours, with details about the prisoners captured from different corps of the Federal army, with the stories told by each of their marches since leaving Cold Harbor on the 12th. The first messenger was Beauregard's aide, Col. Chisolm, who interviewed Lee, lying on the ground in his tent near Drury's Bluff, between 1 and 2 A.M. on the 18th. Lee seemed very placid and heard many messages, but still said he thought Beauregard was mistaken in supposing that any large part of Grant's army had crossed the river. He said also that Kershaw's division was already under orders to Petersburg, and he promised to come over in the morning.

Chisolm was soon followed by Col. Alfred Roman, but he had to leave his messages, as Lee's staff would not disturb him again. About 3 A.M., Maj. Giles B. Cooke arrived and insisted upon an interview. He brought further statements by prisoners which, laid before Lee, thoroughly satisfied him that Grant's army had now been across the James for over 48 hours. The following telegrams, which were immediately sent, will indicate his change of view.

"June 18, 3.30 A.M. Superintendent R. & P. R.R. Can trains run to Petersburg? If so, send all cars available to Rice's Turnout. If they cannot run through, can any be sent from Petersburg to the point where the road is broken? It is important to get troops to Petersburg without delay."

"To Gen. Early, Lynchburg.
"Grant is in front of Petersburg. Will be opposed there. Strike as quick as you can. If circumstances authorize, carry out the original plan or move upon Petersburg without delay."

At the same time, orders were sent Anderson for Field's division and the corps headquarters and artillery to follow Kershaw's division into Petersburg. Kershaw arrived there about 7.30 A.M.; the rest of us about nine.

We must now return to Smith's column, which we saw start to Petersburg, about 16,000 strong, at daylight on the 15th, with about eight miles to go, 2500 of the command being cavalry, 3700 of them colored troops. Beauregard awaits them in the lines of Petersburg which encircle the city, about two miles out, from the river above to the river below, a development of about 10 miles. The intrenchments had no abattis or obstructions in front and consisted only of a small outside ditch and a parapet, with platforms and embrasures for guns at suitable intervals. As Beauregard expected Hoke's division about dark, every moment of delay was valuable. To prolong it, he used the old device of sending forward a regiment of cavalry and a battery. These delayed the approach for about three hours, at the expense of a gun captured. The march was then resumed, and about 9 A.M. the head of the column came to the zone of felled forest in front of the intrenchments. Beauregard, fortunately, had a good supply of guns and ammunition which he used freely in preventing the enemy from establishing his batteries or moving his troops within sight, and it was 1.30 P.M. when the column was deployed. Smith had still to make his reconnoissance, and this occupied him until 5 P.M. But it had been efficiently made, for he learned that our infantry was stretched out in a very thin line, and it led him to decide that his charge should be made, not with a column, but with clouds of skirmishers. Another hour was taken to form the troops, and at 6 P.M. all would have been ready, but it was now found that the chief of artillery had sent all the horses to water, and it required an hour to get them back. Tall oaks from little acorns grow! By such small and accidental happenings does fate decide battles! Petersburg was lost and won by that hour.

At 7 P.M., the guns returned and opened a severe fire, to which the Confederate guns did not reply, reserving their fire for the columns which they expected to see. These never appeared, but instead, the cloud of skirmishers overran the works and captured the guns still loaded with double canister and defended by only a skirmish line of infantry. Hink's colored division, which made the charge, lost 507 killed and wounded from the fire of the skirmishers. It captured four guns and 250 prisoners. Lines of battle followed, and by 9 P.M. occupied about one and a half miles of intrenchment, from Redan No. 7 to No. 11, inclusive (counting from the river below), getting possession of 16 guns. Hancock's corps had arrived on the ground during the action, and, when it was over, at Smith's request it relieved his troops. Smith had been informed of the approach of reënforcements to both sides, and he thought it wiser to hold what he had, than to venture more and risk disaster. Kautz's cavalry had been kept beyond the intrenchments all day by Dearing's cavalry and a few guns, which fired from the redans in the vicinity of No. 28. About 6 P.M., hearing no sounds of battle from Smith, Kautz withdrew, with a loss of 43 men, and went into bivouac.

After the fighting began, Beauregard had recognized that he

would need every available man to defend the city, and he ordered Johnson to leave only Gracie's brigade in his lines, and to come to Petersburg with the rest of his division. Johnson brought about 3500 men, which, with Hoke, gave Beauregard in the morning an effective force of about 14,000 infantry. During the night he built a temporary line, throwing out the captured portion, while his efficient chief engineer, Col. D. B. Harris, laid out and commenced a better located permanent line at an average distance of a half-mile in the rear.

On the 16th, Hancock was in command, and the 9th corps arrived on the field, giving him about 48,000 effectives. He devoted the day to attacks upon each flank of the broken line and succeeded in capturing one redan, No. 4, on Beauregard's left, and three, Nos. 12, 13, and 14, on his right.

On the 17th, the fighting began at 3 A.M. and was continued until 11 P.M. The attack at three was conducted by Potter's division of the 9th corps, and was a complete surprise. Extraordinary precautions had been adopted to make it so. No shot was fired. Canteens had been packed in knapsacks, and all orders were transmitted in whispers. The Confederates were so exhausted, by their incessant fighting by day and working by night, that they were sound asleep, with arms in their hands, and double canister in their guns. Only a single gunner was waked in time to pull a single lanyard before the enemy swept over and got possession of Redan No. 16, with 4 guns and 600 prisoners. Nowhere else during the long day were they able to make any headway.

The 5th corps had now arrived and one division of the 6th. About dark in the afternoon, Redan No. 3, on the left, had been taken and held temporarily by Ledlie's division of the 9th corps. Gracie's brigade, which had just come in from Bermuda Hundreds, was put to charge them, and drove them out, capturing over 1000 prisoners. After the fighting ceased, Col. Harris superintended the withdrawal of the troops from the temporary line to the new location which had been prepared in the last 48 hours.

At 4 A.M. on the 18th, a general advance was made by the 2d, 5th, and 9th corps, the 6th and 18th supporting in reserve. The ground in front of the points which had been assaulted was thickly strewn with the Federal dead, and the slight trenches, from which they had fought so long and desperately, were filled with the slain there had been no opportunity to bury or remove. A few deserters or prisoners were picked up, and from them Meade learned that Beauregard's whole force had been but two divisions and Wise's brigade, now reduced by heavy losses, but trying to occupy a hastily constructed line a half-mile, more or less, in the rear. This information was conveyed to all the corps commanders, who were ordered to press forward vigorously and overwhelm our lines in their unfinished condition.

No army could ask a more favorable chance to destroy its antagonist than was here presented. Their whole army was at hand, and the reënforcement of Longstreet's corps, even now coming to Beauregard, was not over 12,000 men and was still about three to five hours away. The little which was accomplished during the whole day is striking evidence of the condition to which the Federal army had now been reduced.

At first, much time was lost in driving in our pickets, and in efforts to arrange for simultaneous assaults by the different corps. Meade himself at last fixed upon twelve o'clock, and ordered each corps at that hour to assault with a strong column. By that time Kershaw's division had relieved Johnson's, taking its place in the trenches. Hoke, Wise, and none of the artillery could be relieved until after dark, without unwise exposure of the troops. Field's division took position in the trenches on Kershaw's left, but it did not become engaged.

Humphreys states that about midday the 2d corps made two assaults, "both repulsed with severe loss." Later Meade again ordered —

"assaults by all the corps with their whole force, and at all hazards, and as soon as possible. All the corps assaulted late in the afternoon, and at hours not widely apart: Birney with all his disposable force; Nott from the Hare house . . . supported by one of Gibbon's brigades; Barlow on Mott's left, — but were repulsed with considerable loss. Burnside found the task of driving the enemy [it was but a picket force] out of the railroad cut a formidable one, and, assaulting, established his corps within a hundred yards of the enemy's main line. . . . Warren's assault was well made, some of Griffin's men being killed within 20 feet of the enemy's works, but it was no more successful than the others. His losses were very severe. . . . On the right, Martindale advanced and gained some rifle-pits, but did not assault the main line."

On the Confederate side, the day was not considered a day of battle, but only of demonstrations and reconnoissance. None of our reënforcements were engaged, the only fighting done having been by Hoke's division and Wise's brigade, who, under Beauregard, had already borne the whole brunt of the four days and three nights. The official diary of Longstreet's corps says of the day : —

"We arrive in Petersburg and Kershaw relieves Bushrod Johnson's division, Field taking position on Kershaw's right. A feeble attack is made in the afternoon on Elliott's brigade."

No official report is given of any brigade except Hagood's, which describes only skirmishing, and one attempted charge on our extreme left, "which never got closer than 250 yards."

It was necessary to wait until night before Beauregard's artillery could receive its plaudit of "Well done! good and faithful servants," and be relieved by the fresh battalions of Longstreet's corps. Of all the moonlight nights I can remember, I recall that Saturday night as, perhaps, the most brilliant and beautiful. The weather was exceedingly dry, the air perfectly calm, with an exhilarating electrical quality in it. The dust rose with every movement and hung in the air. The whole landscape was bathed and saturated in silver, and sounds were unusually distinct and seemed to be alive and to travel everywhere. It was not a night for sleep in the trenches. There was a great deal to be done at all points, to strengthen and improve them, and every man was personally interested in working at his immediate location.

In spite of all pains, the drawing out of old guns and approach of new was attended with sounds which wandered far and with luminous clouds of dust gradually rising in the air. Then the enemy would know we were moving and there would come crashes of musketry at random and volleys of artillery from their lines. Then our infantry would imagine themselves attacked, and would respond in like fashion, and the fire would run along the parapet to right and left, and gradually subside for a while, to break out presently somewhere else. I was accompanied by Lt.-Col. Branch, a Col. of artillery of Beauregard's army, a very competent and gallant officer, unfortunately killed in 1869 by the falling of a bridge near Richmond.

Grant did not renew his assaults on the 19th, but expressed himself satisfied that all had been done which was possible, and he now directed that the troops should be put under cover and have some rest.

Humphreys writes : —

"The positions gained by the several corps close against the enemy were intrenched, and the two opposing lines in this part of the ground remained substantially the same in position to the close of the war."

In brief review, it must be said that Grant successfully deceived Lee as to his whereabouts for at least three days, and thus, at the most critical period of the war, saved himself from a second defeat, more bloody, more signal, and more undeniable than Cold Harbor. For, if Beauregard alone, with only 14,000 men, was able to stop Grant's whole army even after being driven by surprise into temporary works, what would Lee and Beauregard together have done from the strong original lines of Petersburg? Grant, personally, was at that period not abstemious, and that his troops knew of it [perhaps sometimes exaggerating facts in speaking of it] was known, even to the Confederates, from the stories of prisoners captured at Cold Harbor. Such a defeat in case of any disaster, with such rumors afloat, would have cast a baleful back-light over the campaign, even to Spottsylvania and the Wilderness. He was now able to base a *quasi* claim to victory in establishing himself within the lines of Petersburg. But all the odium of repeated defeats would have been heaped upon his campaign, had it terminated with a final and bloody repulse.

All this had been changed by his well-planned and successfully conducted strategy. The position which he had secured was full of great possibilities, as yet not fully comprehended. But, already, the character of the operations contemplated, removed all risk of serious future catastrophe. However bold we might be, however desperately we might fight, we were sure in the end to be worn out. It was only a question of a few months, more or less. We were unable to see it at once. But there soon began to spring up a chain of permanent works, the first of which were built upon our original lines captured by the skirmishers the first afternoon, and these works, impregnable to assault, finally decided our fate, when, on the next March 25, we put them to the test.

Of this period following the battles of Cold Harbor and Petersburg, the future historian may find something to say. By all the rules of statecraft, the time had now arrived to open negotiations for peace. There would no longer be any hope of final success, but there would still be much of blood, of treasure, and of political rights, which might be saved or lost. The time never came again when as favorable terms could have been made as now. For it was the hour of the lowest tide in Federal hopes. It remains a fact, however, that for many months, even until the very capture of Richmond, both the Confederate army and the people would have been very loth to recognize that our cause was hopeless. Lee's influence, had he advised it, could have secured acquiescence in surrender, but nothing else would. His confidence in his army, doubtless, for some months delayed his realization of the approaching end. Even when he foresaw it, his duty to his government as a soldier was paramount, and controlled his course to the very last.

And there is this to be said. In every war there are two issues contended for. First, is the political principle involved; which with us was the right of secession. The second is prestige or character as a people. Conceding our cause, did we defend it worthily, history and posterity being the judges?

We lost the first issue; and the more utterly it was lost, the better it has proved to be — for ourselves, even more than for our adversaries. Without detracting from their merit, but displaying and even enhancing it, we have gained the second by a courage and constancy which could only be fully developed and exhibited under the extreme tests endured, and by the high types of men who became our leaders. Is not that end worthy of the extreme price paid for it, even to the last drop of blood shed at Appomattox? I am sure that to the army, any end but the last ditch would have seemed a breach of faith with the dead we had left upon every battle-field.

The Federal casualties for Petersburg and for the campaign are given as follows: —

June 13 to 18: killed 1,298, wounded 7,474, missing 1,814, total 10,586. May 5 to June 18: killed 8,412, wounded 44,629, missing 9,609, total 62,750.

No returns exist for Beauregard's losses, but they have been estimated at: killed, 500, wounded 2200, missing 2000, total 4700. The losses among the general officers were severe on both sides, being of Confederates: killed 8, wounded 15, captured 2, total 25, and of Federals: killed 6, wounded 8, captured 2, total 16.

CHAPTER XXII

The Mine

The Petersburg Trenches. Wilson and Kautz's Cavalry Raid. Their Rout on the 29th. Early's Demonstration toward Washington. The Mine at the Elliott Salient. Extent of the Tunnel and Galleries. Its Ventilation. Countermines. Plans for a Federal Charge to follow the Explosion. Movements of Hancock. The Explosion on the 30th. The Crater. Failure of the Federal Assault.

OUR first days in the Petersburg trenches were exceedingly busy ones. From June 19 to 24, a daily entry in my note-book was "severe sharpshooting and artillery practice without intermission day or night." Our whole time was spent in improving our lines and getting our batteries protected and with good communications. Never until in this campaign had the enemy used mortar fire in the field, but now Abbot's reserve artillery regiment of 1700 men brought into use 60 mortars ranging from 24-Pr. Coehorns to 10-inch Sea-coast, which caused us great annoyance, as we had to keep our trenches fully manned and had no protection against the dropping shells. Fortunately, I had ordered some mortars constructed in Richmond about two weeks before, and they began to arrive on June 24, and were at once brought into use. They were only 12-pounders, but were light and convenient, and at close ranges enabled us to hold our own, with less loss than might have been expected. The cannoneers in the batteries, and the infantry in the lines who were exposed to this mortar fire, managed to build little bomb-proofs, and a labyrinth of deep and narrow trenches in rear of the lines. Abbott's siege-train also included six 100-pounder, and forty 30-Pr. rifles, besides their regular field-artillery. Many of the heavy calibres were mounted on the permanent forts, erected in the outer line already referred to.

These constituted a sort of intrenched citadel, consisting of

ʼisolated forts connected by infantry parapets with ditches and abattis, and impregnable to any assault. Here a small fraction of the army could securely hold its line for days, and continue to threaten Petersburg, leaving the rest free to extend lines on the south or to threaten Richmond on the north. Meanwhile, in front, their offensive system of trenches and redans was pushed as close as possible to ours, and we were constantly menaced with assault, should we weaken our garrison.

One point in our front, called Elliott's Salient, was recognized as particularly weak. The edge of the deep valley of Poor Creek, approximately parallel to our general line of works, here approached within 133 yards of the salient, which was held by Pegram's battery, Elliott's brigade occupying the adjacent lines. Along the near edge of the valley, the enemy built strong rifle-pits, with elaborate head-logs and loopholes, from which a constant fire was kept up upon our works. In the valley behind was ample room for an unlimited force, which could be collected and massed without our knowledge, and would have but 133 yards to advance under fire to reach our works. We soon managed to place obstructions in front of the parapet at this point and watched closely, confidently expecting that the enemy would here begin soon to make zigzag approaches as in a siege.

On June 22, Grant sent Wilson's and Kautz's divisions of cavalry upon a raid against the Lynchburg and Danville railroads. On the same day, the 2d and 6th corps were stretched out to the left with the intent of reaching the Weldon R.R., and perhaps even to the road to Lynchburg.

Lee, advised of this movement, sent A. P. Hill with Wilcox's and Mahone's division, supported by Johnson's, to meet it. With Wilcox's division, he obstructed the advance of the 6th corps so effectively that it failed to reach even the Weldon road, by at least a mile. With Mahone's and Johnson's divisions, he passed through a gap carelessly left between the 2d corps, which was swinging around to its left, and the 6th, which was advancing, and struck Barlow's division of the 2d in the rear. Barlow's and Gibbon's divisions were both badly defeated, losing four guns (which were turned upon the fugitives), several colors and about 1700 prisoners. Mott's division was also routed but retreated so precipitately as to lose few prisoners. Hill returned at night to his intrenchments, and the next morning the 2d corps reoccupied the lines from which it had been driven and the 6th corps formed on its left obliquely toward the Weldon road.

Wilson and Kautz were followed in their raid by W. H. F. Lee's division of cavalry which, however, was unable to prevent the tearing up of the Lynchburg R.R. from near Petersburg to Burkeville, and of the Danville road from Burkeville south to the Staunton River. Here the bridge was defended by local militia who were intrenched with artillery. The river was unfordable, and Lee, attacking in the rear, the Federals decided to rejoin Grant at Petersburg by a circuit to the east.

Unfortunately for them, Hampton's and Fitz-Lee's divisions had just returned from the pursuit of Sheridan's cavalry to Trevillian's Station, where they had had a drawn battle on June 11 and 12. These divisions, aided by W. H. F. Lee's, which had continued in the pursuit, and by two brigades of infantry under Mahone, fell upon Wilson and Kautz on the 29th at Ream's Station and routed them with the loss of 1500 killed, wounded, and captured, and all of their artillery (12 guns) and their wagon-train. They finally made their escape across the Blackwater, burning the bridge behind them, and thus cutting off pursuit by Hampton and Lee. They reached the James at Light House Point on July 2.

They had been absent 10 days, had marched over 300 miles, and torn up 60 miles of railroad. The tracks, however, were soon repaired and traffic restored by all the lines. By the Weldon road, however, it soon became necessary to halt the trains short of Petersburg, and to wagon by a roundabout road into the town.

Between July 6 and 9, Grant had found it necessary to send the three divisions of the 6th corps to Washington to oppose Early and Breckenridge. These, whom we saw sent by Lee, from Cold Harbor, to check Hunter's advance upon Lynchburg, had reached Lynchburg before him. Hunter feared either to attack, or to retreat by the way he had come. After a pause of two days he started, on June 19, through W. Va. via the Great Kanawha, the Ohio River, and the Baltimore and Ohio R.R. to Harper's Ferry. This left the valley open. Early at once moved down it to demonstrate against Washington. The only force available to oppose him was Wallace's command from Baltimore, with Ricketts's division of the 6th corps, which was the first to arrive. Early had crossed the Potomac at Shepherdstown and moved through the passes of South Mountain. On July 9, he attacked and defeated Wallace on the Monocacy. The next day he moved upon Washington, Wallace being driven toward Baltimore.

Never before, probably, had Washington been as bare of troops as when Early arrived before it on the afternoon of July 11. But there were regular garrisons of infantry and artillery at many of the permanent forts, — District of Columbia volunteers, regiments of Veteran Reserves, many miscellaneous detachments at the camp of instruction, and about 2000 organized employees of the quartermaster's department, — in all over 20,000 men. These troops alone, without aid, could have defended the city indefinitely and forced Early to undertake a siege. That night, there arrived the two remaining divisions of the 6th corps, and 6000 men of the 19th corps, under Emory, from New Orleans.

In the afternoon, Early had reconnoitred, and, in consultation with his officers, had ordered an assault in the morning. It is scarcely credible that he would have made more than a demonstration, for any real attack would have been but a bloody farce. In the night he heard of the arrival of the troops and in the morning could see them. He did not attack and that night he withdrew, marching to Leesburg, where he recrossed the Potomac. Grant had intended, on Early's repulse, not only to bring back the 6th corps to Petersburg, but also to bring down the 19th. Had he now carried out those intentions, it is likely that Lee would have brought down Early. It was Lee's policy, however, to fight for time and delay matters by division, rather than to hasten them by concentration. So he left Early in the Valley, where his presence would be a constant menace and would neutralize more troops than his equivalent elsewhere.

On June 30, I became convinced that the enemy were preparing to mine our position at the Elliott Salient. At that point, incessant fire was kept up by their sharpshooters, while a few hundred yards to the right and left the fire had been gradually allowed to diminish and men might show themselves without being fired at. That indicated that some operation was going on, and for several days I had expected to see zigzag approaches started on the surface of the ground. When several days had passed and nothing appeared, I became satisfied that their activity was underground. On my way home, I was that day wounded by a sharpshooter and received a furlough of six weeks to visit my home in Ga. On my way to the cars next day, I was driven by Lee's headquarters, where I reported my belief about the mine. There happened to be present Mr. Lawley, the English correspondent of the *London Times*, who was much interested and asked how far it would be necessary to tunnel to get under our works. I answered about 500 feet. He stated that the longest military tunnel or gallery which had ever been run was at the siege of Delhi, and that it did not exceed 400 feet. That it was found impossible to ventilate for any greater distance. I replied that in the Federal army were many Pa. coal miners who could be relied on to ventilate mines any distance that might be necessary, and it would not do to rely upon military precedents. It proved that my suspicion was correct.

It was June 30 when I guessed it. The gallery had been commenced on June 27. It was undertaken, in opposition to the advice of all the military engineers at Federal headquarters, by Lt.-Col. Pleasants of the 48th Pa. regiment, a coal miner, who saw the opportunity which the situation offered. A gallery was successfully extended 511 feet, with two branch galleries at the end, to the right and left, each 37 feet long. These branch galleries were charged with gunpowder in eight parcels of 1000 pounds each, connected by open troughs of powder to be fired by safety fuses coming through the tamping and along the gallery.

His method of ventilation was very simple. When the tunnel had penetrated the hill far enough to need it, a close partition was built across it near the entrance with a close fitting door. Through the partition on the side of this door was passed the open end of a long square box, or closed trough, which was built along on the floor of the tunnel, conveying the fresh outside air to the far end of the tunnel, where the men extending it were at work.

To create a draft through this air-box, a fireplace was excavated in the side of the tunnel, within the partition, and a chimney was pierced through the hill above it. A small fire in this chimney place, and the outside air would pass through the air-box to the far end of the tunnel, whence it would return and escape up the chimney, taking with it the foul air of the tunnel. This tunnel was finished July 17, the galleries on the 23d, and the mine was charged and tamped on the 28th.

Lee, on receipt of my message on July 1, ordered our engineers to start countermines at the Elliott Salient. Two shafts were sunk about 10 feet and listening galleries were run out from each. Unfortunately, the shafts were located on the right and left flanks of the battery, and the enemy's gallery passed at a depth of 20 feet under the apex, and was so silently built that our miners never knew of their proximity. Had they detected it, they would have hastened to explode what is called a *camouflet*, an undercharged or "smothered mine," which does not disturb the surface, but caves in adjacent galleries.

By July 10, our miners had done enough work, had it been done at the apex of the salient, to have heard the enemy, who would have been directly beneath them. Work was not only kept up, however, on the flanks, but at two other positions farther to the left, known as Colquitt's and Gracie's salients, countermines were also begun; at Colquitt's on the 10th and at Gracie's on the 19th. All four of our mines were constantly pushed until the 30th, when the explosion occurred, the total length of our galleries being then about 375 feet. Of the two galleries on each side of the mine, one, which was unoccupied, was destroyed by the explosion. In the other, the miners were at work, but, though much shaken up, the galleries were not crushed and the miners climbed out and escaped.

Meanwhile, in spite of predictions of failure, the mine had been constructed, and though we were known to suspect it, and our countermining operations could be heard, it was now determined to delay the explosion until preparations could be made to have it followed by a grand charge, supported by the concentration of a great force, both of infantry and artillery. That it might be the more effective, Grant determined to combine strategy with main force, and first endeavor to draw a large part of our infantry to the north side of the James. At suitable points, he had already built signal-towers overlooking our lines, and some of our most important roads; and now the artillery officers were directed to prepare specially to concentrate fire upon every gun in our lines which could be used for the defence of Elliott's Salient. In obedience to these instructions, Humphreys reports, "heavy guns and mortars, 81 in all, and about the same number of field-guns," were prepared with abundant ammunition.

At Deep Bottom, Butler maintained two pontoon bridges across the James, with part of the 10th corps on the north side, under cover of his gunboats and ironclads. Of course, we had to maintain a moderate force in observation, which, under Gen. Connor, was located near Bailey's Creek. Grant could cross both the Appomattox and the James and go from his lines around Petersburg to Deep Bottom by a march of 12 miles, all of it entirely concealed from our view. Lee could only send troops to meet him by a march of 20 miles.

On the afternoon of July 26, Hancock with about 20,000 infantry and Sheridan with two divisions, about 6000 cavalry, were started to Deep Bottom. It was expected that this force, aided by the 10th corps, would surprise the Confederate brigade (Conner's), and would then make a dash toward Richmond. Sheridan was directed also to endeavor to cut the railroads north of Richmond. During the night, this force crossed the river, and, at dawn on the 27th, moved upon our lines and captured four 20-Pr. Parrotts in an advanced position.

It happened that Lee had noted activity of the enemy in that quarter. Wilcox's division was already at Drury's Bluff, and, on the 24th, it and Kershaw's division were sent to reënforce Conner. This force made such a show that Hancock, finding it there before him, did not deem it wise to assault their line. On their left, Kershaw even advanced against Sheridan's cavalry and forced it to retreat. It took a position behind a ridge, where it dismounted a considerable force armed with the Spencer magazine carbines. Kershaw unwisely attempted a charge and was quickly repulsed, losing 250 prisoners and two colors.

On hearing of Hancock's crossing on the morning of the 27th, and that prisoners had been captured from the 2d, 10th, and 18th corps, Lee immediately sent over W. H. F. Lee's division of cavalry and Heth's infantry of Hill's corps. Later in the day, he arranged to have Field's division of infantry withdrawn from his trenches at dark, to follow during the night, and Fitz-Lee's cavalry the next morning. President Davis was also advised, and on the 29th the Local Defence troops in Richmond were called out to the defence of the Richmond lines. These troops were never called out except in the gravest emergencies, which indicates the importance Lee attached to the demonstration.

But it was only a demonstration designed to be abandoned, if it failed to make a surprise of our lines at Deep Bottom on the 27th. As this became fully apparent on the 28th, orders were issued from Deep Bottom to prepare the mine for explosion on the morning of the 30th. Orders were also given for the 2d corps with a division of the 18th corps and one of the 10th to return and take part in the assault. Sheridan's cavalry was also to return, and passing in rear of the army to take position on its left to threaten our extreme right and prevent our reënforcing the vicinity of the mine. The explosion might have been arranged for the afternoon of the 29th, but the morning of the 30th was chosen, as it permitted the placing of more heavy guns and mortars for the bombardment, which would follow the explosion, as well as preliminary arrangements, such as massing the troops, removing parapets and abattis to make passages for the assaulting columns, and the posting of pioneers to remove our abattis and open passages for artillery through our lines. Depots of intrenching tools, with sandbags, gabions, fascines, etc., were established, that lodgments might be more quickly made, though the pioneers of all regiments were already well supplied with tools. Engineer officers were designated to accompany all columns, and even pontoon trains were at hand to bridge the Appomattox in pursuit of fugitives. Finally, Meade personally impressed on every corps commander the importance of celerity of movement. Briefly, no possible precaution was omitted to be carefully ordered, and the success of the Deep Bottom expedition, in drawing Lee's forces to that locality, had exceeded all expectations.

On the morning of the 30th, Lee had left to hold the 10 miles of lines about Petersburg but three divisions (Hoke's, Johnson's, and Mahone's), about 18,000 men, most of the rest of his army being 20 miles away. Hoke and Johnson held from the Appomattox on the left to a little beyond the mine. Mahone held all beyond, one brigade being four miles to the right. The 2d, 5th, 9th, and parts of the 10th and 18th, with two divisions of Sheridan's cavalry, 16 divisions in all, near 60,000 men, were concentrated to follow up the surprise to be given by the explosion under Johnson's division. That it should be the more complete, for two days no heavy guns or mortars had been fired, that the Confederates might believe that the Federals were preparing to retreat.

Everything now seemed to be working exactly as Grant would have it, and it is difficult to entirely explain how the attack came to fail so utterly. Several causes coöperated which will be presently referred to, but among them was the same cause which, on May 12, nullified the Federal surprise at the Bloody Angle at Spottsylvania. Too many troops had been brought together, and they were in each other's way. On a smaller scale, in the assault of Fort Sanders at Knoxville, three Confederate brigades got mingled in the assault, which at once lost its vigor, though it did not retreat until after receiving severe punishment. The brigadier in command, on this occasion, ascribed his failure to the presence of the two other brigades who should have been upon his flanks.

The assault was to be led by Ledlie's division of the 9th corps, a selection made by lot, and a very unfortunate one, as Ledlie and Ferrero, who commanded the colored division, which was to follow Ledlie, both took shelter in a bomb-proof, where they remained during the entire action. The mine was ordered to be fired at 3.30 A.M., but the fuses had been spliced and when first fired, failed at the splice. After an hour, an officer and sergeant entered the tunnel and relighted the fuse. The explosion occurred at 4.40. As the sun rose about 4.50, the delay had been advantageous, as it gave daylight for the movements of the troops and for the artillery fire.

The explosion made a crater 150 feet long, 97 feet wide, and 30 feet deep, the contents being hurled so high in the air that the foremost ranks of the assaulting columns, 150 yards away, shrank back in disorder in fear of the falling earth. The bulk of the earth, however, fell immediately around the crater, mingled with the debris of 2 guns, 22 cannoneers, and perhaps 250 infantry (nine companies of the 19th and 22d S.C., which had been carried up in the air). Quite a number of these who fell safely were dug out and rescued alive by the assaulting column. Some, not yet aroused, were lost, covered up in the bombproofs of the adjacent trenches by the falling earth. This formed a high embankment, as it were, all around the crater, with one enormous clod, the size of a small cabin, perched about the middle of the inside rim, which remained a landmark for weeks. A high interior line, called a trench cavalier, had been built across the gorge of the salient enclosing a triangular space, and the left centre of this space about coincided with the centre of the explosion. The parapets were partially destroyed and largely buried by the falling earth.

Into this crater the leading division literally swarmed, until it was packed about as full as it could hold, and what could not get in there, crowded into the adjacent trenches, which the falling earth had caused to be vacated for a short distance on each flank. But, considering the surprise, the novelty of the occasion and the terrific cannonade by 150 guns and mortars which was opened immediately, the coolness and self-possession of the entire brigade was remarkable, and to it is to be attributed the success of the defence. This was conducted principally by Col. McMaster of the 17th S.C., Gen. Elliott having been soon severely wounded. The effect of the artillery cannonade was more a moral effect than a physical one, for the smoke so obscured the view that the fire was largely at random, at least for one or two hours, during which it was in fullest force. The effort was at once made to collect a small force in the trenches upon each flank, and one in an intrenchment occupying a slight depression which ran parallel to our line of battle some 250 yards in rear of it, the effort being to confine the enemy to the crater and the lines immediately adjoining. The multiplicity of the deep and narrow trenches, and the bomb-proofs in the rear of our lines, doubtless contributed to our success in doing this on the flanks, but there was also decided lack of vigor and enterprise on the part of the enemy, which permitted us to form barricades, which were successfully defended to the last.

Meanwhile the reënforcements to the storming column, instead of spreading to the flanks, massed outside of our lines in rear of the storming column, which had made no further advance, but had filled the crater and all the captured lines. Several efforts were made to advance from time to time, but the first were feeble, and could be checked by the remnants of the brigade under McMaster, until two regiments of Wise's brigade and two of Ransom's were brought up from the left. With their aid, the situation was made safe and held until about 10 A.M., when Mahone arrived at the head of three brigades of his corps, drawn from the lines on our right. A regiment of Hoke's from the left also came up later.

In the meantime, a few of our guns had found themselves able to fire with great effect upon the enemy massed in front of our lines. The left gun in the next salient to the right, occupied by Davidson's battery, was in an embrasure which flanked the Pegram Salient, but was not open to any gun on the enemy's line. This gun did fearful execution, being scarcely 400 yards distant. It was fired by Maj. Gibbes commanding the battalion, for perhaps 40 rounds, until he was badly wounded, after which it was served by Col. Huger and Haskell, Winthrop, and Mason of my staff, and later by some of Wise's infantry. A hot fire was turned upon it, but it was well protected and could never be kept silent when the enemy showed himself.

Five hundred yards to the left was a four-gun battery under Capt. Wright of Coit's battalion, in a depression behind our line, and masked from the enemy by some trees. But it had a flanking fire on the left of Pegram's Salient and across all the approaches and a number of infantry of Wise's brigade could also add their fire. Wright's fire was rapid, incessant, and accurate, causing great loss. The Federal artillery made vain efforts to locate him with their mortar shells which tore up the ground all around, but could never hit him or silence him.

Besides these, a half-dozen or more of Coehorn mortars, under Col. Haskell, from two or three different ravines in the rear, threw shell aimed at the crater. And, finally, 600 yards directly in rear of the mine was the sunken Jerusalem Plank road, in which I had placed Haskell's battalion of 16 guns about the 20th of June, and he had been kept there ever since, without showing a gun or throwing up any earth which would disclose his position. He had suffered some loss from random bullets coming over the parapets at the salient 500 yards in front, but it was borne rather than disclose the location.

This morning, on one occasion, a charge was attempted by the colored division, part of which was brought out of the crater and started toward the Plank road. Then Haskell's guns showed themselves and opened fire. The charge was quickly driven back with severe loss among its white officers. A single private, with his musket at a support arms, made the charge, running all the way to the guns and jumping into the sunken road between them, where he was felled with a rammer staff. Meanwhile, our guns across the Appomattox on the Federal right, and from our left near the river, had kept up a reply to the Federal cannonade to prevent their concentration opposite the mine. Lee and Beauregard had early come to the field, which they surveyed from the windows of the Gee house, where Johnson made headquarters, on the Jerusalem Plank road, near Haskell's guns. Hill had gone to bring up his troops.

On the arrival of Mahone, he at once prepared to attack, and had formed Weiseger's brigade, when a renewed attempt to advance was made from the enemy's lines on our left of the crater. He at once met this by a counter-charge of Weiseger's with a portion of Elliott's which drove the enemy back and which caused the retreat from the rear of their lines of many who had been sheltered within them. These suffered severely by our fire from the flanks as they crossed the open spaces behind, under fire from the guns upon both flanks and infantry as well.

This retreat under such severe fire was seen in the Federal lines, just in time to put a stop to an attack upon our right flank, about to be made by Ayres's division of Warren's corps, which had been ordered to capture the "one-gun battery" on our right, as they called the one at which Gibbes had been wounded.[1]

There was very little infantry supporting this gun, or able to reach it, without exposure. Ayres's attack would probably have been successful. He was about to go forward, when Meade directed all offensive operations to cease. Wright's brigade arriving about half-past eleven, Mahone made a second attack, which was repulsed with the aid of the Federal artillery bearing upon the ground.

Between 1 and 2 P.M., Sanders's brigade having arrived, and also the 61st N.C. from Hoke, a combined movement upon both flanks of the crater was organized. Mahone attacked on the left, with Sanders's brigade, the 61st N.C. and the 17th S.C.; Johnson attacked on the right with the 23d S.C. and the remaining five companies of the 22d, all that could be promptly collected on that flank.

This attack was easily successful. Mahone has stated that the number of prisoners taken in the crater was 1101, including two brigade commanders, Bartlett and Marshall.

The tabular statement of the Medical Department gives the Federal casualties of the day as: killed, 419; wounded, 1679; missing, 1910; total, 4008. Elliott's brigade reported the loss by the explosion as: —

	TOTAL	AGG.	
In 18th S.C. 4 companies	86		About 300 were
In 22d S.C. 5 companies	170		blown up, but a
In Pegram's battery out of 30			small percentage
present	22	278	escaped alive.

Including these, Johnson reports the casualties in his division (Elliott, Wise, Ransom, Gracie), as follows: —

Killed, 165; wounded, 415; missing, 359; total, 938.

[1] Humphreys calls this a two-gun battery. There were two embrasures and two guns, but only one used. The other did not bear where desired.

There are no returns for Mahone's and Hoke's divisions. Hoke's division was composed of Corse's, Clingman's, Fulton's, Hagood's, and Colquitt's brigades, and Mahone's had only three brigades on the field, — Weiseger's, Wright's, and Sanders's. Of these eight brigades, only Weiseger's had serious losses, but there are no reports except for Colquitt's, who, like the rest of Hoke's division, held a portion of the line not attacked. His casualties were 4 killed and 27 wounded. The total Confederate loss is given in the Tabular Statement of the Medical Department as: 400 killed, 600 wounded, and 200 missing, which is perhaps between 200 and 300 too small.

The Military Court censured Gens. Burnside, Ledlie, Ferrero, Willcox, and Col. Bliss, commanding a brigade. They also expressed their opinion : —

"That explicit orders should have been given assigning one officer to the command of all the troops intended to engage in the assault when the Commanding General was not present in person to witness the operations."

There is nothing in the Reports to explain this. Grant sent a despatch to Halleck at 10 A.M., saying that he "was just from the front," and about that time Humphreys reports that Meade, with Grant's concurrence, ordered the cessation of all offensive movements.

CHAPTER XXIII

THE FALL OF 1864

The Situation in August. Hood appointed to succeed Johnston. Evacuation of Atlanta. Capture of Mobile. Reëlection of Lincoln. Battle of Franklin. Sherman's March. Fort Fisher. Conference at Fortress Monroe. Fort Stedman. Movements of Grant. Five Forks. Fort Whitworth and Fort Gregg. Evacuation of Petersburg. Appomattox. Correspondence between Lee and Grant. Conversations with Lee. The Meeting at Appomattox. The Surrender. Visit to Washington. Conversations with Mr. Washburne. Return Home. Record of the Army of Northern Virginia.

GEN. HUMPHREYS writes of the situation in Aug., soon after the fiasco of the Mine, as follows: [1] —

"Between this time and the month of March, 1865, several movements of the Army of the Potomac and the Army of the James were made to the right and to the left, which resulted in the extension of our line of intrenchments in both directions, and caused a corresponding extension of the Confederate intrenchments on our left, and their occupation in stronger force of their intrenchments on the north bank of the James. By this process their lines finally became so thinly manned, when the last movement to our left was made in March, 1865, as to be vulnerable at one or two points, where some of the obstructions in their front had been in a great measure destroyed by the exigencies of the winter."

In other words, attacks upon our lines were now abandoned for a succession of feints, first upon one flank and then upon the other, by which our lines were extended at both ends to the point of breaking. This point was reached in eight months at one or two places, where the Confederates had been tempted by the severity of the winter to burn the *abattis* in front of their breastworks. We will not attempt to follow either these efforts of the enemy, or Lee's aggressive counter-movements, of which

[1] *Virginia Campaign*, p. 267.

there was no lack, though all were attended with much hard fighting.

Besides the heavy casualties of these incessant affairs, which followed each other at short intervals from Aug. 1 to Nov. 1, there was daily sharpshooting and much mortar and artillery practice, which helped swell the totals. Confederate reports are entirely lacking, but losses were fully as heavy in proportion to the numbers engaged, as were the Federal losses; for on several occasions Lee was the aggressor and lost heavily. On one, Oct. 7, on the Darbytown road, Field's division was sent to charge two brigades in breastworks, which proved to be armed with the Spencer magazine-guns. He was quickly repulsed with severe loss, which included Gregg of Texas killed, and Bratton of S.C. wounded. The total Federal casualties for this period, Aug. 1 to Dec. 31, are given as: killed, 2172; wounded, 11,138; missing, 11,311; total, 24,621. The corresponding Confederate losses were probably between 12,000 and 14,000.

It will afford a better view of the situation as a whole to glance at those events referred to by Swinton, where he says: —

"Had not success elsewhere come to brighten the horizon, it would have been difficult to raise new forces to recruit the Army of the Potomac."

The first and most important of the events resulting in "success elsewhere" was President Davis relieving Joseph E. Johnston of the command of the army opposing Sherman at Atlanta, and appointing Hood to succeed him. This step was taken with great reluctance, and under great popular and political pressure brought by Gov. Brown and Sen. Hill of Ga., who claimed that Johnston intended to surrender Atlanta without giving battle. After many reiterations of such charges, Davis was at length led to give a promise to relieve Johnston if, on being asked for some assurance of his intention to fight, he failed to give it. Gen. Bragg was sent to interview him, and after spending two days with him, wired: —

"He has not sought my advice, and it was not volunteered. I cannot learn that he has any more plan in the future than he has had in the past."

Davis then wired to Johnston a direct inquiry, as follows: —

"I wish to hear from you as to present situation, and your plan of operations, so specifically as will enable me to anticipate events."

This was sent July 16, and Johnston replied the same day: —

". . . As the enemy has double our number, we must be on the defensive. My plan of operations must, therefore, depend upon that of the enemy. It is mainly to watch for an opportunity to fight to advantage. We are trying to put Atlanta into condition to be held for a day or two by the Ga. militia, that army movements may be freer and wider."

This reply was certainly not specific, and was considered evasive. It will be remembered that, in April, 1862, the relations between the President and Johnston had been strained to the verge of breaking by the general's reticence as to his plans, and avoidance of interviews, even by galloping to the front on seeing the President approach near the field of Seven Pines. There a crisis was avoided by Johnston's wound and loss of the command of the army.

Now, a very similar issue had arisen, and with it the old and bitter feelings on each side. On the 17th Adjt.-Gen. Cooper wired Johnson: —

"I am directed by the Sec. of War to inform you that as you have failed to arrest the advance of the enemy to the vicinity of Atlanta, and express no confidence that you can defeat or repel him, you are hereby relieved from the command of the Army and Department of the Tenn., which you will immediately turn over to Gen. Hood."

To this Johnston replied that the order had been received and obeyed, and added: —

"As to the alleged cause of my removal I assert that Sherman's army is much stronger, compared with that of Tenn., than Grant's compared with that of northern Va. Yet the enemy has been compelled to advance much more slowly to the vicinity of Atlanta than to that of Richmond and Petersburg, and penetrated much deeper into Va. than into Ga. Confident language by a military commander is not usually regarded as evidence of competence."

It is vain to speculate on what might have happened had Johnston been left in command. Had Lee been commander-in-chief, he would not have been relieved, as was indicated by his restoring Johnston to command on his taking that position in

February. But it is a fact that Johnston had never fought but one aggressive battle, the battle of Seven Pines, which was phenomenally mismanaged.

On the 20th and 21st, Hood attacked Sherman, but was defeated, and after a month of minor operations was finally, on Sept. 1, compelled to evacuate Atlanta. Meanwhile, a naval expedition, sent under Farragut against Mobile, had captured the forts commanding the harbor of that city on Aug. 23. These two events, the capture of Mobile and Atlanta, following each other within a few days, came at perhaps the period of the greatest political depression of the administration. On Aug. 23, Mr. Lincoln had written on a slip of paper: —

"This morning, as for some days past, it seems exceedingly probable that this administration will not be reëlected. Then it will be my duty to so coöperate with the President-elect, as to save the Union between the election and the inauguration, as he will have secured his election on such grounds that he cannot possibly save it afterward."

This paper he folded and had the Cabinet put their names on its back.

The victories came like an interposition of Providence, and proved to be the final turning of the balance in the Federal favor. The Democratic party had nominated McClellan on a peace platform, mistaking the general discontent and depression, for a desire for peace at any price. McClellan himself had repudiated the platform, but, as victory now seemed inclining to the Federal banners, all opposition to the administration died out. At the election in Nov., Mr. Lincoln received 212 electoral votes and McClellan but 21.

The attacks which Hood had made upon Sherman on the 20th and 22d had both been judiciously planned and had stood excellent chances of success. The failure in both cases was from want of strict compliance with orders on the part of one of his corps commanders, Gen. Hardee. To trace it further would bring it home to himself for failure to supervise the execution of important orders — a sort of failure from which even the most eminent commanders have *never* been exempt.

Another and striking example of it attended Hood's next campaign, this time involving practically a death-blow to his army. Having manœuvred to draw Sherman out of intrenchments at Atlanta by moving upon his communications, he succeeded in drawing him as far north as Dalton, and then crossed into Alabama at Gadsden, where he arrived Oct. 20. Here he had hoped to deliver battle, but Sherman declined to follow, and returned to Atlanta, making preparations for the march to Savannah, upon which he set out Nov. 15.

In this event, Hood's orders from the President were to follow Sherman and hang upon his rear. But, with the approval of Beauregard, who had been placed in command of the department, Hood decided, instead, to advance upon Nashville, where Thomas commanded, with an inferior force under Schofield, holding the country to the south. Pres. Davis had not imagined that any demonstration Hood could possibly make upon Nashville would be seriously regarded by Grant. The result, however, proved that it was thought to threaten Ky., and it was considered of such grave importance that Grant had threatened to relieve Thomas for delay in attacking Hood. Grant was actually on his way to Nashville perhaps to do this when Thomas won his victory. So much in explanation of Hood's campaign. The issue at stake was now lost by the non-compliance with orders of Gen. Cheatham, commanding one of Hood's corps.

Schofield had taken position on the north side of Duck River, opposing Hood's crossing. Hood left Lee's corps to demonstrate against Schofield, while he threw a pontoon bridge across the river three miles above and crossed Cheatham's and Stewart's corps which marched to Spring Hill on the Franklin pike, 12 miles in Schofield's rear, arriving about 3 P.M. This place was held by the 2d division of the 4th corps, about 4000 strong; Hood's force was about 18,000 infantry. Hood took Cheatham with Cleburne, a division commander, within sight of the pike, along which the enemy could now be seen retreating at double-quick, with wagons in a trot, and gave explicit orders for an immediate attack and occupation of the pike. Similar orders, too, were given to Stewart's corps, and when Hood found later that nothing was being done, he sent more messages by staff-officers, which also failed of effect. The head of Schofield's infantry arrived about nine o'clock and passed unmolested, except by some random picket shots to which they made no reply. Both Confederate divisions had bivouacked within gunshot of the pike, but no effort was made to occupy it or to cross it. Undoubtedly, here Hood should have ridden to the front and led the troops into action himself. In his book, he calls the opportunity "the best move in my career as a soldier." A few days after, Cheatham frankly admitted his delinquency. It was rumored that both he and Gen. Stewart had that evening absented themselves from their divisions. Both had been often distinguished for gallantry, and Hood now overlooked it, believing it had been a lesson not to be forgotten. Nevertheless, it proved the death-blow to Hood's army.

On the next day, Nov. 30, Schofield took a strong position at Franklin to protect his wagon-trains, resting both flanks on the Harpeth River across a concave bend. His intrenched main line was but a mile in length. It was well protected with abattis, and, 280 yards in front, an entire division, Wagner's of the 4th corps, held an advanced line, with its flanks drawn back nearly to the main line, and also well protected by abattis. His infantry, about 23,000, was a little more than Hood's and was ample to man both lines, and to hold a strong reserve in a well sheltered position close in the rear. One of his infantry brigades, Casement's, was armed with magazine breech loaders. The ground in front was mostly level and open pasture-land, and batteries across the Harpeth could fire upon the approaches.

To assault was a terrible proposition to troops who, during Johnston's long retreat, had been trained to avoid charging breastworks. But Hood saw no alternative, since he had lost the one opportunity of the campaign at Spring Hill the night before. For Schofield was now within a day's march of Nashville. He ordered the attack, and for the credit of his army it must be said that officers and men responded valiantly, and went down to defeat in a blaze of glory. Over 10 per cent of the force engaged were killed outright on the field, over 20 per cent were carried to hospitals with severe wounds, and as many more suffered less severe wounds or were captured. The loss of general officers was unparalleled on either side in any action of the war.

Cleburne, Gist, Adams, Strahl, and Granberrty were killed; Brown, Carter, Manigault, Quarles, Cockrell, and Scott were wounded, and Gordon was captured. Fifty-three regimental commanders were killed, wounded, or captured. The result might have been different, but for three handicaps: 1. Hood, most unwisely, did not precede his charge with a severe cannonade, because the village of Franklin was but a half-mile in rear of his line. The enemy's position was quite crowded, and all his lines were subject to enfilade. It would have severely shaken the enemy, and with little danger to non-combatants, which they could not avoid. 2. The action was not begun until 4 P.M. The sun set at 4.50 P.M. and darkness prevented Hood from getting in two of Lee's divisions. There was no moon. 3. The presence on the field of Casement's brigade with magazine breech loaders. It was said by a correspondent that never before had men been killed so fast as they were during this charge by the fire of this brigade. The action was hand to hand all along the enemy's main line. It was carried for quite a space, at one point, but was restored by a charge of the reserve. At some points men were dragged across the parapets and captured. The battle continued with violence until 9 P.M. and firing was kept up until 3 A.M., when the enemy withdrew from the field, leaving his dead and wounded. Schofield's losses were: killed, 189; wounded, 1033; missing, 1104; total 2326. Hood left 1750 dead on the field and 3800 in hospitals. The slightly wounded and prisoners were about 2000.

His losses in the battle of Franklin made it impossible for Hood to attack at Nashville, but he hoped to fortify and threaten until he was attacked, and then to gain a victory. What a vain hope! Efforts were being made to bring troops from Texas across the Mississippi, which also, *of course*, proved vain. They never even started. His force was now reduced to about 18,000 infantry and 5000 cavalry, with which he took position before Nashville on Dec. 2. Here he intrenched himself and awaited Thomas's attack, which the latter delayed until Dec. 15. By this date he had accumulated a force of over 53,000 men. With these he attacked on the 15th, but with little success and with severe losses at points where he assailed Hood's intrenchments.

On the 15th, the Federals renewed their assaults and during the morning were again repulsed. About 3 P.M., they massed a large force under cover behind a hill about Hood's left centre, and under cover of a heavy fire of artillery made a gallant charge and carried Hood's line, which, seeing the disaster, broke in all directions, and all efforts to rally it failed.

During the night, Hood withdrew, losing 54 guns and 4500 prisoners. There was no return made of his casualties, but he reported them as "very small." Thomas reported: killed, 387; wounded, 2562; missing, 112; total, 3061. Hood made good his retreat to Tupelo, Miss., where his army rested for reorganization on Jan. 10, 1865. In the spring, it was transferred to N.C., where it served under A. P. Stewart and, about 7000 strong, was included in Johnston's surrender. The battle of Franklin had proved its death-blow.

Besides the loss of Atlanta and the destruction of Hood's army, there remains a third sequence of the change of commanders which deserves notice among the "successes elsewhere," preparing the ground for Grant when he again became able to inaugurate a campaign. This was the unopposed march of Sherman from Atlanta to Savannah between Nov. 15 and Dec. 25, with the capture of Savannah on the latter date. It was preceded by the deliberate burning of nearly every house in Atlanta, only the residential portion being spared. This was excused on the ground that "War is Hell." It depends somewhat upon the warrior. The conduct of Lee's army in Pa. presents a pleasing contrast.

It had been hoped that the few troops which could be gathered in Ga., aided by the militia of the State, and by 13 brigades of Confederate cavalry under Wheeler, might effectively harass and delay such a march, but all such expectations proved utterly vain. Though little was said in the press at the time, and our public speakers belittled the achievement, there is no question that the moral effect of this march, upon the country at large, both at the North and the South and also upon foreign nations, was greater than would have been the most decided victory. Already it cast the ominous shadow of Sherman's advance up the coast in the coming spring.

In this connection, there now began demonstrations against Wilmington, which was the last port of the Confederacy holding out opportunities to blockade runners. These came in under the protection of Fort Fisher at the mouth of the river 20 miles below the city. The fort was a formidable one, mounting 44 guns, and had a garrison of 1400 men under Col. Lamb. A military and naval expedition set out against it on Dec. 13, 1864, under Gen. Butler and Adm. Porter in a fleet of 50 war vessels and 100 transports carrying 6500 infantry. The fleet was the largest ever assembled under the Federal flag, and it had been specially intended by Grant that the infantry force should be commanded by Gen. Weitzel. It was never contemplated that Butler should even accompany it. In the expressive language of modern slang he had not only "butted in," and had taken the command from Weitzel, but had devised a new mode of attack upon Fort Fisher. This was to be a disguised blockade runner loaded with 215 tons of gunpowder to be run at night close to Fort Fisher and exploded. It was supposed that this would put the whole fort *hors de combat*. Gen. Delafield, chief engineer, submitted to the War Department a report on destructive effects of explosions of gunpowder in open air, indicating their very limited range. Butler was notoriously a military charlatan, who had been forced upon Grant as commander of the Army of the James by political considerations. During all the summer campaign, he knew and felt his importance, and had been able even successfully to bully Grant himself, who was already under sharp criticism for his terrible losses in battle, and for the rumors in the army of his intemperance.

Early in July, after some preliminary correspondence, indicating a doubt how Butler would relish any interference with himself, Halleck issued an order assigning the troops under him to the command of W. F. Smith, and sending Butler to Fortress Monroe. On receipt of this order, he said to his staff, who were near, "Gentlemen, this order will be revoked to-morrow." The next day, clad in full uniform, he called at Grant's headquarters, where he found Mr. Dana, Asst. Sec. of War. Gen. James

H. Wilson, in a memoir on the *Life and Services of W. F. Smith*, gives the following account of the interview: —

"Dana describes Butler as entering the general's presence with a flushed face and a haughty air, holding out the order relieving him from command in the field, and asking: 'Gen. Grant, did you issue this order?' To which Grant, in a hesitating manner, replied: 'No, not in that form.' Dana, perceiving at this point that the subject under discussion was likely to be unpleasant, if not stormy, at once took his leave, but the impression made upon his mind by what he saw while present was that Butler had in some measure 'cowed' his commanding officer. What further took place neither he nor Mr. Dana has ever said. Butler's book, however, contains what purports to be a full account of the interview, but it is to be observed that it signally fails to recite any circumstance of an overbearing nature."

Not only was the order promptly revoked by Special Orders No. 62, July 19, but Butler's command on the field was extended to include the newly arrived 19th corps, and this disposition of command was still in force when Butler "butted in" to the Fort Fisher expedition, taking his powder boat with him, regardless of Delafield's discussion of the value of powder boats.

The boat was towed into position by Commander Rhind of the Navy who reported placing it "within 300 yards of the northeast salient of Fort Fisher," which bore "west southwest a half west" about midnight of Dec. 23, 1864. It was fired by several lines of Gomez fuse running through the mass of powder and ignited by several devices arranged to act an hour and a half after the ship was deserted. The explosion occurred at 2 A.M., and was supposed by the garrison of the fort to be the accidental explosion of a Federal gunboat. Not the slightest damage was done to the fort, whose garrison remained in ignorance of Butler's plans until published afterward.

On the 24th and 25th, the fort was subjected to a terrific bombardment at the rate of 40 to 50 shells per minute for hours at a time, until the fleet had practically exhausted its ammunition. It had not silenced the fort nor materially damaged it, which, being reported by the land forces who had been put ashore, they reëmbarked without assaulting, on the night of the 26th, and the next day the expedition returned to Fortress Monroe. The casualties in the fort from the fire of the ships were 61, and a greater number were suffered in the fleet from the 662 shots fired by the fort.

Another and a still larger expedition was soon gotten together and despatched against Fort Fisher, but, though his own campaign was still in abeyance, the political situation was now so improved by the "successes elsewhere" that Grant was no longer afraid to exercise his authority, and on Jan. 4, he wrote to Halleck demanding Butler's official head. With a celerity indicative of the pleasure with which both Halleck and Lincoln complied with the request, it was presented to him. On Jan. 7, in General Orders No. 1, "By direction of the President," Maj.-Gen. Butler was relieved from command and ordered to repair to Lowell, Mass.

On Jan. 5, a new expedition, under the command of Porter and Gen. Terry, set sail, carrying about 9500 infantry and a heavy siege-train. It arrived before Fort Fisher and opened fire on Jan. 13, in even greater force than on the previous occasion. A land force of about 7000 infantry was at hand for its defence. Mr. Davis sent Bragg to command it, who made no effort to prevent the enemy's landing. It might have been difficult to prevent him, but to make no effort brought complaint and discouragement. The bombardment was, on this occasion, kept up without intermission day or night, and, instead of being general, was concentrated upon the land defences. On the afternoon of the second day, the palisades and guns of those defences being destroyed and a breach opened, two assaults were made about 3 P.M., one by Ames's division of the 23d corps, about 4500 strong, and one by 2000 sailors and marines from the fleet under Capt. Breese. The latter assaulted the breach, but were repulsed with severe loss. The infantry, passing around and through the palisades, made a lodgment between the traverses, and after seven hours' fighting possessed the fort. When Bragg took command of the land forces, Whiting, who had commanded the whole post before, took command of the fort. He was mortally, and Col. Lamb desperately, wounded in the defence. The loss of the infantry assaulting column was 110 killed, 536 wounded.

During the winter, the Confederate lines about Petersburg had been constantly extended at both ends, it has been already explained how. The troops were extended with them until it was about 37 miles by the shortest routes from our extreme left on White Oak Swamp below Richmond on the north side, to our extreme right below Petersburg. Lee's force at this time was about 50,000 and Grant's about 124,000. Humphreys gives the following brief statement of the Confederate condition: —

"The winter of '64–65 was one of unusual severity, making the picket duty in front of the intrenchments very severe. It was especially so to the Confederate troops with their threadbare, insufficient clothing and meagre food. Meat they had but little of, and their Subsistence Department was actually importing it from abroad. Of coffee or tea or sugar, they had none except in the hospitals.

"'It is stated that in a secret session of the Confederate Congress the condition of the Confederacy as to subsistence was declared to be: —
'That there was not meat enough in the Southern Confederacy for the armies it had in the field,
'That there was not in Va. either meat or bread enough for the armies within her limits,
'That the supply of bread for those armies to be obtained from other places depended absolutely upon keeping open the railroad connections of the South,
'That the meat must be obtained from abroad through a seaport,
'That the transportation was not now adequate, from whatever cause, to meet the necessary demands of the service.' . . .
"The condition of the deserters who constantly came into our lines during the winter appeared to prove that there was no exaggeration in this statement."

In addition to the scarcity of provisions, there was also threatened a deficiency of percussion caps. The supply for the campaign of 1864 had been maintained only by cutting up the copper stills of the country, but they were now exhausted and there was no more copper in sight.

Col. Taylor, in *Four Years with Lee*, writes that during the last 30 days before Petersburg: —

"The loss to the army by desertion averaged a hundred men a day. . . . The condition of affairs throughout the South at that period was truly deplorable. Hundreds of letters addressed to soldiers were intercepted and sent to army headquarters, in which mothers, wives, and sisters told of their inability to respond to the appeals of hungry children for bread, or to provide proper care and remedies for the sick, and in the name of all that was dear appealed to the men to come home and rescue them from the ills which they suffered and the starvation which threatened them. Surely never was devotion to one's country and to one's duty more sorely tested than was the case with the soldiers of Lee's army during the last year of the war."

Early in Feb., there occurred the last of the many affairs on our right flank. Grant had found that we were still hauling supplies from the Weldon R.R. and had sent Gregg's cavalry to destroy it, and tear it up for 40 miles south, and the 2d and 5th corps were sent across Hatcher's Run to guard their rear. Lee, hearing of the Federals outside of their intrenchments, sent three divisions under Mahone, Evans, and Pegram to attack them. There was sharp fighting for two days without material success on either side. The Federal losses were 1474 and probably the Confederate were 1000. Among them, unfortunately, was Gen. Pegram, whose loss was universally deplored. Col. Taylor, under date of Dec. 4, has noted the loss of another brilliant and popular young officer who had been a classmate of Pegram's at West Point in 1854, as follows : —

"Gen. Gracie, who showed such tact in getting Gen. Lee to descend from a dangerous position, was killed near the lines a day or so ago. He was an excellent officer, had passed through many hard-fought battles, escaped numberless dangers, and was finally killed while quietly viewing the enemy from a point where no one dreamed of danger."

Col. Taylor, in a letter, describes the incident referred to as follows : —

" Gen. Lee was making an inspection along the line occupied by Gen. Gracie's troops; the fire of the enemy's sharpshooters was uncomfortably accurate along there and the orders were against needless exposure. To get a good view Gen. Lee mounted the parapet or stepped out in front of the works. Of course all who saw it realized his danger, but who was to direct his attention to it? Gen. Gracie at once stepped to his side. The minnies whistled viciously. Gen. Lee, oblivious to his own danger, quickly realized Gen. Gracie's and immediately removed from the point of danger. That is all but it showed tact on the part of the latter."[1]

[1] Gen. Gracie was killed Dec. 3 by a shrapnel shot from Battery Morton which killed also two others with him. He had just received a furlough to visit his wife and child in Richmond but had missed his train.

I have already said that the fall of 1864 was the period of the war when the Confederate authorities might have made peace with greatest advantage to their people. Had they then offered a return to the Union, they might have secured liberal compensation for their slaves and generally more liberal terms financially and politically than at any other period of the contest. What these concessions might have been was suggested in the conference held at Fortress Monroe on Jan. 30, between Messrs. Lincoln and Seward, and the commissioners sent by Mr. Davis, Messrs. Stephens, Hunter, and Campbell. After this conference adjourned, without coming to any agreement, there were rumors that Mr. Lincoln had offered to pay the South $400,000,000 in bonds as compensation for the slaves, if the South would return to the Union. This was denied by some of Mr. Davis's cabinet, and the discussion brought out informal statements which Mr. Lincoln had made in the conversation which had taken place.

One was: —

"Take a sheet of paper and let me write at the top Union, and you may fill in the rest to suit yourselves."

To this Mr. Stephens had to reply that the power to write that word was the single power which had been denied the commission.

Next, Mr. Lincoln said that he had always felt that slavery having had the sanction of the government as a whole, it was unfair that the whole financial loss of its abolition should be thrown upon the South; that he had always felt ready to vote bonds to compensate her for this loss, and that he had heard as much as $400,000,000 suggested for this purpose.

There was no formal proposition made, for the Conference never reached that stage, but it is well known that until the day of his death, Mr. Lincoln cherished a desire to see the South compensated for the loss of her slaves, and that on Feb. 5, immediately after the failure of the Fortress Monroe Conference, he submitted to his cabinet a proposition to offer the South $400,000,000 in six per cent bonds in payment for peace with the abolition of slavery. His cabinet unanimously disapproved it, to his surprise and chagrin, whereon he dropped the matter, saying sadly, "You are all opposed to me." [1]

"Few cabinet secrets were better kept than this," Nicolay says, but the diary of Sec. Welles refers to it as follows: —

"The President had matured a scheme which he hoped would be useful in promoting peace. It was a proposition for paying the expense of the war for 200 days, or $400,000,000, to the rebel States to be for the extinguishment of slavery, or for such purpose as the States were disposed. This in a few words was the scheme. It did not meet with favor, but was dropped. . . ."

Early in March, Sherman's army moved into N.C. where it was confronted by Gen. Joseph E. Johnston, recalled by the Confederate Congress to command the army composed of the garrisons of Savannah and Charleston, and the remnants of the army of Hood which had been brought over from Tupelo, Miss. It was plain that Lee would soon be forced to abandon Richmond and Petersburg, and take advantage of his interior lines to unite with Johnston, and endeavor to crush Sherman before he could unite with Grant. Before undertaking this, which was felt to be an almost impossible task, however, he determined upon one last effort to break up Grant in his immediate front, in spite of all of his fortifications. He selected for his point of attack Fort Stedman, about a mile from the Appomattox River on Grant's right, and assigned Gordon to command the assault which was to be made Mar. 25. A surprise was relied on to secure Fort Stedman. Three columns of 100 men each, with local guides, were to seize what Gordon took to be three redoubts commanding Stedman on each side; a division was to follow them, and, through the gap thus made, the lines were to be swept in both directions and a force of cavalry was to ride and destroy the pontoon bridges across the Appomattox, and to raid City Point.

Taking advantage of an order allowing deserters to come in with their arms, several pickets were captured, the trench guard rushed, the fraise and abattis cut quickly by a strong pioneer party, and Fort Stedman was assaulted and occupied with two

[1] Told by Nicolay and Hay, X., 137.

adjacent batteries. But the three "redoubts" were found to be only some old open lines at commanding points now unoccupied. Federal infantry presently came in force and killed or captured all of the three columns sent under a misapprehension very likely to occur where earthworks have to be guessed at from imperfect observation. Field's division, which had been ordered over by rail from the north side, was delayed by the breaking down of the train. The column which had taken Fort Stedman was caught like rats in a trap. Humphreys writes: —

"The cross-fire of artillery and infantry on the space between the lines prevented the enemy from escaping and reënforcements from coming to them. Many were killed and wounded trying to get back to their own lines; 1949 prisoners, including 71 officers and 9 stand of colors, fell into Gen. Parke's hands. His loss was 494 killed and wounded, and 523 missing, a total of 1017."

While this fighting was going on, the other Federal corps were ordered to feel the lines in their fronts, it being hoped they might find some weak spots from which men had been drawn for Gordon's attack. Much sharp fighting resulted at many points, the total casualties for the day reaching 2000 for the Federals and 4000 for the Confederates. These attacks, however, everywhere failed entirely of their purpose except at a single point, on the lines of the 6th corps, about nine miles to our right from the point of Gordon's attack. Here, opposite a fort called Fort Fisher, our abattis had been weakened to get in fire wood from the front, and here the enemy were able to make a lodgment within our intrenched picket-line. When Grant's general assault was made at 4 A.M., April 2, this was the spot, and the only one, where at first it was successful. Humphreys states that it was —

"through openings made by the enemy for his convenience of access to the front, Gen. Wright told me that this was the weakest part of all the line he saw, and the only point where it could have been carried. His loss in killed and wounded was 1100, all of which occurred in the space of 15 minutes."

Apprehensive now that Lee might abandon Petersburg and Richmond at any moment, Grant determined to delay no longer, taking the initiative in moving around his right flank. His effective force, by his latest returns, was 101,000 infantry, 9000 artillery, 14,700 cavalry, total, 124,700, with 369 guns. Lee's forces by his latest return, Feb. 28, were 46,000 infantry, 5000 artillery, and 6000 cavalry, total 57,000, from which 3000 should be deducted for desertions in March. In N.C., Sherman was about Goldsboro with about 100,000, against which Johnston in front of Greensboro had, perhaps, 25,000. There was really no need that Grant should have hurried himself, for, though by all the maxims of strategy, Lee should now unite with Johnston and both attack Sherman, his deficiencies in transportation were so great that no such movement was practicable.

On March 27, Sheridan with two divisions of his excellent cavalry with their magazine carbines had rejoined the army, and Grant began to transfer his forces to his extreme left. A single division only, Devens of the 24th corps, was left north of the James. Two divisions of the 25th corps under Weitzel held the Bermuda Hundreds lines. All the rest of the infantry, about 90,000 muskets and the whole of the cavalry, thoroughly organized and abundantly equipped with transportation for rapid motion, on March 28 only awaited Grant's word to launch themselves upon Lee's communications.

On this occasion, Grant narrowly avoided one mistake of previous campaigns made, not only by himself in May, 1864, but by Hooker in May, 1863, and by Lee in June, 1863. He kept his cavalry moving and acting with his infantry instead of sending it off on a raid, having suspended on the 29th orders of the previous day to move against the railroads. It is noticeable, too, that Grant, on this occasion, concentrated practically his entire force in the attack upon our right, whereas, in the fall, he had never attacked upon one flank without some demonstration, at least, upon the other.

On the 30th, Wilcox's division on the north, and Heth's on the south, of Hatchers Run had sharp affairs with the approaching Federals, whom they went out to meet in some cases, but were finally driven back within their lines. The Federal losses for the day were 1780. There are no returns for ours.

Meanwhile, Lee was bringing up Pickett's and Johnson's divisions of infantry, about 6600 men, and two of Lee's divisions of cavalry, about 5760 men, for an expedition against Sheridan. They attacked him on the 31st, and drove him back in much confusion nearly to Dinwiddie C. H. Night ended the fighting, with Pickett so far in advance that he would have been cut off by Warren's corps, during the night, had he waited until morning. But he fell back, and took position in the morning at Five Forks, four miles from our right at Burgess Mills.

Here he made the fatal mistake of halting and proceeding to intrench, as well as the time and the scarcity of intrenching tools would permit. He was four miles away from where other troops could help him or they could be helped by him. He should never have stopped until he had connected with our right flank.

Longstreet writes: —

"The position was not of Pickett's choosing but of his orders, and from his orders he assumed that he would be reënforced."

As it was, in the morning, April 1, Sheridan, reënforced now by the 5th corps, some 15,000 men, followed, and massing a force of cavalry on Pickett's right, with the 5th corps he turned his left flank and routed him, capturing, as stated by Warren, 3244 men, 11 colors, and 4 guns, with a loss of only 634 men. The Federal Gen., Winthrop, was killed, and on the Confederate side Col. Pegram, a brother of the Gen. Pegram killed Feb. 6, and highly distinguished as an artillerist.

This battle was fought between four and six in the afternoon, and Humphreys notices a peculiar phenomenon of acoustic shadows, such as has been spoken of before in telling of other battles. He writes: —

"A singular circumstance connected with this battle is the fact that Gen. Pickett was, all of this time and until near the close of the action, on the north side of Hatchers Run where he had heard no sound of the engagement, nor had he received any information concerning it."

The distance was but little over a mile, and Fitz-Lee and Pickett were in company. Neither were on the field until the action was decided.

Although this action was a complete success, after it was over Warren was removed from the command of the 5th corps by Sheridan, under charges of which Warren was afterward fully acquitted by a Court of Inquiry.

When Grant heard at 9 P.M. of Sheridan's success, he was assured that he must now have Lee's long lines stretched to near the breaking strain, and that the time had come when he could renew his assaults, suspended since the occasion of the mine. With his usual promptness, he ordered the 2d corps, which was near him, south of Hatchers Run, to feel our works in its front at once. The other corps, stretching back to Petersburg, were ordered to cannonade our lines during the night, and, at his favorite hour of 4 A.M., to assault all the soft spots, of which, for two or three days, each corps commander had been ordered to make a study.

The midnight demonstration by the 2d corps waked a heavy fire of musketry and artillery, but produced no other results. The assault of the 6th corps at dawn, however, under Wright, was made at the point where our abattis had been weakened, and the enemy had made a lodgment, on Mar. 25. As before mentioned, here their assault was entirely successful, after incurring a loss of 1100 men. They then turned to the left and swept the Confederate line to its extremity. At the crossing of the Jerusalem Plank road, Parke got possession of an advanced line, with 12 guns and 800 prisoners, but he failed to carry our main line in the rear, and the fighting was kept up all day. At all other points, the morning assaults were repulsed.

After capturing all the works to the south and west, the enemy now turned toward Petersburg, where two isolated works, Forts Gregg and Whitworth, about 300 yards apart, stood about 1000 yards in front of our main line of intrenchments. The rear of Fort Gregg was closed with a palisade, and its ditch was generally impassable. On the right flank, however, a line to connect with Whitworth had been started, and here the unfinished ditch and parapet gave a narrow access to the parapet of Gregg. It was by this route that the enemy finally reached it. It was defended by Capt. Chew of the 4th Md. battery and Lt. McElroy of the Washington artillery, one gun each, and 62 dismounted artillery drivers; portions of the 12th and 16th Miss., under

Lt.-Col. Jas. H. Duncan, and of Lane's brigade under Capt. Geo. H. Snow, 214 men in all. Fort Whitworth was open at the gorge and was held by three guns of the Washington artillery and the 19th and 48th Miss. until the final charge was being made upon Fort Gregg, when, by Lee's order, the garrison was withdrawn.

The defence of Fort Gregg was notable, as was also the attack. The Federal forces were evidently feeling the inspiration of success and the Confederates the desperation of defeat. Several attacks by Foster's division, of the 24th corps, were repulsed. The last, aided by two brigades of Turner's division (while the 3d brigade advanced upon Whitworth) swarmed over the parapet of Gregg and captured, inside, the two guns with two colors. Of the garrison, 55 were killed, 129 were wounded, and only 30 were found uninjured of the 214. Gibbon's loss was 122 killed, 592 wounded, total, 714.

Lee and Longstreet, from the main line of intrenchments, witnessed the gallant defence of Fort Gregg and its final fall. A. P. Hill, aroused by the terrific cannonade and musketry at daylight and riding to join his troops, had been killed by some stragglers of the 6th corps, which, as has been told, had carried our lines and penetrated far inside of them. When Lee, on the night of April 1, had heard of the disaster to Pickett at Five Forks, he had wired for Longstreet with Field's division. This left only Kershaw's division and the local troops to hold Richmond, but Weitzel's force had already been so reduced that no aggressive idea was left him. Had he known of the withdrawal of Field's division, he might have been tempted to make an effort to take the city. On Longstreet's arrival in Petersburg, his troops were hurried to the intrenchments, whence they saw the gallant defence made by Fort Gregg, which had been done under the assurance that "Longstreet is coming. Hold for two hours and all will be well."

When these saw the forts captured, they expected nothing else but that the heavy blue columns and long lines would now move to crush them. But the lesson of Fort Gregg had not been thrown away. Grant recognized that Lee must retreat during the night, and that from his own position he would have the advantage in the start, and he preferred to order things prepared for the march westward in the morning. Lee had already advised Mr. Davis of the necessity of abandoning the lines that night, and, having noted Grant's pause after the capture of Fort Gregg, now, about 3 P.M., he issued the formal orders for the evacuation in time to have the troops begin to move at dark.

My headquarters had been on the Richmond side for some months, and my duty included the command of Drury's and Chaffin's bluffs, and the defence of the river. It happened that on April 2, I had prepared several torpedoes to be placed in the river that night, and early in the morning I went down into the swamp and was detained until late in the afternoon, when the orders of evacuation reached me. Part of my command was to cross the river at Drury's Bluff and part at Richmond. After giving necessary instructions, I rode into Richmond, and took my post at the bridge to see my batteries go by. Many accounts have been given of the scenes in Richmond that night, and I will not refer to them.

The freight depot of the Danville Road was close by the bridge, and I walked into it and saw large quantities of provisions and goods which had evidently run the blockade at Wilmington. I treated my horse to an English bridle and a felt saddle-blanket, and I hung to a ring on my saddle a magnificent side of English bacon, which proved a great acquisition during the next few days. These provisions were intended for Lee's army, and had been sent to Amelia C. H. from Danville, the train being ordered to come on to Richmond to take off the personnel and property of the government. Unfortunately, the officer in charge of it misunderstood his orders and came on without unloading at Amelia. Near my station in the street, a cellar door opened in the sidewalk, and while I waited for my batteries a solitary Irish woman brought many bales of blankets from the freight depot in a wheelbarrow and tumbled them into the cellar. Many fires were burning in the city, and a canal-boat in flames came floating under the bridge at which I stood. I could not see by what agency, but it was soon dragged away. The explosions of our little fleet of gunboats under Admiral Semmes at Drury's Bluff were plainly heard and the terrific explosion of the arsenal in Richmond. About sunrise, my last battalion passed and I followed, taking a farewell look at the city from the

Manchester side. The whole river front appeared to be in flames. Its formal surrender was made to Weitzel at 8.15 A.M.

We marched 24 miles that day and bivouacked at night in some tall pine woods near Tomahawk Church. I had barely gotten supper when I was ordered to join two engineers being sent to find a wagon route for our guns and trains to an overhead railroad bridge across the Appomattox River. We travelled all night in mud and darkness, waking up residents to ask directions, but we finally got the whole column safely across the railroad bridge and went into camp near sundown about three miles from Amelia C. H.

The next morning we passed through the village, where we should have gotten rations, but they did not meet us. They had gone on to Richmond and been destroyed there, as has been told. Here a few of the best-equipped battalions of artillery were selected to accompany the troops, while all the excess was turned over to Walker, chief of the 3d corps artillery, to take on a direct road to Lynchburg. About 1 P.M., with Lee and Longstreet at the head of the column, we took the road for Jetersville, where it was reported that Sheridan was across our path and Lee intended to attack him. We were not long in coming to where our skirmish line was already engaged, and a long conference took place between the generals and W. H. F. Lee in command of the cavalry. It appeared that the 2d and 6th corps were in front of us, but might be passed in the night by a flank march. We countermarched a short distance, and then turning to the right, we marched all night, passing Amelia Springs, and arrived at daylight at Rice's Turnout, six miles west of Burkesville.[1] Here I was ordered to select a line of battle and take position to resist attack, and here we waited for the remainder of the army to come up and pass us, but we waited in vain.

While the 2d corps had closely pressed the rear of the column

[1] During this night's march a widespread and long-continued panic was started by a large black stallion carrying a fence rail swinging to his bridle and running away along the roads on which the troops were marching. The first false alarm started the troops to firing on each other, and this spread and was kept up a long time. Among the valuable officers killed in it by his own men was Maj. Smith, who commanded our Drury's Bluff batteries.

all day, the cavalry and the 6th corps had struck its flank under Ewell at Sailor's Creek. Besides Kershaw's division, this force comprised no veteran soldiers, but the employees of the departments under Custis Lee, the marines and sailors of our little fleet under Admiral Tucker, and the heavy artillerists of Drury's and Chaffin's bluffs, under Col. Crutchfield and Maj. Stiles. This force, though largely composed of men who had never before been under fire, surprised the enemy with an unexpected display of courage, such as had already been shown at Fort Stedman and Fort Gregg, and would still with flashes illuminate our last days. It formed line of battle on the edge of a pine wood, in full view of two lines of battle in open ground across a little stream. It had no artillery to make reply, and it lay still while other Federal infantry was marched around them, and submitted to an accurate and deliberate cannonade for 20 minutes, followed quickly by a charge of the two lines. Not a gun was fired until the enemy approached within 100 yards, showing handkerchiefs as an invitation to the men to surrender. Then two volleys broke both of their lines, and the excited Confederates charged in pursuit of the fleeing enemy, but were soon driven back by the fire of the guns. A second charge of the Federals soon followed, in which the two lines mingled in one promiscuous and prolonged mêlée with clubbed muskets and bayonets, as if bent upon exterminating each other individually. Gen. Custis Lee in his official report thus describes the ending : —

"Finding . . . that my command was entirely surrounded, to prevent useless sacrifice of life, the firing was stopped by some of my officers aided by some of the enemy's, and the officers and men were taken as prisoners of war."[1]

Toward noon, the enemy began to appear in our front at Rice's Turnout, and made demonstrations, but were easily held off by the artillery. Meanwhile, Lee had become very anxious over the non-arrival of Anderson's command (the remnants of Pickett's and Johnson's divisions), and at last rode to the rear to investigate. He did not return until near sundown and with him came fuller

[1] Col. Crutchfield, who was Jackson's chief of artillery, and lost a leg at Chancellorsville, was killed in this action. A graphic and detailed account of it is given in Stiles's *Four Years under Marse Robert*.

news of the battle at Sailor's Creek in which Anderson was also involved. Our loss had been about 8000 men, with six generals — Ewell, Kershaw, Custis Lee, Dubose, Hunton, and Corse —all captured.

One notable affair had taken place on this date, between a small force under Gen. Read, sent ahead by Ord to burn the High Bridge on the Lynchburg road, and Dearing's and Rosser's cavalry. The expedition consisted of two regiments of infantry and about 80 cavalry. They had gotten within a mile of the bridge, when our cavalry, in much larger force, attacked them. Humphreys writes: —

"A most gallant fight ensued in which Gen. Read, Col. Washburn, and three other cavalry officers were killed. After heavy loss the rest of the force surrendered. Gen. Dearing, Col. Boston, and Maj. Thompson of Rosser's command were among the killed."

About sundown, the enemy at Rice's showed a disposition to advance, and Lee soon gave orders to resume our retreat. In the morning we might have gone on toward Danville, but now we turned to the right and took the road to Lynchburg. I remember the night as one peculiarly uncomfortable. The road was crowded with disorganized men and deep in mud. We were moving all night and scarcely made six miles. About sunrise, we got to Farmville and crossed the river on a bridge to the north side of the Appomattox, and here we received a small supply of rations.

Here we found Gen. Lee. While we were getting breakfast, he sent for me and, taking out his map, showed me that the enemy had taken a highway bridge across the Appomattox near the High Bridge, were crossing on it, and would come in upon our road about three miles ahead. He directed me to send artillery there to cover our passage and, meanwhile, to take personal charge of the two bridges at Farmville (the railroad and the highway), prepare them for burning, see that they were not fired too soon, so as to cut off our own men, nor so late that the enemy might save them.

While he explained, my eyes ran over the map and I saw another road to Lynchburg than the one we were taking. This other kept the south side of the river and was the straighter of the two, our road joining it near Appomattox C. H. I pointed this out, and he asked if I could find some one whom he might question. I had seen at a house near by an intelligent man whom I brought up and who confirmed the map. The Federals would have the shortest road to Appomattox station, a common point a little beyond Appomattox C. H. Saying there would be time enough to look after that, the general folded up his map and I went to look after the bridges.

As the enemy were already in sight, I set fire to the railroad bridge at once, and, having well prepared the highway bridge, I left my aide, Lt. Mason, to fire it on a signal from me. It was also successfully burned. In the *End of an Era* by John S. Wise, he has described an interview occurring between his father, Gen. Wise, and Gen. Lee at Farmville at this time, which I quote : —

"We found Gen. Lee on the rear portico of the house I have mentioned. He had washed his face in a tin basin and stood drying his beard with a coarse towel as we approached. 'Gen. Lee,' exclaimed my father, 'my poor brave men are lying on yonder hill more dead than alive. For more than a week they have been fighting day and night, without food, and, by God, Sir, they shall not move another step until *somebody* gives them something to eat.'

"'Come in, General,' said Gen. Lee, soothingly. 'They deserve something to eat and shall have it; and meanwhile you shall share my breakfast.' He disarmed everything like defiance by his kindness. . . . Gen. Lee inquired what he thought of the situation. 'Situation?' said the bold old man. 'There is no situation. Nothing remains, Gen. Lee, but to put your poor men on your poor mules and send them home in time for the spring ploughing. This army is hopelessly whipped, and is fast becoming demoralized. These men have already endured more than I believed flesh and blood could stand, and I say to you, Sir, emphatically, that to prolong the struggle is murder, and the blood of every man who is killed from this time forth is on your head, Gen. Lee.'

"This last expression seemed to cause Gen. Lee great pain. With a gesture of remonstrance, and even of impatience, he protested. 'Oh, General, do not talk so wildly. My burdens are heavy enough! What would the country think of me, if I did what you suggest?'

"'Country be d—d,' was the quick reply. 'There is no country. There has been no country, General, for a year or more. You are the country to these men. They have fought for you. They have shivered through a long winter for you. Without pay or clothes or care of any sort their devotion to you and faith in you have been the only things that have held this army together. If you demand the sacrifice, there are still left thousands of us who will die for you. You know the game is desperate beyond redemption, and that, if you so announce, no man, or government, or people will gainsay your decision. That is why I repeat that the blood of any man killed hereafter is on your head.' Gen. Lee stood for some time at an open window looking out at the throng now surging by upon the roads and in the fields, and made no response."

Well might Lee say, "My burdens are heavy enough!" Gen. Wise had in no way exaggerated them.

Poague's battalion of artillery had gone ahead to the intersecting road Lee had mentioned, and Mahone's division (now assigned to our corps) supported by Poague's guns, took a good position and began to fortify. They held the position all day, being charged in the afternoon, repulsing the enemy and charging in turn. They captured the colors of the 5th N.H., and regained one of our guns which had been overrun by numbers. The enemy, Miles's division, reported a loss for the day of 571. The march of our column was continued under the protection of Mahone's division, with but one slight interruption.

Crook's division of cavalry forded the river on our left and moved toward our train. Gregg's brigade, in the lead, was charged by Mumford and Rosser, and Gregg and a bunch of prisoners were captured, on which the rest of the division was withdrawn. Our march was now kept up all night and the next day until sundown. I rode off from the road, after midnight, with my staff and found a fence corner where we could rest awhile without having our horses stolen as we slept, for I had now had but one night's rest out of six.

After sundown on the 7th, Mahone, still holding the road against the 2d corps under Humphreys, asked a flag of truce to enable him to remove the wounded, left in front of his line when he charged and captured the colors of the 5th N.H. When the reply came, granting the truce for an hour, it brought also a letter from Grant to Lee, as follows: —

"April 7, 1865.

"General: The result of the last week must convince you of the hopelessness of further resistance on the part of the Army of Northern Virginia in this struggle. I feel that it is so, and regard it as my duty to shift from myself the responsibility of any further effusion of blood, by asking of you the surrender of that portion of the Confederate army known as the Army of Northern Virginia.

"U. S. GRANT, Lt.-Gen."

Lee, at that moment, happened to be near Mahone's lines, and within an hour the following reply was delivered to Gen. Seth Williams, the bearer : —

"APRIL 7, 1865.

"GENERAL: I have received your note of this date. Though not entertaining the opinion you express on the hopelessness of further resistance on the part of the Army of Northern Virginia, I reciprocate your desire to avoid useless effusion of blood, and therefore, before considering your proposition, ask the terms you will offer on condition of its surrender.

"R. E. LEE, Gen."

The next day, the 8th, was the first quiet day of our retreat. The 2d corps followed us up closely, but there was no collision. All the rest of the Federal army had taken the more direct road which I had seen on Lee's map, and was marching to get ahead of us at Appomattox C. H. During the day I rode for a while with Gen. Pendleton, our chief of artillery. He told me that some of the leading generals had conferred, and decided that it would be well to represent to Lee that, in their opinion, the cause was now hopeless, in order that he might surrender and allow the odium of making the first proposition to be placed upon them.

But it was thought that Longstreet was the man to make the proposition to Lee. Longstreet had not been consulted, and Pendleton had undertaken to broach the matter to him, and had done so. Longstreet had indignantly rejected the proposition, saying that his duty was to help hold up Lee's hands, not to beat them down; that his corps could still whip twice its number and as long as that was the case he would never be the one to suggest a surrender.

On this, Pendleton himself had made bold to make the suggestion to Lee. From his report of the conversation, he had met a de-

cided snub, and was plainly embarrassed in telling of it. Lee
had answered very coldly, "There are too many men here to
talk of laying down their arms without fighting."

Evidently Lee preferred to himself take the whole responsibility of surrender, as he had always taken that of his battles,
whatever their issue, entirely alone.

Some time in the afternoon he received Grant's reply to his
inquiry as to the terms proposed. It was as follows: —

"FARMVILLE, April 8, 1865.

"GENERAL: Your note of last evening in reply to mine of same date,
asking the condition on which I will accept the surrender of the Army of
Northern Virginia is received. In reply I would say that peace being
my great desire, there is but one condition I would insist upon, namely,
that the men and officers surrendered shall be disqualified from taking up
arms again against the government of the United States until properly exchanged. I will meet you, or will designate officers to meet any officers
you may name for the same purpose at any point agreeable to you for the
purpose of arranging definitely the terms upon which the surrender of the
Army of Northern Virginia will be received.

"U. S. GRANT, Lt.-Gen."

Lee received this late in the afternoon of the 8th. It was
answered from the roadside and delivered to Humphreys after
sundown for transmission to Grant. Lee had but recently been
appointed commander-in-chief of all the Confederate armies,
and he now delays the surrender of his own army in order
that the negotiation may include that of all the Confederate forces under his command. In accomplishing this he
might reasonably hope to secure the best possible terms,
as it would bring instant peace everywhere. His letter was
as follows: —

"APRIL 8, 1865.

"GENERAL: I received at a late hour your note of to-day. In mine of
yesterday I did not intend to propose the surrender of the Army of Northern Virginia, but to ask the terms of your proposition. To be frank, I do
not think the emergency has arisen to call for the surrender of this army,
but, as the restoration of peace should be the object of all, I desire to know
whether your proposals would lead to that end. I cannot therefore meet
you with a view to surrender the Army of Northern Virginia, but as far

as your proposal may affect the Confederate States' forces under my command, and tend to the restoration of peace, I should be pleased to meet you at 10 A.M. to-morrow on the old stage road to Richmond between the picket-lines of the two armies.

"R. E. LEE, Gen."

This letter was received by Grant at Curdsville, a roadside village on the road Lee had travelled, about midnight. It was not answered until in the morning, as Grant did not intend to accept Lee's invitation to meet him at 10 A.M. Grant had doubtless had an early interview in his mind when he sent his second letter, and was probably accompanying the 2d corps, that he might be conveniently near. But he had been recently cautioned from Washington about making or discussing any political terms, and, as Lee's letter seemed to involve a chance of such discussions, he apparently decided to make the proposed meeting impossible by at once leaving that road and riding across to the road being travelled by Ord and Sheridan.

Before starting, however, he replied to Lee from Curdsville, as follows: —

"APRIL 9, 1865.

"GENERAL: Your note of yesterday is received. I have no authority to treat on the subject of peace. The meeting proposed for 10 A.M. to-day could lead to no good. I will state, however, General, that I am equally anxious for peace with yourself, and the whole North entertains the same feeling. The terms upon which peace can be had are well understood. By the South laying down their arms they will hasten that most desirable event, save thousands of human lives and hundreds of millions of property not yet destroyed.

"Seriously hoping that all our difficulties may be settled without the loss of another life, I subscribe myself, etc.

"U. S. GRANT, Lt.-Gen."

Meanwhile, during the afternoon, we had approached Appomattox C. H., two miles beyond which was the junction of our road with the one on which Sheridan and Ord were now approaching, and already the advanced guards of the two forces were in collision. Lee arranged during the evening with Gordon and Fitz-Lee, who had the advance, that they should make a vigorous attack at dawn and endeavor to clear the road.

This was done, and, in evidence of it, a battery of 12-Pr. Napoleons was presently sent in to me, having been captured by a cavalry charge of Robert's brigade. Though this evidenced good spirit on the part of our men, our advance made no progress, and the increased fire told of large forces already in our front. Lee was up at an early hour and sent Col. Venable to Gordon to inquire how he progressed. Gordon's answer was: —

"Tell Gen. Lee I have fought my corps to a frazzle, and I fear I can do nothing unless I am heavily supported by Longstreet's corps."

When Lee received this message, he exclaimed: —

"Then there is nothing left me but to go and see Gen. Grant, and I would rather die a thousand deaths."

Venable writes: —

"Convulsed with passionate grief, many were the wild words which we spoke as we stood around him. Said one, 'Oh, General! What will history say of the surrender of the army in the field?' He replied, 'Yes, I know they will say hard things of us. They will not understand how we were overwhelmed by numbers. But that is not the question, Colonel. The question is, Is it right to surrender this army? If it is right, then I will take all the responsibility.'"

Meanwhile, the march of the army had come to a halt in front, while, for a time, the rear closed slowly up. I had bivouacked near the road, and soon after sunrise I came upon Lee with his staff by the roadside, at the top of a hill. The general called me to him, and taking his seat upon a felled oak, peeled off its bark, and referring to the map we had looked at together on the 7th, he said:[1] —

"Well, we have come to the Junction, and they seem to be here ahead of us. What have we got to do to-day?"

I had been somewhat prepared by my talk with Pendleton, had formulated a plan of my own, and was glad to have a chance to present it. My command having been north of the

[1] I still cherish a rectangle of that Confederate photographic map linen mounted, labelled S. Side James River, and with Lee's autograph upon it. He had carried it in his breast pocket for months, and when he finally rode to meet Grant, Venable took it to burn. I cut off and preserved the outside fold with his label and signature.

James had had no share in the fighting about Petersburg, and but little in the retreat. They had now begun to hear of a surrender, and would hint their sentiments in loud voices when I rode by.

"We don't want to surrender any ammunition. We've been saving ammunition all this war. Hope we were not saving it for a surrender."

I told the general of this and said that if he saw fit to try and cut our way out, my command would do as well as they had ever done.

He answered: —

"I have left only two divisions, Field's and Mahone's, sufficiently or ganized to be relied upon. All the rest have been broken and routed and can do little good. Those divisions are now scarcely 4000 apiece, and that is far too little to meet the force now in front of us."

This was just the opportunity wished, and I hastened to lay my plan before him. I said: —

"Then we have only choice of two courses. Either to surrender, or to take to the woods and bushes, with orders, either to rally on Johnston, or perhaps better, on the Governors of the respective States. If we surrender this army, it is the end of the Confederacy. I think our best course would be to order each man to go to the Governor of his own State with his arms."

"What would you hope to accomplish by that?" said he. "In the first place," said I, "to stand the chances. If we surrender this army, every other army will have to follow suit. All will go like a row of bricks, and if the rumors of help from France have any foundation, the news of our surrender will put an end to them.

"But the one thing which may be possible in our present situation is to get some sort of terms. None of our armies are likely to be able to get them, and that is why we should try with the different States. Already it has been said that Vance can make terms for N.C., and Jo Brown for Ga. Let the Governor of each State make some sort of a show of force and then surrender on terms which may save us from trials for treason and confiscations."

As I talked, it all looked to me so reasonable that I hoped he was convinced, for he listened in silence. So I went on more confidently: —

"But, General, apart from all that — if all fails and there is *no hope* — the men who have fought under you for four years have got the right this morning to ask *one* favor of you. We know that you do not care for military glory. But we are proud of the record of this army. We want to leave it untarnished to our children. It is a clear record so far and now is about to be closed. A little blood more or less now makes no difference, and we have the right to ask of you to spare us the mortification of having you ask Grant for terms and have him answer that he has no terms to offer. That it is 'U.S., Unconditional Surrender.' That was his reply to Buckner at Fort Donelson, and to Pemberton at Vicksburg, and that is what is threatened us. General, spare us the mortification of asking terms and getting that reply."

He heard it all so quietly, and it was all so true, it seemed to me, and so undeniable, that I felt sure that I had him convinced. His first words were: —

"If I should take your advice, how many men do you suppose would get away?"

"Two-thirds of us," I answered. "We would be like rabbits and partridges in the bushes, and they could not scatter to follow us." He said: "I have not over 15,000 muskets left. Two-thirds of them divided among the States, even if all could be collected, would be too small a force to accomplish anything. All could not be collected. Their homes have been overrun, and many would go to look after their families.

"Then, General, you and I as Christian men have no right to consider only how this would affect us. We must consider its effect on the country as a whole. Already it is demoralized by the four years of war. If I took your advice, the men would be without rations and under no control of officers. They would be compelled to rob and steal in order to live. They would become mere bands of marauders, and the enemy's cavalry would pursue them and overrun many wide sections they may never have occasion to visit. We would bring on a state of affairs it would take the country years to recover from.

"And, as for myself, you young fellows might go to bushwhacking, but the only dignified course for me would be, to go to Gen. Grant and surrender myself and take the consequences of my acts."

He paused for only a moment and then went on.

"But I can tell you one thing for your comfort. Grant will not demand an unconditional surrender. He will give us as good terms as this army has the right to demand, and I am going to meet him in the rear at 10 A.M. and surrender the army on the condition of not fighting again until exchanged."

I had not a single word to say in reply. He had answered my suggestion from a plane so far above it, that I was ashamed of having made it. With several friends, I had planned to make an escape on seeing a flag of truce, but that idea was at once abandoned by all of them on hearing my report.

At this time the negotiations had been definitely broken off by Lee's second letter. The meeting which this proposed had been declined by Grant in a letter now on its way to Lee, but not yet received. He had told me Grant's terms as if he knew them, but later he felt some uneasiness lest Grant might not feel bound by his offer after it had once been declined. Longstreet, in *Manassas to Appomattox*, mentions his apprehensions on this subject, but states that he, from personal acquaintance with Grant, felt able to assure Lee that there would be no humiliating demands, and the event justified that assurance.

About 8.30 o'clock Lee, in a full suit of new uniform, with sword and sash and an embroidered belt, boots, and gold spurs, rode to the rear, hoping soon to meet Grant and to be able to make the surrender. Instead, he learned of Grant's change of route and was handed Grant's letter, dated that morning, and declining the interview. He at once wrote a reply as follows, and asked to have it sent to overtake Grant on his long ride.

"April 9, 1865.

"General: I received your note of this morning on the picket line whither I had come to meet you, and ascertain definitely what terms were embraced in your proposal of yesterday with reference to the surrender of this army. I now ask an interview in accordance with the offer contained in your letter of yesterday for that purpose.

"R. E. Lee, General."

While this last message was being prepared, a messenger riding like the wind dashed around a curve, and seeing Lee, and having but one arm, with difficulty stopped his horse nearly 100 yards beyond. All recognized the rider, Col. John Haskell of Longstreet's artillery, and, as his horse was checked, Lee went to meet him, exclaiming: "What is it? What is it?" and then, without waiting for a reply: "Oh, why did you do it? You have killed your beautiful horse!"[1]

[1] Haskell's horse was well known in the army for its beauty and speed. It had been led all the way from Richmond on the retreat, with a view to making an escape in case of a surrender, which intent had now just been abandoned, as already told. The horse recovered and was sold to a Federal officer for a handsome sum in gold.

Haskell explained that Fitz-Lee had sent in a report that he had found a road by which the army could escape, and that Longstreet had ordered him to overtake Lee, before he could send a note to Grant, and to kill his horse to do it. Longstreet, in his book, says that Haskell's arrival was too late, that the note had gone. But Humphreys's narrative shows that Col. Whittier, who took the note, witnessed Haskell's arrival before the note was finished. Lee, however, had not credited the report, and a later messenger soon came to say that the report was a mistake.

When Field's division had been halted by the flag of truce, Humphreys's corps was within a half-mile, and under his orders it soon appeared to be making preparation for a further advance. Field, meanwhile, went to intrenching. Grant had instructed Humphreys not to let the correspondence delay his movements.

In Longstreet's front Gordon had all the morning been engaged with Sheridan, and firing, both of musketry and artillery, was still in progress. Lee had at first neglected to give authority to ask for a truce, but later sent it to Gordon who sent Maj. Sims of Longstreet's staff to request one. Sims met Custer who had himself conducted to Gordon, and demanded the immediate and unconditional surrender of the army, which Gordon refused. Custer said: —

"Sheridan directs me to say to you, General, if there is any hesitation about your surrender, that he has you surrounded and can annihilate your command in an hour."

Gordon replied: —

"There is a flag between Lee and Grant for the purpose of surrender, and if Gen. Sheridan decides to continue the fighting in the face of the flag of truce, the responsibility for the bloodshed will be his and not mine."

On this, Gordon says, Custer rode off with Maj. Hunter of Gordon's staff, "asking to be guided to Longstreet's position." Finding Longstreet, he made the same demand for immediate and unconditional surrender. I have told of this scene elsewhere [1] more at length, but did not know until the recent publication of Gordon's book, that it was Custer's second attempt that morning to secure the surrender of the army to himself. Longstreet

[1] *Century*, April, 1903.

rebuffed him, however, very roughly, far more so than appears in Longstreet's account of the interview.

Meanwhile, in our rear, more serious trouble threatened. The 2d corps, closely followed by the 6th, began to advance. Lee, who was still awaiting between the lines Grant's reply to his letter (which had over 15 miles to go, and did not reach Grant until 11.50 A.M.), sent by his staff-officers two earnest verbal requests to Humphreys not to press upon him, as negotiations were going on for a surrender. Humphreys, under his orders, felt unable to comply, although the second request was very urgent. He sent word to Lee, who was in full sight on the road, within 100 yards of the head of the 2d corps, *that he must withdraw at once.*

Lee then withdrew, and the 2d corps continued to advance, and deployed in front of Field's intrenchments, and the 6th corps also deployed, on the right of the 2d, ready to assault. At the critical moment when this assault was about to begin, it was suspended by the opportune arrival on the ground of Meade. Meade had read Lee's letter to Grant of that morning, and he took the responsibility of sending Lee a letter granting a truce of one hour, in view of the negotiations for a surrender. This letter was delivered at Field's lines, and, Humphreys says, was received by Lee between eleven and twelve o'clock. This truce may have been prolonged, for it must have been as late as 1 P.M. before the message sent by Babcock from the front, to be presently told of, could have been started.

Meanwhile, during the morning, and before the first flag of truce was sent, Longstreet had directed me to form a line of battle on which all of our available force could be rallied for a last stand. I got up all the organized infantry and artillery in the column, and took up a fairly good position behind the North Fork of the Appomattox River. To our left the enemy was still extending his lines, and some of my battery commanders were anxious to expend on them some of the ammunition they had hauled so far, for the firing had not yet ceased. But I knew that Lee would not approve an unnecessary shot, and not one was fired from our line.[1]

---

[1] The last cannon shot was fired from Gordon's lines under orders to cease firing, conveyed by Maj. W. W. Parker of Huger's battalion. It was fired

When the truce in our rear was for the time arranged, Lee returned to our front and stopped in an apple orchard a hundred yards or so in advance of our line where I had some fence rails piled under a tree to make him a seat.[1]   Here Longstreet joined him, and they again discussed the chances of Grant's making some humiliating demands.   Humphreys's refusal to recognize Lee's presence between the lines as constituting a truce, while awaiting the reply to Lee's proposal to surrender on Grant's terms, and the reluctantly allowed single hour of truce as the alternative of instant battle, naturally made them, perhaps, suspicious.   Few in either army yet knew of the liberality with which Grant was prepared to treat us.   The general temper had been illustrated in the fight at Sailor's Creek by the Chaffin's Bluff battalion, under Stiles, who tried to insist upon fighting to the last ditch.   Even Lee and Longstreet, under the present circumstances, could not feel confidence in their hope that he might not demand unconditional surrender.   So as they sat together under the apple tree awaiting the coming of Grant's messenger to summon Lee to the conference, silence gradually fell between them.   The conversation dropped to broken sentences, and there were occasional long silences between them.   The last thing said was by Longstreet to Lee, as Grant's messenger was seen approaching.   It was : —

"General, unless he offers us honorable terms, come back and let us fight it out."

Grant's messenger was Col. Babcock of his staff, who had ridden ahead for eight miles with the reply to Lee's last note. Less formal than the previous correspondence had been, and using for the first time the customary terms of courtesy, it conveyed assurance that no unpleasant surprises were to be expected.   It read : —

by a section under command of Lt. Wright of Clutter's battery.   The battery was one of McIntosh's battalion of the 3d corps and was commanded by Lt. McIntosh, a brother of Col. McIntosh.

[1] Within two days this tree was cut down for mementoes and relics and the roots dug up.   This was begun by the Confederate soldiers and finished by the Federals.

"APRIL 9, 1865.

"GEN. R. E. LEE, Commanding C.S.A:—

"Your note of this date is but this moment, 11.50 A.M., received. In consequence of my having passed from the Richmond and Lynchburg road to the Farmville and Lynchburg road I am at this writing about four miles west of Walker's Church and will push forward for the purpose of meeting you. Notice sent to me on this road where you wish the interview to take place will meet me.

"Very respectfully, your obedient servant,

"U. S. GRANT, Lt.-Gen."

After reading this note Lee said that he would ride forward to meet Gen. Grant, but that he was apprehensive lest hostilities might begin in the rear on the termination of Meade's truce. Babcock accordingly wrote requesting Meade to maintain the truce until orders from Grant could be received. To save time this was taken at once through our lines by Col. Forsyth of Sheridan's staff, who was accompanied by Col. Taylor, Lee's adjutant.

The meeting, by strange coincidence, took place in the house of Maj. Wilmer McLean, who had owned the farm on Bull Run on which had occurred the first collision between the two armies at Blackburn's Ford on July 18, 1861, and who also owned the farm and house used for similar purposes to-day, as told in the account of that battle. Lee was accompanied to the meeting only by Col. Marshall, his military secretary, and a single courier, who held their horses during the two or three hours consumed. A quiet dignity characterized Lee's bearing throughout the scene, and on the part of all Federal officers present there an evident desire to show only the friendliest feelings. The formal proceedings were limited to an exchange of notes, Grant's note being as follows:—

"APPOMATTOX C. H., VA.,

"April 9, 1865.

"GENERAL: In accordance with the substance of my letter to you of the 8th instant, I propose to receive the surrender of the Army of Northern Virginia on the following terms, to wit: Rolls of all officers and men to be made in duplicate, one copy to be given to an officer to be designated by me, the other to be retained by such officer or officers as you may designate. The officers to give their individual paroles not to take up arms against the government of the United States until properly exchanged, and each company or regimental commander sign a like parole for the men of their commands. The arms, artillery, and public property to be parked and stacked and turned over to the officers appointed by me to receive them. This will not embrace the side arms of the officers nor the private horses or baggage.

"This done each officer and man will be allowed to return to his home, not to be disturbed by United States authority so long as they observe their paroles and the laws in force where they may reside.

"U. S. GRANT, Lt.-Gen.

"GEN. R. E. LEE."

This was accepted by Lee in the following note: —

"HEADQUARTERS ARMY OF NORTHERN VA.,
"April 9, 1865.

"GENERAL: I received your note of this date containing the terms of the surrender of the Army of Northern Virginia as proposed by you. As they are substantially the same as those expressed in your letter of the 8th, they are accepted. I will proceed to designate the proper officers to carry the stipulation into effect.

"R. E. LEE, Gen.

"LT.-GEN. U. S. GRANT."

Some conversation had accompanied the preparation of the letters in which Lee had explained that our cavalry had been required to furnish their own horses, and it was very desirable that they might be allowed to retain them, that the men might plant crops for the summer. Having been in public service they were legally captured property, but Grant cordially yielded the title, not making it part of his terms, but instructions were given all quartermasters to allow all claims of horses as private property without question. Gen. Lee expressed much pleasure at this concession, saying to Grant: —

"This will have the best possible effect. It will be very gratifying and will do much toward the conciliation of our people."

Grant's commissary was also ordered to immediately deliver to Lee 25,000 rations. The conference then terminated, and Lee rode back to his camp. As he was seen approaching the artillery commands were formed by the roadside with instructions to uncover in silence as he passed, but the line of battle which had been maintained all day, seeing the movement of the cannoneers, broke their ranks and overwhelmed all with a great crowd, wrought to a high pitch of emotional affection for its beloved leader of the cause now forever lost. With alternate cheers and tears they flocked around him so that his progress was obstructed, and he presently stopped and made a few remarks to the men, after which he was allowed to pass on to his camp. He told the men that in making the surrender he had made the best terms possible for them, and advised all to go to their homes, plant crops, repair the ravages of the war, and show themselves as good citizens as they had been good soldiers. This was but the second address which he ever made. On his way to Richmond at the beginning of the war, as his train passed Gordonsville, he was called upon for a speech and responded briefly, advising his hearers not to lounge about stations, but to be putting their affairs in order for a long and bloody war, which was sure to strain all their resources to support it.

The firing of salutes was soon begun in the Federal camps and the playing of bands, but Grant requested that all such demonstrations be suppressed, which was quickly done.

Without any further mention of the subject it was assumed as a matter of course, by Grant, that our paroles would protect every one who surrendered from political prosecutions, and he had it so arranged that each one was furnished with an official copy of Gen. Orders No. 43, issued from the headquarters of the 24th corps, which had a printing press along. It read as follows : —

"By agreement between the officers appointed by Generals Lee and Grant to carry out the stipulations of the surrender of the Army of Northern Virignia, the evidence that an officer or enlisted man is a paroled prisoner of war is the fact of his possessing a printed certificate, certifying to the fact, dated at Appomattox C.H., April 10, 1865, and signed by his commanding officer or the staff-officer of the same.

"All guards, patrols, officers, and soldiers of the United States forces will respect such certificates, allow free passage to the holders thereof, and observe, in good faith, the provisions of the surrender that the holders shall remain unmolested in every respect.

"By command of Maj.-Gen. Gibbon,

"EDWARD MOALE, Lt.-Col. & A.A.G."

Our paroles had printed across the ends "Paroled Prisoners' Pass" in some ornamental work between top and bottom lines, the paper being about three inches by eight. Mine read: —

"Brig.-Gen. E. P. Alexander, chief of artillery, 1st corps A.N.V. of Ga., a paroled prisoner of the Army of Northern Virginia, has permission to go to his home and there remain undisturbed with four private horses.

"W. N. PENDLETON, Brig.-Gen. & Chief of Artillery."

After the assassination of Lincoln, there came a wave of bloodthirsty resentment over the administration, which found victims both among the innocent and the guilty. Powerful influences sought to involve Lee and others among his officers in the destruction they planned. They sought to read into the terms given by Grant a single word "military," that the immunity promised might read that paroled prisoners should not be disturbed by U. S. "military" authority so long as they obeyed the laws in force where they resided. Then they hoped that "the hanging might begin." Gen. Lee was already indicted for treason by a grand jury summoned in Norfolk, early in June, 1865. Grant immediately notified President Johnson that no man protected by his parole could be interfered with, and this effectually stopped all such proceedings.

The report of our ordnance officers on the morning of the 9th had shown only 7892 organized infantry with 75 rounds of ammunition and 63 guns with an average of 93 rounds. The infantry were directed to march out and stack their arms and retire. The Federal officers then took possession.

I was directed to form all the guns and caissons in single column along the road, that the Federal officers might then conduct it to their camps. The artillery horses had already been out of rations for some days. The Federal officers had reported their own supplies of forage exhausted. With a heart full of sympathy for the poor brutes, I formed the column on Tuesday, April 11, and left them standing in the road, which they filled for about a mile. The next morning I bade good-by to Appomattox, and as I rode off from the scene I saw the mournful column of artillery still standing in the road unattended, but with many of its poor horses now down in the mud and unable to rise.

Grant had left Appomattox on the 10th, after a call of courtesy on Gen. Lee, in which he had suggested that Lee might serve the cause of peace by a visit to N.C., where he might see President Davis and Gen. Johnston. But Lee felt that the surrender had made him but a private citizen and without authority, and he naturally avoided even the appearance of wishing to interfere, and declined to go.

At that time Brazil was going to war with Paraguay, and, fearing that I might find difficulty in getting employment as a civilian and being already so far on my way, I determined, before returning to Ga., to go to Washington, D.C., and interview the Brazilian minister as to the chances of a position in the Brazilian army. So from Appomattox I started on April 12 for Washington, sending my horses to Ga., by friends, and joining a mixed party of Federals and Confederates riding to Burkesville, where we could take a train. The party had an escort of cavalry, and included Hon. E. B. Washburne of Ill., well known as the special friend of Gen. Grant, and Confederate Maj.-Gen. Wilcox of Ala. In the course of the ride Wilcox and I had a conversation with Mr. Washburne, which impressed us both deeply at the time, and which, I am sure, I can even now repeat without material variation.

In common with all of Grant's army, the officers and soldiers of our escort and company treated the paroled Confederates with a marked kindness which indicated a universal desire to replace our former hostility with special friendship. All Federal privates would salute our uniforms, horsemen and teamsters would give us the roads, and in all conversations with officers or men special care would be evident to avoid painful topics. At one time, when the three mentioned were riding together, Mr. Washburne asked us, —

"What, in your opinion, will now be the course of your other armies? Will they seek to prolong the war, or will the surrender of Lee be accepted as ending it?"

We both answered that we had no doubt of the latter course being followed by the remaining armies, nearly as fast as the news could reach them. And we then said to him: —

"The question will not be what are we going to do, Mr. Washburne, but what is Mr. Lincoln going to do?" "Well; gentlemen," said he, "let me tell you something. When the news came that Richmond had fallen, and that Grant's army was in a position to intercept Lee's retreat, I went up to the White House to congratulate Mr. Lincoln, and I had the opportunity to have a talk with him on this very topic. Of course, it would not be proper for me to violate Mr. Lincoln's confidence by disclosing any details of his plans for restoring the Union, but I am going to make you a prophecy.

"His plan will not only astonish the South, but it will astonish Europe and foreign nations as well. And I will make you a prediction. Within a year Mr. Lincoln will be as popular with you of the South as he is now with the North."

As soon as we were alone together, we compared notes as to what Washburne could have meant. In view of our poverty it could only have meant that in some way the South would receive money. In view of the lack of any other plausible excuse for paying it to us, and of the arguments used by him at the Fortress Monroe conference why the South should be compensated for the emancipation of the negro, I have ever since felt convinced that Lincoln, in that interview with Washburne, recurred to his well-known wish to do that act of justice to the South, and that Washburne believed that he would now be able to accomplish it with the prestige which success in the war would bring, and with the spread of the good feeling already inspired in the army by Grant's act of generosity. Unfortunately, and without fault of her own, the work of an assassin, only three days later, changed everything, converting into gall the very milk of human kindness in every breast, and blasting the South with a whirlwind of resentment, the effects of which will not disappear for generations. But one of its first effects was one for which I will ever remain grateful. It made it utterly impossible for me to go to Brazil. I called on the Brazilian minister in Washington on the 18th, while the President's body was lying in state in the White House, and the streets swarmed with angry crowds ready to mob any one known to be a Confederate. His Excellency kindly advised me to give up all ideas of Brazil, and to take myself out of Washington City with the least possible delay. This I was fortunately able to do, with one narrow escape from a detective, who saw something suspicious in my five hundred dollar Confederate boots and blue soldier's overcoat dyed black. But I was able to elude him, and take a train to New York whence I sailed to Port Royal, S.C. Thence via Savannah and through the country ravaged by Sherman, with many delays and difficulties, I made my way to my boyhood's home at Washington, Ga., where my wife and family were.

This place was now on the only route of travel possible between the eastern states of the Confederacy and the Gulf States. Through it passed, not only President Davis with his family, but the whole Confederate government, which here disbanded, and beyond this point became fugitives, and also the entire débris of all the eastern armies whose homes lay west of the Savannah River. I, therefore, anticipated that I would here meet Mr. Davis, and would be able to give him more news than had reached him by the land route he had travelled, on which there were but few and disjointed pieces of railroad in operation, and no through telegraph lines nor mail service.

So not only was I full to overflowing with important information, but in my talk with Gen. Lee on the morning of the surrender I had gotten to appreciate the spirit of dignified submission in which he was meeting what had befallen him, and was advising the same course to all. As I recalled what he had said about my proposition to disperse the army in the woods and bushes, —

"that the only dignified course open to him would be to go and surrender himself to Gen. Grant and take the consequences of his actions,"

I felt a passionate longing to repeat that conversation to Mr. Davis, and to beg him to take advantage of the opportunity opened to him by the government's offer of a reward of $100,000 for his capture as concerned in the assassination of Lincoln. It seemed to me to offer the only dignified escape from his perilous and impossible position as a fugitive, that, with the example of Lee's approval of such a course before him, he would welcome the opportunity to go to the nearest Federal officer and surrender himself and demand a trial on the charge of complicity in the assassination.

But it was not to be. I am not sure whether or not the news of the rewards being offered for his apprehension ever reached Mr. Davis, before his capture on May 10 in Southwestern Ga.   I had lost twenty-four hours in leaving Savannah by my horse shying at a dead mule by the roadside, and breaking my buggy, and that loss brought me to Washington, Ga., on May 5. Mr Davis had left Washington on May 4 with a small escort of friends, planning to make his way across the Mississippi and to carry on the war with forces to be raised there.   It was the disappointment of my life, even though in later years and after the death of Mr. Davis, Mrs. Davis has assured me that nothing could have ever induced him to thus abandon the cause of the Confederacy.

But he would have seen before him the parting of the ways, and down the road of dignified submission even to injustice, wrong, and robbery, as we still conceive it, he would have seen the figure of Lee preceding him and calling upon all to follow.

Who knows but what he might have been moved to do so?

The Federal casualties in the closing operations from March 29 to April 9 are shown in the following table: —

CORPS	KILLED AND WOUNDED	MISSING	TOTAL
2d	1394	630	2024
5th	1919	546	2465
6th	1542		1542
9th	1548	161	1709
24th	714		714
Cavalry	1151	339	1490
Total	8268	1676	9944

The Confederate casualties, of course, can never be accurately known.   In killed and wounded they were probably about the same as the Federal losses, but the captured or missing would be much greater.

The following table gives the total numbers of officers and enlisted men paroled on April 9: —

	Officers	Men	Total
Lee and Staff	15		15
Longstreet's Corps	1,521	13,312	14,833
Gordon's Corps	695	6,505	7,200
Ewell's Corps	19	268	287
Cavalry Corps	132	1,654	1,786
Artillery Corps	192	2,394	2,586
Miscel. Detachments and Civilian Employees	288	1,361	1,649
Total	2,862	25,494	28,356

Gen. Humphreys states that of the troops surrendered only about 8000 had arms. The miscellaneous detachments included the remnants of the Naval and Heavy Artillery battalions, provost guards, departmental employees, and some odds and ends of troops.

I cannot bring my narrative to a close without a brief summary of the record made by the Confederate Army of Northern Virginia in the two years, nine months, and nine days during which it was under the command of Gen. Robert E. Lee, from June 1, 1862, to April 9, 1865. In this brief period of a thousand days, with inferior numbers, poorly equipped and but badly supplied with food and clothing, it fought seven great campaigns, against six picked generals of the enemy, as follows: —

> 1st against McClellan before Richmond.
> 2d against Pope before Washington.
> 3d against McClellan in Maryland.
> 4th against Burnside before Fredericksburg.
> 5th against Hooker on the Rappahannock.
> 6th against Meade in Pennsylvania.
> 7th against Grant before Richmond.

This last campaign endured for eleven months, during which the guns were scarcely silent a single day. Lee's army at its greatest numbered less than 85,000 men. It put *hors de combat* more than 262,000 Federals within the period mentioned.

The following figures are from the official archives, in the War

Record Office in Washington, showing the Federal numbers killed, wounded, and missing in each campaign, with a deduction of 2000 from the first for the casualties occurring before June 1, 1862.

CAMPAIGNS	DATES	AGGREGATE LOSS
McClellan	June 1, 1862, to Aug. 8, 1862	22,448
Pope	June 26, 1862, to Sept. 2, 1862	16,955
McClellan	Sept. 3, 1862, to Nov. 14, 1862	28,577
Burnside	Nov. 15, 1862, to Jan. 25, 1863	13,214
Hooker	Jan. 26, 1863, to Jan. 27, 1863	25,027
Meade	June 28, 1863, to May 4, 1864	31,530
Grant	May 4, 1864, to April 9, 1865	124,390
	Aggregate	262,141

These figures include nothing for Longstreet's corps at Chickamauga and Knoxville, it having been detached from Lee from Sept. 1, 1863, to April 30, 1864. They would add many thousands to this list of casualties could they be included.

Briefly it may be said that Lee, in a fight to a finish against heavy odds, prolonged the struggle for a thousand days, and put out of action, in the meantime, more than three of the enemy for every man in his own army at its maximum of strength. Scarcely in the history of Napoleon's twenty years in power can the record of such fighting as this be paralleled.

The number of the enemy placed *hors de combat*, in the Grant campaign alone, are said to double the losses inflicted upon his opponents by the Duke of Wellington in all his battles in India, Spain, and at Waterloo. No modern European war has approached this for carnage.[1] Even in the recent conflict between Russia and Japan, where the armies were of immense size and the weapons of peculiar power, one is almost amazed after read-

[1] Grant's Casualties were subdivided as follows :

Killed	Wounded	Missing	Total
15,139	77,748	31,403	124,390

The losses of the Japanese in the Port Arthur Campaign, in killed and wounded only (excluding losses from sickness) as given by their chief medical officer, were 65,000. Corroborative data from various sources confirm the figure. Losses of the Russians have not been published.

ing the popular accounts to find the killed and wounded among the Japanese in the siege of Port Arthur largely exceeded by those of Grant in his last compaign. Bravery in battle is the religion of Japan, and the whole nation is a religious unit. It is encouraging to realize that the loyalty to his flag and country of the Anglo-Saxon has shown itself capable of enduring equal tests of devotion.

It would be strange indeed if in critically reviewing the details of Lee's rapidly conducted campaigns we found no instances of grave errors of judgment when brought to the test of being viewed in retrospect. We do find them, and have not hesitated to note and to criticise them as frankly and freely as he himself would have done had he lived to write his own memoirs. No more intimate idea can be gained of his personal character than can be had from the study of his attitude upon such occasions.

Knowing how quickly and clearly he must have recognized mistakes after making them, and how keenly he must have felt them, one can appreciate the greatness of mind with which he always assumed the entire responsibility; either frankly saying to his men, as at Gettysburg, "It is all my fault," or, as at the "Crossing of the James," passing over whatever had happened in silence, without any attempt to impute blame elsewhere, or any apology, excuse, or even a spoken regret.

This was equally the case when the fault was altogether that of others, as his official reports amply testify. The same mental poise which inspired the unparalleled audacity of his campaigns gave him the strength to bear, and to bear alone and unflinching, even through the closing scenes of the surrender, the burden of his great responsibility. Surely there never lived a man who could more truly say: —

> "I am the master of my fate,
> I am the captain of my soul."

INDEX

621

INDEX 629

511, 514, 518 *et seq.*; at North Anna, 529, 530, 531, 532, 534; plans for attack at Cold Harbor, 535, 536 *et seq.*, 546, 547, 549, 550 *et seq.*; mine at Petersburg, 565, 567, 571, 593, 597, 600, 602, 603, 604, 605, 606, 608, 609, 610, 611.

Lee, W. H. F., 189, 285, 375; Petersburg, 562, 567.

Leyden's battn. art'y, 480.

Liddell, Col., mortally wounded at Antietam, 251.

Lightfoot, Lt.-Col., 262.

Lincoln, Abraham, loss of confidence in Gen. McClellan, 58; Valley Campaign, 101, 172, 175; unwise selection of Pope as commander, 176; appoints Halleck commander-in-chief, 177; effect of Proclamation of Emancipation of Gen. McClellan, 276; he visits the army, and his words to McClellan, 277; relations with McClellan, 278; disagreement with McClellan, 281; orders Halleck to relieve McClellan, places Burnside in command of the army, Porter relieved, succeeded by Hooker, 282, 286, 314; relieves Burnside of command and assigns it to Hooker, 316; 373, 377, 577, 587.

Local Reserves, 550.

Lockwood's brigade at Gettysburg, 407.

Long, Col. A. L., 108, 390; "Memoirs of Lee," quoted, 416.

Longstreet, Gen. James, at Bull Run, 22, 23, 24, 29, 32, 46 *et seq.*; in command of division of Johnston's army, 59; at Williamsburg, 67 *et seq.*; at Seven Pines, 74, 75, 76 *et seq.*; Seven Days' Campaign, 115, 118 *et seq.*, 134, 139; Malvern Hill, 157, 160, 161 *et seq.*; in command of Wing, 175; made Lt.-Gen., 176; ordered to proceed to Gordonsville, 183; Clark's Mountain, 187, 189, 191, 195, 201; joins Jackson, 203, 206, 209, 210, 212, 213, 214, 216, 220, 228, 232; Antietam, 249, 251; made Lt.-Gen., 279, 281, 285, 286, 287; at Fredericksburg, 302, 312; encamped above Fredericksburg, 317, 319; arrives in Petersburg on his way to rejoin Lee, 364, 365; at Culpeper, 372; leaves Culpeper, 374, 375, 377 *et seq.*; at Gettysburg, second day, 397; Gettysburg, 403, 404, 405, 407, 411, 412, 415, 416; "Manassas to Appomattox," quoted, 416, 421, 423, 424, 432, 460, 461, 466, 480, 481, 484,

485, 486, 490, 491; casualties, 439, 448, 547, 491, 492, 497, 498, 556, 593; battle of the Wilderness, 503, 504, 505; wounded, 506, 523 *et seq.*; at North Anna, 529, 530, 535; wounded, 536, 547, 550.

Magruder, Gen. Joseph B., at Bull Run, 44, 48; at Yorktown, 63; defences at Williamsburg, 66; at Seven Pines, 75, 76, 89; Seven Days' Campaign, 123; the pursuit, 134, 135, 137, 138 *et seq.*; Malvern Hill, 157, 162 *et seq.*

Mahone, Gen. Wm., 88, 162, 164; brigade of infantry at Crampton's Gap, 233, 234; Antietam, 261; at Chancellorsville, 325, 352; Gettysburg, 400, 401; battle of Wilderness, 505; Spottsylvania, 513, 514, 518, 538; Petersburg, 561, 568, 570, 571, 572.

Malvern Hill, battle of, 156 *et seq.*

Manassas Depot, destruction of, 195.

Manassas Second (Second Bull Run), 200; casualties, 201; arrangement of opposing armies, 203–204; casualties, 219.

Manigault, Gen., 461, 462, 475; account, 476–477, 478, 479.

Mansfield, Gen. J. H. F., commands 12th corps, Antietam, 250, 251; killed, 255.

Marshall, Maj., 109.

Marye's Hill, assault of, 301, 302.

Maryland Campaign, Table of Confederate Casualties, 273, 274; Federal, 275.

Maurin, battery of, at Fredericksburg, 303.

Mayne, Capt., at Bull Run, 24.

McCall, Gen., 108, 153, 155.

McCandless, Gen., at Gettysburg, 405, 433.

McClellan, Gen. Geo. B., in West Virginia, 14; in Virginia, 55 *et seq.*; advance on Richmond, 59; defeat at Gaines Mill, 60; at Fortress Monroe, 63; Yorktown, 65; pursuit of Johnston, 66; McDowell's army assigned to, 71 *et seq.*; Valley Campaign, 97, 101; Seven Days' Campaign, 111, 112, 114, 123 *et seq.*; Seven Days' Campaign, the pursuit, 133, 138; reason for severe criticism of, 139; Malvern Hill, 169, 170, 171; recalled to Washington, 172; lack of enterprise and audacity, 178; leaves Harrison's Landing, 185; assigned command of troops, 223–224, 229; at Sharpsburg, 243; ac-